The Roman West, AD 200–500

This book describes and analyses the development of the Roman West from Gibraltar to the Rhine, using primarily the extensive body of published archaeological evidence rather than the textual evidence underlying most other studies. It situates this development within a longer-term process of change, proposing the later second century rather than the 'third-century crisis' as the major turning point, although the latter had longer-term consequences owing to the rise in importance of military identities. But in many areas more 'traditional' forms of settlement and display were sustained, to which was added the vocabulary of Christianity. The longer-term rhythms are also central to assessing the evidence for such aspects as rural settlement and patterns of economic interaction. The collapse of Roman imperial authority emphasised trends such as militarisation and regionalisation along with economic and cultural dis-integration. Indicators of 'barbarian/Germanic' presence are reassessed within such contexts and the traditional interpretations questioned and alternatives proposed.

SIMON ESMONDE CLEARY is Professor of Roman Archaeology at the University of Birmingham. His particular area of interest in Roman archaeology has always been the later Roman period and the transition to the Middle Ages, and he has excavated on several sites of this period in Britain and south-west France. He is the author of *The Ending of Roman Britain* (1989) and, with Ray Laurence and Gareth Sears, *The City in the Roman West, c. 250 BC – c. AD 250* (2011).

The Roman West, AD 200–500

An Archaeological Study

SIMON ESMONDE CLEARY

CAMBRIDGE UNIVERSITY PRESS
Cambridge, New York, Melbourne, Madrid, Cape Town,
Singapore, São Paulo, Delhi, Mexico City

Cambridge University Press
The Edinburgh Building, Cambridge CB2 8RU, UK

Published in the United States of America by Cambridge University Press, New York

www.cambridge.org
Information on this title: www.cambridge.org/9780521196499

© Simon Esmonde Cleary 2013

This publication is in copyright. Subject to statutory exception
and to the provisions of relevant collective licensing agreements,
no reproduction of any part may take place without the written
permission of Cambridge University Press.

First published 2013

Printed and bound in the United Kingdom by the MPG Books Group

A catalogue record for this publication is available from the British Library

Library of Congress Cataloguing in Publication data
Esmonde Cleary, A. S. (A. Simon)
The Roman West, AD 200–500 : an archaeological study / Simon Esmonde Cleary.
    pages   cm
Includes bibliographical references and index.
ISBN 978-0-521-19649-9
1. Rome – History – Empire, 284–476.   2. Rome – History – Germanic Invasions,
3rd–6th centuries.   3. Romans – Europe, Western.   4. Europe, Western – Antiquities,
Roman.   5. Rome – Antiquities.   6. Archaeology and history – Rome.
7. Archaeology and history – Europe, Western.   I. Title.
DG311.E76   2013
937′.06–dc23
                                                                                        2012027743

ISBN 978-0-521-19649-9 Hardback

Cambridge University Press has no responsibility for the persistence or
accuracy of URLs for external or third-party internet websites referred to
in this publication, and does not guarantee that any content on such
websites is, or will remain, accurate or appropriate.

Contents

List of figures [*page* vi]
Acknowledgements [xiii]
A note on places and maps [xv]

Introduction [1]

1 Prologue: the third-century crisis [18]

2 The military response: soldiers and civilians [42]

3 Reshaping the cities [97]

4 Christianity and the traditional religions [150]

5 Emperors and aristocrats in the late Roman West [198]

6 Rural settlement and economy in the late Roman West [264]

7 The economy of the late Roman West [303]

8 Breakdown and barbarians [338]

9 The fifth century and the dis-integration of the Western Empire [395]

10 Epilogue: AD 200–500, a coherent period? [455]

Bibliography [483]
Index [522]

Figures

1.1 Map of coin hoards closing in the 250s from Gaul and Germany (redrawn with permission after Dr P. Haupt 2001: Karte 48)   [*page* 38]

1.2 Map of coin hoards closing with issues of Postumus (260–8) from Gaul and Germany (redrawn with permission after Dr P. Haupt 2001: Karte 50)   [39]

2.1 Military installations along the Rhine, in northern Gaul and south-eastern Britain in the fourth century (map prepared by Henry Buglass)   [47]

2.2 Krefeld-Gellep forts and cemeteries (redrawn after Pirling 1986: Abb. 30)   [51]

2.3 Distribution of crossbow brooches in Gaul, Germany and Britain (redrawn with permission after Dr E. Swift 2000a: Fig. 16 [part])   [59]

2.4 Crossbow brooch from Lankhills, Winchester (photograph courtesy of Oxford Archaeology)   [60]

2.5 Late Roman fortifications at urban sites in northern Gaul and Germany (map prepared by Henry Buglass)   [62]

2.6 Cologne, the third-century *Römerturm* (photograph: author)   [63]

2.7 Xanten, the late Roman defences within second-century *colonia* (redrawn after Otten and Ristow 2008: Abb. 387)   [64]

2.8 Périgueux, the late Roman walls (photograph: author)   [65]

2.9 Jublains, plan of the first-/second-century city and the late Roman blockhouse and defended enclosure (redrawn after Naveau 1997: Fig. 18)   [66]

2.10 Jublains, south side of the late Roman defended enclosure (photograph: author)   [67]

2.11 Bavai, plan of the first-/second-century forum with the late Roman walls around it (redrawn after Faider Feytmans 1957: *dépliant*)   [69]

2.12 Amiens, plan of the late Roman defended area (river courses modern) (redrawn after Bayard and Massy 1983: Fig. 113)   [71]

2.13 Metz, Saint-Pierre-aux-Nonnains, the third-century basilican building from the north-west (photograph courtesy of Professor Guy Halsall)   [74]
2.14 Late Roman hilltop defended enclosures in north-eastern Gaul and the Rhineland (map prepared by Henry Buglass after Brulet 1990: Carte/Beilage 4; Cüppers 1984: 323; Hunold 2011: Karte 1)   [77]
2.15 Distribution in Gaul, Germany and Britain of the commands of the *comes sacrarum largitionum* (Baf, Bar, G, Li, M, T), the *magister officiorum* (A, Bal, C, Lo, Sa, Sc, Sp) and the *magister militum praesentalis a parte peditum* (PrL, PrS) – none of these officials had subordinates or installations in Iberia (map prepared by Henry Buglass)   [92]
3.1 Amiens, areas occupied in *c.* 250 (upper panel) and *c.* 270 (lower panel) (river courses modern) (redrawn after Bayard and Massy 1983: Fig. 112)   [108]
3.2 Arles, distribution of monuments in the fourth century (with permission from the Ecole Française de Rome and Professor M. Heijmans; plan prepared by Henry Buglass)   [109]
3.3 Bordeaux, the 'Palais Gallien' amphitheatre, west face (photograph: author)   [119]
3.4 Périgueux, the 'Tour de Vésone' temple (photograph: author)   [120]
3.5 Le Mans, west walls showing patterned decoration (photograph: author)   [125]
3.6 Périgueux, nineteenth-century engraving of the Porte de Mars (Caumont 1870: 206)   [126]
3.7 Spain, urban defences in the northern part of the peninsula (map prepared by Henry Buglass)   [127]
3.8 Lugo, the late Roman walls (the upper part with windows is modern) (photograph: author)   [128]
3.9 Barcelona, the walls: lower part Augustan, upper part and towers late Roman additions (photograph: author)   [131]
3.10 Late Roman urban defences in southern Gaul (map prepared by Henry Buglass)   [132]
3.11 Saint-Bertrand-de-Comminges, the early fifth-century wall with wall-top (photograph: author)   [133]
3.12 Mérida, the 'Casa de los Mármoles' fourth-century urban residence (redrawn after Alba Calzado 2005: Fig. 3)   [138]
4.1 Geneva, location of late Roman churches (redrawn with permission after Professor C. Bonnet 1993: 20–1)   [154]

4.2 Geneva, development of the episcopal complex from the fourth to the sixth century (redrawn with permission after Professor C. Bonnet 2006: Fig. 55) [154]
4.3 Trier, plan of fourth-century Christian double basilica (redrawn after Wightman 1970: Fig. 8; Cüppers 1984: 162) [157]
4.4 Plan of baptisteries in Provence (redrawn with permission after Professor J. Guyon 2005: Fig. 12) [160]
4.5 Fréjus, the baptistery (photograph: author) [161]
4.6 Riez, the baptistery (photograph: author) [162]
4.7 Tarragona, martyr church in the amphitheatre, from the north-east (photograph: author) [163]
4.8 Toulouse, decorated sarcophagus (photograph: author) [167]
4.9 Distribution of Christian tombstones in the West, AD 300–750. (Map prepared by Henry Buglass with permission after figures in Dr M. Handley 2003: Ch. 1) [169]
4.10 Bar charts of the rising Christian 'epigraphic habit' in Gaul and Spain (redrawn with permission after Dr M. Handley 2003: Figs. 2.1 and 2.2) [169]
4.11 Barcelona, the episcopal complex (redrawn with permission from Dr J. Beltrán de Heredia Bercero 2002: 75; Bonnet and Beltrán de Heredia 2000: 224) [172]
4.12 Tarragona, the Francolí and Parc Central Christian complexes (redrawn with permission after Dr J. López Vilar 2006: Fig. 270) [173]
4.13 Rouen, western part of the Christian basilica (redrawn after Lequoy and Guillot 2004: Fig. 281) [176]
4.14 Cologne, the Saint Gereon complex (redrawn after Verstegen 2006: Taf. 13) [177]
4.15 Villa Fortunatus, plan, with development of church (redrawn with permission after Dr A. Chavarría Arnau 2007: Figs. 51 and 52) [182]
4.16 Torre de Palma, Christian basilica (redrawn with permission from Dr J. Hale after Maloney and Hale 1996: Colour Fig. 17) [183]
4.17 Centcelles, plan (redrawn after Schlunk and Hauschild 1978: Abb. 184) [183]
4.18 Carranque, plan of mortuary complex (redrawn after Fernández-Galiano 2001: 72) [184]
4.19 Loupian, plan of church and baptistery (redrawn after N. Duval 1995: 48) [186]

4.20 Vandoeuvres, plan of villa with Christian area (redrawn with permission after Mr J. Terrier 2005: Fig. 6)   [188]
4.21 Ribemont-sur-Ancre, plan of sanctuary complex in the second century (redrawn after Agache 1978: Fig. 36)   [192]
4.22 Ribemont-sur-Ancre, the principal temple and annexes in the fourth century (redrawn after Brunaux 2009: Fig. 77)   [193]
4.23 Châteaubleau, the temple complex in the early fourth century (redrawn with permission from Mr F. Pilon after Parthuisot *et al.* 2008: Fig. 2)   [194]
4.24 Matagne-la-Grande, early-fourth-century temple complex (redrawn with permission of CReA-Patrimoine / Université libre de Bruxelles – Cedarc / Musée du Malgré-Tout de Treignes, after Cattelain and Paridaens 2009: Fig. 11)   [195]
5.1 Trier, plan showing buildings of the palace complex (redrawn after Cüppers 1990: Abb. 511)   [201]
5.2 Trier, the 'Basilika' from the west (photograph: courtesy of Dr R. White)   [202]
5.3 Trier, plan of the Kaiserthermen (redrawn after Nielsen 1990: Fig. 98; Wightman 1970: Fig. 6)   [204]
5.4 Trier, the Kaiserthermen from the east (photograph: courtesy of Dr R. White)   [205]
5.5 Trier, the 'Langmauer' enclosure and associated villas (redrawn after Cüppers 1984: Abb. 152)   [208]
5.6 Pfalzel, plan of the villa (redrawn after Cüppers 1984: 321)   [209]
5.7 Arles, 'Baths of Constantine' with basilica on the southern side (redrawn with permission from the Ecole Française de Rome and Professor M. Heijmans after Heijmans 2004: Fig. 139)   [210]
5.8 Córdoba, the La Cercadilla complex (redrawn with permission after Dr R. Hidalgo Prieto 1996: Fig. 3)   [213]
5.9 Carranque, the residence (redrawn after Fernández-Galiano 2001: 88)   [216]
5.10 (Montréal-)Séviac, plan of the villa (redrawn after Balmelle 2001: Fig. 298)   [218]
5.11 Montmaurin, plan of the villa (redrawn after Fouet 1969: Fig. 23)   [220]
5.12 Montmaurin, colonnaded internal court (photograph: author)   [221]
5.13 São Cucufate, plan of the villa (redrawn with permission after Dr Chavarría Arnau 2007: Fig. 112)   [222]
5.14 Chiragan, plan of the villa (redrawn after Joulin 1901: Pl. III)   [229]

x   List of figures

5.15 The Missorium of Theodosius (with permission from Bridgeman Art Library)   [232]
5.16 France, distribution of fourth- and fifth-century mosaics (redrawn with permission from Maison Ausonius after Balmelle 2001: Fig. 19)   [246]
5.17 Loupian, plan of the villa in the early fifth century (shaded areas: mosaics) (redrawn after Pellecuer and Pomarèdes 2001: Fig. 10)   [249]
6.1 Saint-Germain-lès-Corbeil, plan of the villa in the fourth century (upper) and the fifth century (lower) (redrawn with permission from Professor P. Van Ossel after Ouzoulias and Van Ossel 2001: Figs. 12 and 13)   [274]
6.2 Ile-de-France, development of occupation across time in the areas surveyed (redrawn with permission from Professor P. Van Ossel after Ouzoulias and Van Ossel 2001: Figs. 1 and 3)   [276]
6.3 Ile-de-France, creation and abandonment of sites across time in three areas surveyed (redrawn with permission from Professor P. Van Ossel after Ouzoulias and Van Ossel 2001: Fig. 9)   [277]
6.4 Vert-Saint-Denis, plan of the fourth-century settlement (redrawn with permission from Professor P. Van Ossel after Van Ossel and Ouzoulias 2000: Fig. 5)   [278]
6.5 Saint-Ouen-du-Breuil, plan of the fourth-century settlement (redrawn with permission from Professor P. Van Ossel after Van Ossel and Ouzoulias 2000: Fig. 9)   [280]
6.6 Berry, development of occupation across time in the areas surveyed (redrawn with permission from FERACF after Gandini 2008: Fig. 41)   [283]
6.7 Berry, creation and abandonment of sites across time in the areas surveyed (redrawn with permission from FERACF after Gandini 2008: Fig. 42)   [284]
6.8 Berry, sizes of site by century (redrawn with permission from FERACF after Gandini 2008: Fig. 45)   [285]
6.9 Provence, development across time of types of site by area surveyed (redrawn after Raynaud 2001: Fig. 6)   [288]
7.1 Histogram of number of shipwrecks in the Mediterranean by century (redrawn after Professor A. Wilson 2009: Fig. 9.2)   [314]
7.2 Histograms of number of shipwrecks in the Mediterranean by 25- (upper) and 20-year (lower) periods (redrawn with permission after Professor A. Wilson 2009: Figs. 9.5 and 9.6)   [316]

7.3 Distribution of Argonne products (including those produced in the Paris Basin) (redrawn with permission after Professor P. Van Ossel 2011a: Fig. 5) [320]

7.4 Distribution of *Eifelkeramik*/Mayen ware (redrawn with permission from Professor R. Brulet after Brulet *et al.* 2010: 422) [321]

7.5 Distribution of *terra sigillata hispánica tardía* (TSHT) (redrawn after Reynolds 2005: Map 6) [324]

8.1 Alzey fort, fourth-century (black) and fifth-century (outline) structures (redrawn with permission after Professor J. Oldenstein 1986: Abb. 2) [346]

8.2 Toulouse, 'Visigothic' sites in the north-western part of the city. (A) Saint-Pierre-des-Cuisines; (B) Hôpital Larrey building; (C) Notre-Dame-de-la-Daurade (with permission from the Ecole Française de Rome) (redrawn after Martin 1727: Pl. IV; Pailler 2002: Figs. 166, 169 and 189) [362]

8.3 Notre-Dame-de-la-Daurade, plans and view of the interior before demolition (redrawn after Martin 1727: Pl. IV) [363]

8.4 Spain, 'Duratón' grave goods of Ripoll López's *Nivel 2* (with permission from Professor G. Ripoll López, 2001: Fig. 1) [366]

8.5 Distribution of early medieval horse burials in Europe (redrawn with permission after Professor M. Müller-Wille 1996: Abb. 146) [384]

9.1 Tarragona, main Christian areas in the fifth century (map prepared by Henry Buglass) [403]

9.2 Arles, rue Brossolet, fifth-century occupation (redrawn with permission from the Ecole Française de Rome and Professor M. Heijmans after Heijmans 2004: Figs. 207–209) [406]

9.3 Arles, fifth-century occupation round curved end of circus (redrawn with permission from the Ecole Française de Rome and Professor M. Heijmans after Heijmans 2004: Fig. 224) [407]

9.4 Mérida, the 'Casa de los Mármoles' residence as subdivided in the fifth century (redrawn after Alba Calzado 2005: Fig. 6) [412]

9.5 Toulouse, rue Sainte-Anne, development of street and occupation from the first to the end of the fifth century (redrawn with permission from the Ecole Française de Rome after Pailler 2002: Fig. 149) [419]

9.6 (Montréal-)Séviac, fifth- to seventh-century Christian installations in the south-eastern angle of the villa (redrawn after Lapart and Petit 1993: Fig. 115) [421]

9.7 Marolles-sur-Seine, plan of fifth-century occupation (redrawn with permission from Professor P. Van Ossel after Van Ossel and Ouzoulias 2000: Fig. 4) [430]

9.8 Congosto, plan of fifth-century occupation (redrawn after Quirós Castillo and Vigil-Escalera Guirado 2000: Fig. 6)   [442]

9.9 El Bovalar, plan of settlement (redrawn after Gurt i Esparraguera and Palet Martínez 2001: Fig. 11)   [445]

9.10 Lunel Viel, Roman and later settlement and cemetery sites (redrawn after Raynaud 1990: Fig. 2)   [447]

9.11 Roc de Pampelune, plan of settlement and defences (redrawn after Schneider 2007: Fig. 7)   [448]

Acknowledgements

This book has been long in the making. The conventional piety would be 'too long', but in fact the extended gestation has worked hugely to its advantage. Above all this has been because of the enormous increase in publications bearing on the subject matter of this book over the last decade and more, ranging from detailed considerations of individual sites or classes of material to more synthetic publications on such topics to regional or national surveys up to general works of synthesis setting agendas and intellectual approaches. The reader will see time and again how these have contributed to the evidence base and to the thinking in this book. They have made possible a work utterly different in scale and complexity to the one I set out to write some twenty years ago. In addition, in this time I have been privileged to undertake fieldwork in south-western France, to attend conferences across the area of the late Roman West, but above all to get to know a whole series of thoughtful, stimulating and generous colleagues, tolerant of my linguistic inadequacies and of my peculiar perspectives and ignorances formed across the Channel. Many of their names appear in parentheses in the chapters that follow, either as the authors of publications cited or for giving me access to unpublished material and ideas under the rubric 'pers. comm.': to these and to all other colleagues both on the Continent and in the United Kingdom who have helped inform, educate and correct me, my sincerest thanks.

The main writing of the book took place during a year's sabbatical in 2008–9, part funded by the University of Birmingham under its study leave provisions and part funded as a period of matching leave by the Arts and Humanities Research Council. The final, if delayed, appearance of this book is, I hope, recompense for their investments, which I acknowledge with great gratitude.

The draft of the book that appeared in 2009 was patiently read through by Chris Wickham, who combined his usual support and kindness with many observations large and small that have substantially improved both the content and the form of the work: to him my particular thanks, and again I hope this finished work is some recompense. Two 'anonymous' referees of the draft and of the revised version for Cambridge University Press also made a number of very useful observations, which I have incorporated in the appropriate places.

A book such as this needs illustrations, for in archaeology a picture can indeed be worth a thousand words. The preparation of the line illustrations was undertaken by Henry Buglass, who with good humour and an artist's eye transformed the various photocopies and sketches I gave him into the maps and plans that are a real ornament to the book. Graham Norrie likewise took charge of digitising and preparing the photographic material and of making sure that it all matched his exacting standards before being confided to the publishers. I am also very grateful to the various authors and bodies that have allowed me to reproduce photographic or line illustrations, sometimes unmediated, sometimes used as the basis for redrawn images.

The various staff of Cambridge University Press who have been involved in advising on the preparation of the book and in seeing it through the press have been immensely tolerant and supportive, above all Michael Sharp, who accepted the idea of the book and oversaw its appearance many years later.

I would like to conclude with a vote of thanks to the various schoolmasters who over a period of some ten years inculcated in me a thorough grounding in the grammar and syntax of French and later Castilian Spanish (as well as Latin and Greek), allowing me not only to read these languages and their cousins such as Catalan, Italian and Portuguese, but also not to be afraid of foreign languages but indeed to delight in the thought worlds they reveal.

A note on places and maps

This book contains the names of hundreds of sites, find spots and so on. Many appear on the maps, but many more do not. So in order to help the reader locate them, I have tried at their first appearance (at least) to give the modern national administrative unit in which they lie (such as a French *département* or a Spanish *provincia*), the only exceptions being major sites such as a Barcelona or a Cologne, where such information seems to me otiose.

The base maps, prepared by Henry Buglass especially for this book, show the coastlines to either side of the North Sea as they were (approximately) in the late Roman period after the Dunkirk II marine transgression.

Introduction

What is the justification for yet another book, and a fairly fat one at that, on the subject of the late Roman Empire in Europe, specifically western Europe, a field already jostling with other publications? After all, in anglophone scholarship the last decade alone has seen a series of major publications that chronologically or geographically cover this period and area, indeed usually ranging more widely. On one bookshelf alone in my office I can find a selection of these. There are general and illuminating textbook-style introductions to the period such as Roger Collins's (1991) *Early Medieval Europe 300–1000*, Stephen Mitchell's (2007) *A History of the Later Roman Empire AD 284–641*, John Moorhead's (2001) *The Roman Empire Divided 400–700*, and the 'terrible twins' of 2005, Peter Heather's *The Fall of the Roman Empire: A New History* and Bryan Ward-Perkins's *The Fall of Rome and the End of Civilization*, two books that in their sizes, their approaches, their types of evidence and their intellectual frameworks show how much divergence there can be in studying this period. Other recent, wide-ranging works include another 2005 publication, Chris Wickham's massive and already massively influential *Framing the Early Middle Ages: Europe and the Mediterranean, 400–800*. More immediately concerned with the Western Empire are Guy Halsall's (2007) *Barbarian Migrations and the Roman West 376–568* and Matthew Innes's (2007) *Introduction to Early Medieval Western Europe 300–900: The Sword, the Plough and the Book*. On a more sanguinary note there are two recent works that bear upon the area under consideration in this book, Michael Kulikowski's (2007) *Rome's Gothic Wars from the Third Century to Alaric*, and Chris Kelly's (2008) *The End of Empire: Attila the Hun and the Fall of Rome*. These are just some of the publications of the last decade or so. Behind them lie such seminal works as A. H. M. Jones's (1964) *The Later Roman Empire 284–602* or Peter Brown's (1971) *The World of Late Antiquity: From Marcus Aurelius to Mohammed*, the works that for the anglophone world opened up the study of the period, made it into a thriving field of intellectual endeavour and conditioned much of its growth over the better part of half a century. Apart from such single-author works there are of course the great multi-author works such as Volumes XII (2005), XIII (1997) and XIV (2000) of

The Cambridge Ancient History covering respectively the periods 193–337, 337–425 and 425–600. And this is just the English-speaking world – indeed just the British part of that world. Similar developments have taken place in the modern countries that lie within or overlap with the territories of the Western Roman Empire, some of which will appear in the course of this book, as well as in the English-speaking world elsewhere, especially North America (one thinks, for instance, of scholars such as F. X. Gearey or R. Mathiesen).

So why then another book in an already crowded field? The simple answer is that all the books above are about history and this book is about archaeology. The books above take as their evidence base the written sources, be they narrative history or chronicles or hagiography or laws or the acts of Church councils or other classes of written object such as inscriptions or coins. This opens up huge resources for interrogation but also constrains that interrogation partly because of the inbuilt biases of literary form or the personal biases of authors, but more importantly because of what the written sources that survive do not deal with. There are enormous areas of life and death in this ancient world that simply cannot be approached from the written evidence that has come down to us. And because of this the questions to be asked and the analyses to be undertaken are circumscribed by what that evidence is concerned with and can reasonably be asked to tell us about. Of course, many of the authors listed above are well aware of archaeological evidence and what it can offer; in ways that, for instance, A. H. M. Jones famously was not. The most sustained use of archaeological evidence is that by Chris Wickham, who uses it throughout his major work and shows a sophisticated understanding of its strengths and weaknesses. Nevertheless, it is largely there to supplement textual evidence, and the questions posed and the approaches used in the book remain ones that are essentially text-driven. Moreover, he employs only certain parts of the archaeological record, principally those to do with economic structures over time, and to an extent social structures also, rather than using the full range of archaeological evidence, since that is not his purpose. Guy Halsall and Bryan Ward-Perkins also use elements of the archaeological record in the context of what are also still text-driven approaches. Though the latter ranges more widely through the archaeological repertoire, this is still using parts of it rather than a systematic consideration of all the domains of archaeological evidence available. Ward-Perkins's book has attracted much discussion for its moralising title. On the whole I avoid offering such judgements, but, equally, I have to say that I do not see that more than a handful of people (some kings and bishops) were better off at the end of the fifth century than had been their equivalents at its start; on the other hand, a great many people were certainly worse off in many ways, and not just the crudely financial. One book that might be thought to deal with much the same area and period as the present work is Ellen Swift's (2000) *The End of the Western Roman Empire: An Archaeological Investigation*. It is indeed based on archaeological evidence, but a very restricted compass of that evidence, the material culture relating to dress and thus to 'ethnicity' and mobility. It does this very well and its analyses will be very valuable later in this book, but it does leave much scope for treatment of other domains of archaeological evidence. The title of Richard Reece's (1999) *The Later Roman Empire: An Archaeology AD 150–600* also suggests something that has anticipated this book, but in fact it also has a restricted compass, concerned mainly with the material culture of the late Roman elite; it does this in his usual clear-sighted and stimulating fashion, but again leaves scope for other approaches. Likewise, Jeremy Knight's (1999) *The End of Antiquity: Archaeology, Society and Religion AD 235–700* covers much the same geographical area as this book and makes much use of archaeological evidence, but its core is to do with the creation of a Christian archaeology across the West and how to interpret the significance of the sites and monuments.

So the prospectus for this book is that it is a first attempt to move a wide spectrum of the archaeology of the late Roman West centre stage, and to try to discuss the area and period in terms of its archaeology and come to conclusions based on the archaeological evidence rather than the textual evidence, or the textual evidence augmented by some of the archaeological evidence. This is what some might term its unique selling point. The evidence used is mainly settlements, burials and artefacts; the evidence from areas such as osteology, palynology and other palaeo-environmental disciplines figures far less often. The broad outline of what this book sets out to do is given by its title; uninspiring but accurate. It is an attempt to provide an overview of developments in the western part of the Roman Empire from the end of the second century AD to the start of the sixth, an overview based on the archaeological evidence and its various possible interpretations. The reasons for these geographical and chronological limits are outlined below.

Of course, all that textual history has taught us cannot be 'unlearnt', nor should textual evidence be ignored, nor am I a 'rejectionist' who thinks that all historical evidence should be set aside and the purity of archaeology preserved, but the ways in which historical evidence and narrative will be used here and articulated with each other need to be set out. At a 'grand narrative' level, it is pretty much impossible to unthink questions such as 'decline and fall' or 'Germanic settlement' and the origins of the successor states, and they will make their appearance here, but considered from a starting point in the archaeology, which may well not take the same routes or get to the same destinations as the texts. At another level of discourse, there are things we know about through the textual record which we would be hard put to it to derive from the archaeology. Examples of this that play an important exegetic role in various chapters of this book are the *Notitia Dignitatum* (Chapter 2), Christian ideas about the dead (Chapter 4), the nature and role of *paideia* (Chapter 5), or the operations of the late Roman tax system with its consequences for the wider economy (Chapter 7). These again will all be taken into consideration, but as providing a series of models for the archaeology, rather than as preordaining structures into which the archaeology has to fit whether it wants to or not: history as archaeology's bed of Procrustes (or older Ugly Sister with the glass slipper). On occasion, particular items of textual evidence will be used, but only where they clarify what was happening in a way that archaeology of its nature cannot. I am all in favour of drawing on as wide a range of evidence as possible to study the past; the wider the range of evidence, the wider the range of perspectives and the richer the consequent analyses and discussions. But this can only be done if the proper nature of each discipline, its particular protocols of analysis and synthesis, and its strengths and weaknesses are understood and respected. Because the development of the disciplines of archaeology and of history accorded to history the chronological priority, in periods such as this with a relatively abundant historical record, archaeology has all too often been used as the handmaid of history. What this book seeks in part to do is to try to emancipate archaeology from the role of servant by establishing the sorts of evidence that archaeology can bring to debates about this area of the human past and also the parameters within which this evidence and its analyses can be interrogated, especially by practitioners of other disciplines. In this way archaeology and history (and all the subdisciplines within them from palynology to palaeography) will each be able to contribute its own perspectives. Sometimes these perspectives will be in harmony; sometimes they will disagree or even flatly contradict each other. This last possibility is perhaps where really interesting progress is to be made.

Coverage and approaches

The book's main area of study covers the region from the Strait of Gibraltar to the Rhine; that is its definition of the 'Roman West'. It thus encompasses the whole of the Iberian peninsula (though not the small area of western North Africa, Mauretania Tingitana, that administratively formed part of the *diocesis Hispaniarum*); that peninsula will sometimes be referred to as the Iberian peninsula, sometimes as Spain, because the latter is in English a generic appellation for the peninsula, even if it does subsume modern Portugal into its larger neighbour. What are now France and much of the Benelux countries will appear under the name of Gaul, since that is also a common usage among anglophone scholarship, largely in order to avoid simply equating the Roman provinces north of the Pyrenees with modern France. 'Germany' or 'the Rhineland' will be used interchangeably for the Roman provinces of Germania. The work will also on occasion deal with Britain, where the archaeology of the island provides complements, comparisons or contrasts to the mainland areas of the West. It is not an attempt to rewrite the archaeology of Britain in the fourth and fifth centuries, but those whose main focus of study is insular may nonetheless find developments on and arguments relating to the Continent to have relevance to the study of Britain. This definition of the 'Roman West', of course, excludes the historic heartland of the empire, Italy. The exclusion of Italy is entirely pragmatic; to have dealt with it at the same level of detail and argument as the other areas would have enormously lengthened the book (to say nothing of the time needed for researching and writing it); it would also have posed the problem of how to deal with the giant incubus that was the city of Rome. This definition also means that the areas of central Europe lying outside the Rhine and upper Danube frontiers are only dealt with in passing. It might be objected that developments crucial to what happened west of the Rhine had their origins there, and this is true enough: indeed, this work makes use of the concept of a zone on both sides of the Rhine. But as well as the pragmatic reason again of not overextending an already very large field of study, it is the contention here that the central concern of this work is the areas that had for several hundred years formed part of the Roman Empire and thus had become different from areas that had remained outside the empire. The West as defined here is big enough already, if not too big.

The period AD 200–500, which does not respond to more traditional periodisations of the Roman Empire or of antiquity, needs some explanation. The year AD 200 was very purposefully chosen to break with the convention of starting works on the later Roman Empire or late antiquity in around AD 300, after the storms of the third century had been successfully navigated. This latter is an essentially historiographical tradition, justified in part by a change in the number and nature of the narrative sources at the end of the third century but more especially dictated by the contrast of the relatively stable political and military situation from the accession of Diocletian in 284 with the political and military instability of the preceding half-century. The years either side of 300 really do seem to the historian to mark a *temporum renovatio* in a way that the years either side of 200 simply do not. But much more importantly, since this is a work based on archaeology and not text, AD 200 was chosen because it lies at the threshold of a period of major change in the archaeological record, one commencing well before any 'third-century crisis' and marking the end of an archaeological period stretching from at least the first century BC, with AD 200 marking (in round numbers) the transition to a period with important differences from what went before. AD 500 essentially marks the end of this archaeological period, not only with the loss of most of the Roman political, economic and cultural superstructure but also with the putting in place of important changes in the basic settlement forms, social and economic formations, and thus the nature of the archaeological record. So it will be a central argument of this book that the period AD 200–500 is in certain significant senses an archaeological 'period' with its own internal patterns that are in important respects (though not all respects, of course) different from what came before and after. This argument will be considered in much more detail in the Epilogue, Chapter 10, once all the evidence that forms the core of this book has been laid out. It is thus a period which, because it is defined by the archaeological record, does not accord well with the conventional historically derived periodisation, allowing us to re-evaluate perceptions of late antiquity in the West. This is largely why the term 'late Roman' has been preferred since the three centuries here do not encompass the whole of what is normally thought of as 'late antiquity', but instead are the period when the West either was still part of the Roman Empire or was still very strongly influenced by its continuing presence, politically, socially, culturally and economically.

Having laid out the geographical and chronological fields of this book, we now need to turn to the methodological and theoretical approaches that will inform the work. Since the area and period to be studied have a considerable chronological and geographical extent and saw the lives and deaths of millions of people, the archaeological record thus created exhibits enormous variability. In order to avoid the Scylla of overgeneralisation where the macrolevel of the big picture risks obscuring multiple variations and realities, and the Charybdis of overspecificity where concentration on the microlevel of those same variations and realities risks obscuring how they may interrelate at a macrolevel, the big picture, I propose to employ a number of exegetic categories that allow for variation but also hold those variations in relation to larger-scale analyses that articulate the particular with the general. The categories are as follows: periodisation, regionality, integration/disintegration, identity and materiality. These have been chosen as they respond to recurring and important aspects of the archaeological record.

Periodisation

This aspect relates to how the period defined above in an essentially descriptive way may be used more dynamically to structure and explain the processes observable over the three centuries concerned. As was stated above, it is a contention of this book that the period from the late second/early third centuries to the late fifth/early sixth centuries is a time span which has a logic that makes it, to a significant extent, internally coherent and thus distinct from what went before and came after. It will be argued that it is a period where the archaeology shows episodes of relatively rapid change at beginning and end framing a time of relative stability. The evidence and justification for this position will be presented in the Prologue and Epilogue chapters, Chapters 1 and 10. But the idea of a period of some three centuries within a longer span evokes the ideas of Fernand Braudel (1972) and the *Annales* school in history and archaeology (Braudel 1972; cf. Bintliff 1991), especially since this book will have a certain amount to say about the Mediterranean. Archaeologists have tended to favour some of the concepts and analyses of Braudel's approaches, since archaeology is much better adapted to recognition of more drawn-out change in the *moyenne durée*, the medium term measured in centuries, than to that of the rapid happenings of *histoire événementielle*; to recognition of the cumulative processes of the collective than to the actions and motives of the individual. But these ideas need to be used more than descriptively. This book will draw on the *Annales* tradition by, in particular, using its insights in trying to relate the period which is its central concern and may be classed as partaking of the character of the *moyenne durée* to the longer term and the shorter term. The longer term will concern itself with fundamental constraints, principally agricultural resources, systems and productivity, along with features such as geography and communications, which time and again return to condition what humans can achieve in this pre-industrial area (see especially Chapters 5 and 6). The shorter term will be the preserve of *histoire événementielle* and the *conjonctures* this produced and which fed through into alterations in the *mentalités* conditioning human actions in the more medium term. This is the area where political, military or other events altered people's perceptions of the state of the world and how to react to it, or where short-term cultural events fed through into overall cultural formations over a more extended time span. The changes at the opening and closing of our period here can be seen as *conjonctures*, where relatively rapid and short-term changes impacted strongly upon *mentalités*, resulting in and represented by defining changes in the archaeological record.

Finally, a Braudel-style approach makes it incumbent upon the writer to explain how a period of the *moyenne durée*, such as the one studied here, articulates with the preceding and succeeding periods within the structures and rhythms of the *longue durée*. Thus the *conjonctures* act upon and modify existing structures so as to create new ones, linking the period that is our focus here to longer-term developments, and contributing to these developments rather than being partitioned off from what went before and what came after.

How these *conjonctures* impacted on existing patterns and how this fed through into modifications in the creation of the archaeological record take us into a methodological area where Braudelian analyses have long been criticised for lack of clarity, with the articulation between *histoire événementielle* and the associated *conjonctures*, on the one hand, and their interaction with the *longue durée* and existing structures of the *moyenne durée*, on the other hand, not being fully worked through and characterised. In large measure, this can now be analysed through the application of some of the theories put forward by Anthony Giddens (1986 in particular) relating to the reflexive dialogue between 'structure' and 'agency'. Again this approach is one that archaeologists find fruitful because of the ways in which it responds to the nature of their evidence and the timescales at which it operates. This book opens and closes with two periods when the existing structures were subject to a great deal of 'feedback' from those agents that operated within them, resulting in profound modifications to those structures over a relatively short period of time (of the order of inside of a century in each case, fast in terms of archaeological change). These changes operated not only at the level of 'structures' in their role as conceptions of social or cultural order, but also at the level of the physical structures from which people/agents learnt their roles and within which they carried on their lives. Major changes in these structures, both as organising concepts and lived environment, characterise both the thresholds at the beginning and the end of the period discussed here. Ideas such as 'lived environment' and its role in constituting the individual and the group and their praxis recall the *habitus* of a Bourdieu-style analysis (Bourdieu 1977, 1984), a concept that will be invoked in discussions of major aspects of the built environment such as towns and villas and their roles in constituting the individual and transmitting structures of thought and praxis, but that also clearly relates to other aspects of the generation and internalisation of elite behaviour in particular and is displayed here in the correlates of elite culture and 'taste' (Bourdieu 1984), a major exegetic category for this book. But as is also a major axis of discussion here, these forms and their expressions change markedly in this period, so the causative factors (e.g. Christianity, militarisation) which modified the behaviours of individuals and groups and fed back into and changed their existing structures also need to be identified and their impacts characterised.

Regionality

Given the large geographical area covered here and the fact that it encompassed a wide range of climatic zones, landforms, natural resources and communication patterns, it is only to be expected that there would be a range of regions identifiable. At this physiographic level, we are dealing with the factors of the *longue durée* such as climate and resources that conditioned the patterns of human activity since the last retreat of the ice. As we shall see, particularly in Chapter 5 and to an extent in Chapter 6, these factors continued to shape certain aspects of human activity right through the period under consideration here. Overlaid onto this was a whole array of human regionalities conditioned by aspects such as ethnicity, language, and social and political structures operating in the *moyenne durée* and then acted upon by shorter-term events, in particular the processes of the incorporation of different regions into the Roman Empire and their response (especially those of their elites) to the threats and opportunities thus opened up to them. At one level, regions will be used here in an essentially descriptive fashion, identifying areas where the archaeology appears to have a degree of coherence, particularly if that coherence sets the area apart from its neighbours. It will also become clear that there are a number of regions that recur with some frequency in the chapters that follow (for instance, the Paris Basin, the south-west of Gaul, the south-east of Gaul, Catalonia, the northern Meseta, the Guadalquivir valley), regions defined not only by a coherence in the past but also by the quantity and quality of archaeological work in the present. But over and above these largely descriptive and pragmatic uses of the idea of the region, there are some more dynamic aspects of the concept. It will be argued that though the Roman Empire was always an empire of regions (and indeed of smaller subdivisions), regions become more visible and important from the later third century on than they had been in the first and second centuries (a trend perhaps most pronounced in Gaul, but perfectly visible in Iberia and Britain also). At one level this is visible in the archaeology of the regional elites, which becomes more differentiated, partly as a result of reactions to the events of the mid to later third century (e.g. northern Gaul), partly as a result, it will be argued, of the degree of relationship with the imperial court (e.g. south-western Gaul, the northern Meseta), and partly because of geographical factors such as the influence of the Mediterranean seaways (south-eastern Gaul, Catalonia) or the geography of the Iberian peninsula. So these regions are not merely descriptive, nor simply the ones that are most archaeologically visible; in the fourth century they were the ones that were becoming increasingly differentiated from their neighbours. This has important repercussions into the fifth century as the overarching political, military and fiscal structures of the Western Empire disintegrated, leaving the various regions to follow different trajectories fashioned by a combination of their fourth-century histories, short-term events through the fifth century and continuing cultural developments over that period with which the various regions interacted in different ways. So regions are not just descriptive conveniences; their inhabitants are central to driving the processes of change visible in the archaeology.

Integration and dis-integration

Leading on from the importance of regions is the complex of ways in which these regions were integrated into the larger system that was the Roman Empire through the third and fourth centuries and the ways in which that system promoted, consciously or unconsciously, the various forms of integration we can trace in the archaeology. Equally, with the collapse of the central political, military and fiscal formations of the Western Empire in the course of the fifth century, how did this dis-integration at the level of the empire itself have knock-on effects leading to other forms of dis-integration down the spatial and political hierarchies? Integration and dis-integration are not only synchronic measures of the ways in which societies were structured and the levels at which they operated, but they are also diachronic descriptors of processes that vitally affected the changing levels of complexity at which those societies could operate. These levels in their turn were major influences on the formation and patterning of the archaeological record, and thus on our interrogation of that record. For the late Roman West, and operating in the direction of integration, there was for two-thirds of the period under consideration the fact that the area formed part of the Roman Empire. The nature of Roman imperialism was such that it promoted, sometimes consciously but often unconsciously, mechanisms of integration. Consciously, of course, the late Roman state strongly insisted on political and military integration, above all through loyalty to the emperor and to legitimating ideologies such as worship of the divinely sanctioned imperial person, worship of the imperial family past and present, and worship of other religious manifestations such as Roma or the imperial *numen*, along with appeals to a sanctified past. In the period considered here, there was, of course, the transition to Christianity as the sole imperially approved and supported religion, which was eventually through its claim to unique revelation to be even more insistently integrative than the manifold traditional religions. There were also ideologies of superiority in relation to peoples not so favoured as to be subjects of the emperor, and thus of the desirability and rightness of the Roman order of things. One of the things that distinguished Roman from barbarian was that the inhabitants of the empire lived in a state governed by law and laws, which (however imperfectly in practice) ordered the relations between humans and between humans and the emperor.

The integrity of the imperial territories, their defence against external threat and internal unrest, was ensured by the army, which throughout the imperial period had been a standing army, its costs underwritten by the state (the taxpayer) and commanded by and loyal to the emperor, who, for all the rhetoric about the divinity of his person and office, was ultimately a military dictator. The presence of military personnel, not only along the frontiers but often deep into the interior, was a feature of the way that the empire of the fourth century operated to maintain its existence. These troops were commanded by an elaborate military hierarchy depending ultimately on the emperor, and they were perhaps the single largest and most distinctive occupational group in the empire, a group which was bound together by an organisational common identity (see Chapter 2). To ensure the continuance of the army and the loyalty of the troops, the late Roman state had inherited and built on another powerful integrative system – the fiscal complex of revenue and expenditure, largely geared to supporting the army, upholding the emperor and paying for the bureaucracy that administered both. This system brought in its train important integrative mechanisms for the wider economy, as will be outlined in Chapter 6. But it will be argued, starting in Chapter 2 and again in Chapters 8 and 9, that the military had an important effect on elite culture. A contention of this book will be that as time went on the elites of the empire increasingly chose to represent themselves in ways derived from military power and the vocabulary of its representation. The elites increasingly became militarised, both in how they operated and in what was expected of them, and also in how they conceived of and expressed their status. This can be clearly seen from the late third and through the fourth century in northern Gaul (and occasionally and to a lesser extent elsewhere), and from the beginning of the fifth century this spread south of the Loire as the combination of increasing military instability and the increasing presence of 'barbarian' peoples, whose elites were essentially warrior elites, made military prowess and performance more and more important. By the end of our period, the vocabulary of military ideology and self-representation is pretty much universal in the settlements, burials and material culture of what had been the Roman West.

Alongside this increasingly important military rhetoric of power was another integrative nexus which derived clearly from existing 'civilian' assumptions about elite status and self-representation. As has been extensively demonstrated, the expansion of Roman military and political control had been succeeded from the end of the first century BC by the creation and diffusion of a set of cultural norms about what it meant to be a citizen of the Roman Empire, and in particular how the myriad local aristocracies of the empire could redefine their status in terms of what they perceived as desirable, Roman-style behavioural norms. This led to the considerable degree of cultural integration in the first and second centuries AD, familiar to the archaeologist through non-military settlement types such as cities and villas, building types both public and private, cultural practices such as religious observance or the use of inscriptions, or material culture such as dress and self-(re)presentation. The forms of cultural expression taken by regional and other elites will be central to the arguments of Chapters 3 and 5 for the fourth century and Chapters 8 and 9 for what came after. Such phenomena, of course, not only expressed the identity claimed by their user but also helped shape the next generation through its being schooled in the *habitus* produced by them. These cultural manifestations are also well known to vary significantly in different regions. This demonstrates an important point about the use of the term 'integration': it is most emphatically not a synonym for 'homogenisation', something the late Roman state could not have enforced, even if it had wished to – an idea that in fact probably never entered anyone's head.

Let us turn now to dis-integration. The reverse of this coin of integration, particularly evident for the fourth century, is the dis-integration during the fifth century (the term 'dis-integration' here being analogous to but preferred to Wickham's [2005] 'involution'). This dis-integration first and most evidently affected the central organs of the Western Empire with the progressive enfeeblement of the imperial office itself, both reflected in and accelerated by the collapse of the army and military power of the Western Empire. This had been provoked and was promoted by the loss of imperial territory (and thus manpower and tax revenues) to various incoming 'barbarian' peoples, who progressively seized more imperial territory, ultimately destroying first of all the Romans' ability to recruit and support forces loyal to the emperor and then the office of Western emperor itself in 476. Economically, the knock-on effects of this could be significant, with marked downturns in both the volume and range of the movement of goods and thus of commercial activity as a result of the dis-integration of the economic structures that had been provided by the state, but, as we shall see (Chapters 8 and 9), this could vary greatly and perhaps surprisingly by region. Culturally, the arrival and increasing dominance of these peoples posed problems both for the existing Roman provincial elites and for the new peoples themselves. To judge by the archaeological evidence, the material cultures of the Germanic peoples seem to have been less fully formed and distinctive than might be thought from the relatively monolithic and homogeneous impression given by (Roman) writers when referring to 'Franks', 'Visigoths', 'Vandals' or whomever. In turn, these peoples found themselves in contact with established hierarchies and elite practices, which clearly affected the choices they made about their self-representation. So, on the one hand, there were modifications to Roman provincial elite practice as the old imperial models progressively became impotent and new rulers established themselves, and, on the other hand, the incoming peoples had to adapt themselves to the populations and practices they found already in place. Since Germanic elite male culture seems to have been based very much on warrior status and martial prowess, this fed into the militarisation of some Roman elites that was, as noted above, already under way and encouraged it among elites that had until then held to the traditional civil rhetoric of status display. It also meant that 'Germanic' martial material culture acquired great significance as a mode of self-representation among peoples and elites who were not themselves 'German'. This last – and the whole concept of 'German-ness' – brings us onto the territory, of course, of the various discourses about 'identity', in both the general arena of postmodern debates over the construction of identities and the more specific debates arising from the more general ones concerned with the construction of 'barbarian' or 'Germanic' identities in the late- and post-Roman world and what the statements of ethnic identity and affiliation made, above all in burial, meant at the time.

Another feature of the collapse of imperial power and the substitution of the power of the new Germanic political entities, 'kingdoms', was a shift in the nature and expression of power. Under the imperial system, power had ultimately been 'public', in that the use of military or other force was supposedly restricted to and sanctioned by the organs of the imperial system. This is not, of course, to deny that there was a great deal of 'private' power and violence wielded by landowners and others, but that coexisted with and was subordinate to the 'public' power of the state. Both the army and the other sinews of war, such as taxation, pay and supply, were at the disposal of the emperor, and indeed emperors were very suspicious of any too great use of 'private' power, particularly if it might threaten imperial control. Brigandage, riot or revolt (as defined, of course, by the imperial power) tended to attract retribution and suppression. Archaeologically, it is noticeable, for instance, how few 'private' fortifications – that is, fortifications other than at military or urban sites – there were. But in the fifth century, with the collapse of the state, we see increasingly the 'privatisation' of power, through the transfer of military force to warlords of various sorts, some of them nominally loyal to the emperor or the imperial system, some of them Germanic rulers, and some operating what to all intents and purposes were private armies, protection rackets or both. Not only was the small scale of many of these operations another measure of dis-integration, but that dis-integration also shows increasingly in the archaeology of fortifications and burial, where expressions of a military or warrior ethos had taken over from the old, civilian expressions of power that had characterised the elites of the Roman Empire, whose involvement in public military power was not central to their self-definition – and self-representation. Their identity and its projection had now come to depend on other considerations.

Identity

Identity has been a 'hot topic' in archaeology over the last twenty years or so, arguably nowhere more so than in the field of what the ethnic identities ascribed to various 'barbarian' or 'Germanic' groups who entered the territories of the Roman Empire in the fourth and fifth centuries meant (to barbarians or to Romans), how they were constructed and how the material record (particularly objects but also structures) may or may not represent these 'non-Roman' identities. But equally within and across the populations of the empire, there was a huge range of possible identities to be expressed, be it by gender, age or status; by occupation or occupational group (e.g. the army); by 'ethnic' identity within the empire ('Spaniard',

'Syrian'); or by religious affiliation. As the work of the last couple of decades has shown, any individual was the intersection of a number of different identities, each of which would assume greater or less emphasis depending on the circumstances within which he or she was interacting with others ('situational' identity). Moreover, with the exception of certainly genetically conditioned features such as gender (by and large, some rare syndromes excepted, though gender is also socially constructed), appearance (malleable to an extent), and physical and mental abilities or disabilities (compensatable up to a point), identities were also fluid and could be (re-)constructed. Previous identities could be modified or suppressed and new ones created or assumed, though this might well require negotiation with others since identity is not only self-created ('emic') but also externally ascribed ('etic'). One of the most familiar forms of the assumption of new identities in late antiquity illustrates this very well: the conversion of an individual to Christianity, a combination of internal ('emic') re-forming and external ('etic') acceptance by the Church. The nature and processes of transmission or acquisition of 'barbarian' identity have been much contested in modern scholarship (and probably at the time also), and will be more fully laid out and discussed in Chapter 8. What concerns us more here, therefore, is to establish that 'identity' was and is a central concern of the way human beings imagine themselves and structure their relationships with other human beings. In order to do this, they habitually adopt visual (sometimes also aural or olfactory – more rarely tactile or gustatory) markers of the identity/ies to which they wish to lay claim. The effects of this in the creation and patterning of the archaeological record are enormous, encompassing major classes of archaeological evidence such as the plans and uses of settlements and buildings, the types and uses of objects (material culture), the use of natural environments and products (e.g. diet), and the statements made through funerary deposits about the identities claimed for the deceased, and these effects will be met with time and again through this book, though perhaps most evidently in Chapters 2, 3, 4 and 7.

Materiality

All the variables discussed above, chronology, regionality, integration/disintegration (political, economic, cultural) and identity, fed through into the creation of the archaeological record and the patterning of its materiality. The archaeology encompasses settlement types and functions, building types and functions, material culture (objects), burials and other funerary evidence, and palaeo-environmental evidence (seeds, pollen, animal bones, sediments and much more). These are very unevenly distributed by type and geography in the modern fieldwork and literature. Sometimes this is a reflection of formation processes in the past – for instance, where a particular type of structure, object or burial rite was or was not used; sometimes it is a reflection of preservation and recovery – for instance, the survival of pottery over textiles or, until recently, the preferential recovery of masonry over timber structures; sometimes it is a reflection of modern research or political and cultural agendas – for instance, the importance accorded to Christian sites and material; and sometimes it is a reflection of the date of development of techniques and thus their integration into major discourses – for instance, faunal or sedimentological analyses, which have still to be accorded their proper worth. All of these biases will influence the contents of this book, and wherever I am conscious of them (and there will be blind spots) I will try to flag up them and their consequences.

Biases and lacunae

Other biases simply reflect my personal knowledge and abilities. For instance, I am much more at home (in descending order of [in]competence) in French; Spanish (Castilian); other Iberian languages such as Portuguese, Catalan or Galician (but emphatically not Basque); and Italian than I am in German. My own fieldwork experience has also coloured what I know about. Apart from Roman Britain, my main fieldwork projects have been in the south-west of France (late Roman Novempopulana), and this may show; fortunately, it is a rather crucial area in several important respects for the period and questions covered in this book. I have tried by assiduous use of the bibliographies of books and articles to widen my research knowledge, but there will remain lacunae some of which are real, and some of which are an artefact of my ignorance. But equally it has become clear to me that there are regions and areas of the Roman West where the databases for types of archaeological sites or materials are simply more extensive and better studied than for other areas. Because of this, time and again I come back to regions such as the north and centre of Iberia, south-western Gaul, south-eastern Gaul, northern Gaul, and the Moselle and central Rhineland (and, be it added, Britain, which actually has some of the best evidence in the entire West). It is also worth pointing out that because this is a book operating over a wide area and a considerable time span, it has necessarily to take a fairly broad-brush approach. On the one hand, this can mean that there is not room to consider evidence at what one might term the 'micro level' – for instance, there is little about small areas, what the French would call *pays*, which, of course, to most of the people most of the time were the scale of existence that concerned them. Instead, what this book will try to do is identify and discuss the larger frameworks conditioning life and death in such *pays*. Nor can there be detailed discussions – for instance, typological or palynological; the principal arguments from these have to be recycled from more detailed publications. On the other hand, because for some classes of evidence (for instance, churches and villas) there can be so much evidence that even to try to comprehend it all would be impractical, I have adopted the approach of using key sites or areas that are good examples of the type in which to ground more general discussion. It is hoped that this has the merit of showing how certain classes of evidence are constructed and function in reality rather than in the abstraction of a catalogue approach that inevitably results in a series of unconnected bits and pieces.

So there will inevitably be lacunae in what follows. This will sometimes be because of the uneven incidence of the evidence, but all too often it will be because of weaknesses in my knowledge of the literature. If I have ignored key sites or important publications, this should be taken as a sin of omission arising from my ignorance; it should not be taken as a sin of commission, my passing judgement on the work of other scholars by passing over it in silence. This book is a first attempt at synthesising a huge amount of data in a number of modern languages and from within a whole range of exegetic frameworks that take a large number of theoretical perspectives. If on occasion it falls down on the job, well, that is unavoidable. I just hope that having such a book rather than not having it will make its faults seem venial rather than mortal, and if colleagues wish to point me towards what I have missed and where I might improve on what is in here, well, maybe I could think of an updated and improved edition, or else I could take up some of these ideas, as well as develop others I have not had the space to consider here, in subsequent publications on the hugely complex and endlessly fascinating archaeology of the area and period that is the Roman West AD 200–500.

1 | Prologue: the third-century crisis

The imperial crisis of the third century

On 11 September in (probably) 260, Marcus Simplicius Genialis, acting in the stead of the governor of the province of Raetia, and along with his army, dedicated an altar to the goddess Victory and erected it in the provincial capital Augsburg, where it was rediscovered in 1992. The inscription on the altar commemorated a victory won by Genialis, commanding the army of Raetia with supporting troops from Germany and a provincial militia, in which they defeated a war band of Semnones/Iuthungi who had penetrated into Italy and were returning to their homelands north of the Danube with 'many thousand' Italian captives, who were freed as their captors were slaughtered in great numbers (Schallmayer 1995). This monument takes us straight into some of the defining features of the third-century crisis of the Roman Empire as it was seen at the time and has been seen since by modern historians. Most obviously, there is the external military crisis exemplified by the existence of hostile peoples with sufficient manpower to undertake substantial offensive action against the empire, and their ability to penetrate the frontier defences on the upper Danube, cross the Alps and pillage unopposed in northern Italy, carrying away 'thousands' of Roman citizens and probably also much portable loot. Less obviously, there is the internal military and political crisis signalled by the emperor, whose name Genialis records as consul for the year: Postumus. Postumus was the first of a series of local emperors who ruled most of the area that is the concern of this book between 260 and 274, rulers who had been proclaimed by local military and civil elites to try to bring order to an increasingly serious military situation. Indeed, the Augsburg inscription is evidence that, at least temporarily, Postumus ruled in Raetia as well as Gaul, Germany, Spain and Britain. The Augsburg altar therefore encapsulates two of the main aspects of what has been seen both by commentators at the time and by modern scholarship as the 'third-century crisis' of the Roman Empire: external threats to military security and internal political instability. To these, modern scholarship has normally added financial and economic turbulence. The purpose of this chapter is to look at the ways in which this perception of there being a crisis in the mid to later third century has influenced the way we have constructed our master narratives for the period between the Antonines (late second century) and the Tetrarchy (late third century), how these have constrained our view of events in the West, and whether other approaches are possible, especially if we concentrate on the archaeological evidence without its being required to fit into a predetermined historical account of events and their causes.

Let us start by examining the traditional markers of the third-century crisis: external military threat, internal dynastic instability and financial turbulence. First of all, the principal cause of this instability, especially from the middle of the third century on, was the growing external threat and the increasing tempo of invasions across the frontiers, culminating in the 250s, 260s and 270s when in the East the renascent Persian (Sassanian) Empire undertook regular and damaging invasions into Roman territory, and in Europe there was a chronic succession of incursions by peoples largely of Germanic stock across both the Danube and the Rhine (for description and analysis of the military problems of the empire, see Luttwak 1976: 130–54). Essentially, this meant that for the first time in centuries the Roman army no longer had the upper hand in the choosing of when and where it would take the offensive; increasingly it was on the defensive and responding to events. These events were coming to happen simultaneously on different frontiers far removed from each other, requiring the division of the emperor's attention and of his armies, rather than the concentrated application of force against a single chosen foe that had characterised the Roman warfare of the first and second centuries AD. In that earlier period also, emperors such as Trajan or Marcus Aurelius when mounting major campaigns could afford to assemble huge expeditionary armies by withdrawing large numbers of troops from other provinces. In the third century this was seldom possible, since to strip one area of the frontiers to bolster another was to invite invasion of the weakened province. Thus emperors had to use detachments of units and provincial armies, known as 'vexillations' after the *vexillum* or military standard at their head, meaning that the forces they assembled were seldom of the scale of a century earlier. This in its turn compromised the Romans' ability to take the initiative or to mount campaigns that eliminated a threat rather than just repelling it for the time being.

Since, secondly, these invasions and incursions impacted upon different army groups and provincial populations when the existing 'legitimate' or 'central' emperor was coping with a crisis at the other end of the empire, the response was often the proclamation by the army and provincial elites of a new emperor to try to safeguard regional interests. So one of the other defining features of narratives of the third century is the breakdown in the systems of orderly imperial succession and a consequent proliferation of pretenders to the purple, the more successful of whom are now viewed as 'legitimate', and the less successful as 'usurpers' ('Why doth treason never prosper? Because if it prosper none dare call it treason'). Previously, legitimacy of succession had been ensured by a combination of dynastic structure, military support and senatorial acquiescence, and on those occasions where military support was used to impose a new emperor, senatorial approval was sought and the new ruler retrospectively inserted into the imperial dynasty. But after the assassination of Severus Alexander in 235, these three criteria progressively became out of step. Emperors tried to designate their successors and senatorial recognition remained a strategy for claiming legitimacy, but increasingly it was the regional armies that made and unmade emperors at will, promoting new claimants to the throne; these claimants were, often enough, senior military commanders under the emperor they dispatched so as to take his place. This chronic instability also meant the individual emperors rarely reigned long enough for them either to see a son grow to manhood or to train up a successor, let alone establish a dynasty with a recognised succession. Thus arose a toxic combination of external pressure and internal faction, with the Roman armies spending time and manpower they could ill afford on fighting each other as much as the invaders. As emperors increasingly became warlords (and vice versa), their absolute priority was the defence of their own position and that of the empire, and what was effective in this replaced constitutional nicety, with the senate increasingly displaced from its former positions of military and provincial command. In these ways the military and political instabilities fed off each other, and the provinces of the empire suffered at the hands of barbarian invaders and passing Roman armies. Central and defining features of the Roman system had become dysfunctional, and were 'in crisis'.

Rather different is the third of these markers, the evidence for fiscal and financial crisis during the third century, a nexus of evidence that has then been assimilated to the imperial crisis. In part it was caused by the escalating costs of empire, in particular paying the army as its pay rates escalated under Septimius Severus (193–211) and Caracalla (211–18) without there being any matching increase in the state's structural resources with which to pay, the result being increased exactions and the debasement of the coinage (cf. Duncan-Jones 1994: 15–16). The debasement of the silver coinage had begun back in the second century but accelerated considerably under Commodus (180–92), Severus and Caracalla, leading to more and more coins of lower and lower value being struck. Among other things, this resulted in a situation where increasing quantities of money of declining value chased a probably stable quantity of goods – in the modern world, the classic conditions for inflation and its attendant economic instability. In addition, the minting of the gold coinage, the 'reserve currency' of the Roman state, became more and more sporadic and the coins more variable in weight and sometimes the fineness of the gold (for discussion and graphs for gold and silver, see Burnett 1987: Ch. 6). Linked both with this and with the military crisis was the evidence for spates of coin hoarding, which could be seen either as evidence for periods of external threat or as evidence for the financial instability, with the deposition of quantities of high-value and, more especially, low-value coin (cf. Haupt 2001 – see below for a more detailed discussion). In the traditional view, another pointer to economic dislocation was the evidence for the decline in the long-distance supply and trade routes from the Mediterranean out to the armies on the frontier and for the disappearance of major industries such as the samian pottery producers of central and eastern Gaul (cf. King 1981). Taken together, these crises in military effectiveness, imperial legitimacy, and financial, fiscal and economic coherence made up the 'third-century crisis' as described in the texts, ancient or modern.

In both the ancient and the modern literature, the 'crisis' has been implicitly likened to a medical crisis, a point at which the patient would either succumb to or recover from a disease (cf. Reece 1981); this was a crisis from which, as the ancient sources acknowledged, the empire at times seemed unlikely to pull through but from which it did eventually recover, though the patient would never be the same as before. Harsh medicine was administered by a succession of Balkan generalissimo emperors in the latter part of the century, with the empire recuperating through the relatively long, stable reigns of Diocletian and Maximian in the Tetrarchy of 285–305 and, after a period of renewed civil war, the long reign of Constantine I (306–37, sole emperor from 324), who re-established the dynastic principle, his family prolonging the dynasty to 363. Nevertheless, to this day, the third century continues to be seen as a watershed dividing the narrative of continuing expansion, prosperity and stability that characterises the 'High Empire' or 'Principate' of the first and second centuries from the reverse of all these in the decline and fall of the 'Late Empire' or 'Dominate Empire'. In very large measure this responds to the perceptions of people writing at the time or very shortly afterwards; writers of the second half of the third and the early fourth centuries saw the events of the third century as a crisis, from which the empire emerged profoundly changed (for an analysis of the ancient sources and the picture they present, see Witschel 1999: Ch. 2, Sect. 1). Until recently, modern writers on the period, educated in and often dependent on these ancient literary sources, have tended to follow the line peddled by the ancients of the third century of a catastrophe, not just in the general modern sense of a calamity, but in the more specialised, original meaning of the word as an overturning, a period in which the old forms and certainties were dissolved and replaced by new, less satisfactory ones.

The problem of such an approach is, first, that this tends to elide cause and effect by reducing both the processes and the reasons for change simply to the events of that half-century or so, and in particular to warfare, be it invasion from beyond the frontiers or internal wars of imperial succession. Second, it thus tends to telescope what will be argued throughout this book to have been longer-term processes commencing before the 'crisis' and continuing after it. The 'third-century crisis' all too often has acted as a *deus ex machina*, apparently explaining all change, but in fact absolving writers from the need to tackle the much more laborious task of explaining what was actually going on. Furthermore, the traditional view of the third century has left modern historiography struggling with an unacknowledged problem: the third century all too often acts as a 'firewall' or a 'cut-out' between those histories and historians that concern themselves with the High Empire, on the one hand, and those whose concerns lie in the Late Empire or late antiquity, on the other hand. Those working on the High Empire can and often did and do close their studies at the beginning or end of the Severan dynasty (193–235), absolved from venturing any further; those dealing with the Late Empire or late antiquity start with Diocletian and the Tetrarchy (284–305) or with Constantine I (306–37), as if it were with *tabula rasa*, and are thus permitted largely to ignore the antecedents of their period of study. It is invidious to name names, but just to substantiate the proposition, one may point to two recent (and excellent) English-language surveys of earlier and later Roman history, Martin Goodman's *The Roman World 44 BC—AD 180* of 1987 and Stephen Mitchell's *A History of the Later Roman Empire AD 284-641* of 2007. This attitude is, though, changing, for instance, with publications on the third century as a whole by workers such as Christol (1997) in French, Witschel (2004) in German or Potter (2004) in English. And there were always exceptions. Volume XII of the Second Edition of *The Cambridge Ancient History* runs from 193 to 337 (Bowman, Cameron, Garnsey 2005): its predecessor ran from 193 to 324. But even for these works it can be argued that they isolate the third century, and it thus still marks a caesura in imperial history. It is not this book's remit to try to undo the consequences of this convention for the writing of Roman history; it is necessary, though, to point out the existence of this convention and the way in which it has fragmented the historical endeavour.

It is, though, this book's remit to consider the effects of this historical practice on the way in which the archaeology of the third century in the West has been studied and to try to correct any deformations it may have introduced. The historiographic traditions concerning the 'third-century crisis' have influenced the ways in which the archaeology of the third century has been studied, especially through the notion of 'crisis' as the dominant discourse and with the middle and latter part of the century being the time of most important change. The historiography of modern treatment of the period of 'crisis' is as yet weakly developed (for a digest of some of this literature, see Witschel 1999: Chs. 1 and 2, Sect. 1), but time and again in the following chapters we shall meet instances of where changes in the archaeology are attributed to the 'crisis' or the 'invasions', so specific modern authors will not be cited here in what would be an invidious process. But it is a central contention of this book that the threshold of 'accelerated change' (to use the term *beschleunigter Wandel* of Witschel 2004: 252) in the archaeological record lies not in the mid to late third century, but the better part of a hundred years earlier, from the later second century. Therefore, as will be argued in the succeeding chapters, trajectories of change were already established by the time of the crisis and in progress for reasons, it will be proposed, to do with longer-term economic and cultural developments in the West generally. The historically recorded crisis (or, better, crises) will have interacted with and influenced the activities that created the archaeological record, but they will have modified already existing trajectories of change rather than setting them in motion. Indeed, it is certain that some of the changes already under way will have affected the course of events in the mid to later third century and the way in which they are analysed today (for instance. the ways in which developments in urban functions and fabrics or in the coinage and currency are now read through the prism of 'crisis', despite their originating significantly earlier), so our notions of 'crisis' or 'change' need to consider developments over the period as a reflexive rather than unilinear complex of processes.

The third-century crisis in the West

With the standard, historical view of the third century dominant, those working in the developing archaeology of the Western provinces of the Roman Empire naturally enough tended to interpret the third century, particularly the second half of the century, in terms of 'crisis', and sought manifestations of the structural crises of military effectiveness, imperial legitimacy, and financial and economic coherence at the regional or local scale. That external threat and invasion and thus military weakness and also the internal crisis of the imperial succession had their impact on the West was clear. The period of crisis (for a narrative history, see Drinkwater 1987: Ch. 1) was seen as starting with the assassination of Severus Alexander in 235 at Mainz, where he was responding to the first major incursion across the Rhine. In the 250s, 260s and 270s, the literary sources tell of a series of more and more devastating incursions, deep into Gaul and, according to one (not terribly reliable) source, as far as north-eastern Spain (for the literary sources, see Drinkwater 1987: Ch. 2). In addition to the external military reverses, there were internal dislocations. From 260 to 274, Britain, Gaul, the Rhineland and, intermittently and partially, the Iberian peninsula were under the control of the series of emperors based in Gaul, the 'Gallic Empire' mentioned at the outset of this chapter. Their rise to power was a textbook example of how these usurpations occurred. In the late 250s, the Alamanni again menaced the Rhine frontier and the emperor Valerian sent his son Gallienus to hold the line. With the capture of Valerian by the Persians in 259, Gallienus hurriedly left for the East, leaving his young son Saloninus as representative of the dynasty. In this crisis the army and the aristocracy of Gaul needed more than a boy; they murdered Saloninus and proclaimed in his stead Postumus, a commander of proven ability. He reigned for eight years before being deposed in his turn, and after an obscure period of pretenders to the Gallic throne, Victorinus emerged in control, lasting two years before being deposed in favour of the Tetrici, father and son, who in their turn surrendered to the emperor Aurelian, who had entered Gaul with a large army. That the external threat was not effectively countered is suggested by historical accounts of serious crossings of the Rhine under Postumus, who also took the decision to abandon the *Agri Decumates*, the re-entrant of land between the upper courses of the Rhine and Danube conquered nearly two hundred years before. Very probably these reverses led to Postumus's downfall in a military coup. His eventual successor Victorinus may also have gone the same way. The surrender of the Tetrici was unusual in not involving a bloody termination of the usurping regime, above all of its leaders (they suffered no worse than exile). Aurelian's successor Probus is recorded as having had to campaign in Gaul in 278 to restore seventy *civitates* that had been devastated by the Alamanni. Some fifteen years later the Western Augustus Maximian is said to have won a series of crushing victories over the Alamanni and others and imposed terms, but even then the military threat from across the Rhine did not go away. With such a litany of invasion and civil strife, it is not surprising that the intellectual framework for study of the period reflected this, with the notion of crisis unchallenged, and, indeed, study of this crisis was the definitive approach. This became established as the absolute orthodoxy in the modern historiography of France, Germany and Spain. As study of the material evidence for the West in this period developed, it is equally unsurprising that workers should have sought to identify the effects of the crisis in the archaeology. This intellectual framework did, though, given rise to a major methodological problem, particularly in France and Germany; because the invasions were an article of faith, they were given as both the date and cause of changes in the archaeology in the second half of the third century without further consideration of the dating evidence and whether or not the evidence warranted this explanation.

The principal types of evidence that scholars used to identify an archaeological crisis in the mid to late third century were as follows: massive changes to the form and fabric of the major cities along with a decline in the largely urban phenomenon of setting up inscriptions; the (near) disappearance of lesser urban centres; the abandonment of villas; the atrophying of the long-distance trade networks with the Mediterranean and of some of the major industries, particularly ceramics, associated with these networks; and spates of coin hoarding dating to this period. These types of evidence were most readily observable to modern workers in the area of what had been Gaul and Germany, and it was there that this paradigm was developed and elaborated. It was more difficult to observe analogous trends in the Iberian peninsula, but partly because of the textual construct of the 'crisis del impero' and partly because the development of thinking about the archaeology of the third century lagged behind that north of the Pyrenees, the Gaul/Germany model was followed there, and the 'crisis' became embedded in the study and explanation of the period. The most widely recognised archaeological markers of the third-century crisis – changes to major cities, villas and trade – will all be dealt with in much greater detail in the chapters that follow (esp. Chapters 2, 4, 5, 6 and 7), and so will only be briefly characterised here in order to outline the 'traditional' view. There will then be a longer consideration of the evidence for and possible meanings of the episodes of coin hoarding since these are important in themselves and also relate to some of the evidence that will be considered in the following chapter.

In AD 200, the majority of the cities of the West had been sprawling, undefended places, studded with impressive public buildings and monuments, the residences of the nobility and the workshops of the artisans, and surrounded by mausolea and tombs. In the fourth century the cities of northern Gaul consisted of a tiny proportion of their former area, and they were surrounded by thick, high walls apparently safeguarding imperial officials rather than civic councils, walls which reused much of the stonework of the now demolished civic buildings and monuments and the now dismantled mausolea and uprooted tombstones, attesting to the disappearance of civic values and of family continuity, with little or no evidence of the former place of the cities as centres of population and culture, or their former role as centres of manufacture and trade. The causal link between these radical transformations and the barbarian invasions was seen as buttressed by the reference to the emperor Probus having liberated seventy cities from the invaders (*Historia Augusta*, Probus XV.3). At the time these arguments were being formed, the only dating evidence available was the presence of dated inscriptions, which ran down into the first half of the third century, along with some milestones of the Gallic Empire. This again brought the available construction dates for the defensive circuits into the date range of the great invasions of the 260s and 270s, so the view took root that the cities had been ravaged by the invaders and out of the ruins the Romans had constructed these walls as a belated response. Any signs of burning were pressed into service as evidence for the sacking and burning of the city concerned. These views were developed in the later nineteenth and earlier twentieth century, a period at which French workers could well have been predisposed to pass value judgements on the destruction of Gallic civilisation by Germanic barbarians from across the Rhine. Because of the impressive scale of these north Gaulish fortifications, they tended to be taken as the archetype of the late Roman city in the West, to which other cities should conform. And indeed many of the cities of the southern half of Gaul and of regions of Spain, as well as Italy, did acquire late Roman defensive circuits, though not always exactly to the pattern of those in northern Gaul.

Through the third century the practice of setting up inscriptions to invoke the gods, record imperial and civic patronage, and commemorate the dead fell away sharply. This was again seen as an indicator of the loss of traditional values, particularly by generations of workers raised on the primacy of the text and to whom the near disappearance of a whole class of texts central to the study of the provinces was very evident. It also resonated with the evidence from fourth-century imperial legislation inveighing against the unwillingness of the curial class to shoulder the expense and responsibility of administering their cities and providing the traditional benefactions (e.g. Jones 1964: Ch. 19). More recently, the decline in epigraphic commemoration has been reassessed, leading to a less 'catastrophist' view of this process. The setting-up of inscriptions is now appreciated to be a matter of social fashion, with pronounced chronological patterning and regional variation. The patterns of and reasons for the changing 'epigraphic habit', famously characterised by MacMullen (1982) and since refined (e.g. Meyer 1990; Woolf 1998: Ch. 4), have been argued to reflect factors such as anxiety about status, either in periods of transition or among people in socially marginal positions or incomers to a region (e.g. Hope 2001), with statements of position and status serving to establish a claim to respectability for the persons commissioning the inscription and their family. Thus it is argued that Roman citizens would wish to assert that status, especially on tombstones, partly to establish their superior status but also because of the legal consequences in succession law. Alternatively, Woolf (1998: Ch. 4) points to the large numbers of inscriptions from southern Gaul and elsewhere under the High Empire set up by freedmen, the classic social parvenus attempting to buy their way into social structures which otherwise marginalised them. The argument is that from the early third century, as the age of transition had passed and as from AD 212 all freeborn subjects of the empire became citizens, such claims to status and position became less and less problematic and thus less and less worth inscribing (cf. Kulikowski 2004: 33–8), and so some forms of dedicatory inscription and tombstones became otiose. It is also likely that other forms of self-representation became more important to the formerly inscribing classes. So rather than being an index of civic decline, the tailing away of the 'epigraphic habit' probably has far more to do with social transformations and the arenas for making statements about social standing. So the numerical decline in the 'epigraphic habit' cannot be read across into a value judgement of decline in Roman-style urbanism or cultural values. Furthermore, as we shall see in Chapter 4, there was actually a resurgence in inscribing, particularly of tombstones, in the fourth and fifth centuries as Christians took to the practice, again perhaps unwittingly expressing anxieties about the place of the new faith.

The 'small towns' or *agglomérations secondaires*, the secondary religious, residential and commercial roadside centres, particularly common under the High Empire in Gaul and Germany, have also traditionally been considered to have been destroyed or abandoned in the second half of the third century. If one looks at the tables showing duration of occupation produced for recent syntheses (e.g. Bénard *et al.* 1994: 256–60; Petit *et al.* 1994; Rorison 2001: Ch. 5), the great majority of the periods do not continue past the second half of the second century. Time and again, the reason is given as *'invasions germaniques'*, and any occurrence of fire debris is pressed into service as evidence of violent destruction, even in regions well away from the Rhine; it would be invidious to name individual instances of this, but many of the papers in Petit *et al.* (1994) still show the influence of this framework. Given that such settlements under the High Empire seem, in Gaul at least, to have been a more or less ubiquitous phenomenon and to have acted as some sort of level of administrative, economic and social intermediary between the principal cities and the rural population, their postulated disappearance was seen as having longer-term significance for the settlement hierarchies of Gaul over and above the shorter-term event of their abandonment. More recent research and publication has been seriously calling into question whether there was such a widespread, uniform phenomenon with such a simple cause (cf. p. 140), but that this notion should so long have held sway is an index of the way in which the historical narrative profoundly shaped the interpretation and presentation of the archaeological data.

A similar point can be made for villas and other rural settlement types, particularly in the regions near the Rhine. For generations of earlier workers there, the notion of widespread destruction of villas in the second half of the third century at the hands of invading barbarians became an *idée fixe*. A litany of sites in modern-day northern France, Belgium and Germany was held to exhibit evidence of violent destruction, usually by fire, which was then blamed on invaders from across the Rhine (cf. Van Ossel 1992: Tab. 20 – though note that he is emphatically not accepting the traditional causation). The problems with this framework have long been evident. There are seldom precise indications of how much of a villa was consumed by fire, let alone what caused that fire. The dating evidence was all too often assimilated to the narrative of Germanic invasions rather than allowed to speak for itself. We shall review the more recent work on this problem in Chapter 5, but again the point here is the degree to which it influenced much earlier work and contributed to the 'catastrophist' view. Nevertheless, even more recent archaeological work such as that of van Ossel (1992) for northern Gaul generally and of other workers (e.g. papers in Ouzoulias *et al.* 2001) has shown that substantial restructuring of rural settlement patterns between the second century and the fourth did take place in many regions, and a range of explanations for this will need to be factored in in Chapter 5, possibly including violent destruction.

The argument to do with the 'decline' in economic activity and long-distance trade is slightly more complex but essentially similar in the analyses of its causation. In the first and second century there is abundant evidence for the existence of a substantial movement of goods from the Mediterranean regions up to provinces such as Germany and Britain as well as the interior of Gaul. The best direct evidence for this is the presence of large quantities of amphorae on sites in these provinces, particularly of forms such as the Dressel 20 oil-container from southern Spain (Baetica) (e.g. Laubenheimer 1990: 111–34; Laubenheimer and Marlière 2010). Other evidence comes from the pattern of distribution of other ceramics that clearly travelled along with the amphorae (e.g. Greene 1979; Vilvorder in Brulet *et al.* 2010: Ch. 21) as well as the series of inscriptions that relates to the participants in this movement of goods (cf. Middleton 1979). Since the goods in question were largely *garum* (fish sauce), olive oil and wine, this was seen as evidence not just for the creation of a considerable degree of economic integration, but also for the integration of the north-western provinces into a wider nexus of Mediterranean ('Roman') taste. The gradual disappearance of this network in the early third century was seen as another index of the disruptions caused by the insecurities attendant on the Germanic penetrations into the interior of Gaul. Linked with this was the disappearance of the largest, most widespread and most studied ceramic industry in Gaul, *terra sigillata hispánica tardía* or samian (Brulet *et al.* 2010: Chs. 1–7). From the second half of the second century and on into the first half of the third century, the main centres of production of this fine, red-gloss pottery lay in the Rhineland and north-eastern Gaul at major sites such as Rheinzabern (Brulet *et al.* 2010: Chs. 5–7). These centres did not outlast the third century, and, not surprisingly given their location, they were seen as having fallen victim to violent destruction at the hands of invaders. As with the amphorae and related products, this disappearance was held to mark not only an economic but also a cultural dislocation, since *terra sigillata hispánica tardía* had been the most complex and most widespread ceramic industry in both its manufacture and distribution; also its forms and decoration were clearly derived from Mediterranean repertoires. Again, we now understand that the explanation of barbarian destruction is oversimplified (cf. King 1981), as we shall see further in Chapter 7, but it is clear how the older view formed part of the archaeological notion of the 'third-century crisis'. Major cities, lesser towns, villas, manufacture and trade will all be reassessed in later chapters; the point here has been to establish the ways in which the predetermined historical narrative impacted upon study of the archaeology and for so long deformed it significantly. This is not to say that there was never any Germanic invasion, nor that there was never destruction as a consequence of such invasion; again, possible instances of this will be explored in later chapters. It is, though, to say that it is not the only, indeed not the most likely, explanation in most cases, and this 'invasion hypothesis' has often involved doing violence to the dating evidence, thus obscuring longer-drawn-out processes and causes of change.

The arguments outlined above may seem like a classic piece of revisionism, an attempt to argue away a long-held view and to replace it with a radically different interpretation. This is not the purpose of this approach. Instead, it is an attempt to show that all the various strands of evidence which have in the past been twisted into a single thread of argument need to be teased out again and re-examined in terms of their own protocols of study and interpretation. In particular, the various forms of archaeological evidence need to be assessed in their own terms rather than forced to conform to an agenda predetermined from the historical sources. Questions need to be posed about the ways in which archaeological evidence can and cannot be interrogated about historically attested invasions, and alternative explanations of archaeological phenomena need to be considered, working from archaeological principles. If this is done, then, as seen above, the traditional archaeological props to the textual narrative become seriously deficient, and more convincing and more interesting explanations of these archaeological data can be put forward instead. Nevertheless, the textual tradition is unanimous in seeing the mid and later third century as a period of crisis for the empire and in seeing invasions across the frontiers as a defining aspect of this crisis. Moreover, specific dates, invaders and regions are given in which these invasions took place, and this cannot all be put down to a desire to construct a moralising argument. Given that different authors in the 250s, 260s and 270s consistently refer to major invasions across the Rhine, serious enough to lead to the abandonment of imperial territory in the form of the *Agri Decumates*, and that emperors such as Postumus (260–8), Probus (276–82) and, later, Maximian (295–305) are all credited with major campaigns against the Alamanni and other Germanic tribes, there is no reason to doubt serious disruption along the Rhine and into the interior of Gaul. Despite the reservations voiced above, can archaeological evidence for this disruption still be identified, what was the nature of these 'invasions', and what form would evidence for hostile activity take? Can we now indulge in some neo-revisionism and try to reinstate in part the notions of invasion and destruction, but this time based on more reliable archaeological evidence and perhaps not so tied to particular dates?

How might such events be manifested in the archaeology? The Augsburg altar may point the way by showing us what the invaders were after. The altar specifies human booty, presumably destined to slavery or perhaps ransom. We may also reasonably posit portable loot. So are we able to identify such episodes in the archaeology? A possibility is finding Roman loot back east of the Rhine. One such hoard may well be that from Hagenbach in Rheinland-Pfalz (Bernhard *et al.* 1990), where it looks as if a boat laden with booty sank in what was then a branch of the Rhine. Among the booty was a series of inscribed, silver, votive leaves, and analysis of the names on them (Gorrochategui 1993) suggests they may originally have come from sanctuaries in the central French Pyrenees. If so, this again demonstrates the ability of raiding parties to penetrate deep into imperial territory in the absence of any internal Roman forces to interdict their movement. But without this hoard, there would be no indication of trouble in that area of Aquitaine in the later third century. There is certainly a large quantity of Roman material, including precious metal coinage, from east of the Rhine and dated to the third century, but mainly from funerary contexts, so it is difficult to tell whether it arrived as booty or as diplomatic gifts, let alone whether it was buried with the person who originally acquired it (cf. Böhme 1974).

More equivocal, of course, is the evidence from destruction deposits at Roman cities and other sites, because of the range of reasons why timber-framed buildings might catch fire. At the more certain end of the scale for hostile destruction, one may point at an area of the Krefeld-Gellep cemeteries (Pirling 1986: 38–41) which contains what seem to be the bodies of men fallen in battle in the middle of the third century. Another site which does seem to have been destroyed in the mid 270s is that of Speyer in the Rhineland, where a general destruction level has been excavated, revealing quantities of human remains (Bernhard 1994). But there is then a sliding scale of certainty. For instance, the city of Augusta Raurica (Augst) on the upper Rhine was conventionally thought also to have been destroyed in the Alamannic incursions of 259–60 and replaced in the early fourth century by the riverside fort of Kaiseraugst. More recent work (cf. Schwarz 1998) shows instead more than one episode of destruction and gradual militarisation of the area. The earliest major destruction horizon, probably in the later 240s, is attributed to an earthquake, with possibly a subsequent military post under later Kaiseraugst. The next major destruction horizon, associated with human skeletons and military equipment, dates not to the *Alemanneneinfall* of 259–60, but rather to the mid 270s and might well relate to an Alamannic invasion attested to at that date, but equally could possibly relate to the passage of Aurelian's army in 273–4 to subdue the Gallic Empire. Thereafter the high point in the old city, 'Kastelen', was fortified, before being abandoned in favour of the new strong point of Kaiseraugst around 300. This well-studied instance shows how careful archaeologists need to be over dating and even then how difficult it is to ascribe causation with any certainty. A study of the archaeology of Metz in the third century (Dreier 2011) again shows major changes in the fabric of the city with evidence for a fall in the population levels, the destruction of some buildings by fire and the probable fortification of the main amphitheatre by the digging round it of a ditch before the core of the city was defended by the construction of walls towards the end of the third century. Even when all prudence is exercised over the causes of these phenomena, particularly the fires, it does seem likely that there was at least one episode of violent destruction (Dreier 2011: 171). Both Augst and Metz were near the frontiers, so it is perfectly plausible that they should have been attacked in one of the historically attested episodes of barbarian invasion or Roman civil strife. But lying deep into Gaul, another city with good excavated data is Arles (Heijmans 2004: Ch. 2), where on a number of peripheral sites, both to the north of the Rhône in the area of Trinquetaille and to the south of the walls in such areas as the Jardin d'Hiver, large, well-appointed residences with mosaics and marble were burnt down in the early 270s and then not reoccupied or rebuilt. The date range of the material recovered would allow all these events to be contemporaneous, and obviously it is then tempting to attribute them to the invasions of the mid 270s, but in fact it is impossible to be categorical on this point. Episodes of destruction there are, but nothing diagnostic, such as the remains of people who had suffered a violent death, to suggest hostile action rather than accident. Again, the purpose of this brief discussion is not to deny that there were occasions when cities suffered violence at the hands of either Germanic or Roman invasions; it is just to caution against an easy equivalence of fire deposits and their causation by warfare. After all, as has been pointed out (e.g. Witschel 2004: 259–60 and references), instances of fires, sometimes consuming large areas, are well known in the archaeology of the first and second centuries at many Roman cities in the West (including, famously, Rome itself in 64). Without textual reference to invasion or other warfare, armed destruction is hardly ever invoked to explain these instances; instead the vulnerability to fire of cities constructed largely or in important part in timber is regularly deployed. The contrast in the exegetic frameworks is marked.

Coin hoarding

There remains one complex of material that has often been used to 'demonstrate' the reality of the external threat and internal troubles of the West in the mid to later third century and that requires closer attention here; this is the evidence from coin hoards. In the Western provinces, particularly in Gaul, Germany and Britain, there was a steep rise in the quantity of such hoards from the middle of the third century and through the second half of the century (for distribution maps and discussion, see Haupt 2001). It was not just the quantity of hoards that increased steeply but also the number of coins in the hoards, in some cases reaching into the tens of thousands. So in terms of both quantity of hoards and quantity of coins, these decades can be shown to deviate strongly from the 'normal' incidence of hoards. The emperors represented in these hoards were above all those of the 260s and 270s, the emperors of the Gallic Empire of 260–74 (Postumus, Victorinus and the Tetrici) and the corresponding 'central' emperors such as Gallienus (260–8), Claudius II Gothicus (268–70), Aurelian (270–5) and Probus (276–82). These were, of course, the emperors whose reigns spanned the years for which we have the most vivid textual accounts of repeated Germanic incursions into Germany and Gaul, and possibly even Spain. With Blanchet's (1900) publication *Les trésors de monnaies romaines et les invasions germaniques en Gaule*, the link between these spates of hoarding and their causation by the threat or actuality of the historically attested Germanic invasions was made explicit. This hypothesis was followed by many subsequent workers, even to the extent of using the distribution of hoards to trace the invasion routes in a sort of join-the-dots exercise (e.g. Johnson 1976: Figs. 1 and 2). At first sight, this link is very seductive, but subsequent work on the nature of and reasons for hoarding and on the monetary history of the Roman Empire means that we must take a more nuanced view, one not wedded to monocausal explanations. In order to assess the validity of any claim to explain the pattern of coin hoarding in any region at any period, certain basic processes need to be taken into consideration before any interpretation can be more or less plausibly based on the data. Reece (2002: Ch. 3) has laid out basic parameters: it is necessary in particular to look at the processes of hoard assemblage and the processes of hoard non-recovery, for both of these condition the pattern of coins in hoards and that of the hoards themselves that we have today. Once these parameters have been examined and analysed, then hypotheses may be proposed in order to explain the observed patterns of hoards as we have them now.

At the period we are considering, hoards come in various metals and denominations, principally gold (rare) and the progressively debased 'silver', which by the 260s and 270s often had less than 5 per cent silver mixed with a copper-based alloy, the resulting coin often referred to by numismatists as 'billon'. The hoards also sometimes contained components other than coins, such as jewellery. There are also hoards which contained no coins or in which coins were a small component; these are largely of silver plate and other objects and will be considered below. The implicit conventional view is that hoards were put together at short notice (e.g. under threat of invasion) by withdrawing as much coin as was needed or available from the circulating coin pool and depositing it. While this might be a reasonable scenario for hoards containing relatively small numbers of coins, for hoards containing thousands or tens of thousands of coins, it is much more difficult to see how hoarders could have laid hands on that many coins in short order, unless they were themselves professionally involved with large quantities of coin – for instance, as part of the state's fiscal personnel or as money changers and 'bankers'. In fact a number of hoards from both Britain and the Continent have recently been 'excavated' under laboratory conditions and shown to consist of several 'lots' of coin added to the hoard or put into the container in separate events (e.g. Estiot 1996: 61–3). Thus we should no longer assume hoards to be a uniform 'job lot' withdrawn from the circulating coin pool and put together in one go but, rather, possibly the result of a series of decisions, not necessarily all with the same rationale. In this way, a single such hoard may actually comprise a number of smaller hoards of varying dates and assembled over a considerable period of time. A variant of this is that a 'hoard' may consist of a number of containers in close proximity, so that either its assembly or its deposition may have been the result of a number of separate events.

The hoards that we have today are those that were not recovered in antiquity but have been recovered in modern times. This may seem a statement of the obvious, but it has implications. It implies that the hoards we have are part of a larger, unknowable whole and that they have been selected for us by processes of non-recovery that we will have to think about (the Blanchet-style view, of course, was that the owners were killed or fled and so could not recover them). It therefore implies that what we have may be a skewed sample of what was originally deposited at the period we are considering, but also that this period may itself be an abnormal and artificial 'peak', because in other periods hoards may have been more thoroughly recovered. It also means that of the hoards deposited and recovered in antiquity and of the hoards deposited, not recovered and not yet found by us, we cannot speak. Another consequence of the more systematic and detailed examination of hoards is that we can be more confident of the date of minting of the latest coin in the hoard. As we shall see below, hoards retrieved some time ago may have been misdated because small numbers of later coins did not register amid the huge volumes that made up the bulk of the hoard.

Having laid out some considerations about how hoards were assembled in the first place and how they were not recovered in antiquity – that is, 'what' these hoards are – we need to consider possible scenarios for the 'why' – what reasons may we adduce for their assembling, deposition and non-recovery, bearing in mind that these can normally only be hypotheses. The main heads under which we may consider these hypotheses are as follows: the monetary/financial context, the political context, the religious context and the military context. The monetary/financial context argues essentially that hoards were deposited because the coins in them were either (1) worth saving, or (2) not worth throwing away. For (1), as noted above, the first half of the third century saw a progressive, relatively rapid debasement of the silver coinage from somewhat under 50% silver to under 10%, and less by 260. Under such circumstances with the coinage visibly depreciating, Gresham's law ('bad money drives out good') comes into effect; there is good evidence that some hoards of the first half of the third century were assembled out of older coinage with a higher silver content than at the time of the assembling (sometimes one or two later, poorer coins in the hoard give this away). For (2), we come on to the 'peak' of the 260s and 270s with hoards comprising thousands or tens of thousands of coins, but mostly of low intrinsic value and very probably low face value also. These are the 'radiate' and 'barbarous radiate' issues, so-called either because the official issues portrayed the emperor's head with a crown of solar rays ('radiates'), or because they ('barbarous radiates') were imitations of the official, radiate issues (they are also called, particularly by workers on the Continent, *antoniniani*). These official issues and their imitations were overwhelmingly of the emperors of the 260s to early 270s, and they contained very little silver and were often crudely engraved and struck (especially the 'barbarous' ones) on flans of decreasing size and variable shape. Then came a point where the monetary/financial and the political contexts intersected. In 274 the Gallic Empire was surrendered to the emperor Aurelian. In the same year Aurelian reformed the currency to try to improve the intrinsic worth and the acceptability of the coinage; this included raising the silver content of the coins. This meant that the circulating radiate and barbarous radiate coinage was no longer in line with the denominations and silver content of the new currency and might not have been negotiable against it, or only at a heavy discount. This could well have been the context for the thesaurisation of these coins, sometimes in huge numbers. No longer legal tender, they still had a little intrinsic value, though generally not enough silver to make it worth the difficulty of recovery with the then available technology (Reece 1981: 86), and, of course, they were still recognisably coin. So setting them apart for some possible future use may have been the best option, certainly preferable to destroying them. Thus the great spate of hoarding coins of the Gallic Empire, and of contemporary 'central' emperors, which has, ever since Blanchet, been seen as an indication of the threat or the actuality of invasion, may in fact tell us more about the monetary and political factors affecting the coinage of these decades.

There is also an argument from hoard type. If the causative mechanism for hoarding was invasion or the fear of invasion and the purpose was to safeguard wealth ('savings' or 'value' hoards), then it is odd, on the one hand, that the majority of (unrecovered) hoards were of the low-value radiate and barbarous radiate issues and that, on the other hand, hoards of gold and silver coinage representing real intrinsic as well as face value were not the principal form of hoard (unless they were all recovered). Indeed, silver hoards of this period, generally of plate or jewellery, not coin, were not common in Gaul (Hobbs 2006: 37). What may have put paid to the coinage of the Gallic Empire as negotiable specie was the reign of the emperor Probus (276–82), when the coinage of the Gallic emperors was demonetised, and large quantities of the inferior coinage of the legitimate emperors Gallienus (260–8) and Claudius II (268–70) were shipped into Gaul to replace it (Estiot 1996: 61–2 with the example of the hoard of Saint-Maurice de Gourdans where the excavated 'lots' of the hoard show this succession), so the radiates and their imitations did continue to circulate, and, of course, a coin remained negotiable with those who were prepared to accept it, whatever the state may have said. That this spate of hoarding was essentially to do with the quality of the coin and the political and monetary changes from 274 explains also why such hoards occur not only in Gaul but also in Britain, which was not, so far as we know, threatened militarily at the time but which also yields large numbers of such hoards, some of them very large (cf. Robertson 2000: Figs. 14 and 15), something that the Blanchet-style invasion hypothesis had never satisfactorily explained. Some particularly large coin hoards of the period have been suggested (Estiot 1996: 63) even to have been the product of state calling-in of these coins. This quite complex interplay of factors points up the importance of gaining the most accurate possible terminal date of the minting of the coins that make up the hoard. Thanks to modern 'excavation' of hoards and to re-examination of older finds, it is clear that the conventional dating of so many hoards to the 260s and early 270s may be erroneous; some hoards have a small number of coins minted up to a decade later. To take an example, re-examination of the hoard from Waziers (Nord, France) of 3,617 coins, whose dates of minting closed in 274–5, has shown that there was also one coin minted in 281

(Delmaire 1995: 22), so, among other things, the presumed link with the invasions of the mid to late 270s during the reign of Probus could not be sustained. How many existing hoards would detailed examination show to close later than was supposed by earlier workers?

So far we have been discussing coin hoards and interpretations based on factors relating to their place in the monetary system. It is worth noting that there are some other types of hoard for which other possible motives for deposition may be advanced. There are a small number of hoards of precious objects, mainly silver plate and silver objects such as busts of deities, that date to the mid to later third century from sites such as Chaourse (Aisne) (Baratte 1989: 111–37), Notre-Dame-d'Allençon (Maine-et-Loire) (Baratte 1981), or Rhetel (Ardennes) (Baratte 1989: 161–74), traditionally interpreted as having been deposited as a result of the military insecurity of the later third century. While this is possible, other theories such as ritual deposition can be entertained. The problem is that what little is known about the circumstances of deposition of the treasures does not suggest any particular religious or cultic link either in the material itself or in the place of deposition. Were such a hoard to be found concealed at a religious site or in ways that emphasise its religious nature (for instance, its content), then a ritual explanation would be more easily sustained. The same holds good for coin hoards which have been recovered from religious sites, most probably deposited as votive offerings. While a ritual explanation may serve to explain individual hoard depositions, as an explanation for widespread 'peaks' in hoard deposition it becomes more difficult to sustain since it requires a convincing explanation as to why such a fashion should have come into being for a short period over a wide area (e.g. Gaul and Britain in the 260s/270s), and to date no such explanation has been forthcoming. There is also the disjunction in metal types to be factored in. The silver treasures mentioned above were clearly intrinsically valuable, quite apart from the added value of the quality of the craftsmanship of the objects. Most coin hoards of the same date are remarkable for the poor quality of the pieces contained in them, though it could be argued that they were being used as a 'token' offering to the gods. The 'ritual' context is one that must always be borne in mind for individual hoards, but as a generalised explanation it does not yet convince.

Does the threat context still have any validity, even if a Blanchet-style simple connection between hoard deposition and Germanic invasion has clearly been debunked? Clearly, people did conceal hoards in times of invasion or threatened invasion; one has only to think of the well-known case of Samuel Pepys in 1667 (cf. Kent 1974: 189), though that example gives much pause for thought about how Pepys' hoard would have been interpreted if recovered by a modern archaeologist. Again we must consider Reece's (1981: 84–7) strictures on how to identify patterns of hoarding that may be susceptible to such interpretation. Such a pattern needs to show a marked chronological or geographical deviation, a 'peak', compared with what came before and after, and what was going on in contiguous regions. As we have seen above, by and large much of the hoarding used by Blanchet and his successors can be more satisfactorily explained by other causative agencies. It is noticeable that hoards closing in the 240s, 250s and into the 260s (Haupt 2001: Karten 46–9) have a distribution that also favours the Seine–Rhine area (Figure 1.1). There is then a 'peak' at the end of this period in the West which is markedly aberrant, that of hoards closing (Figure 1.2) with issues of the Gallic emperor Postumus (260–8) (Haupt 2001: Karte 50). These have a pronounced geographical concentration in northern Gaul from the Seine valley eastwards with a particular emphasis on the area of the Scheldt basin. This is the sort of pattern that could be interpreted in terms of a threatened or actual invasion, though the lack of comparable hoards in the Rhineland poses awkward questions as to why

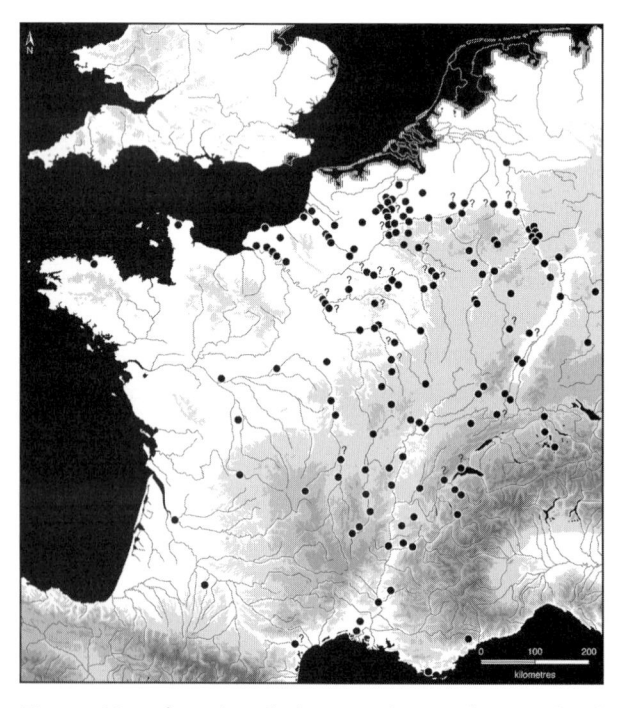

Fig. 1.1 Map of coin hoards closing in the 250s from Gaul and Germany

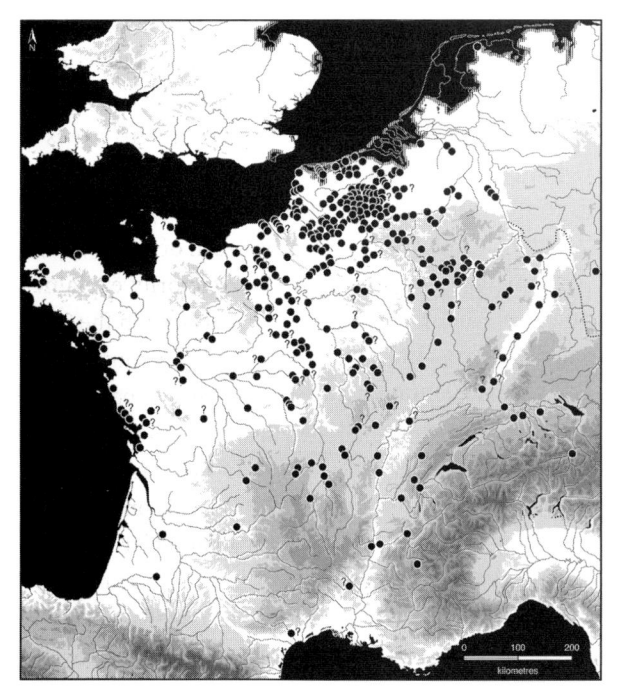

Fig. 1.2 Map of coin hoards closing with issues of Postumus (260–8) from Gaul and Germany

the actual frontier zone was not behaving in the same way. When all allowance is made for monetary factors, there is still a tendency for this area along and behind the frontier to see a heavier incidence of hoarding, or rather of the non-recovery of hoards, in the decades either side of the middle of the century. As stated earlier, the revisionist views on the traditional markers of third-century 'crisis' are not meant to deny that there were episodes of raiding or more serious invasion (as on the Augsburg altar), but only that such incursions should not be seen as the only mechanism for change in the third century and that they need to be examined in other lights. The same is true for hoarding; the preceding discussion is designed to widen the interpretative scope of our consideration of patterns of hoarding and to suggest other, perhaps more plausible explanations than 'threat' hoarding. But it is not to deny that hoards could be and were buried for such reasons: there remain biases in the distribution of hoards in Gaul from the middle of the third century on which could correspond to threat, actual or perceived: these consistently come from the region from the Seine valley across to the Rhine.

One further point: questions of debasement, monetary instability, copying and hoarding have traditionally, if implicitly, been seen from the point of view of the producer, the state, with consequent negative value judgements. Certainly, they would have caused difficulties where payment in coin was the norm; in the Roman world this was in particular done for the army. But on the other hand, given the low and intermittent supply of what seem to have been relatively high face-value coins, large sections of the economy and population of the West had, until this period, probably functioned largely without the use of coin (cf. Walker 1988 for quantification of the [low] level of monetisation in first- and second-century Britain). But seen from the point of view of the consumer, the provincial population, another judgement is possible. In the second half of the third century, for the first time an abundant coinage of relatively low intrinsic and face value came into being (substantially supplemented by local imitations), and some hoarders clearly had been able to amass considerable numbers of these pieces. What we may well be seeing is the creation of a situation where coin became a medium of day-to-day exchange for goods of relatively low value, thereby in fact facilitating exchange and increasing the level of economic activity. This use of low-value coin and of imitations was to continue as a feature of the fourth-century economy, and will be touched on more fully in Chapter 7.

Discussion

This chapter has not sought to reopen the whole body of evidence, analysis and interpretation for the third century. But it has tried to show that there are features of the third century and more particularly of its modern study that have to be recognised in order to understand the way in which the study and interpretation of the archaeology has developed and continues to be influenced. Only once these features have been identified and can be discounted can the archaeology seek to break free from a pre-existing interpretative straitjacket and establish its own perspective on what was happening in the third century and how that fits into longer-term trends in the centuries to either side. The essential point is, of course, that the ancient textual sources give a pretty much unanimous view of the century, particularly its second half, as a period of unalloyed disaster and crisis for the empire. This agenda was accepted and developed by much modern scholarship, colouring the study of the entire period. The study of archaeological sites and material developed within and out of this tradition and thus expected to find signs of destruction and catastrophe. In this it was for a long time successful; indeed, it remains so to this day in some works. But a reaction has set in and much of the archaeological evidence that formerly was bent to serve the catastrophist interpretation has been re-evaluated in the light of questions more suitable to the elucidation of such types of evidence. Nevertheless, as stated more than once in this chapter, one must be careful not to go too far in the other direction and create a scenario in which the archaeology simply opposes itself to and denies the historical consensus of the ancient texts (however tempting it might be so to do). It has to be allowed that there are features of the evidence, such as the restructuring visible at the cities of northern Gaul, at the secondary urban centres, at villas, in rural occupation patterns and in the incidence of coin hoarding, that could be related to external invasions and internal civil wars. And for most of these the evidence tends to cluster in the northern half of Gaul, in the region from the Seine to the Rhine. So though archaeology may have great difficulties in identifying the short-term, *événementielle*, occurrence of warfare and destruction, it may be better at discerning the more medium-term patterning of evidence that speaks both of such events and also of reactions to them. It is this that in part lies behind the presentation of evidence and the analyses that constitute the next two chapters.

2 | The military response: soldiers and civilians

This chapter explores the ways in which the relatively short-term *histoire événementielle* of the mid to late third century had longer-term impacts on the society and values of the areas nearest the frontiers with consequent major changes in the nature of the archaeological record, changes that need both to be appreciated and critically evaluated. In the consideration of the third century, it was argued that there has in the past been a disproportionate and unhelpful emphasis on 'crisis' as both process and explanation of change in that century. But it was, nevertheless, also accepted that there may well have been a military crisis in the Rhineland and northern Gaul, difficult to detect in the *archéologie événementielle* of the period, with the partial exception of the spates of hoarding in the 260s and 270s, above all in the area between the Loire and the Rhine. It was also suggested that the most telling evidence in the archaeology for the existence of such a military crisis might well be its consequences and aftermath, particularly in the much greater visibility of the military and of military-style activities and personnel all across the Loire-Rhine region. This is what in part this chapter sets out to demonstrate.

It will be argued that this period sees the start of one of the major threads in this book, the growing importance of military-style identity and self-representation, certainly for the elites, and probably also for others. This sets in train what may briefly if somewhat oversimply be characterised as the 'militarisation' of the aristocracies of the Western Empire, a process that, starting in northern Gaul and the Rhineland in the later third and fourth centuries, was to gather pace and become near universal across the West in the fifth century. This chapter puts forward the idea that the response to military instability (or the perception thereof) in northern Gaul and the Rhineland in the later third and on into the fourth centuries was changes in the imperial army itself in this region and also in the *mentalités* of the aristocracies of the region, and that the result was an archaeology dominated by installations and paraphernalia expressive above all of military power, either that of the late Roman state and army or that of those who took their lead from these new expressions of power. Accordingly, the chapter will seek first to describe and explain the changes to what we think of as the official imperial army, and will then go on to explore the ways in which the priorities of defence and military preparedness impacted on areas and settlements that archaeology has traditionally seen as 'civilian', most especially the cities, before looking at other aspects of the archaeology, such as burial and rural settlement, which will be argued to attest to the importance of the links with the army and with military practice.

One of the consequences of the repeated military disruptions and campaigns of the second half of the third century is that the army would have gained a more prominent place in the experience of the civil population of the north of Gaul. From the end of the first century, the great bulk of troops in the West had been withdrawn from the interior and stationed on the frontiers of the provinces. The main supply routes, particularly the Rhône–Saône–Moselle–Rhine axis would still have seen a lot of military comings and goings, as also would the axis up through northern Gaul to Britain. Military personnel were probably also a fairly familiar sight in the interior in relation to the gathering and transport of supplies, as the items of military apparel from many towns attest to. But by and large the interior of the Western provinces was a demilitarised zone in that it did not hold permanent garrisons; military personnel were transitory. With the developments in the third century, the army would have been much more regularly seen in the interior, perhaps in pursuit of invaders or in transit elsewhere, but also probably on a longer-term basis as the safeguarding of resources and supplies became more pressing. This was in all probability particularly the case in the regions close behind the frontier line, and the process can to a certain extent be traced in the archaeology as *burgi* start to appear away from the line of the Rhine. Moreover, the emperors of the mid to late third century, be they 'legitimate' or the local 'Gallic' variety, were increasingly military strongmen surrounded by an ever more militarised retinue. This carried over into the fourth century where the rhetoric (sometimes even the reality) of the emperor as successful military leader, which had always been central to the legitimation of the reigning emperor and the imperial office more generally, now became the yardstick against which holders of the imperial office were judged. In these ways one can argue that the army became more central to civil life in the frontier provinces and for the elite increasingly a source of power, authority and advancement. So both 'official' and 'unofficial' manifestations of military or militarised behaviours need to be understood not just in terms of the army but also in terms of the army as a model for the elites of the region, above all from the late third century on in northern Gaul and the Rhineland.

The imperial response

Whatever the modern perceptions of the immediate nature and effect of the Germanic incursions of the mid and later third century, it can be argued from the archaeology that they resulted in a deal of dislocation and reordering of the Rhine frontier in the medium term. This period in the later third and, particularly, the earlier fourth century also saw major changes in the composition and deployment of the imperial army. This in turn impinged on a medium-term process whereby the arms, armour and equipment of the army had been changing away from those familiar from the first and second centuries towards something very different in the fourth century. All of these and their manifestations in the archaeology will now be considered, both for their own sake and for the effects they were to have on the civil population, particularly in northern Gaul during the fourth century and more widely later on. But before considering them in detail, it is worth laying out what it was that we may consider to have set the army and its personnel apart from the rest of the population in the Roman West and allows us to use words such as 'army' or 'military' as a shorthand to designate a distinct functional and social grouping, particularly since it is a central argument of this chapter that military practices and representation spilt over into the 'civilian' world in ways that can make the distinction archaeologically ambiguous.

A standing army, such as the Roman army under the High Empire and the Late Empire, has an existence, continuity and associated practices that create a separate identity for it and its members. Institutionally, a standing army and its constituent units have a continuity of existence preceding and outlasting the military careers of any of its individual members or the uses to which individual emperors might put the army. For the Roman army specifically, it has been pointed out (James, S. 2001) that there probably was no such thing as *the* Roman army but rather a series of regional or provincial armies, a trend which, as we shall see below, probably became more accentuated under the Late Empire. Nevertheless, there was a commonality of shared interest and identity among the soldiers and in addition a lot of cross-posting of individuals and units, so links were maintained and innovations and practices disseminated. Institutionally also, the late Roman army was distinct from almost all other institutions and inhabitants of the empire in that its installations and equipment were underwritten by the state and its members paid, fed, equipped and armed by the state. This in itself would have created very profound distinctions in the minds both of the soldiers and of the civilians whose tax-renders paid for them. Other institutional differences included the legal privileges long enjoyed by the soldiery, with the competence only of military courts in cases involving soldiers: abuse of these privileges and immunities had long been a source of discontent among the civilian population. The individual soldiers serving in the army internalised these differences from the moment they entered the army, partly through formal observances and partly through informal practice, these constituting a military *habitus* distinct from that of the civilian world around them. The *sacramentum* (military oath) administered on enlistment, the presence of the *imagines* of the emperors, and the parades and rituals observed on imperial anniversaries would have created, reiterated and emphasised the personal link between the emperor and his troops and the loyalty owed by the soldiers to the imperial person, a loyalty recalled every time a soldier handled his pay as the coins bore the image and likeness of Caesar. The cycle of these rituals and the specifics of the daily military round, such as the ways in which the day was structured and marked (e.g. by trumpet calls) and associated activities such as fatigues and guard duty, would also have fashioned a specifically military sense of time and how it was structured and divided, structures again with a degree of commonality across a regional army if not more widely. The existence of units and their representation by standards would have fixed another level of loyalty, that to the unit, and have fostered *esprit de corps* both in the soldier's unit and by contrast with other units. Within the unit the subgroups to which the soldier belonged, the officers and the command structure would have served as a form of family to men divorced from their natural families. It is clear that soldiers felt an empire-wide bond with each other, their *commilitones* (fellow soldiers) (James, S. 2001: 79), a term invoked by emperors when addressing the army. This was expressed in a number of ways that both made clear their belonging to the 'imagined community' (James, S. 2001 drawing on Anderson 1991) of the soldiers and their distinction from civilians. One distinction that appears infrequently in the archaeological record but must have been important in day-to-day terms was the use of a distinct language – in the West, the *sermo militaris*, a form of Latin that not only acted as a *lingua franca* for soldiers from different ethnic and linguistic backgrounds but also emphasised their solidarity and exclusion of outsiders. More recognisable in the archaeology is the presence of distinctive forms of self-representation, particularly through clothing, proclaiming their military identity, their solidarity with their *commilitones* and probably also their specific unit identities (for instance, the unit shield-designs depicted in the *Notitia Dignitatum*). This was not just a matter of specifically martial aspects such as shields and weaponry, which might not all have been worn on a regular basis, but also more day-to-day items of apparel such as dress (including fabric, cut and colours), fittings such as belts and brooches, and other items such as (hobnailed) footwear, as well as aspects of personal appearance such as hairstyle and being bearded or clean-shaven. All of these were ways which in themselves and by their day-to-day use or by repeated participation helped mould in the minds of the soldiers their distinctive military identity and signified their difference from (and doubtless their assumed superiority to) the civilian population. For the latter, soldiers would probably have been instantly recognisable by sight (and possibly by sound and by smell) in the street; they were probably to be avoided and daughters locked away. Nevertheless, military style was an expression of a major focus of power in the empire and therefore a ready-made vocabulary for those who wished to define themselves as powerful and to express their power visibly (cf. Gardner 2007). In the later third and fourth centuries, it is possible to recognise elements of all the institutional and personal factors that made the Roman army and its soldiers distinct and distinctive. What happened to this complex of signifiers in the fifth century is a major question that will be addressed in Chapter 8.

It is also important to note that the preceding paragraph has rather played to the old stereotype of the army as a self-contained, male community, separated by the walls of its forts from the civilian population, even those such as family members, slaves and traders who might actually be in day-to-day contact with soldiers. Late Roman soldiers had wives and families, and they may have had attendants, grooms and servants (slave or free). Their forts certainly attracted civilians of greater or less moral uprightness. An important focus of research recently, particularly in the anglophone world, has been the nature of these wider military communities and how they might be recognised in the archaeology (e.g. Goldsworthy and Haynes 1999; James, S. 2001), though this focus has often been on the first and second centuries. Gardner (2007) has made an important contribution to getting this process under way for the later period. Nevertheless, the extent to which male soldierly identities formed those of their civilian contacts, perhaps particularly their womenfolk, remains very under-explored, but will be referred to at points below and again in Chapter 8.

However, it is time to start to assess the archaeological evidence for the Roman army and in particular for military identity in the built environment and in personal self-representation, in order to understand both the nature of the late Roman army and how its vocabulary of power might be transmitted to and appropriated by civilians wanting to use that vocabulary to make statements about themselves. The following sections will deal first with the constructions and installations within which the army was based and which served both to defend the empire against external threat and to ensure the regime's and the army's hold over the provinces and populations of that empire. It will then move on to examine the archaeological correlates of being a soldier, particularly in areas such as dress and accoutrements.

Military installations: forts and frontiers

We start with the systems of fortifications referred to by the shorthand of 'frontiers' (a concept discussed more fully below, p. 54), beginning with the long-established military zone along the Rhine and then moving on to the new installations either side of the North Sea and the Channel (Figure 2.1). With the abandonment in the 260s of the *Agri Decumates* to the east of the upper and middle Rhine, a whole new military zone had to be created along the left bank of the river in what had for a century and a half been a largely civilian area. This in fact proceeded very gradually, with only a few new forts on the stretch of the upper Rhine to the north and south of Strasbourg even a hundred years after the abandonment of the *Agri Decumates* (Johnson 1983: 250–6; Schönberger 1969). It should be remembered, though, that, prior to its

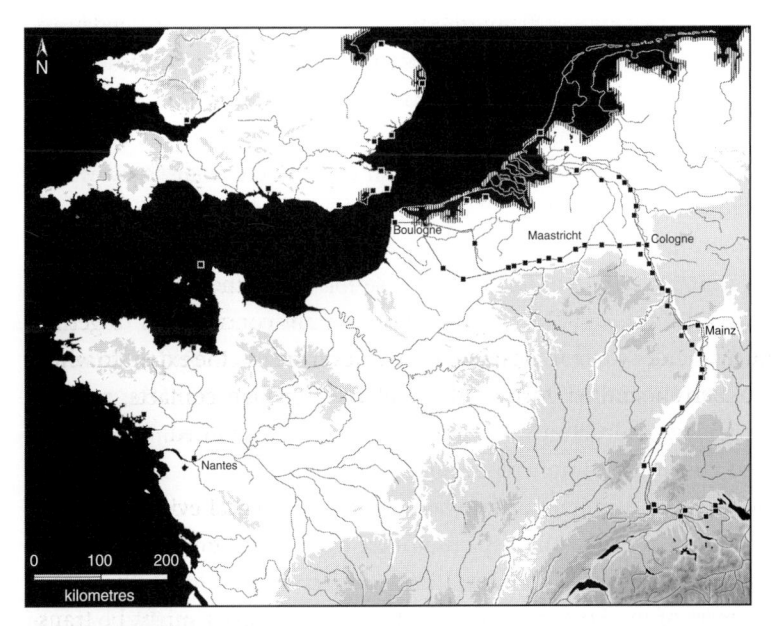

Fig. 2.1 Military installations along the Rhine, in northern Gaul and south-eastern Britain in the fourth century

canalisation in the nineteenth century, the course of the upper Rhine in this area, the Altrhein, consisted of a broad, meandering, uncontrolled river in a wide, swampy flood plain, not easy to approach or cross. It was upstream and downstream of this zone, in modern-day Switzerland and from the Mainz area downriver, that the Rhine was easier to approach and cross, and thus it is in these areas that we see concentrations of forts and smaller blockhouses (*burgi*). In the south, in modern Switzerland, on the uppermost Rhine and through to the upper reaches of the Danube, was a series of heavily defended strongpoints on the 'Roman' bank of the river, suggesting a perception of very real threat from the southern end of the Rhine–Danube re-entrant and/or a desire to block the approaches to the passes over the Alps into Italy (to prevent a repeat of raiding of the type attested to on the Augsburg altar). Likewise, to the north of the plain of the Altrhein where the river again became easier to approach and cross, the long-standing military zone of the lower Rhine saw considerable (re-)construction of forts and *burgi* from the area of Mainz as far as roughly the modern border between Germany and the Netherlands. Downstream of this, evidence for military occupation of what had been the forts along the lowest stretches of the Rhine is sporadic, with the evidence from only Meinerswijk and Maurik (Van Es 1994: 64–6) standing in stark contrast to the many forts of the second century along this stretch of the river. Moreover, at the Rhine mouths and to their south, there was dislocation as a result of the Dunkirk II marine transgression, a process which significantly altered the coastline of north-western Gaul. Militarily, this is reflected in the abandonment of all Rhine installations downstream of Maurik, and down the coast to the south-west the creation of the new fort at Oudenburg (Mertens 1972) to help safeguard the Strait of Dover. The area between the sea to the west, the river Maas (Meuse) to the east and south of the lower Rhine – Toxandria – seems gradually to have been less and less under direct Roman control, becoming instead the base for the Salian Franks discussed below (p. 376).

The character of late Roman military fortifications along the Rhine has been extensively studied at the level of the individual site and of the zone as a whole (Bridger and Gilles 1998; Johnson 1983: Ch. 11; cf. von Petrikovits 1971), so rather than simply repeating the material there presented, it would be more useful to highlight certain features common to the zone in order to gain a sense of the new military order. One striking feature is the range of sizes, shapes and types of fortification. Rather than the relatively standardised forts of the High Empire, which were essentially fortified bases of operations for units of a limited range of sizes and types, the installations of the later empire show much more individual variation, tailored to their particular defensive function and also probably reflecting much greater variation in the type and size of units. This accords well with work showing that the units of the late Roman army seem not to have had standardised forms or complements, even though the types of unit names (e.g. *cohors*, *cuneus*) that recur often in the literary sources give an impression of uniformity. Nor is there any longer standardisation of the shape of forts, *castra*. Some, such as Alzey (Oldenstein in Cüppers 1990: 302–3) or Bad Kreuznach (Rupprecht in Cüppers 1990: 321), were laid out square, with regularly spaced projecting towers and gates in the middle of the sides. Altrip (Bernhard in Cüppers 1990: 299–302), on the other hand, was trapezoidal even though of the same Valentinianic date as proposed for Alzey, so no chronotypology can be confidently established (von Petrikovits 1971: 185). Others, such as Boppard (Wegner in Cüppers 1990: 344–6) or Kaiseraugst (Drack and Fellmann 1988: 411–14), were rectangular. In general, there does seem to have been a preference for rectilinear plans for forts, but other sites, such as Bitburg (Cüppers 1990: 336–7), were more irregular in shape because adapted to the local topography. The style of military architecture is also well known and well understood (Johnson 1983: Ch. 2), with its emphasis on thick, high walls, plentiful external towers and small, defended gateways, an architecture designed to withstand both sudden attack and longer-drawn-out sieges or periods when the surrounding area might be in the hands of invaders, protecting the personnel and materiel gathered inside the defences. The variability in internal buildings is also remarkable. In place of the uniform and distinctive type of barrack block familiar under the High Empire, there is a considerable range of structures, with almost each fort having its own internal plan and buildings. Occasionally, as at Köln-Deutz (Precht in Horn 1987: 513–16), there is a regular series of buildings reminiscent of the habits of earlier times. But more usual is the sort of mix of buildings to be seen at a site such as Alzey, where there is a series of buildings along the inside face of the walls in a sort of casemate arrangement (common at other sites also), these consisting largely of rooms which may well be accommodation for the troops, and other buildings, including a bathhouse, in the interior of the fort. From these it is extremely difficult to reconstruct the size and structure of the unit in garrison, a fact which accords with the other evidence (cf. Elton 1996: Ch. 3) we have for the unit sizes and structures of the late Roman army being much less standardised than were those that we like to imagine (rightly or wrongly) for the early imperial army. This also means that whereas a fort of the early imperial period, in its appearance, layout, hierarchy of spaces and accommodation, served both to differentiate the military lifestyle from the civilian and to promote the idea of the soldiery as an 'imagined community' across the empire, late Roman forts, or at least their internal arrangements and buildings, were far less homogeneous, suggesting that local and unit identities and loyalties may have developed alongside any loyalty to the army as an institution. It is also possible that what we call forts may at times have held units of the regular army, at times more irregular units such as *foederati* (see below p. 79), or even at other times a civil population, given the difficulties of distinguishing between these groups on strictly archaeological grounds (cf. Gardner 2007: esp. Ch. 3; see also discussion below, p. 80). And, as we shall also see, there are sites that we conventionally regard as civilian (such as towns in northern Gaul) that actually are difficult to distinguish, on the grounds of the fortifications, building types and finds, from sites regarded as military. One resource which has yet to be exploited to the full is that of burials. The cemeteries attached to late Roman forts in the Rhine corridor have by and large not been the object of systematic excavation. One important exception is that at the fort of Krefeld-Gellep (*Gelduba*), where the long-term excavations under Renate Pirling (Figure 2.2) have yielded an enormous database of burials starting in the later Roman period and running down into the seventh century, to which we shall return in later chapters (for a summary and bibliography of the earlier part of the project, see Pirling 1986). On the Channel coast, the fort at Oudenburg has another useful, though far smaller and shorter-lived, cemetery that has been excavated (Mertens 1977). These findings will be used in due course (p. 343) to analyse the differing components of the fort's population.

As well as the garrison forts, there were also the smaller installations now generically referred to as *burgi* (sing. *burgus*). These were principally sited to protect lines of communication such as the Rhine itself or roads, but sometimes also to safeguard particular installations or resources in the interior. They normally consisted of a fortified enclosure, sometimes with a blockhouse or strongpoint inside the enclosure to house a small garrison. The group on the upper Rhine in what is now Switzerland has already been referred to; it most probably served to supervise legitimate passage along and across the river and to deter illicit crossings. Others on the lower Rhine between Mainz and Cologne served as defended landing places, again showing that protection of movement *along* the river was as important as the control of movement *across* it. Nor was it foreseen that movement across the river was only to be by potential foes. Several forts on the 'Roman' bank of the Rhine had bridgehead forts on the 'free' bank, of which Köln-Deutz, constructed by Constantine I, is the best known (cf. Carroll 1997), with

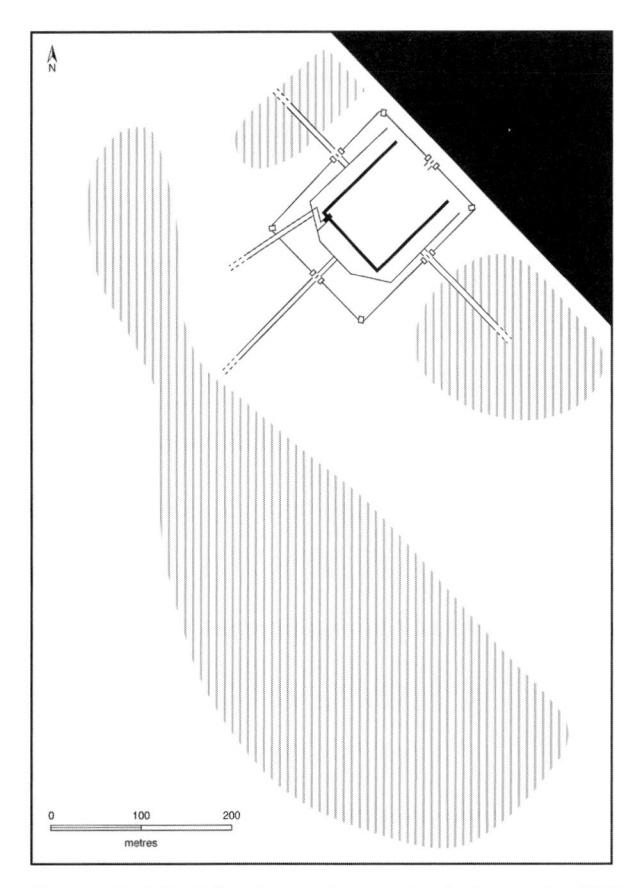

Fig. 2.2 Krefeld-Gellep forts and cemeteries (redrawn after Pirling 1986: Abb. 30)

others at sites such as Kastell over the river from the major centre at Mainz or at Whylen opposite Kaiseraugst. The purpose of these was not only to protect and supervise the bridgehead but also to ensure that Roman troops could enter Germany at will, as they did down to at least the reign of Valentinian I, who campaigned into Free Germany. Apart from along the Rhine, the other main system of *burgi* lay along the road west from Cologne through Maastricht and Tongeren to Bavai, which could ultimately link through via Courtrai and Tournai to Boulogne and Britain. The *burgi* consisted (Brulet 1995) of ditched enclosures with few traces of internal structures, though a couple later had towers constructed in them. Generally, they lay to one side of a roadside settlement of the High Empire, though few of these have yielded any evidence of occupation beyond the late third century, which was probably also the date of construction of the *burgi*. There is no evidence as to whether they were permanently garrisoned or just formed a series of strongpoints usable by official traffic and travellers along the road. The purpose of this fortified road has been debated. Some have seen it in combination with the series of *burgi* on the Maas downstream of Maastricht as an internal frontier or line of control, penning the Salian Franks into Toxandria. Others have seen the fortified road line as a safe-guarded, strategic communications axis linking Cologne and the Rhine garrisons with the garrisons either side of the Channel and with those in Britain. It could, of course, have fulfilled both functions

The importance of Britain and of safeguarding communications with the island as well as protecting the littorals can clearly be seen in the strings of new fortifications constructed on either side of the southern part of the North Sea and along the north and south sides of the Channel, the 'Saxon Shore'. The best known and most impressive forts are those on the British side guarding many of the major estuaries and inlets from the Wash round through the Strait of Dover to Portsmouth Harbour, and they were constructed from the early to the late third century (Pearson 2002). So the 'Saxon Shore' was not a unitary, planned system; rather, the name is a retrospective grouping of these forts into a single 'system' imposed by the *Notitia Dignitatum* and set down when, to judge from the archaeology, several had already been abandoned. This makes the origins and purposes of individual forts and of the 'system' very debatable (cf. Pearson 2002: Ch. 6); nevertheless, a unified military command did at some point come into being under the *comes litoris Saxonici per Britannias* (*Not. Dig. Occ.* XXVIII). Interestingly, the *Notitia* lists for the two commands on the Gallic side of the Channel, the *dux tractus Armoricani et Nervicani* (*Not. Dig. Occ.* XXXVII) and the *dux Belgicae secundae* (*Not. Dig. Occ.* XXXVIII), both put 'in litore Saxonico' (on the Saxon Shore) at the end of their first entries, making explicit the link with the other side of the Channel. The installations of the Gallic shore are much less known than their British counterparts, such as Alet near Saint-Malo, seemingly a defended headland; others, such as Oudenburg (though not in the *Notitia* lists), were very comparable to the British sites (see papers in Maxfield 1989). On the subject of Britain, it is worth mentioning that the northern bounds of the province were still secured by Hadrian's Wall and the forts to its south under the command of the *dux Britanniarum* (*Not. Dig. Occ.* XL). The unit titles along the wall listed in the *Notitia* are unusual in that they are for the most part old-style *cohortes* and *alae* rather than the newer title types, suggesting that the units concerned had stayed put there since the turn of the second and third centuries (though their composition and structure had probably altered significantly; see Bidwell 1997: Ch. 4).

The titles of the commanders mentioned in the preceding paragraph would have sounded bizarre to the ears of a second-century Roman and are thus an index of the changes that took place in the organisation and command of the army, especially under Constantine I (306–37) and his successors. These changes had in large part been brought about by the exigencies of the warfare of the third and early fourth centuries, in particular the need to try to preclude invasion or to deal with it if it happened, and the need for individual emperors to have their own personal military forces. By the end of the third century, the itinerant emperors travelled accompanied by an entourage, called in Latin a *comitatus*. Part of this was necessarily a military retinue, partly for the safety of the emperor's person and partly so that the emperor could bring effective military pressure to bear. At the turn of the third and fourth centuries, these seem largely to have been units and vexillations from the provincial armies and bearing the traditional types of unit title (Duncan-Jones 1978). By a law of 325 (*Cod. Theod.*VII.20.4), such troops now held a higher status and a new title, *comitatenses*, clearly showing their origins in the imperial retinue. By the time of the compilation of the *Notitia Dignitatum* at the end of the fourth century, the bulk of the *comitatenses* appear to be what we refer to as regional field armies, under the command of a *comes* or a *magister* (Hoffmann 1969). These may have originated in the *comitatus* of the various emperors of the fourth century, such as the sons of Constantine I, who ruled in particular areas of the empire, with these units remaining in those areas after the deaths of their emperors. Those units in direct personal attendance upon the emperor were qualified with the title *palatinus* or *praesentalis*, indicating that they were attached to the imperial palace or served in the presence of the emperor. In the West (cf. Hoffmann 1969), the *Notitia* records a major field army in Gaul (under the *magister equitum per Gallias*) and smaller ones (possibly of recent creation) in Spain (under the *comes Hispaniarum*) and Britain (under the *comes Britanniae*). By contrast, those units that did not form part of the new higher-status field armies were now committed to frontier defence – hence their generic name of *limitanei* (from *limes*, a frontier) or *ripenses* (from *ripa*, a riverbank where so many frontiers lay). As well as the profound changes in the overall structure of the army, there is a plethora of new unit titles such as *vexillatio* or *cuneus* (wedge, a cavalry formation) or just *numerus* (unit) recorded in the *Notitia*, attesting to the disappearance of the old-style units such as legions and cohorts in the furnaces of the external and civil wars of the later third and early fourth centuries, and their recasting in the mould of the new model army. In addition, there were paramilitary peoples such as the *laeti* and *foederati* discussed in more detail below (p. 79), essentially formations of 'barbarian' warriors serving alongside units of the regular Roman army and subject to Roman generals. One feature common to both the *comitatenses* and the *limitanei* is their essentially regional structure under a series of territorial commands, reinforcing the suggestion made above that army structures were increasingly viewed as local as much as part of empire-wide institutions.

It is important to emphasise that all these changes – new army structures, new unit types and new fortifications – developed or were put in place gradually, sometimes *ad hoc*, rather than as a considered, centrally directed scheme, as was once influentially suggested by Luttwak (1976: Ch. 3) with his concept of a purposeful plan of 'defense-in-depth' whereby, even if the frontier defences were penetrated, the fortifications in the interior served to interdict enemy movement and to deny them supplies as well as facilitating Roman response through the existence of a series of strongpoints that were also supply depots. This analysis could only be arrived at by taking the end product of the changes of a hundred years or more at the end of the fourth century and reading these retrospectively as a unitary plan rather than as a series of local and regional responses to particular circumstances. The idea has been comprehensively dismantled by Whittaker (1994: Ch. 5), who, among other things, showed that the Roman ideology remained one of offensive warfare and the right to rule even if defensive measures had also to be taken. Whittaker also argues for the important concept of a frontier not so much as a line on the map, or as a 'moral barrier' dividing civilised from barbarian, as a 'zone' where there were populations who, whatever their political affiliations, were in day-to-day contact and thus had much more in common with each other than they did with, for instance, on the Roman side, those in Italy or Egypt, even if they were ruled by the same emperor. This echoes the concept put forward by Böhme (1974) for a *Mischzivilization* either side of the Rhine, where Roman military personnel and civilian populations interacted with Germanic groupings such as the Franks and Alamanni, and these latter were themselves profoundly shaped by contact with the political, military and economic structures of the empire and by its material cultures. The recent emphasis in anglophone scholarship (e.g. Goldsworthy and Haynes 1999; James, S. 2001) on the army not as a separate, self-contained entity but rather as the framework from which depended a whole series of other individuals and communities (wives, children, grooms, slaves, innkeepers, traders and prostitutes) fits in well with such a perspective. In this view the army articulates a whole series of groups or communities at different levels on both sides of the Rhine. This in turn brings into play questions of military and military-related identities (cf. Gardner 2007), particularly perhaps for men from east of the Rhine who nevertheless spent important parts of their lives serving in the Roman army and whose archaeological manifestations will be considered below (p. 78). But, as will be argued below, such identities were also important for others, probably including men who had never served in the army in the sense of having belonged to a regular unit and been on the payroll.

Weaponry, armour and military dress

Another important alteration in the archaeological record of the military is the profound changes in weaponry, armour and other equipment that took place through the third century, with the result that the soldier of the fourth century had a very different appearance to his second-century predecessor (Bishop and Coulston 2006: Chs. 7 and 8; Feugère 1993: Ch. 10). It is necessary to have some idea of these changes and the resulting equipment, not just to understand the army but also because it is some of this material whose symbolism was appropriated outside the army proper, demonstrating the importance of the rhetoric of military and state apparel as a marker of status. The sources of evidence are varied. There are representations of soldiers in a variety of media. Some of these are rich, high-status items such as the silver plate showing the emperors Constantius II (337–60), (probably) Valentinian I (364–75) and Theodosius I (379–95) accompanied by soldiers (Toynbee and Painter 1986: Pls. IX*b*, *c*; X*a*). Since these troops are in such close attendance upon the person of the emperor, they are probably to be seen as members of the *scholae*, the personal bodyguard, and details of the soldiers on the dish of Constantius II and on the great, silver Missorium of Theodosius I from Spain (Almagro-Gorbea *et al.* 2000: 190) (cf. p. 232), such as the hairstyle and neck rings, suggest they may be of Germanic origin, comparable with the herm busts of Germanic youths from the balustrade around the imperial villa at Welschbillig north of the imperial residence at Trier (Wrede 1972). Other, less-high-status media of representation can also be found, such as representations of soldiers on glass beakers (Harden 1987: 234). The military tradition of erecting tombstones depicting the deceased had declined enormously by the fourth century compared with the first and second, but there are a few tombstones of this late date such as that of the *imaginifer* (bearer of the imperial portrait) Valerius Januarius from Amiens (Bayard and Massy 1983: 249; *Corpus Inscriptionum Latinarum* [*CIL*] XIII.3492), showing him in his military garb. Then, of course, there are the finds of actual military equipment. As yet, they have not been subjected to the same level of study as has the equipment of the first and second centuries. This is gradually changing, but it does mean our knowledge is not as systematic as we would like. One important problem is that the incidence of military material in different types of archaeological deposit is still unclear. In part this is to do with the manufacture of the objects, most of which were probably produced in the state arms factories (*fabricae*) situated near the frontiers (see p. 92), but what types of material were produced at which *fabrica* and when is as yet only very dimly apprehended. Other factors must have involved features of the 'life' of material such as whether it was made of valuable materials or not, its commonness or rareness, its fragility or robustness and whether it was recyclable. Yet another set of factors governing the selection of material must have been whether it was singled out for purposive deposition, as in graves or in votive deposits (see the comments below on the Scandinavian bog finds), whether it was 'lost' or discarded in the normal course of events, or whether it is found, for instance, in a state that may suggest it was damaged and had been taken out of circulation for recycling. So we have very little idea of what sorts of 'filters' have operated to select the small proportion of the totality of late Roman military equipment to come down to us and therefore of how representative the material may be; it may well be highly unrepresentative. Added to that, we do know that the further filter of taphonomy, conditions in the soil, will have greatly affected survival – above all, influencing the non-survival of organic material such as leather and textiles (i.e. all clothing and much equipment) and wood (see the comments below on the non-survival of much to do with archery) except in unusual conditions such as waterlogging. So the following remarks can only be offered as a provisional outline.

We look first at armour and weaponry, the items most clearly tied to a soldier's martial character and functions (see also James, S. 2011, a hugely important work which there has not been time to assimilate here). The familiar forms of high-imperial helmet, with large cheek pieces and deep, flaring neck guard, had given way to types that for the ordinary soldiers were considerably more utilitarian and were easy to construct (perhaps reflecting volume production in the state *fabricae*), consisting essentially of an iron two-part or four-part bowl to which simple cheek pieces and neck guard could be attached, and which were worn over a simple, round felt or fabric cap the *pileus pannonicus*. For the officers, helmets were increasingly elaborate, not to say vulgarly ostentatious, with the most elaborate having the bowl set with glass and semi-precious stones and a raised crest-ridge (probably holding plumes) running fore and aft (such helmets are shown being worn by the emperor himself on some coins) (Klumbach 1973). All depictions of shields and finds of shield parts show that the oblong, curved legionary shield of the High Empire had dropped out of use and that all soldiers now were equipped with a circular or oval shield with central boss; the chapters of the *Notitia Dignitatum* relating to senior military officers such as the *magister militum praesentalis* (master of the soldiers in the [imperial] presence – *Not. Dig. Occ.* V) show shields painted with a variety of designs and, to judge by the unit titles appended to these representations, these were shield designs identifying the different units. Body armour now consisted of either chain mail (*lorica hamata*) or scale armour (*lorica squamata*), with the scales sometimes simply wired together horizontally onto a backing tunic, or sometimes more elaborately wired together vertically also so that a weapon could less easily penetrate between the scales (James, S. 2004: 110–39; cf., most recently, Bishop and Howard-Davis 2009). Scale armour sewn to horse blankets was also used to protect the mounts of the new, heavily armoured shock cavalry of the Late Empire, the *catafract(ari)i* or *clibanarii*, developed in the East in response to their Persian counterparts but also attested to in the West (Mielczarek 1993). The famous plate or segmental armour of the High Empire, the '*lorica segmentata*' does not seem to have been made much after the middle of the third century, though representations in the *Notitia Dignitatum* suggest continuing use of the construction technique, but now for limb guards rather than for body armour proper (Bishop 2002: 91). Likewise, the most familiar Roman offensive weapon of the Republic and High Empire, the short stabbing sword of the infantry, the *gladius*, seems largely to have fallen out of favour, being replaced by the longer slashing sword, the *spatha*, always the preferred weapon of the cavalry. The changes in sword types and shield forms, particularly the abandonment of the oblong shield and the *gladius*, presumably reflect changes in ways of fighting, in particular replacement of the very close-order infantry formations characteristic of the early periods in favour of more open battle lines. A shafted weapon retained from the earlier period was the well-known *pilum* with its pyramidal head and long, iron shank, but it took its place alongside a variety of spear types and an innovation in the form of a small, lead-weighted throwing-dart, the *plumbata* or *martio-/mattiobarbulus*. Archers also continued to be an important element of late Roman forces (more so, to judge by the *Notitia*, in the East), but by their very nature wooden bows and arrow shafts rarely survive in the archaeological record (though iron arrowheads do), so it is very difficult to form an impression of the frequency of such weaponry in the West. The finds of weaponry and other equipment deposited in bogs in southern Scandinavia, as at the Danish sites of Nydam and Illerup Ådal (Ilkjaer 2000 and references), do, though, give an invaluable impression of what such weapons looked like. These bog finds also demonstrate the interaction of Roman and 'barbarian' military identities through the ways in which captured Roman weapons have been reworked with local fittings, showing how they became incorporated not only into these non-Roman panoplies but also, presumably, into the warrior ideologies of these societies. This is of a piece with the finds of Roman-produced equipment in graves east of the Rhine, suggesting that the occupants had served in the Roman army and this remained an important part of their identity, or else that access to Roman goods was a mark of prestige. So depictions of Roman soldiers in a variety of media from within the empire, as well as finds of armour and weaponry both within and without the empire, give us an appreciation of what the late Roman military might have looked like.

Armour and weaponry were, of course, central to the functions and identity of soldiers. But probably more commonly encountered both by soldiers themselves and by those who came into contact with them were the items of 'everyday' military apparel such as clothing and the accoutrements that went with them, such as brooches and belts. Chief of these was the belt (*cingulum*), broad and equipped with buckles and decorative plates of varying degrees of elaboration and fineness, including examples in precious metal for officers, belts which, of course, marked out the soldiers even when in 'mufti'. Because of their ubiquity and importance, these belt fittings have been subjected to a great deal of study, which has allowed the construction of a chronotypology of this material (cf. Böhme 1974; Sommer 1984; Swift 2000a). It is clear from the distribution of this material principally in the frontier zones, and from textual references from other representations in visual media, that these belts were a prime signifier of being in the service of the late Roman state, above all the army, but also the bureaucracy, which was regarded as a paramilitary organisation, service in it being referred to as *militia* (military service), and joining it and retiring from it were referred to as 'putting on the belt' and 'laying aside the belt' (*cingulum sumere* and *cingulum ponere*). There is also the delightful tomb painting from Silistra in the Balkans showing his attendants bringing a late Roman civil servant his formal wear, including a broad belt with metal fittings (cf. Brown, P. 1971: Figs. 17–20). He is brought his cloak with its coloured patches presumably signifying his rank and fastened with a common type of late Roman brooch called in English scholarship a 'crossbow' brooch (cf. Swift 2000a: Ch. 2 for a summary of the literature and references to the extensive, largely German-language publication on the subject). These brooches (Figure 2.3) were made in a variety of metals and have a wide distribution along the Roman side of the riverine frontiers, the Rhine and the Danube, and in Britain, showing their link with the militarised areas of the European provinces

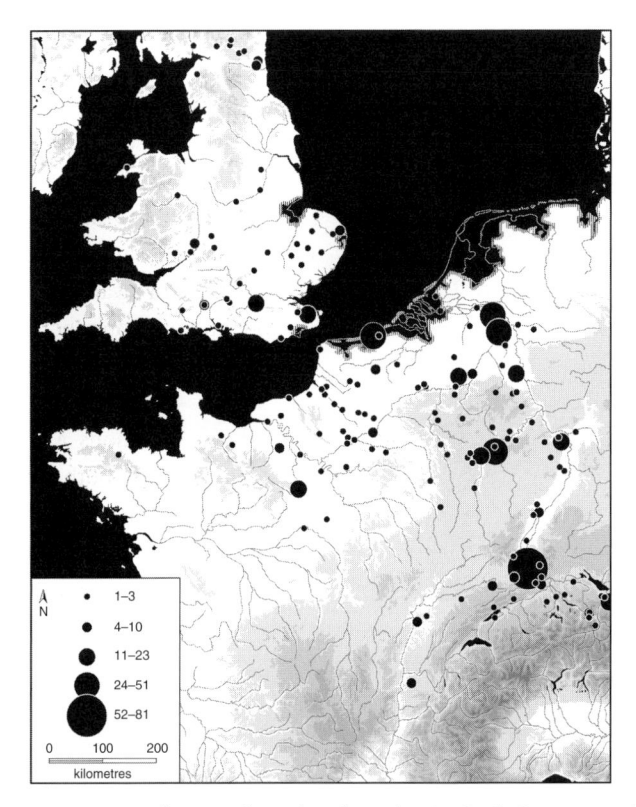

Fig. 2.3 Distribution of crossbow brooches in Gaul, Germany and Britain

(Figure 2.4). A tiny number of surviving examples are of gold and these sometimes bear imperial inscriptions, an example from Niederemmel near Trier commemorating the tenth anniversary (*decennalia*) of the accession of Constantine I (cf. Cüppers 1984: 113–14); one can imagine this being presented to a senior officer or official by the emperor himself in a court ceremony. A scarcely larger number are of silver, but with the precious metal examples there may be problems of under-representation, as very probably they preferentially ended up in the melting pot, and also were very seldom selected to go into graves. Most, therefore, are of copper alloy (which seems to have been thought suitable for funerary use), though there are clear gradations in such matters as whether they were solid or hollow cast (the latter must have been worn with lighter materials), the number of decorations (including probable imperial portraits, the Christian chi-rho symbol, good-luck invocations – Figure 2.4) and whether or not they were gilded. Another indicator of the power and prestige associated with this item of dress is afforded by its representation on the 'consular diptych of Stilicho',

Fig. 2.4 Crossbow brooch from Lankhills, Winchester

an ivory plaque depicting (it is generally argued, though the diptych is anonymous) the military strongman of the Western Empire in the opening years of the fifth century, whose cloak is clasped by an elaborate form of the brooch (cf. Volbach 1976). Sadly, we have very little surviving evidence for the tunics, long johns, cloaks and other items of military clothing that mosaics, paintings and other media show existed and to which texts sometimes refer. These representations do allow us to say that very important visual information was conveyed by such things as the nature of the fabric used, decorative elements including coloured patches, and quite possibly the colour the item was dyed, quite apart from the metal elements. Since so little actual textile survives from the Western armies and not much more representation, we can know only that we do not know. But elements such as style and colour may well also have influenced civilian clothing if it was trying to imitate the vocabulary of official power and rank.

The militarisation of northern Gaul

The previous sections outlined the nature of the evidence for the 'official' army in the late Roman West. Now we move on to related questions to do with the extent to which military practice and culture influenced and was appropriated by civilian elites in their quest for means to underpin and display their status. First of all, it is clear that military personnel were present in the interior of northern and, to a lesser extent, central Gaul, both in what may have been purely military installations and at types of sites that we have conventionally categorised as 'civilian', especially the cities. Secondly, there is the phenomenon of the wider adoption of military markers in the population at large in what might be termed an 'unofficial' fashion. This is not only militarisation *sensu stricto* insofar as it concerns the extent and disposition of 'official' military dispositions and installations of the region, but also *sensu lato* in the evidence for military influence on the civilian population of the region through military-style installations, military demands on the economy, and, importantly, the adoption of a military vocabulary for statements of power and authority by the elite (and the concomitant downgrading of traditional means of elite expression such as the villa). The related and long-standing question of the presence of people of Germanic origin in northern Gaul and its significance will also be considered in the context of developing understanding of the analysis of funerary archaeology and of metalwork types. The archaeological evidence will be supplemented as appropriate by epigraphic material (principally tombstones) and textual evidence, in particular the *Notitia Dignitatum*.

Late Roman 'forts', that is, installations holding a garrison of the regular army, are identified because they can be shown to be such by inscriptions or by the lists of units in garrison at named places in the *Notitia Dignitatum*, or because they lie along the Rhine and are similar in plan and buildings to known army installations, as discussed in the previous chapter. But there were many other fortifications in northern Gaul and the Rhineland in the fourth century and much other evidence such as weaponry, belt fittings and brooches which all bear military links and significance. In this chapter these will be considered as characterising what was termed above as military *sensu lato* in that either they represent the provision of 'rear echelon' facilities and bases for the army complementary to its garrison forts, or they probably, to a greater or lesser degree, represent private power and force, as opposed to the installations and personnel of the regular army under state control. Such archaeological evidence will be considered under the principal headings of urban fortifications, hilltop fortifications, burials and the material from them. Consideration will also be given to changes in the pattern of rural settlement and settlement types from the second century onwards and their meaning for the economic and social structures of the region in the fourth century. The epigraphic and documentary evidence for military and state involvement in the region will be considered to complement the archaeological evidence. This will then lead to the concluding discussion and arguments about the nature of the Loire-Rhine region in the late third and fourth centuries.

Urban sites and urban fortifications

The region between the Rhine and the Loire sees the largest concentration of late fortifications at what had been, or maybe continued to be, urban sites in the Western provinces (Figure 2.5), apart from the special case of Britain (see below, Chapter 3, p. 135). In this region a small number of cities had received defences under the Early Empire as a mark of their prestige, and developments at them in the fourth century need to be considered first. In some cases their early imperial importance carried over into the Late Empire. Thus the circuits at the *coloniae* of Trier and Cologne were maintained through the Late Empire, among the largest in the Western Empire. Trier became a principal imperial residence in the West, along with Milan, from the late third century, so it received exceptional attention and resources as manifested in the great complex of imperial buildings to be considered in Chapter 5. Cologne remained the major military command centre for the lower Rhine, with its wall circuit maintained and refurbished,

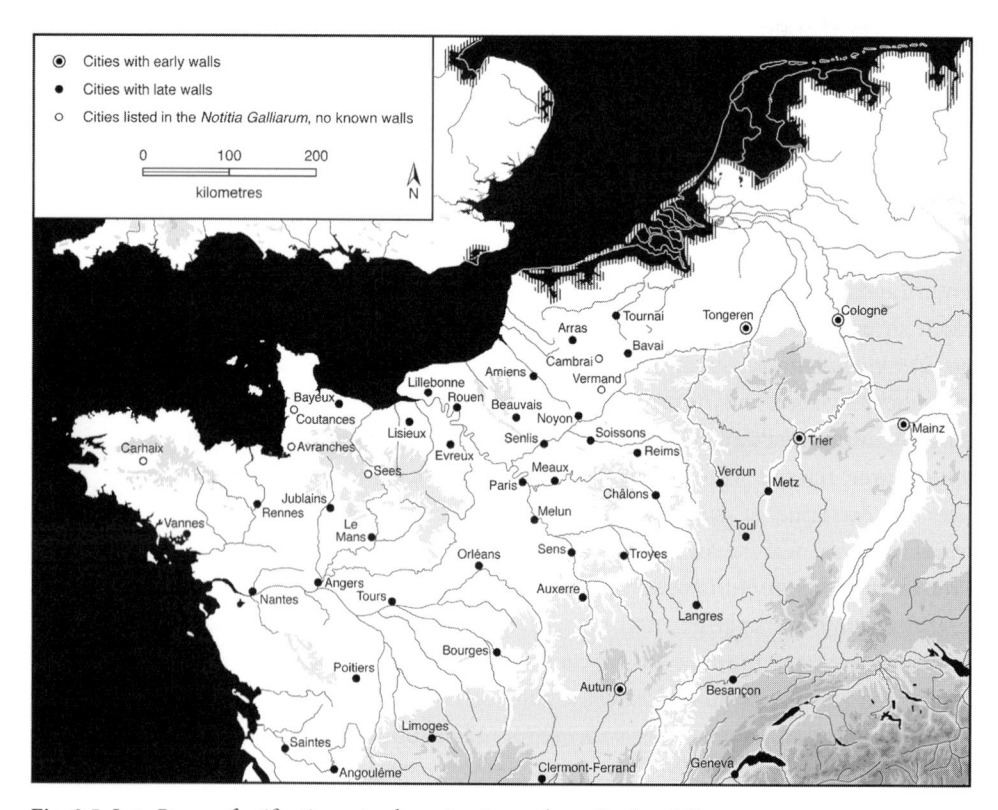

Fig. 2.5 Late Roman fortifications at urban sites in northern Gaul and Germany

Fig. 2.6 Cologne, the third-century *Römerturm*

especially, for instance, the north-western tower of the circuit, the so-called *Römerturm* (Figure 2.6), which had elaborately patterned facing as did other towers (now disappeared) on the circuit (Gans 2006). The eastern end of the bridge over the Rhine was defended by a new fortification, Köln-Deutz, of the Constantinian period, the bridge and river front of the city dominated by the huge *Praetorium*, probably the residence of the governor or possibly of the military commander, with a formidable octagonal tower in the centre of the powerful façade (Precht 1973). By contrast with these major imperial cities, at the Trajanic *colonia* of Xanten and the former *Colonia Ulpia Traiana*, now simply *Tricensima*, the early second-century defences were given up in favour of a much smaller, heavily defended circuit enclosing the central area of the earlier town (Figure 2.7), dating to the early fourth century and containing stabling in the excavated area (Otten and Ristow 2008). This was presumably part of the installations of the garrison listed at the site, *legio XXX* (hence *Tricensima* – Thirtieth), suggesting that Xanten may no longer have had a civilian population within its walls (though the

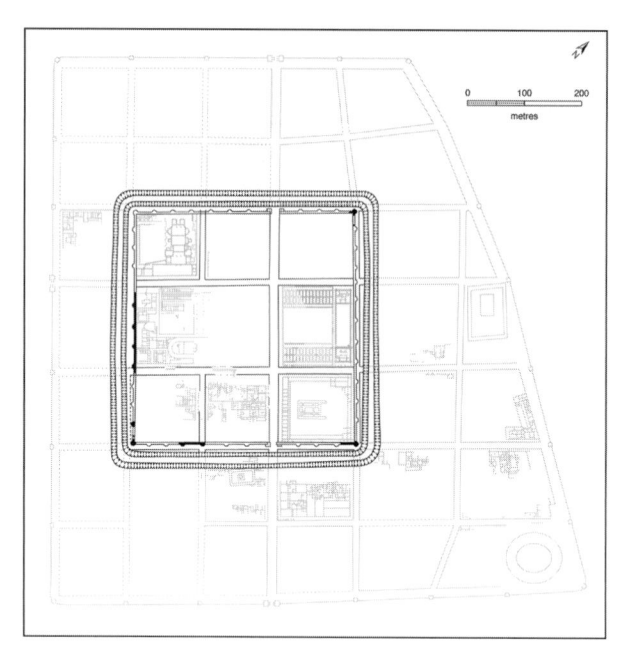

Fig. 2.7 Xanten, the late Roman defences within second-century *colonia*

area of the present Dom to the south may have housed a civilian settlement). Further up the Rhine at the capital of the former Germania Superior, Mainz, the civil town had been given walls in the later third century, enclosing the river front and then running upslope to join the eastern face of the defences of the legionary fortress on top of the hill (Rupprecht in Cüppers 1990: 458–61). Back from the Rhine, at Tongeren/Tongres a reduced circuit was constructed in the upper part of the town, enclosing only about one-third of the area within the earlier walls (Raepsaet-Charlier and Vanderhoeven 2004). The huge earthwork defences at Reims dating to the Augustan period seem long since to have been abandoned (cf. Neiss and Sindonino 2006). Further south but still in the old Lugdunensis and linked to the military north by its arms factories (*fabricae*) (see below, p. 92), the extensive Augustan wall circuit at Autun is claimed to have been given up in favour of a 10-ha. defended enclosure formed by walling off the southern spur of the earlier defences, though the existence of and dating for this enceinte remain uncertain (Rebourg 1993: 55).

This small number of earlier fortifications was to be overtaken by the new-build walls of the later third and fourth centuries. In the nine late Roman provinces coterminous with the old Belgica, Lugdunensis, and Germaniae Superior and Inferior, there were some thirty sites which under the High

Fig. 2.8 Périgueux, the late Roman walls

Empire had been the undefended centres of *civitates* and under the Late Empire were equipped with fortifications of classic late Roman type (Figure 2.8) with thick, high walls and projecting towers, with the lower courses built of reused large stones from earlier public buildings or monuments and tombstones and milestones (cf. Reddé *et al.* 2006). This compares with only some ten of this type in the rest of Gaul. The dated inscriptions reused tend to provide a *terminus post quem* of the later third century, often the Gallic Empire (260–74), and thus earlier workers saw them as a response to the Germanic invasions; a monumentalised piece of shutting the stable door after the horse had bolted. More recently, well-dated stratigraphic sequences have become available at a number of sites, and these show that the process was much longer drawn out and more variable than the earlier generalising explanations would allow. It should be noted, though, that the dated sections of walls excavated are always a small percentage of the total length of the wall circuit, so one must be judicious about extrapolating the dating of small sample areas to the whole circuit. These circuits were often major undertakings which could have been erected quickly (especially with military assistance), but equally could have taken some time to complete. As with the frontier fortifications, there are very considerable variations in size, form and date, some of which may be associated with regional or functional groupings, and these will be further considered at the appropriate point below. In the following discussion, the military aspects of these sites will be emphasised. This is not to ignore the powerful symbolic role of urban defences as a status monument under the Late Empire, nor is it to ignore the evidence for non-military activities; these will be dealt with in Chapter 3. The emphasis is rather to integrate them into the overall thrust of argument of this chapter relating to militarisation.

An emblematic example of what might happen to an urban centre is provided by the case of Jublains in the west of Gallia Lugdunensis (Naveau 1997). Under the High Empire, this had been the principal centre ('*civitas capital*') of the Aulerci Diablintes and had consisted essentially of a temple complex, baths and theatre/amphitheatre, the elements elsewhere characteristic of a major Gallic sanctuary complex, but here equipped with a street grid and a forum (Figure 2.9). The area of the street grid seems never to have been fully built up, and the limited excavation across the site also suggests

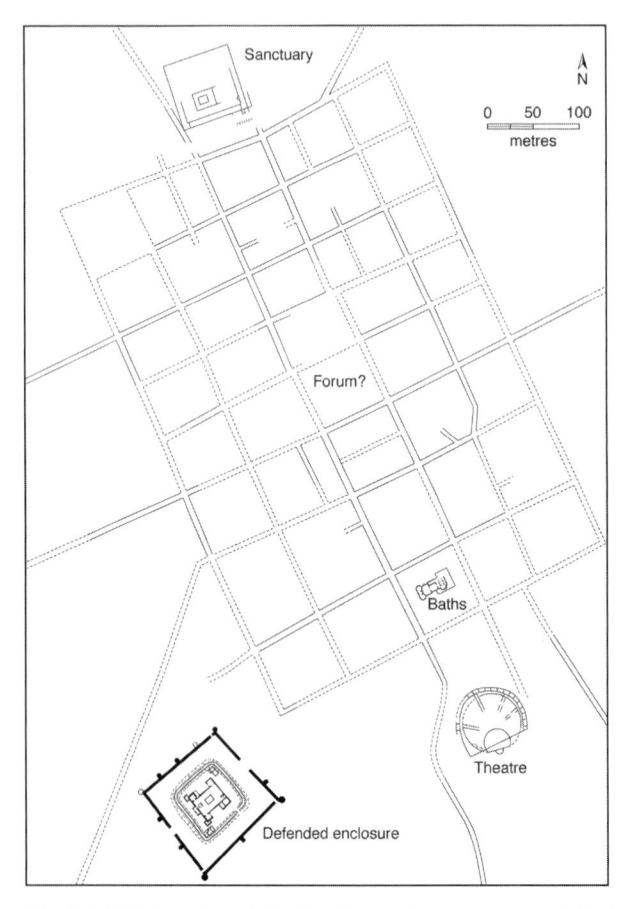

Fig. 2.9 Jublains, plan of the first-/second-century city and the late Roman blockhouse and defended enclosure

that from the later second century on occupation declined in extent and intensity (Bocquet and Naveau 2004), with little fourth-century material. But a major, new building was constructed just outside the south-western angle of the street grid, probably at the start of the third century. A large, stone-built, rectangular structure around a central courtyard, with a large entrance way and with projecting towers at the ends of the long sides, it is thought to have been a secure storehouse (Rebuffat in Naveau 1997: 186–7). Probably around the 270s, it and two small, outside bathhouses were enclosed within an earthwork defence. A little later, this was replaced by a substantial, rectangular defensive circuit with projecting towers (Figure 2.10). This may well never have been finished, and there is no good evidence that it was occupied in the fourth century. Taken together, the sequences in the gridded area and the fortified area suggest that Jublains as an urban centre was in progressive decline by the end of the second century. But it still had an important function, proclaimed by the storehouse as a secure centre for the storage of supplies, possibly the grain render of the *civitas*, but perhaps also gold from the area (there is a small late Roman strongpoint or *burgus* at Rubricaire south of Jublains in the zone of the gold deposits). This was emphasised by the successive fortifications at the end of the third century. But both the old urban area and the storehouse seem to have been redundant in the fourth century. Jublains is still listed as a *civitas* in the *Notitia Galliarum* in the early fifth century, but was never the seat of a

Fig. 2.10 Jublains, south side of the late Roman defended enclosure

bishop and was probably absorbed by the neighbouring *civitas* of the Aulerci Cenomani centred on Le Mans. So here we have a late 'urban fortification', in that it is at a '*civitas* capital', but which is in fact a testimony to the demise of Jublains as an urban centre; this also raises questions about what is meant by a *civitas* in the *Notitia Galliarum*.

Jublains was not a one-off and thus unrepresentative. Another site to raise interesting questions of status and function is Arras (*Nemetacum*), under the High Empire the capital of the Atrebates. In the later third century, a roughly rectangular circuit of walls was constructed in the centre of the occupied area enclosing some 8 ha. On the series of sites along the rue Baudimont in the north-western part of the walled area was a remarkable sequence. Since the early third century, this had been the site of a sanctuary of Attis and Cybele; this was demolished around 375 and a totally different sanctuary erected over part of the site, consisting of an offering pit with three human skulls at its centre, the pit protected by a timber shelter. Around this were further deposits, including human and animal remains and weapons and utensils. The excavators (Delmaire 1994: 138) suggest, on the basis of the atypical rites represented and of some finds of material originating east of the Rhine, that the sanctuary may be 'Germanic'. Most of the interior of the walled area was ravaged by fire in the 380s (cause unknown), and on the rue Baudimont sites new buildings were constructed, interpreted as barracks of traditional form (Delmaire 1994: 138–41). It would seem that a unit of the regular army was now stationed at Arras. The other late building is known to be an apsidal hall, originally part of a bathhouse near the site of the medieval cathedral. This is often interpreted as a church, but since the apse was heated by a hypocaust, the structure is perhaps more likely to be part of an episcopal complex (a reception room?) than a church. Clearly, late fourth-century Arras had an important military aspect, and the *Notitia Dignitatum* (*Occ*. XLII.40) lists a *praefectus laetorum Batavorum Nemetacensium, Atrabatis* (commander of the Nemetacensian Batavian [from the lower Rhine] *laeti* at *Atrebatis* [Arras] – the *laeti* being Germanic peoples serving in the Roman army; see below), so the modern use of the word *castrum* (fort) for the fortified area may well be appropriate.

East of Arras lay the capital of the Nervii, Bavai (*Bagacum*), with one of the more remarkable wall circuits of the Late Empire. Under the Early Empire, Bavai had been endowed with a forum complex on a pharaonic scale, raised on a high cryptoporticus. The monument seems to have been completely out of proportion with the relatively modest area occupied and the buildings of the town of the first and second centuries, a town which by the third century was contracting in area with buildings abandoned

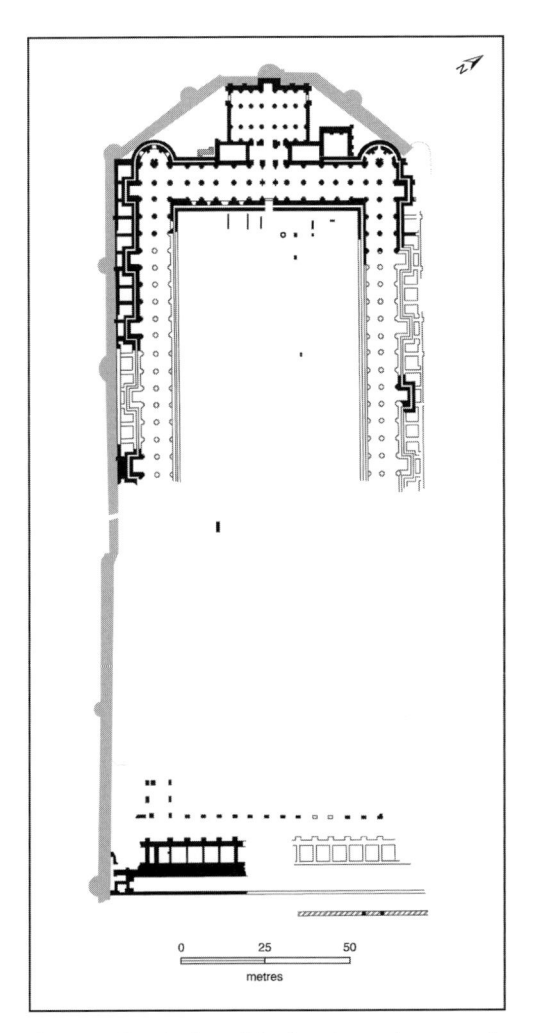

Fig. 2.11 Bavai, plan of the first-/second-century forum with the late Roman walls around it

(Loridant 2004: 77–8). In the late third century, the forum complex was surrounded by a defensive ditch and its outward-facing openings blocked up. This was in preparation for the addition of a defensive wall to the outside face of the forum massif (Figure 2.11). This was strengthened by a second, thicker wall with projecting towers, normally dated to the first half of the fourth century, but the presence of certain pottery forms elsewhere dated to the second half of that century suggests a Valentinianic date for the upgrading of the circuit (Loridant 2004: 78–9). At the same time, there appears to have been a rectangular extension to the circuit on the eastern side of the forum. The original fortification comprising the forum was not only small, some 2 ha., but encumbered with the structures inherited from the forum, so it cannot have been an 'urban' fortification in the sense of defending a town or city; it was a military strongpoint and anchored one end of the fortified road westwards from Cologne. Moreover, the *civitas* of the Nervii was in the fourth century known as the Camaracenses after Cambrai (*Camaracum*), which must have replaced Bavai as 'capital', so the latter would have lost its administrative importance as well. Sadly, hardly anything is known of Cambrai under the Late Empire. A little to the north of the Bavai–Cambrai road lay the site of Famars (*Fanum Martis*) (Delmaire 1990: 210–39), under the High Empire a secondary centre with a substantial bathhouse. In the third century the bathhouse seems to have been used as a storehouse; it burnt down with grain, peas and groups of coins inside it in the Constantinian period. Subsequently, a fortification was constructed, partly against the bathhouse, enclosing 1.8 ha. The *Notitia Dignitatum* (*Occ.* XLII.39) gives it as the site of a *praefectus laetorum Nerviorum*, so it, too, would seem to have become a military strongpoint. East of the reduced Tongeren/Tongres, the passage of the river Maas for the Cologne–Bavai road was ensured by the new fortification, probably of the early to mid fourth century, at Maastricht (Brulet 1990: 84–7), where a rectangular area of some 2 ha. was walled, with a probable bridgehead fortlet on the other side of the river at Wyck. The only building known from the interior of the defences is a large storehouse in the southern half. Whether Maastricht should be seen as a 'town' or a 'fort' is entirely unclear, testimony to the blurring of categories going on in northern Gaul. Other transfers of 'capital' in the area were those of the Menapii from Cassel (*Castellum*), in an area rendered unviable by the Dunkirk II marine transgression (Delmaire 2004: 45), to the former secondary site at Tournai (*Turnacum*) on the crossing of the Scheldt, where a square area of some 13 ha. was walled, and of the Viromandui from earlier St-Quentin (*Augusta*) back west to the major late Iron Age *oppidum* at Vermand itself.

A somewhat similar situation to that at Bavai can be seen to the southwest at the main town of the Ambiani, Amiens (*Samarobriva*), which under the High Empire had had a similarly monumental forum complex, made all the grander by the addition at its western end of a large, stone-built amphitheatre (Bayard and Massy 1983: Ch. 4). The third century saw progressive contraction of the occupied area at the city, to judge from the distributions of the coins of successive emperors (Bayard and Massy 1983: Ch. 8) (cf. p. 108). At the construction of the walls, probably in the earlier fourth century, the massif of masonry comprising the forum and amphitheatre

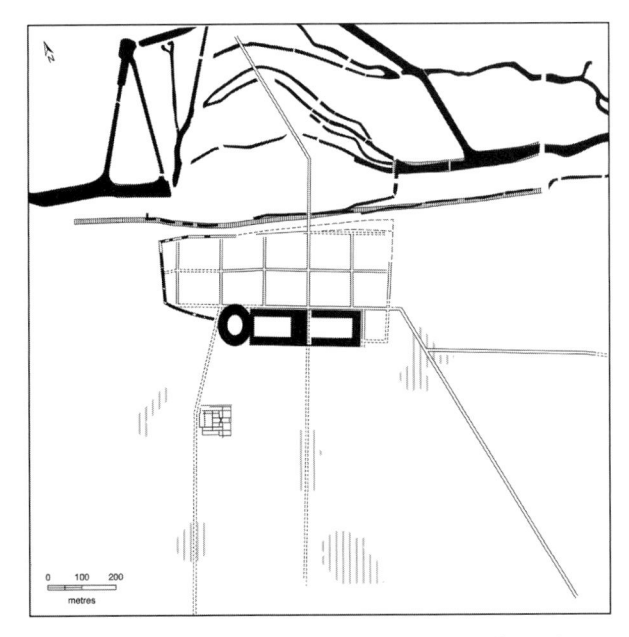

Fig. 2.12 Amiens, plan of the late Roman defended area (river courses modern)

formed most of the southern side of the circuit (Figure 2.12), though, unlike Bavai, it was not just a matter of this complex; an area between the forum/amphitheatre and the river Somme to the north was also enclosed (Bayard and Massy 1983: Ch. 9), making a total fortified area of 20 ha., as opposed to the 140 ha. or so of the street grid of the High Empire. Like Bavai, Amiens had seen substantial contraction. From late Roman Amiens come four military tombstones: the first is (*CIL* XIII.3493) of Valerius Durio, a *circitor* (junior officer) of a unit of *catafractarii* (armoured cavalry); the second (*CIL* XIII.3495) of Valerius Zurdiginus, a *decurio* (officer) of a unit of *catafractarii*; the third (*CIL* XIII.3492) of Valerius Januarius, *imaginifer*, of a *numerus* (unit) of Ursarienses (cf. p. 91); and the fourth (*CIL* XIII.3494) of the cavalryman Valerius Justus, who belonged to a *schola provincialium*, which appears not to be a regular army unit but perhaps more a local force or militia. Amiens appears more than once in the *Notitia Dignitatum*, once as the place of origin of the unit of *equites catafractarii* Ambianenses then (*c.* 395) campaigning in Thrace (*Not. Dig. Or.* VI.36); it seems likely that this is the unit with which Durio and Zurdiginus had served. It also appears (*Not. Dig. Occ.* IX.39) as the site of two *fabricae* producing swords and shields for the army; evidence for metalworking in the eastern part of the former forum complex has been linked with this (Bayard and Massy 1983: 253). As at

Arras so at Amiens, the army was clearly a major, even predominant, element in the fourth-century city in a way quite unlike its second-century predecessor.

It is evident that in Gaul north of the Somme at a number of places that had been urban under the High Empire and at a number of other places also, the archaeological evidence for the late Roman period is that they had become either purely military centres or places with a very strong military component. Indeed, if one were to look simply at the plan of the fortifications, the internal buildings and the artefact assemblages, it would be very difficult indeed to state that they were significantly different from those from forts of the regular army such as Alzey or Köln-Deutz, reflecting the point already made about the fluidity of military identities. The great majority of these sites seem to be related to the safeguarding of the principal communications routes, especially the Rhine–Britain axis. But similar observations may be made about some 'urban' sites south of the Somme also, particularly in the area of present-day Normandy. The regular, rectilinear plan is also a feature of some other urban fortifications such as Bayeux, Evreux and Lisieux (Johnson 1983: 87–8), sites at which urban use and occupation seem to have been winding down through the third century and at which there is little evidence for fourth-century civil occupation (Fichet de Clairfontaine *et al.* 2004; cf. Gauthier and Fixot 1996: *passim*). Indeed, these are sites reminiscent of Jublains in that even under the High Empire there is no evidence for intense urban activity. One may cite in addition Rouen, certainly a flourishing urban site under the High Empire but where a central core of only just over 15 ha. was enclosed by a strong wall, archaeomagnetic dating from the bricks in one section of the walls giving a late third-century date (Lequoy and Guillot 2004: Ch. 5). The circuit of the walls approximated to a square and elsewhere might be seen as a purely military site. Interestingly, these military-looking 'urban' sites in Normandy lie in what was the area of the command of the *dux tractus Armoricani et Nervicani*, raising again the question of a civil or of a military vocation for their fortifications and the areas within them.

There were, of course, many other fortified sites in the northern to central parts of Gaul which had under the High Empire been the principal towns of the *civitates*, places such as Paris or Reims, each of which demonstrates different aspects of urban development during the later Roman period (cf. Van Ossel 2011b). The evidence for Paris is relatively abundant (Busson 1998). The Ile de la Cité was defended by a wall enclosing a lentoid area of some 9 ha., and a dendrochronological date from an associated structure suggests that the wall dates to the early fourth century (Busson 1998: 402).

Little is known of what lay within the defences, save a large, basilican building in the northern part of the area, immediately east of the main north–south road inside the gate to the bridge over the Seine. The function of this structure is uncertain. It was long thought to be an early church, but this idea is now discounted; its function as a large storehouse is more likely. But the main part of the Roman city of *Lutetia*, capital of the Parisii, had always lain south of the river on the left bank. The limited evidence from this zone suggests that Paris, too, saw a progressive shrinkage of the inhabited area through the third century and on into the fourth (Busson 1998: 76-7). In the later period, the monumental Cluny Baths were still standing, but whether they still functioned as baths is doubtful. There are some traces of occupation with material of fourth-century date from the slopes down to the Seine, but little compared with the material from inside the Ile de la Cité walls, let alone compared with the second century. Whether Paris retained any significant civilian population is debatable; it could have been another military-dominated strongpoint (and it served as a winter base for the Caesar Julian during his campaigns in Gaul in the later 350s).

Reims (*Durocortorum*), capital of the Remi and principal town of Gallia Belgica, had a street grid covering some 200 ha. by the end of the second century, by which time it seems to have been built up. When the walls came to be built, they enclosed 55 ha., a large area in comparison with most other late defended towns in Gaul, but only some 25 per cent of the second-century area. Unfortunately, there is as yet insufficient evidence to trace developments through the third and earlier fourth centuries. Thanks to a series of recent excavations, though, the construction of part of the late wall circuit can now be dated to the two decades 330–50 (Neiss and Sindonino 2006: 95), significantly later than the traditional date range. This means that all through the troubles of the third century and well into the fourth century Reims remained an open city, and this despite the fact that at some time it came to house three of the *fabricae* dedicated to producing clothing and equipment for the army (see below). Major baths at Reims were completed as a gift to the city by Constantine I (*CIL* XIII.3255), reinforcing the evidence for the city as important to the imperial government, and the evidence for the size and decoration of fourth-century houses within the city walls and outside (Neiss and Sindonino 2006: 104–8) suggests an out-of-the ordinary concentration of population and wealth, presumably a function, at least in part, of the imperial installations there.

Between Reims and the imperial residence at Trier lay the important city of Metz, which also demonstrates similar developments (Halsall 1995: esp. Ch. 7; cf. Dreier 2011). Walls, probably of the early fourth century, enclosed

Fig. 2.13 Metz, Saint-Pierre-aux-Nonnains, the third-century basilican building from the NW

an area of 72 ha., among the largest areas delimited by late walls in Gaul. Within the wall circuit was the large, fourth-century basilica later to become the church of Saint-Pierre-aux-Nonnains (Figure 2.13). While it is associated with an earlier public baths, it is not certain whether the basilica acted as a new *palaestra* to the baths, or whether it should be compared with the great, imperial basilica in neighbouring Trier (p. 202), and was thus an official, administrative building. Elsewhere within the walls there is evidence from a number of sites of continuing excavation to the mid fourth century or later, and outside the walls the 'Grand Amphithéâtre' remained in use into the fifth century, if not necessarily as an amphitheatre (p. 427). Again, the position within and links to the imperial hierarchies of government were crucial for the overall prosperity of the city.

The overall argument about the nature of urban sites between the Loire and the Rhine should be clear enough. Apart from Trier, Cologne and possibly Metz, none exhibited the sort of civic monumentality characteristic of the Early Empire, which was designed to replicate an essentially civilian urban culture. Instead, these sites clamorously proclaim their military affiliations. Some, indeed, such as Jublains or Bavai, had probably ceased to have any civilian population worth the name and had become simply military strongpoints. Others, such as the sites in Normandy, may well have gone down a similar route; indeed, their urbanism under the High Empire seems always to have been superficial and rather odd. Even those sites where there was at least room for a continuing civilian population, such as Amiens or Reims, had a major investment in military and military-related personnel and installations, and they were, of course, to become physically dominated by their great, new wall circuits. One question that we have not so far considered is that of who paid for and built these wall circuits. It is impossible to be certain because we have no epigraphic evidence, such as inscriptions over the gates, to tell us. But it has just been argued that these defences are often much more to do with protection of imperial installations, materiel and personnel than of urban populations. In this case it would not be unreasonable to argue that these walls were constructed at state behest, though whether directly by the state is more questionable. It might be that there was input from the army (the resemblance of some of these 'urban' fortifications to defences at Rhineland sites has been remarked upon). Some support for this may be gained from the constructional similarity of groups of fortifications in the same area, such as Beauvais, Soissons (Johnson, S. 1983: Ch. 5) and, indeed, the Normandy group of Bayeux, Evreux and Lisieux. These resemblances argue more for common plans and workforces than for individual initiatives. Another argument in favour of command by some organisation at a higher level than the individual *civitas* may be the sheer scale of these defences and the huge volumes of material they consumed; again this would seem to argue for an organisation capable of commanding huge resources. But even so it may well have been that the state commanded and then devolved the construction to the individual *civitates*, since, apart from the army, it had no mechanisms for undertaking such projects. Similar arguments are deployed in the next chapter in relation to other groups of defences in the West, particularly that in north-western Hispania (p. 127). In that chapter it is also argued (p. 132) that the presence of the ten or so defensive circuits of this north Gaulish type that lie south of the Loire can be explained again in terms of imperial considerations such as safeguarding supply routes. The involvement of the local government structures and of the elites may explain why these fortifications also have a pronounced element of monumentality and display.

If the monumental style of a city of northern Gaul in the second century was an index of its function as a nursery for citizens of an essentially civic type, then the monumental style of a city in the same region in the fourth century showed its function as training ground for the new soldier-citizens formed to sustain and defend the empire. Indeed, this book argues (more particularly in the following chapter) that a central function of a city is to produce citizens of the type desired by the society of which it is an expression (cf. Laurence *et al.* 2011). The form a city takes and the buildings with which it is endowed are not just passive reflections of the civil and civic values prevailing in the society that constructed them, but also an active ingredient in (re)producing a citizen of the type wanted by that society: hence the differences in building types and ideological structures between, say, a classical Chinese city and a Spanish colonial city even if both are laid out on grids of streets. It will be an important contention both of this chapter and of Chapters 3 and 8 that the cities of the late Roman West need to be analysed and discussed with this precept in mind. The creation of fortified urban sites during the later third and fourth centuries in northern Gaul and subsequently in other areas of the West was not simply a passive reflection of the military needs of the time. These sites were also the places in which generations of their inhabitants (for those that retained civil populations) were brought up and formed, and the fortifications were a significant constituent of the active creation of these 'new model citizens' – a suitable military epithet.

One last point. It is clear that the area in which these new-style fortifications and 'urban' sites are clustered, the region between the Loire and the Rhine, more particularly the Seine and the Rhine, is also the region in which in the preceding chapter it was argued that for all the revisionism about the 'third-century crisis' there may nonetheless be some archaeological evidence for military instability (p. 39). In this case, then, it may be that what these fortifications show us, among other things, is the region most touched by the troubles of the third century and in which the imperial authorities responded by imposing a network of fortifications and military garrisons designed to counter any possible repeat and to back up the watch on the Rhine.

Hilltop fortifications

The forts, *burgi*, fortified towns and other places considered above were not the only fortifications in the Rhine-Loire area, though they seem to have been in some sense 'official' or an expression of 'public' power, in that they were constructed either by the military authorities or by civic authorities (the latter probably at the behest of or with the aid of the military). There is another type of late fortification which needs to be taken into account here, the hilltop circuits west of the central Rhine (Figure 2.14). There is a larger group of about 60 on the territory of the present Federal Republic of Germany in the hilly country to either side of the Moselle, the Hunsrück to the north and the Eifel to the south (Gilles 1985 is basic; for an update, see Gilles 1998), connecting through to a smaller group of some 25 in the east of

The militarisation of northern Gaul 77

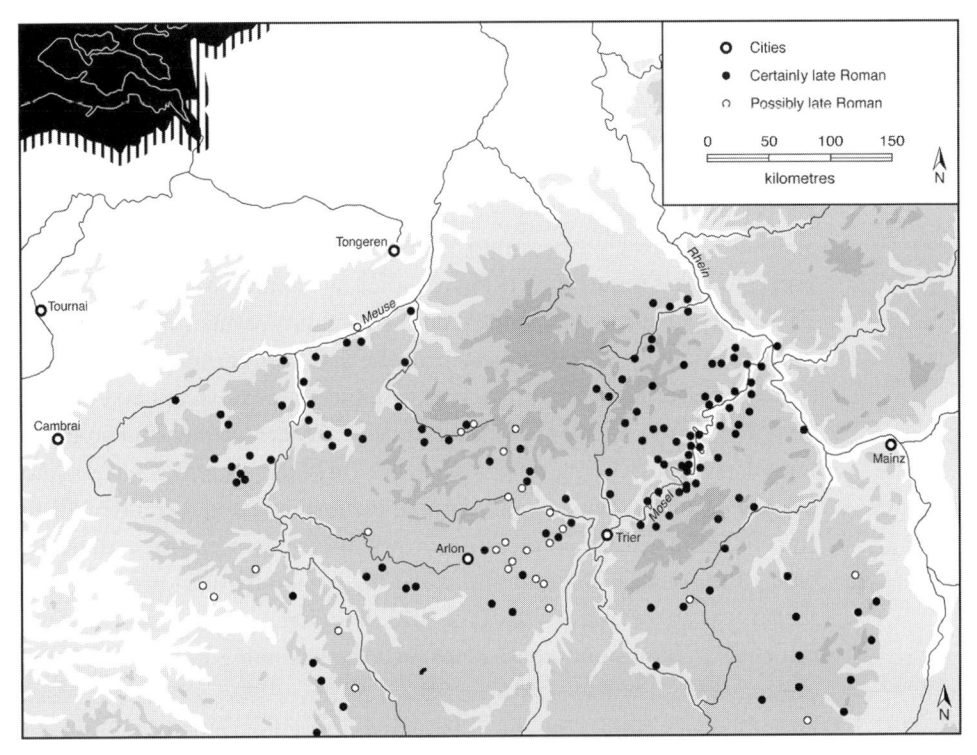

Fig. 2.14 Late Roman hilltop defended enclosures in north-eastern Gaul and the Rhineland

modern Belgium, north-west of the Hunsrück in the Condroz and round the upper valley of the Maas/Meuse (Brulet 1990: 153–91). Hilltop fortifications were rare elsewhere in Gaul, so the concentration in these regions east of the middle and lower Rhine has been seen as a reaction to the fact that these areas lay on the main invasion axes across the middle Rhine for the Alamanni; moreover, just to the north lay the Salian Franks in Toxandria, whom the literary sources portray as troublesome – witness the expedition against them by Julian in 358 (Ammianus Marcellinus, *Res Gestae* XVII.8) – though how much this was not because of a real threat from the Franks but was rather a display of imperial muscle by the young Caesar is a question that has recently been posed (Drinkwater 1996). These fortifications were in stone and normally encircled the hilltop, though some simply barred the neck of a spur (as at the classic site of Furfooz), and were mostly under 1 ha. in area, though some were larger, up to 7 ha. at Nismes in Belgium. Those where excavation has taken place have yielded dating material for their construction ranging from the later third century to the middle of the fourth. A crucial feature of a number of these fortifications is that cemeteries have been excavated outside them, and the contents of some of the graves raise important questions about the identities of the occupants. The classic site of this type is that of Furfooz, with the fortification of the Haute-Recenne (Brulet 1978), where a well-built, mortared stone wall cut off the spur in the later third century. Outside the walls lay a bathhouse. The site is thought to have been abandoned in the mid fourth century (supposedly as a result of the historically recorded Alamannic incursions in the 350s), before being put back into commission with a second, outer wall, the ruins of the bathhouse now being occupied by a cemetery (Nenquin 1953). This cemetery, uncovered in the nineteenth century, contained a number of burials with grave goods suggestive of the presence of military personnel, perhaps of Germanic origin, such as weapons (swords, spears and knives) and fittings from more or less elaborate belt suites for the men and brooches for the women, including types such as the *Tutulusfibel* or the *Armbrustfibel* (see below, p. 85), held to be of German manufacture and therefore indicative of a German (female) presence. Brulet (1978) therefore proposed on the basis of the quality of the masonry and the bathhouse of the earlier phase that it was an 'official' fortification with a military garrison, and that the cemetery of the second phase betokened the stationing here of Germanic personnel (*laeti* or *foederati* – see below) by the military authorities. More recently, a very similar pairing of a hilltop fortification with a cemetery with weaponry, belt suites, etc., has been discussed, at Vireux-Molhain in the French Ardennes (Lemant 1985: esp. discussions by Böhme: 76–88, 131–3), where a triangular fortification encircled the top of a hill with the cemetery on a lower but still prominent hill to the south. The fortification dated to the first half of the fourth century, and excavations in its interior revealed traces of burning in the middle of the fourth century, dated by a hoard of bronze coins of the House of Constantine and therefore again proposed to be a result of the Alamannic incursions of the 350s. The cemetery dates to a reoccupation in the later fourth to early fifth centuries and contains some cremations, very rare by this date in Roman provincial burial practice but common east of the Rhine, and also burials with weapons, belt suites, *Armbrustfibeln* (though no Roman-produced brooches) and other objects of Germanic types, though, interestingly, little Germanic female material. From good examples such as these and the more partial evidence from other sites, a narrative has emerged of the creation of 'official' or of 'private' hilltop fortifications of the late third/early fourth century (the division largely being on the criterion of the quality of the masonry – good quality, mortared against rougher drystone) that were destroyed in the Alamannic invasions attested to by the historical sources for the first half of the 350s (though why the Alamanni should have bothered to destroy such sites, or why the destruction should not have been the work of the Roman army of reconquest under Julian is not made clear) and then reoccupied in the later fourth century as the base for a group of Germanic military personnel and their wives (though children's graves seem curiously rare).

These fortifications and cemeteries were therefore usually linked more with the requirements of imperial defence than with civilian concerns, positing a pattern of the placing of Germanic warriors, *foederati*, in purpose-built fortifications to safeguard the attack corridor from across the central Rhine. It was thus a manifestation of 'public' power. An alternative view, less favoured but worth considering, is that these were instead expressions of 'private' power, the creation by local elites of fortified centres of residence for themselves and their followers, replacing the earlier aristocratic vocabulary of display such as the villa. These were much more militarised locations of residence and means of self-representation resulting from the military shocks of the third century and the continuing threats of the fourth, to say nothing of the greater importance of the regular army in this area. Were this the case, then it would be remarkable that such 'private' fortifications were permitted in large numbers so close to the imperial residence and major imperial administrative centre at Trier, which was an expression of the 'public' power of the state. Crucial in attempting to determine such questions is the material from the associated cemeteries and how it is to be analysed.

Burials

The burials with weapons, belt suites, brooches and female accoutrements at these hilltop sites are in fact part of a much larger question which needs to be addressed. Traditionally, graves containing weapons and the often associated graves where the deceased were accompanied by dress fittings (brooches, buckles, strap ends and the like – of types either originating east of the Rhine or in 'Germanic' taste) have been assimilated to the documentary evidence, particularly from the *Notitia Dignitatum* (see below, p. 90), for the settlement in the fourth century of Germanic peoples from east of the Rhine across northern and central Gaul (Böhme 1974 gives the fundamental catalogue, typology and discussion and takes a strongly 'Germanist' position, maintained in later publications [such as Böhme 1985, 1996]; Sommer 1984 updates the catalogue and typology). This settlement was argued to be either that of *laeti* (surrendered peoples with an obligation to supply recruits to the Roman army) or that of *foederati* ('barbarian' peoples operating under treaty with the Romans); given the date and relative wealth of some of the burials, they came to be felt to be more likely those of *foederati* rather than those of the lower-status *laeti*. The burial rite was seen as 'German' because of the presence of weapons, which was seen as the prerogative of warrior Germans rather than as characteristic of the Roman provincial population, supposed to have been banned from bearing arms. This meant that the metalwork, especially brooches, with clear parallels outside the empire, was 'Germanic' and so therefore were the people buried with it. The other metalwork, particularly the belt suites but also the weaponry, was by extension considered as 'Germanic' or in 'Germanic taste', even if produced inside the empire, and therefore considered as a marker of ethnic identity. Besides the hilltop fortifications and cemeteries just discussed, similar burials have been found at a variety of sites, including forts, urban sites, villas and other rural settlements, or simply rural cemeteries whose wider context is unknown. Such metalwork was also to be found outside imperial territory, to the east of the Rhine (Böhme 1974; cf. Swift 2000b: 88–97), where its presence was taken to be the result of the 'Germanic' style and use of the material, reinforcing its ethnic significance. Implicit in these arguments was a sort of prefiguring of the events of the fifth century when the Germanic peoples, the Franks from Toxandria in the north and the Alamanni and others from east of the Rhine, were to destroy Roman political and military rule, replacing it with their own kingdoms. The presence of Germanic peoples in the fourth century was taken as anticipating, even aiding, the process of the replacement of Roman by German power.

More recent research has reviewed, on the one hand, the context of the burial rite, the significance of the metalwork itself and its stylistic origins and affinities. On the other hand, wider methodological concerns about funerary practice and burial have undermined earlier, easy assumptions about equating burial practice with ethnicity. This has gone hand-in-hand with questions about how individuals were self-aware agents in the portrayal and reshaping of their identity, and also the dialectic between the deceased, those performing the funeral and burial, and any intended audience (cf. Theuws 2009: 293–7), wherein a variety of statements could be made that either reflected properties of the deceased in their lives, properties the deceased had wanted reflected, or properties thought appropriate to the deceased by social convention, or else reflected properties that were reshaped by the living who performed the burial in ways they found useful in the context of the theatre afforded by funerary rites. All this has questioned the underpinnings and assumptions of the traditional, 'ethnic' narrative, opening the way to a wider and more nuanced interpretation of these sites and their material. So, it is necessary to review the outlines and main conclusions of this work.

First of all, we consider the burial rite. There is nothing particularly 'Germanic' about the predominant rite in these cemeteries, inhumation with or without grave goods – indeed, quite the reverse (for a first attempt at deconstructing the traditional burial narrative for northern Gaul, see Halsall 1995, and, more recently, for summaries of his developing position on the subject, see Halsall 2000, 2007, 2008). If one looks at the burial rites in use in Germany east and north of the Rhine during the third to fifth centuries, or Later Roman Iron Age (LRIA), the majority of them used cremation for the disposal of the body; inhumation was rare and the one site where it was common, the Leuna-Hassleben complex of north-western Germany, was also associated with quantities of Roman imports in the richer burials, suggesting that the elite in this area were in fact using Roman-derived burial goods and practices to express their status. This preference for cremation is an important factor in explaining why there is a disparity in the incidence of this material west and east of the Rhine, as it is much less common on the eastern side of the river; it does not survive in cremation burials, unlike the situation to the west of the Rhine. West of the Rhine, inhumation had become the predominant burial rite of the indigenous Gallo-Roman population by the fourth century, cremation having been phased out between the late second and late third centuries (Raynaud 2006; Tranoy 2000; Vidal 1992). Though the deposition of grave goods was not common, it did exist, so there was no prescription against it (least of all at this date by Christian doctrine, cf. p. 164), and, of course, inhumation favours the survival of grave goods much more than does cremation (unless, as is increasingly the case with the excavation of cremations, careful measures are taken to sift any surviving pyre debris from the burning place or from the grave for the vestiges of material consigned to the flames with the deceased on the pyre). This again emphasises the importance of taking into account burial rites when analysing the distribution maps of the object classes in this period.

Second, there is the question of 'weapon burials'. From about the middle of the fourth century, some burials in northern Gaul were accompanied by items designated as weapons, thus giving rise to the terms *Waffengrab/ tombe à armes*/weapon burial or grave. These burials were widely distributed across the north of Gaul (Böhme 1974: Karte 19), though, significantly, they were far less common east of the Rhine (of the 83 Böhme lists, only some 15 come from outside Roman territory, though variation in burial rite between cremation and inhumation may be a factor here), suggesting that they may not be part of a particularly 'Germanic' tradition; indeed, some could be the graves of Germans who had served as Roman soldiers and returned home to be buried in a way derived from Roman provincial (including military) practice, thus emphasising what may have been a defining aspect of their life course. Even within northern Gaul, these burials were strongly concentrated between the Seine and the Rhine, and a more recent distribution map of such burials (Böhme 1985: Fig. 75) shows only 17 out of 99 south and west of the Seine. The types of weapons involved are principally arrows, axes, lances/spears and knives. As noted above, this was felt to be something inappropriate to Roman provincial civilians, since they were largely forbidden to carry arms, and furthermore the rite had no antecedent in the provincial funerary repertoire. The source for this innovation was therefore sought in a people where warrior status, the bearing of arms and thus the importance of weaponry as symbolic of status (male, adult, free) were deemed central. The 'early Germans' were seen as a warrior race whose menfolk were defined above all by their fighting prowess. Thus weapon burials were interpreted as the graves of Germanic warriors living and dying within the Roman Empire.

This model has for some time attracted criticism on the grounds that there was nothing ancestral to this burial rite east of the Rhine, so reasons for its appearance should be sought in Roman Gaul. Halsall (1995, 2000, 2007, 2008) has argued powerfully that this burial rite (and others in the same 'package' such as the deposition of dress fittings) was a response to social stress and the consequent need to define social position more clearly; he proposes that this was done in part through assuming the signifiers of official Roman, particularly military, status. A variant of this was proposed by Whittaker (1994: Ch. 7), who argued essentially for a two-way process whereby military groups ('Germanic') were settled on the land (as *foederati* or something similar) and thus had both martial and land-owning responsibilities, as expressed through their burial rite; conversely, as Roman state power weakened, landowners increasingly had to offer protection to their dependants and started to turn into warlords. The simple point that the distribution map of these weapon burials strongly suggests that they were in fact an innovation taking place within northern Gaul itself rather than imported into it has also been strongly supported by Brather (2008: 432–8). A powerful critique of the traditional assumptions, their reinterpretation and the fundamentals on which these were based has been offered by Theuws (2009; cf. Theuws and Alkemade 2000). First of all, he notes that the designation 'weapon' is often debatable (some graves contain no more than knives) and that the impression the term gives of the military or martial is unfounded. Furthermore, if one refines the chronology of these burials, major differences appear. The earliest type of 'weapon burial' dating to the second half of the fourth century is characterised by arrows (probably with bows, whose elements rarely survive), axes, spears/lances and sometimes knives, but, emphatically, not by swords, shields or helmets. Furthermore, a review (Kazanski 1995) of such 'weapons' from northern Gaul has shown that in fact few of them can be stated with confidence to originate from Free Germany, rather than from the Roman traditions of weaponry, or to belong to types widely distributed across Europe. Swords and shields only appeared in a tiny number of burials from right at the end of the fourth century, with sword burials only becoming more widespread (and then not very common) from the middle of the fifth century. In relation to the 'weapon burials' of the second half of the fourth century, Theuws (2009: 305–9) noted that the 'weapons' chosen are ones that do not fit well in a military context or interpretation; instead he suggests that what we are seeing is equipment more suited to hunting. Given that hunting (as we shall see in Chapter 5, p. 242) was an activity of prestige, linked to aristocrats and in many ways definitive of their status, this suggests an entirely different interpretation of these 'weapon graves' as those of leaders of their communities defined in part by this aristocratic pastime. It is interesting to note that similar interpretations had also recently been advanced for the rather similar 'weapon burials' of the Duero tradition in central and western Spain (see below, p. 88). Theuws (2009: 309–14) also notes that burials of this type have very localised distributions in the interior of northern Gaul between the Seine and the Rhine, distributions that do not map onto the distribution of the regular Roman army or of the related *praefecti laetorum* overseeing groups of settled barbarians supplying young men to the imperial forces. It is also worth noting that 'weapon burials' were not an especial characteristic of the few excavated fort cemeteries of the fourth century such as Krefeld-Gellep (Pirling 1986) or Oudenburg (Mertens and van Impe 1971), again suggesting that such burials elsewhere are not of military personnel as such but rather of people adopting what they perceived as military-style status markers. Theuws (2009: 309–14) suggests that these may therefore be the burials of incoming groups with their leaders (not necessarily 'barbarians' or 'Germans') settling on lands available because of the disruptions of the latter part of the third century. It is a bit difficult, though, to see why this should only have occurred the best part of a century after the disruptions.

Another innovative feature of the burial practice here is that the distribution of the belt elements and brooches in these furnished male and female graves shows that the bodies were clothed at burial, or at least had clothing placed with the corpse, rather than being shrouded, as seems to have been the majority rite. This has been interpreted in ethnic terms, as the transfer to inhumation of a 'Germanic' practice of laying out a body for cremation clothed, though this practice again is one that it is very difficult to demonstrate as having actually been characteristic of Germanic populations east of the Rhine because either such evidence would not survive the process of cremation, or, even if it could be demonstrated that there had been dress items on the pyre, it would not be possible to state their positioning with relation to the corpse. And in parallel with the uncoupling of the burial rite from an automatically 'Germanic' context has been a reassessment of important classes of metalwork, showing that they were in fact of Roman provincial manufacture and not produced for a particularly 'Germanic' taste (though the decorative style was later to have an important impact on the development of the decorative styles of objects produced outside the old imperial frontier from the fifth century). The main focus of study has always been the belt suite, the various elements that went to decorate the distinctive, wide belts of the fourth and fifth centuries; surviving examples are almost always of copper alloy, though some rare pieces in gold or silver attest to the splendour of the apparel of senior officers (cf. Böhme 1974; Sommer 1984). One consequence of the amount of study lavished on these objects is that their typological sequence and the broad date ranges for the different types have been established with a degree of certainty. The decorative style of these pieces – particularly those of the type known as 'chip-carved' (*Kerbschnitt*) – because they were often found east of the Rhine and because of their influence on later Germanic metalwork, was held to be in 'Germanic' taste and thus their wearers to be Germans. It is now appreciated that in fact this material was produced in Roman state *fabricae*, particularly in Pannonia on the Danube bend, but also in northern Gaul, for distribution to servants of the late Roman state, in particular soldiers and administrators (who ranked as a paramilitary force). These pieces thus say nothing about the ethnicity of their wearers but quite a lot about their wearers' relation to the imperial power. A similar argument can be adduced for the other common metalwork type from these graves, the brooches, of the type referred to above (p. 59) and known in English as the 'crossbow brooch' and in German as *Zwiebelknopffibel*. These also were produced in the state *fabricae* (Swift 2000a: Ch. 2), again often in Pannonia (Types 1 and 3/4) but also probably in northern Gaul (Type 2). Representations in art, such as the tomb painting from Silistra (Bulgaria) (p. 58), show them being worn by a state official in combination with a decorated, wide belt. Again, their significance was not for the wearer's ethnicity but for his function and rank. The finding of such material in fourth-century burials in northern Gaul, the Rhineland and Britain shows the presence of men about whom their official status (military or imperial official) was an important claim to be made in death. But belt suites and brooches on their own could mean either a soldier or an official (of whatever ethnic origin).

Other burials from cemeteries which contained male 'weapon graves' and other types of burial were those with other classes of brooch such as the *Armbrustfibel* (confusingly, this translates as 'crossbow brooch' but must be distinguished from the type mentioned above – to achieve this here, the term will be left in the German), the 'equal-armed brooch' (*Gleicharmigefibel*), the 'tutulus brooch' (*Tutulusfibel*) and the 'saucer brooch' (*Schalenfibel*), as well as other items of apparel such as elaborate hairpins, earrings and other jewellery (for typology and discussion, see Böhme 1974: Ch. 1). Apart from their incidence in Gaul, the distribution area of the four brooch types mentioned above was a small area between the lowest courses of the Elbe and the Weser (cf. Böhme 1974: Karten 1–3, 5–8), which is also where most of the male 'weapon graves' east of the Rhine were located. This has again been taken to argue for the persons buried with this material to have originated in the Elbe–Weser area and to have moved to Gaul. In fact, though, more recent study of the origins and development of this material – for instance, the type of *Tutulusfibel* known as the Cortrat–Oudenburg type (Halsall 2000: 171–2) – suggests in this case that its homeland was again on the 'Roman' side of the Rhine, though in the area of Toxandria, so whether the makers of these objects saw themselves as 'Roman' or 'Germanic' is very problematic. A further development of this is, of course, the prestige of Roman goods beyond the frontier, such that not only was Roman-manufacture metalwork regularly found there (Böhme 1974: *passim*), but also there was even a small-scale production of imitations of a Roman buckle type in the former *Agri Decumates* (Sommer 1984: Sorte 1, Form C, Typ F, Gunzburg variation; cf. Swift 2000b: 89–90). The overwhelming presence of the empire, the renown of its army and the prestige of its culture in their turn open the possibility that some north Gaulish burials with only Roman-manufacture belts, brooches, etc., may have been of ethnic Germans wishing to make statements about their assimilation to and place in the imperial system. Nevertheless, in this case there is a strong argument that the direction of movement must be reversed and the Elbe–Weser group of material seen as having belonged to persons from that area who had been to or lived in Gaul, returned to Free Germany and happened to practise a burial rite where such personal adornments were important and were preserved for archaeologists.

There is general agreement that the burials with these classes of brooch and other jewellery represent burials of women, like the male dead, clothed at burial. Given that they were burials of women, it is likely that these women accompanied their menfolk, and it has been proposed that in some cases their burials should be associated with male burials alongside them, as seems likely, if unproven. In the case of burials whose links with the Elbe-Weser area suggest they may have been of Germanic origin (even if the accompanying objects are no longer so definitively 'German'), it would then be that some of the male burials with weapons/belt suites/brooches were of German origin; this is entirely reasonable given the evidence from the texts generally for the increasing use of Germanic troops in the Roman army in the late fourth century and the specific evidence of the unit titles of formations stationed in northern Gaul listed in the *Notitia Dignitatum* (see below). But even if some of these burials were of men and women of Germanic extraction, this does not invalidate the arguments against the simple equation of certain types of metalwork and Germanic ethnicity. As Theuws (2009: 314–15) has pertinently asked, was the ethnicity of the deceased something that those conducting the burial necessarily thought worth making a statement about? A partial way out of this world of distorting mirrors will be through systematic application of techniques such as mitochondrial DNA and stable-isotope analysis now coming on stream, which may tell us something about the descent or childhood environment of the person sampled. Mitochondrial DNA analysis, which identifies the line of maternal descent, could identify individuals or groups at variance with the bulk of the local population, though, of course, genetic descent need not be the same as claimed identity (genetic 'Germans' could have spoken Latin and been buried to look 'Roman', and vice versa). Stable-isotope analysis, on the principle that the minerals absorbed into the bone during childhood leave different 'signatures' according to the geology of the region in which the childhood was spent, will only identify first-generation incomers; their offspring raised in Gaul would look 'Gallic'. These techniques are discussed further in Chapter 8, p. 392.

Clearly, the idea that burials displaying certain characteristics, such as containing 'weapons', belt suites and/or brooches of Roman manufacture, necessarily indicated a German ethnicity for their occupants can no longer seriously be sustained. This is not to deny that some who went to their long home in such graves with such equipment may have been of Germanic extraction – it is much more likely than not that some were. But many of such burials probably were those of men and women of other extractions, most probably Gallo-Roman. This would match the evidence of the burial rite, which has been argued to be essentially that of the provincial, Gallo-Roman population, or possibly of non-Gallo-Romans who had assimilated to local funerary practice. In this case, how then may we seek to interpret the range of burial types in northern Gaul largely of the later fourth century furnished with essentially Roman-manufacture material? The answer would appear to be essentially that these are mostly the burials of Gallo-Romans but demonstrating interesting developments in their funerary statements. One of the weaknesses of traditional approaches was that they 'cherry-picked' certain burials or aspects of burials out of their wider contexts of burial and grave goods in fourth-century northern Gaul, and these things now need to be replaced in those contexts. The overwhelming majority of burials in individual cemeteries (be they at urban, rural or military sites) and across northern Gaul as a whole continued through the fourth century to be simple inhumations with no grave goods. Even for the minority of burials which did contain grave goods, the majority of these were clearly of Roman manufacture and consisted largely of vessels, either of pottery or of glass, with occasional other goods such as coins. Even in the grave groups with belt suites, brooches or 'weapons', these objects often were a minority of the objects committed to the earth with the corpse. From this evidence alone it would be difficult to conclude that we are dealing with anything other than minority variations on the normal Gallo-Roman burial rite. But some men were having their importance displayed in part through the elaboration of the burial ritual by the deposition of quantities of objects, and in part by being accoutred in objects declaring the importance to them of links with the officers and officials of the Roman state – perhaps more with the military than with the bureaucracy. A preferred locus and mode of elite display had been displaced to the military-style burial, betokening the militarisation of the markers of aristocratic status (for further consideration of this, see Chapter 5, p. 262). The blurring of 'civil' and 'military' as categories is also emphasised by Willems (1989) in his entitling a paper on the late Roman 'weapon grave' from the villa at Voerendaal (Limburg, Netherlands) 'An Officer or a Gentleman?'. It is also noteworthy that in these groups with a preference for burial in this manner, a minority of the female burials stand out also for the quantity and range of dress items buried with the dead. This would seem to argue that these women had a particular importance. This could be that they played a more powerful social role generally, but perhaps, more specifically, they were important for their part in transmitting identity, with a strong element of matrilinearity in these groups. Finally, it is worth noting here that burials with similar material, especially the belt suites and crossbow brooches along with some knives, but not the axes, bows and spears found in northern Gaul, have also been found in late Roman cemeteries in Britain such as Lankhills, Winchester (Clarke 1979). In that case the most elaborate graves with metalwork were linked by the excavator with burial rites in the central Danube area rather than Free Germany, though more recent stable-isotope work has not shown any simple correlation of non-normative burial rite with incomers from the Continent, least of all any from central Europe (see below, p. 392). Many of the burials according to the 'Danubian' rite have isotopic signatures local to Winchester (though here again the 'second-generation' problem must be acknowledged).

There was one other area of the West with a marked tradition of burial involving the deposition of weapons and dress accessories, in particular belt fittings. This was the northern part of the Iberian peninsula, especially the northern Meseta, home of the 'Duero' tradition of burials with accompanying 'Simancas' brooches and knives (cf. Aurrecoechea Fernández 2001). These cemeteries, many excavated some time ago under less-than-ideal conditions, contain a range of burial types, but mostly relatively simple inhumations. Some of these are accompanied by pottery, glass or metal vessels, and other material, some of it gender-specific such as hobnailed shoes for men or long, iron pins with women. Such dating evidence as there is suggests that the burials start in the second half of the fourth century if not earlier. Among these burials are a small number with brooches, belt suites and weapons (axes, knives, spears/lances). Because of the general geographical overlap between the distribution of these burials and that of the military units listed for northern Spain in the *Notitia Dignitatum* (cf. Chapter 3, p. 129) and because of the typological similarity of some of the personal adornment and weaponry to those from north Gaulish and Rhineland sites, it was argued that these were the burials of Germanic military personnel serving on some internal *limes Hispanicus*. More recently, particularly with the idea of a *limes Hispanicus* progressively discredited, attention has been drawn to the wider contexts of the other burials in the cemeteries, the sites with which the cemeteries may be associated and the overall distribution of this burial custom, leading to some referring to them as *'cementerios tardohíspanos con ajuares'* – that is, 'late Spanish cemeteries with grave goods' – an accurate if periphrastic title. Based on his excavations on the cemetery of Albalete (Cuenca), Fuentes (1989) noted that the brooch/belt/weapon graves were only part of a range of burial possibilities. Other graves included other tools and utensils, some agricultural and some artisanal.

He, like Theuws (2009) for northern Gaul, also noted the functional ambiguity of the 'weapons', which were not incontestably for warfare but could have been for other activities such as, in particular, hunting. On the basis of this, he suggested that men engaged in a variety of activities held status which was displayed in their burials. Since then the excavation of the graveyards around the villa of La Olmeda (a particularly lavish and important villa, one of whose mosaics is a high-quality mosaic of the hunt) has shown that these were of the 'Duero' type, associating this type directly with a high-status civilian site. It is now argued that this type of cemetery represents social and functional gradations within the civil population, quite possibly among the retinue of a *dominus*. The presence of material resembling that found on north Gaulish/Rhineland sites is argued to be the product of blending elements of indigenous Spanish funerary practice with material expressing the prestige of the military personnel stationed in the northern Meseta and the northern littoral (Aurrecoechea Fernández 2001: 226–9). According to this argument, we have a situation similar to that in the northern part of Gaul, where elements of the population had become 'militarised' by contact with regular troops. For northern Spain this debate still requires more data and more reliable data and perhaps more awareness of the theoretical debates on identity as expressed through dress and funerary practice; nevertheless, the possibility of a sort of 'independent invention' of a militarised status with its status markers is intriguing.

So far, this chapter has argued that a range of different types of archaeological evidence normally studied separately is better understood in combination as the expression of a landscape and a society that were increasingly dominated by or making use of expressions of military power. This took the form of fortifications, of which some are linked with units of the regular army ('forts'), others are at places which had been but were not necessarily any longer urban, and were probably constructed for essentially military purposes, possibly by the army itself ('city walls'), and yet others seem to have been a localised response, possibly more 'unofficial' than the other two categories ('hilltop fortifications'). Moreover, finds of metalwork produced in state *fabricae* are common at occupation sites of all types in the interior of northern Gaul, well away from the frontier zones. A considerable amount of this material also comes from burials, many of which have in the past been interpreted along simple ethnic lines as the graves of incoming 'Germans', male and female. As has been seen, it is now better to regard these as the burials of people who, the men especially, used material derived from the military repertoire as a way of demonstrating their leadership; military dress had become part of the rhetoric of power. So between the Loire and the Rhine, and more particularly the Seine and the Rhine, much of the archaeology of power had become increasingly bound up with the Roman state and its self-representation, above all the military. In addition to this, it is very probably the case (and this will be discussed further in Chapters 6 and 7) that much of the economy of northern Gaul was subordinated to military requirements, either through the provisioning of the army with foodstuffs and other raw materials or through the production of finished goods for the military, be it in the state *fabricae* or in private workshops and manufactories.

Military dispositions and the *Notitia Dignitatum*

Given the ways in which the archaeological evidence is tending, it would be sensible to adduce here the evidence for military dispositions in Gaul and the Rhineland contained in the pages of the *Notitia Dignitatum*, as a complement to the archaeology. The *Notitia* is, of course, a problematic document in terms of its purpose, date of composition and relationship to realities on the ground (Goodburn and Bartholomew 1976; Hoffmann 1969). It does, though, provide an impression, however blurred, of the overall dispositions of Roman forces somewhere in the later fourth to early fifth century and can thus be used to supplement and gloss the information from the archaeology. The formal frontier army commands are well enough known and have already been mentioned. On the central Rhine was the *dux Moguntiacensis* (*Not. Dig. Occ.* XLI) with his forces; the *comes Argentoratensis* (*Not. Dig. Occ.* XXVII) was based at Strasbourg though with no forces listed; the tiny command of the *dux Sequanici* (*Not. Dig. Occ.* XXVI) with his one unit was probably at Besançon. Then there is presumably a missing leaf that would have given the command in Germania I on the upper to middle Rhine. Next we have the *dux Belgicae II* (*Not. Dig. Occ.* XXXVIII) with a small command on the Gallic side of the Strait of Dover; the *dux tractus Armoricani et Nervicani* (*Not. Dig. Occ.* XXVII) with his string of posts along the Normandy coast and also exercising authority over Aquitania I and II, Lugdunensis II and III, and Senonia. In Britain, the *comes litoris Saxonici per Britannias* (*Not. Dig. Occ.* XXVIII) held the command of the south-eastern coast, and the *litus Saxonicum* is also, as noted above, specifically evoked in the two coastal commands in north-western Gaul, demonstrating the close links to be expected between the two sides of the Channel, which have traditionally been rather underestimated because of separate national traditions of study (cf. Johnson, D. E. 1977; Maxfield 1989). These are, of course, the officers and named units of the regular frontier forces, the *limitanei* or *ripenses*, charged with holding the Rhine frontier or protecting the seaways of the Strait of Dover and the Channel. The *Notitia* lists give the garrison posts of these units, and the majority of them can be identified with known sites (there are other military sites known to have been in garrison, especially along the Rhine, but this is a comment on the problems of the *Notitia*; it is a snapshot). It is interesting to note that the *dux tractus Armoricani et Nervicani* has listed among his installations Rouen, Avranches, Coutances, Vannes and Nantes, which under the early empire had been cities, but which, as we have seen in the case of Rouen, may by the fourth century have been more purely military. The command of the *dux* covered the area of what is now Normandy, which contained 'urban' fortifications that in fact closely resemble attested military sites (see above, p. 72).

As well as the *limitaneus* commands of Gaul, there was also a large force of the *comitatenses*, the mobile field army, under the *magister equitum per Gallias* (*Not. Dig. Occ.* VII.63–110 for the infantry units; 167–78 for the cavalry). The problem with these troops is that though their unit titles are given, unlike for the *limitanei* no base is specified, and as yet we are uncertain how to identify such units and their personnel in the archaeology, with the occasional exception, such as the helmet of an officer of *VI Stablesia(ni)* from Deurne in Holland (Braat 1973) (a unit frustratingly, if typically, not listed in the *Notitia*). Late Roman laws in the *Codex Theodosianus* suggest that the *comitatenses* could be billeted on the civilian population – perhaps this is reflected by the probable comitatensian tombstones at Amiens. The suggestion by Böhme (in Lemant 1985: 132) that the late fourth-century 'Germanic' soldier graves associated with the hilltop fortifications of the Rhineland were part of the *comitatenses* as yet lacks substantiation. Nevertheless, given that the threat to Gaul came from across the Rhine frontier, it is highly likely that a significant part of the comitatensian troops should have been quartered in northern Gaul and the Rhineland.

In addition, there are the formations listed under the *magister militum praesentalis a parte peditum*, a senior infantry commander in attendance upon the imperial presence (*Not. Dig. Occ.* XLII). For Gaul, it lists (XLII.13–24) a small number of naval units on the rivers of the interior (including at Paris) and the coasts. More importantly, it lists (33–44) the locations of the prefects of a series of groups of *laeti*, peoples of Germanic origin settled in the interior of the empire and under an obligation to supply recruits to the

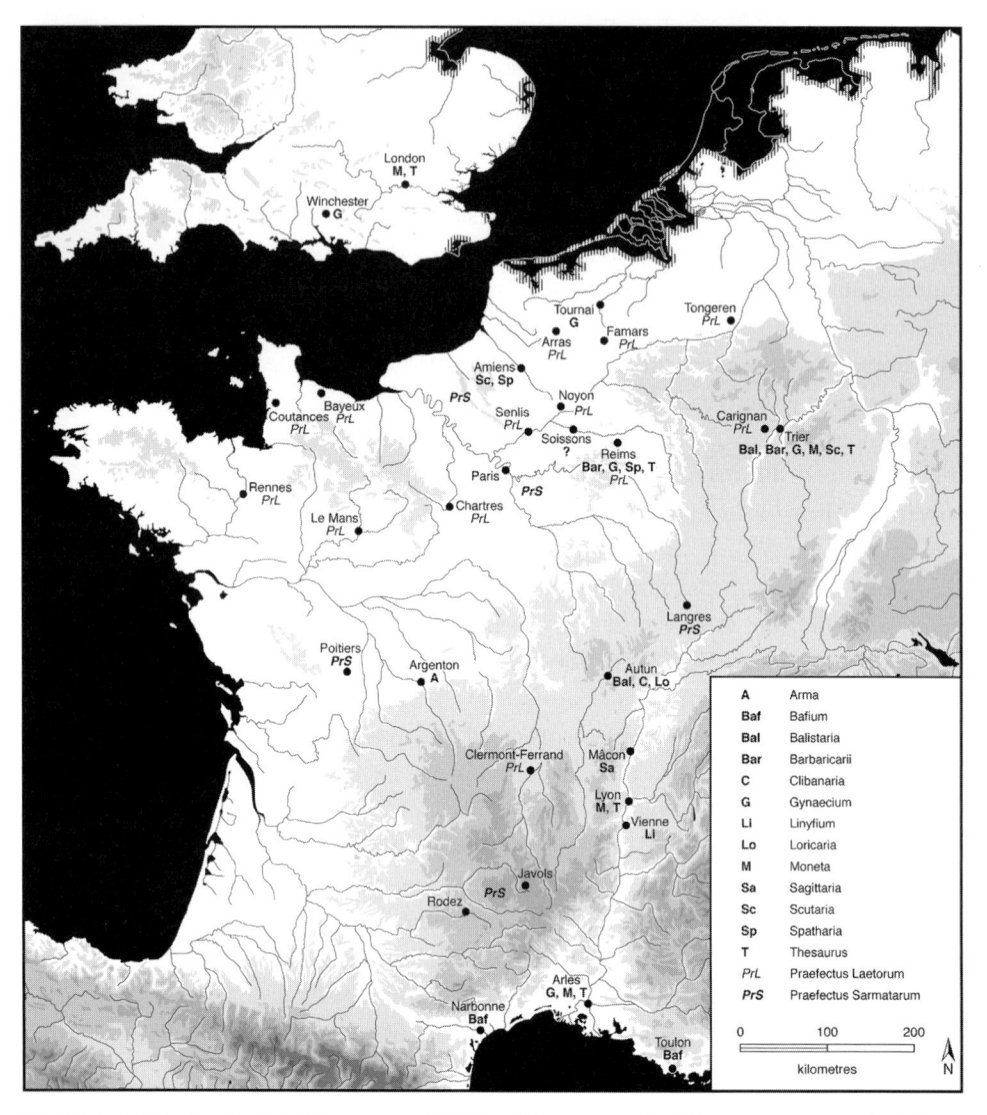

Fig. 2.15 Distribution in Gaul, Germany and Britain of the commands of the *comes sacrarum largitionum* (Baf, Bar, G, Li, M, T), the *magister officiorum* (A, Bal, C, Lo, Sa, Sc, Sp) and the *magister militum praesentalis a parte peditum* (PrL, PrS) (neither of the first two officials had subordinates or installations in Iberia)

Roman army (Figure 2.15). These are listed overwhelmingly in the provinces between the Loire and the Rhine, though it should be noted that the list is incomplete, so the bias in distribution may in part be a result of the loss of information for other provinces. Later in the list (64–70) come the units of *Sarmatae gentiles*, troops from the eastern part of the Danube stationed in Italy and in central and northern Gaul (the manuscript breaks off, probably depriving us of further locations in Gaul, and perhaps also Britain). Two of the entries (66, 67) state that the Sarmatians were stationed 'from Chora as far as Paris' and 'between Rennes and Amiens', suggesting a dispersed and rural presence.

The *Notitia* also gives us, in the list of the *magister officiorum* (*Not. Dig. Occ.* IX), the locations of the state *fabricae* producing the weaponry and other equipment for the army (Figure 2.15): *ballistaria* (artillery – Autun and Trier), *clibanaria* (cavalry armour – Autun), *loricaria* (armour – Autun), *sagittaria* (arrows – Mâcon), *scutaria* (shields – Amiens, Autun and Trier), *spatharia* (swords – Amiens, Reims), *arma omnia* (all weapons – Argenton) and something (now lost) at Soissons. In addition, the list of the *comes sacrarum largitionum* (*Not. Dig. Occ.* XI) gives the *fabricae* for the production of clothing: *gynaecia* (weaving mills – Arles, Lyon, Reims, Tournai, Trier and that at Autun transferred to Metz, as well as the one in Britain), the *linyfium* (for linen – Vienne) and the *fabricae barbaricariorum* (elaborate officers'/ officials' gear 'in the barbarian style' – Arles, Reims and Trier), as well as the mints and treasuries related to his fiscal responsibilities. Even if the *Notitia* has its problems, the dispositions of troops and the locations of *fabricae* given for Gaul show as clearly as the archaeology that between the Loire and the Rhine were stationed large numbers of troops, often in cities or former cities, as well as a series of state-funded factories.

Conclusions

So if we place side by side a range of different types of evidence, concerning military installations, 'urban' fortifications, hilltop fortifications, burial practices, higher-status grave goods and the *Notitia Dignitatum*, all point to the same conclusion, that in the fourth century the area of Gaul between the Loire and the Rhine, but more particularly from the Seine to the Rhine, became a zone deeply marked by the presence of the military. Is it legitimate to speak of this as a 'militarised zone' behind the frontier proper? It is, if we accept that we are not talking about a region that only held military personnel or only served the needs of the army, but rather of a region where the army and its needs were ever-present controlling factors in the fourth century in a way they had not been in the second. In part there was militarisation *sensu stricto* through the construction of forts, strongpoints, storehouses and other military installations, along with the stationing of military formations, be they units of the regular *limitanei* and *comitatenses*, of Germanic and Sarmatian federate troops or even of provincial militias.

But it was also militarisation *sensu lato* in that the dominance of the social and economic structures of the area by the military and by military requirements meant that the local elites adapted their calibration of social position to that of the military and adopted the language of military position and its expression through dress and thus into their burials. The landscape within which they lived was equally deeply marked by the exigencies of military power, be it in the increasing number of fortifications large and small all across the area, including many at places which under the High Empire had been purely civilian and urban (Bavai or Jublains being epitomes of this), or be it in the downgrading of the manifestations of traditional, civil aristocratic expression not only at the towns but also in the countryside.

There is the corollary to the increasing importance of the army and military-related economic activity and status display. If the 'militarisation' of the Loire-Rhine region had entailed the creation by the local elites of a new language of status and display based on the army, what had become of the means of status display characteristic of the High Empire, in particular the rural status marker, the villa? The developments in the countryside of northern Gaul are considered in some detail in Chapter 5, but here I wish simply to concentrate on the one aspect, namely the place of the villa as expression of landed wealth and status and of a certain concatenation of ideas as to how an aristocratic lifestyle should be conducted. The countryside of the centre and north of Gaul had been studded with villas as an expression of integration into Roman-style aristocratic norms, albeit that the particular forms the villas took were often heavily influenced by existing settlement forms (cf. Woolf 1998: Ch. 6). Some areas, such as Picardy, exhibited remarkable concentrations of villas of varying size (Agache 1978). By the fourth century the picture was very different (cf. Van Ossel 1992 for the most convenient conspectus of evidence). Across swathes of central and northern Gaul, villas had been abandoned, an abandonment starting as early as the late second century and rarely accompanied by destruction (see Chapter 5). The result was that in much of the Loire-Rhine region by the fourth century there had been a sharp quantitative decline in the number of villas, and in those that remained there had been a marked decline in the scale and quality of the buildings and fittings. Often the evidence suggests that it was the more workaday elements of the complex that survived, those concerned with the production and processing of surplus, rather than the main residence. The evidence would seem to point again to the priority of military requirements rather than civilian display in the countryside of late Roman northern Gaul (Van Ossel 1995). It was only really in the region around the imperial residence at Trier and to an extent around the important Rhineland city of Cologne that villas are found in any number and to any level of opulence during the fourth century. It is also worth noting that these were also the areas where monumentalised tombs in the earlier tradition were to be found, as in the example of Weiden bei Köln (Fremersdorf 1957) still in use in the late period. Clearly, and this is discussed further in Chapter 5, the proximity of the supreme imperial power stimulated a particular and rather conservative form of aristocratic display, but this in its turn simply serves to emphasise the decline in such traditions elsewhere in the region. Again, the evidence points to the militarisation of the aristocratic *mentalité* and its expressions in northern Gaul as the medium-term consequence of the much greater prominence of violence and the army through the third century and thereafter. This is not so say that villas disappeared altogether across the rest of northern Gaul – there is growing evidence for the presence of a number of villas (cf. Van Ossel 1992, 1995). But in terms both of the quantity of villas and of their size and elaboration of plan and decoration, they show a marked decrease in comparison with the second century. One argument that may be put forward for this is that villas no longer played as central a role in aristocratic display and self-promotion as they had in the earlier period. The means of such display had now widened to encompass such things as military-style accoutrements and had also been displaced to new forms of burial rite. It should be clearly understood that this is not to say that the exploitation of the countryside had declined to match the decline of the number of villas; the evidence is that it was still open and cultivated (e.g. Van Ossel and Ouzoulias 2000), but the surpluses rendered to the landowners were being deployed in other ways alongside the reduced role for the villas.

But these transformations are also equally clearly marked by their absence south of the Loire. In the southern half of Gaul, fortifications, especially at cities, were much rarer in the fourth century, and those that existed were often linked either to provincial capitals or to the longer-distance supply routes. Examples of this include Tours, where the *castrum* in the north-eastern part of the earlier city dates to the 370s, just the time when the city was promoted capital of the new province of Lugdunensis III (Galinié 2007: 359–61), or Dax, on the road between northern Spain and Bordeaux (cf. p. 131), where the walls may date to the mid fourth century or later (Garmy and Maurin 1996: 122). The weaponry, belt suites and brooches so widespread in the north, particularly in burials, were almost entirely absent south of the Loire (this, incidentally, is why Böhme's great survey stopped at the Loire, there was no point in his going further [Böhme

1974: 2], so the fall-off on the line of this river is real and not an artefact of Böhme's choice of study area). Thus the negative distributions south of the Loire emphasise and confirm the positive distributions between that river and the Rhine (or Elbe); the Loire–Rhine region really was different both from what was happening to the south of the Loire and from its second-century self, and what had made it different was the extent to which the army, military exigencies and the resulting emphasis on martial modes of representation had marked the landscape and society between Loire and Rhine and had altered the society and its *mentalités* in this region in the medium-term response to the 'crisis' of the third century, which seems to have touched this region above all.

3 | Reshaping the cities

Introduction

The Roman Empire was an empire of cities: it was through cities that the empire was administered and taxed, it was through the cities that the cultural formations of the Roman world were displayed and reproduced, and it was through cities that many of its economic structures operated. The centrality of cities and their populations to the life of the empire was recognised at the time; it is also a staple of modern scholarship, in which cities are often taken as a metonym for the success or failure of the whole Roman imperial enterprise. This has given rise to major debates about the nature of Roman cities, both within Roman society specifically and more generally as instances of the urban phenomenon. In this chapter we shall be looking at developments at 'cities'; that is, the larger urban sites that were administrative centres. The lesser centres – from the British 'small towns' to the French *agglomérations secondaires* – pose much more of a problem, one that will be considered later on (p. 140).

The debates about the role of cities within Roman society have been largely dependent on the viewpoint of the participants and the types of evidence that they have used to support their views. Thus the political historian would look at cities as expressions of the interaction of the requirements of the state for the good governance (and taxing) of the populations with the interests of the urban elites, particularly the landed aristocracy, and to an extent the commercial groupings. Based not only on narrative histories but also on evidence such as administrative and commercial documents or epigraphy, such historians tended to an 'institutional' view of the city, a place of local government within the wider framework of the empire, but also the arena within which local concerns and interests manifested themselves in politics through institutions which might be variously titled associations (tending to good order) or factions (subversive of good order). Historians oriented more to the visual and basing themselves on the materiality of the city might regard the Roman city more as a place for the reproduction and expression of a particular culture through the medium of the layout of the city, its public buildings and monuments, their adornment through architectural idiom and materials, their embellishment with statuary, and the civic attitudes and activities that not only produced these buildings and their embellishments but were also in their turn reproduced by them. An economic historian might be more concerned with the role of Roman cities in articulating and developing the Roman economy. Traditionally, such study would have been based on the surviving documentation directly or indirectly concerned with production and commerce. Increasingly, it is now based also on the archaeological evidence of artisan or industrial activity, and of manufactures such as pottery, for indications of the sale and direction of production and distribution. Allied with this would be the economic impact of the city on its hinterland (however defined) for the raw materials for its feeding, for its housing and for its industries. A demographic historian, using the evidence not just of the documentation but also of such things as types of housing or the evidence of osteology for reconstructing past populations with their age and disease profiles, might see cities as nucleations of population in a range of occupations and with varying levels of nutrition and exposure to trauma with all that implies for morbidity and mortality as distinct from that of the rural population. At least the economic and demographic approaches had the virtue of making the human population and its needs central, thus helping to avoid the reification of 'the city' as an entity in itself rather than as a collection and expression of humans. It was recognised that the Roman city could not be studied in isolation but had to be studied in relation to its productive and demographic hinterlands and linkages and also to other cities with which it was often in direct competition, either at the level of elite emulation and competition or at the level of popular rivalry (as in the famous case of Pompeii and Nuceria).

For reasons largely to do with the primacy of text in these debates, both as regards the chronological primacy of the texts being there long before archaeology and as regards the traditional primacy of the written word in academic discourse, the argument for the Roman city as essentially a political and cultural rather than an economic entity gained great force. This was where it impinged on more general considerations of the urban phenomenon, being presented and used as a 'type' of city, one most influentially formulated as the 'parasitic' type of antiquity, a characterisation most closely associated with Moses Finley (e.g. 1973: Ch. 5) but in fact going back further than that to the arguments of, for instance, Max Weber. In this model the Roman city lived off its hinterland without returning anything like the economic value extracted to support it (a surplus product of empire). It was able to do this because those powers that be in the society which had command of economic surplus in the form of tax (the state) or rent (the elite – later also the Church) chose to expend these resources on this culturally conditioned phenomenon – the institution which, as Aristotle famously said, separated humans from beasts. Though cities provided certain non-economic services (for instance, education, entertainment or law), the returns to the wider population these represented were held to be marginal, but only if one accepts the premise of this economic cost-benefit analysis. Crucially, Roman cities were argued to have developed only a low level of economic activity either in the acquisition and transformation of primary materials into finished goods or in the marketing of finished goods brought in from elsewhere, the latter an aspect of the argued low level of economic activity and innovation characteristic of antiquity. Yet, at the same time, cities required foodstuffs (particularly grain), building materials (stone, clay and timber), textiles and other materials such as leather for clothing and shoes, fuel (especially firewood) and, of course, their human populations and labour force. All this, of course, allowed the construction of the 'type' of city characteristic of antiquity, perhaps especially the Roman period, that could be contrasted with the commercially driven and entrepreneurial formations of the Middle Ages leading on to the development of capitalism in early modern Europe, subsuming the arguments about 'types' of cities into even larger arguments about the socio-economic bases and forms of society (for a more extended discussion and critique of these arguments, see Horden and Purcell 2000: Ch. 4).

Mention of Horden and Purcell's major work raises the question of their dismissal of the city as an 'essential' category of settlement or even as an heuristic device, for which the arguments are presented in that work (2000: Ch. 4). In outline, they argue that the functions that went on in a 'city' can also be found in the surrounding countryside. Given, as they justifiably argue, that the city cannot be understood without reference to its hinterland and that by and large what went on in the city had important similarities to what went on in that hinterland and elsewhere, then the city and what went on in it were not a phenomenon ontologically different from other types of settlements and activities: they should be understood only as parts of a wider system, not as distinct from it and not therefore as a phenomenon ontologically and epistemologically distinct from their wider cultural, economic and political context (to summarise but not, I hope, misrepresent arguments presented at greater length and much more subtly by them [2000: Ch. 4]). Archaeology has always tended to view the city as essentially different because of certain demonstrable and quantifiable qualities, so the city (wherever and whenever) was quantitatively and qualitatively different from the not-city. The city was a fixed geographical location containing a denser population than elsewhere. That population mainly, if not exclusively, performed non-agricultural functions and so could not feed itself and was provisioned by agriculturalists. Non-economic functions and services such as the administrative, legal or educational could be performed elsewhere, but probably rarely were. Cities marked a greater concentration of religious specialists, generally operating from temples or churches as substantial as, if not more than, any other in their region. Likewise, economic functions such as manufacture and marketing could be and were performed elsewhere, but they occurred at cities in concentrations greater than those detectable in the countryside; thus, city-based economic activities in relation to the percentages of the rural and the urban within a given population overwhelmingly favoured the latter, and the city-based elements were both more numerous and more diverse and at the same time concentrated and interacting in a small physical area with great connectivity between different participants in any *chaîne opératoire*. The material expression of cities was also on scales, in forms and of types not paralleled in the countryside. Yes, in the West one can find theatres, occasionally fora, and other monument types that are habitually found in cities out in the rural areas, but this does not of itself make cities indistinguishable from the country. Yes, aristocrats functioned on their country estates as well as in town, and the layout and décor of their residences in both locations were often similar, but this does not mean that the two arenas were identical; indeed, that they felt it necessary to have a town house as well as a rural villa argues that they saw cities as different and important. For these reasons (many of which, it will be noticed, are particularly recognisable in the archaeology), the idea of the city will be retained here not simply as an heuristic device but also as an 'essential' category: cities were different.

Moreover and specific to the Roman-period city, in Europe it was a phenomenon coterminous with the Roman Empire; peoples outside the Rhine and Danube military zones were happy to get by without cities, operating the functions which the Romans concentrated in cities across a range of settlement and location types, perhaps in a way more like the model proposed by Horden and Purcell. To be able to make this statement itself means, of course, that the Roman city was a distinct and distinguishable (if variable) settlement type, for its absence to be recognisable. Not surprisingly, archaeologists have been more amenable to the ideas proposed by Martin Carver (1993) that Roman and medieval cities constituted 'arguments in stone' (and timber, be it added) where the physical remains of these places and of their materiality were placed centre stage, a thesis which sits well with the one expressed in this chapter and elsewhere (see below, p. 147) of cities as places for producing citizens and thus not only physically reflecting but also actively conditioning the forms urban society took. It is such ideas that will be more central to the arguments developed below.

Views of the late Roman city

The discourse about the late Roman city has tended up to the present day to reflect the apprehension of the Roman city as more to do with political and cultural formations and so with a weakly developed economic character and functions. This was greatly accentuated by the perception of the late Roman city (perhaps especially in the West) as in 'decline', shrinking in area and thus in the potential for productivity while at the same time being increasingly dominated by walls and churches and thus by military and religious functions and personnel rather than civic society. The conventional view also proposed, on the basis of fourth-century legislation against *curiales* (municipal councillors) who failed to fulfil their civic duties and of the decline of the raising of inscriptions, always closely linked to the urban elites, a decline in the 'institutional' character of these towns – that is, their role as political centres – with the place of the former councils increasingly being filled by imperial provincial governors and imperial civic *curatores*. This in its turn was held to be reflected in the decline of the 'epigraphic habit' as the civic elites who had been responsible for the euergetistic projects named on the inscriptions withdrew from the traditional arenas of competitive display. Thus cities in the late Roman Empire in general, but perhaps particularly in the West, were held increasingly to be shadows of their former glories, abandoned by their elites, with their splendid monuments increasingly cannibalised into their new, shrunken wall circuits and their remaining populations reduced in number, vitality and prosperity.

Given that major changes are clearly visible in the physical reality of towns in the Western provinces over the period from *c.* AD 200 to *c.* 400, it is entirely reasonable that the meaning of these changes has attracted much debate and generated an extensive literature on the nature of the changes and their significance for urban life and thus for the vitality of the empire as a whole (cf. Liebeschuetz 2001 for a magisterial survey and equally magisterial bibliography). The last quarter-century or so has seen a steady move away from simple, Gibbonian views of 'decline and fall' to ones characterised by words such as 'transformation' in English, '*mutation*' or '*étiage*' (ebbing) in French, '*Veränderung*' in German and '*transformación*' in Spanish. All of these terms clearly have an agenda of moving away from linear and teleological descriptions and analyses to something which appreciates that the cities of a society taken together or a particular city on its own could serve different purposes manifested in different physical forms at different times. Alongside this, there has been growing appreciation of the importance of regional histories, processes and choices, as, for instance, in the cities of late antique North Africa (e.g. Lepelley 1979–81), where different processes were at work from those visible in Spain (e.g. Kulikowski 2004), or in Gaul (Duby 1980: Pt. IV), or within a region of Gaul (Maurin and Pailler 1996). This has resulted over only the last fifteen years or so in a number of publications, mainly the proceedings of conferences, where the titles show the redrawing of the terms of debate, such as the following: *Towns in Transition* (Christie and Loseby 1996), *La fin de la cité antique et le début de la cité médiévale* (Lepelley 1996), *The Idea and the Ideal of the Town Between Late Antiquity and the Early Middle Ages* (Brogiolo and Ward-Perkins 1999), and *Towns and Their Territories Between Late Antiquity and the Early Middle Ages* (Brogiolo *et al.* 2000), the last two publications resulting from the large, EU-funded 'Transformation of the Roman World' project, which had its own agendas (cf. Ward-Perkins 2005: 174). In conclusion, we may also list *Die Stadt in der Spätantike – Niedergang oder Wandel?* (Krause and Witschel 2006). Not only do these volumes seek to situate themselves within the wider context of the debates about 'late antiquity', as they developed over much the same period, but most of them also link explicitly through to the Middle Ages, indicating that these late Roman towns lie at the roots of medieval Europe (the titles, interestingly, show little desire to link back to the earlier Roman period – another example of the *tabula rasa* afforded by the third century). These volumes are also marked by the increasing use of archaeological evidence as it became more and more available. Nevertheless, the agendas in them and the sources used to frame the debates are overwhelmingly textual. To this extent, they represent less of a break with tradition than they may have wished. Moreover, because of the reliance on textual evidence (including such things as inscriptions, saints' lives and official documents), the focus is very often on 'institutional' aspects such as municipal institutions or municipal culture, such as *collegia* or games and other evidence of popular civic life such as the circus factions. Very often, such agendas respond much better to the conditions of the cities of the East where the documentation is much richer, with the cities of the West (especially away from the Mediterranean littoral) an add-on where they have useful evidence; the work by Liebeschuetz (2001) is itself a good example of this, and none the worse for it.

Here a rather different approach will be taken, as always based on the archaeological evidence, backed up by textual material where that usefully complements the archaeological evidence. This means that the focus will be more on the evidence for the activities attested to at these sites through their physical structures and remains, and how they are distinct from those at other classes of site and thus still distinctively urban places. Inevitably, given the nature of the evidence, questions such as the vitality or otherwise of municipal institutions will be much less the dominant theme of the discussions. This chapter will concern itself principally with the cities of Gaul south of the Loire and of the Spanish peninsula, with remarks on the situation in Britain in respect to these two areas. Chapter 2 dealt with many of the allegedly urban places between the Loire and the Rhine, particularly with the evidence for their increasing militarisation in the later third and fourth centuries and was not concerned as much with other aspects; these aspects will be alluded to in the context of developments of the areas which are the focus of this chapter and will be brought into the final discussion. First of all, there will be a consideration of whether there are overall trends to be identified in urban development in the West from the later second century independent of any 'third-century crisis', in particular questions of the diminution in occupied area and other aspects of urban life such as the decline in the epigraphic provision from the later second century onwards and what this may say about the longer-term cycle of urban development in the West through the first half of the first millennium AD. Then the evidence for the developments in urban form in southern Gaul and Spain largely in the fourth century will be characterised, beginning with a consideration of the fate of the suite of public buildings and monuments inherited from the High Empire and then looking at the evidence for the new public monumentality of cities in the later period – that is, essentially walls and churches. The limited corpus of private residences and other private buildings will also be considered. It will be proposed that despite important regional differences, this area as a whole exhibits certain broad similarities in urban form and culture, ones which are markedly different from those to the north of the Loire and ones also which suggest a much greater degree of continuity in 'classical' urban life, with a greater persistence of established urban form and building provision, and thus presumably a greater persistence in institutional, cultural and economic formations than was possible in northern Gaul. Our understanding of cities in the late Roman West has been too much shaped by the sheer physical presence of the late defences between Loire and Rhine, and this has resulted in a view of how late cities in the West developed that is too bound up with the expectations created by what happened in this particular region to the detriment of our understanding of cities in the rest of the area. This will not be to deny that the military exigencies of the period had their effects on these cities, but they did not determine urban form and experience in the way they did further north.

As mentioned in Chapter 2, the theoretical stance in this chapter will be that towns were not just passive reflectors of social structures and values inherent in the societies that created and used them, but rather were actively involved in creating citizens and thus reproducing the desired and developing forms of society (cf. Laurence *et al.* 2011). Cities created citizens. Those who laid them out and over time accumulated the sets of public and private buildings that constituted them were concerned not only to create a set of places or '*loca*' that reflected how their own society worked along axes such as age, gender and status, but also to ensure that these *loca* should pass onto and inculcate into new citizens (immigrants and children) the societal values they favoured. Thus the physical forms of the city and of its constituent public and private buildings and spaces were not just a passive reflection of society but also active constructors of identity. In the terminology of a Bourdieu-style analysis, they provided the *habitus* within which the citizen was constituted; in terms of a Giddens-style analysis, they were the 'structures' (physical and mental) within which their inhabitants were 'agents', whose actions fed back into the 'structures' and altered them, consciously or unconsciously, over time. The changes in the size, layout, accoutrements and function of cities between *c.* AD 200 and 400 have a lot to tell us about how views of what it was to be a citizen of the Roman Empire were undergoing radical transformations. What do towns of *c.* AD 200 tell us about their roles in social and ideological replication, and what do the subsequent changes tell us about the modification of social and cultural structures and the new forms which townspeople were creating and how those in their turn acted upon the creation of urban society and values?

The second and third centuries

By the end of the second century, those cities between the Strait of Gibraltar, the Rhine and Hadrian's Wall which held any superior administrative status had invested themselves as best they could with the public trappings of what they perceived as Roman urbanism (cf. Laurence *et al.* 2011). These attributes are familiar enough to us today, though not all cities possessed all of them and some were comparatively rare. Nor were they exclusive to the cities; some lesser centres equipped themselves with some of the monument types as a statement of their ambition and perception of their place within the Roman world. The attributes included a regular street grid (or at least paved and maintained streets); buildings expressive of civic status such as the forum and basilica; religious structures such as temples and their precincts, and other sanctuaries; public baths of varying size and lavishness of appointment, with their attendant aqueducts and sewerage systems; monuments for public entertainments such as amphitheatres, circuses, odeons and theatres; walls, more as a show of status than a defence; and other paraphernalia such as arches. These were expressive of a range of attributes within the Roman political and cultural world: the power of the local elite, as expressed in the self-government of a city and through its material correlates the forum and basilica with their statues and inscriptions, or walls expressive of superior civic status; participation in Roman-style religious observance and practice as expressed through temples and sanctuaries, either on the familiar, Graeco-Roman model or local adaptations; acceptance of Roman cultural values (or local understandings of them) as expressed in places of spectacle such as circuses, theatres and amphitheatres and the performances that took place in them; and Roman-style care and grooming of the body in the baths with their associated social life, all going to produce the local version of the Roman citizen identity (male, female, children). All of these were predicated upon an idea and ideal of the 'public citizen'; they were places where all classes of citizen (occasionally also both genders) could participate in the activities that went on in them and interact with other citizens, including those at the upper end of the power/wealth spectrum. It was therefore an urban society with public political values, ones that the form of the city and its buildings and public spaces were devised to reproduce. This was predicated on the notion that the elite would be prepared to channel its disposable surpluses into these places, investing in the physical and other trappings of Roman-style urbanism through acts of culturally conditioned benefaction – euergetism.

Power, religion and culture were all clothed in the Mediterranean-style architecture of the types of monument and their adornment. But it is this material expression that has engendered major historiographical problems. At one level this is because it is the architectural language which was reanimated during the Renaissance and remains to this day expressive to us of power and worth, thus predisposing us to view its presence as an index of success and its disappearance or absence as an index of 'decline' or 'failure'. Moreover, acquiring these monuments was a long-drawn-out process, and the period when these cities attained the fullest range of this monumental equipment was also the period when they attained their greatest extent, the later second century. Understandably, this came to be seen in a teleological light, with the state of affairs at the turn of the second and third centuries as the 'natural culmination' of the process of urban growth and monumental embellishment. Equally understandably, the observable subsequent shrinkage of the occupied area of cities and the disuse and/or demolition of their civic monuments came to be seen as a falling away from the high ideals of Gibbon's 'fortunate age of Trajan and the Antonines'. The reason for this falling away was, of course, traditionally ascribed to the problems of the mid to later third century, either directly as in north Gaul and the Rhineland or indirectly as in Spain. But there is an alternative viewpoint, the one preferred here, which sees the later second-century city not as a benchmark but as a historically contingent phase, and the third and fourth centuries not as a 'decline' but as the creation of a new form of urbanism that responded better to society's changing priorities and ambitions, one that was also in part a comment on later second-century overstretch. Changes there certainly were in the size, public buildings, 'epigraphic habit', building stock and material culture of these cities, but these arguably began in the later second century, suggesting that the flowering of Roman-style urban culture at this period contained the seeds of its own alteration, and they then continued to produce a third-century form of the city, which in turn mutated into the more familiar fourth-century form.

The cities of southern Gaul and Spain in the third century

Both the archaeological and the textual evidence for the urban pattern in Gaul point to a remarkable degree of stability from the second into the fourth century. The archaeology shows activity in the fourth century at almost all of the places known to have been the centre of a *civitas* by the end of the second century, even if, as was seen in the previous chapter, what was going on at that time may not have been what we would term 'urban'. Recent reviews of the textual evidence for the administrative hierarchy (Beaujard and Prévôt 2004, esp. the map on p. 34; Loseby 2000) show only some four *civitates* to have disappeared before the end of the fourth century, and another four in the fifth century. Six *civitates* saw their capital moved (particularly in northern Gaul, cf. p. 62), but remained as entities. On the other hand, several new *civitates* were created by the subdivision of existing, large *civitates*, principally, but not exclusively, in the south-west. The lists of *civitates* in the fifth-century *Notitia Galliarum* show overwhelmingly more similarity to than difference from the situation in the second century.

But such locational and institutional stability can mask the extent to which the material evidence shows major change in the form and functions of these cities. In the discussion in Chapter 2 (pp. 62–76) of the places in northern Gaul which under the High Empire had been the centres of *civitates*, it was noted that at several of them excavation has yielded evidence that their occupied area was in decline from the earlier part of the third century. A particularly well-documented case is that of Amiens (Bayard and Massy 1983: 214–20, esp. Fig. 112), where by the middle of the third century many of the peripheral *insulae* of the street grid had been abandoned (Figure 3.1). In about 250, there was a major fire, which traditionally would have been attributed to a 'barbarian invasion', but the excavators see no evidence for this as the cause. But after the fire only a relatively small area at the core of the old street grid was now occupied, little larger than the area to be enclosed by the walls early in the following century. Other sites in northern Gaul, such as Bavai and Paris, all show a progressive decline in occupation through the third century, while to their west sites such as Jublains and several of the *civitas* centres of present-day Normandy, such as Lillebonne or Vieux (Fichet de Clairfontaine *et al.* 2004), show little sign of occupation by the end of the third century, as we saw in Chapter 2. Further south, there is evidence from the excavations at Tours (Galinié 2007: 355–63) that much of the large, gridded area of the High Empire on the south bank of the Loire was no longer occupied by the end of the third century. To the south-east, in the Massif Central, the early imperial site at Javols (Ferdière *et al.* 2009: 185–6) saw a progressive decline through the third century, with the site abandoned and the centre eventually displaced to Mende. Further south, into Provence, a similar pattern can be detected with a certain amount of evidence that shrinkage was already under way from the early third century, well before the construction of wall circuits. The best evidence comes from a series of cities in southern Gaul, in particular Aix-en-Provence, Arles, Nîmes and Vienne.

The best-documented instance is that of Arles (Heijmans 2004: Ch. 2), already mentioned in Chapter 1 (Figure 3.2). Across the Rhône and north of the city centre, the area of Trinquetaille had during the second century become a suburb of well-to-do residences decorated with floor mosaics and marble detailing. In the second half of the third century, all the buildings excavated in this zone of the city were consumed by fire. South of the city centre a similar pattern has been observed, with a series of rich *domūs* being destroyed by fire towards the end of the third century. On none of these sites was there reuse

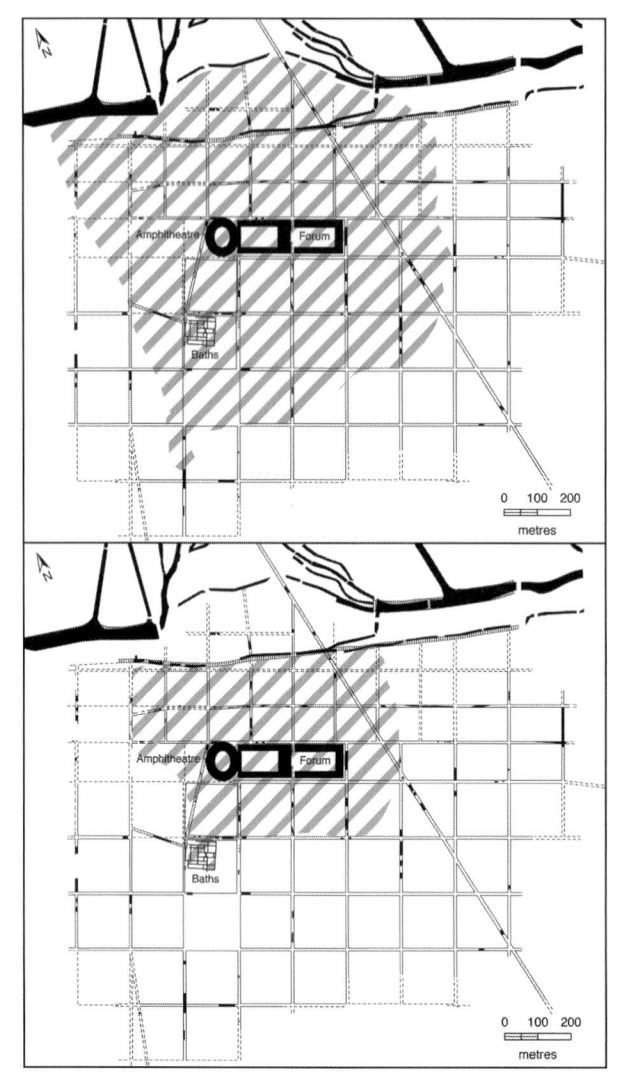

Fig. 3.1 Amiens, areas occupied in *c.* 250 (upper panel) and *c.* 270 (lower panel) (river courses modern)

until the fourth century, and that reuse was sporadic (for Trinquetaille, often funerary). The circumstances of this widespread destruction and abandonment of the peripheral quarters of the city have naturally provoked considerable debate. The traditional view was that the buildings were burnt during a Germanic invasion, be it that in 260 or that in 275 (often blamed on the Alamannic king Crocus mentioned by Gregory of Tours some four centuries later). The dating evidence from the more recent excavations suggests a *terminus post quem* of 260, but with some imprecision over how long after.

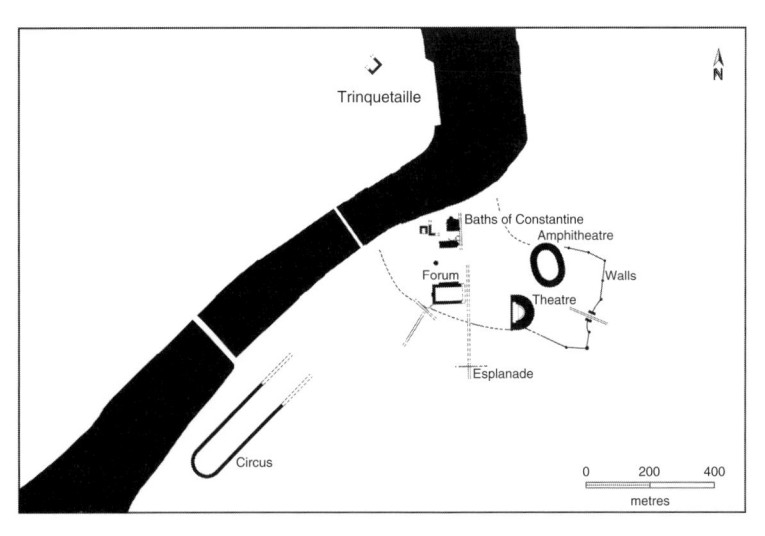

Fig. 3.2 Arles, distribution of monuments in the fourth century

This can allow either general contemporaneity of the conflagrations or for different sites to have burnt down at slightly different times. What is striking, though, is the fact that none of these sites was reoccupied and rebuilt (as had happened on the esplanade site south of the walls after destruction by fire in the 190s) but remained abandoned. As Heijmans notes (2004: 42), this means that in the quarter-century between 250 and 275 the urban fabric of Arles had undergone profound modification, with large areas around the core of the city being abandoned.

The evidence from the other towns of the lower Rhône valley is comparable if less stark. If we work from north to south, at Vienne the extensive suburb of Saint-Romain-en-Gal on the west bank of the Rhône across from the city centre saw a gradual, progressive abandonment of both the private housing and the public bathhouses in the area through the third century (Leblanc and Savay-Guerraz 1996), and by the end of that century what had been a densely built-up and thriving area of the city was largely deserted. The dating evidence suggests that this was gradual though weighted towards the second half of the third century, with both pottery and coins showing a steep decline in numbers and an absence of fourth-century types. Some buildings bore traces of fire, but it could not be established whether this happened before or after they were abandoned. At Aix-en-Provence, the late second-century city had spread beyond its Augustan wall circuit with the construction of a number of large, well-appointed houses. Through the course of the third century, these houses on the periphery were progressively abandoned and demolished. The excavator (Nin 1996) notes a complex of probably related processes: the zones abandoned were on the edge of the built-up area and consisted principally of spacious residences. By contrast, the areas closer to the centre of the city and less pretentious housing seem to have fared better; but even there the picture is one of the upkeep of structures, particularly large residences, built in the second century, rather than the construction of new buildings. This last and the abandonments seem to speak of a more general slowing of the dynamic of development in the city. A similar picture is developing for Nîmes (Monteil 1996a), where the abandonment of large houses on the periphery of the city seems to have been starting as early as the later second century, particularly on the upper slopes of the town. On the flat ground of the city centre, occupation continued through the third century, though even there a deceleration in the laying of mosaics may attest to a certain weakening of the urban dynamic.

Elsewhere in this area the evidence for individual towns is weaker (cf. Heijmans 2004: 31–5), though none show any growth after the end of the second century. Even though the percentages of the urban areas considered are tiny (of the order of 2 per cent), there is a consistency in what evidence we have. Why this region should show this consistent pattern is unclear, but it may be that having benefited economically early on from the establishment of the long-distance commercial axis up to the Rhine armies, the withering of this commerce (cf. p. 29) adversely affected the economic basis of the towns of the lower Rhône valley. Unfortunately, there are as yet no surveys available for the south-western region of Gaul, and the available evidence is too patchy to form any conclusions (Balmelle 2001: 96–7). There may have been shrinkage at major centres such as Limoges, Périgueux, Poitiers and Saintes, but often this seems to be a projection back of the reduced areas defended in the fourth century. Saint-Bertrand-de-Comminges (Esmonde Cleary 2007a: 92–5), though, seems to have continued at pretty much its second-century extent, and there is little evidence of major recession of the inhabited area at Bordeaux before the imposition of the defences around the port.

South of the Pyrenees, likewise, it is difficult to be certain about the situation at individual towns, let alone whether there was a consistent pattern. The review by Bowes and Kulikowski (2005) of the Spanish historiographical tradition in writing about late Roman Spain has shown that this was much influenced by a perception of urban decline from the 'golden age' of the second century consequent on the presumed third-century barbarian invasions, and thus tended to privilege evidence for 'decline' and the writing of a pessimistic view of urban development, a tradition which echoed the long-standing tradition in France, where the third-century invasions were seen as a crisis from which even the towns of southern Gaul never fully recovered. A further strand in this weaving of a tale of 'decline' was the fall-off in the 'epigraphic habit', which was taken as an index of decline of the forms of civic self-representation and of the civic functions and values commemorated on inscriptions. In fact, as Kulikowski (2004: 33–8) shows, this is a hugely oversimplified and linear reading of a complex situation. The uptake and subsequent deployment of inscribing in Spain had always been strongly influenced by geography, chronology and settlement type. So also was the abandonment of the practice. Kulikowski argues that widespread inscribing on stone was in the longer perspective a time-limited activity, one promoted by social and cultural conditions where identities were uncertain and changing and therefore needed to be 'fixed' in stone. In the West this was above all in the first to early third centuries, a period of rapid change in social and cultural norms and structures (cf. Woolf 1998: 98–105). In this scenario, from the second half of the second century on, regions and social groups in Spain no longer found inscribing on stone necessary or useful, so they stopped commissioning such monuments, but at differing times and at different rates. This does not, of course, mean, as previous workers imagined, that the civic and religious activities and posts that had previously been mentioned on inscriptions ceased to operate; it is more that it was no longer felt necessary to memorialise them on stone. So the numerical decline in inscribing is no longer read across into urban 'decline' more generally; in a way, it is rather that it is really the peak in the 'epigraphic habit' that needs elucidating. It will be noted in the next chapter (p. 168) that the late Roman upswing in the 'epigraphic habit' of the fourth century on is similarly associated with a time of social uncertainty, specifically with the establishment of Christianity as a major force in people's lives and deaths.

Two recent publications (Kulikowski 2004, 2005) have reviewed the evidence for the development of towns from the third to the fifth centuries in Spain, but even these remain wedded to an institutional view of developments in the towns of the peninsula, largely, as the author admits, because of the lack of good archaeological evidence from a sufficient number of sites to be able to write an archaeology of the period. This matches other publications emanating from the peninsula itself (e.g. papers in Arce and Le Roux 1993 – despite the best efforts therein of Sillières and of Le Roux himself). One may point to individual instances such as the abandonment of the Pyrenean town of *Labitolosa* (Magallón *et al.* 1995) in the far north and major changes to the fabric and functions of the sanctuary town of *Munigua* in the far south (Schattner 2002), but so far the research has not been undertaken to offer a systematic survey of what happens town-by-town and region-by-region, and when. While it is not yet possible here to offer an overview based on a range of instances, as has just been done for Gaul, some individual examples will be mentioned below when looking at the fate of particular monument types inherited from the High Empire (p. 114).

A fairly consistent pattern seems to be emerging, for Gaul at least, of the progressive shrinking of the occupied area of cities, starting as early as the late second century in some cases and more generally visible from the first half of the third century. This is, of course, a chronology unconnected with the trouble and strife of the mid to later third century, though that period may have accelerated change, so the causes of this trend of abandonment need to be sought elsewhere. It is noticeable that at all the examples cited above there is a regularity to the pattern of abandonment; it starts in the peripheral area of the city, normally the most recent to be built up. It would seem that the high spring tide in construction by the later second century had reached its peak and begun to ebb, and that the latest areas to be occupied were the most susceptible to changed conditions. The solution may in large part be that the cities had become overextended, probably in relation to the carrying capacity of their economic catchment areas, and probably aggravated by the fact that the urbanism represented at the end of the second century was one of prestige monuments and residences erected in competitive emulation by the prosperous families of a city, thereby putting all the more pressure on the economic base generally and on the particular family more specifically. In Chapters 6 and 7, we shall examine other evidence for a general realignment of rural settlement and of economic activity, which often exhibits a downturn in intensity from the peak attained by the later second century in a pattern suggesting overstretch and over-exploitation of the rural economy and the colonisation of marginal lands that could not sustain the pressure. If so, then it may be that the cities of the later second century, rather than representing a peak of development not just in extent but also in the quality of their monuments and residences and in less tangible euergetistic expenditures such as games and feasts, represented a form of civic hypertrophy, brought about by several generations of ever more intense competition in a sort of 'potlatch' consumption of surplus, leading to a sudden and unpredictable breakdown.

The economic structures of the cities and the place of the cities within the wider economic structures of the empire will be the specific concern of Chapter 7; in this chapter, it is the administrative and cultural changes and functions of the late Roman city in the West that are our concern. Therefore, the groundwork of the physical evidence from the cities of the third and fourth centuries needs to be laid, starting with what happened to the monuments and other buildings inherited from the High Empire, and then looking at the tradition of urban fortifications, residences and other private buildings, before discussing the significance of the changes and the new types of urban form to which they led. One major reconfiguration, the archaeology of the developing importance of Christianity, will, though, be left to the next chapter – otherwise, this chapter would be immensely long and overburdened.

Public buildings and monuments

The cities of Spain and southern Gaul for the most part remained unfortified until well into the fourth century or later, perpetuating their overall plan as established under the Early Empire. This discussion will therefore begin with a consideration of what happened to the public buildings and monuments inherited from the second century and what this may signify for the political and cultural institutions they represent. The discussion will then move on to consider the new types of public monuments, the walls and churches, with their effect on and significance for urban form and culture. The discussion will close with a brief overview of the evidence for private housing and other activities at the cities. The discussion will focus on Spain and southern Gaul, but relevant evidence for Britain will be adduced to contextualise some of the developments there.

First of all, it should be noticed that through the third and fourth centuries the urban street systems, be they formal grids or something less rigid, were conserved in use. This implies some sort of centralised control ensuring the upkeep of the physical structure of the streets (evidence for remetalling) and preventing the colonisation of these public spaces by private constructions. This last was, of course, as we shall see in Chapter 9, to be a feature of the fifth century and on, marking an important break with established municipal norms and leading in some cases to major recasting of the urban fabric – in MacDonald's (1986: Ch. 2) terms, the 'armature' conditioning the overall structure and pattern of urban forms. The maintenance of street systems suggests not only a controlling authority willing and able to undertake it, but also a continuing urban ideology wherein the types of public space, movement and interaction afforded by streets mattered. To pass through or to move around the city either on foot (two or four) or in wheeled vehicles, to access public and private buildings leading off the streets, to participate in processions and other ceremonies along the streets, and to interact with other people were activities and qualities that were still central to the way of life of the citizens, albeit tempered by age, gender, status and time of day or night.

Within the urban area defined by the streets, and usually central within it, the forum/basilica complex has always had a special place in creating perceptions of the change from the High to the Later Empire because of its perceived role as an expression of civic autarchy. It was thus an index of the persistence or failure of such civic identity and of the commitment to urban life of the curial class. The evidence for the civic monuments of Spain is sparse and largely negative. Excavations on fora have been rare, restricted to towns such as Astorga, *Complutum* (Alcalá de Henares) and Valencia, where such evidence as there is of change of use comes rather in the fifth century than the third or fourth, though at *Complutum* there is clear evidence for a grandiose, new civic complex at the turn of the third and fourth centuries (Rascón and Sánchez 2000). On the other hand, at *Baelo* in the south, there is evidence that the forum was being colonised by smaller, probably private structures by the later second century, as was the *macellum* also, before it collapsed and was not rebuilt. At *Emporiae* in the north-east, a similar pattern of colonisation of public space can be observed also from the second century. The overall pattern of maintenance is repeated in southern Gaul (Heijmans 2006a: 30–4) where excavations at towns such as Aix-en-Provence, Arles and Nîmes in the south-east also suggest maintenance through the third and fourth centuries with change coming about only in the fifth. Further west, at towns such as Bordeaux and Périgueux, the construction of the new wall circuits left the forum area outside the defences, but one cannot assume that the complexes ceased to function; at Bordeaux, the 'Piliers de Tutelle' monument, which may have been part of the forum complex, remained standing until the eighteenth century, and at Périgueux the huge, circular main temple, the 'Tour de Vésone', next to the forum stands to this day, and its recently discovered sister at Cahors may well also have been standing in the later Roman period (Rigal 2004). This is hardly a firm basis for argument, but, such as it is, it does not support the idea of a systematic abandonment of the centres of civic political identity until late in our period, and it suggests that these cities still had a concept of municipal government and of public life through the fourth century. In Britain, there is more excavated evidence that reveals a diverse pattern (Esmonde Cleary 1989: 71–2); for every London, Silchester or Wroxeter where the forum does not outlast the third century, there is a Caerwent, Caister-by-Norwich or Cirencester with evidence for repair and maintenance, suggesting no common pattern but rather redefinition of civic space as, when and if required. This seems to fit with the wider pattern for the West, one where fora and basilicas were maintained if still felt suitable, but could also be left to degrade, be converted to some other use, or be suppressed. In these latter cases, civic authority and administration must still have been exercised from somewhere, and it will be suggested below (p. 136) that they may on occasion have been displaced into the 'private' setting of aristocratic houses.

The fate of public baths in Gaul and Spain in the third and fourth centuries is rather different, with such evidence as there is for an overall pattern telling more of disuse and demolition, though not uniformly so. In Spain, the new civic complex at *Complutum* was constructed at the expense of the existing baths, and the baths at Ecija (*Astigi*) were disused in the fourth century, with sculpture deposited in the *natatio* (Romo Salas 2003: 292–5), and baths seem to have gone out of use at Toledo, Valencia and Zaragoza. They did, though, remain in use at Gijón (Fernández Ochoa and Zarzalejos Prieto 2001), and inscriptions record the restoration of the *thermae Cassiorum* at Lisbon (*CIL* II.191) and the *thermae montanarum* at Tarragona (*CIL* II.4112) in the fourth century (cf. Kulikowski 2004: 112). For southern Gaul, two recent surveys (Bouet 2003a, 2003b) show that in the south-east there was abandonment and demolition of public baths by the end of the third century at Arles, Fréjus, Nîmes, Vaison-la-Romaine and Vienne (Saint-Romain-en-Gal). In the south-west, there is the case of the destruction of the rue des Frères-Bonies baths at Bordeaux by the construction of the walls. On the other hand, there is some evidence for the maintenance of baths, notably in the south-west at Saint-Bertrand-de-Comminges (Aupert and Monturet 2001: 94–7) and in the south-east at Marseille, the Place Villeneuve-Bargemon baths. With the exception of the 'Baths of Constantine' at Arles (cf. p. 210), which are exceptional due to their likely imperial links, urban baths constructed in the fourth century tend to be very modest in scale and may sometimes be linked to the episcopal complex of the town. In Britain, likewise, there is a general picture of decline in the size and upkeep of public baths – for instance, at Chichester, Exeter, Lincoln, London and Wroxeter – but mirroring this, there were numerous urban baths built in the fourth century, but more modest in scale and attached to the town houses of the wealthy. A similar pattern may also be discerned in Spain, though the evidence from the towns is less compelling than from Britain (García-Entero 2005). But, on the other hand, there is extensive evidence from both urban and rural sites for the construction of new, domestic bathhouses, sometimes to complex plans and with the use of marble and mosaic (cf. García-Entero 2005: Ch. 3, for Spain; Bouet 2003a, for south-eastern Gaul; Balmelle 2001: Ch. 3, Sect. 3, for south-western Gaul). The general pattern seems to be one of increasing disuse of the large, public baths inherited from the first and second centuries, but, on the other hand, a growing emphasis on private baths attached to elite residences. The reasons for this are debated. A simple, functional explanation, and one which, after anything up to two hundred years of existence for many of these bathhouses, has strength, is that the large, public bathhouses were too complex and costly to maintain, and that repeated heating of their structures to relatively high temperatures may well have taken its toll on their masonry. Allowing the fires to go out and the structure to cool and then reheating it would probably have been even more deleterious. Baths were not only expensive to construct and to maintain their structural integrity, but also required expensive heating in the long term. Evidence that this may have been a contributory factor is found in a law in the *Codex Theodosianus* (XV.1.32) remitting one-third of their confiscated revenues to the cities for various purposes including heating the baths. There is also the problem of maintaining the water supply, especially in calcareous regions where the channels of aqueducts were prone to narrowing and blocking as calcium carbonate precipitated out of the water.

But a very telling piece of evidence that there was more to it than simple functionalism is the concomitant change from large, publicly accessible complexes to smaller, more private bath suites attached to the urban residences of the elite (cf. García-Entero 2005: Ch. 3, for Spain; Bouet 2003a, for south-eastern Gaul; Balmelle 2001: Ch. 3, Sect. 3, for south-western Gaul). This replacement may very well represent changing views on the proper location of bathing, with the aristocracy starting to put physical and social distance between themselves and their social inferiors and displacing bathing into their houses (which might also help explain any disinclination to help fund the public baths). This may also match the displacement of civic functions into the 'private' sphere. The evidence of the many private baths of the period shows clearly that bathing was still an integral part of life, perhaps especially so for the aristocracy. Since bathing had always been one of the central activities by which Roman identity was established and proclaimed through the effects bathing had on appearance, odour and so on, the maintenance of the habit of bathing is important. If one turns to the fifth-century letters of Sidonius Apollinaris describing life (however idealised) at his country estate of *Avitacum* in the Auvergne, bathing was for him clearly part of aristocratic social activity at the appropriate hour of the day to prepare him and his guests for the main meal of the day. So bathing remained a crucial activity for defining physical and social identities, but it no longer needed the great public bathhouses of the earlier period. Since these can also be read as having been an instrument and expression of public life and solidarity across the urban population, given that everyone used the same facilities, their disuse can also be understood as an index of the fragmentation of earlier civic ideals. Developing Christian beliefs may have impacted on bathing culture also (cf. Yegül 2010: Ch. 11). The Church did not forbid bathing as such; indeed, it had its own baths at episcopal complexes, perhaps showing how bishops saw themselves as a form of aristocrat or were of aristocratic lineage themselves. If bathing was for hygienic or medicinal purposes, then it was permissible. But if it tended to titillation of the senses and sensuality in general, then it was seen as an occasion of sin, particularly if associated with pagan activities such as the gymnasium. The consequences of changes in social fashion, the behaviour of the elite and possibly the growth of a Christian ethos of bathing for the great public bathhouses were thus often dire. The exception was where the emperor stepped in (Arles and Trier); since major baths had become an established element of the vocabulary of imperial largesse, at Rome above all, so major baths remained a necessity for cities with imperial residences. Public baths, therefore, rather than expressing some simple, linear 'decline', are in fact a very good case study of how changing perceptions of the nature and expression of the citizen were reflected in the physical equipment of the city.

In contrast with the baths, other monumental buildings for leisure and spectacle such as amphitheatres and circuses seem to have been much more favoured. There is, however, an archaeological problem, since, though it is easy to recognise the disuse of such a monument if it has buildings constructed across the arena or track or has its seating dismantled, it is much more difficult to prove continued use since the evidence for this is essentially negative, a lack of evidence for disuse. Is an amphitheatre with no positive evidence for maintenance or restoration continuing in use, or has it been abandoned? In Spain, amphitheatres, which in the Early Empire had not been much taken up as a form of civic monument in Spain, seem finally to have overtaken theatres as the preferred setting for *spectacula*; the theatre at Cádiz was disused by the end of the second century (Kulikowski 2004: 95 and references), the amphitheatre at Tarragona (cf. p. 163) was restored with material taken from the theatre in the early third century (TED'A 1990: Ch. 3, Sect. 2), and the theatre at Zaragoza was converted into an amphitheatre by modifying the *orchestra* and front seating to form an arena, probably at the turn of the third and fourth centuries.

The theatre and temple of the imperial cult outside the eastern walls of Córdoba seem to have been abandoned by or in the fourth century (Ventura *et al.* 1998: 99), though provincial governors still used the forum for dedications to the House of Constantine (Stylow 1990). At Mérida, the amphitheatre bears an inscription attesting to a restoration under Constantine I in 335, and only two years later, in 337, an inscription recorded major works at the circus of Mérida to bring it back into full use. Mérida by this date was the capital of the Diocese of the Spains and clearly attracting patronage from senior officials; indeed, the fact that the two inscriptions recording the restoration of major monuments are only two years apart suggests a coordinated campaign of *mise en valeur* of the monuments of the city's distinguished past, thereby linking the Constantinian diocesan capital to its Augustan origins. In general, amphitheatres in Spain seem to have continued in use through the fourth century. The evidence from circuses such as that at Tarragona is that they, too, were still in business (Humphrey 1986). A similar pattern seems to be visible in southern Gaul, with the majority of theatres, amphitheatres and circuses remaining in use through the third and fourth centuries (Heijmans 2006a: 38–9).

In south-eastern Gaul, major monuments such as the circus at Arles, the theatre at Aix-en-Provence or the amphitheatre of Orange all seem from recent excavations to have been used down to the end of the fourth century. Likewise, in south-western Gaul, amphitheatres at cities such as Agen and Bordeaux were still in use; indeed, at Bordeaux substantial parts of the 'Palais Gallien' amphitheatre survive to this day (Figure 3.3). At Périgueux the amphitheatre was incorporated into the defences, but that does not preclude its still being usable, as may have been the huge amphitheatre at Saintes, despite some of its stonework being reused in the defences. At sites such as Saint-Bertrand-de-Comminges and Toulouse, the theatres may well have continued to function. Britain was never well endowed with stone-built theatres and amphitheatres – indeed, its theatres were very few (Canterbury, Colchester and [?]Cirencester), and though its amphitheatres were more numerous, they tended to be relatively small and constructed in earth and timber (Wacher 1995: Ch. 2). Nevertheless, the evidence, such as it is for the urban amphitheatres, does not indicate the disuse of those at Carmarthen, Chichester and Cirencester before the end of the fourth century, though the theatre/amphitheatre at Verulamium seems by the end of that century to have become a rubbish dump. Only the amphitheatre at Dorchester seems to have passed out of use, perhaps as early as the second century. So little is known of theatres in Britain that it is not possible to be certain, though that at Canterbury seems still to have been standing in

Fig. 3.3 Bordeaux, the 'Palais Gallien' amphitheatre, west face

the early medieval period. So across the late Roman West, amphitheatres, theatres and circuses continued to be maintained, and probably used, down into the late fourth century. Amphitheatres would have suffered from the imperial legislation restricting and then banning gladiatorial spectacles. Theatres had always had a close link with the traditional religions and so may have fallen foul of the growing Christian influence. Circuses, on the other hand, had become very much linked with imperial munificence and the imperial presence, and this ideology seems in some measure to have transferred to kings in the West when there was no longer a Western emperor. This must mean that through the fourth century inhabitants of the cities where such installations were maintained and used must on occasion have gathered to witness the combats, performances and races, with all the religious and imperial imagery and ceremonial that accompanied them, instilling in them civic and imperial values based on those of the traditional civic community.

More contentious is the fate of the temples of the traditional religions, since discussion of this topic has been bound up with assumptions about the part Christians played in the disuse of temples and whether the buildings were converted into churches. The methodological problem posed for theatres and the like is even more acute for temples: though one can identify demolition or collapse, whether a temple was being used or not up to that point is very difficult to establish, and the circumstances under which it was

Fig. 3.4 Périgueux, the 'Tour de Vésone' temple

demolished or allowed to fall into ruin are, likewise, almost impossible to reconstruct from archaeological evidence, except in a few, exceptional cases. Of course, famous instances of surviving temples in Gaul, such as the Maison Carrée at Nîmes, the Temple of Augustus and Livia at Vienne, and the 'Tour de Vésone' at Périgueux (Figure 3.4), show that some temple buildings did survive in the long term; but what purpose(s) they served and at what point they ceased to be used for the worship for which they had been built are entirely obscure (at Nîmes the Maison Carrée seems to owe its preservation to having in the early Middle Ages become the seat of civic authority, the Consuls, not to being converted into a church, which did not happen until the seventeenth century). One of the few detailed excavations of a major temple has been on the *capitolium* of Toulouse, where the temple structure was systematically dismantled at the turn of the fourth and fifth centuries, with some of its materials being recarved on site. The temple podium remained, but the area around it was completely reorganised with new streets and buildings colonising the former open spaces of the temple precinct. In the Middle Ages the church of Saint-Pierre-Saint-Géraud occupied the temple podium, but the date at which it was constructed remains unknown, for all that it has been proposed as successor to the church dedicated to Saturninus mentioned by Venantius Fortunatus (*Poems* II.8), probably in 567 (Boudartchouk *et al.* 2002). Not far from Toulouse, the main forum temple at Saint-Bertrand-de-Comminges and its precinct were demolished, probably again at the turn of the fourth and fifth centuries, the site of the eastern wing of the *peribolos* being overlain by a small bathhouse (Badie *et al.* 1994: 62–8). In Spain, likewise, it is not possible to identify general trends, certainly not of suppression of the temples of the traditional religions (Alemany 2006), and, as in Gaul, there are survivals, such as the 'Temple of Diana' at Mérida or the temple at Evora. In Spain, as in Gaul, it is necessary to review the evidence and circumstances on a case-by-case basis. The earliest dated instance of the suppression of a major temple seems to be at Tarragona, where the hilltop imperial temple was replaced in the course of the fifth century by the episcopal group (see below, p. 403). But, otherwise, suppression or conversion to a different use (including for Christian worship) seems on the whole to be a phenomenon of the sixth century onwards, though whether by then such temples were any longer being used for the traditional religions remains a very open and largely insoluble question. A central problem is to what extent the suppression of these temples can be attributed simply to a religious motivation, or instead to the patterns of the disuse of monuments and the colonisation of public spaces that were a feature of the fifth century in this region and which will be discussed in more detail in Chapter 9.

Overall, it can be argued that Spain, southern Gaul and Britain in the third and fourth centuries are characterised by a general continuity of the structures and probably the functions of the public buildings constructed by the end of the second century, though, admittedly, the evidence is as yet only impressionistic. This is not to claim that all such structures continued unchanged; as we have seen, some few do appear to have been given up, but more general is a pattern of modification, restoration and adaptation down to the end of the fourth century. It is also worth noting that the street grids also seem to have been maintained and kept clear of 'parasitic' structures through the fourth century, arguing for both a degree of continuing municipal control and an ideology of the form and pattern of the city, especially since this would have continued to give these cities an appearance recognisably descended from that of the High Empire. There were still fora, temples, baths, theatres, amphitheatres and circuses, and since all of these were substantial and imposing structures (even if in varying states of maintenance or disrepair), their presence in and impact on the urban landscape and texture would have remained formative of the experience of these cities. So across these regions, the suite of public buildings and monuments expressive of the civic status and ambitions of the High Empire remained to a considerable degree intact. This also suggests that the civic values of these cities and the sorts of citizens they were geared to replicate also remained much more stable than has often been envisaged because of the over-concentration on the 'walls and churches' model of late urbanism, one that, it will be argued later (p. 433), is anachronistic south of the Loire for the fourth century and only developed fully in the latter part of the fifth century. Therefore, in the fourth century, cities over much of the Roman West (Britain included) remained expressions of 'civilian' political and cultural formations, visibly descended both in their materiality and thus in their ideology from those of the second century. Nevertheless, from the later fourth century and with increasing frequency in the fifth, the new monumental expression of the militarisation of civic values, walls, did become more common as major modifiers of urban topography and ideology and thus of the types of citizen produced, and it is to them and their part in the change from a late classical to a late antique form of urbanism that we must now turn.

Urban fortifications

In Chapter 2, a specific tradition of 'urban' fortifications was considered, that in central and northern Gaul. Here the subject of the nature and significance of urban defences in the Roman West more generally will be addressed before examining the evidence for urban defences at towns outside northern Gaul. In the first and second centuries, some towns in the Western provinces were provided with defences (see Esmonde Cleary 2003 for Gaul, Germany and Britain; Pfanner 1990 for Spain), and it is clear from their incidence that their provision was closely linked with questions of civic status and urban monumental display rather than strictly military or defensive considerations, making the point that the ideological context of urban defences was status and display. The one divergent region was Britain, where the number and form (the extensive use of earthworks) of urban defences were exceptional in the West prior to AD 200 (cf. Esmonde Cleary 2003: 79–84), though still clearly linked to status and with ambitions for monumentality – for instance, in the form of the stone-built gates. As was seen in Chapter 2, from the second half of the third century, the provision of walls started to become general in northern Gaul and the Rhineland and to an extent in central Gaul. In Britain earthen defences were progressively replaced in stone through the third and fourth centuries. The first decades of the fifth century saw the extension of defences into areas where they had hitherto not been common, such as south-western and south-eastern Gaul and parts of Spain, and these will be further considered below. There is clearly, therefore, a great deal of chronological and regional variation, with the areas of southern Gaul, Spain and Britain, which are our focus in this chapter, exhibiting marked regional characteristics.

The military purpose of these fortifications at the level of the individual town, and more generally at the level of the regions where fortifications were widespread, cannot be doubted. At the level of the individual town, these fortifications were created to be effective against the then-existing forms of attack and siege, either by the barbarians, who seem from the literary accounts rarely to have been able to mount an effective assault on a defended town, or by the rather more efficient Roman army itself, which was equipped with siege weaponry. So their function was evidently in part purely military: the safeguarding of whatever lay within them. Many towns, more especially in southern Gaul and the Iberian peninsula, also contained large residences and artisan premises. The defended area also came to be the preferred location for episcopal complexes (see below, p. 152), but the creation of intramural churches was, overall, clearly subsequent to the construction of the defences, so it cannot be linked to their original purpose. The function of groups of defended towns is also one that has been linked with the installations of the state, particularly as has been argued for northern Gaul, but this will also be argued for northern and western Spain. This argument sees a major purpose of defences as the protection of supplies and materiel collected as part of the *annona* system during their transit from where they were raised to where they were to be used.

It is a truism that in the late antique world urban defences were intimately connected with urban status, as they had been under the High Empire. The original appearance of many or most of these wall circuits supports this view, as does the scale of some, like the walls of Lugo in north-west Spain (below). These are monuments which, in terms of the outlay of labour, material and money, easily match and often surpass, the urban status monuments of the High Empire. Moreover, in a variety of media, such as manuscripts, mosaics, painting and precious metals, walls were the standard depiction of the town (Bertelli 1999; Bisconti 1989; Deckers 1989; Rickert 1989). This is reinforced by textual sources, where again walls appear either as a metonym for 'town' (e.g. the *muri Elusae* to denote the town of Eauze by Claudian [*In Rufinum* I. v.37]), or as the defining feature of the town, as in Cassiodorus's phrase from the sixth century, '*et ornatus pacis . . . et bellorum necessitas*' ('an ornament in peace . . . and indispensable in war') (*Variae* 1.28.1), neatly encapsulating both the monumental and the symbolic roles of walls, or that of the seventh-century Isidore of Seville: '*urbs ipse moenia sunt*' ('the walls are the very town') (*Etymologiarum Libri* II.xv.1.2). So walls were not just functional; they were also monumental and symbolic. A late antique town would have seen its walls as expressive of its status and pretensions just as an earlier town would have seen its forum or amphitheatre; likewise, a lack of walls would have indicated inferior rank. So when we examine and discuss the incidence of urban defences across the Western provinces or their presence at specific towns, it is important not just to assess their military capacities and significance, but also to situate them within the changed ideological framework of towns and their self-representation in the late Roman world.

Even for northern and central Gaul, whose urban defences were presented in Chapter 2 largely in terms of their military functions, these arguments have validity. It is clear that considerable care was taken over the construction of these walls, with an eye to their presenting an impressive, monumental appearance. Despite the view propounded by earlier workers that these circuits were constructed in haste as a response to the barbarian invasions, in fact their workmanship shows little sign of pressure. Unlike walls clearly built as a hasty response, such as the Herulian walls at Athens (Frantz 1988), where architectural *spolia* were reused higgledy-piggledy, the reused stones in the lower parts of many Gallic walls were carefully laid, adjusted and disposed so as to hide their original function and give the appearance of newly quarried stone. The facing of the main part of the walls in small block work (*petit appareil*) with cordons of bricks was carefully laid and regular; indeed, at Le Mans, different-coloured stones were used to give a patterned effect (Figure 3.5). Gateways were often picked out in some way and given special emphasis, as by architectural framing. A useful instance is the gates at Périgueux, where the east gate (the *Porte de Mars*) was in large ashlars (Figure 3.6; cf. Figure 2.8 for the walls at Périgueux), as were its flanking towers, also decorated with pilasters (Garmy and Maurin 1996: 146–8). It is also important to remember the sheer scale of these undertakings in terms of the volume of material used – for instance, in walls in

Fig. 3.5 Le Mans, west walls showing patterned decoration

Gaul which could be 5 m and more in thickness and more than 10 m in height, requiring a considerably greater volume of material and of labour than the monuments of the High Empire. So the central and northern Gaulish defences fit into the discussion on urban monumentality in the Late Empire, showing that whoever commissioned them, civic authorities, the army or the state acting through either of these, still appreciated the need to present the site in the approved monumental vocabulary. It is perhaps significant that it is at places such as Le Mans and Périgueux that particular attention to monumentality was to be found; further away from the Rhine frontier and the coasts, they may have retained more urban functions and population than some other places further north and east. Dey (2009) has also drawn attention to other wall circuits, such as those at

Fig. 3.6 Périgueux, nineteenth-century engraving of the Porte de Mars

Angers, Nantes and Rennes, which share with Le Mans, though not so pronouncedly, a taste for polychrome decoration. He suggests that this was because the walls, probably imperially financed, and, in particular, the gates were seen as a suitable backdrop for the ceremony of the *adventus*, the emperor's formal arrival at a city, at which a formal panegyric praising the emperor, his warlike qualities and his liberality to the city might be intoned. It is unfortunate for testing this hypothesis that so few gates of this period have survived (those at Le Mans itself are long gone), but one might point to the example of the Porte de Mars at Périgueux cited above. Even if the emperor himself proved not to be a frequent visitor to western Gaul, provincial governors and other even higher officials would visit and might, with the imperial *imagines* arrayed alongside them, be an acceptable substitute for their imperial master.

Late Roman urban fortifications in Spain

The most recent reviews of the evidence for walls from Spain (Brassous 2011; Fernández Ochoa and Morillo Cerdan 2005) list up to twenty-four cities with proven late Roman wall circuits. Some are refurbishments of early imperial defences – Barcelona, Gerona, Mérida, León and Zaragoza (the development in this period of other early circuits at towns such as Tarragona or Valentia is unclear) – with Astorga, Braga, Gijón, Iruña and

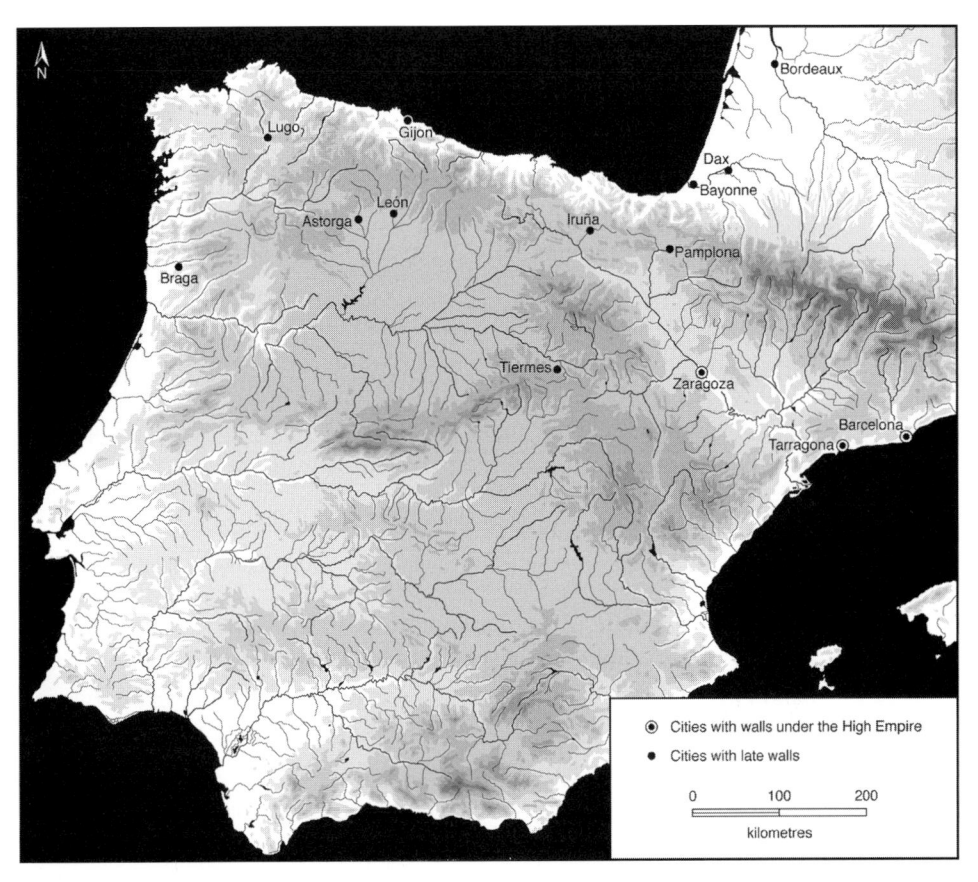

Fig. 3.7 Spain, urban defences in the northern part of the peninsula

Lugo as new constructions (Figure 3.7). The sites at Burgo de Osma, Cáceres, Caparra, Càstulo, Chaves, Coimbra, *Conimbriga*, Coria, Elche, Evora, Inestrillas, Pollentia, Sagunto and Tiermes have been claimed to have late Roman fortifications, but the evidence for them is much less certain. The most distinctive and best-known group is that in the northwest, Cantabria and Galicia, comprising Astorga, Braga, Gijón, León and Lugo, with Gijón and Iruña associated but not of exactly the same type. The five similar sites are distinguished by relatively long circuits studded with close-set, projecting, semicircular towers (defined by Richmond 1931; see also the papers in Rodríguez Colmenero and Rodà 2007). The most remarkable of the series are the walls of Lugo (Figure 3.8) sited on a hilltop and enclosing some 34 ha. (Rodríguez Colmenero 2007), an area corresponding roughly with the earlier occupied area. The walls themselves, fronted by a wide ditch, were built of the local schist with some granite and some reused stonework from earlier structures. They are up to 8 m thick and survive

Fig. 3.8 Lugo, the late Roman walls (the upper part with windows is modern)

from 8 to 12 m high. Along the front of the walls is a series of semicircular towers ('*cubos*') 10–13 m in diameter, with a similar distance between each pair of towers. At each tower, there is an entrance in the rear face of the wall (curiously, well above the then ground level) giving access to a staircase, which then bifurcates to either side up to the wall walk. Unfortunately, the wall-top and the upper parts of the towers were removed in the Carlist wars of the nineteenth century to facilitate the deployment of artillery. The gates were framed with large blocks of carefully cut and laid pale granite to give them a monumental appearance, again pointing up the importance of gates as places to impress travellers and welcome high officials. Recent excavations suggest a date of construction at the turn of the third and fourth centuries for the circuit at Lugo (González *et al.* 2002). This was an enormous undertaking, financially and logistically, and even today, lacking its upper works, the circuit remains immensely impressive and a testament to just how monumental these defensive circuits could be (indeed, leading to the circuit being inscribed as a World Heritage Site in 1995). The sheer scale of these walls and the resources that would have been needed to construct them have led to the suggestion that they were created with official aid.

At León, a fortress since the Flavian period of *legio VII Gemina*, the early imperial fortress wall was thickened by the addition of a late third-century wall with projecting towers, though not as massive nor as close set as those at Lugo. A similar towered wall, *c.* 3.70 m thick, was constructed at Astorga, enclosing an area of 26 ha., as also a wall at the lesser known town of Braga enclosing 39 ha., and also the wall defending the peninsula that dominates the port of Gijón, an area of 16 ha. (Fernández Ochoa 1997). As at Lugo, where there have been recent excavations, the dating evidence suggests construction at the turn of the third and fourth centuries. Here we have a group of defences geographically circumscribed, architecturally very similar and all lying within the same date range. A site which may well be related is that of Iruña, between Galicia and the Pyrenees, where 5-m-thick walls with semicircular towers enclosed an area of 11 ha. Richmond (1931) also attributed the towered walls of Zaragoza to this group, but more recent research suggests that the walls originated under the Early Empire, though the visible fabric may be the result of late imperial remodelling of the defences (cf. Fernández Ochoa and Morillo Cerdan 2005: 320).

The traditional explanation for this spate of wall construction was the supposed Germanic incursions into northern Spain *c.* 270, but that was before good archaeological dating was available, and this pushes the date of construction a generation or so later. Moreover, the scale of the walls and the care taken over their construction suggest something more considered than a hasty response to invasion. More recent discussions have pointed to the importance of the natural resources of the region. Though Galicia had contained important gold workings under the High Empire (hence the presence of *legio VII Gemina*), this seems to have come to an end by the mid third century (Domergue 1990), though there may have been some small-scale, later production round Lugo and in the Asturias. On the other hand, the region was rich in agricultural resources, both grain and animal. Another exceptional feature is the abundant milestones and other evidence for the maintenance and improvement of the road network in northern Spain in the second half of the third century and into the fourth (Iglesias-Gil and Muñiz Castro 1992), with over one hundred fourth-century milestones from Galicia and northern Portugal (Caamaño Gesto 1997), showing the importance not only of the defended strongpoints but also of the communications system linking them. A hypothesis has been put forward (e.g. Díaz and Menéndez-Bueyes 2005; Fernández Ochoa and Morillo Cerdan 2005) that the rationale for all this was that the northern part of the Spanish peninsula became an important source of supplies, *annona*, for the Roman state, with materiel being collected, channelled along the road through Iruña and then over the western Pyrenees and up the road through southwestern Gaul, defended by the fortified sites at Bayonne and Dax, to the important entrepôt of Bordeaux for onward transmission to the armies by land or by sea. Documentary support for the importance of northern Spain to the late Roman state comes from the *Notitia Dignitatum*, which lists a series of military units in the region (*Not. Dig. Occ.* XLII.25–30), not only *legio VII* at León, but also units at Lugo (*cohors Lucensis*), Paetonio (*cohors II Flavia Pacatiana*), Iuliobriga (*cohors Celtiberae*) and Iruña (*cohors I Gallica*) as well as the as yet unlocated *cohors II Gallica*. For a long time, the explanation for these military dispositions was sought in an unproductive debate about an hypothesised internal frontier or *limes Hispanicus*, but their presence is much more likely to be explained by the need to safeguard the supply routes. To take the hypothesis one stage further, the construction of other fortifications in the west-central part of the peninsula, such as at Caparra, *Conimbriga* and Norba, has been seen as an extension of this system to draw upon the resources of this region also, funnelling them north to Galicia and then east to Gaul (cf. Díaz and Menéndez-Bueyes 2005: 277–86). Unfortunately, many of these central-western wall circuits remain dated only by supposed historical causation such as the presumed third-century invasions, so the precise sequence of urban defence and its rationale(s) are as yet irrecoverable. The scale of construction at towns such as Lugo has suggested to some that the walls were actually built by the army; while this cannot at present be demonstrated, it is perfectly likely. But the idea that the north-west Iberian fortifications were constructed by the army has been challenged by Brassous (2011), who points out that evidence for such military construction is difficult to come by more generally across the empire. He favours a more 'civic' explanation for the construction of this monument type, as elsewhere, and it is worth noting the fact that at Lugo and at other places such as Astorga and Braga the defences enclosed the area occupied at the time of their construction. So they are not just citadels, and at Lugo the occupation within the walls seems to be civilian, so this may argue for the civic communities having influenced the laying out of the circuits and the circuits having been part of the civic expression of these places. This is similar to what seems to have been happening in Britain also at the same time. Nevertheless, the evidence for the upgrading of the road system and the fortification of a number of urban centres across central-northern and north-western Iberia from the later third century remains striking and is not really paralleled elsewhere in the peninsula.

Apart from the Galician group and the possibly related sites in west-central Spain, the evidence for urban fortifications elsewhere in the peninsula is scanty. One partial exception concerns sites in modern Catalonia, particularly Barcelona and Gerona. In the late third century or first half of the fourth century, the existing Augustan walls of Barcelona were massively thickened and roughly doubled in height to 9 or 10 m. As high again was a series of closely spaced towers with large, arched openings in their upper stories (Figure 3.9). This constituted a very impressive set of fortifications

Fig. 3.9 Barcelona, the walls: lower part Augustan, upper part and towers late Roman additions

standing on an eminence overlooking the major port of the north-eastern seaboard of Spain and communications with Gaul and Italy (for a summary of knowledge of the walls of Barcelona, see Puig and Rodà 2007). On the road between Barcelona and the crossing of the eastern Pyrenees lay the city of Gerona (*Gerunda*), where a triangular hilltop area of just under 5 ha. was defended around AD 300 by a 2-m-thick wall of massive masonry founded on a late Republican predecessor, with no towers but with strongly defended gateways (Nolla 2007). Another pre-Roman fortification at Sant Julià de Ramis, 5 km north of Gerona, was put back into commission to guard the road, and further north again, the Panissars pass over the Pyrenees passes was defended by the *Clausurae* of Les Cluses (Castellvi *et al.* 2008). Thus the importance of the eastern route over the Pyrenees matched the care given to that at the western end of the chain.

Late Roman urban fortifications in southern Gaul

The development of urban fortification in southern Gaul, essentially the diocese of the *Septem Provinciae*, differs markedly both from what we have seen for central and northern Gaul and Spain and from what we shall see below for Britain. In general terms, there is little evidence for a general pattern of provision of defences of similar type (Figure 3.10). In the

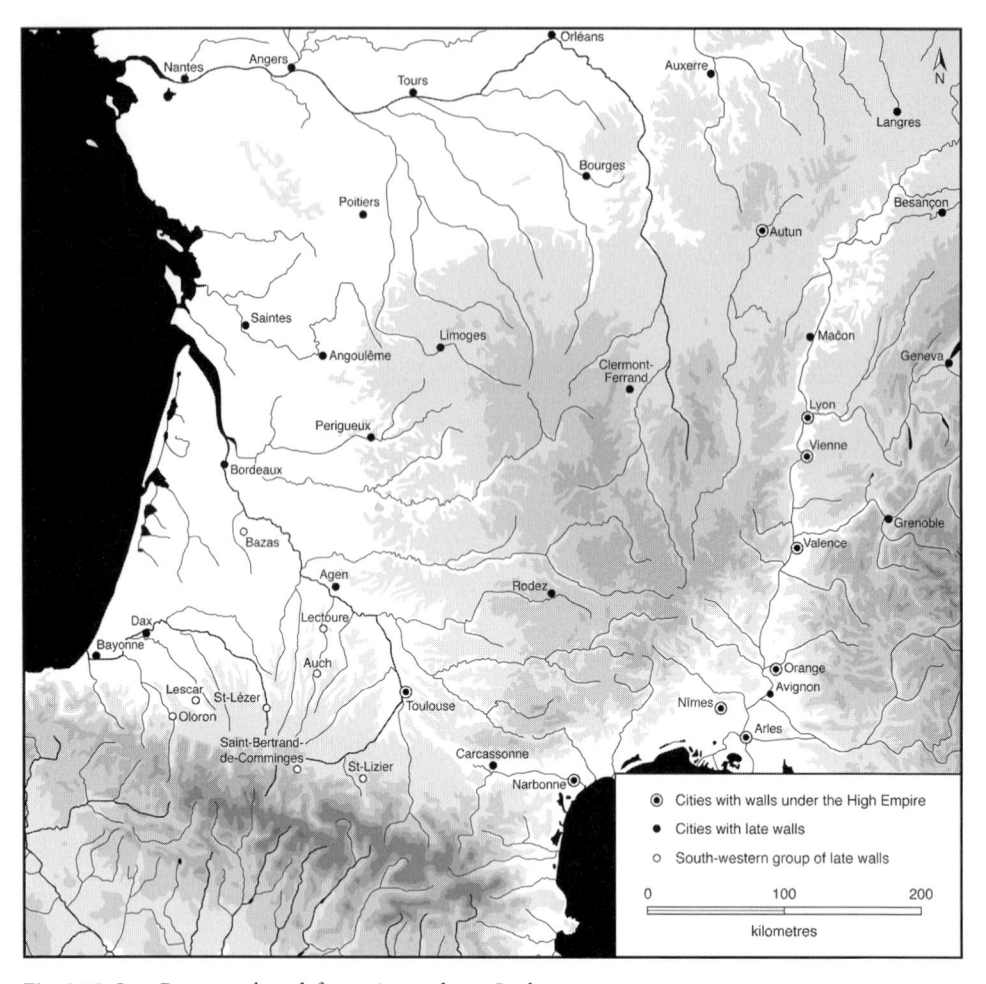

Fig. 3.10 Late Roman urban defences in southern Gaul

south-west, south of the Loire, there are very few fortifications of the 'classic' late Roman type in Gaul. The three wall circuits between the Pyrenees and the Garonne, Bayonne, Dax and Bordeaux, have already been mentioned in connection with the hypothesis of safeguarding the route of the Spanish *annona*, an idea also favoured by French workers (Maurin 1992). Between the Garonne and the Loire valley, there were only official-style circuits at Bourges, Périgueux, Poitiers, Rodez, Saintes and Limoges. The first three of these plus Limoges could be seen as securing the routes up from Bordeaux and the grain lands of the south-west towards the frontier zones (for instance, the reference by Ammianus Marcellinus [*Res Gestae* XVII.8.1] to Julian's having to delay the start of campaigning in 358 while awaiting the arrival of grain from Aquitaine), but these circuits are few in number with long gaps between, suggesting that if the safeguarding of materiel was one of their functions there was little perception of threat.

There is also the local group of urban defences in Novempopulana consisting of the sites of Auch, Bazas, Lescar, Lectoure, Oloron-Sainte-Marie, Saint-Bertrand-de-Comminges, Saint-Lizier and probably the related military site of Saint-Lézer (the *castrum Bigorra* of the *Notitia Galliarum*) characterised by their positioning on hilltops, their small size and their relatively thin walls with no foundation courses of reused stonework (Esmonde Cleary 2004). All bar Auch and Saint-Bertrand seem to have been the principal centres of late creations of *civitates*, and the scale of their defences suggests a local importance only. Indeed, their small size and the lack of evidence for major buildings within the walls, in particular at the newly promoted sites, have been used to argue (Esmonde Cleary 2004: 186–8) that these places were essentially *cités administratives* rather than the more familiar type of Roman city with a range of administrative, social and commercial functions. So the defences here may be showing us interesting evidence for what the authorities at the time (imperial? provincial? municipal? Visigothic?) required from a 'city'. The only well-dated circuit of the group is that at Saint-Bertrand (Figure 3.11), where the construction of the walls can now be dated to the first third of the fifth century (Esmonde Cleary and Wood 2005: 181, 291–2). Otherwise for the south-west, there are the poorly known and understood circuits at Angoulême, Clermont-Ferrand and Cahors.

Fig. 3.11 Saint-Bertrand-de-Comminges, the early fifth-century wall with wall-top

A recent review of the evidence for urban fortifications in south-eastern Gaul (Heijmans 2006a) has shown clearly that here there was a series of defences, albeit as yet poorly known at the level both of the individual site and of the region. Several cities had been endowed with walls in the first century, almost all of them *coloniae* (cf. Esmonde Cleary 2003: 72–5), and at one of them, Toulouse, it appears that the Augustan circuit remained in use, augmented by the addition of a wall along the Garonne riverside (Baccabrère and Badie 2002), though its date is debated. Otherwise, to stay in the province of Narbonensis I, at Narbonne, there is a well-known, if undated, reduced (15–20 ha.) circuit built in large, reused ashlars. At Nîmes, stretches of a late Roman wall founded on reused stonework has been found in the area of the amphitheatre, and Béziers has also yielded elements of what may be a late, reduced circuit. Of course, the most famous wall circuit in this province is that of Carcassonne, the kernel of the present later medieval triple circuit as recreated in fairy-tale form by Viollet-le-Duc in the nineteenth century. This was the only one of these circuits built on the central/north Gaulish model with foundation courses of reused large blockwork and several semicircular towers, though its situation on a hilltop and restricted area resemble more the circuits of Novempopulana (Letterlé 2001). Its date can now be ascribed to the middle of the fourth century. Also of the very reduced area seen at Carcassonne and in Novempopulana was the circuit at Clermont-Ferrand, in due course to be so valiantly if vainly defended by its bishop Sidonius Apollinaris (Provost and Jouannet 1994). Running up the Rhône valley were some other defended cities. From south to north, these were Arles, where a wall defending the southern side of the city has been confirmed but not yet dated (Heijmans 2004: 83–111); Avignon, where elements of a circuit of reused large blocks have been recovered, dating probably to the middle of the fourth century; and Die, in the valley of the Drôme, a tributary of the Rhône, which was provided with a towered wall circuit in the third century enclosing the unusually large area of 23 ha. Further north, it is likely but not proven that Vienne, ancient capital of the huge *civitas* of the Allobroges, received a reduced circuit in the centre of the city. Two towns that became capitals of territories carved out of the *civitas* of the Allobroges, Geneva and Grenoble, certainly did have reduced circuits of the later third century, the latter dated by a gate inscription of Diocletian and Maximian. On the other hand, other old and prestigious towns such as Orange and Valence have yielded no trace of late walls. In the neighbouring province to the east of Narbonensis II, linking the Rhône to Italy, the only proven urban defences lie far up the valley of the Durance at Gap, with a defended area of only 2 ha. at the centre of the town. Heijmans (2006c: 72–4) suggests that several of the circuits in the south-east may be as late as the earlier fifth century and constructed in the face of the Germanic invasions of that period, but, on present evidence, this must remain speculative and reasons related to the display of civic status should not be set aside.

Southern Gaul overall shows little evidence for a coherent pattern of the provision of defences, throwing into relief the situation north of the Loire where the coherence suggests high-level forethought. In both the south-west and the south-east, a number of cities probably remained unfortified until at least the end of the fourth century and possibly well after. In the south-west, a case can be made for the provision of 'classic', official Gaulish defences at a small number of sites in order to safeguard the transmission of the *annona* out of Spain and Aquitaine. There is also the group of atypical, hilltop defences in Novempopulana whose context remains debatable but which gives unexpected insights into the nature of the fifth-century 'city'. For the south-east, there is as yet no evidence for regional or subregional groupings, to judge by the form and build of the known wall circuits; at present, they look more like the actions of individual communities, quite possibly as acts of civic monumentalisation as much as for defence. It is possible that the cities along the *via Domitia*, Nîmes, Béziers (?) and Narbonne, may also have served to guard that road linking Italy to Spain, though in that case late defences at principal cities between the Rhône and Italy, such as Aix-en-Provence, might be expected.

Urban defence is one area in which Britain demonstrates regional variation, setting it apart from southern Gaul and Spain. The majority of cities and many of the 'small towns' had received defences in the second century, usually in earthwork (Esmonde Cleary 2003, 2007b). In the course of the third and fourth centuries, almost all of these had a stone wall built into the front of the earthwork; thus, of the cities maintaining the relatively generous areas enclosed, none were reduced in size, unlike what happened in northern Gaul and the Rhineland. Indeed, the few cities defended for the first time at this date, such as Canterbury, enclosed the large areas characteristic of established British practice rather than the reduced areas normal across the Channel. But Britain was not completely out of line with practice elsewhere in the West; similar, relatively generous wall circuits enclosing most of the then occupied area were also a characteristic of the urban defences of northwestern Spain constructed at the turn of the third and fourth centuries. Where Britain was more exceptional was in the importance accorded to the second-rank urban settlements ('small towns'/*agglomérations secondaires*) through the provision at the core of some thirty or so of them of a defended area. Comparison with cognate settlements elsewhere in the West argues that such places in Britain were still of significance and continued to act as an intermediate level of settlement.

All in all, in Spain, southern Gaul and Britain, the provision of urban defences was not a major, ubiquitous defining feature of urban development in the late Roman period, in contrast to northern Gaul. Yes, there were regions where provision of defences in the third and fourth centuries was commonplace, notably Britain (for historical reasons) and north-western Spain, but equally there were regions, including much of Spain and much of southern Gaul, where towns were either left undefended or were only defended relatively late, around the turn of the fourth and fifth centuries. This suggests that there was little top-down interest on the part of the late Roman state in requiring the construction of defences (for an opposing view, see Luttwak 1976: Ch. 3); some specific counter instances, in particular related to the exploitation of Spanish resources, have been argued, but these are a minority of all cities in the peninsula. In that case, there must be a strong argument that the provision of urban defences should be seen, in important part, in the light of urban monumentalisation under the Late Empire, cities adopting the new vocabulary of status as suited them. Nevertheless, the small areas generally enclosed do suggest that this civic ambition was tempered by an appreciation of the practicalities of defence and that the (over-)ambitious, status-driven, long circuits of the Early Empire were no longer sensible.

Domestic architecture

As we turn from public monuments and buildings to the private sphere of housing and commercial premises, the staples of the private building stock of the Roman town of the High Empire, the picture is very fragmentary, but there is enough to get some sense of what cities in this super-region consisted of apart from their walls and churches. At the level of the houses of an individual town, there is a scatter of information for south-eastern and south-western Gaul, with a little evidence from Spain. Because the evidence from the villas of the late Gaulish and Spanish countryside is so much fuller, discussion of the significance of the plans and decoration of elite housing will be held over to Chapter 5.

A recent study of the peristyle house in Gaul, the most elaborate of urban residences in plan, has shown that these were essentially a phenomenon of the first, second and early third centuries, with few surviving beyond the middle of the third century (Vipard 2007: esp. 267–71). Though their demise is no longer to be laid at the feet of 'barbarian invasions', there is certainly a change in the location and nature of elite residence at this period. In the south-west of Gaul, it may well be that this was displaced to the rural context of villas. But it is difficult to argue this for other areas, as will be seen in Chapter 5, so it may be a marker of more profound mutations in the nature of urban society, as seems to be the case across the West more generally. For Gaul, it is the south-west that has yielded the best evidence for the plans and appointments of a number of rich, late, urban residences (Heijmans 2006b), particularly at Bordeaux (Balmelle 1992), where the Ilot Saint-Christoly house was clearly a major *domus* with a number of mosaic floors. South of Bordeaux, in Novempopulana, there is evidence for large urban residences with mosaics at the provincial capital of Eauze, at Auch and at Dax, but above all at Saint-Bertrand-de-Comminges, where a number of major residences were maintained and refurbished into the fourth century (Sablayrolles and Beyrie 2006: 340–67, 372–90). This group of rich, late, urban residences in Novempopulana should clearly be related to the major group of rich, late, rural residences in the same province, and this again will be discussed further in Chapter 5. Outside Novempopulana and Bordeaux, there is evidence that a large, centrally placed residence of the Early Empire at Périgueux (rue des Bouquets) was still occupied through the fourth century, but otherwise there is as yet little urban excavation from other sites to fill out the picture.

A recent review of the evidence for urban housing in south-eastern Gaul has shown a distinct absence of new residences or decorative elements such as mosaics to match those of the south-west (Heijmans 2006b: 49), though at some towns such as Fréjus, Marseille or Nîmes the presence of later deposits or traces of occupation within *domūs* constructed in the second century shows that these could still have been in use in the fourth century – sometimes this late occupation is of a lower standard of materials and care than had been the case earlier (Heijmans 2006b: 50). Arles tends to be a somewhat exceptional case, with more evidence for the construction of relatively large residences (Heijmans 2004: 350–3), though, as will be seen in Chapter 5 (p. 210), Arles was among the most important towns of Gaul in the fourth century with a possible imperial residence in the earlier part of the century and a concentration of state officials, including the transfer there at the turn of the fourth and fifth centuries of the seat of the Praetorian Prefect of the Gauls. Other, more modest housing has been found by excavation at some of the more important cities of the southern half of Gaul, such as Aix-en-Provence, Arles, Bordeaux and Toulouse, attesting to a different stratum of urban society and activities, probably more artisanal in character (Heijmans 2006b: 50–1). Elsewhere in central Gaul, the evidence is much more sporadic, though one may point to examples such as the 'House of Balbus Iassus' at Autun (Rebourg 1993: 103–9) with its mosaic and *opus sectile* floors.

In Spain, there has been little systematic excavation of urban housing of the late antique period, in part, perhaps, because of the long-standing perception of the demise of the classical Roman city from the third century, with a corresponding emphasis on the more magnificent remains of the villas of the period. Thus, a very recent review of the evidence for Spain (Arce *et al.* 2007) essentially had to confine itself to three sites. The most important recent excavation of urban housing has been at Mérida on the Morería site immediately inside the riverside stretch of the walls (for a convenient summary, see Alba Calzado 2005). In the fourth century, part of the site was occupied by a residence of some pretension, the 'Casa de los Mármoles' (Figure 3.12), arranged round a central, colonnaded courtyard paved in black and white *opus sectile*. At the opposite end from the entrance was a large, rectangular room with apse, presumably a reception and dining

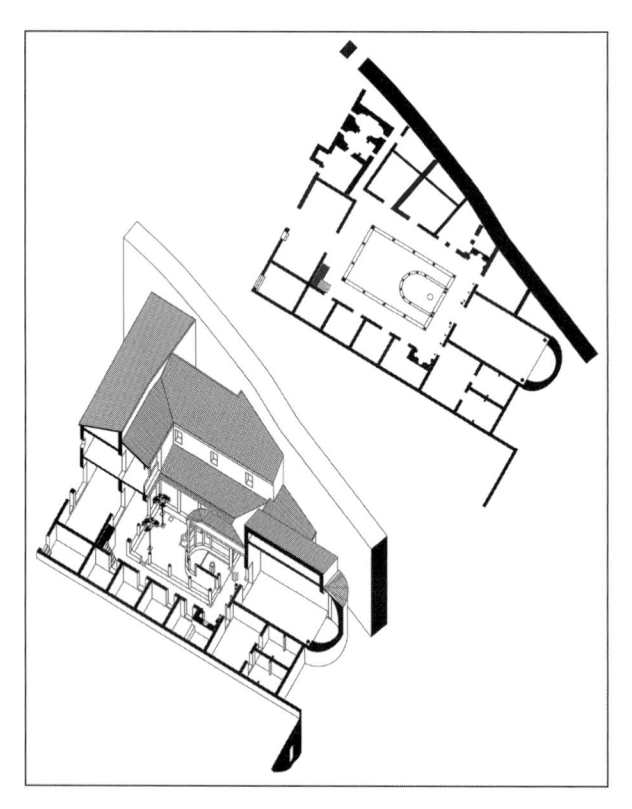

Fig. 3.12 Mérida, the 'Casa de los Mármoles' fourth-century urban residence

room. It opened off a transverse corridor with apses at each end, a much scaled-down version of the sort of arrangement to be seen at the palace at Trier and the great residence of La Cercadilla outside Córdoba (see Chapter 5). Opposite the reception hall and projecting into the courtyard was a square chamber with a central fountain and marble lining the floor and walls, the chamber terminated by a semicircular setting of columns with a floor also in black and white squares. This would have provided a very cool and elegant vista for anyone in the main reception room, or could have been used for dining itself. Other rooms opened off the long sides of the courtyard, and the house had its own baths and latrine. Though on a fairly cramped site, the complex had been carefully thought through and elements such as the apsidal reception hall and the fountain chamber showed a familiarity with the forms of aristocratic architecture current in the fourth century (cf. Chapter 5, p. 224). Unfortunately, there is little comparable domestic architecture from Spain yet available to set alongside the Morería house (cf. Kulikowski 2004: Ch. 5, 2005). There is also the question of whether, as Mérida was the administrative capital of the *diocesis Hispaniarum*, the entire Iberian peninsula (plus Mauretania Tingitana), it was exceptional because of the concentration of senior officials and thus its residences may not be representative of wider trends in Spain. Otherwise, one may point to the Calle Bisbo Caçador site inside the southeastern walls of Barcelona, where there is part of a courtyard house with its own baths and with mosaic floors, a floor in marble *opus sectile* and wall paintings. This remodelling of an existing house dates to the fourth century (Arce *et al.* 2007: 314–16). The third example is the more modest town of *Complutum* (Alcalá de Henares) in the centre of the peninsula, where the fourth century saw the refurbishment and aggrandisement of a number of houses, including the 'Casa de Hippolytus' with its mosaics and bathhouse, and the 'villa' of El Val with its semicircular courtyard (García Moreno and Rascón Marqués 1999).

Urban archaeology on the late Roman towns of Britain has been more systematic, and has yielded a picture that increasingly shows the administrative centres still to be densely inhabited from the later third into the first half of the fourth century, with both large residences, often of some architectural pretensions and equipped with such markers of superior status as private bath suites and mosaics, and a range of more modest dwellings, on the evidence of hearths, ovens and so on, of artisan as well as residential character (Faulkner 2000b; Perring 2002). This would suggest that despite the declining provision of public buildings and monuments as outlined above, Romano-British towns continued as centres of aristocratic use, with perhaps the administrative functions now displaced into residences, and of economic and social activity. It may be that future excavation in southern Gaul and Spain will show a similar pattern there also; certainly, what little there is seems to fit this pattern. The more modest, artisan buildings of fourth-century Britain at present stand somewhat isolated. There is as yet little comparable evidence from the towns of southern Gaul or Spain. There is evidence from individual cities such as the *garum* factory at Barcelona (Beltrán de Heredia Bercero 2002: 58–62), but no consistent evidence base or pattern, so it is not easy to establish the extent to which these towns remained centres of manufacture and commercial activity. Better evidence, perhaps, is that of the distribution patterns of pottery and other materials discussed in Chapter 7, strongly suggestive of city-centred patterns of distribution if not manufacture, and which at the moment must stand proxy for evidence from the towns themselves, though this is likely to emerge in due course.

One question about these urban residences that ought to be drawn out relates to the suggestion made earlier in this chapter that what had been 'civic' and 'public' functions that had originally been performed in the sphere of 'public' buildings, such as the forum and basilica, came to be displaced to the more controllable setting of the 'private' house. Of course, as will be more extensively considered in Chapter 5, 'public' and 'private' are polarities that were not strictly separated in the Roman world. A function of the Roman aristocratic house had always been to receive visitors, either the relatively large number of clients let into the atrium at a morning *salutatio* or the smaller numbers of equals and superiors received further into the house as a mark of their superior social status (Wallace-Hadrill 1994), and this was also true of the late Roman house (Ellis 1994). The apsidal reception rooms and other important rooms marked by mosaics and other embellishments would have been entirely suitable for such functions, as were their country cousins, so one may envisage them being used by a powerful *curialis* or an appointed imperial official, such as a *corrector*, to administer the city and its *civitas*.

Lesser centres

A widespread feature of the urban pattern of Britain, Gaul and Germany down to the third century was the 'small town' or *agglomération secondaire* – what will here be termed a secondary centre (Burnham and Wacher 1990 for Britain; Petit *et al.* 1994 and Rorison 2001 for Gaul). Usually sited at transport nodes such as where a road crossed a river or at the junction of two or more roads, these secondary centres seem to have discharged roles that were largely religious and economic, to judge by the building types consistently found at them. The majority of the buildings are of the 'artisan' type, combining the commercial functions of shop and workshop with living accommodation. The evidence for heat-using processes, particularly metalworking since its evidence survives well in the archaeology, points to artisan activities, either transforming primary resources or fashioning finished items and repairing them. The evidence for the presence of finished goods of local fabrication (such as pottery) and for goods traded over longer distances has led to the general acceptance that these centres had an important commercial vocation as lesser market centres between the larger cities, servicing the rural populations. The near ubiquitous presence at these centres of temples likewise suggests an important facet of their place in the settlement pattern. The extent to which these sanctuaries were the reason for the centre coming into being (as was certainly the case at some of the major rural sanctuaries of Gaul), or were a response to the existence of the centre is something that has yet to be determined by a larger number of well-excavated examples.

Coming through into the later third century and fourth century, there is, unfortunately, no detailed synthesis of the evidence from these sites for this period (a brief summary is in Rorison 2001: Ch. 5), though there are a number of regional publications (Bellet *et al.* 1999; Bénard *et al.* 1994; Fiches 2002; Galinié and Royo 1993; Maurin 1992; Petit *et al.* 1994: *première partie*). In all of the studies, the overwhelming focus is on the first century BC to the early third century AD, and the later Roman period is treated very cursorily. At one level this is because the 'third-century crisis' still casts a long shadow over study of these sites, not only appearing as an explanation of observed 'decline' at them, but also being expected and actively sought (and, not surprisingly, often found). The diagrams of occupation created show this third-century threshold very clearly (e.g. Petit *et al.* 1994: *première partie*). Sometimes at sites near the Rhine such as Dalheim (Luxembourg), there is epigraphic evidence for just such destruction (Krier 2011), though it should be noted that there is no clear archaeological evidence for the 'violence of the barbarians' mentioned in an inscription at the site. But, at another level, it does seem to be the case that there were profound changes to the extent and intensity of occupation at these sites and to the activities that took place at them from the mid third century onward; the evidence for abandonment of areas of the settlements, for individual structures and for the cessation of artisan activity is too generalised across Gaul and the

Rhineland and too well documented in the archaeology simply to be the result of modern perceptions of the period. This therefore suggests that the sorts of functions that the centres had performed under the High Empire were no longer required in the later period. This seems particularly to have affected the commercial side of their activities, since it is the artisan buildings that overwhelmingly were abandoned. As we shall see in Chapter 6, commerce continued at various levels in the later Roman period across the West, so it was not the activities that ceased but their expression through this sort of settlement. Were the activities simply displaced to the major cities, or were there other rural centres, such as sanctuaries or perhaps villas that took over such functions? At present it is not possible to say. But it is worth noting that evidence for continued if reduced occupation and activity is increasingly coming to light from excavations – for instance, in south-west Gaul (cf. Boudartchouk 2005; Colin 2008, both concerned with Christianisation of the region but showing that some of the sites concerned were such secondary centres). It may be that the apparent cessation of activity at these centres will need in future to be reassessed, as it is shown that there was fourth-century occupation at such sites, but, equally, what that occupation was and what part these sites played in the economic, religious and social landscape will need to be reassessed also.

Discussion

At the start of this chapter, various characterisations of the Roman city were outlined: the institutional/political version, the politico-cultural version, the economic version and the demographic version. It was shown that these could be subsumed into wider debates positing the ancient city as a particular 'type' of city, marked by being 'parasitic' on its society rather than a motor of that society's development. In this discussion we shall draw out the main lines of argument from the various areas of evidence and debate summarised above. The evidence and discussion above clearly show that cities remained a necessary and defining feature of much of the Western Empire through the third and fourth centuries and on into the fifth (and, equally, remained something deemed entirely unnecessary beyond the Rhine and Danube, *Mischzivilization* or no), but, equally, they clearly show that there was huge variation by region and by period. There is far less impression of formal and cultural homogeneity than there had been under the High Empire, where the layout of cities and the provision of public buildings and monuments seem to have been more homogeneous, suggesting a more coherent view of how to express civic status and ambitions on the part of the elites over a wide area (cf. Laurence *et al.* 2011). Different regions were reinventing the Roman city to suit their purposes, one of the many ways in which regionalism becomes more pronounced in this period. Given all these variations, what can usefully be said in the way of general argument that does not run the risk of operating at such a level of generalisation as to be platitudinous? One approach is the classic archaeological one of classification and hierarchisation, in order to define similarities and differences and thus to reduce hundreds of individual instances to manageable groupings. This continues to have its long-established value of giving heuristic categories to think with and about. Here, four groups will be proposed, two with a small number of examples, two with larger numbers. These are as follows: cities with important imperial connections; cities exhibiting important continuities with the High Empire (essentially the cities of southern Gaul and Spain – and Britain); the new, militarised cities of northern Gaul; and the late, 'minimalist' cities, largely in south-western Gaul.

Most prominent in terms of area and monumental equipment and variety of functions, but certainly not in numbers, were those cities with direct and regular connections with the imperial presence and the highest echelons of the imperial administration; these are cities linked into the super-regional networks of power and officialdom. For our area this was, above all, Trier, and, to a lesser extent, Arles (these are discussed more fully in Chapter 5), which were comparable with other major imperial centres such as Milan or in due course Constantinople. The imperial equipment of such cities in the form of palace complexes, with their audience halls, residential quarters, major baths, churches and circuses, set a standard which other cities would note and to which they might aspire, much as the architecture and appointments of the imperial residences set a standard for the residences of the aristocracies (cf. Chapter 5). One of the features of both Trier and Arles was that these imperial residences were set within cities whose existing monuments were curated and refurbished as part of the projection of imperial power and magnificence, so to that extent they promoted the active maintenance of the built heritage from the High Empire (as also did the imperial legislation inveighing against the despoiling and degradation of the buildings and adornments of cities referred to above). The monumental past was therefore itself an active instrument in the construction of the identity of major cities rather than just an incidental legacy of former years, and new complexes were physically related to the old, one of the ways in which the fourth century was shaped by the second. This attitude is visible above all at Rome, but the attitude applied to other major centres. Because of this, one may see something of the same attitude in the echelon of major administrative centres, the diocesan capitals. Trier and Arles, of course, also acted as such capitals, and in the case of Arles this may have been an important strand in its urban development through the fourth century. The capital of the diocese of the *Hispaniae*, Mérida, shows very similar patterns, in particular with the restoration of the theatre under Constantine I and the refurbishment of the circus in the 330s. The other evidence for the city in the fourth century, particularly residences such as the 'Casa de los Mármoles', also gives an impression of an out-of-the-ordinary level of prosperity and investment. As for the capital of the *Britanniae*, London, our picture is at present impressionistic, but within the long wall circuit, at the end of the third century augmented by the river wall, has been discovered a series of fourth-century mosaics and parts of residences which would fit well with Mérida or other similar towns, suggesting that fourth-century London with its suite of imperial administrative and financial officials may have been more vibrant than it is often presented as being. One other city that might be mentioned in the same breath, though not a major administrative centre, is Metz (cf. Chapter 2, p. 74), which had at least one major civil complex constructed within its relatively large circuit of walls. The extensive area and the curation of older monuments along with the furnishing with new ones echo, on a smaller scale, Metz's near neighbour Trier, and the reasons for Metz's exceptional fourth-century appearance must surely lie in its siting on the main route to the imperial residence and the model that that residence represented.

Apart from this small group of cities, there was the much larger group of cities across southern Gaul and Spain which did not acquire the classic monuments of the late city, walls and churches, until the end of the fourth century or later. Despite their numerical preponderance, these cities have tended to be much less visible in the literature. In part this was because few of them had or have a good series of excavated sites on which to base individual analyses, let alone an attempt at synthesis. But it is also, of course, because of the traditional fixation on walls and churches, thus inevitably discounting other manifestations of urbanism. As noted above, at these cities the determining structure or 'armature' of the classical, Roman city continued to operate, the street grid or system, implying both an authority that was concerned and able to maintain it and an urban ideology that saw it as integral to the self-presentation of urban and civic space, with a continuing gradation between 'public' and 'private'. Again as noted above, a considerable number of these cities also maintained buildings and monuments inherited from the second century such as theatres, amphitheatres and circuses. This is particularly noticeable in Spain, but it also applies across southern Gaul, even at cities such as Bordeaux, which had a restricted wall circuit imposed but where major, earlier monuments such as the 'Piliers de Tutelle' and the 'Palais Gallien' amphitheatre were maintained, and similarly in the case of the 'Tour de Vésone' temple at Périgueux, which was also left standing (Lauffray 1990). This active maintenance should surely be read in the same light as at the imperially influenced cities such as Mérida. It was a part of the self-perception of the cities concerned to invoke their heritage of earlier monuments as well as to conserve the street systems, so an important element of their civic ideology was that in part they regarded themselves as maintainers of what they saw as the urban values of earlier times. So it can be argued that in this southern half of the Western provinces there was a greater continuity through the fourth century in urban form and ideology than has often been allowed, even if the elites were less likely to record this epigraphically. There is also some evidence that the cities of the old Narbonensis and from the Mediterranean littoral of Spain (e.g. Aix-en-Provence, Marseille, Narbonne, Barcelona, Tarragona, Valencia and Cartagena) were particularly vigorous, so integration into the Mediterranean economic and cultural cycles may have been an important 'connectivity' as well as that linking cities to the imperial court. It is here also, as places with active links to the earlier imperial past, that the cities of Britain fit, with the considerable degree of maintenance of their street grids and of the old-style public monumentality, augmented in this case with the newer, monumental wall circuits. We know more about their private residences and artisan buildings than we do generally about their Continental counterparts, but these can be read as a development through from the later second century rather than an innovation in the later centuries.

There is clearly another major category, the militarised 'cities' of northern Gaul described and discussed in Chapter 2; one may prefer to call them 'fortress cities'. This is not the place to iterate everything said in Chapter 2, but if one is following a classificatory approach, then this class needs to be flagged up, and, of course, it is one that often took a very different view of the monuments of the High Empire by reusing them as the core for later fortifications, as we saw at places such as Amiens and Bavai, or through the incorporation of stonework from civic and funerary buildings and monuments into the new walls, as and when they came to be constructed. We have very little information as to how the spaces within these defences were organised. Were there streets? The evidence from analogous sites such as Kaiseraugst strongly suggests that there were. Were there other 'public' spaces? What was the building stock of these places? Was it dominated by state-related installations such as official residences and barracks, as apparently at Arras, or major storehouses as at Paris or Maastricht? Or were there also urban residences of the type we have seen further south? But given the small areas enclosed by most of these defences, it is difficult to envisage the sort of physical appearance of the southern cities. In terms of phenomenology, of the intersection of the physical environment with mental perception, these 'fortress towns' must have had a very different character: to live in them was to experience a very different view of urbanism. Even at cities such as Amiens and Bavai where major earlier monuments such as the forum on its cryptoporticus had been retained, they had not been curated as an active link with the past but had rather been reworked and redefined as subservient to the new monumentalism of fortification. In terms of the (re)production of social structures and values in their citizens, these were cities of the present with little use for the past.

But the example of Périgueux, mentioned earlier, argues for a more nuanced approach even at some of these 'fortress cities' to the south of the Loire. Here many earlier monuments were clearly dismantled and their stonework formed the lower courses of the new fortifications. Yes, these walls incorporated the existing amphitheatre, a highly defensible structure, but was it still kept in commission for spectacle? One might ask the same question of the amphitheatre of Tours, also sitting aside the wall circuit. As noted, the major public complex of the 'Tour de Vésone' temple was maintained, and it appears that so was a set of baths in the area of the medieval cathedral and another to the south of the temple complex. It can clearly be argued that the suppression or maintenance of existing monuments at Périgueux was a highly selective and therefore ideologically driven process; indeed, the amphitheatre physically became part of the main new civic monument, the walls, thus uniting old and new. So here we may have a case where the new urbanism of the small 'fortress town' was imposed upon but also negotiated within the fabric of a continuing city of southern Gaul. One might also argue something similar for Bordeaux, where it is clear that the defended area around the river harbour lay alongside the old city centre, some of whose monuments were clearly still extant. A similar case may be made for Saintes, where, even if some earlier monuments were cannibalised into the new walls, others such as the amphitheatre and the 'Arch of Germanicus' existed alongside the walls. The juxtaposition of a city essentially of the old 'classical' type with a relatively large area and curating some of the major monuments of its past with a small 'fortress city' arguably emphasises the novelty of the latter and that it owed its existence to the priorities of the state rather than the concerns of the local community.

But a very different approach to what constituted a city was taken by the unusual and therefore interesting group of late *civitas* capitals in Novempopulana in the deep south-west of Gaul, where in the first half of the fifth century a series of *civitates* created in the fourth or fifth centuries acquired 'capitals' (e.g. Oloron, Saint-Lizier) consisting simply of a hilltop fortification enclosing a small area with no evidence for civic monumentality beyond the walls themselves – indeed, little evidence for any activity outside the walled nucleus. Similar installations were created also at existing 'old-style' *civitas* capitals such as Auch and Saint-Bertrand-de-Comminges, and at the latter at least the area of the earlier city continued to be occupied for a time alongside the new hilltop defence (Esmonde Cleary 2007a: Ch. 5). Clearly, the definition of a 'town' for whoever decreed the creation of these places was now very stripped down and functional. Something of the same attitude may be visible in south-eastern Gaul at roughly the same period. Over the three hundred years from the early second to the early fifth century, the nature and perception of Roman urbanism had altered out of all recognition.

What this classificatory approach has emphasised is that there was no one response to developments in the third and fourth centuries nor one common model of urbanisation, certainly not before the walls-and-churches stereotype of the fifth century. Clearly, then, there was a variety of possible perceptions of urban form and function, and this must be related closely to the analytical framework proposed here of cities as 'machines' (in a Le Corbusier-type sense) for producing citizens. The four classificatory groups examined above can be collapsed essentially into two overlapping types, which themselves were to become more homogenised in the fifth century (see Chapter 9). One type is that represented by the 'imperial cities' and the cities of southern Gaul, Spain and Britain, and the other by the cities(?) of northern Gaul and of Novempopulana. The first of these groups exhibits a considerable degree of continuity with the 'classical' past in the overall layout of the city, in its lack of fortifications, and in the survival to a greater or lesser extent of the old civic monuments and religious precincts and buildings. So far as can be told, in many cases this represents the conscious curation of these monuments (even if in a progressively more degraded state) rather than simply their physical survival without their old functions and significance. If this conscious curation was the case, then we see a purposive ideology of maintenance of tradition. As will be argued also in Chapter 5, tradition was and is not a passive replication of the existing state of affairs 'because it was there' but rather an active and positive strategy with an ideological purpose of staking a claim to the glories of the past and its cultural and moral superiority. Negatively, it also has the purpose implicitly or explicitly of denigrating more recent trends and tendencies, perhaps as to be found north of the Loire – it is noticeable that Ausonius does not include any militarised northern city in his 'Order of Noble Cities' (*Ordo Urbium Nobilium*), and his poem on the Moselle (*Mosella*) opens with his relief at seeing Trier because it reminds him of Bordeaux after journeying through 'trackless forest'; for all that this last is part hyperbolic stereotype, it may also reflect the poet's own perspective. If the classical past was being actively curated and exploited, then, presumably, the citizens being created in these classicising cities were expected in part to reflect the old Roman civic virtues and values, or at least those elements of them as understood and found acceptable by the elites of the fourth century. Thus fora may still have represented the importance of administrative and legal activity and the identity of the community as expressed by statues of its former leaders along with those of its new imperial masters and their governors. This may be the ideological context for the mentions of continuing spectacles of the traditional type in circus and amphitheatre to be found in the literary sources (cf. García and Rascón 2001; Landes and Carrié 2007), recalling the practice of the earlier empire, though, of course, these had acquired their overlay of distinctively late Roman concern with ceremonial and status display: tradition is mutable. In such ways citizens of a recognisably classical Roman stripe could be reproduced, perhaps a better testimony to the continuation and vitality of municipal institutions than that derived from the sparse literary sources for the West and a corrective for views of these cities which telescope their chronology and define them too much by the (late) arrival of walls.

Walls, though, were the defining feature of the cities of northern Gaul in the course of the fourth century as of north-western Spain, and then also of the cities of south-western Gaul in particular in the earlier fifth century. These represented a very different perception and evocation of citizenship, already discussed in Chapter 2 (p. 75), but which can be summarised as the (male) citizen in arms. The citizen who grew up and lived in these places with their huge sets of walls, their military personnel and garrisons, their visual language of military-style dress and adornment, and the threat (real, imagined or imperial rhetoric) of invasion from across the Rhine was being called to a very different relationship with the empire and with Rome's past, one that harked back to the centrality of military service and of warfare in the creation of the Roman citizen and to the soldier as the noblest Roman of them all.

So far this discussion has been concerned with what might be termed the politico-cultural city as expressed (or argued) in its public buildings and monuments. More difficult to synthesise is the disparate and patchy evidence for the city as economic entity. Was the late Roman city, even more than its High Empire avatars, a demonstration of Finley's model of the 'parasitic' city or instead of Horden and Purcell's (2000: 101) 'against *villes*' stance? This will be considered more fully in Chapter 7, but it is worth making a few points here. For northern Gaul, the evidence is contradictory. On the one hand, the excavated evidence shows few artisan buildings and little evidence for manufacture. On the other hand, it is at several of them that the state invested to create the *fabricae*, one of the areas in which the ancient world came closest (though how close?) to the capitalist-industrial idea and practice of mass production: note that the state did not create *fabricae* other than at places it categorised as cities (whatever their contemporary reality in terms of size, buildings and population). In southern Gaul and Spain, as stated above, there is at present little evidence for large-scale industrial activity, certainly in comparison with the areas given over to such things as surviving public monuments, churches and fortifications. It is also noticeable to the archaeologist that the deposits in late Roman cities are relatively 'clean' in terms of the debris from industrial processes, certainly by comparison with their medieval successors (cf. Carver 1993: Ch. 3), and while this may in part be explained by differences in rubbish-disposal regimes, it is, in more important part, expressive of a qualitative difference in the intensity of artisan activity between the two periods. Though, as we shall see in Chapter 7, the archaeological evidence demonstrates that late Roman cities did have a role in commerce, it was often of items not fabricated at the cities themselves such as pottery. In this respect late Roman cities did differ from the 'type' of medieval cities, the latter being seen as primarily geared to manufacture and marketing, with the manufacture taking place *in situ* rather than at rural locations. In fact, this urban/rural synthesis had always been a feature of the way the Roman economy worked, certainly in the West, and one must not allow moralising arguments freighted with concepts of 'progress' to cause the medieval structures to be seen as 'more advanced' and thus 'better' than the Roman way of doing things. They did things differently there.

In sum, the city remained as a central and defining feature of the late Roman West, but one that was highly variable in its physical manifestations, in its functions and in its population according to its location, status and date. Indeed, it is questionable whether the concept of 'the Roman city' existed any longer (if it ever had) except at the very general level of 'a city within the territory of the Roman Empire'. These cities must now, therefore, be approached on a city-by-city and a region-by-region basis rather than subsumed to some overall model of what a late Roman city 'ought' to be.

4 | Christianity and the traditional religions

This chapter is going to be the wrong way round. It is going to devote most of its space first of all to a religion that for most of the period, possibly all the period, was in numerical terms the religion of a minority of the population. It will after that have relatively little to say about the whole complex of deities and religions that were followed by the majority of the population. The bulk of the chapter will concern itself with the archaeological evidence for Christianity, in the West a parvenu religion that depended ultimately for its widespread adoption on the patronage of the emperors and the ways in which their examples and decrees were increasingly followed by the local aristocracies. This is not to say that conversion to Christianity was simply a matter of political calculation; clearly, many people (even emperors) believed in it deeply. But it is to make the point that without imperial sponsorship its spread and ultimate success would have been far slower and have taken very different forms. But most people for most of our period did not follow the religion of the 'pale Galilean'; they adhered to the traditional deities and practices of the Roman state, of other Mediterranean cults, and, overwhelmingly, the myriad gods and spirits of local place and practice. In this work these will be subsumed under the term 'traditional religions', a term I prefer to 'paganism' or 'polytheism' or other attempts at brief descriptors of the existing religious conformations, and one which I owe to Duffy 1992, in whose work the term is elaborated and discussed in ways that make evident its usefulness, though not exact similarity, in this context. But for reasons that will become clear below, we have little evidence for and little discussion of these deities and cults across the late Roman West. Because of its subsequent centrality to European civilisation, the development and spread of Christianity has long been a field of major scholarly endeavour, almost always by scholars from one of the Christian confessions. While this has enormously enriched our knowledge and understanding of these transformative processes, it has meant that an inverse amount of time and effort has been expended on the traditional religions; often it seems they are only there in order to be triumphed over by the new religion and are not worth serious consideration in their own right. So because of this evidential inversion, it makes more sense to start with the relatively coherent picture for Christianity before moving on to the much more fragmentary and less easily synthesised evidence for the traditional religions.

Christianity

One of the defining features of late antiquity anywhere in the Mediterranean basin and its hinterland was the gradual conversion of the Roman Empire to Christianity, expressed both in the acceptance of Christianity as the 'state religion' and in the growing numbers of individuals converted to the faith. It is a spectacular example of how profoundly a shift in *mentalités* could reshape the religious, social and cultural outlook of all classes of peoples over a huge area – a shift unconnected with and not to be predicted by the rhythms of the *longue* or the *moyenne durée*, though to have massive consequences for the manifestations of the latter. This was because Christianity developed and expressed a whole series of ideological views, ritual practices and religious identities of which a number of important aspects were at variance with those of the traditional religions. This means for the archaeologist that Christianity materialised itself in a range of distinct and distinctive ways. Initially, the impact was greatest at the cities, where it transformed major aspects of topography, buildings and spatial arrangements, in large part through the creation of new features such as Christian places of worship, but also in part by the consequent dereliction or obliteration of important features of the pre-existing cities, often though not exclusively to do with manifestations and performance of the traditional religions. Because of this, the contribution of Christianity to the development of the cities of the late Roman West has been accorded separate treatment here, though in the final part of the chapter there will be a discussion of the ways in which Christianisation of the city related to other facets of the development of the city in this period across the West in order to bind Chapters 3 and 4 together (developments at the lesser towns and in the countryside will be considered in Chapters 5 and 6). One of the features of the new Christian identity, at the level both of the individual believer and of Christian communities, was Christians' very strong sense of belonging to an 'imagined community', partly through the formal hierarchical structures of Christianity, and partly through attempts at defining Christian belief, doctrine and behaviour either at the level of empire-wide ('ecumenical') Church councils or at the more regional versions held in the West once Christianity became a permitted religion (*religio licita*), starting with the Council of Arles in 314. But this sense of inclusion was also generated by the reciprocity of membership of church communities across the empire, promoted by such developments as pilgrimage. These meant that there was a considerable degree of similitude in the physical manifestations of the new religion as it inserted itself into existing cities, first of all conditioned by their existing fabrics and then coming increasingly to alter them to suit Christian ideologies.

Churches

The single most important impact of Christianity on the physical form and materiality of the late Roman city in the West, as elsewhere, was the construction of churches, the new form of major religious building, designed for the enclosing of clergy and congregation, and, along with certain subsidiary structures (most notably baptisteries), destined to express the developing sacramental practice of the Christian communities. The most important Christian monument in any town with a bishop was the bishop's church with its baptistery and ancillary buildings, what in French is referred to as the *groupe épiscopal* and is here referred to as 'the episcopal complex'. The episcopal church was generally of basilican form with an apse. The basilican form was adopted by the Christian Church after the persecutions ended and the religion was declared *licita*, lawful, and something larger and more imposing than a house church created for a small congregation within a domestic setting was needed At one level this was a functional decision, given that Christianity was a religion which required congregational worship within a building rather than the more external forms of public worship typical of traditional Graeco-Roman cults and of existing religious practice in the Western provinces; the basilica was an existing building type which could accommodate large numbers of worshippers, dependent simply on the size of the building. But at a more symbolic level the basilica also had resonances that were appropriate in a Christian setting. The traditional, civil basilica (and its military counterpart) was the *sedes iustitiae*, the seat of justice, where lawsuits were heard and justice dispensed; the transition to divine rather than human justice was easy to make. On the tribunal at the end of the basilica, sometimes framed by an apse, sat the magistrates and judges, the *iudices* (or in a military setting the commanding officer), so the placing there of the altar as the sign of the presence of the Judge Eternal was entirely natural, and ranged on a bench (*synthronon*) around the inside of the apse would have been the bishop and his clergy. In the fourth century another use for the basilican form was as the setting for the presence of the emperor, as in the great basilica of the palace at Trier (cf. p. 202), and the emperor was increasingly seen as the instrument of the Christian God's purpose, as well as possessed of his divine *numen* and religious office in the traditional religions. So the established semiotics of the basilica would have been easily understood in their new Christian manifestation. To illustrate this, rather than create a catalogue that is to a degree an abstracted version of actuality, the example of an important, recently excavated site will be taken to demonstrate several types of evidence in a real setting: this is the exemplary series of excavations by Charles Bonnet and his team undertaken between 1976 and 1993 underneath and around the medieval cathedral of Geneva and at other churches in the modern city (cf. Bonnet 1993, 2006). Then wider issues raised by the Geneva case study will be explored, before consideration of the archaeological evidence for the development of urban Christianity in specific cities and areas of the West.

Geneva

Geneva in the early-imperial period was a *vicus* of the huge *civitas* of the Allobroges centred on Vienne. In the later third century, it was probably raised to the status of *civitas* in its own right and at the end of that century, it was enclosed within a rectangular circuit of walls 3 m thick delimiting an area of 5.5 ha. on top of a spur overlooking the south side of the western end of Lake Geneva and the outflow of the river Rhône (Figure 4.1). In the north-eastern part of the walled area lay an existing, large, courtyard house. In the 350s the western part of the south range of this house was demolished to make way for the new, public church of the bishop with its subsidiary buildings, the whole completed by 370 (conceivably taking the place of an existing house church in the demolished part of the house). At the core of the complex was the church (Figure 4.2), a rectangular building, with an eastern apse and entered by a door almost in the centre of the south wall; the church was constructed in *opus africanum*, and since this technique was rare in Gaul but common in the Mediterranean lands, the builders presumably came from well to the south of Geneva. The apse and the eastern extremity of the main building were reserved to the altar and the clergy. A partition divided the main chamber/nave opposite the main door, so those entering would have to choose either the western half of the nave or the eastern. A little to the south of the church was a baptistery, consisting of a rectangular chamber with an eastern apse of three-quarters of a circle. Set into the floor in the north-western part of the chamber was a rectangular basin, presumably for the actual baptism (at this period administered to adults and by a bishop); the eastern part of the chamber and the apse were divided off, presumably for the use of the officiating bishop, his clergy and

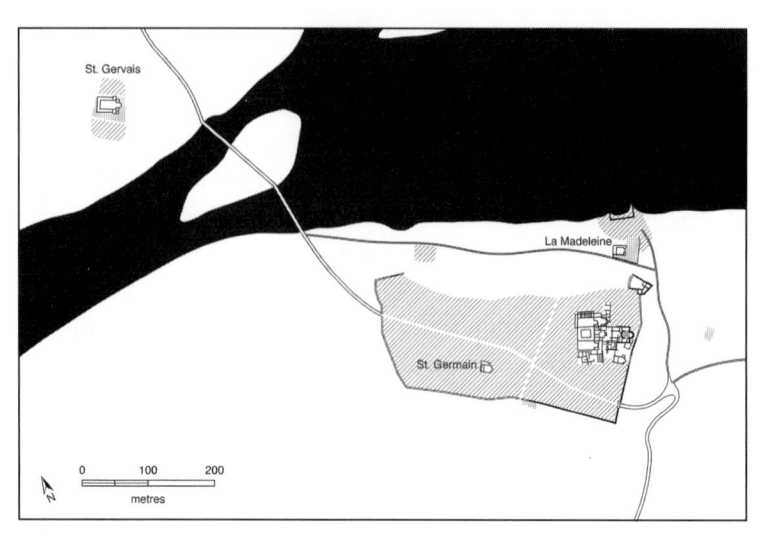

154 *Christianity and the traditional religions*

Fig. 4.1 Geneva, location of late Roman churches

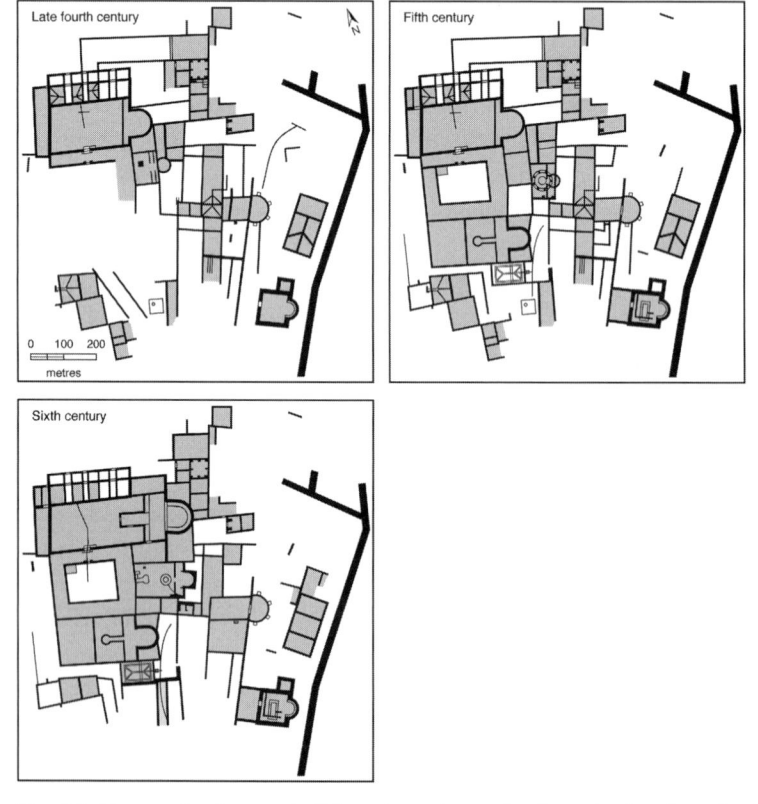

Fig. 4.2 Geneva, development of the episcopal complex from the fourth to the sixth century

attendants. A corridor along the western side of the church led to a series of heated rooms, probably accommodation for the clergy and household (*familia*) of the bishop, and there were further rooms to the east of the church along with the remaining part of the earlier house.

Around the year 400, the complex was substantially remodelled and enlarged. South of the church was constructed a colonnaded courtyard or *atrium*, with on its southern side another church of very similar plan and dimensions to the existing one to the north. Like the earlier church, the apse and the eastern part of the nave were separated off and reserved to the clergy: projecting out into the nave from this enclosure was a walkway (*solea*) leading to a polygonal *ambo* for the reading of biblical texts. A new baptistery was constructed in the centre of the range to the east of the courtyard, which linked the two churches. It was of similar plan to the earlier baptistery (which now served as a vestibule to it), a rectangular chamber with a small apse, but it now had an octagonal basin in the centre of the main chamber surmounted by a *ciborium* or canopy supported on eight columns around the basin. As in the earlier baptistery, the eastern part was marked off for the bishop and clergy. East again of the baptistery were other rooms, one of which may have been a large refectory for the communal meals of the clergy, with evidence for butchery between it and the bishop's residence. In the area between these rooms and the eastern defensive wall lay the bishop's residence, including a large heated room, probably a reception/dining chamber, with a small apsidal chapel closing the complex to the south, presumably for the private use of the bishop. South of the southern church were other rooms architecturally linked with the episcopal complex.

By the end of the fifth century, there had been further modifications to the complex, of which three should be noted. First, the northern church was enlarged by the demolition of the original apse and the prolonging of the nave eastwards and the construction of a new apse, bringing the total length of the building to 43 m. The apse and the eastern part of the nave continued to be reserved for the clergy and from the western side of the enclosure a structure projected into the nave, consisting of two walls, of which the southern contained a tomb under a niche (*arcosolium*). This arrangement, an elaborate form of *solea* soon after embellished with columns, is suggested to be for processional or choral rituals, different from the *solea* and *ambo* of the southern church. Second, to the south, the baptistery was completely reconstructed. It was extended to the west, more than doubling its size, and so that it now opened directly off the *atrium*. A new octagonal basin was constructed to the west of the previous one, again surmounted by a *ciborium* (the foundations reusing carved stonework from its predecessor, giving some idea of the architectural decoration of that period). The new, deeper apse and the eastern part of the main chamber were again reserved to the clergy, now with enough room for an altar. Inside the main, western door was a small *solea* and *ambo* arrangement, with traces of a second *ambo* next to the *ciborium*. Clearly, the ceremonies of baptism had become much more complex and more public. Third, south of the eastern part of the south church was constructed a large, heated reception room, whose floor was covered in a mosaic in geometric patterns. The whole complex was maintained, altered, rebuilt and extended through the next seven centuries, but here we must restrict ourselves to these initial phases.

The cathedral is not the only church in and around Geneva to have been excavated to reveal its late antique predecessor (cf. Bonnet 2006 and Figure 4.1). In the central part of the town lies the church of Saint-Germain, a simple apsidal structure yielding fragments of a screen datable to the end of the fourth or the beginning of the fifth centuries. At the foot of the northern side of the plateau, outside the walls and near the port, was the church of La Madeleine (Bonnet 1977), probably of the same general period. It lay in a cemetery area and had originated as a small chapel (*cella memoriae*) to commemorate a particular burial. The interior of the chapel soon filled up with burials, and western and northern extensions were built to accommodate more burials. North-west of the walled area and on the other side of the uppermost course of the Rhône was the church of Saint-Gervais (Bonnet and Privati 1991), in an area which had also earlier been used for burials, with stonework from a large, fourth-century mausoleum reused in the church. Constructed in the course of the fifth century, the church consisted of a rectangular nave with eastern apse and flanking chambers to north and south of the east end of the nave; overall, it was of similar dimensions to the north church in the episcopal complex, large for such a church. Under the apse was a crypt approached by a staircase from the east end of the nave. An impression in the wall plaster suggests the original presence of a tomb oriented north–south, and the most likely function of the crypt was as the shrine to an important burial. Another north–south burial of this phase lay in the north-western angle of the nave. The church was subsequently enlarged to north, west and south and became a major focus for burial, including some in high-status tomb types. As well as the funerary churches and burials, Geneva has also produced eleven early Christian inscriptions (Handley 2003: 5). Geneva thus provides a good case study of most of the important types of evidence for the impact of Christianity on the urban fabric of the late Roman world, types of evidence

Double churches

The first major rebuild at Geneva endowed it with a second basilica matching the first, an example of a relatively common but as yet imperfectly understood phenomenon, the double church (cf. Duval, N. and Caillet 1996 for a consideration of the term and different national perspectives). A major problem is that the term 'double church' covers a wide geographical area, and a number of different relationships between the churches in terms of their plans (side by side? in a line?) and relative chronology, and it often involves working backwards from later (often Carolingian) configurations and documentary evidence to seek explanations. This discussion will therefore limit itself in the first instance to double churches demonstrable archaeologically and dating before the end of the fifth century, discussing the various relationships between the churches before considering what these pairings may mean. Double churches can be most satisfactorily identified as two churches of comparable scale (i.e. one is not simply subordinate to the other) placed alongside each other (either close together as at Trier or further apart as at Geneva) as parts of a unified architectural composition. The great double church at Trier (Figure 4.3) will be mentioned again briefly in Chapter 5 as

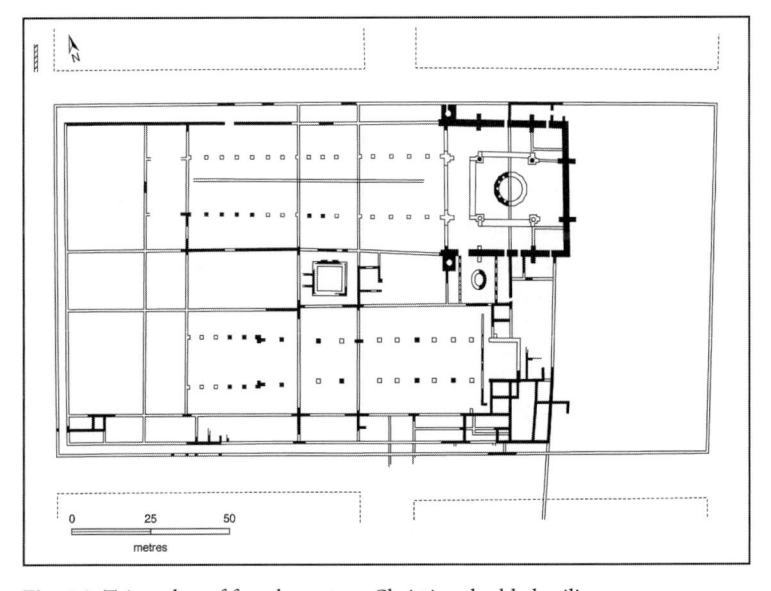

Fig. 4.3 Trier, plan of fourth-century Christian double basilica

part of the palace complex (p. 203), but deserves fuller treatment here. The excavations after the World War II in the bomb-damaged cathedral (Dom) and the Church of Our Lady (Liebfrauenkirche) immediately to its south revealed that the later medieval structures overlay two huge basilicas of the fourth century, of comparable dimensions and plan (the southern basilica being somewhat longer and narrower than the northern), with a baptistery in the space between them. Excavation under the northern basilica showed that it replaced part of the original Constantinian palace and dated to the years after 326. The northern basilica was substantially rebuilt in the second half of the fourth century, being extended eastwards and furnished with a monumental, internal, pillared structure enclosing a dodecagonal setting, perhaps for a major relic, the pillars presumably supporting a canopy or *ciborium*. It was long assumed that the two basilicas were contemporaneous, but more recent analysis of the post-war records (unfortunately, never fully published) suggests that in fact the southern basilica may be a little later than the northern, though this leaves the question of whether, even so, the pair was envisaged from the start (Piva 1996; Weber 1996). Based on arguments developed for the double church at Aquileia in northern Italy and taking into account the position of the baptistery between the two basilicas, the argument is that Trier was a double church where one church (the northern) was for the baptised and the other (the southern) for those under instruction on the faith (catechumens), who would then pass through the waters of baptism from one basilica to the other. Unfortunately, such early sources on liturgy as there are lend no credence to such an arrangement, catechumens being instructed where suitable, including in the episcopal church (cf. Piva 1996: 59–60). Other suggestions for the provision of two major churches have included that one was for everyday use and the other for the use of the bishop, especially at festivals; that they had different dedications, often one to a martyr and the other to the Virgin Mary (based on later practice, as at Trier); and that they were for seasonal use in summer and winter (based on Carolingian practice in Italy). None of these explanations has won general support, due in large measure to the lack of late Roman evidence for any of them. Another possibility, seen in the evidence for the development of the whole of the episcopal complex at Geneva, is the all-too-human urge to aggrandise and to elaborate places of importance; thus, the provision of a second major church was perhaps for differing liturgical functions, as well as the enlargement of the baptistery, and to provide chapels, creating larger spaces for congregational worship as the size of the Christian community grew, and also providing more complex and impressive settings for processional liturgies. Now that it appears that the basilicas at Trier may in fact not be contemporaneous but built at different times, such an argument could apply to these as well. It should also be noted that double churches were by no means ubiquitous, with concentrations in Palestine and Syria, central North Africa, the north Balkans, northern Italy and, in the Western provinces, in Gaul, but not in Spain, Germany or Britain; this suggests even more that instances of the practice need to be viewed in the light of individual circumstances and regional practice.

Baptisteries

The baptistery at Geneva is similar to many other baptisteries in the Western provinces, albeit that they vary in size and elaboration of fittings. The essential element was a basin where the candidate could stand for the bishop to perform the baptism. Since in this period the norm was adult baptism, a sunken basin, often with a raised step around the rim, would have been a convenient arrangement. Baptisteries, therefore, are normally to be found at urban, episcopal churches, and would come into their own for the baptism ceremonies, particularly at Easter. The group of baptisteries preserved in Provence (Figure 4.4) shows the variations possible, from the huge building at Marseille (Guyon in Duval, N. 1995: 142–6), through the still-standing examples attached to the episcopal churches at Aix-en-Provence (Fixot *et al.* 1985), Fréjus (Figure 4.5) (Février and Fixot in Duval, N. 1995: 155–64) and Riez (Figure 4.6) (Barruol in Duval, N. 1995: 85–93), to the tiny baptistery inserted into a former bathhouse at Cimiez (Février in Duval, N. 1995: 103–8). All have in common the central basin, usually octagonal, surmounted by a *ciborium* on pillars (as at Geneva), enclosed within a building which, in the case of the examples cited above (bar Cimiez), was further embellished with internal niches. A similar baptistery has recently been excavated outside the medieval cathedral at Grenoble, nearer to Geneva, dating to the latter part of the fourth century (Baucheron and de Montjoye 1996), as has a more elaborate version with chambers radiating from the sides of the octagon at Limoges (Denis 2006). South of the Pyrenees, the same form was in use – for instance, as excavated at Barcelona (Godoy Fernández 1995: 202–7). Given that baptisteries were designed for use on only a few occasions each year, this may be another instance of elaboration for its own sake and as an expression of the growing confidence and wealth of the Christian community rather than in response to any specific liturgical need.

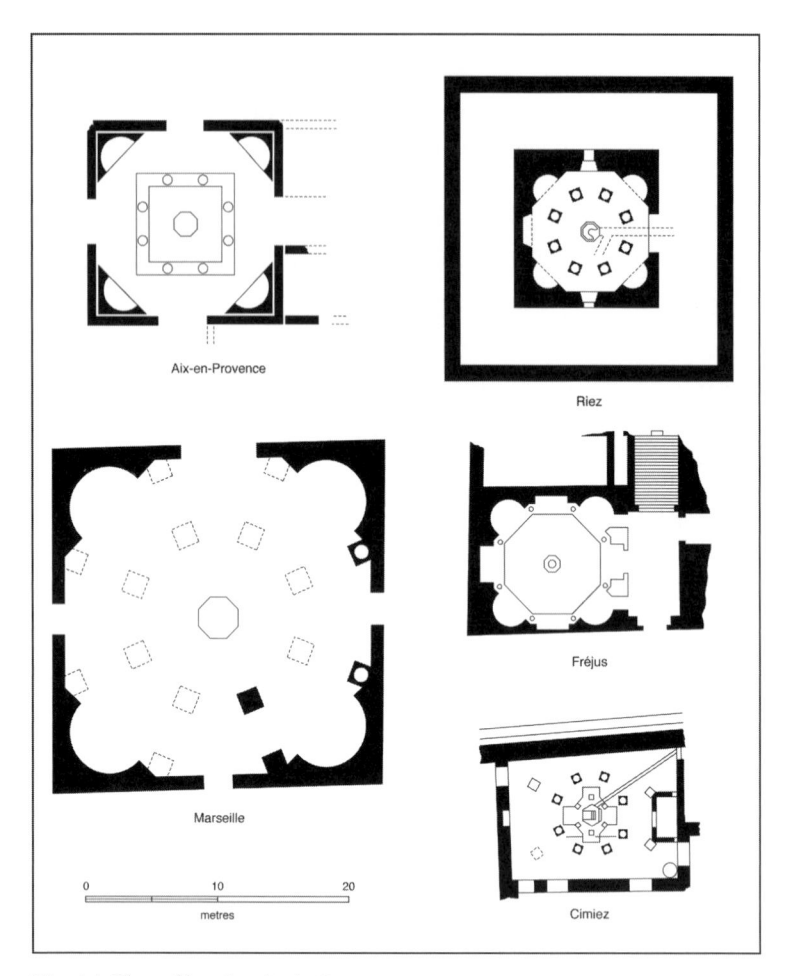

Fig. 4.4 Plan of baptisteries in Provence

Burial

The most radical break with the urban past, and one with consequences for urban form stretching well into the next millennium, was the change in the beliefs and *mentalités* concerning the relationship between the living and the dead, as exemplified by the location of the dead and the placing of Christian cult buildings with respect to the dead (for instance, at Geneva the churches of La Madeleine and Saint-Gervais). The traditional religions and the legal prescriptions of the Roman world enjoined a strict separation between the living and the dead. The corpse was an unclean object and brought ritual pollution upon those who came in contact with it. Even once

Fig. 4.5 Fréjus, the baptistery

the dead had been cremated or inhumed and the appropriate purificatory rites performed to reintegrate the living into the wider community, both the physical remains and the place where they lay remained ill-omened. This ideological distancing of the dead from the living was matched by a physical distancing, with burial being required to take place outside the occupied area. It was not only people who were polluted by contact with the dead, but also cult buildings and the rituals performed at them; temples were defiled by the presence of a corpse and had to be purified. Thus, by and large, there were no places of public worship in the areas ascribed to the dead.

Fig. 4.6 Riez, the baptistery

Individual tombs or family plots might have simpler or more elaborate provision for gatherings, rituals or meals on the appropriate festivals, but these were within the context of private funerary ritual and commemoration rather than of public worship. In general terms these prescriptions and proscriptions were observed in the Western provinces, leading to the familiar location of urban cemeteries along the approach roads to the town.

But the Christian disposition led to a complete breakdown of these separations and the patterns they created in urban form. Archaeologically, this is marked by two related phenomena: the appearance of churches in cemetery areas and the penetration of the spaces of the living by the physical remains and associated rituals of the dead: these are the physical manifestations of major changes in perceptions of death, the dead, and the meaning, symbolism and place of the physical remains of the dead. The start of the transformations is normally visible first in the cemeteries, with the marking of particular burials as 'special' by the construction over them of a simple chamber, or by the construction of a chamber and the deposition in it of one or more burials. These structures then were augmented by enlargement and/or the addition of supplementary elements, the whole coming to take on the familiar form of rectangular nave with or without aisles and an eastern apse – a building for public, congregational liturgies of commemoration. The 'foundation' burial either remained *in situ* and had a major feature such as the altar overlying it, or was removed and reinstalled, for instance, in a purpose-built crypt as at Saint-Gervais, Geneva. The church became a focus for burial, both inside the building and clustered around it, clearly influenced by a desire to be near the primary burial. Such a collocation of a cult building and the dead would have been unthinkable in the traditional religions. The reasons for this change in attitudes to the dead can be reconstructed from the textual sources and are well known. Christianity developed the belief that the physical remains of those who had lived a holy life and/or died a death as witness (Gk. *martyros*) to the faith were themselves impregnated with holiness and also acted as a channel of divine grace (the 'very special dead' of Brown, P. 1981). Their place of burial was marked by a structure (*cella memoriae* or *memoria*), and sometimes the place of martyrdom by a *martyrium*, within which commemorative rituals and gatherings could be held, such as the church constructed within the amphitheatre of Tarragona (Figure 4.7) commemorating the martyrdom of the bishop Fructuosus and the deacons Augurius and Eulogius. As the size of the Christian community grew and/or as did the renown of the holy person enshrined, so the church building became larger and more magnificent: the rapid development of the shrine of Saint Martin, bishop of Tours, in the cemetery to the west of the walls of Tours is an excellent example; it grew from the small structure erected by his successor to the great basilica of a century later (cf. Pietri 1983). The view grew that burial close to the holy ones (*ad sanctos*) could obtain for the deceased a share of their holiness and grace. However much a high theologian such as St Augustine might argue

Fig. 4.7 Tarragona, martyr church in the amphitheatre, from the north-east

that this was an erroneous view (in the *de Cura pro Mortuis Gerenda*, 'On the Care to Be Had for the Dead', *Retractationes* II.64), the evidence of the placing of the dead, of their tombstones and of many other texts shows clearly that this is what the generality of Christians believed (Duval, Y. 1988). Nevertheless, these churches still lay in the extramural cemeteries characteristic of classical Roman urban form.

This veneration of the physical remains then had another consequence in establishing the transgressive pattern of Christian disposal of the dead. Through the fourth century, but particularly in the latter part of the century, and on into the fifth, the cult of the saints developed greatly, as they became intercessors between the earthly and the heavenly kingdoms (Beaujard 2000). But it was not only the saint in the abstract who was potent; the physical remains of the saint also were deemed efficacious, leading to the increasing veneration of relics. Originally, these were parts of the bodies of the saints themselves, and later on even things which had been associated with them such as clothing; eventually, even a piece of cloth which had been placed in contact with the relics (*brandea*) was held to be imbued with the divine power. Patrons of churches such as bishops and lay notables sought to have a relic or relics in their church – for instance, under the altar. Thus pieces of the dead not only had become objects of worship in themselves (a concept and practice repugnant to believers in the traditional religions), but also had transgressed the boundary between the spaces of the dead and of the living (in strict archaeological terms, an interesting example of post-mortem manipulation of human remains with secondary reburial) and had become a focus of devotion within a cult building. Because of the common belief in the efficaciousness of burial *ad sanctos*, people sought to be buried near the relics, at first probably those who had the clout to ignore the ancient prescriptions against intramural burial, but later on the more general populace. Thus the placing of the dead among the living was negotiated and legitimised and became a regular practice, with intramural burial being one of the most characteristic of the changes in urban form between the town of classical antiquity and its Christian, medieval successor.

The question of whether there was at this date a specifically Christian burial rite is one that has been much discussed, particularly in the light of the development of what was later to be known as 'Christian burial', involving the east–west inhumation of the body without grave goods. The problem is that this has tended to impose a predetermined agenda on the subject and to abstract and isolate a particular presumed group of burials from the broader context of developments in funerary practice, rural as well as urban, in the late Roman West. As has already been noted in discussion of burial in northern Gaul in Chapter 2, there are broad trends visible in burial practice from the third to the fifth centuries, such as a preference for inhumation over cremation, an east–west orientation and a decline in the practice of depositing the types of grave goods familiar under the High Empire (including pottery and other vessels), and these were happening to a chronology independent of the widespread adoption of Christianity in the West (cf. Morris 1992; Tranoy 2000: 129, 140–4). Here, the evidence for burial at undoubtedly Christian sites such as churches will be briefly assessed against the question of whether there is a distinctively Christian rite of burial identifiable in the archaeology or in the texts. The archaeological evidence from the excavation of burials in and around churches shows that in fact there was at this date no requirement for east–west burial. For example, at Saint-Gervais, Geneva, the focal burial seems originally to have been placed north–south, as was the earliest burial elsewhere in the church, in the north-western angle of the nave, and anyway the other burials were aligned not with the compass but with the long axis of the church, which actually lies south-west to north-east (Bonnet and Privati 1991: 20–4). At some churches, burials outside the east end are oriented with respect to the curve of the apse, as at the recently excavated funerary basilica at Maguelone (Raynaud 2006: 143). There was, though, an overall preference for a generally east–west orientation, but this was also the case at cemeteries, both urban and rural, where there is no good reason to suppose they were predominantly Christian (cf. Raynaud 2006). Grave goods are a regular component of burials associated with churches at this date; clearly, there was no prohibition on placing offerings with the Christian dead or with sending them to the next world clad in the belts and brooches of this one. This again chimes with the evidence from the generality of burial at the period that the deposition of grave goods in the familiar form of vessels was decreasingly practised, but the presence of items of apparel possibly suggest displacement of observances to this area of funerary practice. And, as in many traditional burial rituals, it was the observances at the hour of death, after the soul had gone forth and in the funerary liturgies that really mattered; the deposition of the corpse was the end product of a sequence of rituals no longer visible to the archaeologist. The archaeological indications about grave furnishings (or not) are consistent with the evidence of the texts that in the fourth and fifth centuries the Church had yet to develop a theology of how burial was to be effected, and that what we think of as 'Christian burial' was a construct largely of the seventh century, when ideas of the simple and holy life and its outward manifestations were carried over into the grave (cf. Paxton 1990: Ch. 2, esp. 62–3). The deposition of grave goods was not seen as problematic; rather it was despoiling them from the tomb that exercised Christian commentators (cf. Effros 2002: 41–69). More important were the correct treatment of the corpse before, during and after burial, and the rituals and liturgies which enfolded the deceased (cf. Paxton 1990: Ch. 1), together with the beliefs they expressed. Nor does it appear that Christians at this period were much concerned to maintain exclusivity in their burial spaces; the idea of a 'Christian cemetery' is one that has been constructed by archaeologists in the face of the lack of textual evidence for any legal or customary ban (Johnson 1997). Christians and adherents of the traditional religions could be buried in the same cemetery; blood may have been thicker than the waters of baptism, and family relationships may have been more important in the structuring of cemeteries than religious affiliation, as also may have been the plots owned by particular *collegia* or burial guilds. Indeed, from this point of view, the Church itself could be seen as a form of *collegium*. Clearly, burial *ad sanctos* would mean much more to a Christian, so it may well be that such cemeteries were essentially Christian-only spaces, but there is no certainty on this point, and on what criteria would the burial of a non-Christian in such a cemetery be detected, given that the forms which burial took were so alike for Christians and non-Christians? To adapt the words of Paul-Albert Février (1987: 289), at this date there is a conceptual distinction to be made between 'the burial of a Christian' and 'Christian burial', rather than anachronistically conflating the two.

Commemorating the dead: sarcophagi, mausolea and tombstones

If Christianity was a religion that held that all were equal in the sight of God, this was not a view that necessarily commended itself to the elites of the late Roman world, to whom matters of status and degree and the ways in which these were displayed were of the utmost importance. Thus there were ways in which a burial might be embellished to demonstrate the importance of the occupant. The most widespread of these were sarcophagi and tombstones. The transition from cremation to inhumation as the dominant burial rite in the West, starting in the second and essentially complete by the end of the third century, meant that the coffin or sarcophagus could be a site for statements about the relative status of the deceased, with the wealthy and aristocratic appropriating them as vehicles for conspicuous display from the end of the second century (cf. papers in Elsner and Huskinson 2010). The more elaborate sarcophagi, above all those with sculptured decoration, make sense only if they were exposed to view in a mausoleum, funerary church or other accessible setting (Figure 4.8). Sarcophagi could be

Fig. 4.8 Toulouse, decorated sarcophagus

in a variety of stones, from locally available limestones and sandstones to the much more prestigious marble. It was more usually marble that was the medium for decorated sarcophagi, with at least one long face being sculpted, in the more elaborate examples in two registers. Sometimes, as at Arles, there was a flat lid with a deep front edge carrying another register of decoration. In these examples the sides and rear were left undecorated, showing that they were placed into a mausoleum in such a way as only to present the front face, quite probably in an *arcosolium* or niche. Other types were sculpted on all four sides and had a decorated lid, suggesting that they were free-standing within the funerary structure containing them. Initially, the sculpted scenes depicted scenes from traditional mythology or activities such as warfare or hunting, proper to their aristocratic milieu. In the later third and fourth century, this tradition was adapted to show scenes from the new, Christian mythology, though depictions of traditional mythology persisted, either because of the religious affiliations of their patrons or because the learning thus expressed within contemporary aristocratic culture (cf. p. 244) was greater than their strictly religious connotations. Unfortunately, because most of the surviving elaborate sarcophagi of this period had an afterlife as containers for significant medieval cadavers (principally saints and bishops), very few survive *in situ*; known examples of mausolea have usually been despoiled of their sarcophagi, and churches have often had their more spectacular sarcophagi reused. Instead, there are groups of decorated sarcophagi from important cities such as Arles or Tarragona, which have tended to be studied from art-historical or iconographic perspectives. Many excavated fourth- and fifth-century cemeteries at towns such as Lyon, Mérida or Trier have yielded mausolea, generally simple, rectangular, semi-subterranean chambers into which coffins and sarcophagi were inserted, quite probably family mausolea. Some of these were later to become the focus of funerary churches (e.g. Saint-Just, Lyon; Santa Eulalia, Mérida; Saint Severin, Trier).

Tombstones were more mundane, and their epitaphs told of a wider social spread of the Christian faithful, and their beliefs and practices (for an excellent, recent study, see Handley 2003). They usually opened with the name, and often the rank or status of the deceased (lay or clerical), stating in a variety of ways that they were now at peace (Handley 2003: Ch. 2). There was then often an indication of the age at death (cf. Handley 2003: Ch. 4), characteristically given as *plus minus* 'more or less' since it was of lesser import than what follows next, the date on which they passed from this world to the next – their heavenly birthday. Often the tombstone bore explicitly Christian decorative motifs such as the chi-rho, alpha and omega, or doves either side of a vase or *cantharus* (in reference to the *refrigerium*, the state which the soul had entered and also a commemorative meal of the same name), so even the unlettered would understand these to be the burials of Christians. Handley (2003: Ch. 1) provides quantified data for the study of the incidence of these inscriptions in Iberia, Gaul and the Rhineland between 300 and 750 (a rather different date range from the one in this work, but used here nonetheless), mustering a grand total of 4,198 examples, to which one might add one from Britain (the lack of such inscriptions from late Roman Britain when this 'epigraphic habit' was firmly established elsewhere in the West during the fourth century is telling). The geographical distribution is given in the map (Figure 4.9), showing a general bias towards the provinces nearer the Mediterranean, but with a significant grouping in Belgica I and the Rhineland. The incidence of these monuments was overwhelmingly urban, accounting for some 55% of inscriptions from Iberia and just under 70% for Gaul (Handley 2003: 4–6). Arles, Lyon, Mérida Tarragona, Trier and Vienne all have more than one hundred such inscriptions, one of the attributes that marks them out as particularly important urban centres in this period. The chronological pattern can also be established (Handley 2003: 11–14), Gaul and Iberia developing in parallel (Figure 4.10), with few tombstones before AD 300, and increasing steadily through the fourth and fifth centuries.

In the West, the erection of tombstones, common in the first and second centuries, had, as noted in Chapter 1, declined sharply through the third century to near extinction by the fourth, so this revival in the practice

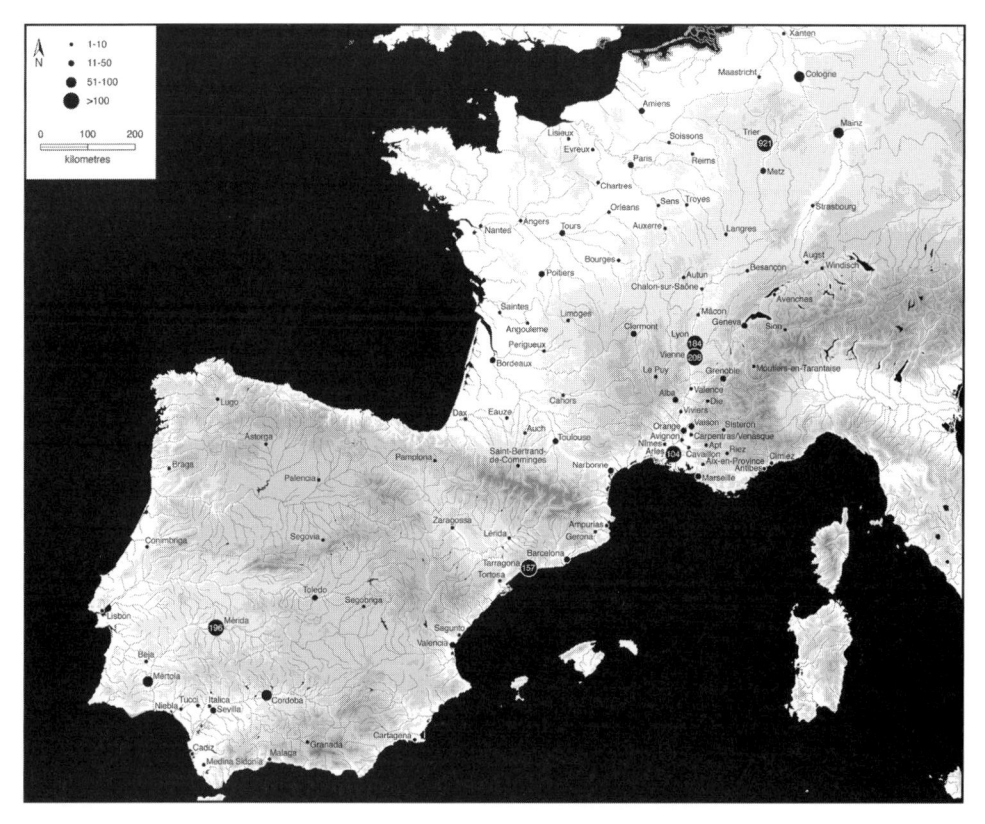

Fig. 4.9 Distribution of Christian tombstones in the West, AD 300–750

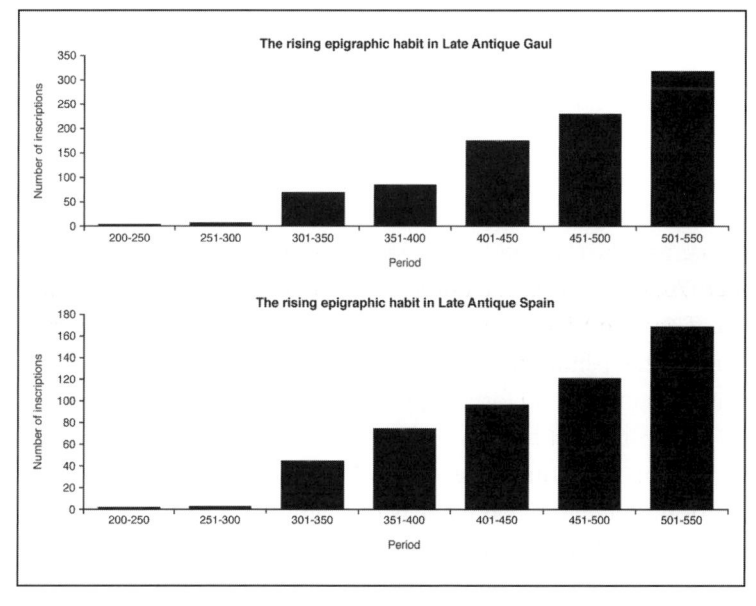

Fig. 4.10 Bar charts of the rising Christian 'epigraphic habit' in Gaul and Spain

(though never to earlier levels) needs some thought. Clearly, the curve in part reflects the legitimisation of Christianity from early in the fourth century and its growing numerical and social influence thereafter, with both ecclesiastical and lay status being recorded to aid the memory of the living by keeping the departed in mind. But the growing power and respectability of the Church was something that had to be negotiated internally by the Christian community, so new forms of commemoration and new ways of drawing attention to the particularly influential in life or the particularly holy in life or in death had to be established, and the tombstone would do this. Moreover, the increasingly powerful Church was a latecomer and not always a particularly well-liked one, so it would need to make its mark also among the followers of the traditional religions. The fact that there was no parallel renaissance in the practice of epigraphic commemoration among the followers of the traditional religions may suggest that the need to commemorate and the insecurities this may betray lay more within the Christian community.

Christianity across the West

Here we shall turn from somewhat abstract discussions of general features of the impact of Christian beliefs and practices on the cities of the late Roman West to more specific considerations of how these were manifested, first south of the Pyrenees in Iberia, and then to the north of the Pyrenees in Gaul and the Rhineland. The churches and other buildings of Christianity have been the subject of considerable research in all areas of Iberia, southern Gaul and Britain. Both the nature of the evidence and modern traditions of study on either side of the Pyrenees have led to significantly differing perspectives on the development of Christianity in Gaul and in Iberia. In twentieth-century Spain, Catholic Christianity became central to the concept of Spanishness (*hispanidad*), particularly under the Franco regime (Bowes 2005: 3–9), with parallel developments in Portugal under Salazar. This meant that the questions of the origin and early development of Christianity in the peninsula were so bound up with questions of national identity and destiny that the former questions came to be studied in a rather different way from elsewhere in Europe. Particularly important was the appropriation of Theodosius I (emperor 379–95), of Spanish origin, as a precursor of the fervent if gloomy piety of Counter-Reformation and later Spain, though, as has been recently shown (McLynn 2005), there were many more important influences on Theodosius than his province of origin, which he possibly left as a child to accompany his father, the general.

Spanish scholarship since the death of Franco has reacted against the traditional view by asserting the similarity of early Christianity and its monuments in the peninsula to those elsewhere in the late Roman world, and the publication of major surveys (Godoy Fernández 1995; Martínez Tejera 2006; Schlunck and Hauschild 1978) has made the topic much more accessible to study. In France, the study of Christian origins also had strong links through the nineteenth and twentieth centuries with the Catholic Church and Catholicism as a determinant of French culture (Barral i Altet 1991; Février 1991), but the French Revolution and its anticlerical tradition meant that there were other ways of looking at Gallic Christianity. Moreover, the study of early Christian sites and monuments in France itself was associated both with the development of the study of the early Middle Ages – the archaeology of the Merovingian period (Barral i Altet 1991: 361–4) – and with the development of the archaeology of Christianity in France's North African colonies (Frend 1996: Chs. 5 and 6), meaning that it could never be as introspective as was the case in Spain. As for Spain, there are now recent, comprehensive corpora for Gaul, in this case on the impact of Christianity both on urban topography and on the physical remains of churches and other Christian material (Duval, N. 1995, 1996). The intellectual history in Britain was very different, with Protestantism being the dominant religious tradition, but Protestantism was itself fissiparous, and with Catholic emancipation in the first half of the nineteenth century, what developed was dispute between the different Christian traditions as they sought to validate their own claims to primacy through appeal to the vestiges of Roman Christianity (Petts 2003: Ch. 1). But since the archaeology of Romano-British Christianity was and remains very sparse, this dispute was rather of the nature of bald men fighting over a comb.

Spain

As yet there are few intramural episcopal complexes from the Iberian peninsula to set alongside examples such as Geneva. The best-studied example is that at Barcelona (Bonnet and Beltrán de Heredia 2000), where, within the northern angle of the walls (Figure 4.11), lay a large *domus*, altered to receive a baptistery, whose earliest form has been lost to subsequent rebuildings. In the fifth century the baptistery was rebuilt with an octagonal basin, with *ciborium*, within a square building. A three-aisled structure on a different orientation abutted its northern side, originally interpreted as a basilican church, but more recently argued to be the bishop's reception hall (*aula*), with the church as yet unexcavated under the existing medieval cathedral church. To the

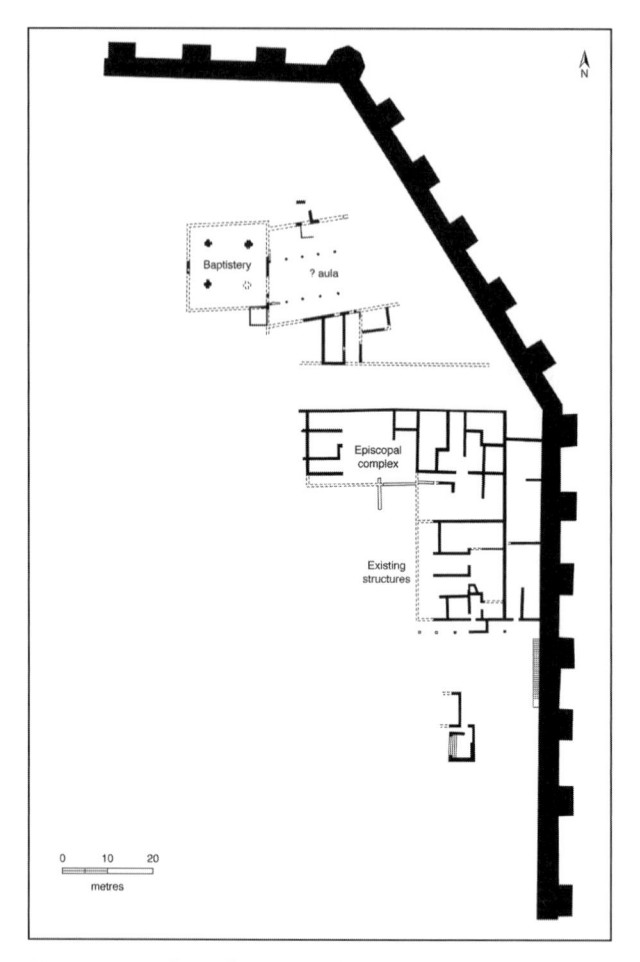

Fig. 4.11 Barcelona, the episcopal complex

north-east, parts of an existing *domus* were remodelled, presumably as part of the episcopal residence, down into the fifth and sixth centuries, including a subsidiary church or chapel with reliquary, and with eventually a small cemetery being inserted into a former open space. The other major, recent excavation in the area of an episcopal complex has been that at Valencia (Ribera and Rosselló 2000) on the Almoina site to the east and north-east of the medieval cathedral and overlying the forum and possibly *macellum* of the Roman city. These latter were demolished in the fifth century and succeeded by an intramural cemetery and a well, along with two later chapels, one a cruciform funerary chapel added to the presumed eastern end of the episcopal church. These sites apart, no episcopal group has been excavated, though at

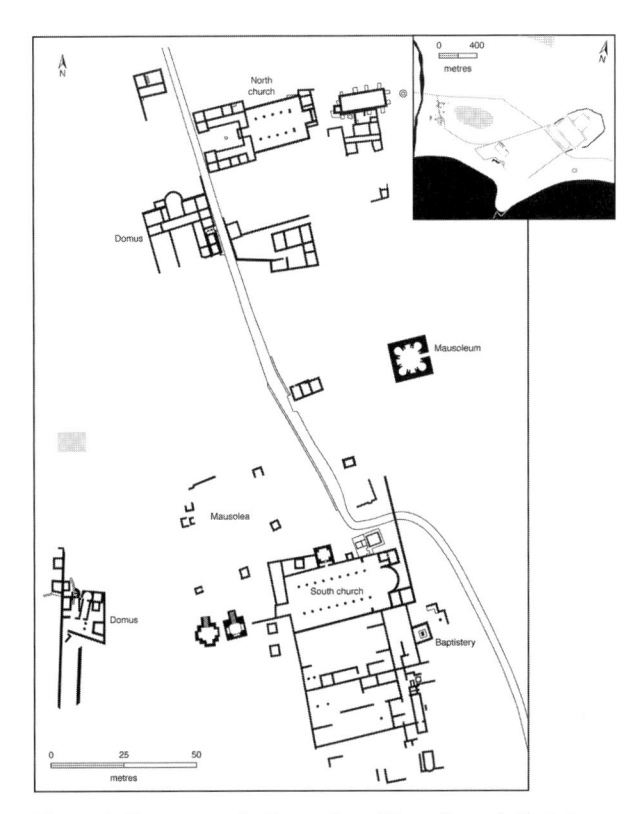

Fig. 4.12 Tarragona, the Francolí and Parc Central Christian complexes

sites such as Tarragona the location of the episcopal church is known (see Chapter 9, p. 403).

Instead, the archaeology of early Christianity at Iberian cities is dominated by the remains of *martyria* and other cemetery churches (cf. Bowes 2005: 194–5). The best known of these is the complex of churches around Tarragona, consisting of the basilica of Francolí west of the city (Figure 4.12), dedicated to the martyred, third-century bishop Fructuosus and his deacons Augurius and Eulogius, whose place of martyrdom in the amphitheatre was itself, as noted above, to be commemorated by a *martyrium* (TED'A 1990). The Francolí basilica was a large, mid-fifth-century, three-aisled church with a mausoleum on its northern side and a later baptistery as part of a range of buildings attached to the southern side; this was clearly a church designed for large congregations and for public ceremonials including, latterly, baptism. To the north-east lay the more recently discovered church of Parc Central, an aisled basilica with atrium, associated with a residence and agricultural dependencies (Alemany 2006).

Its proposed interpretation as an urban monastery is far from certain. The basilica of Santa Eulalia at Mérida is as well known as the Tarragona complexes (cf. Kulikowski 2004: 236–8). It originated as a small, east–west, rectangular mausoleum with eastern apse. The area became a focus for burial, and another mausoleum was built to the west, with a southern apse and crypt. These were destroyed in the latter part of the first half of the fifth century (supposedly in the Suevic siege of 429, though there is no independent, corroborative evidence), but the cemetery remained a focus, and at the end of the fifth century a large, new basilican church was built, its eastern apse enclosing the original mausoleum. The corpus of urban churches in Iberia dating to before the end of the fifth century is as yet very small. Textual references to bishops and churches at various towns in the fourth century make it likely that there are more to be discovered, but the disjunction between the earliest textual dates and the archaeological evidence for intramural episcopal complexes has led a number of Spanish workers to suggest that the earliest episcopal churches in the Iberian peninsula may have been cemetery churches, with the move inside the walls happening later. This emphasis on the role of the martyrs in the formation of early Iberian Christianity accorded well with the place in more recent Spanish Catholicism of the witness of the martyrs. It is, though, a view which has attracted criticism from the French tradition of study (e.g. Guyon 2005, delivered originally to an Iberian audience), which prefers to see the episcopal complex as an essentially intramural phenomenon, albeit in many cases in Gaul not before the fifth century, as we increasingly understand to have been the case in Italy also (cf. Cantina Wataghin 2003). A complementary argument is that the fourth-century episcopal site may still have been in a house church, as possibly at Barcelona or Geneva, and thus much less visible to the archaeologist.

Gaul

In his recent overview of urban churches in the southern half of Gaul, Guyon (2006) has shown that north of the Pyrenees also the process of implantation of churches was geographically patchy and generally took place no earlier than the very end of the fourth century, and more usually in the fifth. The well-known episcopal complexes of this part of Gaul, such as Aix-en-Provence, Fréjus, Marseille or Riez, with their elaborate baptisteries all date to the fifth century, often quite late (see Duval, N. 1995), and there is the textual evidence for the dedication of the cathedral of Narbonne in 445. Somewhat different is the basilica in the area with a regular street grid in Saint-Bertrand-de-Comminges in the south-west (Guyon 2003), a church built in a still-occupied area of the town, but not the episcopal church. Just outside the *Septem Provinciae* but clearly to be considered alongside these churches is Lyon, where Sidonius Apollinaris's description (*Epistulae* II.10) of the dedication of the new episcopal church by Bishop Patiens (and graced by a verse inscription composed by Sidonius) dates to the mid fifth century. Parts of this church have been excavated along with the late fourth-century baptistery to its north (Reynaud 1998: Part II, Ch. 1). At Lyon also, there have been important excavations on the extramural church commemorating Saint-Just implanted in an existing cemetery and incorporating an apsidal mausoleum. The first church is difficult to date, but probably does not predate the late fourth century (Reynaud 1998: Part I, Ch. 2), with the nearby church of Saint-Irénée probably later still (Raynaud 1998: Part I, Ch. 4). Even at so important a town as Arles, it is difficult to find much evidence for a church before the later fourth century – probably it may be found in the south-eastern corner of the defended area (Heijmans 2004: 281–9). The examples cited above are the best known archaeologically and can stand for the longer list of less-well-evidenced churches.

The archaeological evidence for fourth- and fifth-century urban churches, as opposed again to sixth-century churches, in the northern half of Gaul and in Germany is much less coherent. Textual sources, conveniently gathered in the various volumes of the *Topographie chrétienne des cités de la Gaule*, make it clear that bishops were progressively installed in the cities of central Gaul during the fourth century and on into the north in the later fourth and fifth centuries. But archaeological traces of their episcopal complexes are almost entirely lacking, The one important exception is Rouen (Lequoy and Guillot 2004: 257–60), where, at the turn of the fourth and fifth centuries, a 15-m-wide basilica with a nave at least 35 m long (the eastern parts of the church are inaccessible under medieval structures) was built over an existing house, whose bathhouse, most curiously, was preserved standing against the west façade of the new church (Figure 4.13). Excavations further south hinted that there may have been another church, giving a double church. The date of the construction would fit with its having been the responsibility of the late fourth- to early fifth-century bishop Victricius, disciple of Martin of Tours and militant evangeliser of northern Gaul. Another probable fourth-century complex is to be found at Reims, where there is the site of a church with a baptistery and traces of other structures, presumably the episcopal complex (Neiss and Berry 1998). Indeed, the installation of episcopal complexes in northern Gaul and the Rhineland

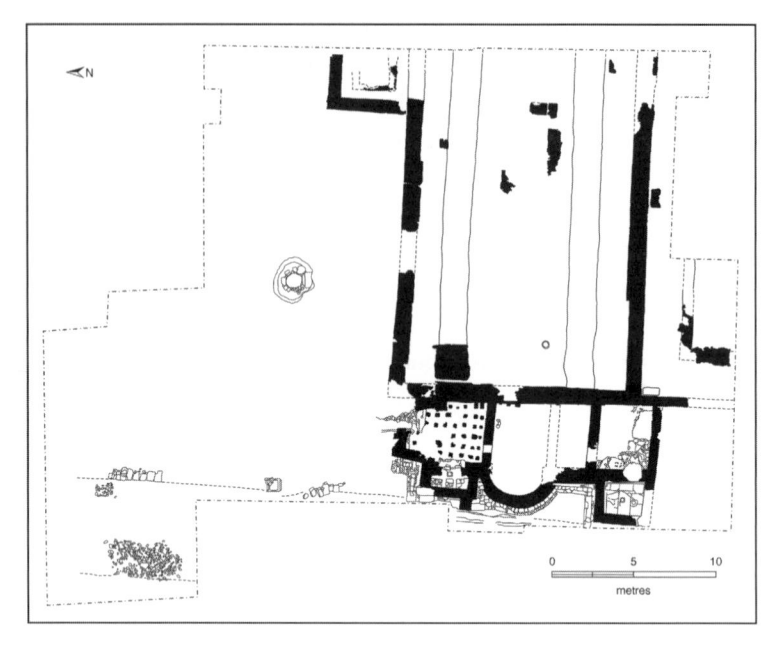

Fig. 4.13 Rouen, western part of the Christian basilica

may well have been a relatively slow process, one made more obscure by the chances of survival and excavation.

The Rhineland

Cologne provides a good example of this (Krings and Will 2009). Textual sources indicate a bishop from at least 314, sufficiently powerful to call a synod in 346. Yet, the excavations under the cathedral (*Dom*) show a relatively modest basilican church that cannot with certainty be dated to the fourth century and which seems only to have acquired a baptistery to its east at the end of the fifth century (Ristow 2009). Yet, in the later fourth century, an extraordinarily ambitious cemetery church was erected in the northern cemetery of the city, the present-day St Gereon (Verstegen 2006). This was in the form of a decagon (Figure 4.14), elongated along its east–west axis with a narthex and atrium to the west and the eastern bay projecting in an apse. The other eight bays consisted of a series of semi-circular niches opening onto the main vessel of the church. These niches would have been covered by semidomes, with some form of dome covering the central space. This mastery of form and construction, as well as rich decoration in marble from across the Mediterranean as well as polychrome

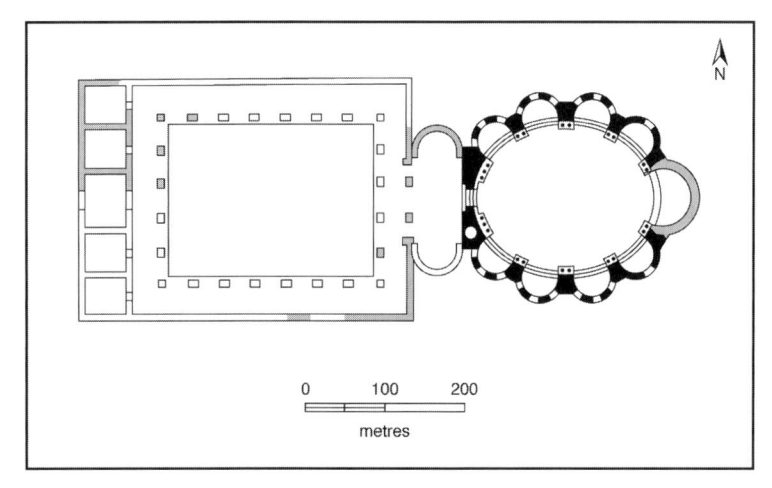

Fig. 4.14 Cologne, the Saint Gereon complex

and gold-glass mosaic, places St Gereon among the most sophisticated buildings in the fourth-century West. Clearly a cemetery church, its original dedication is not known, but its architectural and decorative ambition are striking and argue for a patron of the highest social standing and of great wealth. Cologne also had further cemetery churches such as St Severin to the south (Päffgen 1992). Other well-known cemetery churches in the Rhineland include the fourth-century *memoria* of Sts Cassius and Florentius to the south of the fortress at Bonn (Horn 1987: 370–2) or the *memoria* and associated structures and burials under the medieval Dom at Xanten, south of the reduced fortified area that constituted fourth-century *Tricensima* (cf. p. 63) (Bridger 2008). It is also important to note for the Rhineland the presence of churches in some military bases, such as those at Boppard, probably of the fifth century (cf. Cüppers 1990: 345–6). Further up the Rhine, there was a church in the fortification at Kaiseraugst dating to the fourth century (cf. Drack and Fellmann 1988: 412–14).

The Church and the city

Both north and south of the Pyrenees, it is clear that the development of Christian buildings and thus any Christian topography took place relatively late in our period, not really getting under way before the opening of the fifth century at many towns in Gaul and Spain, approximately the same time as some were being provided with walls, thus marking the transition to the typical status monuments of late antiquity and expressing human and episcopal church was constructed over part of the former forum, but only after the latter had been abandoned and partly dismantled for a considerable time. In southern Gaul at Aix-en-Provence, the episcopal complex overlay and may have reused structural elements of the forum, but again whether this was convenience or ideology is difficult to determine. Not far away at Marseille, the fifth-century episcopal complex was constructed over an urban residence. Nor is there any consistency in the extent and nature of the reuse of architectural elements from earlier structures; indeed, a number of major churches seem to have been constructed from newly quarried stone. So a simple, causative link between the demise of public buildings and monuments of the High Empire and the building of churches is, on present evidence, impossible to sustain. There is also the problem that any Christian urban topography has tended (as with so much to do with the archaeology of Christianity at this period) to be seen very much in isolation. In fact, of course, it had to develop within an already existing religious topography of the city concerned, the topography of the existing cults, and buildings and burial grounds of the traditional religions. The existence of these and their influence on the positioning of the newcomer deserves much more attention than has been given to date.

Nevertheless, and to reprise a theme of the discussion in the preceding chapter, how did the profound changes in the nature of major public monuments related to the advent of Christianity impact on the nature of the citizens produced in these physical milieus? The disuse and destruction of the public spaces constituted by temples and their precincts, fora, civil basilicas and other publicly accessible spaces, along with the statuary, the epigraphy and the activities performed in these buildings and spaces, marked the end of one type of citizen. The development of churches as the major buildings for the gathering of the community under the leadership of the bishop and in the context of the Christian liturgy and belief systems must necessarily have given rise to a very different type of citizen and of civic political and communal life. The linking together of the new intra- and extramural churches in the stational liturgies and in the processions articulated by them (Esmonde Cleary 2005; Loseby 1996) will not only have created the new conceptual geography of the Christianised town and its links to the community of all believers living and dead, but will also have involved the 'forgetting' of those elements of the former urban form no longer deemed useful for or consonant with good Christian practice or with developing the thought world of the good Christian citizen.

Christianity in the countryside

Discussion so far has concentrated on the substantial evidence for the introduction of Christian cult into the cities of the West; this reflects the chronological primacy of these developments as well as the institutional importance of bishops and urban churches in the developing Church in the West. But Christians lived in the countryside as well as in the cities, and gradually they, too, began to create and construct places of worship and burial to cater to their religious needs and aspirations. The period covered here sees a broad pattern, the appearance of places of Christian worship and burial associated with private properties in the countryside, generally villas; these therefore were largely an expression of private patronage by Christian landowners. This is the context for rural Christianity that will be our main concern here. Towards the end of our period, in the later fifth century, we start to see the creation of churches serving other types of rural communities – a process that later was to develop into the more formal parish system of the Middle Ages but which lies outside the date range of this work.

The evidence for Christianity at villas in the fourth and fifth centuries is much stronger for Spain than for Gaul and Germany, thus reversing the situation with regard to the cities (cf. Bowes 2005). The evidence from Britain conforms more to the Spanish than to the Gallic pattern. In Spain the evidence is biased towards mausolea and funerary churches, since these are more readily recognised structurally or by their accompanying cemeteries. Identification of chapels or oratories in the main residential building is very much dependent on the survival of liturgical fittings or of decorative schemes; for the latter, the British villa of Lullingstone (Kent) is the *locus classicus* (Meates 1979) not only of such a scheme but also of how the chance survival of the wall plaster fallen from an upper room demonstrated that there had been a Christian oratory, which would otherwise simply have escaped detection. For Spain, there is the example of the site of the Villa Fortunatus (Huesca). The villa (its name comes from a mosaic bearing the name *Fortunatus* with a chi-rho in the centre) was a large courtyard residence. At some time, perhaps in the first half of the fifth century, some of the rooms at the south-western angle of the courtyard were modified (Figure 4.15) to create a T-shaped liturgical space with aisles to the nave and a narthex at its southern end. There were subsequent internal modifications, including the creation of a crypt, before a major rebuild in, probably, the sixth century, by which time the villa building itself had been abandoned, the church thus mediating between antiquity and the Middle Ages (Godoy 1995: 227–37). So far this is the only clear example of the creation of a

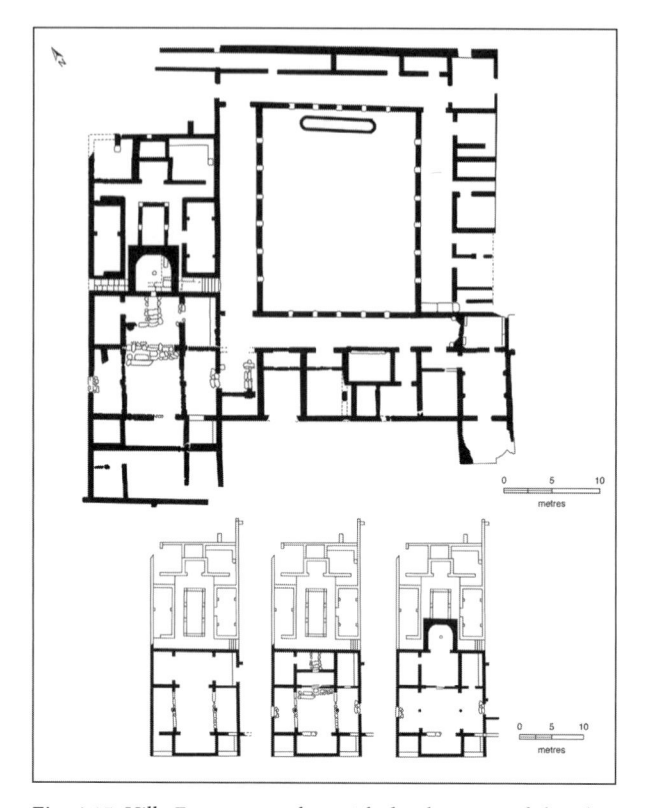

Fig. 4.15 Villa Fortunatus, plan, with development of church

church within the existing structures of a villa. In Portugal at the villa of Torre de Palma (Alto Alentejo), a Christian basilica (Figure 4.16) was constructed over part of the villa in the second half of the fourth century (Maloney and Hale 1996), lying east–west with nave and side aisles and an apse at each extremity. This is a large and elaborate plan for a rural church at this date, more reminiscent of an urban basilica, and its presence here is a puzzle.

More common in Spain than churches within villas is the evidence for mausolea and burial churches. Perhaps the most famous supposed example of this is the villa of Centcelles (Tarragona) a few miles east of the city of Tarragona (see Arce 2002a for full documentation). A circular, domed chamber formed part of a wing of a lavish villa (Figure 4.17), apparently acting as a sort of vestibule, and leading off it another chamber of an elaborate polylobate plan. It is preserved to full height, and the interior surface of the cupola bears the remains of an elaborate mosaic of figures against a background of gold-glass tesserae. The decoration consists of two

Christianity 183

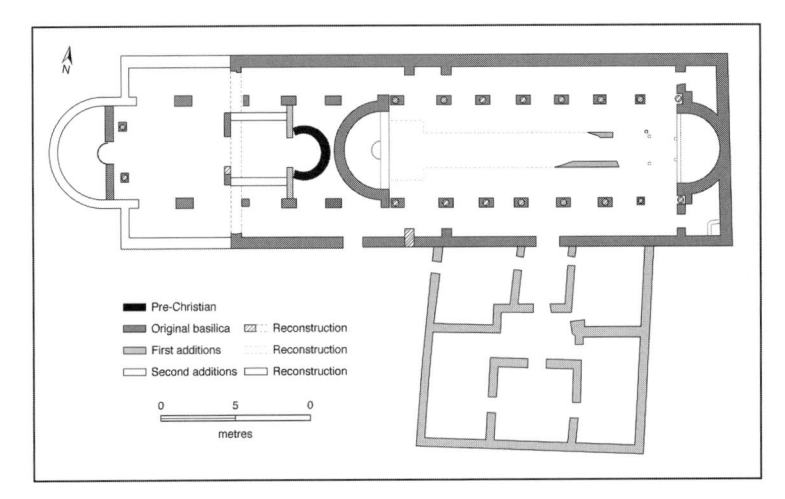

Fig. 4.16 Torre de Palma, Christian basilica

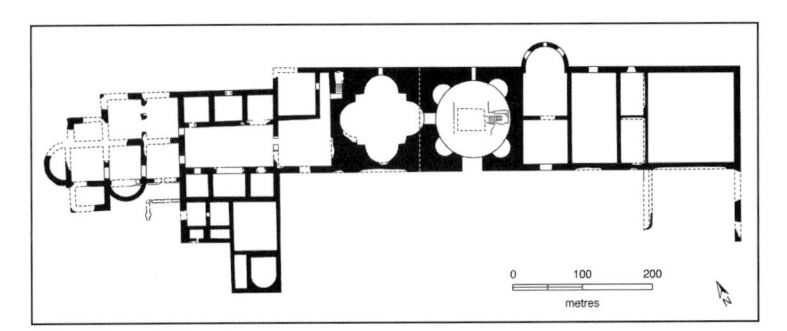

Fig. 4.17 Centcelles, plan

main registers of panels separated by columns with human figures and other subjects in the panels, which may well be biblical scenes such as Noah's ark. The two main registers are separated by a strip of geometric decoration, and below the outer register is a continuous band with hunting scenes. Excavated into the floor of the chamber is a crypt, probably for burial. This was long considered a high-status mausoleum, and even suggested as the burial place of the emperor Constans after his assassination at Elne just north of the eastern end of the Pyrenees, but more recent research (Arce 2002) has thrown serious doubt on this traditional interpretation. The crypt has been shown to be a later addition, and it has been pointed out that other late Roman aristocratic mausolea in Spain stand apart from the residential building. It seems more likely that the structure was originally an elaborate

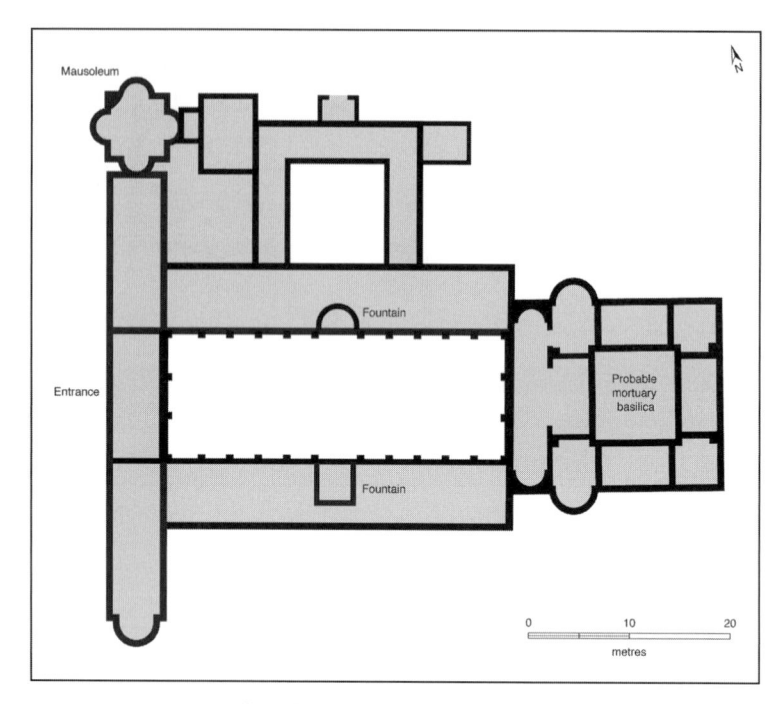

Fig. 4.18 Carranque, plan of mortuary complex

vestibule in a rich villa, and its funerary vocation was a later change of use. Even so, the ownership of the villa, its purpose and the iconographic scheme of the cupola remain a focus for debate (Arce 2002, 2006; Sotomayor 2006). If Centcelles can no longer be accepted as a mausoleum, then the palm for the most elaborate Spanish villa mausoleum may pass to the villa of Carranque (Fernández-Galliano Ruiz 2001). The villa is considered as a whole in the next chapter (p. 216), but here attention is directed to the mausoleum complex (cf. Bowes 2005: 218–27). It consists of a rectangular colonnaded courtyard entered by a monumental entrance (Figure 4.18). Off the main court opens another leading to a tetraconch chamber which also forms one end of the principal façade of the complex. At the far end of the main court was a cross-in-square building with an elaborate narthex. The main volumes of the building were covered with vaults and domes turned in brick. As well as being of considerable architectonic ambition, this building has yielded hundreds of fragments of coloured marbles from all across the Mediterranean basin as far as Asia Minor and Egypt, including purple porphyry (García-Entero and Vidal 2008), attesting to great wealth and long-distance connections on the part of the proprietor. Unfortunately, there is no certain indicator of the use of the complex. It has been proposed as a mausoleum, based on the cross-in-square plan of the imperial mausoleum of the Holy Apostles at Constantinople and a possible link through the postulated ownership of Carranque by the late fourth-century praetorian prefect of the East, Maternus Cynegius (Bowes 2005: 225–6), but on the present evidence this theory, attractive though it may be, cannot be sustained. Other than these two elaborate, tantalising, but ultimately unproven examples, there are some half-dozen other villa sites with late Roman mausolea associated. There is no consistent plan, the forms ranging from rectangular, apsed buildings at La Alberca (Salamanca) (Schlunk and Hauschild 1978: 112–14) or Marialba (León) (Godoy 1995: 334–7) to the centrally planned octagon of (Las Vegas de) Pueblanueva, originally holding marble sarcophagi (Schlunk and Hauschild 1978: 129–31). The most elaborate plan was that of the mausoleum at La Cocosa (Badajoz), rectangular on the exterior but with the interior consisting of a series of apsidal spaces, the easternmost containing a marble sarcophagus. Glass tesserae recovered show that the decoration must have been elaborate (Schlunk and Hauschild 1978: 11–12). One may also point to the probable conversion of the *nymphaea* at the villas of São Cucufate (discussed in more detail in the next chapter, p. 221) and Milreu in modern Portugal into mausolea, though whether Christian from the outset is now not provable. Though the dating of some of these monuments can be imprecise, they seem most probably to date to the late Roman period, probably from the later fourth century into the fifth.

North of the Pyrenees, rural churches are not common for the fourth and fifth centuries. The best examples lie in south-eastern Gaul, where they become more common from the sixth century (cf. Codou 2000, 2005a, 2005b). Most elaborate is the site of Saint-Maximin(-la-Sainte-Baume) (Var), where a probably late Roman mausoleum has long been known under the medieval basilica (Février in Duval, N. 1995: 175–80). More recent excavations have revealed that it lay next to a church probably of the fifth century, to which was added in the sixth a baptistery, suggesting an important late Roman centre, perhaps an estate church and family mausoleum. West of the Rhône is the exceptional site of Loupian (Hérault), where, some 800 m from a major late Roman villa (cf. p. 249), lay a 35-m-long basilica with along its northern flank a series of chambers, of which the central one was a baptistery with a hexagonal basin (Figure 4.19). The complex dates from the late fourth or more probably early fifth century (Pellecuer in Duval, N. 1995: 47–50). The presence of a baptistery at a rural site at this date is most unusual, given that it is generally an urban

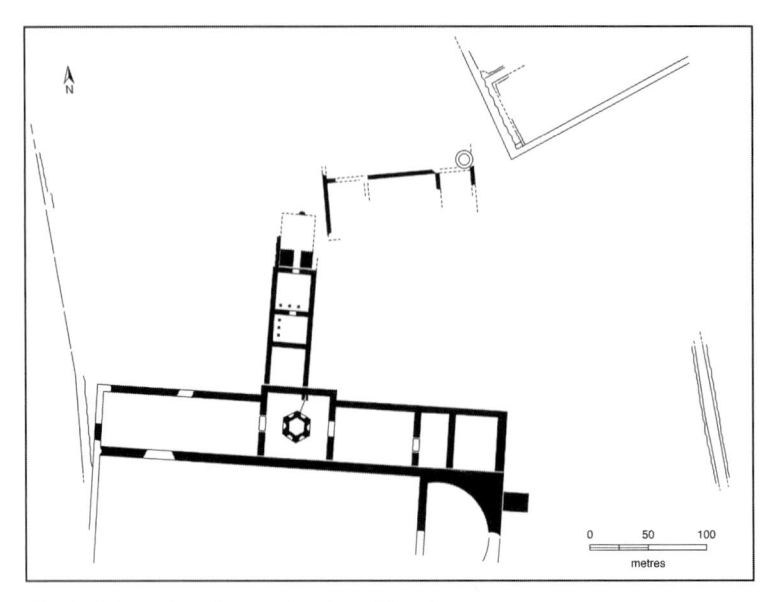

Fig. 4.19 Loupian, plan of church and baptistery

monument forming part of the episcopal complex. This and the size of the church may suggest that the person responsible for its construction was very well connected indeed; quite possibly, it was the proprietor of the nearby villa. If so, it would seem to be the same sort of church as at Saint-Maximin, and perhaps also La Torre de Palma in Iberia. Before leaving Provence, mention must be made of the remarkable '*pierre écrite*' in the *commune* of Saint-Giniez (Alpes de Haute Provence) to the north-east of Sisteron. Here at the entrance to the long defile of the Saint-Giniez valley is an inscription on the rock face set up by Claudius Postumus Dardanus, praetorian prefect of the Gauls in the early fifth century, and his wife Nevia Galla, recording how the road was improved by cutting back the mountain and that the property was defended with walls and gates. The name of the property is given as Theopolis, the city of God. It may thus be one of that class of villas used by a group of like-minded aristocratic souls as a place to live a communal life of prayer and contemplation at a remove from the world. Perhaps the best known of this class of aristocratic religious community in Gaul is the estate of *Primuliacum*, where the historian and hagiographer Sulpicius Severus says he established such a group. The site of the villa has not been located, though it would seem to be somewhere in the south-west, in Novempopulana. In the south-west (Colin 2008: esp. Ch. 7) also are some archaeological instances of the Christianisation of villas, particularly the fifth-century oratory with baptistery installed in the villa at (Montréal-) Séviac (Gers) (cf. p. 218) and the baptismal basin excavated under the church of Martres-Tolosane near the enormous villa of Chiragan (Haute-Garonne) (Boudartchouk 2005: 138–41). Slightly different is the case of another enormous villa, that of Valentine (Haute-Garonne), where there was a fourth-century mausoleum with marble sarcophagi, which developed into a cemetery church (Colin 2008: 55–80), and from which came the long and elaborate verse epitaph of Nymfius, dating to the turn of the fourth and fifth centuries. This is one of the few demonstrable instances of villa mausolea in late antique south-western Gaul, as opposed to Spain. Nevertheless, the presence of so many carved and figured sarcophagi from southern Gaul (not just the south-west) in the fourth and fifth centuries must argue for mausolea, since the decorating of them only makes sense if they were to be placed where they would be displayed and visible. (The lack of carved sarcophagi in Britain is an area where the island differs from aristocratic practice in southern Gaul and Spain.) Between Valentine and Séviac was the site at La Gravette, L'Isle-Jourdain (Cazes in Duval, N. 1996: 155–9), an *agglomération secondaire*, where, from the fourth century, there was a simple rectangular church with rectangular apse associated with a walled burial ground. In the fifth century this was remodelled and another church containing a baptismal basin constructed to its south-east. The significance of this site is that here we see a church associated not with the great villa of a rich, landed aristocrat but serving a much more modest population on a major road. Unfortunately, we do not know at whose instigation this church was constructed. Once away from the south-east and south-west of Gaul, rural churches that can be confidently ascribed on the basis of their archaeology to the fourth or fifth century are much rarer, though sporadic textual references show that they did exist, as in Sidonius Apollinaris's mention in a letter (*Epistulae* V.15) of dedicating a baptistery for a certain Elafius at a *castellum*, possibly Chastel-sur-Murat (Cantal) (Boudartchouk 2006). As we shall see in Chapter 9, the growth in occupation at hilltop fortified sites was a feature of the later fifth century, so the appearance here of a new class of rural churches is to be expected. The long-term work in the canton of Geneva with which this chapter began also furnishes some archaeological evidence for the Christianisation of the countryside around Geneva itself (Terrier 2005), with the example of the villa at Vandoeuvres (Figure 4.20), to which was added at the very end of the fourth century a small, rectangular chapel, used from the start for burial, adjoining a small room that since the first century had probably had a religious purpose. To the north were other structures of uncertain use.

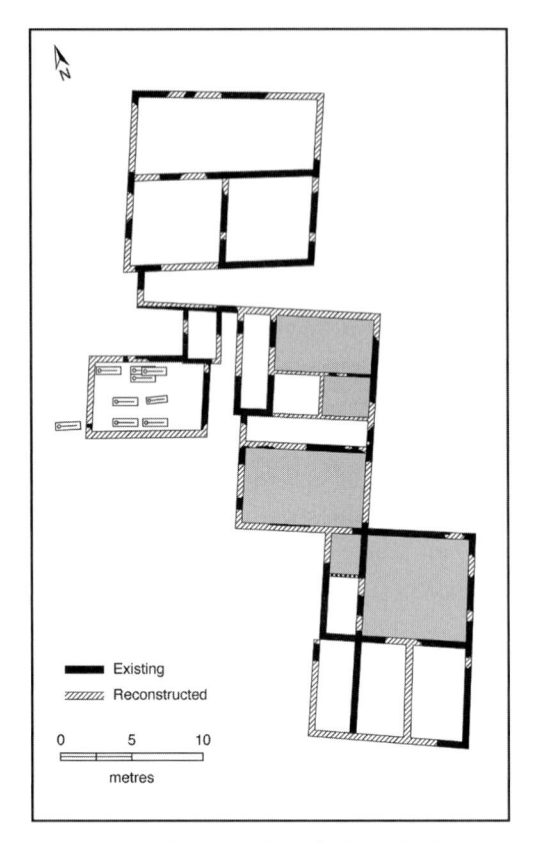

Fig. 4.20 Vandoeuvres, plan of villa with Christian area

Other church structures in the area seem to date from the sixth century and later. This matches the evidence from a series of other regions of Gaul and beyond that a denser system of rural churches, often not associated with villas, was a development of the sixth century onwards (Delaplace 2005).

There is one last topic on the spread of Christianity in the West in the fourth and fifth centuries that needs to be addressed and that has been adumbrated above: monasticism. From the fourth century on, groups of Christians gathered in order to live a communal life of religious observation, prayer and study. Sometimes these were essentially aristocratic enterprises as with Sulpicius Severus and his community at *Primuliacum*. Sometimes they were established under the aegis of a bishop wishing to have a spiritual retreat from the more secular concerns of his office. The classic site for this is Marmoutier, a little upstream from Tours and on the other side of the Loire, where Martin of Tours' biographer, Sulpicius Severus, tells us that the bishop founded a retreat with twenty-four followers. Research on the caves under the remains of the great abbey church destroyed during the French Revolution has revealed nothing datable to the late Roman period (Lelong in Duval, N. 1996: 103–5). Nor is there anything certainly of this period at the other proposed Martinian foundation at Ligugé south of Poitiers, where the remains of the church overlying a large late Roman villa cannot with certainty be pushed back before the sixth century (Février and Duval in Duval, N. 1996: 278–83). But the site that dominates all discussion of early monasticism in Gaul is that of Lérins, one of the Hyères isles off the south coast of Provence east of Toulon. Founded in the third decade of the fifth century by the aristocrat Honoratus, who was fleeing the troubles in northern Gaul, it soon became an aristocratic community of ascetics with a wide network of contacts across southern Gaul and further afield. Lérins monks soon became highly desirable as bishops and other leaders of the Church and, unlike some of the other aristocratic communities, Lérins enjoyed a continued existence under the leadership of a succession of strong heads. Lérins became to its members an 'imagined community', or, in the words of a recent review of the evidence, *un lobby* (Heijmans and Pietri 2009) of great importance. Since they were responsible for generating a significant amount of the Christian writings of fifth-century Gaul, the island community was seen at the time and has been seen ever since as the most important cradle of monasticism in the West outside Italy. Be that as it may, or may not, there is little from the recent structural survey and excavations on the island that elucidates the physical form of the community in the first century of its existence (Codou 2009), least of all the monastic cells that the *Vita* of Honoratus tells us were the accommodation on the island (Hilarius of Arles, *Vita Sancti Honorati* 17.1), so it cannot be used to give us a template for what a monastic or eremitical community should look like. Lérins has taken us into the Christian future of Gaul at the end of the fifth century as the evangelisation not just of the urban but also of the rural population gathered pace. And this chapter so far has shown how the long-term study of the texts and the archaeology of the development of Christianity in the West has yielded a remarkable harvest of knowledge and understanding: there may be many gaps to fill in the archaeology, but the overall framework for the study is firmly in place, and all new discoveries can be placed into a coherent context. The archaeological correlates for the formation of Christians, their initiation, their participation in public and private worship, their burial and the commemoration of the 'very special dead' can all be identified and discussed.

The traditional religions

The same cannot be said for the archaeology of the traditional religions, which needs to be considered now. The neglect of the traditional religions is one of the posthumous triumphs of late Roman Christianity in the West. Most modern scholarship has seen two agents for the destruction of these religions. The first is the Germanic invasions of the third century, thought to have resulted as much in the destruction of temples and sanctuaries as of towns and villas, particularly in the regions nearest the Rhine. The other is evangelising bishops, above all Martin of Tours in the second half of the fourth century, whom Sulpicius Severus presents on more than one occasion as having destroyed pagan shrines and other places of worship such as trees. His successors such as Victricius of Rouen carried on the 'good' works, though it took some time, since Caesarius of Arles (*Sermones* 53) in the first half of the sixth century was still having to admonish those in his flock who not only did not destroy temples but even rebuilt them. But the view that the main narrative is that of the triumph of Christianity with the traditional religions largely there to be dismantled and suppressed has enormously biased study in favour of Christianity and away from considering the other religions among which and among whose adherents early Christianity and Christians in the West had to make their way. This is true not only of Gaul but also in large measure of Spain, where it has again been the spread and ultimate victory of Catholic Christianity that for a long time was almost the sole preoccupation of workers on religion in the Iberian peninsula in late antiquity. Britain, though, has long had a different tradition of understanding the subject. At least as far back as 1966, when Lewis published his diagram of the dating for Romano-British temples (Lewis 1966: 140–2), it was appreciated that the majority of temples in the island continued in use through the later third and fourth centuries – indeed, that some were not founded until then. Subsequent work has done nothing to disturb that pattern; a larger number of sites with better-studied stratigraphy and dating material have served only to confirm it. The only historically derived narrative was a liking for the idea of a 'pagan revival' under Julian (361–3), though, as has subsequently been realised, there is no archaeological warrant for such a scenario (e.g. Petts 2003: 42).

Because of the prevailing intellectual tradition on the Continent, there has been no recent systematic attempt to assemble and assess the archaeological evidence either for activity at sites established under the High Empire or for new foundations from the later third century onwards (a state of affairs kindly if depressingly confirmed to me by William van Andringa). For Gaul, an outline characterisation of the topic published some years ago (Fauduet 1994: 120–4) showed that, whereas 57 sites were claimed to have been abandoned in the third century, 120 remained in use through the fourth and in some cases into the early fifth century. There is an entirely proper caution against assuming that sites where the only evidence for late Roman use is fourth-century coins were necessarily still in religious use; nevertheless, the figures are striking. The incidence of this evidence for fourth-century use was not uniform geographically; the highest level of survival was in the south-east with over 75% survival in Provence and the Rhône valley, and over 50% survival in large swathes of the centre, north and west of France and, interestingly, in the German *Land* of Rheinland-Pfalz right on the Rhine frontier. What form these sites took in the fourth century is less certain and more variable, and might perhaps be approached by a variety of examples from a particular region of Gaul, anecdotal though this approach may be, to show the range of possibilities known to date.

One of the most famous and most extensively excavated religious sites of Roman Gaul is that of the huge sanctuary complex of Ribemont-sur-Ancre (Somme), 20 km east of the city of Amiens (Brunaux 2009). By the early third century, this consisted of a complex of buildings stretching down a slope with the principal temple at the top looking down a long trapezoidal court (like the plan of many villas in the area), flanked by subsidiary structures and with a theatre and a major set of baths on the axis running down from the temple (Figure 4.21). Extensive modern excavations on the temple and its surrounding porticos have shown that these structures were systematically dismantled down to their foundations in the course of the third century, but that these foundations were then reused to construct new superstructures on exactly the same lines; this is certain for the porticos and very probable for the temple (Brunaux 2009: 139–52). In addition, a new 'processional way' was constructed in front of the temple, defining an area with what was probably an altar base (Figure 4.22). There is no trace here of destruction by fire or other violent means. Instead there is an unexplained demolition of the principal sanctuary, only for it to be rebuilt shortly afterwards (there was no build-up of material between the foundations and the new walls on top of them). So through the latter part of the third century and much of the fourth century, the temple complex retained much the same architectonic form and massing as it had a century earlier, even if the decorative schemes (sculptural and painted) were less accomplished than in the second century. The coin list for the site closes with issues of the House of Valentinian (360s–380s), so it looks as though the sanctuary was

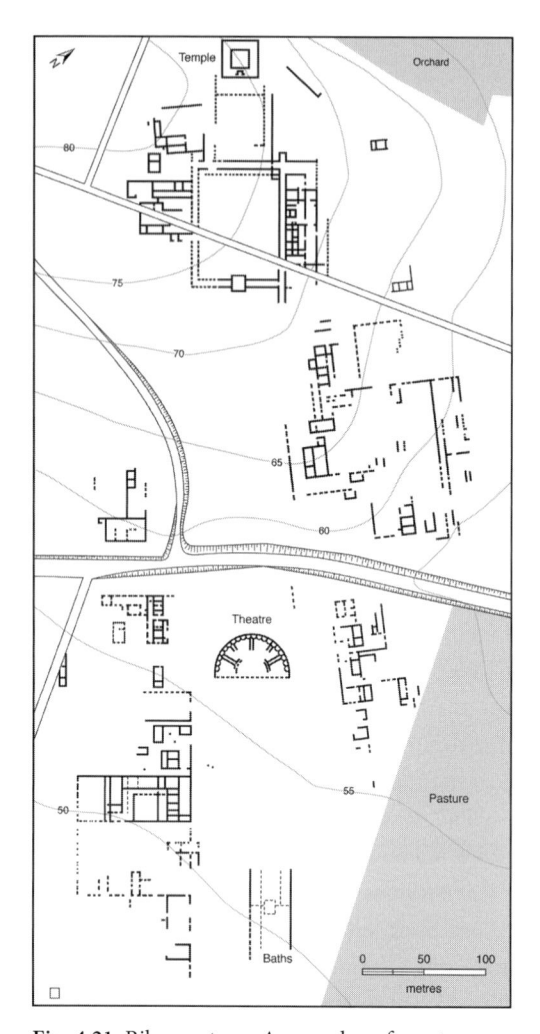

192 Christianity and the traditional religions

Fig. 4.21 Ribemont-sur-Ancre, plan of sanctuary complex in the second century

frequented until at least the last quarter of the fourth century. Clearly, here, we have no simple tale of destruction at the hands of invading Germans or evangelising bishops, but rather a major change in the history of the structures alongside what seems to be a broad continuity of use.

Recent excavations on other major temple complexes show a similar pattern of continued, if modified, occupation through the later Roman period. The major sanctuary at La Bauve, just outside the city of Meaux (Seine-et-Marne), like Ribemont, shows modifications to the temple and other structures in the later Roman period, but essential continuity of use (Magnan 2000). This also seems to be the story at the large complex at

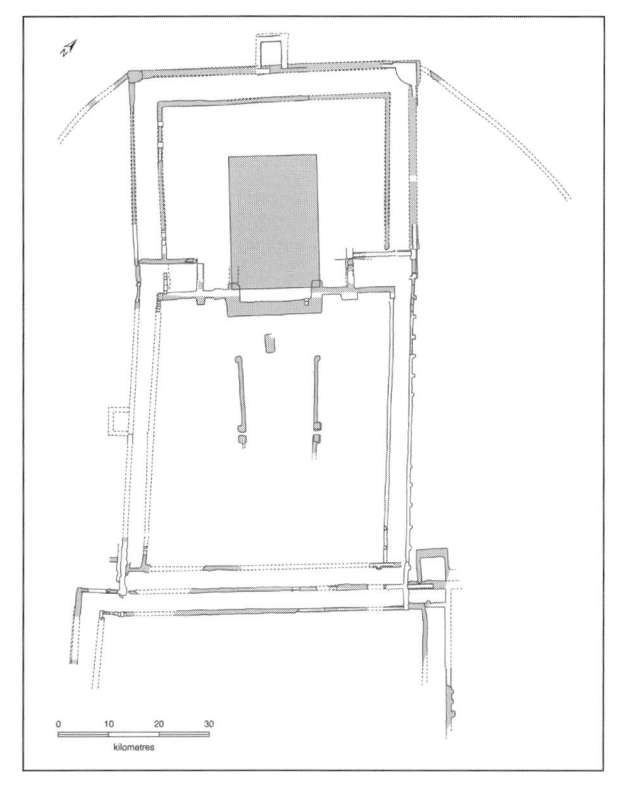

Fig. 4.22 Ribemont-sur-Ancre, the principal temple and annexes in the fourth century

Châteaubleau (Seine-et-Marne) to the east of Meaux (Pilon 2008); indeed, the main suite of sanctuaries does not reach its greatest number until the first half of the fourth century (Figure 4.23), when the line of buildings is linked to form a single complex, and the enclosure walls and colonnade reach their most elaborate form (Parthuisot *et al.* 2008). Some 70 km to the south-west, the temple at the *agglomération secondaire* of Jouars-Pontchartrain (Yvelines) in the third century likewise saw the rebuilding of the temple and the restructuring of the precinct and other parts of the complex, but the numismatic evidence shows clearly that it remained in use down to the end of the fourth century (Blin 2000). This is a rather random selection of instances from broadly the same region of north-central Gaul, united essentially by being recent excavations, but what they all have in common is that they show that temples and sanctuaries established in the first and second centuries AD (if not earlier) continued in use through the later third and fourth centuries at least undiminished in extent and in some cases not reaching their full architectural development until this period.

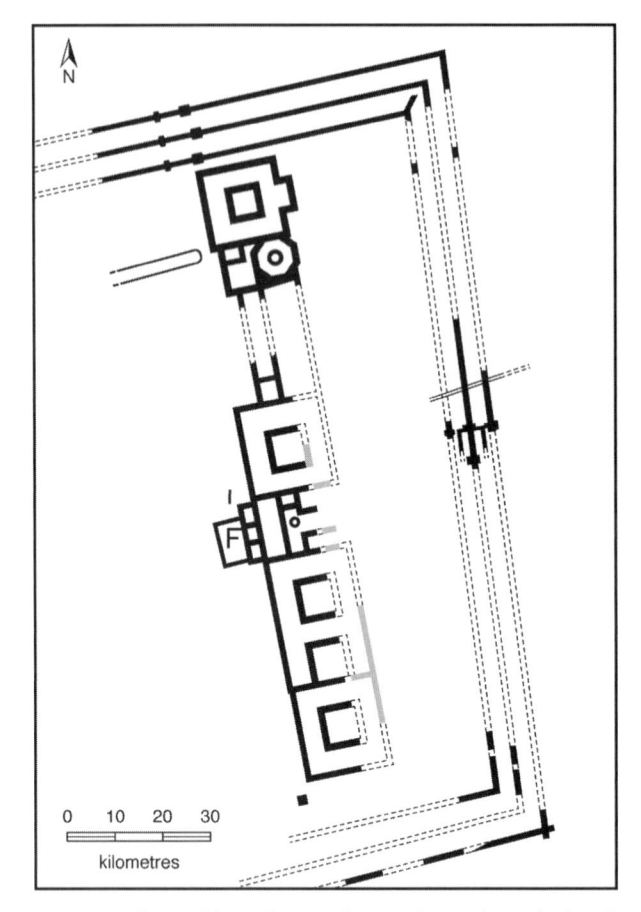

Fig. 4.23 Châteaubleau, the temple complex in the early fourth century

More striking still is the evidence from the site of Matagne-la-Grande (Namur) in the southern part of the province of Germania II (Cattelain and Paridaens 2009). The site consisted of two 'Romano-Celtic' temples and a subsidiary structure within a walled precinct (Figure 4.24). East of the precinct stood two other subsidiary structures. The recent excavations on this site showed clearly that it was constructed *ex novo* and on a site with no evidence for preceding religious activity in the first quarter of the fourth century. Probably in the 350s the temples were embellished, and the southern side of the precinct wall was turned into a monumental porticoed façade with main entrance and a corner pavilion, while another small temple was constructed to the east of the precinct at about the same time. The angle pavilion was the focus of the deposition, presumably votive, of a large number of coins of the later fourth century, and the numismatic evidence

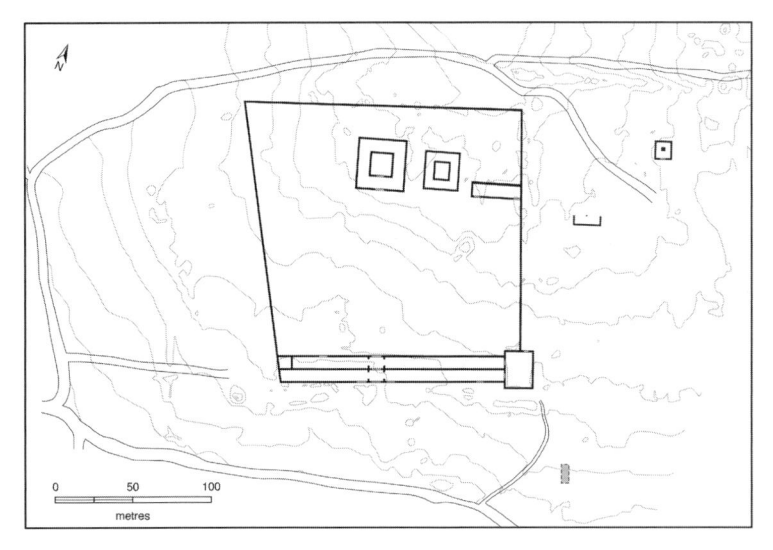

Fig. 4.24 Matagne-la-Grande, early-fourth-century temple complex

suggests that the site continued in use down into the first half of the fifth century (Doyen in Cattelain and Paridaens 2009: 52–89). The foundation date and the overall date range for the use of the site lie in flat contradiction to the accepted chronology for sites of the traditional religions in the north of Gaul. But there is another temple site some 3 km to the south-east at Matagne-la-Petit which also seems to have been in use through the fourth century (Cattelain and Paridaens 2009: 127). Some 40 km to the north-east in the roadside settlement of Liberchies was a temple building constructed at the turn of the third and fourth centuries and embellished and frequented through the fourth (Brulet *et al.* 2009). The two Matagne temples lay in a microregion where there is good evidence for continued occupation of villas and other sites and for cemeteries through the fourth century (Cattelain and Paridaens 2009: 123–7), demonstrating an island of settlement little touched by the 'barbarian invasions', the Franks or the incursions of the mid fourth century – a salutary example. Of course, the chronology of the temple site would occasion little surprise had it lain in Britain. But the possibility that in Gaul there were new temple foundations in the later third and fourth centuries is clearly one that must be taken seriously.

In parallel with the lack of systematic study of temple sites, there has been no systematic consideration of other aspects of religious practice such as votive offerings. As mentioned above, there is evidence for deposition of coins at Matagne-la-Grande, as there was also in the temple complex at

Jouars-Pontchartrain (Blin 2000: Fig. 11d) with again an angle room near the main entrance being a particular focus of deposition. A recent survey of the archaeological evidence for cult practice as well as for sanctuaries in the northern part of Burgundy (Kasprzyk 2005: 319–34 – I am grateful to Dr Kasprzyk for sending me a copy of his thesis) shows that occupation and use continued at a number of rural sanctuaries throughout the second half of the third, the fourth and on into the fifth centuries; of the twenty-nine in the study, only four show no sign of use in the first half of the fourth century. The evidence for cult practice likewise shows strong persistence, especially the votive deposition of objects. A particular feature of this last is the sharp rise in the deposition of coins at a number of temples from the first half of the fourth century. That this was not manifest from the later third century on shows that it is not just an artefact of the greater availability of low-value coinage; it seems to be a new emphasis in the means of religious expression at this time. The figures seem to show that temples at the cities and lesser centres of the study area passed out of use towards the end of the fourth century, whereas rural sanctuaries seem to have fared better with twelve out of sixteen sites still frequented in the third quarter of the century. So the evidence from this small area is consonant with that from further north; once a detailed study of sites and assemblages from the sanctuaries of the traditional religions is undertaken, it is clear that the majority of them were still in use through the second half of the third and much of the fourth century, even if the scale and nature of the complexes and their cults had changed. This then raises the fascinating question of the persistence (or not) of these sites into the fifth century, and presumably leaves the fifth century and on into the sixth as the real focus of the 'battle for the souls' of the bulk of the population of Gaul.

South of the Pyrenees, the position is, if anything, even more obscure. In part this is because the Iberian peninsula seems to have lacked the widespread rural temples and sanctuaries that characterised the countryside of Gaul, Germany and Britain. In fact, rural places of worship are very rare in Spain (cf. Keay 1988: Ch. 7), though votive altars and other inscriptions to indigenous deities are common enough in the west and north of the peninsula. Known temples, therefore, are overwhelmingly urban. A review of the textual and archaeological (such as it is) evidence (Alemany 2006) tends to show that there is little or no evidence either for the disuse of temples or for their destruction or conversion to Christian use in the period covered by this book. One possible exception is suggested by the fact that the cathedral at Tarragona overlies the courtyard of the imperial cult complex, but there is no positive evidence that the cathedral deliberately succeeded to any possible temple rather than just colonising an available space. Other than this, there is currently little that can be said about the archaeology of religion in late Roman Spain.

As will be seen from the rather dismal litany above, our knowledge of the traditional religions, their places of worship and their cult practices in the later third, fourth and fifth centuries across the West is very deficient (largely with the exception of Britain). But as we have also seen, across Gaul and Germany (possibly less so Spain), there must in fact be a great deal of evidence for later Roman (re-)construction at and use of shrines and temples. Likewise, if properly looked for, there would also doubtless be plenty of evidence for religious practices such as votive deposition. It is just that this work remains to be done, and, unfortunately, did not fall within the scope of preparing this book.

5 | Emperors and aristocrats in the late Roman West

Introduction

Roman society was intensely hierarchical and driven by competition for the gaining and maintaining of social position; these were overwhelmingly matters for men, with relatively little 'public space' for women. At the apex of this hierarchy was the emperor, who was both autocrat disposing of the power, patronage and massive revenues of the empire and by far the richest landowner of the empire in his own right through the accumulated holdings of the imperial patrimony (the *res privata*). Still very rich, powerful and influential were the members of the senatorial order, the old aristocracy of the Roman state; the financial qualification for entry to the order was substantial, and the expenditure required of those who rose to high office was formidable. As with so many nobilities, descent had come to be a vital marker of status within the order, with a limited number of great families dominating in the city of Rome. The senate might have lost much of its direct military and political power to *arriviste* generals and courtiers, especially from the later third century on, but it remained a social elite with immense influence on aristocratic behaviour and self-representation. Lower down the scales of power and wealth, but still leaders of society in their own regions, came the aristocracies in the provinces, deriving their power from their landholdings and from their descent, but often, as we shall see, augmenting these by service at the imperial court and in the imperial administration. Alongside these nobilities defined by landed wealth and by descent, there were, under the Late Empire, other paths to prominence through service to the emperor, either as a senior civil official or as a military commander. Increasingly, bishops also became a form of aristocracy, commanding the wealth of their churches and more and more the object of imperial favour, until in the fifth century many bishops were drawn from the local nobility. All of these needed ways of demonstrating their superiority over the mass of the people and their place within the hierarchies of wealth, power, education and taste of the late Roman world.

One complex of ways in which aristocrats in the late Roman West could and did represent themselves has already been discussed in Chapter 2 and

Introduction

relates to a military-style vocabulary of rank and power, which seems in northern Gaul to a considerable extent to have come to exist alongside the traditional means of display such as the urban residence and the villa with the cultural assumptions that these embodied. In this chapter the emphasis will rather be on the aristocracies of the southern parts of Gaul and of Spain, where the military symbolism was of little consequence in the later third and fourth centuries, though it was to become more significant in the fifth, as will be discussed in Chapter 9. Here, then, we shall be looking at means of self-presentation that are 'civilian' and derive ultimately from the sorts of aristocratic locations and means of display that had developed in the Western provinces in the first and second centuries AD. If the *mentalités* of the elites of northern Gaul had clearly been significantly affected by the events of the third century, their southern cousins (and those in southern Britain, as we shall see) had responded in ways that emphasised continuity and tradition, albeit that it was tradition as (re-)invented by them. These were the product of a very different set of *mentalités*, which laid much greater stress on cultural than martial values.

Archaeologically, these elites tend to be very visible because the visual was central to the expression of wealth, status and descent, and also because the visual was expressed in ways which survive well in the archaeology. But there were significant variations in the ways in which the aristocracies represented themselves, and it is the purpose of this chapter to look at these various ways and how they impacted on the archaeological record. The chapter will start with an overview of the evidence for the greatest of all aristocrats in the West, the emperors, whose residences both partook of the existing vocabulary of power and status display and served as models for those lower down the pecking order. It will then consider the evidence for forms of elite display in southern Gaul, Spain and Britain – regions where aristocratic display remained 'traditional' in that it was centred on villas and on the furnishings and fittings of the villas, such as mosaics and sculpture, with a strong investment in long-standing Graeco-Roman culture such as mythology. Central to the discussion and understanding of these types of evidence will be the deployment of the concept of *paideia* as a theoretical and analytical framework, demonstrating the ways in which the material correlates observable today can be recontextualised within a world-view where gradations and nuances in the mastery of elite, classical culture were vital in the processes of optimising one's own status while at the same time undermining the claims of others – the 'narcissism of small differences' in Freud's formulation. This will be followed by regional surveys of these three main areas, showing how they can be understood within this exegetic framework. The very different evidence for elites in northern Gaul and the Rhineland will be revisited as a counterpoint to the 'traditional' forms of display of the areas further south and west.

The imperial residences

The crisis in imperial succession and legitimacy during the third century had an important consequence for the West, namely the *de facto* regionalisation of the imperial power as it became normal to have more than one Augustus at a time, each with territorial responsibilities: sole Augusti became rare and even they (e.g. Constantius II in 350–61) often in fact had junior colleagues (Constantius Gallus as Caesar in the East, 351–4; Julian as Caesar in Gaul, 355–60). This meant that residences suitable for the 'Master of the Land and Seas and of Every Nation of Men' (Parsons 2007: 73) had to be constructed, and a number of such residences of the late third and fourth centuries are known across the empire. Some conform to the model of a relatively small, if splendid, fortified residence, such as Diocletian's palace at Split, his birthplace, on the east coast of the Adriatic (cf. Wilkes 1986) or the recently discovered complex in the Balkan interior at Gamzigrad (*Romuliana*), the residence of Diocletian's successor, the emperor Galerius (Augustus 305–11) (Srejović 1993; Srejović and Vasić 1994) – testaments to their builders' military careers – or the less overtly dynastic residence at *Mediana* (Srejović 1993: 169–77). These fortress palaces fed into the representation of the emperor as all-conquering general, scourge of the barbarians and restorer of internal peace. Thus the military power on which each emperor depended was presented as the defining quality of a good and successful emperor (as it had been ever since the days of an Augustus or a Trajan), and the emperor was depicted in the guise of general in statuary and other artistic media, and also frequently and stridently on the coinage, where the emperors not only struck down the enemies of Rome but also trumpeted the virtues of the armies or their foresight (*providentia*) in defence of the empire. It is this strand in the imperial office and image that was more emphasised by the aristocracies of northern Gaul in their adoption of a militarised vocabulary of self-representation. The alternative model was based more on the 'civilian' virtues of the emperors, as materialised most evidently through the imperial residence on the Palatine at Rome, a huge, sprawling complex of colonnaded courts, gardens, and elaborately decorated reception rooms and audience chambers, with all the offices necessary to house and support the emperor, his staff, and his military retinue and bodyguards. It is this model that we find in the Western provinces, principally at Trier and Milan along with, in slightly different fashion, Arles, as well as further afield in the Balkans at such residences as *Naissus* (Niš), *Serdica* (Sofia), Thessalonica and, of course, the 'Great Palace' at Constantinople.

Trier

The largest and most splendid of these residences in the West beyond the Alps was at Trier (*Colonia Augusta Treverorum*) not far behind the Rhine frontier with good communications to the interior of Gaul. The imposing surviving buildings of this palace complex (Figure 5.1) have made it one of the most intensively studied of imperial residences and, to an extent, an archetype for what is to be expected at such a place (Cüppers 1984: 68–74, 139–65; Wightman 1970: 98–123). Trier had been an important city under the Early Empire (Wightman 1970: 71–97) and in recognition of this had been accorded a circuit of walls enclosing the huge area of 285 ha. It was a

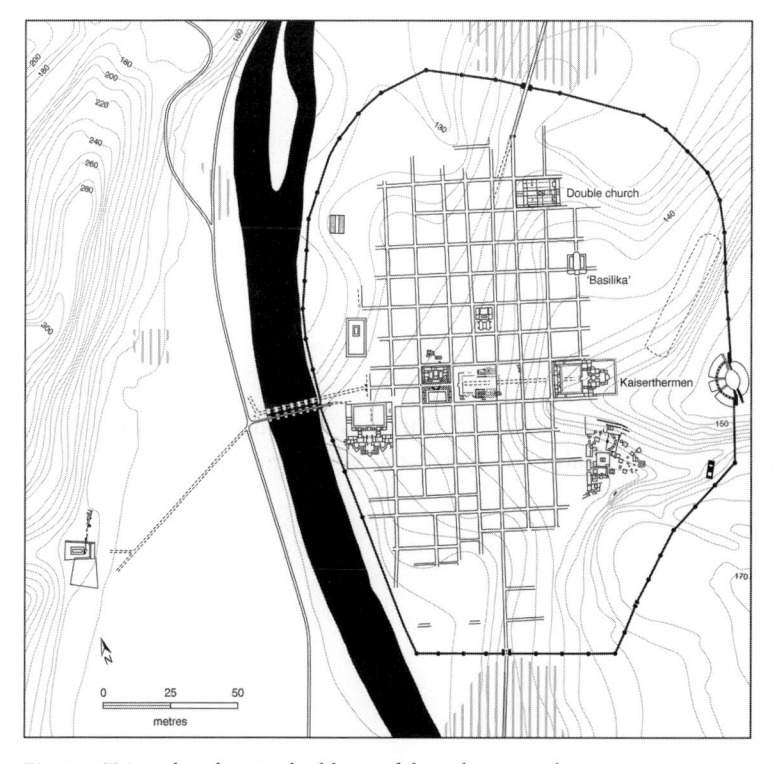

Fig. 5.1 Trier, plan showing buildings of the palace complex

place of importance under the Gallic Empire, the seat of a mint and the find spot of a mosaic naming the future Gallic emperor Victorinus (268–70) when still a tribune of the praetorian guard (of Postumus?). The turning point came under Constantius I (Caesar in the West, 296–305; Augustus, 305–6) and in the earlier part of the reign of his son Constantine I when this usurper made it his principal residence between his proclamation at York in 306 and his departure for the battle of Milvian Bridge and mastery of Rome in 312. The main surviving building of the palace, the 'Basilika', is built of bricks bearing the same stamps as those used in the bridgehead fort of Köln-Deutz (cf. p. 50), which also has an inscription of 310. Excavations on the other major surviving monument, the 'Kaiserthermen', have yielded dating evidence suggesting a similar or slightly earlier date range. The complex of buildings making up the palace stretched all along the eastern side of the central part of the city; it is worth noting that the wall circuit was not reduced in extent as so often happened elsewhere. The complex consisted of a series of structures to house the emperor and the court and for the emperor to discharge the duties and ceremonies of his office. Central to this aspect of the palace was the huge hall (since the nineteenth century a Lutheran church and known as the 'Basilika'), in plan a rectangle 67 m long by 27.5 m wide by 30 m high with a deep apse at the northern end (Figure 5.2) and a long, transverse, apsidal fore-hall at the southern end. Uniquely in the West, the 'Basilika' was built throughout of brick (rather than brick-faced rubble stone). Though now rather stark in appearance,

Fig. 5.2 Trier, the 'Basilika' from the west

there is evidence (Cüppers 1984: 147–54) that originally the interior was richly decorated with architectural detailing, mosaic and stone inlay; furthermore, a subtle trick of perspective was played with the windows of the apse (smaller and set lower than their equivalents in the nave) to make the apse appear more distant, so, clearly, great care was taken over the form and decoration of this building. It must have been the *consistorium*, the formal audience hall (hence an alternative Latin term *aula palatina*) where the imperial presence would be made manifest, with the emperor enthroned beneath the great arch dividing nave from apse (and whose décor has sadly long since vanished) with his high officials and commanders, court and functionaries ranged down the nave in their rich formal attire and gleaming with gold. In such a setting the emperor would receive embassies, proclaim laws and accept the adoration of promoted officials as they received their codicils of appointment, as shown on the Missorium of Theodosius (p. 232), in a display of his quasi-divine nature and supreme power.

The other major surviving structure from the palace is a huge set of baths (never finished or put into operation) at the southern end of the palace quarter and now called the 'Kaiserthermen' (Figure 5.3): this in a city which already possessed one substantial and one enormous set of second-century baths, the Viehmarkt baths and the 'Barbarathermen' respectively. Clearly, such major provision of public bathing facilities was an important aspect of imperial munificence, even if rather outmoded over most of the rest of the Western provinces (cf. p. 115). Later in the fourth century, during the period of residence of Valentinian I (much of 367–75), most of the Kaiserthermen was to be demolished, with the former *tepidarium* and *caldarium* retained, not as a baths, but perhaps as another audience chamber (Figure 5.4). To the east, between the palace complex and the hill of the Petrisberg crowned by Trier's large amphitheatre, lay the circus or hippodrome (Cüppers 1984: 190), constructed in a valley infilled with rubble for the purpose (the proximity of the Circus Maximus to the imperial residence on the Palatine in Rome meant that the circus had long since become a locus for public appearances by the emperor at the lavish games he financed). The last major monument of the palace of which we know is the pair of large, Christian basilicas, the northern of which was the episcopal church, built over the northern part of the palace from the later 320s. As we saw in Chapter 4 (p. 157), the scale of these churches and their date of construction is unique for the West and must be a testament to imperial patronage, either by Constantine I himself (no mean builder of huge Christian churches at Rome and elsewhere) or quite possibly by his mother, the dowager empress Helena, a long-time resident of Trier when she was not

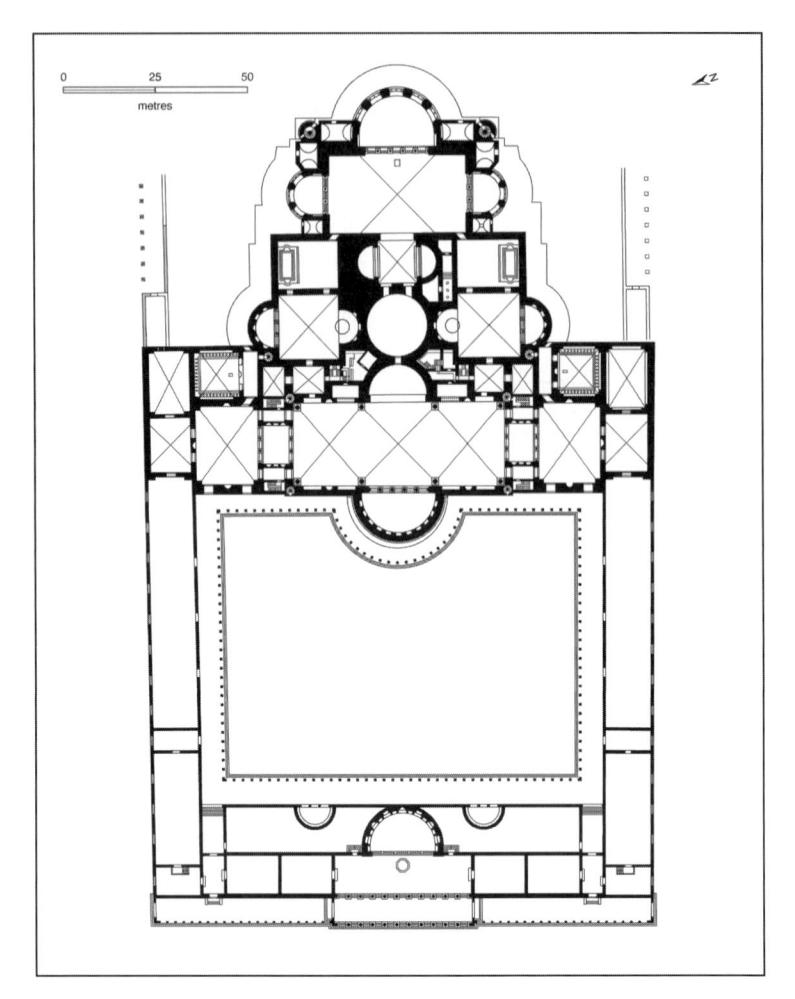

Fig. 5.3 Trier, plan of the Kaiserthermen

off relic hunting in the Holy Land. Even after the departure of Constantine I and the death of his mother in about 330, the imperial palace at Trier saw a resident emperor for long periods in the fourth century – under his son, the Western Augustus Constantine II (337–40); under the latter's brother and killer Constans (340–50); and then again under Valentinian I (364–75, often resident at Trier from 367) and under his son Gratian (375–83). Gratian's assassin and successor Magnus Maximus (383–8) used the city a great deal, but after his suppression Trier never again functioned as an imperial residence, though it remained very important and a great prize for attackers.

Little is known of the rest of the palace, unfortunately for us given its role as the exemplar north of the Alps of the highest grade of aristocratic

Fig. 5.4 Trier, Kaiserthermen from the east

residence. On the model of the original imperial palace, the *Domus Augustana* on the Palatine at Rome, or of other complexes such as those at Milan, Thessalonica or above all the somewhat later 'Great Palace' at Constantinople, the Trier palace presumably consisted of ranges of architecturally complex and ambitious reception rooms and other semi-public spaces set around colonnaded courts along with offices for the imperial functionaries, living quarters for the imperial family, and bath suites and barracks for the imperial bodyguard. These spaces, especially the 'public' areas where officials, embassies and guests were received, would have been richly decorated. Walls and floors would have been sheathed in mosaic or in polychrome cut marble (*opus sectile*). These spaces would have been adorned with statuary, pictures and hangings, doubtless extolling the virtues of the emperor. Furnishings, fixtures and fittings would have been elaborate and ostentatious, with much use of precious metals. In the courtyards and open spaces, the dominance of the emperor over nature would have been exemplified by formal planting and gardens, with fountains and pools fed from aqueducts to emphasise the opulence and control over resources of the emperor. The richly decorated ceiling plaster (Simon 1986) recovered from under the episcopal complex at Trier presumably adorned part of the palace and is a pale reflection of the richness (or vulgarity) that must have been omnipresent in the imperial residence. And it was not just a matter of the physical spaces. These were the vessels for the elaborate rituals and ceremonies of the imperial court, centred above all on the person of the emperor himself, in which matters of degree and precedence were scrupulously observed and reproduced (Kelly 2004; MacCormack 1981), reflecting the proximity of officials and officers to the fount of power, honour and wealth that was the emperor himself. It was in these surroundings and as participants in these rituals and ceremonies that the high officials of the court and their clerks would have moved; many of these officials would have been drawn from the senatorial order and from the provincial landowning classes and would have absorbed a knowledge of what was proper to the housing of the greatest of all men under heaven, and thus what they would want to deploy in their own residences as a reflection of the imperial majesty and as a statement about any career they may have had at court. Many of the aristocratic residences we shall be looking at, as well as those in other parts of the West, such as Italy (Sfameni 2006), exhibit common features of plan and appointments that echo those of the imperial residences.

The imperial presence and the court were not the only bringers of wealth to Trier in the fourth century. Even when the emperor was not in residence, Trier remained one of the most important administrative and economic hubs of the imperial system. From the late Roman register of military and civilian officers and officials, the *Notitia Dignitatum*, we know that the city was the residence of the praetorian prefect of the Gauls, responsible for the civil administration of the entire area under consideration in this book, and of his subordinate, the vicarius of the diocese of the Gauls, and also the governor of the province of Belgica I (the area around Trier). All of these officials had staffs appropriate to their rank; the theoretical complement for each is given in the *Notitia Dignitatum*, and imperial edicts and other textual evidence suggest that in reality these staffs tended to expand well beyond this complement. There were officials of fiscal and financial administrations, such as the head of the state treasury for the diocese of the Gauls and superintendent of the mint, and also the directors of the various *fabricae* at the city, manufacturing a range of clothing, armour, weaponry and other equipment for the army and bureaucracy. Each of these would have had a residence containing formal reception rooms and other spaces; those of senior officials such as the praetorian prefect would have been on a lavish scale. Sadly, we at present have little evidence for them, though they must have taken up considerable areas and modified the layout and appearance of the city to a significant extent. Moreover, all of these officials and enterprises would have brought wealth to the city, paid as they were out of tax revenues, either in coin or in food and fodder allowances. The 'multiplier effect' of this inflow of money must have been considerable on the economy and buildings of the city, though, unfortunately, archaeology has as yet little to say about this apart from the large, late storehouses near the river in the St Irminen district (Wightman 1970: 117–19) and finds of weaponry and equipment from the city (Cüppers 1984: 292–310). Given that from the time of Constantine I onwards the emperors were Christian, it is not surprising that those wanting to get on at court followed this example, with the result that the Christian archaeology of the fourth-century city is the richest in the prefecture (cf. Chapter 4). As well as the great double church linked with the palace, there was a series of churches in the cemeteries outside the gates, commemorating various martyrs and holy bishops (Cüppers 1984: 203–48). These churches were enlarged in the course of the fourth century and equipped with such things as carved stone sarcophagi. These became the focus for burial of the faithful, considerable numbers of whom were memorialised by the largest collections of Christian tombstones anywhere in the West (Handley 2003: 5), several of them stating the rank at court or in the bureaucracy of the person commemorated (Handley 2003: 53). All in all, the imperial presence at Trier raised it above all other cities in the Western provinces, something recognised in contemporary literature such as the *Ordo Urbium Nobilium* of Ausonius, who himself spent many years at Trier as tutor to Gratian and then a senior courtier; he places Trier sixth after the great and ancient centres of Rome, Carthage, Antioch, Alexandria and the new eastern imperial seat, Constantinople.

It was not only at Trier itself that the effect of the emperor and court were felt; its countryside also was marked by their patronage. A number of sites can be associated with the person of the emperor. Not far to the north of the city, a huge tract of land, 220 km^2, was enclosed within a wall built by army detachments, the Langmauer (or Landmauer) (Cüppers 1984: 288–91). In the southern part of this area lay the large and elaborate fourth-century villa of Welschbillig (Figure 5.5), of which little is known save a long pool in front of the main building, surrounded by a series of herms (busts on square pillars) representing among other things, Greek philosophers and young Germans with distinctive 'pageboy' hairstyle and torcs, perhaps referring to the imperial bodyguard (Wrede 1972). This is unique and may suggest that Welschbillig was the centre of the Langmauer estate and an imperial residence. Just downstream of the city on the other side of the Moselle lay the exceptional site of Pfalzel (Figure 5.6), built to a rectangular plan around a courtyard, with projecting towers at the angle and in the middle of the long sides, the ground floor blind to the exterior (Cüppers 1984: 319–22). Though to the outside world a fortification, the remains of floor, wall and ceiling mosaics, marble, and wall paintings show that internally this was a luxurious residence. It was only part of a larger complex of buildings,

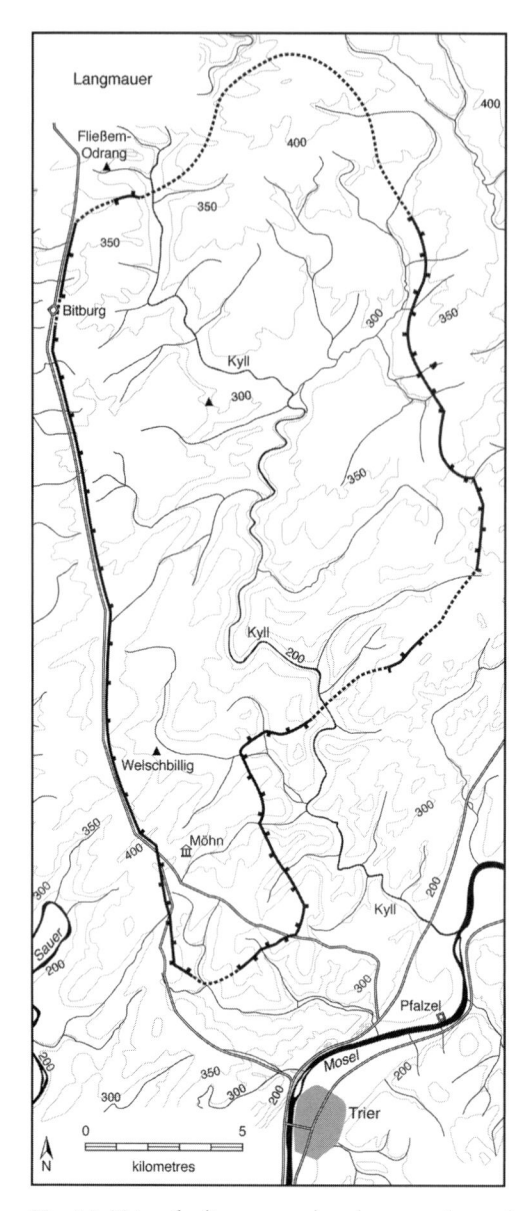

Fig. 5.5 Trier, the 'Langmauer' enclosure and associated villas

with what is probably a set of barracks, suggesting bodyguards. Such a complex calls to mind the rural imperial residences of the Balkans such as *Mediana*, mentioned above. The recent excavation of the upper Rhine site at Oedenburg-Altkirch (Seitz and Sagermann 2005: 204–5) has yielded a Valentinianic fortification to a very similar plan if considerably larger (1.2 ha.

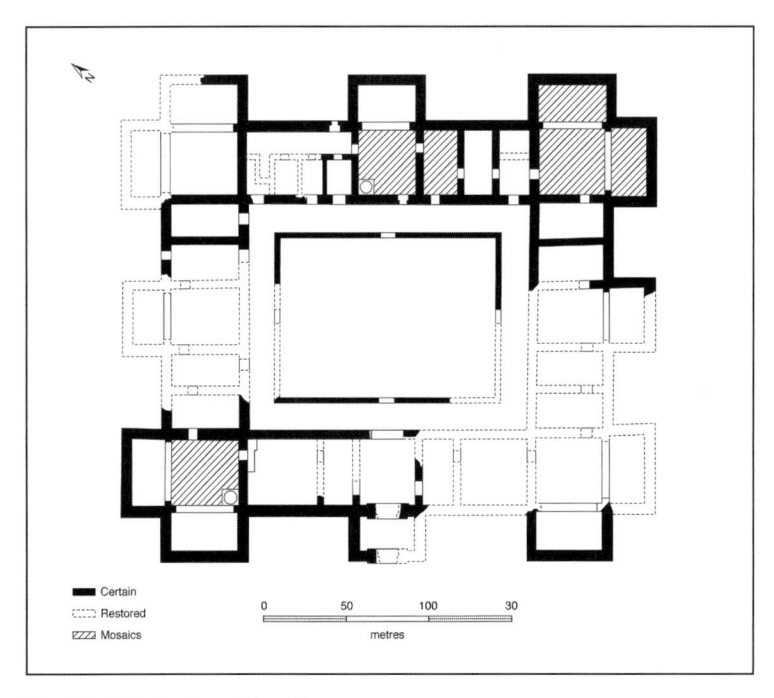

Fig. 5.6 Pfalzel, plan of the villa

as compared with 0.3 ha.), the similarities being so marked that it has been suggested that the two sites were the work of the same architect. Valentinian himself was present at Breisach near Oedenburg-Altkirch in 369. One other site thought probably to be an imperial villa is that at Konz (Cüppers 1984: 310–15), in the centre of the main range of which lay an apsidal reception room; this is thought to be the *Contionacum* whence Valentinian I issued several decrees in 371, one of them only a day after one issued at Trier. As well as these sites, which may well have been in imperial possession and use, the countryside around Trier is notable for being one of the only two areas of northern Gaul in the fourth century where villas were relatively common, the other being the hinterland of Cologne, another major centre of imperial power at the time (Van Ossel 1992: Cartes II, III and VI), as discussed below (p. 260). In both cases, one may posit the wealth of the imperial officials and functionaries as the source of the necessary capital; the way in which this capital was spent, more reminiscent of areas much further south in Gaul and Spain, presumably attests partly to following imperial models, and partly to the desire to maintain the traditional ways of demonstrating wealth and education (cf. p. 242), in contrast to what was developing elsewhere in northern Gaul.

Arles

Trier was exceptional north and west of the Alps. To seek parallels, one has to turn to other major imperial residences such as Milan, Serdica, Thessalonica, or Constantinople. But there were two other Western sites which partook of some of the features of the Trier palace complex and need to be discussed alongside it. The first is Arles, where one of the major monuments of the centre of the city near the Rhône is the 'Baths of Constantine' or 'Palais de la Trouille', a set of large, probably early fourth-century baths of which substantial portions survive intact (Heijmans 2004: 139–60), demonstrating pronounced structural similarities to the 'Kaiserthermen' at Trier. But in a remarkable, recent project it has been demonstrated that immediately to the south of these baths there are the remains of a substantial basilican hall and other structures (Figure 5.7), surviving almost to full height encased within

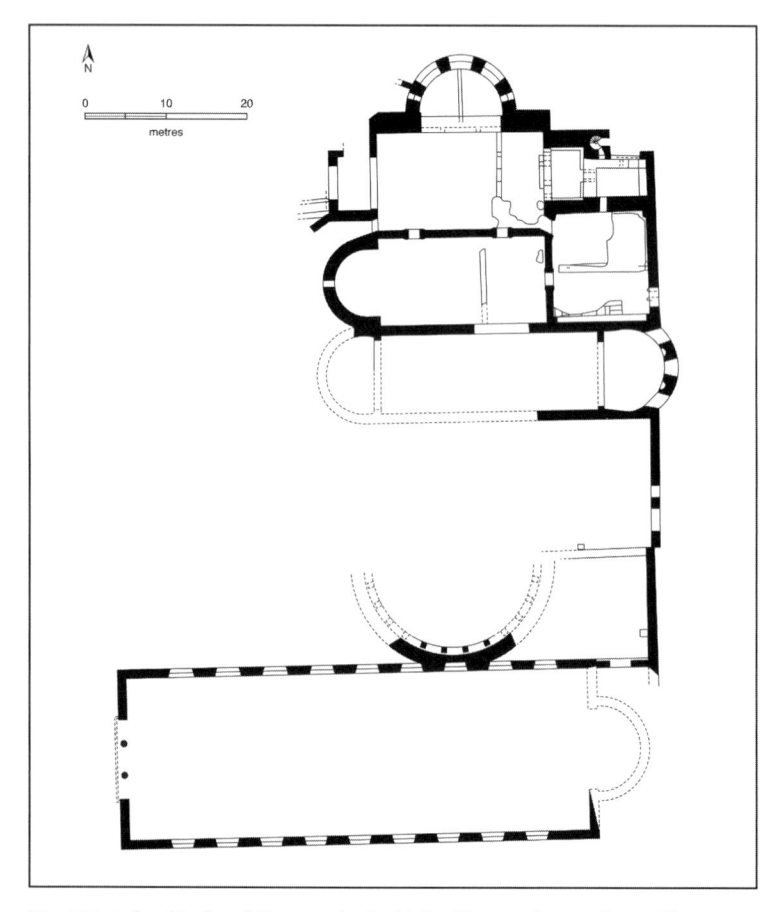

Fig. 5.7 Arles, 'Baths of Constantine' with basilica on the southern side

later structures (Heijmans 2004: 160–94). The basilica was oriented east–west, 57 m in length by some 21 m in width and surviving to *c.* 17 m in height, though originally probably at least as high as the building was wide. It was aisleless and had nine large windows on each side in the upper part of the walls; at the eastern end, there was most probably an apse. Its date is uncertain due to a lack so far of excavation, but structurally it is secondary to the bathhouse and earlier than the construction of a very large apse against the north wall, probably in the fifth century. The function of the basilica remains uncertain; a function as a *basilica thermarum*, a large hall attached to the baths, is unlikely due to the lack of communication between basilica and baths. A function as a church is possible but unlikely since there is no record of a church, let alone such a large one, in the area. The favoured interpretation places it in the same category as the 'Basilika' at Trier, an audience hall; the Arles basilica is almost the same length as that at Trier, albeit somewhat narrower and lower and could well serve as the audience hall for an imperial residence. Arles was briefly an imperial residence at various times under Constantine I and his sons and the city was renamed *Constantina* around 328, probably in connection with Constantine II, born at Arles in 317. Besides the basilica, there is other evidence for large-scale construction work in this part of the city, reaching to the forum to the south of the baths/basilica complex (Heijmans 2004: 222–30), where the temple athwart the north wing had its façade facing towards the basilica rebuilt and flanking colonnades attached; the inscription on the façade mentions Constantine I's wife Fausta (mother of Constantine II), murdered in 326 by her husband along with their eldest son Crispus, giving a *terminus ante quem* for the inscription. Taken together, there are thus grounds for proposing that the central-northern part of Arles was refashioned as a palace quarter under Constantine I, rather as at Trier but on a smaller scale, even if, as it was to transpire, emperors were seldom to reside there. Another possibility is that the basilica was a construction of the fifth century, when the praetorian prefecture had been transferred to Arles from Trier, and the brevity of Constantine I's involvement with the city and such dating evidence as there is may favour this later context.

Arles also had a circus on the south-western side of the city, built in the early second century but with the central *spina* rebuilt and embellished in the late third or early fourth century, possibly including the obelisk (not Egyptian but from the quarries of the Troad in imitation of the Egyptian) now re-erected in the city centre (Heijmans 2004: 239–40). In addition, the Augustan theatre and Flavian amphitheatre were probably still in working order through the fourth century (Heijmans 2004: 238–9). Like Trier but to a lesser extent, Arles also had a concentration of state *fabricae* serving the fiscal authorities and the supply of the army (*thesaurus*, *moneta*, *gynaecium*, and *fabrica barbaricariorum* – treasury, mint, weaving centre, and production of decorated equipment, cf. p. 92). As at Trier, we know little either of the installations of the state or of private buildings of the fourth century, though a range from relatively grand to very simple is apparent (Heijmans 2004: Ch. 6). The development of the religious topography of Arles in the fourth century is still debatable (Heijmans 2004: Ch. 5), but there is a striking concentration of richly decorated marble sarcophagi, probably carved at Arles, from the cemeteries of the Alyscamps to the south-east of the city and that in the Trinquetaille area north of the river. From the latter cemetery comes a particularly elaborate sarcophagus showing the deceased wearing the *trabea*, the dress of a consul. As yet it is not possible to demonstrate the sort of impact on the villas of the lower Rhône valley that one can propose for the region of Trier, probably because the city was not an imperial residence for long enough and did not house the upper echelons of the civil administration in the way Trier did until the transfer of the prefecture at the turn of the fourth and fifth centuries.

Córdoba

The other site and the one most debatable in terms of its function is the recently discovered complex at La Cercadilla, some 600 m north-west of the walls of Córdoba in south-eastern Spain (Hidalgo Prieto 1996). The huge complex stood at the top of the slope up from the river Guadalquivir in a very dominating position. The structural evidence suggests that it was conceived as a unity and constructed in a single operation (Figure 5.8). It was entered from the east, where a rectangular space some 250 m long was flanked by long, narrow buildings whose plan is strongly reminiscent of barrack blocks of the earlier empire with rooms in pairs, an outer smaller and an inner large one. A wall with central gatehouse closed off the western end of this plaza and led into a huge, semicircular court surrounded by colonnades raised on a cryptoporticus. Opposite the gatehouse at the centre of the curve lay an aisleless, rectangular, apsidal basilica 48.5 by 22.5 m, with buttresses along the side walls and round the apse, a plan very similar to that of the 'Basilika' at Trier, which was about twice the size. Opening off the rest of the semicircular portico were rooms, including a much smaller, apsed hall, and small courtyards, and a series of corridors leading back to other buildings including probable baths and reception rooms. The ends of the semicircular portico terminated in rectangular rooms with three apses at one end and other apses down the long sides. Despite heavy robbing of

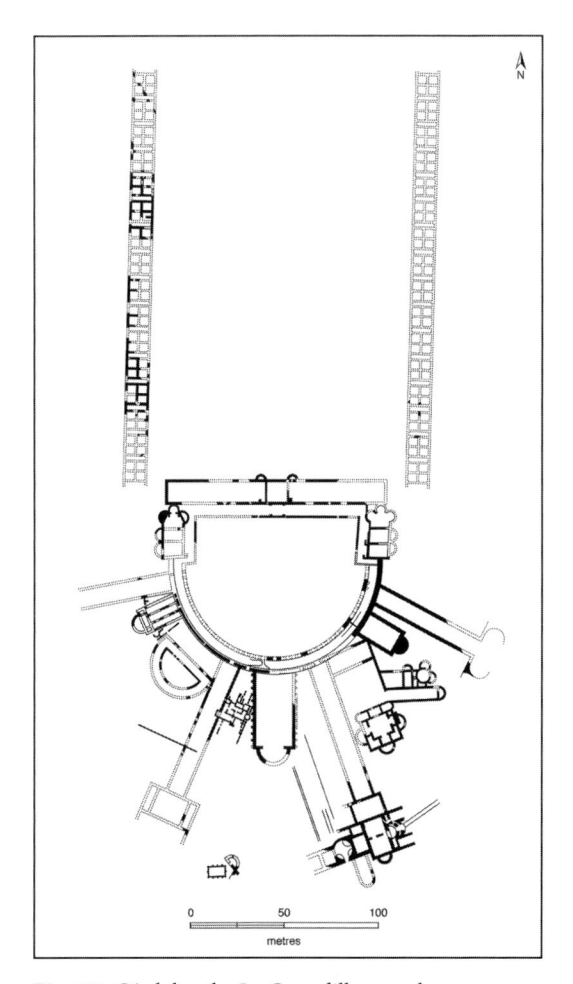

Fig. 5.8 Córdoba, the La Cercadilla complex

materials in the Middle Ages, it is clear that the complex was lavishly decorated. A date in the later third or fourth centuries is given by the material stratified in the construction deposits along with a fragment of an inscription mentioning Diocletian and Maximian and their Caesars, and thus dating between 293 and 305.

It is this inscription that has in part given rise to the controversy over the nature of this vast and ambitious complex. The excavator (Hidalgo Prieto 1996: 104–55) argued that this meant La Cercadilla was an imperial residence, constructed for Maximian when he was on campaign in Spain in the later 290s, and thus antecedent to Trier and other palaces. This has been contested by Arce (1997: 301–2) on the grounds that though Maximian was in Iberia in 296, he was only in passage to North Africa, so there was no reason for him to command the building of a *platium*, and why at Córdoba anyway? Instead, Arce proposes that even if the scale of the complex suggests imperial involvement, it was to provide a residence for the provincial governor based at Córdoba. It has to be said that the scale of the whole enterprise, some 400 by 200 m, sets it well apart from other known examples of gubernatorial palaces of the period (Lavan 1999) or even the wealthiest villas such as Piazza Armerina in Sicily, as does the elaboration of the plan and the size of the semicircular court. The similarity of the plan of the main hall to the slightly later 'Basilika' in Trier is striking, and so is the fact that it is an almost exact match for the main audience hall in the broadly contemporary suburban villa of the emperor Maxentius at Rome (cf. Arce 1997: Fig. 2). If the buildings flanking the entrance plaza were indeed barracks, then that suggests strongly a large bodyguard, proper to an emperor rather than a governor, though similar buildings flank the main approach to the villa at Liédena (Navarra) in north-central Iberia (cf. Arce *et al.* 2007: 201–2), a site not proposed as having any imperial links and where the structures have been suggested as barracks for the estate workforce (or alternatively as storehouses). More recent suggestions that there may be a circus downslope from the La Cercadilla complex (Kulikowski 2005: 60) would fit well with other known imperial residences. But there remains a very valid objection – why should an imperial residence be constructed in this relatively out-of-the-way place? The matter is currently incapable of proof one way or the other, but in view of its scale and plan, it seems appropriate to discuss La Cercadilla alongside imperial residences such as Trier and Arles, even if it is by no means certain that it was of the same imperial class. One other suggestion (Marfil Ruiz 2000: 120–3), that it was the episcopal complex for the city, perhaps connected with the prominent early fourth-century bishop of Córdoba, Hosius, is hard to entertain since the group is unlike any other known episcopal complex, and it is quite unclear how the various parts would have functioned in such a scheme. There is no evidence for specifically Christian material; moreover, at a major church outside the walls, one would have expected a notable concentration of burials, which is conspicuously lacking here until considerably later.

The emperors were the greatest aristocrats of the Roman world, in power, riches and prestige far outstripping even the most ancient, noble and wealthy senatorial *gens*. Nevertheless, their residences and riches properly stand at the head of a consideration of the aristocratic vocabulary of display, on the one hand, because they would only succeed in projecting the awe of the imperial office if they shared in a common vocabulary of display, and, on the other hand, because as the largest and grandest of aristocratic residences with the richest troves of objects, they provided examples for the ambitious and aspirational to follow (this is again why it is so unfortunate that so little is known of the Trier or Arles complexes beyond the major monuments). The size of these complexes; the elaboration of their architectural forms; their use of exotic materials (especially marble) and mosaic; their adornment with sculpture; their mastery of water, not just for baths but also for fountains; and the picture of nature tamed in their gardens and orchards – all these were exemplars for imperial servants such as governors and also for the aristocracies across the West. The next section of this chapter will therefore be devoted to those regions of the West where the aristocracy manifested themselves in ways which in part echoed the splendour of the emperors but also consciously perpetuated settings for and types of aristocratic display long since established under the Early Empire, in particular the villa.

Aristocratic display in Spain, southern Gaul and Britain

The villa as a combination of economic unit and aristocratic residence, expressed in the form of its agrarian and residential buildings, had a long pedigree going back to late Republican Italy. This dual function had been taken up in the Western provinces from the first century on, with some villas emphasising the functions related to the generation of agricultural surplus for profit and showing relatively little investment in status display, whereas others demonstrated a greater predilection for the trappings of wealth such as mosaics (cf. Woolf 1998: Ch. 6, for Gaul; Gorges 1979 and Arce *et al.* 2007, for Iberia; cf. Sfameni 2006, for the situation in Italy). By the fourth century, the rural residence or villa as a *locus* for the display of power and wealth had become a major investment among the aristocracies of certain regions of the West. These were above all south-western Gaul; north-eastern, north-central and south-eastern Iberia; and southern Britain, with other regions participating less intensively. This is one of the clearest examples of the importance of regional variation and how this must structure discussion, rather than implying uniformity or at least a 'norm' which regions lived up to better or worse. Different regions did things differently for reasons inherent to those regions. In the scale, layout and décor of their villas, the regions under consideration here followed imperial exemplars and participated in the wider senatorial and provincial elite culture of the Late Empire. It does, though, need to be said at the outset that we remain much better informed about the residences themselves and their functions than we do about the concomitant agrarian structures, the crops and herds, and how the agrarian economy functioned and was articulated; these matters will be approached in the next chapter (p. XXX). Here we shall look at the layout, plan, décor and movable trappings of the late villa, before considering what their overall distribution signifies. In order to ground the analyses and discussion in reality, the plans of four villas will be considered: Carranque, Montréal-Séviac, Montmaurin(-Lasalles) and São Cucufate, the first and last in Spain, the other two in south-western Gaul, Novempopulana. Each of the four is a much-quoted example and each emphasises different aspects of the complex of possible plan elements.

Carranque

The Carranque villa (Figure 5.9) in central Spain (Fernández-Galiano Ruiz *et al.* 2001) was of very simple plan, a central court surrounded by four ranges of rooms opening onto colonnades around the court. It was entered

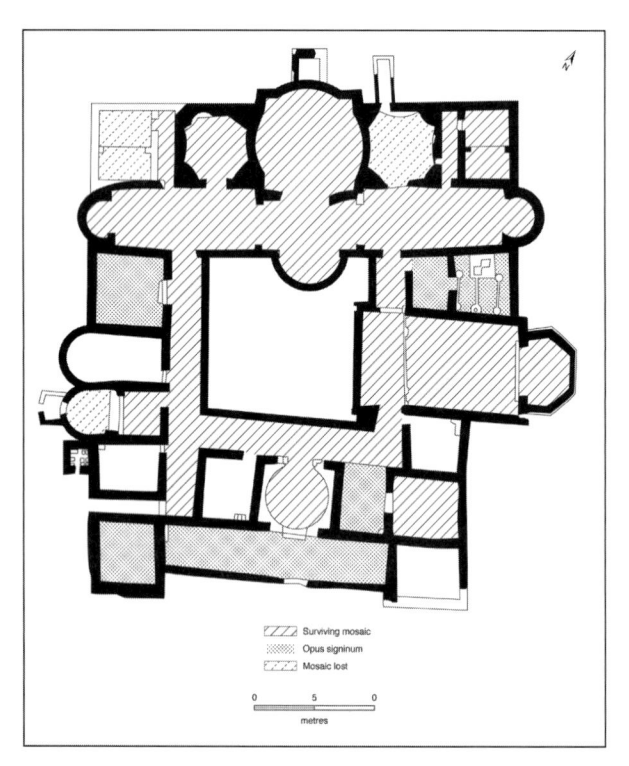

Fig. 5.9 Carranque, the residence

by a doorway in the centre of an entrance façade which led into a rectangular lobby with a circular mosaic. The lobby gave onto the central, colonnaded court of the villa, with at the other end of the court the main suite of reception rooms. On the right, taking up much of the range and with a foreroom projecting into the central court, was a large, rectangular room with a polygonal apse, resembling in plan, but on a much smaller scale, an imperial audience hall as at Trier or La Cercadilla; formal audience by the *dominus* was presumably the function of this room also, which was paved with a mosaic showing the death of Adonis. The reception range consisted of a long corridor or room with apses at each end, forming the third side of the courtyard. In the centre this opened into a large room of square plan, but with the walls consisting of segments of circles rather than being straight, with small niches at the corners; the floor was a mosaic showing the story of Achilles and Briseis. To either side of this were two rooms whose walls were also segments of circles, forming a series of convex walls. These rooms were heated by a hypocaust system. Opposite the door to the central room and projecting into the courtyard was an apsidal structure floored with a mosaic depicting the god Oceanus and with inlet and outflow for water so that the god should be in his element; clearly, this was to terminate the view out from the central room, which was a dining suite. The fourth, south-west range contained two rooms with apses, one heated. The only room other than the main reception rooms whose function can be identified lay in the southern corner between the entrance and the reception hall; a mosaic tells us it was a *cubiculum* (bedroom) and that the owner was called Maternus. It is this that has excited the speculation (Bowes 2005) that the villa with its associated mausoleum complex was built by the Spaniard Maternus Cynegius, praetorian prefect to the emperor Theodosius I, and a noted hammer of the traditional religions (cf. Chapter 4, p. 184); the theory, though attractive, remains unproven. The mosaics paving the villa were among the best in late Roman Spain, but largely in the traditional non-Christian iconography, which has been held to be an obstacle to the villa being that of the pious Christian Maternus, but, as we shall see below, such hard-and-fast cultural oppositions between traditional and Christian owe more to modern preconceptions than to ancient attitudes. The main residence was in fact quite small – the sides of the court measured only some 12 m – but in the sophistication of its architecture, the quality of its mosaics and the use of marbles, it is clear that it was something of a jewel casket. The villa (more specifically the funerary complex discussed in Chapter 4) also boasts a remarkable suite of coloured marbles sourced from across the Mediterranean basin, among them a number from Egypt including

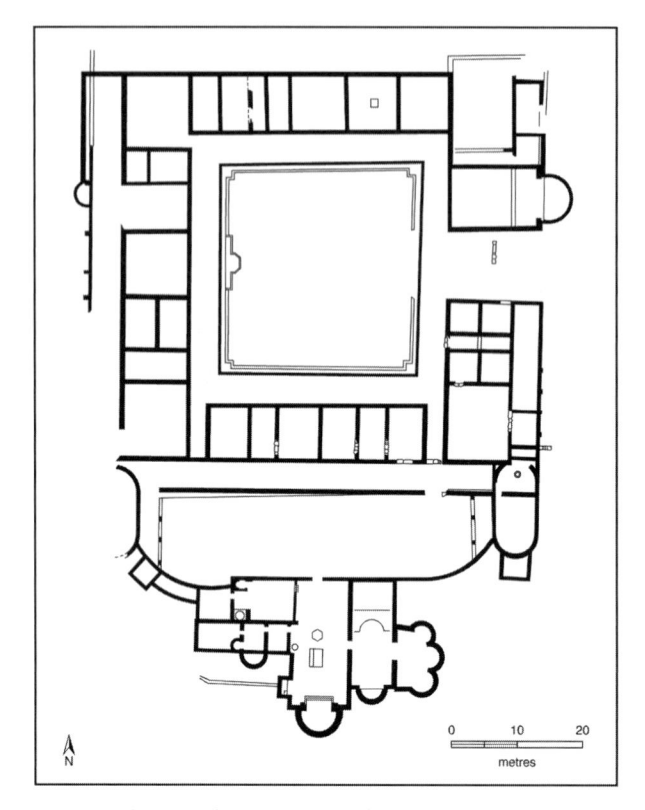

Fig. 5.10 (Montréal-)Séviac, plan of the villa

porphyries along with Aswan granite (García-Entero and Vidal Álvarez 2008). Between the residence and the funerary complex was another structure interpreted as a *nymphaeum*.

Montréal-Séviac

The villa at Montréal-Séviac (Gers) (Figure 5.10) in south-west France, usually referred to as Séviac *tout court*, was similar to that at Carranque in being focused on a central courtyard, here surrounded by a colonnade of columns of Pyrenean marble (Lapart and Petit 1993: 266–83). Though the principal entrance lay in the centre of the eastern range, there was no major room on axis with it, though there was a 'water feature'. Instead, in the north-eastern corner was a major, apsidal reception room of two phases; in the first the reception room lay east–west, and in the second it was enlarged and lay north-south, its plan, like the one at Carranque, recalling the imperial audience halls. The functions of the other rooms, many of them along with the colonnade walks floored in polychrome mosaic, are difficult to identify. But the remarkable feature of the complex is the bath suite (Monturet and Rivière 1986). This lay in an independent building to the south of the main villa, connected to the south range by curving colonnades. Initially built to a very simple plan, during the fourth century it was progressively elaborated until it attained grandiose proportions and a very elaborate plan necessitating vaults and semidomes, with lavish use of marble and mosaic to decorate the interiors. The water supply was most probably brought from a spring to the west of the villa. Through its financial and architectural extravagance, this is clear testimony to the importance of baths as an integral part of the aristocratic way of life, the reciprocal of the decline of major, urban public baths discussed in Chapter 3; for the aristocrat, bathing with friends and guests was part of the daily round of the leisured life, *otium*, and an important locus for social interaction. Séviac was far from the only site in south-western Gaul with elaborate baths; sites such as Castelculier (Lot-et-Garonne) or Saint-Sever, Augreilh (Landes) also have elaborate thermal suites at a remove from the principal buildings. Other baths integrated into the principal residence also show architectural ambition (Balmelle 2001: 178–201). Similar ambition can be demonstrated in some of the larger villas of the Iberian peninsula such as Milreu (Algarve) or La Olmeda (Palencia), or the only slightly less elaborate Torre Águila (Badajoz) or Torre de Cardeira (Beja), all of which were new constructions of the later Roman period rather than remodellings of existing baths, though the evidence for the maintenance and reordering of existing baths also attests to the importance of bathing (García-Entero 2005: *passim*, 2006). As with the Gallic examples, the Iberian ones demonstrated luxury in their appointments such as mosaic floors or marble sheathing, to say nothing of the resources expended to ensure a water supply in such semi-arid conditions, both for bathhouses and, as we shall see next, for fountains.

Montmaurin

Not far to the south-east of Séviac lay the villa of Montmaurin(-Lassalles) (Haute-Garonne) (Figure 5.11); thanks to its excavation and publication by Georges Fouet (1969), this is a classic site for the study of the late Roman aristocratic residence. The complex was arranged around an enfilade of three courts of decreasing size. The first was the entrance court, a semi-circular, colonnaded space (with a water shrine or *nymphaeum*), essentially a scaled-down version of the main courtyard of the La Cercadilla complex. This led to the entrance vestibule and thus through to the middle court,

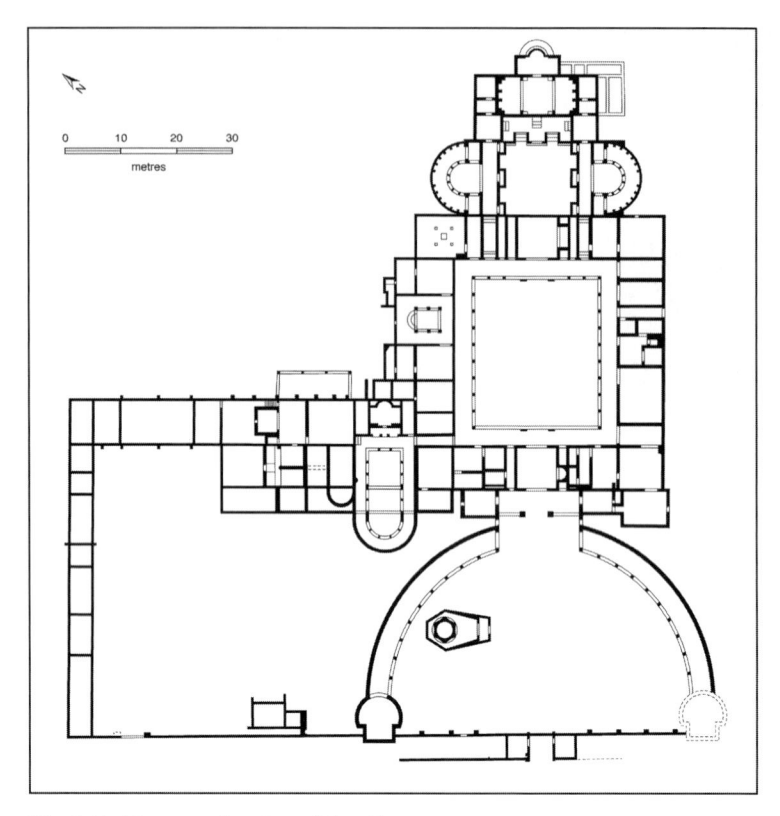

Fig. 5.11 Montmaurin, plan of the villa

round which were ranged a number of rooms, including at least one, on the western side, with an internal setting of columns and open to the sky. The innermost court was the smallest and the most complex. It was possible to pass directly into the court, in the centre of which was a fountain. But the main access ways were to the north-western and south-eastern sides of the court, up flights of steps. These two sides consisted essentially of large, open, colonnaded *exedrae*, so the court would be surrounded by a play of lit and shaded spaces. Further steps led up to the main reception room at the end of the main axis of the villa. The management of space, levels and light in the experience of the visitor is sophisticated and subtle. The axiality of the complex is very evident, the whole logic being of control of access and increasing emphasis on the majesty of the *dominus*. Some persons presumably did not penetrate far beyond the entrance way. Those granted admission to the presence in the inner court would find themselves directed along an axis of increasing intimacy and luxury, finally ascending to the most privileged suite of rooms. In addition to the main, formal enfilade, there was

Fig. 5.12 Montmaurin, colonnaded internal court

another area of the villa. On entering through the vestibule, a visitor turning left could pass through a doorway into another suite of rooms arranged round a small, colonnaded court with exedra (Figure 5.12). Looking down the axis of this court was a relatively small, apsidal, marble-sheathed room (marble was generally more evident than mosaic at this site), perhaps a more private reception room. This suite of rooms also adjoined the baths, access to which may therefore have been restricted to the most favoured, and the baths would also transmit warmth to the suite during the winter. As at Séviac, the control of water was central to the experience, with the fountain in the centre of the inner court and the supply of quantities of water to the baths.

São Cucufate

The villa of São Cucufate (Beja) (Figure 5.13) in Portugal differed from the previous examples in that its spatial arrangement was linear rather than centred on courts, but it shared with Montmaurin, though to a much greater degree, an exploitation of changing levels as a defining device of its articulation (Alarcão *et al.* 1990). The mid-fourth-century rebuild of the villa sought to exploit the rolling character of the site in order to dominate the countryside rather than to adapt to it. The main, entrance façade faced

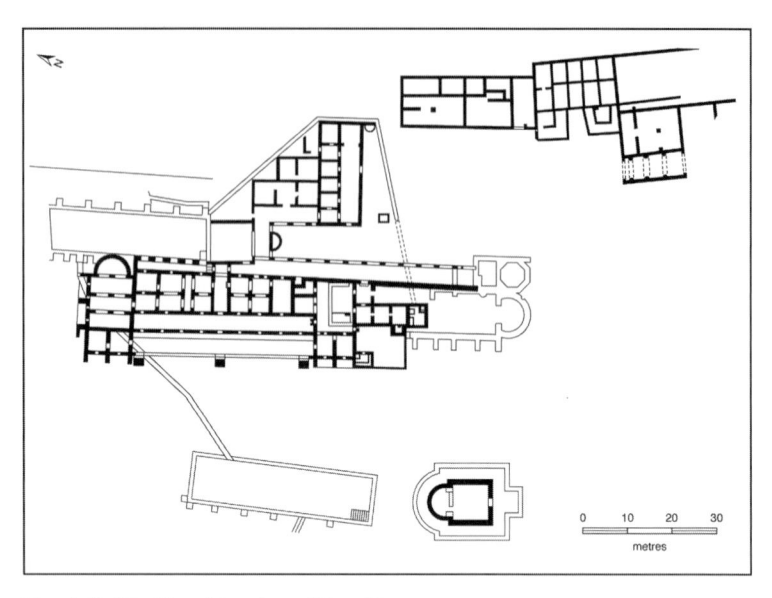

Fig. 5.13 São Cucufate, plan of the villa

south-west and was approached upslope and up flights of steps in a monumentalised version of the 'winged-corridor' façade common in Gaul, Germany and Britain. The central approach led to a passageway through to the eastern side of the complex and the domestic ranges. The most striking surviving feature of the site is the pair of tall arches which announced the presence of an apsidal aula supported by substructures, one of the most grandiose reception rooms of this type anywhere in the West. Immediately east of the apse of the aula and of the north-western half of the main range was a large, rectangular basin for water. In part functional, its waters could be directed to the bath suite and latrines in the south-eastern part of the main range. It was also a demonstration of the control of the dominus over the aridity of the setting, and its reflections would have patterned the eastern façade of the villa. Another, slightly larger, basin lay at the lower level below the entrance façade, with, to its east, a temple consisting of an apsed, rectangular cella surrounded by an ambulatory, all on a low podium. This was quite possibly a *nymphaeum* and one of a regional group of architecturally similar structures known from other villas in the south-western part of Iberia, like the one at Milreu which had mosaics of fish on its podium wall, a piped water supply and evidence for glass mosaic on its vaults. A very similar structure has been excavated at Quinta de Marim, Olhão (Faro), again with evidence for coloured marbles and mosaic (Graen 2005). Attached to the eastern side of this last structure was a square mausoleum, which has led the excavators to propose that the apsidal structure was also a mausoleum, citing mausolea of similar plan known from the villa in west-central Iberia at Los Castillejos (Badajoz) and from the Via Ostiensis, Rome (Graen 2005: 265–8), though it must be noted that there were no burials recovered from the apsidal structure itself. The Milreu example was later to house burials, when it seems to have been converted into a Christian place of cult, with evidence for a baptistery inserted into the ambulatory, a small mausoleum in one angle of the ambulatory and other individual burials. At São Cucufate also, the *nymphaeum* was later to house burials, so it may have been converted into a chapel. As well as the trio of Milreu, Quinta de Marim and São Cucufate, there is the very similar structure from Los Castillejos already alluded to and the probable *nymphaeum* at Carranque, also with a piped water supply and rich decoration.

These four sites exemplify many of the recurrent features of the layout and articulation of aristocratic residences in the later Roman period, urban as much as rural, and which we can now consider more generally as regards both forms and functions. Their overall plan most often combines centrality in the form of arrangement round courts with axiality in the progress from entrance to what are generally identified as principal 'reception room(s)' (a convenient modern term, but one that can overinterpret rooms whose precise function[s] are unknown – see below, p. 237). These reception rooms were very important theatres for the display of the *dominus* to those he wished to impress or awe. One form of ceremonial and its context was that to do with the formal receiving of guests, be they of lower, equal or higher status. For this an appropriate setting would be the long, rectangular, apsidal reception rooms as at Carranque, Séviac and São Cucufate, clearly evocative of the great, imperial *aulae* such as the 'Basilika' at Trier or the axial hall at La Cercadilla. This is one of the clearest ways in which the architectural and ceremonial vocabulary of the imperial residences had been appropriated by lesser potentates and why a knowledge of the imperial residences is necessary to inform our understanding of villa architecture (cf. Gorges 2008; Mar and Verde 2008). Obviously, the role of the proprietor as *dominus* receiving his estate workers or clients, or as host receiving guests, particularly important ones, would impose very different dynamics on what happened, but, unfortunately, these are now unrecoverable through archaeology, though textual descriptions of imperial ceremonial and references to aristocratic codes of behaviour give us some impression of what may have happened.

As well as any ceremonial reception, the entertaining of valued guests to a formal meal was another established way for a host to exhibit his regard for his guests while at the same time displaying his wealth and taste to impress them and to enmesh them in the bonds of reciprocal obligation. A formal meal was one of the main theatres for structured social interaction, then as now often covertly or overtly agonistic, with the physical setting, the furnishings, the reception, service and servants, the quality of the food and drink, and the conversation all serving as an index of the host's status, education and accomplishments (cf. Dunbabin 2003: esp. Ch. 5). Each of these as manifested in the archaeology is worth considering individually and as a component of the whole experience. The physical setting, the room and its decoration and furnishings were of the greatest importance in framing the experience for the diners. Rooms for formal dining took distinctive architectural forms. In the earlier Roman house, this room was the *triclinium*, so called after the rectilinear three-couch settings on which host and guests reclined. In the later empire the couches were often arranged in a semicircular setting, the *stibadium*, around a D-shaped *sigma* table. This arrangement was naturally suited to being placed in a semicircular apse and helps explain the great frequency of apsidal rooms in later Roman residences. A development of this was the adoption of the triconch room, a square or rectangular chamber with apses opening off three of the sides, thus permitting a greater number of diners. These dining chambers commonly were floored in mosaic or, for the very wealthy, in marble *opus sectile*, the places for the couches sometimes being marked by reserved plain panels. The main parts of a mosaic were often elaborately figured, especially with mythological scenes, as a display of both wealth and taste, and possibly the occasion for the formal cultural display of the rhetorical *ekphrasis* (see below). The walls would have been sheathed in marble or, more commonly, richly painted and maybe hung with fine stuffs, as appears in some late antique manuscripts (e.g. Weitzmann 1977: Pl. XIII). There is evidence for painted ceilings; in the richest residences, perhaps ceiling mosaic, especially on the semidome over the apse. There may have been statuary in niches or paintings and other works of art, and some literary mentions of the *abacus* suggest it may have been a piece of furniture for the display of valuable items such as plate. The view outwards from the room could be enhanced by the placing of an architectural or other feature to enhance the perspective by exhibiting the 'nature tamed' of the peristyle garden along with the host's mastery over water expressed in any fountain or pool. More elaborate were instances, as at Carranque or the urban 'Casa de los Mármoles' at Mérida, where a fountain and 'water feature' were placed immediately across the courtyard peristyle from the opening into the room. More elaborate still was the bringing into the room of the water at the southern Spanish villa of El

Ruedo (Córdoba); in the rear wall of the rectangular dining chamber was a feature (a *nymphaeum*?) from which water was piped to a small fountain in the centre of the *stibadium* setting and thence out of the room and into the ornamental basin in the middle of the interior court of the villa (Vaquerizo and Noguera 1997). It has also been demonstrated how different the ambience would be from that of modern rooms because of the necessity of using artificial light, given that the main meal would have started in the late afternoon (Ellis 2007). Lamps, even multiple lamps, would have cast relatively little light, but, on the other hand, this could be used to enhance the theatrical effect by their acting rather as spotlights on the area occupied by the diners and the meal, with the bulk of the room beyond in relative obscurity. The candelabra themselves could also be elaborate display objects, like the silver example from the Kaiseraugst treasure (Guiggisberg and Kaufmann-Heinemann 2003). So, overall, the dining chamber was designed as a highly artificial environment where the host's ability to create a setting far removed from normal daily experience took the guests into a world apart.

As well as rooms clearly intended for dining, such as triconch rooms, the apses of *aula*-style reception rooms could, with a change of furniture, have been used for a *stibadium*. One may note that the most elaborate villas, such as Piazza Armerina in Sicily (Wilson 1983), had both an apsidal hall and a triconch dining chamber, in this case opening off separate courts with the hall in a more 'public' part of the villa. The impulse towards poly-apsidal rooms generated by *stibadium* dining came, by the early fifth century, to result in a specific and rare architectural form, the 'grand dining hall' (Ellis 1994), consisting of a long, rectangular room with two or three paired apses opening off each of the long sides and another apse on the short end opposite the doorway (the *locus classicus* for this form was to be the Hall of the Nineteen Couches in the imperial palace at Constantinople). There is one possible candidate for such a room in the Western provinces, in south-west Gaul at Saint-Rustice (Gironde), where there was a long, narrow room with seven apses; however, it is argued (Balmelle 2001: 196) that both the main vessel and the apses were too narrow for this function and that the subjects of the floor mosaics were of types more usually in this region found in bathhouses (and there is evidence that adjoining rooms may have been heated). How these long rooms were lit normally, particularly those of the *aula* type, remains unclear, but, evidently, the interior impression and expectations of the use of such a room could be radically altered not just by a change of furniture but also by the change from a day-lit reception room to a lamp-lit dining room. What is clear is that the wealthiest villas in the West were built by owners well aware of the current of fashion in layout, room plans and decoration both at imperial residences and at those of the senatorial aristocracy. In addition, the spaces within which such social formalities were played out were not the only way in which the *dominus* proclaimed his wealth and taste; there were other classes of material, often less visible to us now but whose importance at the time would have been considerable.

A measure of the host's wealth and taste would be the reception of the visitors and the attention paid them during the meal by the servants. Clearly, the archaeological evidence for these attentions is limited; nevertheless, they are portrayed in mosaic, wall painting and book illuminations (Dunbabin 2003: Ch. 5, Pls. IX, X, XIII and XVI). The quantity of servants was an increasingly important index of status by the Late Empire. So also was their personal appearance, the most important having elaborately dressed hair, as in the 'Banquet of Dido' in the *Vergilius Romanus* (Dunbabin 2003: Pl. XVI), where the long 'pageboy' haircut of the serving boys is strongly reminiscent of that of the youths on Welschbillig herms (cf. p. 55) or that of the soldiers in attendance upon the emperors on the Missorium of Theodosius (cf. p. 232). Their clothing also could manifest their owner's/master's wealth, particularly through the addition of decorated panels (*orbiculi*) to the tunic. As well as serving the guests at (and possibly after) the dinner, the servants also received them at the start and proffered bowls of water and towels for them to wash their hands before eating.

The archaeological evidence for the food and drink consumed at these occasions is generally rather indirect (cf. Cool 2006). For food, the evidence consists partly of animal bone, where the types and ages of the animals and the butchery marks can tell us something of the meat and fish component of such banquets (meat itself being a sign of extravagance), though since these are usually found in rubbish pits or middens, one cannot be sure what was higher- and what was lower-status consumption and what represented an individual meal (for an analysis of such evidence from the Portuguese villa of Quinta das Longas [Elvas], see Almeida and Carvalho 2005). In addition, there is also the evidence for vegetables and herbs and spices. The latter are important for giving some idea of the range of tastes and flavourings imparted to the food and of the ability of the host to command their availability and his (or his chef's) awareness of current trends. Amphorae can signal condiments such as fish sauce (*garum*). More useful perhaps are representations of food in media such as mosaic and wall painting (Dunbabin 2003: Chs. 5 and 6), which give an impression of how elements such as *hors d'œuvres* or fish were presented, though saying little about either the precise preparation or whether they were served in courses. Amphorae also give evidence of the sources of wine, an indispensable component of a formal meal and also an index, by its source, vintage and rarity, of expenditure by the host. The servants who offered the wine were among the most accomplished of those who waited at table, and the vessels from which and into which they poured were often of considerable luxury, as not only depictions but also actual examples of jugs and cups from late Roman treasures make clear (e.g. Mango 1994). Dunbabin (2003: 162) makes the important point that, compared with hoards of silverware of the Early Empire, those of the Late contain relatively few drinking vessels and much more emphasis is placed on plate, suggesting that the display and presentation of food, or simply the display of large and elaborate plate (see below) had become more important than the service of drink and its accompanying rituals.

During and after the meal, there might be entertainment; some representations of Roman meals include musicians, usually in small numbers, playing quiet and soothing instruments such as the double flute. Other more elaborate entertainments involving more musicians, declamations or tumblers may be supposed but are harder to verify. An important 'entertainment' would be the conversation. This would be the arena for news, political discussions, gossip, and the doings of friends and enemies. It might also take the more structured form of an *ekphrasis* with the host showing off his education and knowledge of the classics by a virtuoso exposition on a mythological or other scene depicted, for instance, on a mosaic, a painting or a piece of elaborately decorated plate (see below for further consideration). This would help explain the importance of such scenes in the fixtures and fittings of the dining chamber and may also help explain why sometimes they are not easy for us to comprehend fully; they were there to impress by their recondite erudition and their 'take' on familiar stories. Clearly, the types of conversation permissible would be influenced by the company – in particular, by whether or not women were present. Representations of late antique dining (Dunbabin 2003: 178–80) are dominated by the menfolk, but some women do appear, sometimes reclining on the *stibadium*, sometimes sitting separately in a chair. So we may surmise that such meals were predominantly all-male affairs, but that women were not excluded. Sidonius Apollinaris, in a letter about his villa at Avitacum in the Auvergne of central Gaul in the mid fifth century, speaks (*Epistulae* II.ii.9) of '*matronale triclinium*', 'the women's dining chamber', raising the interesting possibility of gendered dining. Some elaborate villas do have more than one room that would do service for dining; another possibility, as well as gendered space, is that of seasonal use, especially if one of the chambers were equipped with a hypocaust.

In sum, one must echo the words of Katherine Dunbabin that such late antique banquets were 'a highly codified ceremony, leaving little room for relaxation or diversion' (Dunbabin 2003: 174). Because it was a ceremony, a sequence of events with a prescribed, ritual quality, and because it was codified, the actors knew their places and they knew the rules of the set piece. Within these rules, the host could try to introduce the unique touches that marked him out as a man of power and discernment. The importance of this to the archaeologist is that it provides the frameworks within which the material culture was generated and which allow us to comprehend it within a field of understanding. The depictions and to an extent the tests allow us to see why the archaeology is the way it is.

Furnishings and fittings

This section of the chapter will concern itself with the evidence for other elements of the decoration of late antique aristocratic houses in the West, both in the dining chamber and elsewhere, particularly in areas accessible to visitors and guests, where they might do the good work of communicating the owner's power, connections, wealth and taste.

The nineteenth-century excavations at Chiragan (Haute-Garonne) to the south-west of Toulouse, and not far from Montmaurin, revealed a truly enormous, early imperial villa, still in occupation in the fourth century, with existing buildings modified and additional ones constructed to the new tastes (Figure 5.14), and forming a complex more vast than any of those described above (Cazes 1999: esp. 77–8). In 1826–30, a large pit was excavated in what was later shown to be the north-western part of a probable garden lying between the main residential court and the river; this pit contained huge quantities of broken-up marble sculpture (Cazes 1999: 74–149). Some of this was architectural and attested to the quality of elements such as columns, pilasters and door frames. But the most impressive pieces were from a series of high-relief carvings of the Labours of Hercules, all, bar one, 1.44 m high by 0.88 m wide; where they were originally placed in the villa is unknown, but presumably they lined the walls of a large room or possibly a colonnade or portico. Analysis of these marbles, both of details of the carving techniques and of the stylistic traits (Bergmann 1999; Stirling 2005), has shown that their sculptors had strong links with the long-standing and prestigious school of marble sculpture at Aphrodisias in western Asia Minor, and that these are among the later products of the school. The date of these pieces is debated, with some workers assigning them to the second century and others preferring a later date. In a way this does not

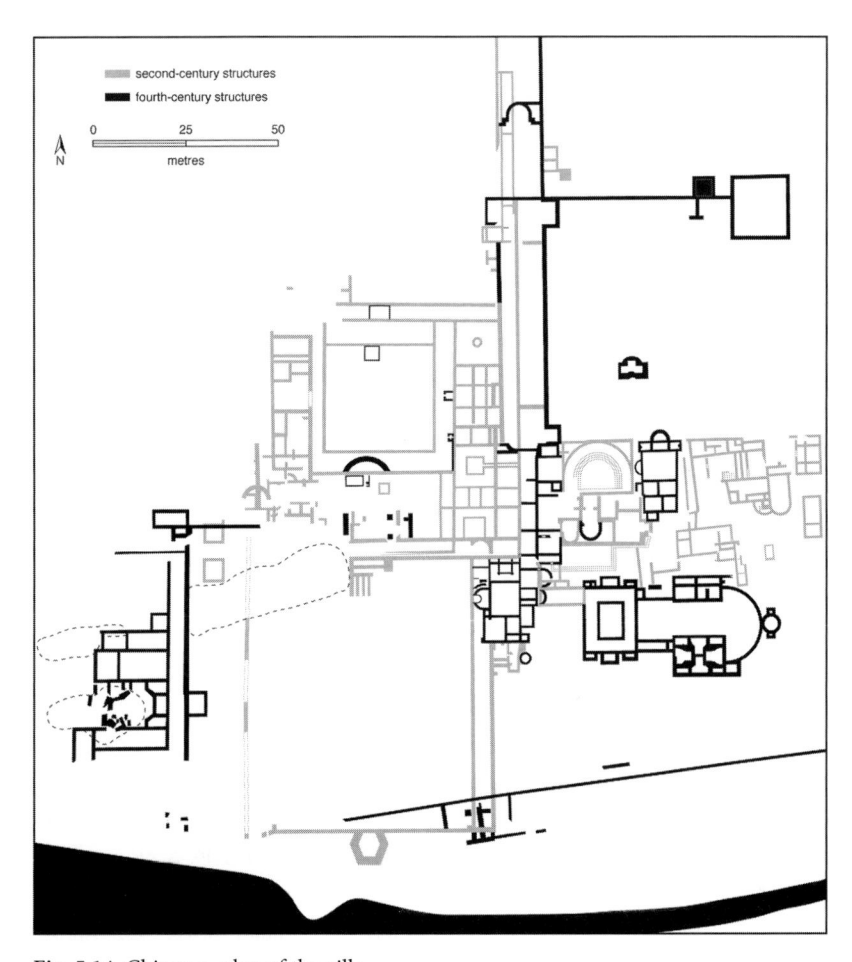

Fig. 5.14 Chiragan, plan of the villa

affect the argument, since it looks as though the pieces were (re-)used in the fourth-century villa. What we know of the stratigraphy of the pits and other features in which they were deposited suggests that this took place at the end of the life of the villa (Stirling 2005: 49–62); thus, even if they were carved in the second century, they were displayed in the late villa and, as we shall see below, the appropriation of earlier sculptures for reuse in the late antique period was an accepted phenomenon. The same sculptors seem also to have been responsible for a series of busts of deities in *tondi* and of Dionysiac creatures along with other single pieces. This is a remarkable testament both to the reach of the Aphrodisias tradition and to the wealth and contacts of the owner of Chiragan. Bergmann (1999: Chs. 5 and 6) suggests that these contacts were mediated through Constantinople, where patrons would find sculptors of the western Asia Minor schools engaged in embellishing the growing capital, though Stirling (2005: 129–30) suggests there may have been sculptors of this school in Rome. Bergmann also suggests (1999: Ch. 1) that other products of the same workshops can be identified from the villas of Saint-Georges-de-Montagne (Gironde) and Valdetorres del Jarama (Madrid) in central Iberia. In addition, Chiragan has yielded a remarkable series of portrait heads of emperors from Augustus and his family through to the end of the third century (with one empress of the House of Theodosius). Were they arranged, as they now are in the Musée Saint-Raymond in Toulouse, in a single line, it would not only have been an impressive sight but it would also have been impressive testimony to the loyalty of the owners of Chiragan and the longevity of their descent. There is also debate as to whether these busts were the result of accretion over the generations or were a single purchase of an existing collection (Bergmann 2007). In fact, both methods of acquisition seem to have been current in the later Roman period in the West, with some sculpture, stylistically, clearly of the period, whereas some was earlier (sometimes recarved to suit the times) and acquired to decorate new-built residences.

So, by chance, we have preserved at Chiragan an example (albeit possibly a top-of-the-range example, since nothing like it survives elsewhere in the Roman Empire) of the quantity of sculpture, architectural and figural, disposed around a grand villa. At one level, literally, this was another register of decoration and one much more at eye level than floor mosaics. But at another level, as will be discussed below, the choice of subjects and the ways in which they were rendered and combined was an expression of the owners' education and culture, one which would be appreciated in particular by the more highly educated and cultured, and therefore probably more important, visitor to the residence. Chiragan must stand as testament to what has disappeared elsewhere. In fact it is not difficult to find plentiful evidence from other villas in south-western Gaul (Balmelle 2001: 228–37). The corpus of evidence for Spain is also growing. In particular there is also the recent discovery of fragments from an ambitious series of sculptures in the architecturally elaborate villa at Quinta das Longas in southern Portugal (Nogales Basarrate *et al.* 2004; Nogales Basarrate and Gonçalves 2004), including divinities and individual elements that suggest a series of mythological characters and cycles. These are all in a high-quality, white marble, whose treatment shows clear links to the Aphrodisias sculptural style. Such links have also been noted for the elements from the villa mentioned above at Valdetorres del Jarama. There is also the evidence for sculptural pieces and programmes gathered in the recent recension of the significant amount of evidence from the villas around Tarragona (Koppel and Rodà 2008). Britain also follows this trend, above all at Woodchester (Gloucestershire) (Lysons 1797), whose large villa seems to have had a sculpture gallery which included several pieces in marble.

Stone architectural elements and sculpture were not the only form of embellishment of wall surfaces; indeed, they were probably at the upper end of the price and quality range. Much more common would have been wall painting, but examples of fourth-century wall painting from domestic contexts are not common for both Gaul and the Iberian peninsula (Abad Casal 1982; Barbet 2008: Ch. 7). A large number of the paintings that do survive betray the desirability of marble facings and *opus sectile* by their attempts to reproduce them in the cheaper medium of fresco painting (e.g. Barbet 2008: Fig. 417). Walls divided horizontally into three registers – dado, main panels and cornice – seem to have remained popular, often with no figured decoration but with swags and garlands, again sometimes echoing originals in stone or marble. Sometimes the principal register was embellished with figured scenes, mythological or other, or with genre landscape or aquatic scenes. Even if we can draw no very general conclusions about trends or preferences, it is important to remember the wall decorations would have been more visually immediate to observers at the time than what was under their feet. So the figured scenes, the mythological ones in particular, must be treated seriously, as they would have formed part of the repertoire of allusive decoration that could be deployed by a patron who wished to demonstrate education. It should also be remembered that there may also have been decoration, sometimes taking human form, in stucco, for which there is evidence from a small number of villas in Spain (Chavarría Arnau 2007: 108) and the probably rather later (late fifth-/early sixth-century) composition of painted stucco figures from the villa of Vouneuil-sous-Biard (Vienne) in south-western Gaul (Sapin 2009), which seem to have been of Christian saints and other symbols. Of course, if the survival of wall paintings is rare, that of paintings, in the sense of scenes or portraits painted on board or some other medium and hung on the wall (and such objects were the focus of Philostratus's demonstrations of *ekphrasis* considered below), is zero. Yet these could be objects of considerable value, particularly those by famous painters.

Furniture also is a very difficult element of the appointments of an aristocratic house for us to appreciate now, largely because the great majority of it was in perishable materials (cf. Croom 2007). Some display pieces were in stone, such as the marble and stone *sigma* tables, of which fragments have been recovered, or stone tabletops or legs. Finds of elements of wooden furniture, or furnishings such as doors, are exceedingly rare, though note the fragment of an oak cupboard door inlaid with bone from a mid-fourth-century well fill at Hayton (E. Yorkshire) in Britain (Hartley *et al.* 2006:

176–7). Otherwise, the best source of information is illustrations, sometimes wall paintings, but also, perhaps more usefully, the manuscript illustrations which begin to become available at this period, albeit most probably produced outside the Western provinces (cf. Weitzmann 1977). For instance, we may point to the banquet scene from the *Vergilius Romanus* (fol. 100v.), probably illuminated in Rome in the fifth century, showing Dido, Aeneas and another figure reclining on a *stibadium* with a foldaway circular table in front of them. The clothing, *stibadium* cover and hangings behind the figures all give the impression of rich fabrics and colours.

Moving to the more portable objects with which an aristocrat would seek to furnish his residence, we may look first at items of plate, of which there is a considerable quantity from the Western provinces. The best-known late Roman object from the Iberian peninsula is the so-called Missorium of Theodosius (Figure 5.15), found in 1847 near Mérida, folded in half in antiquity but not seriously damaged (Blázquez Martinez and Rovira 2000; cf. Leader-Newby 2004: 11–14). It is a silver dish, 74 cm in diameter and weighing 15.35 kg, with a low-relief image of the emperor Theodosius and

Fig. 5.15 The Missorium of Theodosius

his colleagues Valentinian II and Arcadius seated facing the viewer, framed beneath an arcaded pediment and accompanied by German members (identifiable by their hairstyle and torcs as in the Welschbillig herms) of the imperial bodyguard. Beneath the ground line lies a personification, probably of Tellus, the goddess of the earth. Kneeling before and to the (viewer's) left of Theodosius is the figure of an official with his hands wrapped in the folds of his *chlamys* to receive a codicil (document) of appointment from the hand of the senior emperor himself (the official, incidentally, wears a crossbow brooch of the form encountered in Chapter 2). Around the upper part of the field is an inscription linking the dish to the commemoration of Theodosius's *decennalia* (tenth anniversary). It is a member of a class of vessel known as a *largitio* dish, issued as gifts to officials and officers to mark an important imperial event (Kent and Painter 1977; Leader-Newby 2004: Ch. 1; Reece 1999: Ch. 6). This was clearly a display piece, designed to be exhibited where it would impress the viewer with its size and opulence and with the owner's links to the supreme power.

The Missorium of Theodosius is a spectacular example of the large class of silver objects, plate and other material, which must once have been plentiful and of which a sample has survived in hoards such as Corbridge or Mildenhall in Britain; Kaiseraugst on the upper Rhine (Cahn and Kaufmann-Heinemann 1984; Guggisberg and Kaufmann-Heinemann 2003); the Sevso treasure from, probably, the Balkans (Mango 1994); and the Esquiline from Rome (Shelton 1981). It is clear that many of these vessels had not been used, or had been used with extreme care. This particularly applies to the large and elaborate dishes, some of which, such as the large dish from Kaiseraugst, bear cut marks, but many of them bear no trace of use (cf. Hobbs 2010). It is possible that some of the bowls and flagons had been in more regular use, since liquids would leave little trace. Nevertheless, it is still the case that these objects were display pieces designed to be seen and to impress. Where they were displayed is uncertain, but given that most of them are in forms to do with eating and drinking, it is reasonable to think they may have been exhibited in dining rooms, perhaps in cabinets of the type referred to in literary sources as an *abacus* (presumably from the generic resemblance of the frame of the item and its shelves to the reckoning abacus), or on tables as centrepieces or, in some cases, for use. Some pieces, such as those from Corbridge, Mildenhall and Kaiseraugst, bear mythological scenes, whose purpose, as with those on mosaic, will be discussed below. The exact status and significance of such plate has recently been the subject of considerable debate, centring on the worth of the hoards of silver plate that have survived in relation to objects of gold and jewellery, which by and large have not (Cameron 1992; Painter 1993). It is argued that the material that signified wealth and power above all was gold, and that silver was a poor relation. That gold was the statement of wealth *par excellence* cannot be denied; one only has to think of the supposed donation of heavy gold vessels to the churches of Rome by Constantine I to see what an emperor meant by munificence. On a more humble scale, there are the gold objects such as crossbow brooches most probably presented at imperial anniversaries (e.g. Cüppers 1984: 112–14). Nevertheless, silver was a precious metal and if it had no use as a means of displaying wealth, then the objects in these hoards would not have been fashioned; that they were is sufficient testament to their perceived utility as markers of status.

Few other objects in costly materials survive from the Western provinces. Some fragments of ivory from Carranque hint at the presence of one of the other luxury productions of the Late Empire (Volbach 1976; cf. Cutler 1993), and ivory is present also at some ecclesiastical sites – for instance, Geneva – in the form of a *pyxis* or circular box. The evidence of complete ivory objects, especially the elaborately carved 'diptychs' announcing accession to the consulship and other top-rank events and circulated among the senatorial elite, testifies how opulent a material it was and thus how even fragments and small objects had a worth far in excess of what might seem the case at first sight.

More widespread, but again fragmentary, is the evidence of glass, particularly of the luxury end of the range. Plain glass vessels had become very common under the later empire, but a limited number of vessels show a technical sophistication that must have made them very expensive; others were evidently designed to be eye-catching. The most famous type, because of the craftsmanship required to execute them, was the *vasa diatreta* or cage cup, in which the body of the cup, in colourless glass, supported an outer 'cage' of decoration linked to the main vessel by a series of struts (Harden 1987: 238–49). The 'cage' could be entirely or partly in coloured glass, sometimes incorporating good wishes. It should be remembered that the colour effects of such vessels would also change if they were filled with a coloured liquid such as red wine. The fact that these glssses have no foot ring or base must have made them even more impractical, unless supported in some form of stand. Less costly, but still designed to be striking were those types of vessel involving different-coloured glass, complex forms and incised decoration (Harden 1987: Groups G and H). A number of cage cups survive intact because they were deposited in graves, particularly around Cologne and Trier, but fragments of others have been identified by their cage work in south-western Gaul (Hochuli-Gysel 1996). Such vessels must have been prized as much as a conspicuous display of wealth as for their ability to hold liquids.

Much more difficult to assess is the nature and place of objects in perishable materials such as textiles. Mention has already been made above of manuscript illustrations, such as the *Vergilius Romanus* banqueting scene, in which there is a variety of textiles being used as covers and hangings in a range of colours. Many late antique wall paintings of figures show them set in front of hangings or curtains, be they paintings from domestic or funerary contexts, or from those so often divided off as 'Christian'. One may also mention the evidence from Egypt for floor coverings and rugs (e.g. Swift 2009: Pl. I). Rich stuffs and hangings may well, therefore, have been a much more prominent (and expensive) element of décor than we can now easily conceive, much as we are increasingly appreciating the high value of tapestry in the late medieval and Renaissance worlds. In the form of clothing, textiles are well known from mosaics and painted scenes, such as the wall paintings at the oratory at Lullingstone (Kent, Britain) and the cupola mosaics at Centelles and the Bispo Caçador house in Barcelona, which give us some idea of the apparel of the well-to-do. Little actual textile survives from the West, though the range of material preserved from Egypt (e.g. Lorquin 1999) gives some idea of the range of shapes, techniques and colours available there, and the pictorial representations suggest they were available also to the weavers of the West. Important also would have been matters such as the precise textiles and colours, use of which was sometimes limited to particular wearers (such as purple for the emperor), with gradations of clothing reflecting social grades, as, for instance, in the use of gold and jewellery (cf. Janes 1998: Ch. 2). What does survive better in the West is the range of metal fastenings such as brooches and belts, particularly those discussed in Chapter 2 (p. 59) as symbols of office and status in the army and bureaucracy. Clothing was, of course, strongly gendered, with female dress and jewellery another way in which the male aristocrat could display the opulence of his household through the elaboration of the material and colours of the clothes with which his womenfolk were dressed and shod, the quantity, richness and polychromy of their jewellery, and the elaboration of their hairstyles (cf. Swift 2009: Ch. 4). But there was more to it simply than vulgar display, since the clothing of an aristocratic woman should portray her respectable moral character and thus throw added lustre on the husband of such a virtuous wife (Harlow 2004). Again, as with textiles, the best evidence for jewellery and other adornment comes from Egypt rather than the Western provinces, but the dress, jewellery and hair of the Roman-period mummy portraits can stand as proxy for the great ladies and noble children of the late Roman West (cf. Walker and Bierbrier 1997).

Domus and *dominus*

It is time to draw together the strands of the evidence and arguments presented so far to discuss why the late Roman aristocratic *domus* (and/or *villa*) in the West took the form it did and what analysis of that form and its constituent parts can tell us about the ways in which these houses were used, particularly as regards what might be termed their 'public' roles; that is, their functions as the settings for the life of the *dominus*. The last twenty years or so have seen a great growth in interest in how to analyse house plans all across the Graeco-Roman Mediterranean (see Bowes 2010: Chs. 1 and 2 for a brief introduction and bibliography). These have focused very much on questions of household and house functions. The study of the household has sought to elucidate the social structure of housing, using both house plans and the evidence of texts to try to propose what households may have consisted of – nuclear families; extended families; free adult males, females and children; servants (free); and slaves (unfree) – how space was apportioned to them; and how we may try to recognise those spaces through such criteria as room positions, room plans, decoration, and fixtures and fittings. The house-functions approach overlaps with this but could be seen as a more 'political' analysis; that is, one concerned particularly with the 'public' duties and availability of the senior adult male – in Roman terms, the *paterfamilias* or the *dominus*. For late antiquity, much of this analysis has been predicated on the excavated plans of houses from the eastern parts of the empire, but the analyses and insights can be transferred to and complemented by the evidence from the West. In what follows the house-functions/'political' approach will predominate, a reflection largely of the nature of the available evidence, but also of the relatively smaller amount of enquiry that has been invested in the household analysis. It is also appropriate to add, following on from the logic of remarks on the functions of cities made in Chapter 3, that such houses were not just passive reflections of late antique society but were also active participants in the perpetuation of that society by imbuing those who came into contact with them, particularly perhaps the next generation, with the attitudes and values that the houses and what went on in them embodied. The overall sense of what aristocratic attitudes and behaviour consisted of, and of the social and cultural structures, values, and conduct proper to such attitudes and behaviour, was in part transmitted by the arenas in which they were played out in the late Roman *domus*.

Before commencing, some 'health warnings' need to be put in place. First of all, we are dealing essentially with house plans and a very restricted repertoire of furnishing and fittings, above all mosaics, through which to approach questions of room function. We are, of course, also only dealing with ground-floor plans; all manner of things may have gone on in any upper storeys that may be proposed (and for the West they very rarely are). Very often the plan is in fact a palimpsest of alterations (for trenchant comment on this, see Bowes 2010: Ch. 2) that were not recognised by early excavators, or, even if they have been recognised by later excavators, different phases were loaded onto the same plan, producing a potentially ahistorical ensemble. Moreover, the function of many rooms, often the majority, in any house is now unknowable, as the evidence that would have informed an ancient user of the function(s) of the room has long since gone. This leads on to an important final point, that it is increasingly clear that many rooms could serve more than one purpose, the modern functional divisions into 'living room', 'dining chamber' and 'bedroom', were not observed in antiquity; many rooms could be used for any or all of these or more, very often for entirely contingent reasons. Some rooms, of course, did tend to have more or less fixed functions for practical reasons – kitchens, latrines and baths are the obvious examples – but types of rooms of interest to us – and sometimes subsumed, as they have been above, under the term 'reception room' – were much more ambiguous and multifunctional.

Some analyses of late antique housing have characterised the period and consequently its housing as increasingly dominated by hierarchisation and thus the increasing separation of the elite from their social inferiors, resulting in an analysis of aristocratic housing very much in terms of control, and particularly of access (cf. Bowes 2010: 42–54). This is certainly true, and we have seen it in the case of villas such as Montmaurin, where there were several points at which access could be permitted or denied, or Séviac, in which access to different areas of the complex might be structured by the physical form of the villa and the placing of its component elements. But alongside this, one should perhaps employ the model proposed by Wallace-Hadrill. In his analysis of housing at Pompeii and Herculaneum, he sees houses as structured along the axes of public–private, grand–humble (1994: Ch. 1, esp. p. 11). This essentially argues that houses were structured to be penetrated rather than to be exclusive, but that such penetration was clearly structured according to social relationships, particularly those of visitors to the house with the *dominus*. Thus social inferiors would on the whole not be allowed to penetrate very far and could discharge only a limited range of social interactions, whereas more honoured guests would be allowed to penetrate much further and would be invited to participate in a range of activities with their host, and possibly his family. But even this range of activities would be subject to social norms and be much more formal and constrained than much of modern, Western society is used to. Some aristocratic social pastimes could occur away from the residence, such as hunting, but others mark the house strongly, in particular the sociable aspects of bathing and the formal meal as arena for social display. Mention of bathing recalls arguments made in Chapter 3 about the displacement of what had hitherto been 'public' functions and activities into the private context – in particular, 'political' activities, which in the second century would have been carried out in the forum and basilica. In Chapter 3, we saw that the evidence for the maintenance of these complexes over much of the West was at best equivocal. The local *potentiores* (the powerful) could have added the public aspects of administration of a city or *civitas* to the private administration of their personal affairs, both now within the residence. In this case one can easily see how an apsidal *aula*-type of room could well have suited the *dominus* in his role as a local magistrate, dispensing justice and running the affairs of the *civitas*. This would especially be the case at urban houses, but a local lord might well use his villa for similar purposes, possibly at certain seasons of the year. The displacement of bathing from the public baths to the bath suite of the *domus* would thus be part of the same pattern of the 'privatisation' of power and of greater control (not denial) of access to the *dominus*.

One may read this approach off the physical remains of the grand urban and rural residences of the late Roman West. The entrance is usually emphasised, either by its position in a façade and its architectural framing or, in the country, by an entrance court, for which a semicircular plan, as at La Cercadilla or Montmaurin, is particularly characteristic of this period and seems to be a marker of a high-status complex (cf. Balmelle 2001: 147–52). From the entrance, access to and penetration into the complex would have been managed in respect of the social status and business of the visitor. All would at least have caught a glimpse of an internal court, normally rectangular but occasionally circular or octagonal as at two Spanish sites, Baños de la Reina (Alicante) and Valdetorres del Jarama (Madrid) respectively. These peristyle courts not only served a distributive function, allowing controllable access to different rooms or other areas, but also served as spaces to impress through elements such as marble columns and mosaic or marble flooring and views over the formal gardens and fountains the courts contained, which attested to the *dominus*'s control over nature in the form of both plants and of water – for southern Gaul and Spain, the latter would be a precious resource. A few villas, such as Palat (Gironde) in Gaul or, as we have seen, São Cucufate in Iberia, had large, formal pools of water adjoining a principal façade. But it is highly unlikely that the great majority of visitors could wander at will. One may note that the apsidal reception room at Séviac was immediately beside the main entrance, both in its original, more modest, east–west-aligned form and in its greatly extended, north–south replacement (and what did this major amplification and elongation of the *aula* say about its proprietor?), meaning that many visitors did not need or would not be allowed to penetrate any further. At Carranque a visitor would only need to pass round one-quarter of the peristyle to attain the apsidal room and would not need to penetrate as far as the probable dining and reception suite. This restriction of the distance between main entrance and *aula*-style room is a feature also observable at high-status residences elsewhere in the empire (cf. Özgenel 2007). But at Carranque the more honoured guest could have made a half-tour of the peristyle to arrive at the point most removed from the entrance, the dining suite, that extra physical distance representing also a social distance from those not invited to do so. Another element of physical and social distancing is visible in the positioning of the bath suites at many of these complexes. Séviac again affords a good example with the increasingly massive and luxurious baths being positioned separately from the main residence and joined to it by a semicircular colonnaded walkway, recalling the semicircular *cour d'honneur* of a Montmaurin. This distancing of the baths from the main building (not to be read in purely functional terms as removing a fire hazard) can be observed at other villas in south-western Gaul (e.g. Moncrabeau, Valentine), Spain (e.g. Cerro de Villa, La Olmeda), and Britain (e.g. Holcombe, Lufton).

If the functions and positioning of 'reception rooms' and other elements, such as bath suites, that related largely to the discharge of the 'public' and 'political' duties of the *dominus* can be read off the plans and appointments of these chambers, the same cannot be said of the sort of information that would allow us to reconstruct with any certainty the 'household' and 'social' aspects of these residences. One long-standing question about Roman aristocratic houses is whether they contained specific women's quarters (*gyn[a]ecium*) to which adult males who were not members of the family were not admitted, or only seldom, thus keeping women in segregation, or whether it was more a case of well-bred women keeping out of the way of male visitors, unless the latter were sufficiently favoured to be able to meet them. The textual evidence rather suggests the latter, and the lack, so far, of elements of house plans in the archaeology that can confidently and recurrently be identified as women's quarters also rather supports this. Nevertheless, there could have been areas of the house that were principally the women's domain (with their maids and children), and this may account for some of the rooms or ranges of rooms whose functions are otherwise unreadable. The mention cited earlier by Sidonius Apollinaris (*Epistulae* II.2.9–10) in the mid fifth century of a *matronale triclinium*, a women's dining room, does raise the possibility that space in these residences was more formally gendered. This may relate to the provision in some larger complexes of several rooms with apses or other embellishments, another possibility being that dining suites could be duplicated for summer and for winter use. Interestingly, Sidonius's women's dining room adjoins the weaving room and the storeroom, weaving and supervision of household stores being very traditional female accomplishments in Roman society (as viewed by men). Likewise, the position, or indeed the existence, of slave quarters and of areas principally used by slaves is a topic which as yet has hardly been approached; for instance, Balmelle (2001) does not feel able to discuss it, and Arce *et al.* (2007: 56–7, 61–4) can only outline the problem of the existence of and accommodation for dependent labour. For Pompeii and Herculaneum, the identification of such areas is greatly aided by the upstanding nature of the remains, for this demonstrated clearly that in the grander houses it was the treatment of the wall surfaces that would give an immediate sign of the servile nature of a room or area (Wallace-Hadrill 1994: Ch. 3); none of the residences considered here are well enough preserved for this to be possible. That the families resident in these great houses had maids, valets, cooks, servers, grooms and other servants cannot be doubted, though we do not know if they were free or unfree, but how they were accommodated and where they worked and moved around the residence we cannot at present say.

One aspect of the villas in particular is their presence in and impact on the wider landscape. This also is a subject that has received little attention so far, due to the traditional over-concentration on the residential buildings. The impact in terms of the forms and functioning of the agrarian economy will be discussed in the next chapter; here it is the impacts more closely linked to the high-status functions of the villas that will be considered. Above, it was noted that some villas set their baths at a distance from the main building, though still close by. There are a small number of villas where the chances of earlier discoveries and/or more recent work has made it clear that there were detached elements related to the principal residence. Carranque is, of course, a good example for Spain, with its *nymphaeum* and further away the funerary complex. Others such as Torre de Palma (for the plan, see Arce *et al.* 2007: 267) also had a number of detached dependencies that extended the 'footprint' of the villa over a considerable area. In southwestern Gaul, there are instances of villas where separate elements were purposefully disposed in relation to each other to create an ensemble. The villa at Pont d'Oly, Jurançon (Pyrénées Atlantiques), had two sets of elaborate rooms on a common axis of symmetry. To one side of the river Néez was a building with a semicircular *cour d'honneur*, and on the other bank a range of rooms floored in mosaic and with a colonnaded façade to the river. At Nérac (Lot-et-Garonne), the baths were set at a distance from the main residence, on the banks of the river Baïse, with a long gallery extending along the riverbank. Clearly, these villas were responding to and taking advantage of the local topography, particularly the rivers. In Spain there are a number of villas which impact on their local landscape through the use of mausolea (Bowes 2008: 135–46). A good example of this is the villa at Pueblanueva (Toledo), where the great octagonal mausoleum dominated a stretch of flat land west of the villa on the south side of the river Tagus. Likewise, the substantial, probably Christian mausoleum of the major villa at La Cocosa (Badajoz) lay some 250 m away, marking the approach of the villa to those on the road. The remarkable possible funerary complex at Carranque was discussed in Chapter 4, and it is worth noting that it lay near a pronounced river cliff and would have been visible from a large area on the other side of the river. As yet, comparables structures are little known from Gaul, especially the south-west, though the mausoleum close by the great villa of Valentine (Haute-Garonne), with its elaborate verse epitaph to the proprietor Nymfius (Sablayrolles and Beyrie 2006: 471–2), suggests that such things existed – it would be odd if they had not. One may also point to examples such as the hilltop mausoleum in the style of a 'Romano-Celtic' temple at Lullingstone in Britain (Meates 1979: 122–31). Clearly, the mausolea are being used, in ways familiar to archaeologists from funerary monuments of many periods, to declare title to land – above all by reference to the 'ancestors' enclosed within the monument. This does raise the question of whether other structures related to the villa and its proprietors, such as temples or churches, were also being used to mark the landscape of the estate and were in visual and/or ideological relation to the principal residence. As yet we can only note the idea and hope that more systematic work around and away from major villas in the West will eventually allow discussion of this possibility.

One recurrent theme in the decoration of aristocratic residences, be it in mosaic or on silverware, but also in ivory and manuscript illumination, is the hunt. As in so many societies, this had become an aristocratic pastime which allowed the demonstration of manly prowess (*virtus*) as well as allowing a *dominus* to entertain guests, friends and associates in a suitably lavish manner. It would seem that hunting may have become a more important aristocratic activity in the late Roman period (cf. Anderson, J. K. 1985), or at least the number of representations of it and references to it increased. Many of the representations show the activity of hunting itself, principally the driving of game into areas where nets had been set up to contain the game. They also show various kinds of game, and the texts make it clear that the more ferocious the prey, the greater the *virtus* demonstrated in its killing: in the West, boar would seem to be the preferred dangerous opponent. But representations such as the 'Small Hunt' mosaic from the Piazza Armerina villa in Sicily (Wilson, R. 1983: 23, 25), or the central roundel of the 'Great Dish' from the Sevso treasure from, probably, the Balkans (Mango and Bennett 1994: 55–97), show the hunt as the matrix for social interaction, in particular a meal on a temporary *stibadium* under a canopy, with food and drink and even a water heater (*authepsa*). Hunting would have required areas in which it could take place. This raises the question of whether there were 'chases' or 'parks' given over to hunting as in the Middle Ages; if so, there may have been significant areas given over to this activity, a landscape of privilege. In addition, there would need to be game raised, again possibly in specialised areas of landscape such as woodland for boars; there would need to be horses and hounds; and there would also need to be the personnel. In Chapter 2, we noted (p. 82) the recent suggestions for both northern Gaul and central Iberia that local burial traditions in these regions involving knives, spears and occasionally arrows might be interpreted in relation to hunting rather than to warfare. Overall, this activity might have had considerable landscape and social impacts; ones which we at present appreciate only dimly, quite possibly because we have not really looked for them.

As we have looked at a number of aspects of the physical forms and functions of these aristocratic residences and their surroundings, it is now time to look further at the forms of their decoration and embellishment, in particular the choice and deployment of figures and mythological scenes in such media as mosaic and plate.

Aristocratic culture and *paideia*

As was stated at the start of this chapter, we are dealing with a very visual culture. Aristocratic expression and self-representation over much of the fourth-century Western Empire was about display: display in the type of urban or rural residence, its fixtures, fittings, furnishings and materials; display in personal adornment such as dress and in bodily presentation through grooming. At one level, this was a matter of status markers; there was a common social code structuring the range of these markers and their deployment, and the ambitious would naturally seek to decorate themselves and their residences with the most costly and lavish appurtenances possible – gold, silver, marble, mosaic and fine stuffs – financial capital laid out in pursuit of cultural capital. In this way they would transmit clearly to the viewer the status they wished to display, whether it corresponded to their actual rank or was more an expression of aspiration. There was a close relationship between the medium of the material, the decoration chosen and the message conveyed. But there was a more symbolic aspect to this display, particularly where it involved the use of religious, mythological, heroic and other scenes derived from traditional Graeco-Roman culture: this was the way in which objects bearing such representations, as on mosaic or plate, carried coded statements about the education, taste and discernment of the owner.

This is the area of *paideia*, the Greek word denoting 'education', or perhaps it is expressed better by the French *formation*, a more all-encompassing notion of the creation of the adult from the child and the reproduction of the culture through such education (Brown, P. R. L. 1988: Ch. 2). The late Roman version of Graeco-Roman education (Marrou 1965; cf. Kaster 1988) was concerned, first, with mastery of reading, writing and the formal use of the Latin language – that is, 'grammar' – along with knowledge of the writings of the canonical Roman authors such as Vergil. From there some pupils might move on to mastery of 'rhetoric', which included knowing the forms of argument and its conventional vocabulary. Such an education, through the attitudes and manners learnt, allowed its recipients to demonstrate their social position through familiarity with the literary canon and the deployment of classical allusions. This was a long and arduous education, and many did not make it past the 'grammar' stage, though even this marked them out as being literate. But, like all such educations, it was designed to be exclusive, not just in the modern, general sense of the word as pertaining to the few, but also in its literal derivation of shutting out those not initiated into its arts; indeed, it also marked internal gradations of mastery of language, fluency of address, apposite use of devices, examples, gestures and capping of quotations, thus distinguishing the properly educated scion of an established family from the poorer or the incomer with his shakier grasp of these devices. But what it also did was to create a common thought world and set of expectations among those so trained, be they provincial or senatorial aristocrats or the children of parvenu officers or officials, so that when an aristocrat addressed a governor, both knew the rules of the game. This made *paideia* one of the main integrative media for the elite, and it was one within which Christian bishops could operate as much as lay nobles. Moreover, *paideia* was a route to the creation and nurturing of *philia*, long-term bonds of affection and loyalty between members of the elite. This, then, was the mental background archaeologically manifested through the *koine* of house plans, reception rooms where *philia* and *paideia* were deployed, mosaics and their subjects, sculpture, painting, plate and dress, which all expressed the owner's membership of and participation in an empire-wide elite culture.

A further development out of the shared knowledge and assumptions of *paideia* was the importance of the visual arts and their representations of classical mythology, not only passively as depictions but actively as the starting points for the practice of *ekphrasis*. This is best exemplified in the *Imagines* of Philostratus, which is an account of the way a series of paintings (rather than the mosaics dear to archaeologists) in a villa was each used as the basis for a description, narrative and interpretation of the subject matter, by which the eyes of the listeners are opened and the subjects more fully understood, appreciated and internalised (Elsner 1995: Pt. I, Chs. 1 and 2; cf. Elsner 2007). The *ekphrasis* was itself a dazzling display of rhetorical accomplishment, marking out the speaker as a master of all aspects of traditional Graeco-Roman culture and the ability to articulate them in oratorical form and to present them with a wealth of apposite quotation and reference. This may seem to be taking us a long way from the archaeology of the plan and appointments of the late Roman villa, but in fact it gives us the context and the codes within which the villa proprietor operated and made his choices about the layout and décor of his residence. These latter made clear that these choices were an expression of individual agency within the structures of a common vocabulary and were also active elements in his constitution of his image to those viewing it, and thus they were vital to the self-estimation and self-representation of the magnate concerned. Thus, when we come to look at such matters as the choice of subjects for a mosaic, sculpture (as at Chiragan) (Stirling 2005: Ch. 5) or silver plate (cf. Leader-Newby 2004: Ch. 3), *paideia* not only explains why certain subjects (Achilles, Dionysos, Oceanus and Orpheus) were widespread because of their importance in Graeco-Roman myth but also helps contextualise variations and recombinations, including those that do not apparently correspond with the canon of myths and legends as they have come down to us (for instance, on the Corbridge *lanx*). These showed how the aristocrat was playing with and pushing the bounds of the conventions of stories and personages to create something new that was comprehensible to his audience, but they also displayed his ability to manipulate the stock of stories and figures. But more, we may regard these representations as themselves ekphrastic, since in the right hands (or mouth) they could be the subjects of such virtuoso exegetic treatment. Importantly also, *paideia* helps us understand the continued use of mythological and other subjects from the traditional religions in an aristocratic world increasingly Christian, and at specific sites such as Carranque, where a (militantly) Christian owner has been proposed; the traditional *paideia* was the only one there was, so to assimilate oneself to the established means of visual displays of education and taste perforce meant using non-Christian semiotics. But we should not read these through to declarations of religious faith any more than we would with Graeco-Roman mythological subjects in a Renaissance painting; in both cases, it was more to do with artistic convention and vocabulary. Christian theologians were increasingly aware both of the contradiction in Christians being formed in the traditional thought world and of the inescapability of it, coming up with prescriptions as to how to manipulate *paideia* and traditional culture to neutralise the unacceptable bits (cf. Bowersock 1990). Thus we should not view expressions of traditional and of Christian culture as necessarily opposed; they could be held in synthesis. Finally, it should, of course, be noted that what has just been laid out was an ideal, and Ammianus Marcellinus's caustic remarks (*Res Gestae* 28.4) on the philistinism of the expensively educated Roman nobility show that stupidity, laziness and boorishness might account as much for what the modern worker sees as did high-mindedness. So why was this late Roman high culture deployed so unevenly across the Western Empire? Why was it a feature of certain regions and how may we seek to explain why it was those regions where it flourished and not at others?

Regional groupings: Gaul, Spain and Britain

Southern Gaul

So far, the distribution of these indicators of the late aristocratic culture has not been considered, though it should now be clear that the majority of sites mentioned lay in south-western Gaul, and to a much lesser extent in south-eastern Gaul (cf. Carru *et al.* 2001; Pellecuer and Pomarèdes 2001) and the Iberian peninsula. It is the south-west of Gaul that gives the clearest and most detailed evidence for this rich aristocratic culture. Two of the four villas used as case studies earlier in this chapter, Montmaurin and Séviac, lie in this region. So also do others also mentioned for their exceptional size (Valentine) and the richness of their sculptural décor (Chiragan). Others such as Nérac (Lot-et-Garonne) or Pont d'Oly, Jurançon (Pyrénées Atlantiques), have also been mentioned. The excavated plans of others, such as Bapteste at Moncrabeau (Lot-et-Garonne) or Lalonquette (Pyrénées Atlantiques), or the fragments known of Lescar (Pyrénées Atlantiques) or Palat, Saint-Émilion (Gironde), confirm the presence of substantial and richly decorated establishments (cf. Balmelle 2001: catalogue for brief details and plans of these sites). The map published by Balmelle (2001: 72, Fig. 19) of the distribution of fourth- and fifth-century mosaics on the territory of present-day France is truly remarkable (Figure 5.16). Of 130 or so find spots, some 90 (70 per cent)

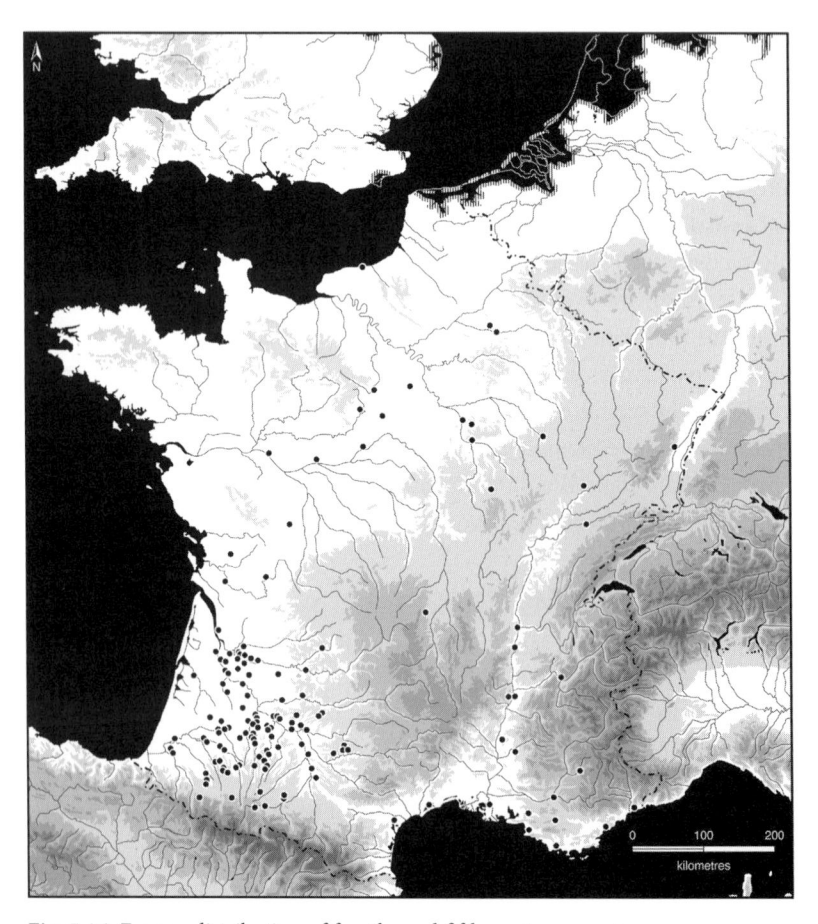

Fig. 5.16 France, distribution of fourth- and fifth-century mosaics

lie between the Dordogne, the Pyrenees and the Carcassonne Gap (essentially the provinces of Novempopulana and the southern half of Aquitania II, fringing into western Narbonensis); the regional grouping could not be clearer, and there is nothing like it from the rest of France, though more recent discoveries in central France (see below) may make the distinctions less absolute. Also, if the map had strayed over the German border into the Trier and Cologne areas, there would have been another, much smaller, group there). It must be recognised that because of the concentration of archaeological work on the grand villas of this region, particularly on the residential areas, we are woefully ignorant of the other forms of rural settlement, be they lesser villas or 'farmsteads', so our overall picture of rural settlement in the region must be very skewed. Nonetheless, it cannot be denied that this was a region marked by large numbers of large and elaborately appointed villas (and some urban residences, see Chapter 3, p. 136), reflecting a rich and competitive regional aristocracy. This was an aristocracy, moreover, that was very much wedded to the traditional means of status display in the Roman West, though the traditions and their architectural correlates had gradually modified over the years.

This is, of course, the region for which we also have ample evidence for a continuing high aristocratic culture in literature, particularly in the works of Ausonius but also of other south-western writers such as Paulinus of Nola, Sulpicius Severus and later Paulinus of Pella. This was an aristocracy whose membership and activities can be traced with some confidence (e.g. Matthews 1975; Sivan 1993), and it is clear that it was linked to the senatorial and imperial orders and wished to emulate the 'traditional' culture to be found there, particularly in the old, senatorial *gentes*. It is no coincidence, as we have already noted, that the area around Trier also boasted some remarkable late villas, harking back to the importance of this type of residence in traditional culture, and in the Trier area actively promoted by the imperial presence (see Balmelle and Van Ossel 2001 for explicit linking of the two areas). Emperors, of course, were not necessarily expected to be leading exponents of *belles lettres*, but it is telling that it was from south-western Gaul, specifically the schools of Bordeaux, that the choleric military ruler Valentinian I summoned Ausonius to act as tutor to his son Gratian in order to ensure that the boy was formed in the grammar and rhetoric of traditional *paideia* and could hold his own in polite society. In the long run, this education and culture did not do Gratian any good when he was hunted down and dispatched by the troops of Magnus Maximus in 383; indeed, the well-educated offspring of the Houses of Valentinian and Theodosius seem almost uniformly to have been rulers enervated by education; they were ineffective and sometimes vicious.

The ascent of Ausonius and his family to positions of high power and wealth as a result of this connection (Sivan 1993: 131–41) is a telling example of the benefits that flowed from the sacred presence, much as Trier shows it for a city. Ausonius's verse is not to modern taste, being seen as too contrived, lacking formal or narrative originality, and with a tendency to the interminable; but it is manifestly ekphrastic, probably particularly so when declaimed and thus approximating to high rhetorical declamation, and with the desire to show off knowledge of recondite classical themes and literature. Moreover, such verse could only have been composed by someone with a rigorous grounding in the Roman literary classics and in the arts of prosody and language; only such a person could have stitched together the *Cento Nuptialis* out of lines and half-lines of Vergil, in the process altering their significance markedly: the importance of *paideia* could not be more manifest. It is important to recognise also that 'tradition' is not the same as inertia, as already argued for cities in Chapter 3. Here we have a positive choice to use 'traditional' forms, be it of dwelling or of literature, as a strategy to demonstrate social and cultural superiority. By seeking to perpetuate an interpretation of classical Roman culture, these aristocrats were consciously aligning themselves socially with the emperor and the imperial court (as we have seen for Trier and the villas around it) and with the senatorial order, guardians of Rome's oldest traditions (or so they liked to imagine), and culturally with the religious and mythological traditions that had helped carry Rome to greatness. That a representative of this cultural tradition, Ausonius, could marshal these literary forms while at the same time adhering to the Christian faith speaks volumes for the ability of traditional *paideia* to hold in creative tension beliefs which look to us as though they should have been mutually antagonistic. Even one such as Paulinus of Nola, who recognised the contradictions, continued to write to his friends across the West in the best Latin, aristocrat that he was, though his old tutor Ausonius was pained that Paulinus could no longer make the sorts of cultural accommodations that Ausonius himself had made.

South-eastern Gaul forms an interesting comparison with the south-western complex. Though there seems no *a priori* reason why the two regions should not be similar, there are, in fact, significant divergences, particularly in the incidence and nature of villas. Surveys of the middle Rhône valley (Ode and Odiot 2001) and of Languedoc (Pellecuer and Pomarèdes 2001; Pellecuer and Schneider 2005; Raynaud 2001) and Provence (Buffat 2011; Carru *et al.* 2001; Trément 2001) all show the persistence of the villa as an

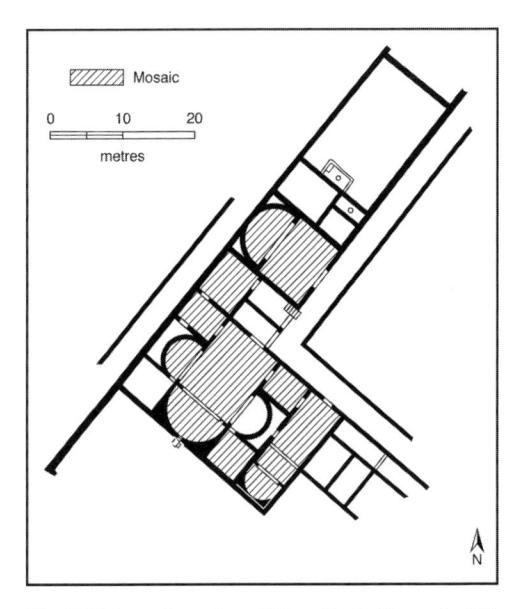

Fig. 5.17 Loupian, plan of the villa in the early fifth century (shaded areas: mosaics)

important, structuring element of the rural settlement hierarchy, even if there had been numerical decline since the later second-century peak. But by comparison with the south-west there is far less evidence of ostentatious investment into elaborate architectural forms, mosaics, marble and other status markers. The most elaborate villa that has been found was that at Loupian in Languedoc (Pellecuer and Pomarèdes 2001: 518–22), where the excavated part of a large courtyard villa of the first century was extensively remodelled in the latter part of the fourth (Figure 5.17), with the creation of a large triconch dining chamber and another apsidal reception room and the laying of a suite of polychrome mosaics covering 450 m^2, whose stylistic links were both with the south-west (some close parallels with Séviac) and, more remarkably, with Syrian mosaic traditions, yet another instance of the artistic connections between eastern and western Mediterranean at this period. Other large villas in the area, such as Saint-André-de-Codols (Gard) near Nîmes or La Ramière (Gard), show architectural modifications such as apsidal reception rooms, but lack the mosaics of a Loupian or the south-west; clearly, the income was directed to other ends, not at present discernible. A similar situation appears to obtain to the east of the Rhône, where the absolute number of villas shows a decline from the late second-century peak, with some substantial establishments but little evidence for investment in south-western-style display, but rather a concentration on the exploitation of the agricultural resources (cf. Buffat 2010), rather as with the Iberian littoral (below). This contrast with the south-west is instructive; *a fortiori*, there was no reason why the south-east should not have shown a comparable surge of ostentation – so far as can be seen, the economic resources were there to permit such expenditure. It could be argued that ownership lay outside the region and that therefore the income was siphoned off elsewhere, but there is no convincing evidence for this, and it might equally well be posited for the south-west. So it looks as if the elites of the south-east did not choose to make the same sorts of statements about how they saw themselves as did their confreres on the other side of the Massif Central. Again this supports the general argument that there was a range of possible strategies for elite display, and that there were regional preferences and traditions rather than homogeneity. What it could well show is that the aristocracy of south-eastern Gaul had fewer links to and less involvement with the imperial court than had those in the south-west and therefore they lacked the cultural incentive to expend their surpluses on this particular form of self-display.

Spain

Traditionally, the historiography of the development of the villas of the Iberian peninsula was one dictated by the literary grand narratives of the third and fourth centuries, with the third century a time of 'crisis' if not of actual destruction, followed by the abandonment of villas occupied under the High Empire (one notes the overall similarity to the then narrative for urban sites), resulting in a fourth-century landscape dominated by a few great *possessores* (including the family that was to produce the emperor Theodosius) living off the labour of an oppressed class of agricultural labourers (often identified with the *coloni* of the texts) and manifested by a small number of grand villas. However, our knowledge and understanding of the late villas of the Iberian peninsula has been transformed by the dedicated work of, in particular, Alexandra Chavarría Arnau, resulting in an impressive list of publications systematising the evidence from the archaeology, epigraphy and texts (now gathered in Arce *et al.* 2007 – including plans of all sites; earlier studies concentrating on particular areas or topics include Chavarría Arnau 1996, 2001, 2004a, 2004b, 2005a, 2005b, 2006a, 2006b; for an English-language summary, see Chavarría Arnau 2004b). Other workers such as Javier Arce and Gisela Ripoll López have also been active in this reassessment of the place of villas in late Roman Iberia (cf. Ripoll López and Arce 2001).

Geographically, three main regions stand out for their groupings of villas. The first is Catalonia north of the Ebro and particularly the littoral. The second is the central and northern Meseta, the basins and tablelands around the upper and middle courses of the Tagus and the Duero. The third is the southern part of modern Portugal from the lower Tagus across to the basin of the Guadiana (Arce *et al.* 2007: Mapa I). Villas occur elsewhere in the peninsula (for instance, in southern Andalusia), but the groupings above comprise the majority of sites. The villas of the eastern seaboard (Chavarría Arnau 1996, 2001) show a range of sizes, complexity of plan and decorative embellishments, with the most substantial bearing comparison with the luxurious establishments of the interior (Abascal *et al.* 2008). There was a group of sites characterised by their architectural sophistication, most notably the villa of Centcelles near Tarragona (cf. Chapter 4, p. 183), where a chamber was modified for use as a circular, domed mausoleum with mosaics of biblical and hunting scenes on the dome. Not far away was the extensive complex of Els Munts, notable for its baths and hydraulic arrangements. Further south along the coast, near Valencia, was the unusual complex of Baños de la Reina (Abascal *et al.* 2000) laid out around a circular peristyle, one of the rooms opening off this having a high-quality *opus sectile* pavement in marble, though even this saw the insertion of functional, agrarian installations. As well as mosaic and marble, there is evidence for sculpture both in marble and in bronze and for other high-quality fittings. From the later third century into the fifth, there was also a tendency in the region to emphasise productive capacity and processes at the expense of the residential and baths areas (Arce *et al.* 2007: 125–9), with installations such as that at Torre Llauder (Barcelona), where eighteen *dolia* were set into the floor of what had been one of the principal reception rooms of the residential part of the villa, smashing through the existing mosaic. These were associated with three large basins, one in the main peristyle. At other sites, there is evidence for the bases of presses for grapes or olives along with decantation basins. At several sites the baths were decommissioned by putting the hypocaust out of use, sometimes removing the *pilae* altogether; it has been suggested that the existing plunge baths would make good decantation basins. Further south, the villa of Sabinillas (Málaga) produced evidence for the processing of marine products. Clearly, agricultural productivity was important, and it may be no coincidence that it was villas in the areas of the peninsula most open to the currents of Mediterranean trade, especially in oil, wine and fish sauce, that were affected (cf. Chapter 7).

The northern Meseta grouping contains some of the best-known and most elaborate villas of late Roman Iberia, such as Cuevas de Soria (Soria) with its large, centrally placed apsidal *aula*; La Olmeda (Palencia), the nearest parallel to Carranque in overall plan, location of principal room (with a large mosaic of Achilles on Skyros and mosaics of hunting scenes), overall abundance of mosaics, and specific features such as the use of walls that are segments of a circle rather than straight; Almenara de Adaja (Valladolid), which is grouped around two courtyards, with two major, apsidal, *aula*-style reception rooms, a triconch, an octagonal room, and one with the interior in a series of arcs of a circle (cf. Carranque and La Olmeda), as well as an extensive series of mosaics (Fernández Ochoa *et al.* 2008); or the major complex at Liédena (Navarra). Perhaps it is also no coincidence that it is from the northern Meseta that come the *cementerios tardohíspanos con ajuares*, considered below with their evidence for a militarised ethos, including crossbow brooches and belt fittings, argued (Aurrecoechea Fernández 2001) to be a representation of the importance of hunting to the aristocratic identity, as outlined above. Of the southern Portugal group, we have already discussed the villa of São Cucufate in some detail and mentioned the related site of Milreu. One might also mention the villa of Torre Águila (Badajoz) with elaborate rooms at the corners of the main peristyle, or that at La Cocosa (Badajoz), or the huge complexes of Torre de Palma (Alentejo) and Cerro da Vila (Faro), or the smaller but remarkably architecturally elaborate site of Quinta de las Longas (Elvas) (Rodríguez Martín and Carvalho 2008). This listing is only an introduction to the remarkable evidence from Iberia now available to set beside that from Gaul (or, indeed, Italy, the eastern Mediterranean or North Africa). Here some commonalities among the Iberian villas and some points of comparison and contrast with their cousins to the north of the Pyrenees will be examined.

The Iberian villa proprietors were clearly as attuned to developments in villa architecture and its significance for the position and representation of the *dominus* as were their Gallic neighbours. The predominance of centrally planned layouts, normally round a rectangular peristyle court, is very marked. So also is the frequency of apsidal reception rooms opening off the central peristyle, most often centrally placed opposite the principal entrance. Other architecturally ambitious forms of reception room are also widespread, including the triconch dining room; evidence for the *sigma* table has been found in some other apsidal reception rooms as at El Ruedo (Córdoba). Large, architecturally sophisticated bath suites are another recurring feature of these late, Iberian villas, along with evidence for the capture, storage and use of water not only for the baths but also for fountains and other 'water-features' associated with the central peristyle of the dining rooms and, in the Portuguese group, for the *nymphaea* at sites such as Milreu, Quinta de Marim and São Cucufate. In the climate of Iberia, this was a striking index of the control of the *dominus* over a recalcitrant Nature. Decoration was at least as lavish as in the Gaulish villas, with extensive provision of mosaic floors, both geometric and vegetal, but also many with scenes from Graeco-Roman mythology quite as suitable for displaying the owner's *paideia* and as objects of ekphrastic virtuosity as those we have seen in Novempopulana. Marble was also widely used for both floors and architectural elements such as wall cladding, as well as for sculpture, as at Valdetorres del Jarama. The general similarity in villa culture north and south of the Pyrenees is patent, showing that both the Gallic and the Iberian nobilities were open to wider influences at this period.

As with Gaul, so with Spain, this high villa culture was highly regionalised, a fact which requires discussion of possible explanations. Evidently, in part, the reasons must start with basic agricultural economics. All these areas were suitable for the production of agricultural surplus, be it crops such as grain, vines or olives, or be it animals such as cattle, sheep or horses. But though necessary, this is not sufficient, since other agriculturally favoured regions did not show the same development – for instance and in particular, the valley of the Guadalquivir in the south of the peninsula, which under the High Empire had become hugely prosperous through intensive oleiculture (see Chapters 7 and 8), yet in the Late Empire supported only a few, not very remarkable villas. A model that may be proposed as part of the answer concerns the relationship of these areas to the imperial fiscal system. We have already seen in Chapter 3 (pp. 129–130) the suggestion that the northern Meseta area and across into Galicia became a major area of surplus production and exploitation by the state from the later third century on, the evidence for which lies in the refurbishment of the communications system, attested to by the many milestones, and in the fortification of the cities of the north and west, the argument being that they safeguarded the extraction of the surplus and its transportation to the western passes of the Pyrenees and thus on into Gaul and up to the military zone of the Rhineland and northern Gaul. The coincidence of this region with that of the northern Meseta grouping of villas seems too close to be due to the operations of random chance, especially since this zone was one where there had been few early imperial villas, so what we are seeing here is a new departure in the later empire. What we may be seeing is a region which, through its involvement in the fiscal structures of the state, generated a significant degree of prosperity through the provision of supplies for profit by purchase over and above the simple tax render. Another exceptional feature of this general region in the late period was a regional fine ware (TSHT), which will be discussed in Chapter 7

(p. 323), and this may again be an index of enhanced economic activity in this region. Something similar could have been the case for Catalonia, with its defended land communications and its sea links to southern Gaul as well as the seaways to and from Italy, but it must be admitted that the evidence for Catalonian (or Languedoc) products travelling far is at present not convincing (cf. Chapter 4, p. 174). At first sight, the southern Portugal grouping seems more difficult to relate to such a model due to its remoteness from Gaul, though less so from the currents of circum-Mediterranean trade through the Pillars of Hercules. But it is important to remember that under the Late Roman Empire the isolated Roman enclave and garrisons of Mauretania Tingitana, in what is now northern and western Morocco, administratively formed part of the *diocesis Hispaniarum*, not of Africa. Could it be that it was the region of southern Portugal, just across the Strait of Gibraltar, that was the breadbasket and warehouse for the support of the units listed in the *Notitia Dignitatum* as serving in Tingitana? So the model links in, and the importance of the imperial fiscal system can clearly be sustained for the northern Meseta and for southern Portugal. It is not so convincing for Catalonia nor yet for south-western Gaul, though there is the one incidental comment of Ammianus referred to above (p. 132) showing that Aquitanian grain could be important, but that was in the exceptional circumstances of supplying an imperial expeditionary force. But given that other regions of Spain were subject to the same fiscal regime, might they not also be expected to have profited from this nexus? After all, villa-poor Andalusia is no further across the Strait from Tingitana than is villa-rich southern Portugal. Is it that in some way certain regions managed to profit more from this system than others? May there have been factors other than the purely economic at work?

Here one might reprise the arguments about the reasons behind the wealth and the particular form of ostentation exhibited in the villas of south-western Gaul, especially those that relate to the linking of the aristocracy of the region into the higher echelons of the imperial service. The argument is that these links enabled the aristocracies of these regions to orient the operations of the state fiscal cycles to their advantage. Either by holding office within the relevant departments of the *comes sacrarum largitionum* or the praetorian prefecture (cf. Chapter 2, p. 92), or by 'influencing' officials and their underlings, they obtained for their home regions the chance to exploit the fiscal system to their advantage by being the preferred areas for the disbursement of state funds in return for surpluses needed by the armies or the central administration. This is plausible but as yet cannot be demonstrated for Iberia as clearly as it can be for the

Aquitanian nobility. Nevertheless, the evidence that can be put together (cf. Arce *et al.* 2007: 43–9) shows clearly the presence of Spaniards in the higher echelons of the imperial service during the fourth century, up to and including the emperor Theodosius I and his family, and such high officials as Maternus Cynegius (whether or not he was the proprietor of the complex at Carranque). Moreover, the Aquitanian Paulinus of Nola married a wife from a prominent Iberian family and spent several years on estates in the north of the peninsula before leaving for Nola, so one should be careful of artificially imposing too much of a division between the southern Gaulish and the northern Iberian elites, along the line of the Pyrenees. So this may be part of the answer – the aristocracies of these regions had manoeuvred themselves into positions of influence at court and in the bureaucracy from which they and their associates stood to gain. A possible complementary group of landowners has been identified by Banaji (2001: esp. Ch. 6) for the East on the basis of the papyrological evidence, but they may be of relevance here. These are the middle- to high-ranking state servants, both military and civilian, who used the wealth accumulated in the imperial service to buy themselves into the landed elite. The evidence for this is primarily from the fifth to seventh centuries, but this may be a testament to the vagaries of the survival and recovery of such evidence. We do not dispose of a comparable body of evidence for the West, but anecdotal evidence such as that relating to men such as Maternus Cynegius, who had risen far in the imperial service from modest beginnings in Iberia; or Rufinus from Eauze in Novempopulana, who rose to be praetorian prefect of the East under Theodosius I (and was the object of a vitriolic diatribe by Claudian, *In Rufinum*); or the senior military officers with barbarian names, all support the likelihood that there was a comparable class of men in the West (it would be almost unthinkable given the structures of Western imperial service that there were not). So as well as the landed aristocracy by descent, there was probably also an aristocracy by imperial service, whose children would, of course, be assimilated to the traditional aristocracy.

But this is a partial answer, because it does not explain why the (ill-gotten) gains of these links were expended in this particular form. Here one must come back to the cultural argument that for ideological reasons the imperial court and the senatorial and provincial aristocracies associated with it chose to display themselves in the ways and for the reasons that have already been demonstrated at some length in this chapter and that have been characterised as 'traditional' (though in fact very innovative). These would also be the modes of display familiar to those who had passed their lives in the upper echelons of the imperial service, especially those in regular attendance upon the person of the emperor. So the efflorescence of elaborately planned and richly appointed villas in certain regions of Iberia, perhaps especially the northern Meseta and southern Portugal, is in part an expression of the relationships of the aristocracies, established or parvenu, of these regions to the imperial power and how those relationships should be made manifest in the old-style *paideia* and its epiphenomena such as mosaics with mythological scenes. In part, it is, of course, also an expression of competitive emulation; once the 'traditional' villa and visual and written cultures were established as the preferred vehicles for aristocratic display and status marking, then inevitably the competitive element inherent in Roman elite culture would mean that these forms of display became the accepted modes of display and competition in these regions, but much less often in others where different social and cultural values prevailed.

Britain

As well as southern Gaul and some regions of Iberia, there was one other area of the Western Empire where the villa culture flourished through the fourth century – southern Britain. That century is seen as the heyday of the villa as economic and cultural system in the island. In a broad swathe following largely the limestone formations from the south coast in Dorset, Hampshire and Sussex, up through Wiltshire and Somerset to the Gloucestershire Cotswolds, Oxfordshire, Northamptonshire and on into Lincolnshire, the British countryside was studded with villas of many shapes and sizes (cf. Perring 2002; Smith, D.J. 1997). The layout, rooms and decoration of some of the grandest, such as those at Bignor (West Sussex) or Woodchester, clearly participated in the same traditions as the grander Continental villas. Some of the more grandiose elements may be lacking or rare; for instance, there is as yet no substantiated effort at an imperial-style *aula*, and triconch reception rooms are very unusual, though there is the example from Littlecote, Wiltshire – note also the elaborate pavilions with their floor mosaics at Keynsham (Somerset). On the whole, bath suites were unadventurous compared with what was on offer at some Continental villas, but some, such as the octagonal plans of those at villas at Holcombe (Devon), Lufton (Somerset) or Teynham (Kent) (Wilkinson 2011), were much more architecturally ambitious, the baths separated from the main building and forming a substantial element of the complex in the way some Continental bath suites were. However, Britain contains a significant proportion of the surviving fourth-century mosaics from the West, some of them of exceptional size and workmanship, such as that from the great, square, pillared reception room at Woodchester (see Neal and Cosh 2002, 2010; Scott, E. 2000), the design of whose border has a direct parallel in a mosaic from a building that formed part of the imperial residence at Trier (Rivet 1969: Pl. 3.32). Britain's cities, as was seen in Chapter 3, were unusual in the West in containing large numbers of relatively elaborate 'town houses', not infrequently equipped with such things as mosaics and private baths. In these respects, both rural and urban, Britain aligned itself very much with southern Gaul and Iberia, demonstrating the persistence of a relatively wealthy class with access to *paideia* in the late Roman fashion and occasionally displaying this knowledge in such things as the Vergilian mosaic at Low Ham (Somerset) or the astronomical allusions on mosaics from Brading (Isle of Wight) (Wilson 2006), eminently suitable subjects for a display of ekphrastic virtuosity.

If we are to follow the logic of the arguments presented above for southwestern Gaul and for certain regions of Spain, such as the northern Meseta, then what we should be seeing is evidence for the linking of the British aristocracy into the imperial service with the consequent expression of these links through the imperially approved vocabulary of display and self-representation. Though late Roman Britain is often studied rather in isolation from the Continent, there is no *a priori* reason why it should not be the case that the British aristocracy had such close links into the imperial system; it is just that we are having to argue from silence. On the economic side, given the proximity of the heavily militarised Loire-Rhine zone, Britain would have been in a very good position to profit from supplying this region, as well as its own smaller version of the same thing along and behind the Saxon Shore system. There is not much direct evidence in the texts, beyond the oft-quoted remark of Ammianus Marcellinus (*Res Gestae*, XVIII.2.3) that Julian restored the granaries on the Rhine used to store grain brought over from Britain, but then that is precisely the right sort of evidence. There is also the ceramic evidence, further discussed in Chapter 7 (p. 322), for the presence of quantities of south British pottery on sites along the Gallic side of the Channel. In a way, it is precisely the villas of late Roman Britain (and equally the many urban residences that distinguish the island) that offer the clearest evidence that, in fact, the island's elites were imbricated with the imperial power, in a way not normally suspected. This, of course, is of a piece with the evidence discussed in Chapter 3 for the towns of late Roman Britain matching more closely those of southern Gaul and Iberia, not the regions immediately across the Channel. So though northern Gaul between the Loire and the Rhine may have been geographically the closest area to Britain, culturally it was at a considerable distance. It is, nevertheless, to the aristocracy of this region and of other regions of Gaul, where the high villa culture of south-western Gaul, parts of Spain and southern Britain did not take root, that we must now turn to round off our discussion of the self-representation of the aristocracies of the West in the later third and fourth centuries.

Central Gaul

As we leave the heartlands of the south-western villa culture in Novempopulana and Aquitania II and travel northwards, the villa, particularly the large, elaborate villa, starts to thin out with remarkable rapidity, but it is still present in certain areas, albeit often in numbers much smaller than in the second century. Nevertheless, the absolute distinction between the south-west and areas of central Gaul will need increasingly to be nuanced. That there are gaps still to fill, by systematic survey of published and unpublished records, aerial reconnaissance and ground survey, is demonstrated by the recent exercise on the territory of the Bituriges Cubi around Bourges, the capital of Aquitania I, to the north-east of the Novempopulana/Aquitania II concentration (Gandini 2008: esp. Ch. 10). The changes through time in the overall settlement pattern and what this may mean for the agricultural exploitation of the area will be considered in the next chapter (p. 283); here the concentration will be on the villa form of settlement and what can be said about its development in the late Roman period, which, it must be said, is almost exclusively based on aerial and ground survey rather than on excavation, so questions about the precise dating of the villas or the nature of their decoration and appointments cannot yet be answered. Changes in the rural settlement pattern starting from the later second century had emphasised the place of the villa in the settlement hierarchy, with lower-order settlements being abandoned and villas surviving (5% of the former survived from the second into the fourth century, but 23% of the latter). Nevertheless, the number of villas fell by 33% over the course of the third century, and new foundations thereafter were very rare. Even so, in the later Roman period, the villa seems to have become a more predominant form of settlement and therefore, presumably, a form of economic exploitation and social and cultural expression in the countryside of the Bituriges Cubi (Gandini 2008: 426). Because of the lack of excavation, few sites can be stated with confidence to date to the fourth century; however, on the basis of its elaborate plan, including a semicircular courtyard, the site at Clion (Indre) (Gandini 2008: 186–7) would seem a good candidate for a major, late villa comparable with those in the south-west. On morphological grounds, others, such as the site at Lissy-Lochay (Cher) and perhaps that at Montlevicq (Indre), may also belong here, and that at Lazenay (Cher) seems to have been at its most elaborate at this period also (Gandini 2008: 187, 247). Clearly, the territory of the Bituriges Cubi lacks the concentration of major villas that characterises Novempopulana and Aquitania II, but, even so, it is equally clearly a landscape where the villa continued to play an important, possibly dominant, economic and social role. Further north, examination of an area of northern Burgundy (Kasprzyk 2003; Nouvel 2009), in the southern part of Lugdunensis Senonia, depended again on aerial and surface survey and remains hampered by a lack of excavation. But it shows again an overall decline in settlement numbers through the third century, particularly the later third, but that villas seem to have suffered less numerically than did smaller establishments. There are again plans known from the air that would not be out of place in the fourth century such as La Chapelle-Vaupelteigne (Yonne), Guerchy (Yonne) or Lucy-sur-Cure (Yonne), the first and last of which have produced evidence such as the presence of mosaic and marble (undated). There is, in fact, a scatter of villas in north-central Gaul with some architectural and decorative pretensions. Further south lay villas such as Escolives-Sainte-Camille (Yonne), Souzy-la-Briche (Essonne) and Suèvres (Loir-et-Cher), all with triconch rooms. Escolives-Sainte-Camille was clearly of some richness in the fourth century and has yielded also official-issue belt fittings (Kasprzyk 2004), showing that we are at the interface between the 'traditional' villa culture and the more militarised aristocratic display of northern Gaul. Another pointer to this may perhaps be the observation (Kasprzyk 2003: 182) that at some sites still occupied in the fourth century there was a retraction in the area of occupation and in the quality of its appointments, and the appearance of timber structures with the masonry ones. This is very similar to what must be the next zone to concern us, northern Gaul.

Northern Gaul

By comparison with the south-west or the south-east of Gaul, in the fourth century the area from the Seine to the Rhine was one with few villas, many of them modest in scale and appointments, presenting a totally different regional facies (Van Ossel 1992 remains fundamental). Not surprisingly, this has traditionally been ascribed to the invasions of the third century having destroyed the villas of the earlier empire, leading to overdrawn pictures of a depopulated, impoverished landscape (see Van Ossel and

Ouzoulias 2000: 133–4). In fact, there were still villas, a few of which shared common characteristics with those we have been examining further south. As stated in the consideration of Trier at the beginning of this chapter, there was a cluster of late villas of some architectural pretensions and decorated with mosaics in the vicinity of the imperial residence on the Moselle. Some, such as Konz, Pfalzel and Welschbillig, have with varying degrees of plausibility been linked directly to the person of the emperor. Others, such as Echternach and Euren, where there are important fourth-century reconstructions, can presumably be attributed to the activities of either palatine or other government officials from Trier who acquired landed estates with the status they attained, or to local families responding to the version of traditional residences visible in the imperial and other residences of the city. Another, smaller group of villas in the 'traditional' style lay around Cologne, another important administrative and military centre at the time.

Outside these particular regions, the overall picture is one of massive change since the second century. This is particularly the case for areas such as Picardy (Agache 1978), where in the second century the number of villas ran into three figures, ranging from modest 'cottages' to huge complexes 250 m long or more at sites such as Estrées-sur-Noye (Somme). There are again problems due to the fact that the overwhelming majority of these sites are known from the air and have not been excavated, but it does seem that many had been abandoned by the fourth century, and that many of those that remained in occupation were considerably reduced in scale compared with the earlier period – for instance, the site at Hamois (Namur) (Van Ossel and Defgnée 2001) or the villa of Dury (Somme) just south of Amiens (Quérel and Feugère 2000). In his survey of the evidence for the Picardy area, albeit conducted twenty years ago, Van Ossel (1992: 98–9) was able to point to a number of sites where excavation had demonstrated continuing occupation into the fourth century or later, even if on a much-reduced scale, with few or no signs of luxury, and often the increasing use of timber for building. So sites continued to be occupied and presumably owned, and agrarian production continued also, but, by and large, these 'villas' were certainly not the theatre for displays of aristocratic self-representation. A similar conclusion may be drawn for much of Gaul north of the Seine (Van Ossel 1992: Ch. 5), suggesting that other than in a small number of privileged areas, such as around Trier and Cologne, the villa, even if it was still a functioning economic concern (cf. Chapter 6), was no longer a preferred *locus* of elite investment for purposes of impressing. This was not a total absence, for there are some fourth-century villas of pretension from this region, but these sites are few and far between, suggesting particular circumstances or proprietors rather than a more general regional vehicle for competitive display. Nonetheless, there are a few villas which recall those further south and they merit mentioning. Perhaps the most impressive was that at Blanzy-les-Fismes (Aisne) with its triconch room floored with an elaborate mosaic of the myth of Orpheus, dating probably to the first half of the fourth century. There were also those at Vieux-Rouen-sur-Bresle (Seine Maritime), with its floors in a brick version of *opus sectile* (Darmon 1994: 83), and Sainte-Marguerite-sur-Mer (Seine Maritime) with eight mosaics, one of them a wall mosaic, as well as fragments of *opus sectile* (Darmon 1994: 106–14). South of the Seine and therefore not far from these last two was the villa at Mienne-Marboué (Eure) with its fine, probably fifth-century mosaic bearing the name of the presumed owner of the property, one Steleco. But to list such a small number of sites with late Roman mosaics simply reinforces the argument that north of the Seine the villa in no way had the same meaning for the aristocracy of the region as it did south of the Dordogne. North of the Seine, other arenas for elite self-representation had opened up, such as the use of military-derived dress, showing the dominance of the state over the civic.

Conclusions

Rather than recapitulate the evidence presented above, it would seem to be more useful to make a couple of points which arise out of that evidence, which recur throughout and which also have importance for the transformations of the fifth century to be discussed in Chapter 9. The first point is the importance of the visual media in presenting and communicating status in this later Roman world. Perhaps because of the traditional reliance on text (itself in origin, of course, an elite visual medium) this aspect has rather been downplayed. It is clear from what has been presented above that in the late Roman world differences of occupation and differences of social degree were each accompanied and signalled by approved codes of dress, personal presentation and physical environment, legible to other members of society. The nature of late Roman society, with its multiple degrees of ethnic, gender, age or regional identities, functional specialisations and social standing, had its visual expressions. The visibility of these various aspects of Roman society transferred well into the archaeological record, and if we focus more on that record than the written one, the importance of visual presentation to an informed readership, both in life and in death, becomes clear. The potential of such data for reconstructing a 'lived experience' or a 'phenomenology' of late Roman Western society is clear and should be a fruitful way forward.

The second point is the integrative nature of late Roman social constructs, in particular those of the aristocracy and the military. Looking across the broad sweep of the West in the fourth century, it is remarkable how much unites the elite self-representation of Iberia, southern Gaul, areas of northern Gaul and Britain, be it in matters of house type, room plan, fixed decoration or portable material culture. Yes, there were regional variations and emphases as one would expect and as is a recurring theme of this work, but these differences worked within a common vocabulary, grammar and syntax of expectations over how these elites portrayed themselves. These were the indicators of the cultural capital gained and expended. The vocabulary was that of the range of status markers available, the grammar was the range of permissible ways in which they could be combined and recombined, and the syntax was *paideia*, the underlying, governing structures of social and cultural formations. This was a visual language, also, which was increasingly taken on board by the Church, since the Church operated in a late Roman milieu and its bishops were increasingly recruited from aristocratic backgrounds. A variant on this was the importance to some elite males, particularly in northern Gaul but sporadically elsewhere, of military self-representation, sometimes perhaps incorporating elements of the German warrior alongside those of the Roman soldier. Things military had, of course, been central to the identity of the Roman male, particularly the elite, since the early Republic, and even though the formal career structures binding military and civilian had been dissolved during the third century, warfare was a central activity of the Late Roman Empire from the emperor downwards. Even the Church, with its rhetoric of the Christian life as a form of *militia*, not to mention bishops with military service under their belts, absorbed some of this ethos.

We may, perhaps, conclude with an example that demonstrates how fluid the construction of such identities might be and how contrary to some of the polarities through which we have traditionally sought to comprehend the period. The villa of Mienne-Marboué was mentioned above for its fifth-century mosaic bearing the name of, presumably, the *dominus*, one Steleco. This was a Germanic name (cf. *Stilicho*), and it is a distinct possibility that he or his immediate forebears had served in the Roman army or as *foederati*. Yet, rather than deploying the semiotics of military or Germanic identity, he had chosen to record himself through that most Roman of media, a mosaic, in a residence of 'Roman', aristocratic type. Steleco or his family had consciously assimilated themselves to Roman-style elite culture and its practices, yet at the same time other elite males – but of Gallo-Roman descent – would have been presenting themselves through the semiotics of the soldier, more particularly the German warrior. Or, yet again, Steleco may have been a Gallo-Roman by descent but given a name whose 'Germanic' significance had largely been lost through mingling of 'Roman' and 'German' populations over the decades. Truly, these identities were 'constructed' and 'situational' rather than innate.

6 | Rural settlement and economy in the late Roman West

In the previous chapter we considered rural settlements, essentially villas, in largely social and cultural terms. But that was to concentrate on specific aspects of the villa at the expense of others, notably the economic, and to concentrate on the villa to the exclusion of other types of settlement and of the population that these housed and of the agriculture that they practised. In this chapter we shall examine the countryside more in habitative and economic terms: what were the settlement patterns, social structures and economic formations of the countryside? The traditional narrative of rural settlement and economy in the later Roman period was simple and derived essentially from textual sources. The High Empire had seen the imposition or creation of a domanial system of exploitation centred on the villa. The villa was not just a cultural symbol of the integration of the elites into the Roman world; it was also an expression of a mode of production responding to the imposition of the imperial system and based on the exploitation of subordinated, peasant labour. In classic Marxist characterisations, this was a slave economy. This economic and social formation was fatally weakened by the 'third-century crisis', which saw the collapse of the villa in many areas (this argument always held true much more for Gaul than for Iberia, but it was principally French workers who structured a debate in these terms at a time when Spanish and Portuguese ones were prevented from so doing) and thus precipitated a crisis in landownership and the system of exploitation. This 'crisis' became assimilated to Marxist debates over the transition from the 'slave' to the 'feudal' mode of production. More recently, with the advent of significant amounts of archaeological evidence and with rethinking of the nature of late antiquity, this schema has been rejected as a gross oversimplification and one which laid far too much stress on a particular settlement type, the villa, at the expense of all others, as well as too much stress on a particular period, the 'third-century crisis', as causative agent at the expense of longer-term developments and perspectives. The view, again text-based, of the late Roman countryside as populated by *coloni* who were little more than tied serfs in an estate system has also been rigorously questioned (e.g. Carrié 1982) and the possibilities of other forms of exploitation achieved through other forms of social structures have been aired.

Therefore, because the subject matter of this chapter will be the medium term, the changes and their significance in human occupation and exploitation of the landscape, a landscape itself conditioned by the long term, this chapter will be the one which most consciously evokes the concepts of the *Annales* tradition of study, or at least the Braudelian generation, with its insistence on the primacy of underlying structures of the *longue durée* and their interaction with the shorter epochs of the *moyenne durée*, with little or no regard for *histoire événementielle* as expressed in questions such as the following: did short-term events, including the 'third-century crisis' or the reaction thereto by the Roman state, intersect directly with the long-term structures producing a new medium-term, or was it more a case of existing medium-term trends continuing, albeit modified? Inevitably, an important element of this discussion will be changes to the number and distribution of villas, partly because of the importance of the settlement type and the class of proprietors it most probably represented, and partly because of the prominence of the villa in the historical and archaeological literatures. What we know, or think we know, about the agrarian systems and economic and social structures of exploitation at the villas will be summarised first. But equally if not more important will be the contribution of our growing knowledge of other types of settlement and their patterns of development across the period. Thanks to archaeology, we now recognise that there was a whole range of settlement and building types in the late Roman countryside and that they represented different types of exploitation (arable, pastoral, mineral, productive and seasonal) and of social groupings as well as different ways of structuring the rural economy and the production and mobilisation of surpluses. To what extent do they have tales to tell that are independent of the particular economic and cultural construct of the villa?

The 'villa economies'

Recently, the evidence for the possible types of agrarian exploitation and the human structures necessary for these has been reviewed for both southwestern Gaul (Balmelle 2001: Ch. 3) and Iberia (Arce *et al.* 2007: Chs. 3 and 5). Both Balmelle and Arce *et al.* are forced to depend on the scattered textual evidence because of the insufficient archaeological evidence to construct an alternative analysis. In part, this lack is because of the tendency for earlier excavators to concentrate on the residential buildings, the *pars urbana*, of the sites at the expense of the agricultural areas and structures. Thus, not only do we know little about the types and plans of the structures that might be found in those parts, but we are also poorly informed on such useful possible sources of evidence as installations, including presses and settling tanks, or on agricultural implements. Crucially, this also means we do not have a dependable suite of environmental evidence on such things as cereal agriculture or animal bones to reconstruct the pastoral regime. Nevertheless, finds and studies from a number of Iberian villas and areas, and, to a lesser extent, from southern Gaul, allow the identification of the materials exploited, even if we cannot as yet approach their relative importance at the level either of the single site or the region. The implements from rural sites in Lusitania, such as São Cucufate, show evidence for cereal agriculture; for viticulture; for presses and decantation tanks, either for wine or for olive oil; for stock raising; for textile production; and for carpentry, as well as for the hunt. All these accord well with the potential of these circum-Mediterranean climatic zones. The predominant product in terms of area and importance was undoubtedly grain, principally wheat, to feed not only the estates but also the towns, to pay taxes and thus to support the imperial superstructure. Other crops such as barley and oats are attested to, which could have gone either to human or animal consumption. The remains of presses and tanks attest to large-scale processing either of the grape or of the olive (more detailed analyses of residues such as grape pips or olive stones are needed to determine which). Both wine and olive oil were staples of the Mediterranean world and could be moved considerable distances, though, unfortunately for modern workers, in this period the wooden barrel (cf. Marlière 2001) seems to have been used in preference to ceramic amphorae in southern Gaul and in Iberia, making it more difficult to track the dispersion of such products away from their places of origin (cf. Chapter 7, p. 314). Nevertheless, the number of presses and other installations detected suggests that the south-west of Gaul, principally north of the Garonne, remained an area of volume production of wine in the fourth century (Balmelle *et al.* 2001), in distinction to all other areas of Gaul, bar one, where production seems to have diminished significantly after the second century (Brun and Laubenheimer 2001: esp. 214–19). The one area of Gaul other than the south-west where viticulture was important – indeed, it had expanded significantly since the High Empire – was the Moselle valley, where recent systematic survey has demonstrated the presence of numbers of wine-producing sites (Brun and Gilles 2001), a phenomenon explicitly linked by the workers to the promotion of Trier to imperial residence. The presence at some of these sites of official-issue metalwork such as brooches and belt suites may attest to state involvement in this industry. The other liquid produced by pressing, olive oil, is less easy to document. It clearly continued to be produced at some Iberian sites (Arce et al. 2007: 80–1) but most likely on a limited scale and certainly nothing like the major industry of Baetican olive oil of the first and second centuries. As we shall see in the next chapter, this industry had been effectively destroyed at the start of the third century, and the region that profited in its stead was North Africa. Indeed, the North African industry seems to have come to hold a dominant position in the supply of olive oil to the littoral of the western Mediterranean during the fourth century and later. In the face of this state-subsidised dominance, other industries such as that in south-eastern Gaul, which was characterised by distribution in the Gauloise 4 amphora (Laubenheimer 1990: 77–110), seem to have gone into recession also. So the evidence, such as it is, for the production of olive oil in southern Gaul and Iberia in the late Roman period probably speaks of the local and regional levels rather than of any significant export trade. But what is common to all these types of production, cereal or fruit, is the creation and mobilisation of large quantities of surplus production over and above that required for the sustenance of the villa and its inhabitants. Some of this may have gone in tax, but much more probably went onto the commercial market to gain income.

The evidence for stock rearing varies regionally in its patterns of the relationship between cattle, sheep or goats, and pigs. One animal which may well have had a particular importance south of the Pyrenees was the horse. This is an animal whose significance is often neglected, but it was particularly important for a state which had a standing army with a large cavalry arm. There are mentions of the raising of horses in late Roman Spain, as, for instance, by the fourth-century veterinary writer Pelagonius (*De Veterinaria Medicina* I.5), who specifically refers to Galicia. Some modern writers have suggested that horses may also have been among the supplies directed from northern Iberia over the Pyrenees to the armies on the Rhine (cf. p. 129). At the villa of El Val (Madrid) in the centre of the peninsula (cf. Arce et al. 2007: 232–6), a range of structures on the northern side of the complex has been argued to be stables, and the site has produced quantities of horse bone, suggesting a specialist role in horse husbandry for this site – whether for the army or the circus we cannot tell. But whatever the precise form of the regimes at individual sites or in particular areas, what is important as a linking economic motif across the 'villa economy' is that it was directed to the production and mobilisation of surpluses on a large scale, and in some cases, such as oleiculture and viticulture, arguably on an 'industrial' scale. Economically, the villa is an expression of the requirement for surplus, and regions and areas where the villa was a widespread form of settlement must have been regions and areas where agriculture was geared to the production of significant surplus.

If reconstructing the agrarian regimes at individual villas, let alone within whole regions, is no precise science, then attempting to reconstruct the social and legal structures of possession for these villas is even more fraught. The general picture derived from the texts, be they narrative or legal, for the Roman Empire of the fourth century was for the importance of alienable and transmissible landed wealth, something we have already encountered in previous chapters. The textual sources paint a picture of landed individuals and families and of their rural residences that accords perfectly well with our understanding of villas in the West at this date, though it must be admitted that that picture is itself in large measure derived from applying the textual sources to the archaeology. Nevertheless, one can well interpret the layout and rooms of a Séviac or a São Cucufate as the residence of a *dominus*, and his family, household and labourers; indeed, it would be quite difficult to do otherwise. But there is an inherent dissonance in trying to identify structures of exploitation and production from the evidence of sites such as villas, which are expressions of expenditure. For what the textual sources also make clear is that Roman landholding was commonly multiple and fragmented, not a single block of land. Aristocrats could and did hold property in more than one locality, in more than one province (as we have seen with Paulinus of Nola and his wife), or, indeed, in many provinces, as her *Life* tells us of Melania the Younger. Thus a particular grand villa, or even group of grand villas, need not have been an economic expression of the prosperity of their immediate environs, but rather of their proprietors' landholdings wherever they may have been, plus, of course, the proprietors' wish to expend their capital and income on the creation and maintenance of this type of residence. Likewise, a modest villa might not be an index of the relative poverty of its proprietor but of his wealth, if it was just the centre of one of his many estates, and its produce and rents were expended somewhere else altogether. Moreover, as the example of Paulinus of Nola and Therasia also shows, estates could be split and recombined on marriage. So also could they be upon the death of a proprietor if, as seems generally to have been the case in the Roman world, a system of partible inheritance was the norm. Property could also be alienated, either by sale or by gift, as Melania the Younger and others did with their property by donating it to the Church.

An allied problem is the nature and legal and other status of the workforce required to exploit these estates. As mentioned above, anachronistic concepts such as the 'slave mode of production' or the 'slave economy' for villas in the Roman West outside Italy have now been largely jettisoned for want of evidence. It is also now appreciated that *coloni* – that is, agricultural workers in direct legal dependency upon their master – were not necessarily the only form of labour force in the fourth-century West, but just one that appears in various more or less problematic texts (Carrié 1982), texts whose analysis also shows that the term *colonus* might mean different things at different times and in different places. Attention has therefore moved more to the archaeological evidence of villa buildings and other settlement types as a way of approaching such questions. Because of the concentration of excavations on the *pars urbana*, the areas where a resident workforce might have been housed have received little and sporadic attention; because of the concentration of excavations on villa sites, settlements at a distance from villas but which may have housed agricultural workers have likewise received little and sporadic attention. In the south-west of Gaul, this has even led some workers to suggest that the villa was a purely residential phenomenon, with the business of agriculture, and its attendant workforce, being located on sites other than the residence. In Iberia, there is the example of Liédena, where the two, long structures outside the main residence, divided into pairs of rooms like early imperial barrack blocks, have been interpreted as lodgings for the workforce, though others prefer to see them as storehouses or working areas (Arce *et al.* 2007: 61). Instead, in a recent review, Arce *et al.* (2007: 61–4) have pointed to the small but growing corpus of surveys and other work in Iberia that has identified rural settlements that comprise groupings of simple residences. Some of these lie close to (less than 5 km from) villas, so they could be hypothesised to be dependent on or associated with such villas. But as she readily admits, archaeology cannot of itself demonstrate juridical or economic relationships; such sites could equally be the centres for a peasantry working the land around the settlement. Or the population of such settlements might owe labour service as well as or instead of rents or other dues to the *dominus* of the villa. The possibilities are manifold and as yet incapable of demonstration one way or the other, but it does bring us to the important topic of how non-villa settlements and the landscapes within which they lay might be interrogated to fill out our picture of rural settlement, economy and society.

Non-villa settlements and economies

As little as ten years ago, it might not have been possible to write this section, and even today it is possible only to a fairly limited extent. Partly this was because of the concentration on the villa, and particularly on the *pars urbana*, both in terms of the expenditure of archaeological fieldwork effort and in terms of exegetic thinking. Partly, it was the correlative of this concentration, the undervaluation and under-exploitation of the place and the contribution of other forms of settlement. This was increasingly recognised and problematised from the 1970s, and projects of survey, excavation and analysis were formulated, but in the nature of things these take a long time to work through both in the field and in the analysis stages. However, a number of teams of workers both north and south of the Pyrenees have been putting in the long-term, and often thankless, labour of survey, excavation, analysis and synthesis necessary to move away from the villa-dominated physical and conceptual landscape towards one scrupulously attentive to the full range of human activity in and impact on the landscape. Much remains to be done, perhaps particularly in the exploitation of palaeo-environmental data; each new survey, each new excavation advances the subject a little. But the questions posed and the methodologies adopted do now allow at least a preliminary sketch of the nature and problems of the data set and the range of questions that may be asked of it, leading to new understandings of the agricultural, settlement and economic landscapes of the period. It is crucially important that these projects allow quantification of the settlement history, not just in crude terms of number of sites occupied but also in terms of numbers of new creations, numbers of continuing sites and numbers of abandoned sites. This would provide evidence for the stability or dynamism of the rural settlement pattern and population, and thereby allow us to move away from a crude elision of a drop in numbers with 'decline'. Questions may also be posed over whether changing numbers are those of essentially similar site types or whether a drop in numbers might, for instance, represent nucleation of a previously dispersed habitat, suggesting that overall population levels may not have changed, but rather that social structures or modes of exploitation and/or ownership changed. This allows for much more nuanced and revealing analyses than do simple, linear and teleological narratives of 'decline'.

Rather than attempt to try to mention large numbers of individual pieces of work often with mutually incompatible methodologies, the approach in this chapter will be to look at geographical groups of projects chosen for the degree of development both of the fieldwork and of the analysis, thus enabling a consideration both of the nature of the data set and of the range of possible approaches. These are as follows: northern Gaul, particularly the Ile-de-France; central Gaul; south-eastern Gaul, particularly the areas to either side of the lower Rhône valley (with an excursus on the south-west); the Mediterranean littoral of Spain; and the valley of the Guadalquivir in southern Spain. The chapter will then conclude with a discussion of possible interpretative models for the countryside, relating chronological developments to a range of economic, social and cultural influences.

Northern Gaul

Our knowledge and understanding of the nature of rural settlement and of the chronology and processes of change in the region of the Ile de France, Picardy and adjacent areas such as Normandy have been revolutionised by the sustained project of enquiry associated above all with Paul Van Ossel, Pierre Ouzoulias and their colleagues, formalised as the research group Diocesis Galliarum. This enquiry has encompassed surface survey, excavation and the exploitation of material culture and environmental evidence. Prior to this work, our picture of rural settlement under the High Empire was dominated by the villa, particularly in the Picardy area, where the aerial survey by Agache in the 1970s (Agache 1978) demonstrated the presence of hundreds of first- to third-century villas of a wide range of sizes along with simpler rural sites. Similar sites, though in less spectacular concentrations, were known or subsequently reported from neighbouring areas or from further afield (e.g. Ferdière *et al.* 2010; Leday 1980). Subsequently, excavation demonstrated that the particular and distinctive layout of these complexes was a reworking of late Iron Age precedents. Agache was firmly of the opinion (1978: Ch. 8) that these villas were destroyed in the crisis of the third century and that the fourth-century landscape was dominated by much simpler structures and settlements peopled by a late Roman version of serfs and prefiguring the villages of the area in the Middle Ages (for a summation of this earlier work, see Wightman 1985: Ch. 11, though she was well aware that the paradigm was shifting). This both derived from and fitted with earlier, historically based views of the period. More recent work has modified the process, chronology and understanding of what happened (Van Ossel 1992 remains fundamental; see also Ouzoulias and Van Ossel 1997, 2001; Van Ossel 1995; see Van Ossel and Ouzoulias 2000 for an English-language summary). What these studies, either recensing older data or based on new material, show is the great regional variability of processes such as site abandonment, survival and creation of new sites. Another very important aspect of the results of this work is that it allows consideration of types of site other than the conventional villa, thus permitting the trajectory for the villa settlement type to be contextualised within a wider series of settlement types and their associated evidence and problems.

For the north Gaulish villa, it is clear, as we have already seen in the specific context of Chapter 5, that the third century was a turning point, with the fourth century showing nothing like the number of villas across northern Gaul and the Rhineland compared with the levels attained by the end of the second century. But it is now equally clear that that turning point did not always lie in the second half of that century, and change could be signalled by abandonment rather than destruction. So any overall discussion of developments in the villa pattern will have to take into account a longer chronological range and wider range of processes than just a short-term 'crisis' marked by destruction. Sometimes, as at some sites in the Forest of Hambach, the change dated to the first half of the third century, whereas for other sites in the same complex it was the later third century (Van Ossel 1992: 69). In other areas in Belgium and France, the end of occupation on some sites dated to the later third century also, but with no trace of fire or violence (Van Ossel 1992: 70–2), as at the well-excavated and well-published villa at Hamois (Namur), where large parts of the villa were simply given up in the later third century, with no evidence of destruction (Balmelle and Van Ossel 2001). Such modifications to the villa pattern raise questions as to whether changes in ownership, exploitation or preferred settlement form (or combinations of these) lay behind the observed changes. On the other hand, in some areas, particularly that around Trier, there was evidence of destruction by fire at a number of villas (Van Ossel 1992: 70). Another well-excavated and well-published example is Echternach (Luxembourg) (Zimmer *et al.* 1981), where there is evidence of destruction by fire in the latter part of the third century, cause unknown. It would therefore be implausible to attempt a discussion of the period that excluded the possibility of the historically attested invasions of the second half of the third century as a causative agent, but, as with other aspects of the north of Gaul discussed in Chapter 2, it is often the aftermath that gives the best guide to the event. Some villas, again Echternach is an example, show a break in occupation in the late third century before reconstruction, suggesting that the 'estate' may have continued as an entity and to have functioned agriculturally even in the absence of its former centre. But as we saw in Chapter 5, the Trier area was then to be the only one in northern Gaul with substantial new villa building in the fourth century, and also on the basis of the reconstruction and maintenance of many villas, the first half of the fourth century was a period of relative prosperity in at least the western half of Treveran territory (Polfer 2001). There was destruction at a number of sites in the lower valley of the Alf, between Trier and Koblenz, but these dated to the 350s rather than a century earlier; historically, this could be associated with the Alamannic incursions of that decade, the usurpation and suppression of Magnentius (350–3), or the campaigns of Julian (355–60). In general, in the areas west of the central Rhine, the evidence is for a secular decline in villa numbers through the fourth century, but with some 55 per cent of villas in the Trierbezirk with good dating evidence showing occupation into the late fourth or early fifth century (Van Ossel 1992: 74). North of the Treveran area and west of Cologne, the Aldenhover Platte seems to have been an area of considerable stability of both villa and non-villa settlement (Lenz 2001).

For the Paris Basin, it has been possible to create balance sheets for the creation and abandonment of sites through time (Ouzoulias and Van Ossel 2001), showing that the third century saw both a rise in the number of abandonments and a decrease in the number of new sites, with greater stability through the fourth century and then another period of abandonment in the fifth. Individual villas, such as Richebourg (Yvelines) (Barat 2003), could show continuity of occupation down into the late third century, with restructuring at that date and continued use into the fourth century. Or it could, as at Bois Rosière (Val-d'Oise), show progressive disuse of the Roman-style structures of a small villa through the later third and early fourth centuries, but continuing occupation into the fourth in timber structures (Poyeton 2003). Otherwise, the fourth-century constructions occasionally took the form of traditional villas, as at Saint-Germain-lès-Corbeil (Essonne) (Petit and Parthuisot 1995; cf. Van Ossel and Ouzoulias 2000: 147), though the fifth-century structures on the site come from a very different tradition of construction (Figure 6.1). Clearly, it would be very foolish to try to write a single narrative of villa 'decline' from such evidence and even more so to posit a single agency such as hostile destruction. Instead, there seems to be a more drawn-out phase of realignment of the rural settlement pattern insofar as it concerned villas. Nevertheless, it is the case that in the fourth century there were, overall, fewer villas in northern Gaul than there had been in the late second century, and they were generally smaller and less well appointed: reasons for these changes will now be considered.

To start with, much work remains to be done at the level of the individual villa to provide reliable occupation sequences and dating. At the level of the region or subregion, it is evident that there are almost as many patterns as there are areas studied. But as stated above, there was an overall drop in the number of villas occupied during the course of the third century, more particularly in the second half of that century. Even without the historical record, the archaeology would attest to significant shifts in the villa

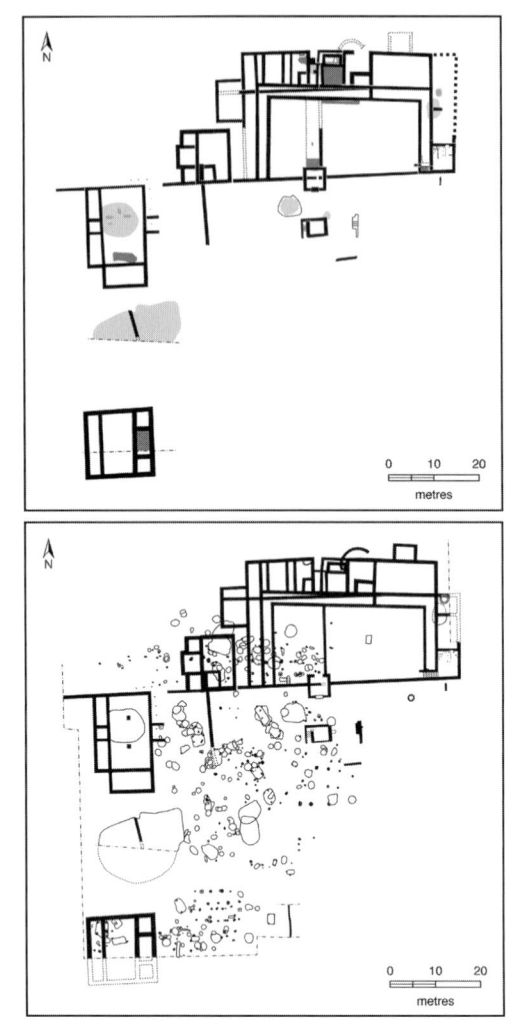

Fig. 6.1 Saint-Germain-lès-Corbeil, plan of the villa in the fourth century (upper) and the fifth century (lower)

settlement pattern, though analysis might focus rather on questions of changes in ownership and exploitation and of preferred settlement type, such as a growth in absentee proprietorship or the decline of the villa as preferred aristocratic settlement. It is worth noting that again the quantitative and qualitative peak of the villa pattern seems to have come at the end of the second and in the first half of the third century, as with the cities of the region (cf. Chapter 2), and the co-'decline' of the cities and the villas may suggest that a realignment of the medium-term economic and social patterns was already under way, quite possibly given greater impetus by a short-term destruction event and the consequent changes in *mentalités*. One other feature of this quantitative decline of the villa between the Seine and the Rhine and the rise to dominance of the non-villa settlement that we shall examine next, is that it contrasts with the pattern we shall be seeing south of the Seine in central Gaul. There, despite a diminution in the number of villas, the diminution in non-villa settlements was even more marked (cf. p. 282), so the pattern north of the Seine will need explanations that also take into consideration the contrast with the region to its south (cf. p. 286). For northern Gaul, it is to these settlements other than villas that we must now turn to fill out the picture for these landscapes.

What follows again leans heavily on the sustained endeavours of the research group Diocesis Galliarum both in the field and in their analyses of the data thus gathered. First of all, it should be noted that in this region we are looking at a dispersed settlement pattern of 'farmsteads', not one of nucleation into village-like groups; this suggests an agricultural system and possibly a landholding system based on the extended family, or else one where extended families worked the lands of more powerful *possessores*, rather than systems dominated by the cooperative peasant economies and societies of the 'village'. Recent surveys in the Paris Basin have shown that, as with villas, the development of the occupation pattern of such settlements can be very variable (Figure 6.2). To take two examples at either end of the possible spectrum, the area of Marne-la-Vallée (Disneyland) to the east of Paris had seen important phases of settlement expansion in the first half of the first century and the second half of the second century, but by the end of the fourth century the great majority of these sites had been abandoned, and the fourth-century landscape appears to have been largely depeopled (Ouzoulias and Van Ossel 2001: 148, based on Daveau 1997), but not, it should be said, abandoned agriculturally. By contrast, in the area of the Pays de France, only some 30 km to the north-west, systematic survey has located 122 sites, of which 65 were creations of the fourth century (Ouzoulias and Van Ossel 2001: 154–6). Recent excavations on the extensions to Charles de Gaulle Airport have shown an even greater density of occupation than that revealed by the survey, though with a much greater representation of earlier sites, meaning the fourth-century peak of creations may be overdrawn but with the density of occupation of that period still valid – a warning of the limits of surface survey. The disparities may in part be explained by the difference in soil types and drainage, as the Pays de France is better arable country than the relatively damp and difficult soils of the Marne-la-Vallée plateau. Between these two extremes, surveys in the areas of la Bassée, Mauldre-Vaucouleurs and Sénart have shown a decline in absolute

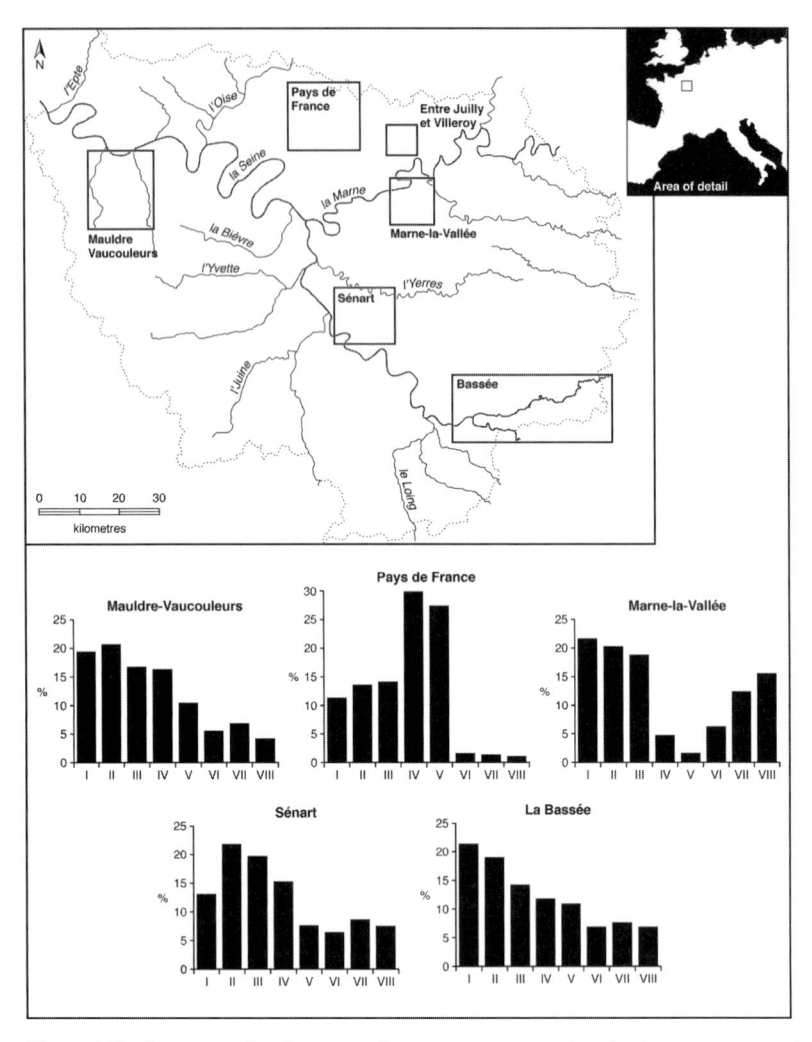

Fig. 6.2 Ile-de-France, development of occupation across time in the areas surveyed

numbers between the second and the fourth centuries, but with no sudden drop in the third and with the fourth-century levels still respectable, though these simple, quantitative histograms can conceal more complex and divergent realities, such as the differing profiles of abandonment and creation between the La Bassée and Sénart survey areas (Figure 6.3) (Ouzoulias and Van Ossel 2001: 148–54; 157–62, esp. Fig. 3, p. 151 and Fig. 9, p. 158). A broadly similar quantitative picture can be seen a little to the south in the Seine–Yonne interfluve, where there was a secular fall in numbers of sites from a peak in the first century through the second to fifth centuries (Séguier 2011: Fig. 3), though with no particular emphasis on the third.

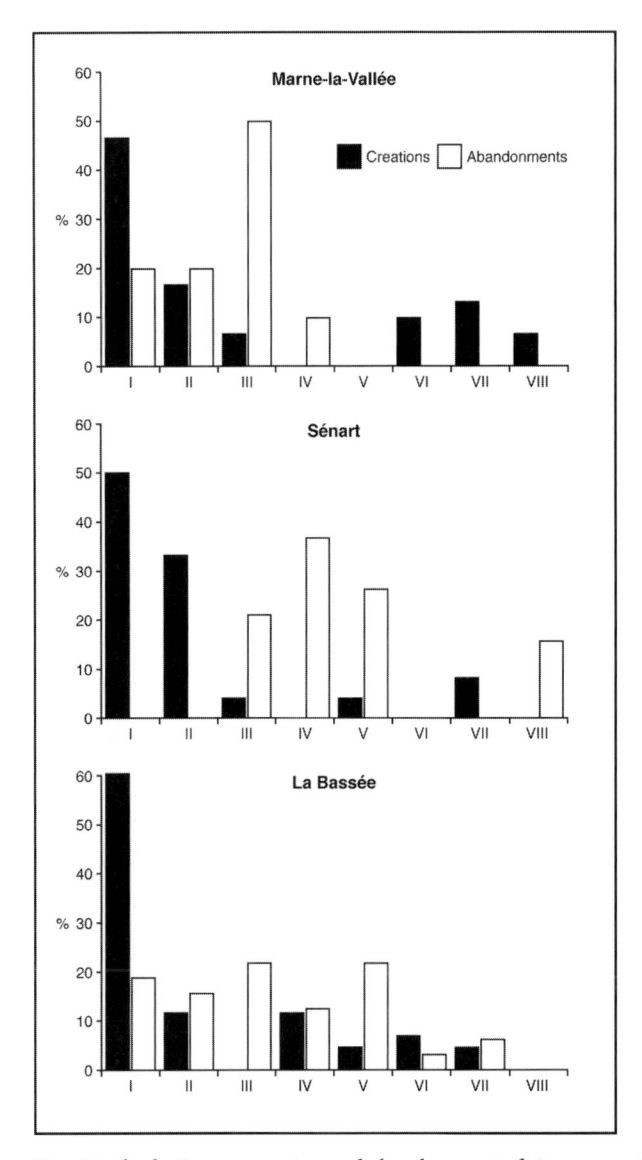

Fig. 6.3 Ile-de-France, creation and abandonment of sites across time in three areas surveyed

On the whole, the pattern seems to be much more of a medium-term cycle with increasing numbers of rural settlements from the late Iron Age into the earlier Roman period and then a settling back through the later Roman period, rather than a precipitous decline in the third century. Such a statement, of course, works at a high level of generalisation, smoothing out differences which can be quite pronounced, as we have seen above; nevertheless, it is a valid general comment.

But fluctuations in numbers of settlements and in their rates of creation or abandonment are not the only changes visible in the archaeological record. There are also changes in the layout of settlement sites and in the plans and materials of buildings on those sites to be taken into account. The counterpart of the decline in the number and elaboration of villas observable across most of northern Gaul is the rise in the number of settlements to more informal plans and with extensive use of timber. Thanks to excavations over the last two decades, particularly in advance of major civil engineering projects such as TGV lines and motorways, there is now a much larger corpus of such settlements and buildings, though still only a relatively small absolute number. A review of the layouts and building types of such settlements (Van Ossel 1997) has revealed that these layouts show much less formal organisation than the villas of the fourth century, let alone those of the second century and their late Iron Age predecessors. Clearly, the rationale of the spatial arrangements of such settlements had broken down. Sites such as Vert-Saint-Denis (Seine-et-Marne) (Koehler 1995; Ouzoulias and Van Ossel 2001: Fig. 14) show, in place of the formal, oriented structure of the villa of the High Empire, a much looser grouping of structures within enclosure ditches (Figure 6.4); a similar pattern can be seen at the site of Marolles-sur-Seine (Seine-et-Marne), with the elements of the fourth-century settlement overriding the more

Fig. 6.4 Vert-Saint-Denis, plan of the fourth-century settlement

regular structure of earlier enclosure ditches. We have already noted the example of Saint-Germain-lès-Corbeil (p. 274). There was little uniformity, either, in the range of structures on these sites. These were normally in wood, set either in post holes or on sill beams, or a mixture of the two (Van Ossel 1997), and ranging from simple, rectangular structures of under 20 m^2 in area to larger, more elaborate structures with one or two rows of internal posts, sometimes with indications of internal subdivisions. The evidence of the tools and of the grain and animal bones points clearly to these being working farms, with economic links to the outside world, as attested to by the presence of pottery and other trade goods.

The change from stone (or at least stone-founded) construction and from the 'Roman' layout of the villa to timber construction and an irregular grouping of buildings clearly indicated to earlier workers a major change in the social and cultural levels of the rural population. This impression was reinforced by the finding at some sites of structures considered to be of 'Germanic' type, leading some workers to propose that the change in construction type and settlement plans was linked to the arrival of Germanic populations in northern Gaul. This was particularly the case with the *fond de cabane* (*Grubenhaus*), or the sunken featured building (SFB), a squarish or rectangular structure represented by a scoop excavated into the subsoil and with one or more post holes in the short sides to carry the ridge pole of the roof. These structures performed a variety of functions (Hamerow 2002: 31–5), often ancillary to larger, rectangular, ground-level buildings. The SFB is a commonplace of fifth- and sixth-century and later settlements in Britain, northern Gaul, Germany on both sides of the Rhine, and the Low Countries, in settlements whose plan, building types and material culture have led archaeologists to associate them culturally with peoples of Germanic origin – Alamanni, Anglo-Saxons and Franks in particular. But the origins of this building type are still debated (Farnoux 1987; cf. Hamerow 2002: 31–5). Most of the fourth-century examples so far found west of the Rhine come from the northernmost parts of Gaul, Toxandria, where Salian Frankish settlement in the fourth century is attested to in the historical sources, and this has been part of the argument for the cultural ascription of this building type.

More recently, a significant site has been found deeper into north Gaul, at Saint-Ouen-du-Breuil (Seine Maritime), in the Pays de Caux north of Rouen (Figure 6.5) (Van Ossel and Ouzoulias 2000: 150–1). The settlement, dating to the second half of the fourth century, consisted of a number of long, rectangular buildings on the same east–west alignment, some with straight sides and some with bowed sides, with associated granaries, SFBs and other structures, suggesting, perhaps, a number of groupings (Figure 6.5). The parallels for the

Fig. 6.5 Saint-Ouen-du-Breuil, plan of the fourth-century settlement

building types, such as the bow-sided, long buildings, the granaries and the SFBs, come from areas associated with Germanic settlement (cf. Hamerow 2002: Chs. 2 and 3). Most of the material culture, principally pottery, was of standard, fourth-century, north Gaulish types, especially the stamp-decorated Argonne ware (Gonzalez *et al.* 2006). There was also a significant presence of black-burnished ware from the Poole Harbour area across the Channel (cf. p. 322). But some of the material is of types traditionally accepted as Germanic, such as brooches, an *Armbrustfibel* and a *Stutzarmfibel* (see Chapter 2, esp. pp. 79–85 for these arguments and more recent caution on simple ethnic identifications of such material). There was also a quantity of handmade pottery in forms and with decoration of Germanic types (cf. Seillier 1994); nevertheless, the fabrics were tempered with flint and quartz, suggesting local manufacture. All in all, the evidence supports the presence at Saint-Ouen-du-Breuil of a population group with contacts, possibly origins, east of the Rhine (though the treatment of the 'Germanic' pottery in ethnic terms as opposed to that of the 'British' pottery in terms of trade and contact is an interesting commentary on how exegetic frameworks for the same class of material from the same site can vary unacknowledged). Given the funerary, textual and other evidence reviewed in Chapter 2 for the presence of 'Germanic' peoples in fourth-century northern Gaul, the discovery of a settlement with non-Roman provincial material should occasion little surprise. But so often the question of Germanic settlement in Gaul in the fourth century has been viewed through the prism of events in the fifth century, so that fourth-century settlers are viewed as the *Wegbereiter*, forerunners, of the Frankish takeover. In fact, Saint-Ouen-du-Breuil can be explained perfectly well in the light of the fourth-century situation, and, furthermore, does not seem to have survived as a settlement much past 400. It should be noted that a similar, long, post-hole building has recently been excavated on the site of Essarts-le-Roi (Yvelines), though the accompanying material culture, principally pottery, seems entirely in the Gallo-Roman tradition (Barat and Samzun 2008), again pointing up the difficulties of characterising 'ethnic' identities in different domains of the archaeological evidence. More generally, the transition to building in timber is no longer seen in ethnic terms as an index of the infiltration of Germanic groups into northern Gaul, but rather in terms of changing social and economic norms, in moving away from the rigid layout of the villa with its accompanying cultural symbolism.

Therefore, as with the villas, so with the 'non-villa' settlements: the Roman-controlled areas between Seine and Rhine saw a countryside still settled and exploited. What had changed since the second century was the balance between the types of settlement, which presumably must reflect changing economic, social or cultural factors. Since in the Roman system the purpose of this agriculture would have been to produce a surplus over and above that required for the sustenance of the rural labour force, and for that surplus to be mobilised to serve the ends of whoever had power over it, these changes pose important questions. Under the High Empire, part of that surplus would have been removed as tax (in coin or in kind), in large part to sustain the armies. But, clearly, part of the surplus had been spent on the construction, embellishment and maintenance of hundreds of villas across northern Gaul, as well as on the public buildings, the private houses, and the goods and services that constituted the cities, along with such things as major rural sanctuaries. Under the Late Empire, this had changed radically. As was discussed in Chapter 2, the evidence that the cities of the Seine–Rhine region remained 'urban' in ways similar to their second century selves is largely lacking; instead the military and other state elements seem to have become increasingly significant. These places did, of course, have one important 'public' monument in the form of walls, but whether the surplus of a *civitas* went directly to pay for this monument, as it would have in the first or second centuries, is not at all certain; the army was supported by imperial revenues more generally. Essentially, there is little evidence that the surpluses generated in this region were deployed to create and sustain the traditional 'civil' forms of social and cultural expression. The few villas, mosaics and other such indicators would have needed only a fraction of the available product. How then to account for the use of these surpluses? One possible model would be that of the 'absentee landlord'; that is, that these territories were still in the possession of aristocratic (senatorial or provincial) proprietors who resided elsewhere, and it was there that they spent the revenues raised in northern Gaul. As was seen in the previous chapter, there is plentiful textual evidence for late Roman aristocrats having estates in more than one region or province, so the surpluses generated in northern Gaul could have been spent in Britannia Prima or Novempopulana. On the present evidence, this is incapable of proof or disproof. An alternative model or partial explanation put forward in Chapter 2 was that the landed elite remained, but that it now chose to represent itself differently, borrowing much more from the new, military aristocracy of the Late Empire than from traditional, civil practice. Another model is that the disappearance of the large majority of villas in the Seine–Rhine region actually reflected the disappearance also of the class of landed proprietors they represented; the upheavals of the second half of the third century to the rear of the Rhine frontier destroyed the existing patterns of aristocratic landholding (cf. Theuws 2009: 309–14). This is a scenario that corresponds with the thesis of increasing 'militarisation' of this region (cf. p. 93), and would therefore see a more direct producer–consumer relationship, with agricultural surpluses going to the armies on the Rhine and in the interior through the medium of the tax-gathering mechanisms, without being mediated through a local, civil aristocracy. This would see the region as more of a military 'procurement zone' than had been the case earlier on. Of course, to choose one or other of these models to the exclusion of the others would be foolish; there are probably elements of all three (and others) involved. But at least this opens up a range of ways of thinking about the question of the near disappearance of 'civil' modes of self-representation in urban and rural buildings.

Central Gaul

In the preceding chapter we touched upon the recent survey work that has been undertaken in areas of central Gaul to the south of the Seine or the Loire, but only as it related to the specific questions of the survival of villas into the fourth century and the types detectable (cf. p. 258). Here this evidence will be recontextualised by bringing into the equation the evidence for developments in the range of other types of rural settlements. As in Chapter 5, the discussion will be articulated around the evidence from the territory of the Bituriges Cubi, since it is this that has been published *in extenso* (Gandini 2008: esp. Chs. 9 and 10), while some other surveys were conducted for doctoral theses that remain unpublished, though papers have appeared on specific areas or topics (e.g. Kasprzyk 2003; Nouvel 2009), and these will be used to supplement the evidence from the area of Bourges. By the middle of the second century, the rural settlement pattern of this area exhibited a range of different sizes, different building plans and different surface markers of prosperity (marble, mosaic and pottery). However, by the second half of that century, the rate of creation of new sites had slowed compared with the preceding centuries (Figure 6.6), suggesting a stabilisation of the settlement pattern, and half of the new creations were villas; at the same period and for the first time, abandonments outnumbered creations of sites (Figure 6.7) (Gandini 2008: 409–13). This trend continued in the first

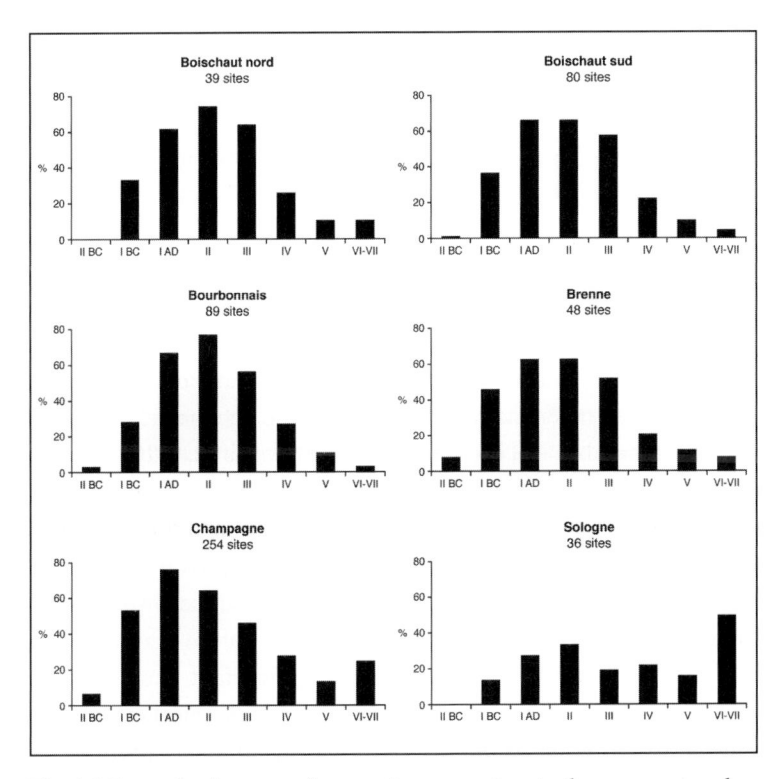

Fig. 6.6 Berry, development of occupation across time in the areas surveyed

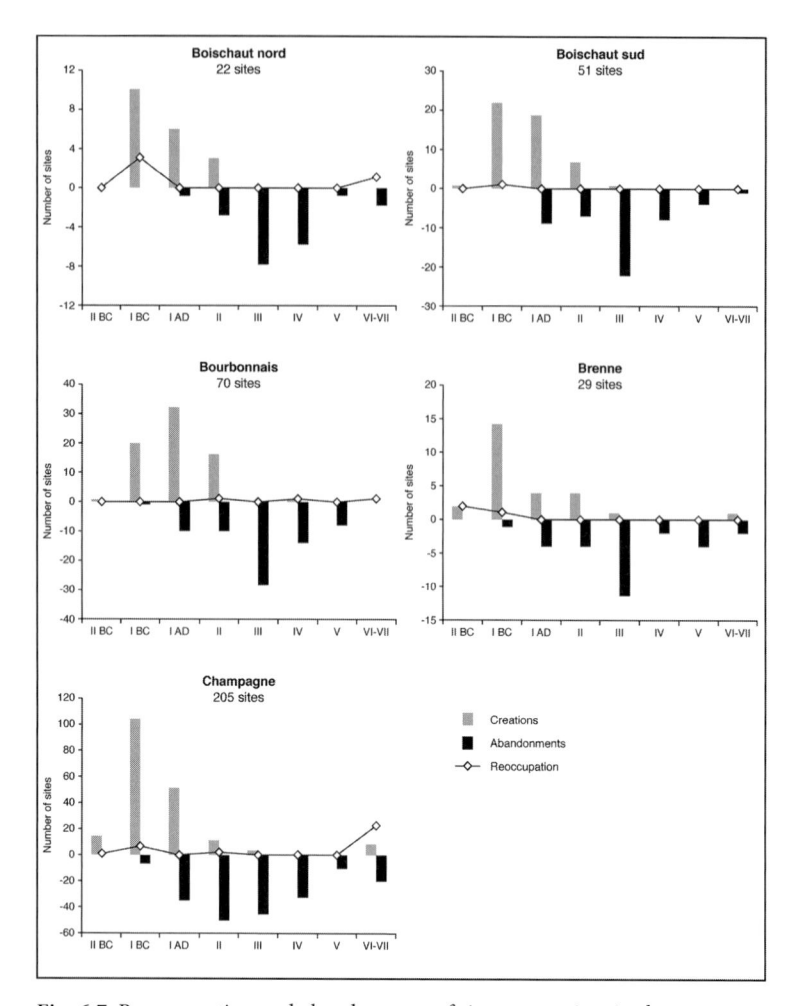

Fig. 6.7 Berry, creation and abandonment of sites across time in the areas surveyed

half of the third century and was accentuated through the second half. These abandonments were not equally shared across the settlement hierarchy (Figure 6.8); the number of villa sites decreased by less than 20 per cent, that of medium-sized sites halved, but the small sites built in timber almost disappeared (Gandini 2008: 413–15). In the fourth century the number of occupied sites was only some 50 per cent of those occupied in the second century, but, as we have just seen, the diminution affected the lower parts of the settlement hierarchy much more seriously, so the nature of rural settlement and society seems to have undergone important modifications (Gandini 2008: Ch. 10). There seem to have been geographical or possibly pedological reasons behind some of this, with, on the one hand, certain areas being almost abandoned and, on the other hand, a preference

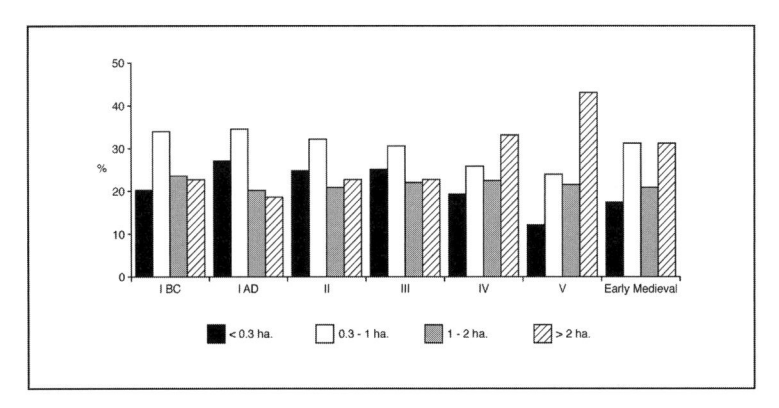

Fig. 6.8 Berry, sizes of site by century

for location near the provincial capital Bourges itself and in the communications corridor of the Cher valley, or else near the secondary centres of Levroux and Saint-Marcel/*Argentomagus* (with its *fabrica*) (Gandini 2008: 422–5). Another series of explanations may be linked to the economic and social exploitation of the territory. The part of the settlement hierarchy which 'benefited' most from these changes was the villas, of which a high proportion remained occupied and which came to be a much more important element numerically within the total of settlements. Are we seeing the concentration of agricultural exploitation, and possibly of rural population onto the villas and thus the development of a largely domanial system of exploitation across the countryside of the Bituriges Cubi? If so, it is interesting to recall that, as yet, few of these villas show the sorts of elaboration characteristic of those further south-west. This may in part be an artefact of the lack of excavation; future excavation may show them more comparable to the Novempopulana/Aquitania II grouping. It may also be that this form of competitive emulation was not one the local elites chose to indulge in, perhaps because they were not so fixated on the imperial and senatorial model of display. The evidence we have for neighbouring areas, such as that of the Senones to the north (Kasprzyk 2003; Nouvel 2009), is comparable. The sites which can be classed as villas (Nouvel 2009: his site class ER3) tell the same tale, of a better rate of survival through the third and on into the fourth centuries at the expense of the smaller, less elaborate site classes ER1 and ER2 (in particular). For the Arverni to the south-east (Trément and Dousteyssier 2001), the proportion of villas surviving from the second to the fourth centuries is exactly the same as that for the Bituriges Cubi at 82 per cent. In all three cases, overall, there was a numerical decline from the levels attained under the second century. But this impacted differentially on the various parts of the settlement hierarchy, with the villa being less affected or more favoured, so that by the fourth century, villas constituted a much more dominant element of the range of rural settlement types. Again, this could be interpreted as the *possessores* setting their hand on more of the productive capacity and surpluses of the territories concerned.

The contrast in the development of the site hierarchy overall and of its different constituents in the region we have just seen compared with that to the north of the Seine is obvious and striking and throws the Seine–Rhine region into even more relief. South of the Seine, the territorial aristocracy was in many areas perpetuated; indeed, it seems to have become more powerful, and apparently it was able to strengthen its hold over rural settlement and productivity at the expense of more modest site types and their inhabitants. In this it matches the pattern we have already to an extent seen in Chapter 5 for the aristocracies of south-western and south-eastern Gaul, regions of Spain and southern Britain. North of the Seine, the inverse seems to have taken place. The settlement hierarchy was dominated by small to medium sites, largely built in timber with little use of stone or formal masonry. Villas had by and large disappeared, and those that remained were usually on a much more modest scale than their second-century predecessors – indeed, sometimes they were little distinguishable from the non-villa sites. The Seine–Rhine region therefore stands out as exceptional, especially given the fundamental richness of its agricultural resources. This supports the arguments put forward in Chapters 1 and 2 that the events of the mid and late third century were very disruptive and in the medium term led to a profound realignment of the economy, society and cultural values, and thus of their expression, between the Seine and the Rhine.

South-eastern Gaul

By contrast, south-eastern Gaul lay far from the frontier, and the textual sources give little evidence of invasion or other disturbance in the region, save perhaps by Crocus and his followers at Arles (cf. p. 107). Nevertheless, it was long accepted that the supposed events of the mid to late third century had led to change in the rural order of things here as elsewhere. As so often, the traditional archaeology of rural settlement in this area had been dominated by the villa, and explanatory models by the 'crisis' of the villa in the third century as an expression not so much of barbarian irruption into the region as of the crisis of the imperial venture and its associated modes of production and display. However, in the 1970s, it became increasingly clear that this was unsatisfactory, yet again because it privileged one settlement type, the villa, at the expense of others, and also because this was a time when fieldwork was beginning to make it clear that there was a lot more to the Roman period countryside than just the villa. This led to the creation in areas of Languedoc and Provence, particularly those to either side of the lower valley of the Rhône, of a long-term programme of systematic survey undertaken with a specific research agenda concerning the changing numbers and forms of rural settlement through time and how these may be interpreted in terms of social structures and as expressions of economic exploitation. As a result of these surveys, undertaken with standardised data-recording systems to allow direct comparison, some 934 sites had been recorded by the end of the European research project ARCHEOMEDES in 1994 (Van der Leeuw *et al.* 2003; see Raynaud 1996 for interim statement and synthesis and Fiches 2002 for a presentation of some of the evidence). As was to be expected, each of the regions surveyed demonstrated its own peculiar pattern; nevertheless, overall trajectories could be established with the individual survey areas as variations on the themes.

Across the areas of Languedoc and Provence surveyed, there was a strong general tendency (Figure 6.9). From the late second century BC, there was a surge in rural settlement and activity, continuing through the first centuries BC and AD and peaking in the first half of the second century. This was marked by increases in the number of settlements, increases in the range of sizes and types of settlement, and increases in the relief and soils exploited (with expansion into the hitherto little settled, more difficult ecological zones such as the *garrigue*), and in due course by the appearance and growth of the villa. Thus these two centuries and more seem to have seen a rapid phase of both intensification and extensification of agricultural exploitation. This is presumably to be linked with incorporation into the Roman Empire and thus into the Mediterranean economic and cultural nexus, stimulating agricultural production and surplus extraction for sale either in the region or in the wider Mediterranean economy. The reciprocal of this was the greater availability of Roman-style imported goods, particularly pottery, incidentally increasing the visibility of these sites to the modern field survey and thus possibly making this upswing more visible. The chronology of this surge in occupation and disposable material culture can be paralleled in the archaeology of neighbouring cities, as perhaps best exemplified by Nîmes (Monteil 1996b: 153–60), which may be where at least some of the income gained was being deployed to embellish the city. A detailed study of the territory of Nîmes (Buffat 2011: Ch. 5, esp. 162–9) shows that in the third century 21 villas were abandoned out of 151 extant at the start of the

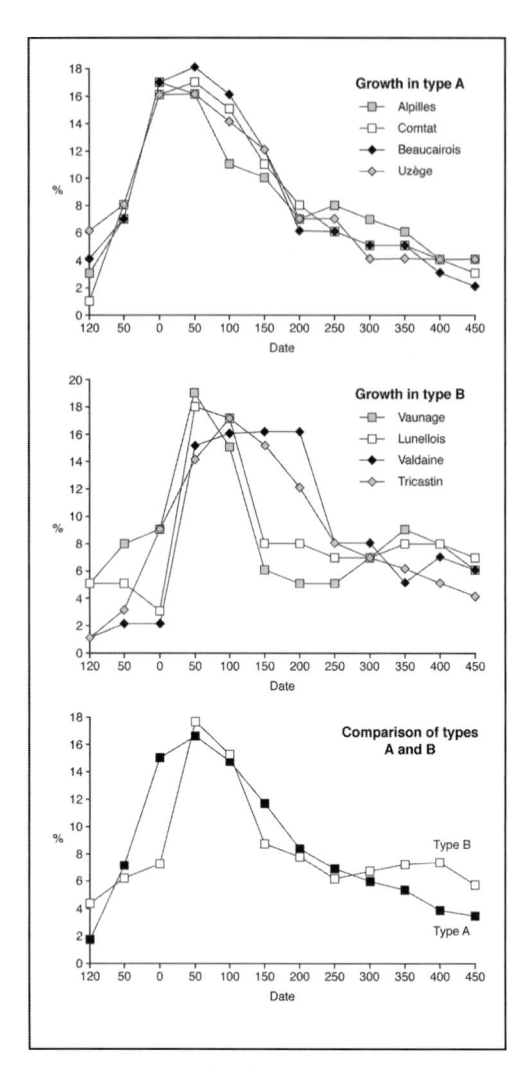

Fig. 6.9 Provence, development across time of types of site by area surveyed

century; that is, 14 per cent – hardly a catastrophe. When one considers that the absolute number of villas abandoned in the second century was greater, 28, representing 15.5 per cent abandonment, then the third century clearly was not a threshold but a continuation of a trend already established. The fourth century saw 27 abandonments, but also 10 probable new villas. But this stability of the pattern of villa occupation took place alongside a pattern of declining numbers of smaller sites (Van der Leeuw et al. 2003: Fig. 33), so what we may also be seeing is the increasing importance of the social and economic landscape of the villa, of the system of exploitation and production it represented, and of its proprietorial class, the *domini*. Elsewhere in the region, from the mid second century, this dynamic of expansion in numbers slowed and changed to a rather different one. Absolute numbers of settlements dropped and there was a tendency to focus back onto a smaller range of settlement types and onto longer-lived settlements at the expense of the dynamic but short-lived types characteristic of the pioneer phase. This could also be accompanied by abandonment of the more marginal areas, such as the Biterrois (around Béziers) (Mauné 1996). So in these areas also the villa may have been imposing itself as the settlement type that articulated the exploitation of the agricultural resources.

A microregional project of survey and excavation to the west of the lower Rhône in the area around Lunel-Viel (Gard) to the south-east of Nîmes (Raynaud 1996) gives a detailed picture of developments (Favory *et al.* 1994; Raynaud 1990). In this later period, the settlement types consisted of small settlements, generally of less than 0.5 ha., and of some larger sites, particularly again the villas and the *agglomérations*, nucleated settlements covering several hectares. At Lunel, the excavated cemeteries reveal evidence for the nucleated population. Where excavated, these two classes of site show a size of population and a range of agrarian and other activities suggesting that, to a considerable extent, they structured the economic exploitation of their zones. In some areas it seems that they also structured the settlement pattern, with villas and *agglomérations* acting as the focus of a grouping of smaller sites. This suggests an hierarchy by function, as well as by size and type, and that the economic basis of the settlements, including the smaller ones, was not autarchic but rather geared to the production and processing of surpluses. This argues in favour of a largely domanial economy and social structure with landed proprietors mobilising agrarian resources and labour in kind, through direct labour and labour obligations, or through rents and other dues. A related pattern can be seen east of the Rhône, where the early imperial surge had also died away from the later second century, but villas continued through the third and fourth centuries in gradually diminishing numbers alongside numerous other smaller settlements (APDCA 1996; Brun and Congès 1996). The presses and storage at these later villas show continuing production of olive oil, albeit on a reduced scale in comparison with the second century. Detailed survey of the area around the late prehistoric and early medieval *oppidum* of Saint-Blaise (Bouches-du-Rhône) and the Etang de Berre north of Martigues showed the long-term dynamics of the peopling of the area, with a secular increase through late prehistory and the early Roman period (Trément 2001). More specifically, it also showed that there was an echelon of non-villa settlements in the fourth century, less intense than under the High Empire (Trément 1999: Pt. III,

Ch. 3), but still suggesting an open and cultivated landscape. Again the presence of villas and the ranking of settlements argue for the funnelling of surplus up the socio-economic hierarchy rather than for a more localised and autarchic pattern.

Clearly, if there was a 'crisis' of rural settlement and economy in south-eastern Gaul, it occurred in the second, not the third century. In reality, it seems not to be a systemic crisis of the rural settlement pattern but rather the culmination of a medium-term upswing in settlement and exploitation and the beginning of the adjustment to a new part of the cycle. What we see is a region, which, for all its microregional variations, had undergone medium-term transformations in its settlement patterns closely linked with the short-term events of incorporation into the Roman Empire. These had in their turn produced not a 'crisis' of subjugation but rather economic and social opportunities with resulting changes in *mentalités* which led to the burst of activity that characterised the Early Empire. This surge then died away, and it is very noticeable that the levels of settlement, both numbers and total occupied area, closely resemble those prior to the surge (cf. Raynaud 1996: 198–204), suggesting that the structures of the long term were reasserting themselves in realigning settlement intensity with the carrying capacity of the agricultural system. This in its turn produced a relatively long period of general stability in settlement numbers and location from the third through the sixth century, with many sites persisting into the central Middle Ages and later (e.g. Lunel-Viel), with the next major threshold of change not until the eighth century. In this period of stability, the villa was still a significant settlement type, and some individual villas such as Loupian and Saint-André-de-Codols were substantial establishments. But the villa was not the only settlement type that structured and controlled the rural economy, so its development and ultimate fate, though of interest, cannot be taken as representative of those of the system as a whole. Instead, if we concentrate on the non-villa settlement types and patterns, we see a situation suggesting that the longer-term structures of agricultural potential and the production based on that were being expressed through long-term exploitation of the landscape by the majority of the rural population, with demand-led adjustments as reactions to the economic superstructures across the period. Perhaps the most important intersection of the medium term with the long term and the consequent change in *mentalités* were that the incorporation of the region into the Roman Empire forever turned its gaze outwards to the Mediterranean both for its economic structures of production and exchange and for its cultural structures, be they the Roman-style expression of the High Empire or the changes wrought by Christianity in the later period.

The Catalonian littoral

A number of systematic surveys have been undertaken in the modern region of Catalonia, particularly along the coastal plain from Empuriès/Ampurias (*Emporiae*) in the north through Barcelona (*Barcino*) and down to Tarragona (*Tarraco*), complementing the longer-standing work on the villas of the area (e.g. Chavarría Arnau 1996, 2006b). As with the work on their south-eastern French neighbours, the individual surveys show variations in the patterns of change over time and in the explanations for this; nevertheless, some overall trajectories can be defined. The evidence for the villas was briefly reviewed in the preceding chapter (p. 250) where it was noted that alongside considerable expressions of wealth there was also consistent investment in agricultural productivity as demonstrated by evidence for wine and olive-oil processing such as presses, storage jars and amphorae. This suggests that there was still a considerable market for these products and that they were, in important part, exploited through a hierarchical, domanial system. As yet, there has been little work on the non-villa settlement of the Mediterranean littoral, though a drop in pottery and thus in the visibility of sites in the later Roman period has been noted in field surveys in Catalonia – for instance, in the area of Barcelona and further north towards Empuriès (Gurt i Esparraguera and Palet Martínez 2001). These observations have been combined with palaeo-environmental evidence, principally pollen, for the Empuriès, Barcelona and Tarragona areas to show that in the fourth century the landscape remained dominated by cereal agriculture, though there was to be a pronounced shift in the fifth century towards a more pastoral agricultural regime (Gurt i Esparraguera and Palet Martínez 2001: 303–11) at the time when the villa sites were contracting or being abandoned (see p. 413 for further consideration of this). Overall, as with the surveys of the lower Rhône basin, the Late Empire saw a diminution in numbers of sites occupied from a peak in the second century. As in southern Gaul, the early imperial peak was the culmination of a phase of expansion of rural settlement beginning in a much earlier, pre-Roman, period. Though it is not yet possible to calibrate the chronology of the contraction in settlement numbers for Catalonia, it certainly does not seem to be an artefact of the third century alone.

More problematic for characterising and discussing the transitions in the later Roman period is the Tarragona survey because of the more than usual difficulties in recognising sites of this period due to the sharp drop in detectable surface remains, particularly pottery (Carreté *et al.* 1995: Chs. 9 and 10; see also Prevosti and Guitart i Duran 2011: Ch. 7, Sect. 5). If one compares raw numbers (Prevosti and Gutart i Duran 2011: 395), there is a fall in the number of sites by just over 50 per cent between the second and the fourth centuries (from 120 to 57). But this is actually part of a longer-term trend through from the first century BC. At that period the settlement hierarchy consisted of small, quite possibly relatively autonomous sites. The first century AD saw the introduction of the villa, both as type of site and presumably as form of agricultural exploitation and social entity. With this came a marked diminution of the number of non-villa sites. The first marked drop in site numbers comes in the second half of the first century, not the third: it was this trend that was continuing into the later Roman period. There were indeed fewer sites overall in the fourth as opposed to the second century, but villas were an important component of the fourth-century settlement pattern (8 as opposed to 39 of the two classes of smaller site combined) and some of those villas were very substantial, such as that at Centcelles (cf. p. 183). So simple numbers are not the whole story. Yes, there may have been an overall demographic decline, but this may have gone along with an increasing concentration of the population there was onto the major domanial sites, the villas, with non-villa sites perhaps in part being 'outstations' of the major complexes. The lack of imported pottery in the hinterland of the city compared with the pottery from Tarragona itself (Carreté *et al.* 1995: Chs. 9 and 10) may therefore be a reflection of the low social status of such settlements; it may also be a symptom of the lack of demand at such sites rather than lack of supply. Such late imported ceramics do occur at the villa sites (Járrega in Prevosti and Guitart i Duran 2011: esp. 180–95), which may have been funnelling produce to the city to feed it and underpin the economic activities that allowed it to import North African, Gaulish and other wares in more substantial quantities than its rural hinterland. At Tarragona and in its hinterland again, as with south-eastern Gaul, we seem to be seeing a medium-term cycle of agricultural expansion and then stabilisation at a lower level linked chronologically with the dynamics of incorporation into the imperial system and the challenges and/or opportunities that posed, in particular the establishment of domanial relations of production as materialised by the villa and its increasing dominance over smaller, less elaborate site types.

The Guadalquivir (Baetis) valley

One of the areas around the Mediterranean most heavily influenced by incorporation into the imperial system was the southern Iberian province of Baetica, comprising the valley of the river Baetis (now Guadalquivir) and the uplands to either side with their Mediterranean and Atlantic littorals. Under the Early Empire, this had become one of the major sources of the olive oil shipped to Rome as part of the system for the alimentation of the metropolis; considerable quantities of oil also were sent north to supply the armies along the Rhine and in Britain. Between the late 1960s and the start of the 1990s, Michel Ponsich carried out a survey of most of the Guadalquivir valley from Andujar, above Córdoba, to Sanlúcar de Barrameda near the river's mouth. The results were remarkable, particularly for the High Empire, when Baetica was one of the principal sources of olive oil for the *annona*, the official supply, of the city of Rome, resulting in a landscape full of evidence for the processing of olives and of the manufacture and use of amphorae on an industrial scale. It is important to remember, though, that this was not a monoculture; even in the principal oleiculture zone between Córdoba, Seville and Ecija (*Astigi*), the olive groves would have been on the higher, poorer ground, leaving plenty of space for cereal culture on the valley floor, diversifying and buffering the produce and labour cycles of the region. The decline of the olive-oil industry in the course of the later second and third centuries will be considered in more detail in the next chapter (p. 399), but for our purposes here the importance of Ponsich's work is that it does give a body of evidence for the later Roman period. This has recently been re-examined in the context of a longer consideration of the late Roman to early medieval period in the region (Carr 2002 – though I do not follow all her analysis). As Carr notes (2002: Ch. 1), Ponsich's survey methodology was not systematic and his categorisations and interpretations can be critiqued. The survey was based on such things as local information and following the course of the main Roman road along the valley or looking in the sides of modern watercourses, rather than the systematic sampling of study areas, a methodology which only developed after Ponsich had started his work. He divided the habitation sites found into four broad categories – *agglomération*, *villa*, *ferme* and *abri*, based on size, nature of material and relation to a watercourse. *Agglomérations* included towns, and *villas* yielded building materials, such as hypocaust tiles or marble, and agricultural equipment, such as olive presses, suggestive of a high-status, productive site. The distinction between *ferme* (farmstead) and *abri* (shelter) was generally on the basis of size and density of the surface scatter and proximity or not to a watercourse. In fact, neither in the size or nature of the surface material nor in the relation to water is there a clear break in the spectrum of sites, so they probably represent something more complex than a bimodal occupation and function pattern, particularly since surface scatters can be a poor guide to subsurface features (cf. Frankovich *et al.* 2000). Despite questions of categorisation and function (which would require systematic sampling by excavation to flesh out), it is nonetheless possible to say something about the pattern and density of later Roman occupation and about change over time from the second century. The distribution of sites of the fourth century (cf. Carr 2002: Fig. 4) shows that there was still a dense network of sites, particularly along the Guadalquivir but also to its south. They represent a range of site types from large villas to much smaller structures, and the presence of presses and decantation basins shows that the processing of olive oil was still important, if no longer at the levels of two hundred years earlier. Baetican olive oil still continued to be exported to Rome, though at very low levels compared with the High Empire, but, on the other hand, it was more common along the Mediterranean coasts of both Iberia and southern Gaul (Reynolds 2005: 383–8). The chronological pattern in which it was the first century BC and the first and second centuries AD that saw a surge of economic activity, as reflected also in the settlement pattern, as Mediterranean trading networks adjusted to the new realities of demand and supply, is one we have encountered before. In this case, from the later second century there was contraction in the export industry and thus in the production regions, but for reasons much more to do with imperial decisions than with any 'crisis' (cf. Reynolds 2005: 371–6). So again the medium-term driver of development seems to be incorporation into the Roman system, which produces the surge and then a settling back to a lower density of settlement and intensity of production, but one still geared to the Mediterranean.

Discussion

In the consideration of the various regional studies discussed above, it was noted that variety was as visible and important as, if not more important than, generalising trends. This discussion, therefore, will not seek to construct any single, all-encompassing rationale for the changes observable in the archaeological record. Rather it will seek to use the insights gained in the different projects to suggest a range of possibilities, all of which most probably interacted with each other; monocausality being inherently very unlikely in the unrolling of human affairs over such a wide area and relatively long time span. General trends with many local variations may be identifiable.

Southern Gaul and Iberia

Let us take first the more Mediterranean areas studied: south-eastern Gaul and the east and south of the Iberian peninsula. It is abundantly clear that there was no 'third-century crisis' in the classic form of a rupture in economic and social developments caused by the irruption into these regions of Germanic invaders from beyond the Rhine. This was an explanatory mechanism deployed in an era before the countervailing evidence of archaeology could be deployed and is now pretty much abandoned. Instead, it is becoming increasingly clear that there was a general tempo of development traceable in the rural settlement archaeology of all these areas, and in northern Gaul also, which operated to a completely different rhythm than that determined by the *histoire événementielle* of the textual sources. In the regions around the western Mediterranean, the crucial threshold appears to be the incorporation into the economic and cultural nexus of the developing Roman Empire in the last two centuries BC, following on from Greek and Etruscan penetration (e.g. Cunliffe 1988). This seems to be the horizon where significant intensification of rural settlement and exploitation becomes visible (admittedly in part, though far from totally, because of the visibility of imported pottery, which also furnished a dating horizon), along with social development such as larger groupings (from the evidence of the coinages) and greater social stratification and hierarchy (*oppida* and the material, particularly imports, from them). In parallel, there would seem to have been intensification, and perhaps some extensification, of the agrarian system. This may have been, among other things, to pay for the import of the prestige goods increasingly necessary for social replication, though it is not necessary to ascribe all change to external motors in the manner of 'core-periphery' models or 'world systems' theory (cf. Woolf 1990); these external motors would have interacted with endogenous factors. With the formal incorporation of the areas into the provincial structures – and particularly from the later first century BC – there were changes in the economic and cultural structures, with displacement of much elite competition to new arenas, in particular the cities and to an extent the countryside in the form of villas. This part of the picture is, of course, very familiar, and the early imperial growth of the cities of Baetica, Tarraconensis and Narbonensis has been much discussed, as, to a lesser extent, has the growth of villas. This expenditure on prestige projects for the community or prestigious private urban and rural residences had to be based, of course, on the extraction of economic surplus, and in the ancient world that meant essentially agriculture: cereal and pastoral agriculture or oleiculture and viticulture. Moreover, the demands of the state over and above those satisfied by taxation provided another incentive to surplus production, as clearly visible in the early imperial West in the *annona* supply to Rome and the supplying of Mediterranean goods to the frontier armies. A further factor was that the imperial system promoted a degree of economic integration and thus expansion (see Hopkins 1980 for the classic statement of cause and effect; Duncan-Jones 1990 for further studies). This complex of influences allows us to construct rationales for the pressure to increase agricultural production through intensification and/or extensification in order to satisfy the demands for surplus with which to meet the demands of the state and, probably more important, to satisfy the culturally constructed desire of the local aristocracies to undertake public benefaction through the embellishment of the cities and to create private luxury in urban and rural dwellings. This pressure may have meant that agricultural production was pushed above the natural, long-term carrying capacity of the landscapes, a tactic that was realisable in the relatively short term but unsustainable in the medium term without innovations in productive techniques or crop types, innovations which do not seem to have occurred.

In Braudelian terms, what we seem to be seeing is the intersection of the relatively short-term event of the incorporation of Iberia and southern Gaul into the Roman Empire with the long-term characteristics of these areas and the creation of a new set of *mentalités* which were to structure the medium-term pattern of settlement and economy supporting a modified social and cultural superstructure. The social superstructure was also one with progressively more pronounced inequalities of command over resources, and was ever more institutionalised as the elite became more and more dominant in the patterns of the agrarian economy and surplus extraction. The markers of that economic dominance were in part the provision for the bulk processing of agricultural produce, visible at villas through presses and oil/wine storage, but also the evidence from amphorae for large-scale movement of bulk products. The acme of this was, of course, the huge surge in the economy and settlement of Baetica engendered by the acquisition of *annona* links to Rome itself (Remesal Rodríguez 1998 and references). But in other areas the effects of economic integration and access to markets were also visible, as, for instance, in the distribution of the characteristic south Gaulish amphora, the Gauloise 4, around the north-western Mediterranean but more into the interior of Gaul and to the Rhineland and Britain, suggesting participation in the state-engendered military supply system (Laubenheimer 1990: 77–110), and demonstrating a profit-driven production on some scale. Villas were also the expression of the cultural formation of this society, with the desire and social pressure to expend resources on Roman-style status markers tied to the dissemination of Roman-style aristocratic culture. But if this was the 'upswing' of a medium-term cycle, what happened to change the pattern from the second through to the fourth century?

If one of the principal drivers of the upswing was economic, the pressure to create greater disposable surpluses, then we might look for economic retrenchment or realignment. Without trespassing too far on the subject matter of the next chapter, such retrenchment can be detected in several of the regions we have studied. Again, the extreme case was Baetica, where the loss of state patronage for the *annona* of Rome caused a significant downturn in the internal economic structures and external profile of the region (see further p. 399). The case for Tarraconensis is much less clear; the evidence of the amphorae imported into and exported from this province (cf. Keay 1984) suggests that there was no disruption of the sort that hit its southern neighbour, but, on the other hand, there does seem to have been a downturn in the course of the third century. Much the same seems to be true for Narbonensis, which, like Tarraconensis, was less dependent on state-engendered trade for its profitability; the Gauloise 4 continued to circulate in the north-western Mediterranean down into the third century, but in declining quantities. So there may have been a certain lessening of the pressure from the export trade to maximise surpluses. Another contributory factor may have been the changes in *mentalités* discussed in Chapter 3 in the towns of southern Gaul and Iberia, where the peak in the development of the classic, Roman-style city (as we think of it) came in the second half of the second century or the opening decades of the third. Thereafter, there was a clear downturn in public munificence as indexed by the construction of new buildings and monuments and the epigraphic record, both in general and specifically as regards the recording of acts of euergetism. In Chapter 3 (p. 106), it was argued that these changes witnessed a change in *mentalités*, with the drive to monumentalism and benefaction characteristic of the High Empire slackening and the provision of the monuments, spectacles and benefactions this entailed tailing away. This may have been partly due to the escalating costs of such competitive display, perhaps producing almost a 'potlatch' situation where the consumption of resources for its own cultural sake was becoming ruinous. It was also argued that, perhaps as a consequence of this, the elite were transferring their displays and markers of status more to the private sphere of their residences, urban or rural. In the cities of Narbonensis, and perhaps Tarraconensis, the third century saw a process of contraction of the occupied areas. Another factor may be the problem alluded to above, that whereas the intensification of production above the normal capacity of a region is feasible in the short term, it is unstable and probably unsustainable over a longer period as factors such as soil exhaustion, erosion and overgrazing take their toll, particularly in semi-arid landscapes with pockets of good soil interspersed with more fragile areas (often the more upland) of thinner, poorer soils. Some of the results of the ARCHEOMEDES project in Narbonensis (Van der Leeuw et al. 2003) suggest that soil impoverishment and erosion can be identified in the middle imperial period. As noted above, there is evidence for a retreat from the less favourable agricultural areas in this region from the second century, in a sort of 'last-in, first-out' pattern. So, we may hypothesise a bundle of interrelated physical, economic and cultural factors, particularly for Narbonensis and Tarraconensis (the economic factor hugely magnified in Baetica). Over-exploitation of the agricultural carrying capacity of these regions may have weakened their ability to produce the surpluses necessary to sustain the economic interaction outside the regions and the cultural expenditure inside the regions. The cycles of competitive emulation within cities between families and also between cities through the provision of public buildings, monuments and benefactions may have become progressively more unsustainable, particularly if the agricultural underpinning was less and less able to sustain it. This then provoked a reaction among the elite against this form of competitive display, diverting them instead into forms of status marking that may have been both less costly and more personally rewarding. As noted in particular in considering the evidence from Narbonensis, the graphs of rural settlement seem to show that after the early imperial surge in numbers and distribution there was a return to the sorts of numbers and density that had obtained before the surge, suggesting that the natural, longer-term capacity of the land was reasserting itself. But as we have also seen, this capacity was perfectly capable of sustaining through the later Roman period a quantity and range of settlement types suggesting continuing exploitation of a variety of ecological zones and also a hierarchy of sites indicating an extractive economy with surpluses available, after tax and other requisitions, for expenditure by the controlling elites. In Narbonensis this often took the form of villas, albeit not as lavish as in the south-west. A similar argument can be put forward for Tarraconensis, where the survey and analysis of the non-villa settlement pattern is not yet quite as fine-grained as for Narbonensis, but in Tarraconensis there is also evidence for an increase in overall numbers of villas and in the lavishness of some of them in the later period (Chavarría Arnau 1996, 2006b), again arguing for a continuing, domanial system of exploitation in this region. If the scheme here proposed is an approximation to the economic and social processes at work in these Mediterranean regions over much of the first half of the first millennium AD, then we may have an understanding of why the observable archaeology is patterned the way it is and of why the chronological element of that patterning was operating to a rhythm other than that of the conventional, text-based 'third-century crisis'.

Central and northern Gaul

In considering the evidence for third- and fourth-century developments in the rural settlement and economy of the central northern part of Gaul, it was clear that there were important differences within this area and by comparison with southern Gaul and Iberia, in particular in the fate of villas as a crucial element of the rural settlement hierarchy and an elite status marker. But we may also ask whether the sorts of analysis of economic, social and cultural factors just undertaken for southern Gaul and Iberia may not also have some merit in understanding developments in this large region. At the level of the villa, which is the site type for which we have the most information, there are lessons to be learnt. Under the High Empire, villas had become a widespread component of the rural settlement hierarchy. They ranged in size from the enormous, as at Haccourt (Liège), to the much more modest, as at Cléry-sur-Somme (Somme) (Agache 1978: Fig. 29), but were most often distinguished by their plan of a domestic range (*pars urbana*) looking along a rectangular or trapezoidal court flanked by smaller, largely agricultural buildings. Some of the larger examples had mosaics and other evidence for a certain luxury, but in the main these villas give the impression of being largely geared to farming and the production of surplus. It has become clear that their distinctive plan is a representation in the Roman style of an overall site layout and a disposition of buildings which go back to the later Iron Age in the second and first centuries BC. Unfortunately, because of the long concentration of research on villas, we as yet know very little of other types of settlement in the landscape and of how these might relate to the pattern of villas. More generally, there is again an economic, social and cultural pattern similar in overall contours to developments in Narbonensis, namely an intensification of activity and expenditure of resources on display in the later Iron Age. In part this seems to have been stimulated by access to goods from the Roman world, though developments in a range of archaeological evidence types suggest important social and cultural restructurings independent of contact with the Roman world.

After the Caesarian conquest, and particularly from the Augustan period onwards, we see the rapid development of the trappings of Roman-style society and culture, particularly with the creation of the cities and their embellishment; Amiens at the centre of the Picardy villa area is a particularly good and well-studied example (Bayard and Massy 1983). In the countryside the construction of villas commenced in the first century AD, but it was the second century that saw the peak in numbers and sophistication. The presence of long-distance trade goods such as amphorae, samian ware, glass and metalwork attests to the importance of economic integration, as does the volume of more local pottery productions and other material; by the end of the second century, the cities and villas of northern Gaul were saturated with consumer products, attesting to a sort of 'consumer revolution' as a result of political and economic integration and the changing cultural preferences of the elite (see Woolf 1998: esp. Chs. 5–7 for full discussion of these trends). But, as we saw above, this surge starts to weaken and fall back from the early third century onwards so far as it concerns the villas; it declines at different rates in different areas, but overall is marked by a lack of new foundations and a gradual diminution in the number and elaboration of existing establishments. As we saw in Chapter 3, this is also the period when the momentum of urban expansion was checked and started to go into reverse, and again Amiens (p. 108) is a very good example.

As we shall see in the next chapter, the end of the second century and the first half of the third is also the period at which there is a considerable economic restructuring, particularly of the long-distance goods and routes. This provides the wider context in which the changes to the rural settlement pattern should be examined. Clearly, the 'downward' part of the cycle was under way from the first half of the third century, well before the main episodes of invasion and disruption. Again, it should be understood that this does not seek to deny the reality of the invasions (albeit archaeology is ill-equipped to detect the actual short-term events) and their possibly catastrophic impact on individual sites. Rather it is to suggest that they acted upon existing trajectories, quite probably accentuating them. But it is difficult to suggest, for instance, why invasions should have caused the abandonment of the distinctive north Gaulish villa layout in favour of the much looser groupings of the later third and fourth centuries; there would seem to have been a separate process at work whereby the spatial rationales behind this style of layout became redundant. Indeed, it is difficult to tie the general phenomenon of villa disuse and abandonment to the invasions, since the chronology shows a process stretching for a hundred years and more from the first half of the third to the first half of the fourth century: individual sites very probably were destroyed, but not all. What the short-term events of the invasions may have done, as suggested in Chapter 2, was to change the *mentalités* of the inhabitants of northern Gaul, particularly the elites, acting on an already existing trajectory away from the forms of expression characteristic of the second century, and instead creating new concepts of status display, in particular through the militarisation of this element of society and of its means of representing itself in the archaeology. But the evidence for both elite and non-elite rural settlement in the fourth century by comparison with the second, suggests a regression to a lower level of settlement activity, as suggested for southern Gaul. Although we cannot as yet read this through onto the pattern of agricultural exploitation, there seems to be no analogue to the abandonment of less-favoured soils and environments further south. Indeed, the regional and microregional patterns for northern Gaul considered above could be used to argue that the productive capacity of the landscape and agrarian regime remained at a reasonably high level, and this is what might be expected given the demands of the army on the Rhine and in the interior of northern Gaul, and of other state employees for food and other supplies to be met either through taxation or through purchase over and above the tax render. Further south, in central Gaul, there appears to have been a contrary process under way, with a considerable degree of stability in the villa element of the settlement hierarchy, but much more impermanence in the simpler, less durable site types lower down the hierarchy. These trends were already visible from the end of the second century, even if they did accelerate in the third. Again, as with northern Gaul, the productive capacity of the region may not have altered very much; what did change was the social structures within which that exploitation was carried out, with apparently a move to a tighter control exercised by the upper echelons of the provincial aristocracies.

As with Narbonensis and Tarraconensis, so with central and northern Gaul, there were medium-term developments under way well before the 'crisis' of invasion and destruction, developments probably to be linked to a cycle of agrarian and economic intensification/extensification starting before the Roman conquest and peaking in the second century AD before starting to fall back again. These developments may in part have been linked to over-exploitation of the carrying capacity of the land (though probably much less so than further south) and in part were very probably linked to over-exploitation of the social and cultural capacity of the elite to sustain the status-markers of the Early Empire. Instead they had started to devise other paths before they were forcibly rerouted by the impact of the events of the second half of the third century, pushing them into new routes, ones closely linked to the military character of the late Roman state in this region, which continued to be vulnerable all through the fourth century. Important elements of this discussion have concerned the overall trajectory of economic development in the West and its impact on the underlying agricultural regimes of these provinces, and through these their rural settlement patterns and settlement types. We now need to look more closely at the trajectories of economic development across the Western provinces in the later Roman period, particularly the extent to which they promoted integration of the various regions.

7 | The economy of the late Roman West

Introduction

This chapter is really the second leaf of a diptych about the economy, of which the preceding chapter is the first leaf. It will therefore be concerned not with the underlying agrarian economy of the West as considered in Chapter 6, but with the ways in which the considerable and sustained surpluses generated by that economy were expended. The topic of the (late) Roman economy is one that has been very extensively studied both by historians and by archaeologists, who have used textual, numismatic and archaeological evidence to approach a range of questions about structure and scale in the Roman economy (to use Duncan-Jones' 1990 title). Because of the nature of the evidence to be used here, the archaeological, certain approaches to such questions will be privileged since they are the ones for which such evidence can most readily be analysed and deployed. These approaches are strongly conditioned by the nature of the proxies for economic activity available to the archaeologist. The emphasis is on proxies with good quality of preservation in the archaeological record and that are also preserved in large quantities, making them susceptible to analysis in terms of economic activity. The material that survives in greatest quantities and has long been used as the chief proxy for economic activity is, of course, pottery, because of our ability very often to identify its source and to date it with some precision through its association with coinage or other independently datable material or phenomena. From these data can be constructed maps of geographical distribution and graphs of chronological distribution, permitting observations of the volume, directions and changes through time of the distribution(s) of individual types of products or of groups of products. A limited range of other materials, such as marble, has been sufficiently well characterised to allow similar geographical and chronological distributions to be plotted. Unfortunately, many of the other common classes of archaeological material such as glass and metalwork cannot be tied to particular sources of material or manufacture through physical or chemical analysis since in both these cases the material was frequently melted down to be refashioned into new objects, thus mixing items from differing origins. On the other hand, stylistic analysis of such material can still be of use in pinning down areas of manufacture, as, for instance, with certain classes of dress adornment (Swift 2000a, 2010), or with 'schools' of certain artistic productions, such as mosaics or sarcophagi, though these latter were *de luxe* products for the elite, whereas pottery has the enormous advantage of a much wider social and functional range in its use. There is, though, one class of metalwork that we can tie back to its places of origin and which clearly had enormous economic importance – coin. Found in enormous quantities (especially the low-value copper-alloy issues) across the West, and with its mint marks providing places of manufacture, this is the one class of material from the Western Empire that can be placed alongside pottery as a source in trying to reconstruct economic activity. By contrast, another very common class of find on sites, environmental evidence (think of the millions of pieces of animal bone, pollen grains, and the millions of crop seeds and weed seeds), is, as yet, less revealing in this context because of the difficulty of identifying where grain or other plant remains originated unless they contain markers (such as weed seeds) of very specific environmental zones, and equally the difficulty of identifying the origins of the animals represented by their bones, though, in due course, programmes of analysis, such as that using stable isotopes (see below, p. 392), might be able to identify beasts moved over longer distances.

This means that the discussions here will be self-limiting as to the aspects of the economy that pottery and other similar archaeological material can usefully be analysed in terms of; that is, in essence, the aspects concerned with the movement of goods in larger or smaller quantities across longer or shorter distances over time and the extent to which these observed distributions can be used to reconstruct the mechanisms and rationales by which the late Roman economy operated. It also means that certain other ways of modelling the Roman economy or certain major questions that have recently been posed by historians of ancient economy (e.g. Bowman and Wilson 2009; Scheidel and Friesen 2009; Scheidel and von Reden 2002: esp. Chs. 11 and 12; Scheidel *et al.* 2006: especially Introduction) will not be directly addressed here. These are, above all, questions concerning whether in the imperial period the economy of the lands constituting the Roman Empire increased in size and whether *per capita* incomes increased. To argue that the economy increased in size would be to propose that the political unification of the empire brought about structural changes, such as economies of scale, improved technologies, improved communications, and improved financial and banking practices, that permitted or encouraged developments that would otherwise not have been possible. The alternative position would essentially be that the creation of such a huge political unit simply aggregated a series of pre-existing economic formations that continued to operate at much the same scale as previously, even if surpluses were in part redirected, and that there was no general uplift in income and prosperity (whatever might happen to individuals). The sorts of evidence and argument to be deployed here will not address these questions directly, though, given the area and period under consideration here, it would be extremely difficult to dispute that the size of the economy overall had done anything other than contract markedly by the end of our period, and that *per capita* incomes had fallen, particularly for the elites (cf. Wickham 2005: Ch. 4). Instead, this chapter will concentrate on the archaeological data with a particular problem in mind: to what extent was the economy of the later Roman West integrated and at what levels and scales? That is, what does the evidence for longer- and shorter-distance contacts and larger- and smaller-scale movements of goods tell us about the extent to which either the later Roman West had remained a series of regional or subregional economies determined by geographical and resource constraints with little to unite them, or it had, by contrast, created an economic superstructure which to some extent linked these more local economies, generating a scale of economic enterprise which would not have occurred otherwise? It must be stated at the outset that 'integration' is not a synonym for 'homogenisation'. This discussion in no way seeks to argue that the Roman economy was a unitary system across the empire or that there was a single 'Roman economy'; there manifestly was not and the degree of regional variation will be central to the treatment. As so often in archaeology, the model thus created of economic interaction can and must, to some extent, stand proxy for social and cultural formations – their nature, range in time and space, and complexity – so it needs to be set alongside some of those we have already examined in earlier chapters.

Given the scale of the Roman Empire, it inevitably encompassed a wide range of climatic zones and resource types, both agrarian and others such as minerals. This also inevitably meant imbalances of resources between particular areas and regions, both in the long term because of structural differences in the availability of particular resources, or in the short term because of factors such as crop failure or warfare, both of these creating the motivation to offset these disparities through exchange. But also, given the scale and geography of the empire and the pre-industrial means of locomotion (wind, river currents, animal traction and human carriage), the movement of goods, particularly the more heavy or bulky ones, was physically the trouble or because these would otherwise have been unavailable. This is, of course, schematic – artisans could also have been merchants, merchants could have been anything from itinerant pedlars or chapmen to entrepreneurial middlemen, and surplus could have been in kind or in cash – but the focus of the process remained the objects traded and the profit to be made. Reciprocity, on the other hand, was concerned much more with social than with financial profit and generally took the form of gift exchange within semi-ritualised social settings such as marriage or, among the elite of the late Roman world, the holding of office, with all the social obligations created and discharged by such transactions – and even apparent discharge could in fact create new obligations (see Chapter 5 for other aspects of this social network). The functioning of reciprocity has been extensively anatomised by anthropologists from Mauss (1954) onwards, resulting in the strong argument that much pre-industrial economic activity was embedded in social relations rather than being the product of the 'free market'; this is now known as the 'substantivist' position of Polanyi (1957) and his followers. Redistribution, on the other hand, was the extraction of economic worth by social superiors from social inferiors under a number of guises such as render, rent, labour obligations and tax, all resting ultimately on the ability to coerce; the product was spent by those to whom it was due on what they pleased with no expectation of reciprocity. This was the basis of many of the economic formations of the Roman Empire, whether the extraction of rent, tribute or other 'payments' in kind by the elite or the imposition of taxes and other obligations by the state; this has been characterised as the 'tributary mode' (Wickham 1984). Again, it is possible to be over-schematic; these categories of market, reciprocity and redistribution were by no means mutually exclusive. There were variants of each which incorporated elements of the others (cf. Wickham 2005: 694–6). Nevertheless, they will be used here as heuristic categories to structure description and discussion.

The relevance of these broad categories to the analysis of the late Roman economy is that they allow the articulation of a series of 'forms' or 'levels' of economic activity, each characterised by the predominance of one or other category of economic activity – these are forms that have a degree of acceptance. The one most visible in the archaeological record – it appears also in the textual record and was both the largest single economic structure (which is not necessarily the same as the largest section of the economy) and one on which others to a greater or lesser extent depended – was what will be termed here the 'political economy' (sometimes called the 'imperial economy'). Partly linked with this, as we shall see, was the 'market economy', which does not, at present, require much in the way of formal explanation, though its manifestations in the archaeology can be more tricky to identify, making very difficult any judgement as to the relative volume and importance of the 'imperial' and of the 'market' economies (the latter perhaps being a better claimant to the title of largest section of the economy), particularly since the latter was really the aggregate of many, many individually quite small-scale formations. Redistribution was again the foundation of what has been termed the 'prestige economy', the use by the elites – higher-level elites such as members of the senatorial order or lower-level ones such as civic aristocracies – of revenues from their landholdings to finance their preferred forms of conspicuous consumption, though, of course, this could also feed into the 'market economy' through purchase of goods and services and would also have been characterised by a considerable degree of reciprocity between individuals and families, from personal gifts to more socially structured expressions such as the dowry. Last, but in the aggregate certainly not the least, was the 'peasant economy', much of it reciprocal through social networks within and between adjacent settlements and areas, evening out inequalities in the distribution of resources (oil, wine and metals) or particular skills (e.g. metalworking) and structuring and reproducing social interactions. The peasant economy was also crucial for the 'market economy', as peasants disposed of surplus in order to have access to more specialised goods and services, and to the 'imperial economy' due to their need to raise coin for fiscal and exchange purposes, which might be done through market transactions.

Super-regional integration: the political economy

Because of its importance and relative complexity, the political economy requires further characterisation so that its impact on the operations of the late Roman economy can be more clearly discerned and understood. This 'economy' was the product of political imperatives operating on the central organs of the Roman state, above all the emperor. First and most important was the imperative of keeping the empire in being through defence against external threat, the maintenance of internal order and the safeguarding of the imperial person, all of these being essentially military matters. This required the existence of a standing army of considerable size for a pre-industrial economy, its provisioning through the *annona* system, its equipping and arming, and its paying in cash. The second imperative was ensuring that politically important groups within the empire did not starve, especially the large and historically significant population of the city of

Rome (and later of Constantinople); this was ensured by the state-funded supply of basic foodstuffs (grain, olive oil and meat) – again *annona*. The third imperative was the discharge of imperial obligations, partly to pay for the bureaucracies necessary to service the first and second priorities, and partly to finance other imperial expenditures such as patronage to individuals (for example, Ausonius and his family), to cities (for example, Trier) and, increasingly, to the Church at Rome, Constantinople, Trier and elsewhere. What this meant in practice was the construction over time of a fiscal system geared to discharging these obligations, through the raising of cash by taxation, through the provision of supplies and their transportation at state (that is, taxpayers') expense, or through some of the cash raised being expended on the purchase of supplies over and above those raised through taxation (*coemptio*). Importantly for a discussion based on the archaeological evidence, this system involved the partial suspension of the normal laws of pre-industrial economic gravity because of political imperatives, in particular through the large-scale transport of bulky and low-value goods over long distances to supply the army or feed the city of Rome (for a clear summary of the textual evidence for the impact of the political economy on the wider economy, see Carrié 1994). There was also the other consequence of the political economy that needs to be borne in mind; of central importance to the functioning of much of the Roman economy was the minting of coin in gold, silver and copper alloy, principally as an adjunct of the fiscal system but also to lubricate many commercial transactions in the market sector of the economy.

The involvement of the state in the supply of the army was, of course, nothing new. The long-distance supply chains from the Mediterranean up to the armies on the Rhine, upper Danube and Britain are very visible in the archaeology, and they and the long-distance commercial networks parasitic on them have been held to be an important aspect of the economic integration and stimulus brought to the West by the fact of empire (e.g. Fulford 1992; Woolf 1992). The transport of Mediterranean goods, particularly olive oil from Baetica in Dressel 20 amphorae, privileged the Rhône–Saône–Moselle–Rhine corridor, as is shown by the distribution not only of the Baetican amphorae but also of Baetican and central Gaulish fine pottery, which rode piggyback on the state-engendered transport system (Greene 1979), and also by the activity of the personnel, shippers (*navicularii*) and middlemen (*negotiatores*) who undertook the transport (Middleton 1979). Equally, the disappearance of this transport of goods was traditionally held to be one of the markers of the 'third-century crisis' and an index of the disruption wrought by the Germanic incursions and probably also the fiscal and financial dislocations reflected in the history of the coinage (cf. p. 329). Linked with this was the disappearance of the great, centralised pottery production centres of the Gaulish red-gloss ('samian') industry, which had flourished through the first and second centuries but did not outlast the third. In fact, as more recent work has shown, these long-distance links were a development largely of the first century AD and on into the second, with the evidence now pointing to the turn of the second and third centuries as the starting point of their progressive atrophy through the first half of the third century. The causes of this are debated. In part it may be that the provincial economies had become more developed over time and thus more able to play a bigger part in the supply nexus rather than relying on imports. But since the shipping of olive oil and wine to the frontier was essentially an expression of the cultural preferences of an army whose legions were, in the first century AD, still largely recruited from around the Mediterranean, it may perhaps be more convincing to argue that, as this element declined with regional recruitment, such tastes dwindled in parallel, leading to a diminution in demand rather than problems with supply. But problems with supply from southern Spain there certainly were from the turn of the second and third centuries, as we shall see below, so here, perhaps, we are seeing a combination of the two. As for the samian industries, decline in quantity and quality of production and scale of distribution can be traced back to the last third of the second century, and it accelerated through the first half of the third, so, in King's evocative phrase when discussing the end of the east Gaulish samian industry, the contribution of any Germanic incursions in the second half of that century was that 'this apparent death-blow was inflicted on a virtually lifeless body' (King 1981: 71). A word of warning: 'samian' and *terra sigillata hispánica tardía* are modern categorisations. High-quality, red-gloss pottery did continue to be made on a large scale, especially in Gaul in regions not far to the west of the east Gaulish centres, but these are now categorised as 'Argonne', not 'samian'. Nevertheless, the 'samian' industries did make extensive use of moulded decorations in a way these later industries did not. It may be that again we seem to have a cycle starting under the Early Empire, increasing through to the middle or later second century, and then going into 'decline'. This is a pattern we have already observed for cities and for regional surveys of rural settlement (Chapters 2, 3 and 6), and we argued that this was a medium-term cycle, and, given that its initial impetus was given by incorporation into the Mediterranean system or into the empire itself, that development reflected the social and cultural values and stimuli of the empire until they became played out in the later third century and new *mentalités* took their place. That economic activities, particularly ones closely tied in to the imperial system, should exhibit similar chronological trends is perhaps not surprising. Imperial intervention in a more targeted and *événementiel* fashion can also be seen at the turn of the second and third centuries, with the evidence that Septimius Severus and his house purposely took action against the olive oil producers of Baetica, partly, probably, for having supported the wrong side in the civil wars of 193–7, and partly in order to benefit the producers in the dynasty's North African homelands (Reynolds 2010). This would certainly have contributed to the demise of the shipment of south Spanish olive oil to the armies on the Rhine and in Britain, though, interestingly, the void thus created was not filled by alternative production areas such as North Africa, suggesting that there was a crisis of demand as well as of supply, as suggested above.

In order to appreciate how the later Roman political economy could operate, the simplest thing to do is to take the example of the best-known and understood element of it to act as a model. The example is that of the nexus represented by the shipping of produce and products from central North Africa (roughly modern Tunisia) around the western part of the Mediterranean basin and into its hinterland. Part of the area under consideration will be the Mediterranean littorals of Iberia and southern Gaul, so this example touches on the provinces under consideration here. The archaeological evidence for long-distance movement of low-value goods in considerable volume is clear enough from the distribution maps and would of itself signal significant and sustained commerce in the western Mediterranean, but this is a case where the textual evidence augments the archaeology by supplying the keys to the mechanism involved. The subject has received a great deal of attention in both the francophone and anglophone literature over the last thirty or so years, particularly as a consequence of the systematic categorisation of the main pottery types involved (for a convenient summary and extensive bibliography, the best guide is the consideration by Wickham 2005: Ch. 11, esp. 708–13). The dominant element of the system in the fourth century was what Wickham terms the 'tax spine' from central north Africa to Rome, supplying the metropolis with grain and olive oil, *annona*, raised through taxation and shipped across the Mediterranean in discharge of fiscal obligations or in return for tax exemptions. Thus did the political necessities of the state create a mechanism for the frequent bulk transport of low-value goods over long distance and, as an unintended consequence, a large-scale transport system that was effectively 'free' in that it was paid for out of tax. Piggyback onto this went other merchandise such as extra oil, red table wares (African red slip [ARS] ware), other pottery, fish sauce (*garum*) and probably also other perishable goods now invisible to us; these goods had little or no cost of transport since the shipping was already paid for, and so they could compete with local products and other imports from a position of advantage. A law of 396 in the *Codex Theodosianus* (XIII.5.2.6) stipulated that such a ship must be back in her home port no more than two years after setting out and that delivery of any *annona* had to be undertaken within the first year. The law clearly takes as a given the prolonged use of *annona* ships for private venture; no wonder then that north African oil amphorae and other products, above all ARS, are such common finds all around the western Mediterranean. The composition of wreck cargoes from this area shows that travel from port to port to sell cargo and take on local goods – cabotage – was a standard form of commerce, and this explains the relatively wide distribution of such material as millstones from Pantelleria, an island on the route from Africa to Sicily (Williams-Thorpe 1988). Clearly, then, market exchange was an important element of this distributive nexus, pointing up both the possible extent and importance of such trade, but also demonstrating that clear distinctions must not be drawn between the political and the market economies – there was a degree of symbiosis. Moreover, the supply of wine, rather than grain or oil, to Rome does not seem to have been part of the political economy, and the sources of wine amphorae were much more diverse, but the market represented by the capital's population still made the trade worthwhile, with the prospect of offloading surplus at other urban markets around the western Mediterranean. A good example of this is the distribution of Calabrian amphorae from the 'toe' of Italy (Arthur 1989) with the emphasis on Rome. So the North African trade, the clearest and best-studied of examples, demonstrates vividly the potential importance of satisfying the state's requirements as a driver for long-distance trade and thus for economic integration at the super-regional level. It is, of course, the clearest and best-studied example because it is so evident in the archaeology and because it is the product of very particular exigencies. The risk, therefore, is to take it as typical of the ways in which the political economy worked and try to impose this model in other regional situations, when, in fact, the North African tax spine could have been atypical. We must be sensitive to variants on the theme of the tax spine or to other possibilities in areas more distant from the central concerns of the political economy such as the city of Rome or the army. Nonetheless, the tax-spine model gives us something very valuable to think with, prompting us to ask whether observed patternings in the archaeology conform to such a model or, if they do not, what else they may be telling us.

A specific type of archaeological evidence which has been much used and discussed in attempting to reconstruct the changing scales and directions of the Roman economy in the western Mediterranean has been that of excavated shipwrecks (e.g. Parker 1992), of which there are now a great number. Like pottery, these are datable and thus their frequency through time can be plotted. Moreover, Roman-period shipwrecks tend to carry amphorae in large numbers, so the origin(s) of the cargo can often be identified with some precision, and the wreck site can give a general indication of where the ship was headed, allowing changes in the patterns of trade over time to be identified also. The well-known graph published by Parker (1992: Fig. 3) shows the number of wrecks recorded from the Mediterranean over a 4,000-year period from 2500 BC to AD 1500 (Figure 7.1); the Graeco-Roman millennium (500 BC to AD 500) predominates absolutely with an enormous upswing peaking at the turn of the eras and an equal downturn thereafter, a downturn starting in the third century AD and accelerating through the fourth and fifth centuries to a nadir in the eighth century. But this graph should give us pause: it takes us as far as the fourteenth and fifteenth centuries, when we know from documentary sources that there was a huge volume of trade across the Mediterranean. If we were to take the Parker graph at face value, we would have to argue that Roman-period Mediterranean trade was orders of magnitude greater than this late medieval commerce, which flies in the face of all the non-shipwreck evidence. As an accurate analysis (Wilson, A. 2009: 219–29) of the variables to be taken into account in

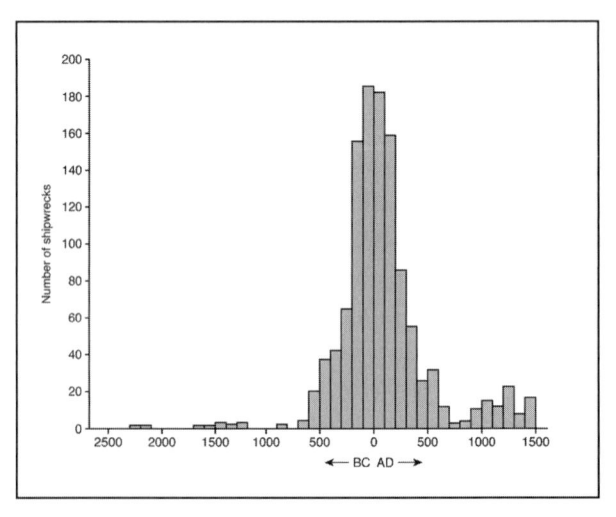

Fig. 7.1 Histogram of number of shipwrecks in the Mediterranean by century

analysing Parker's graph shows, it has long been recognised that what we are essentially dealing with in the Graeco-Roman peak is in large measure an artefact of fashion in containers for the bulk transport of liquids; in the late centuries BC and on into the first two centuries, amphorae were the container of choice, with a decline in their use thereafter, quite possibly as there was a change to a preference for wooden barrels. It is also clear that there were areas and periods of particularly intensive trade (e.g. between Italy and Gaul under the late Republic) that may distort any overall graph. Moreover, amphorae enhance the visibility of the wrecks containing them to modern divers since they both form a noticeable mound and protect large parts of the ship itself. Marble is the only other cargo that has been shown to have a similar effect, but its high cost is more an index of the expenditure of emperors, senators and civic elites (later also bishops) on prestigious building projects, so it is showing us something rather different from amphorae; it was more a part of the 'prestige economy'. Therefore, our perception of amphora wrecks is significantly skewed both in relation to wrecks having more perishable forms of container and in relation to wrecks containing perishable cargoes, above all the great bulk transports used for the transport of the grain *annona* and on which much of the ARS and many of the wine and fish sauce amphorae may have piggybacked. Wilson (Wilson, A. 2009: 228–9) also makes the point that these huge transports may have crossed the open sea rather than hugging the coast, so any wreck way well lie deeper than the depth at which scuba-divers operate. So simply to read a Parker-style graph as a direct expression of increasing or decreasing volumes of trade is to use it for purposes for which it is not (and has never claimed to be) fit. Wilson (Wilson, A. 2009: 219–26) also points out that expressing the graph in periods of a century masks more subtle variations that become apparent if a finer chronological resolution is used (Figure 7.2). What these show is that after the absolute peak(s) in the first centuries BC and AD, amphora-borne trade continued at a relatively high and stable level through the third and fourth centuries before declining again through the fifth century, to settle at a considerably lower level than the third- to fourth-century plateau through the sixth and seventh centuries before the eighth-century nadir. So for the period that is our concern here, amphora-borne trade as measured by number of wrecks continued to be significant and sustained, with a fall-off through the fifth century. What may in due course allow us to refine this analysis is a better appreciation not just of the number of wrecks but also of the size of wrecks across time. For instance, did the fifth and sixth centuries see not only a decrease in number but also a decrease in size of cargoes? At what period did the huge *annona* transports cease to be built and used?

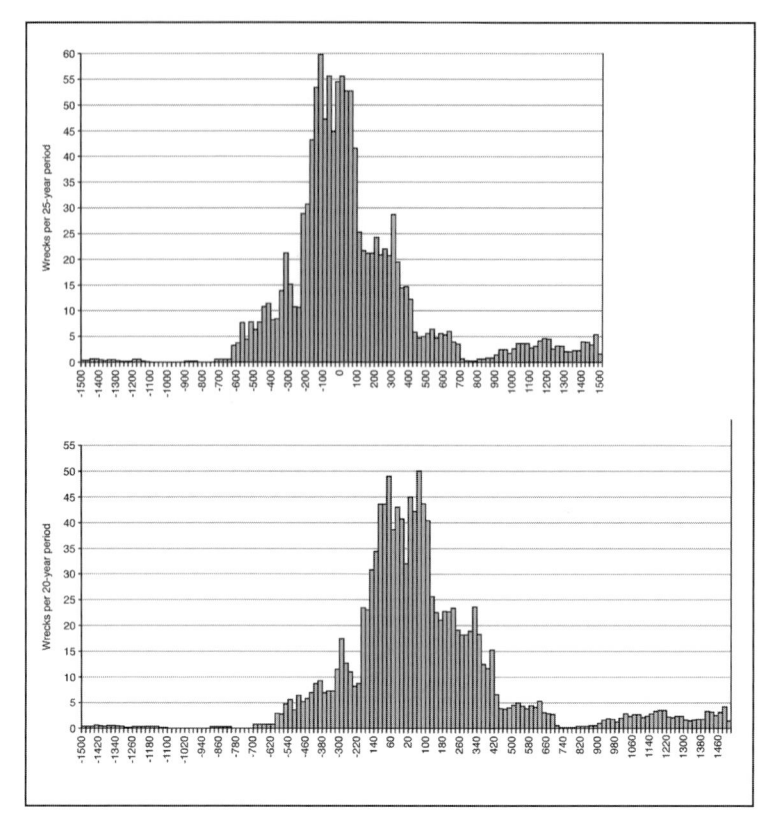

Fig. 7.2 Histograms of number of shipwrecks in the Mediterranean by 25- (upper) and 20-year (lower) periods

The political economy in the West: North African products

Having laid out some general considerations, a particular model and some caveats, we now turn to consideration of a number of examples of economic structures and activities in the West in order to see how well the observed data fit (or not) with the models characterised above. Through this, we may hope to approach the economic structures and processes, in particular the degree to which the economy was integrated over longer and shorter ranges and thus articulated throughout the West above purely local networks of trade and exchange. As stated above, the distribution of North African products comprehended the littorals of Gaul and Iberia; indeed, the rise to dominance of Africa in the provisioning of Rome had to some extent been at the expense of southern Iberia – Baetica – as alluded to in the previous chapter (p. 292). This now needs further consideration in the light of the recent detailed discussion by Reynolds (2010). Until the later second century, Baetican olive oil had formed an important element of the supply to Rome. But the promotion of North African sources by the Severi at the turn of the second and third centuries and changes to the Baetican supply (Reynolds 2005: 376–7, 2010: Ch. 3, Sect. 1) had the effect of diminishing the flow of Baetican exports (oil and *garum*), which show decreasing links to the Rome *annona*, though the presence of the Dressel 23 form shows continuing links. By the end of the third century, there were still links to Gaul and Germany, though in decreasing quantities; this is the continuation of the trend outlined above for the fall-off in the supply corridor from the Mediterranean to the Rhine from the later second century. Even so, Baetican oil and *garum* were still traded, as their presence on Iberian and other sites shows, but the distributions suggest a commercial, market logic rather than the needs of the state. Baetican olive oil and *garum* could also penetrate the full length of the Mediterranean, as far as Alexandria and Palestine, and the *garum* industries enjoyed notable successes nearer home in Iberia and a lively commerce with southern Gaul. Conversely, east Mediterranean products are known from the Mediterranean coasts of Iberia and Gaul, particularly from the second half of the fourth century (Reynolds 2005: 414–18, 2010: Ch. 3, Sect. 2), perhaps a more workaday equivalent of the high-status east–west links demonstrated at villas such as Carranque in central Iberia or Loupian in south-eastern Gaul. Eventually, the diminution in scale and reorientation in nature of the Baetican industries allowed North African goods increasingly to penetrate the markets of the Iberian Mediterranean littoral, so that from the close of the third century they would be the most common non-local wares found at coastal sites and in their immediate hinterlands, with both Tunisian oil amphorae and ARS significant components of ceramic assemblages, particularly at urban sites, which presumably paid for them out of income from the agricultural economy. The experience of Iberia is a useful case study of how short-term events, *histoire événementielle*, such as shifts in imperial favour, could intersect with provincial production to alter radically the volume and direction of commerce. But it also shows the degree to which this all still reflected a considerable degree of integration of economic activity, albeit on a reduced scale compared with the second century.

The evidence from the Mediterranean littoral of Gaul between the Pyrenees and the Alps seems broadly similar to the pattern for Iberia. Excavation at urban sites across this area has demonstrated that African products, both amphorae and ARS, form the largest group of imports for the fourth century, as particularly well documented at Marseille (Bonifay *et al.* 1998; cf. Loseby 1992), Arles and up the Rhône valley as far as Lyon, but also in small quantities westwards through the Carcassonne Gap to Toulouse (Amiel and Berthault 1996). Survey and excavation on the rural sites of Narbonensis have also shown the availability of these products to sites of little pretension as well as at more luxurious sites such as villas (Raynaud 1990: Ch. 4, 2001). The diffusion of these products, be they the liquids contained in the amphorae or the vessels of ARS, in south-eastern Gaul was presumably due again to a combination of the political economy's provision of the means of trans-Mediterranean transport and the market economy, with the oil, fish sauce and other liquid products and the ARS fine wares being bought and sold at the greater urban centres, such as Marseille or Arles, and also probably at the *agglomérations* and so on, to the rural peasantry – a tribute to the integrative effects of the late Roman economic system. On the other hand, the third and particularly the fourth century saw the decline of large-scale, south-eastern Gaulish wine production, if we are to take into account the diminution in production and eventual disappearance of the Gauloise 4 amphora (Laubenheimer 1990: 135–41), the marker for this agroindustry. So North African oil production and its privileged transport network may have out-competed local productions in southern Gaul as it had in Iberia; ARS certainly seems to have out-competed the south-eastern Gaulish *céramique luisante* industry in Provence (Raynaud 1993: 504–10). What this discussion of the distributions of North African amphorae and ARS has shown is the degree of integration achieved as a result of the political economy and the ability of the state to require or subsidise the long-distance movement of bulky and/or low-value goods such as grain or pottery. There was clearly a fiscal and commercial nexus in the western Mediterranean, the littoral in particular, unified by the tax spine from North Africa. It also points up the integration of the 'market' economy into this system. It is also important to see this from the point of view of the consumer, not just the state or the producer, and to appreciate also what this all made available to consumers of a range of social grades.

The political economy in the West: some examples

The North African nexus provides us with a clear and well-evidenced example of the importance of the political economy in driving the form of part of the late Roman economy in the West. But we must be wary of being seduced by the apparently simple character of this nexus and the model it affords for interpreting the archaeological correlates of that economy. It is because this nexus is concerned with the specific question of the politically hugely important population of the city of Rome that we should ask ourselves whether it is typical or may be atypical. Posed in those terms, it is evident that while it provides a convincing explanation for much of what we see around the western Mediterranean littoral, there are large areas of the West that are our concern in this book that were in all probability nothing to do with the supply systems for the city of Rome. So it would be dangerous to assume that a similar system necessarily operated elsewhere. But the West did, of course, contain a significant proportion of another politically extremely sensitive grouping, the army. Might a modified form of the tax spine model be a useful way to think about certain other observable distributions and their relation to the political economy of the later Roman state? Away from the Mediterranean littoral and the clear-cut example of the North African nexus, there are several relatively well-studied pottery types which may respond to analysis in terms of the political economy, but which also demonstrate the importance of the market economy in driving the production, distribution and consumption of these goods.

As was outlined above, the supply of Mediterranean goods to the frontier armies, which had been so important and so visible a pattern in the first and second centuries, had atrophied from the turn of the second and third centuries, quite possibly due to changing personnel and thus tastes in the armies themselves. There is also the distinct possibility that as provincial economies developed they satisfied certain demands more locally and thus engaged in import replacement; the history of the samian industries is a good example of this process. In the fourth century there was a continuing low level of interaction between the Mediterranean and the frontier armies, particularly those on the upper Rhine, but at nothing like the volume or reach of two centuries earlier. But if the long-distance supply of bulk goods had declined, the same was not necessarily the case for demand: there were still substantial bodies of troops along the Rhine, in Britain and in the interior of northern Gaul, as well as other state servants such as administrators and workers in the *fabricae*, all of whom were supplied with basic rations as part of their emoluments. Can this be detected as a factor in the circulation of goods, especially pottery? The most important production for these purposes is that centred on the Argonne region of north-eastern Gaul (Chenet 1941; Van Ossel 1996, 2011a), where from the third century there was large-scale production derived ultimately from the samian tradition and descending from the latest east Gaulish production in forms (especially the Drag 37), with vessels very commonly decorated with stamps of rectangular panels infilled with diagonal lines, a much devolved memory of earlier samian decorative schemes. This production achieved a widespread distribution (Figure 7.3) in northern and north-eastern Gaul, covering essentially the region between the Loire and the Rhine, with outliers to the

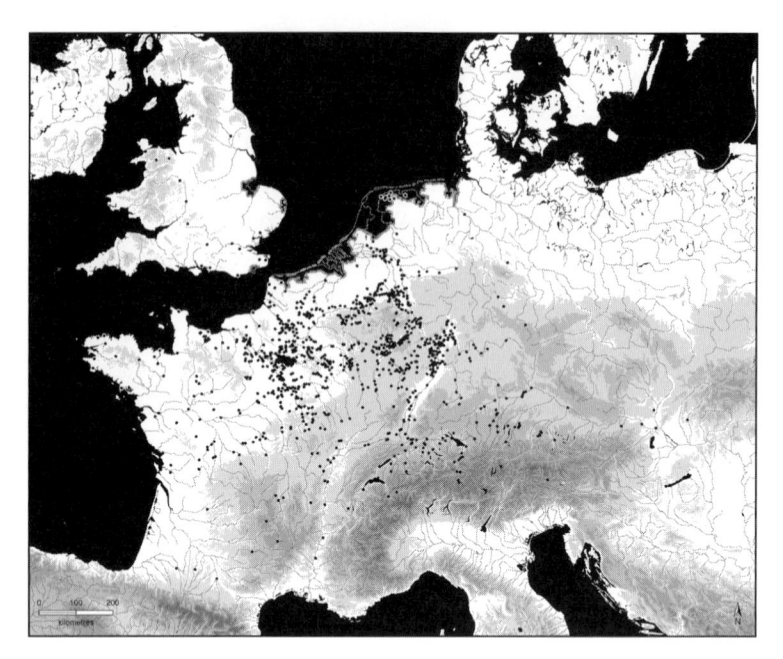

Fig. 7.3 Distribution of Argonne products (including those produced in the Paris Basin)

south of the Loire and across the Channel in south-eastern Britain and further east on both sides of the Rhine and Danube. It occurs on all types of sites: military, urban, rural and cemetery, and is by far the commonest fine ware over this large region. Its presence at the remaining towns of the region, which seem still to have displayed civilian characteristics, such as Amiens, Metz, Paris, Reims and Sens (cf. Chapter 2), at the remaining villas, and at almost all rural sites (see the papers in Ciezar *et al.* 2006; Ouzoulias and Van Ossel 1994; Van Ossel 2011a) argues for market-driven modes of distribution, certainly using urban centres and perhaps more local foci. But Argonne products were also very common at military sites such as forts; at the formerly urban centres such as Bavai, which were by now essentially military strongpoints; at the hilltop fortifications of north-eastern Gaul; and at urban centres housing state servants in *fabricae*, to say nothing of the nexus of military and administrative personnel at the imperial seat of Trier. Some of this may have been obtained through commercial transactions; after all, such sites would have been tempting targets for mercantile networks. But given the time-honoured archaeological role of Roman pottery as a visible proxy for the movement of perishable products, it is very plausible that the distribution of Argonne ware was in part facilitated by the political imperative of army/state servant supply. In this case, grain may

Super-regional integration: political economy 321

well have been the principal product being moved, and, as with the North African tax spine, other goods rode piggyback. The sharp decline in the range and quantity of the Argonne distributions in the fifth century after the breakdown of the imperial system (cf. p. 425) may well be a supporting argument for the part played by that system in the fourth century.

There are other ceramic types in fourth-century northern Gaul which may well also argue for an important military element in their distributions. One example is the rough-surfaced Mayen ware (Redknap 1988: esp. 8–9), also known as *Eifelkeramik*, predominantly lid-seated jars, but also a wide range of utilitarian cooking and tableware forms. It was produced not far to the north-east of Trier, where it was very common, with a distribution (Figure 7.4) closely tied to the Rhine, and it is well represented at

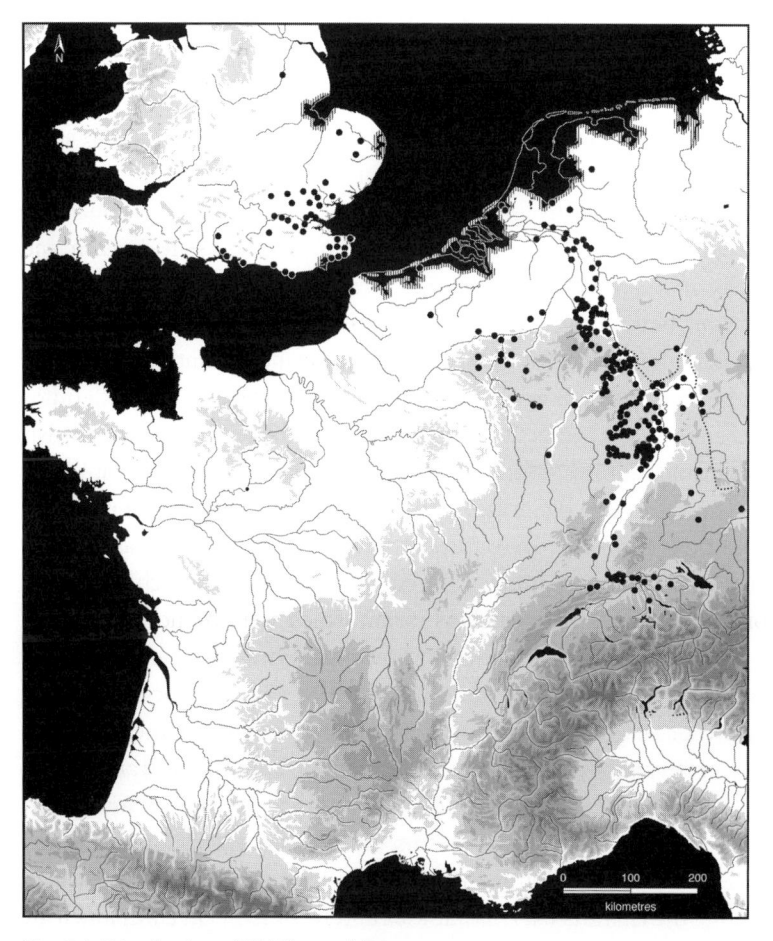

Fig. 7.4 Distribution of *Eifelkeramik*/Mayen ware

military sites along the river, and also comes from military sites and some urban sites in south-eastern Britain (cf. Fulford and Bird 1975). A similar, perhaps imitative ware was the *céramique granuleuse* of the Paris Basin, again relatively widely distributed but with no clear privileging of military sites, suggesting a more purely market orientation in its distribution. Another ceramic occurring on both sides of the Channel was black-burnished ware, a British product from around Poole Harbour. As well as its widespread distribution in Britain itself (Allen and Fulford 1996), its incidence on sites on the Gallic side of the Channel is becoming clearer, with considerable quantities from Cherbourg and some on sites up through Normandy and across the lower Seine into Picardy (where there was a local imitation), along the littoral as far as the fort at Oudenburg and then Aardenburg and the Rhine mouth, and inland as far east as Amiens and the Paris Basin (Adrian 2006; Allen and Fulford 1996: 247–61; D. Bayard pers. comm.; Gonzalez *et al.* 2006); it also was traded sporadically as far as Bordeaux. The reasons for the wide distribution of black-burnished ware in Britain, in particular, and beyond remain problematic: was it the vessels (the jars especially) or was it their contents that were being traded? Without entering into that debate here, one may nevertheless note that in north-western Gaul the distribution covered much the same geographical area as that of the coastal commands of the *dux Belgicae II* and the *dux Tractus Armoricani et Nervicani* as given in the *Notitia Dignitatum*, both commands explicitly linked in the document to the Saxon Shore. So it may be that here we are seeing a military command and supply area, perhaps again with the pottery travelling along with other materiel such as foodstuffs. It has to be said that the pattern on the British side (Allen and Fulford 1996: 255–61) does not show a specifically military pattern (save the large quantities from the Saxon Shore fort at Portchester and quantities from the shore forts at Pevensey and Dover), but more a regional, market-type pattern centred on the road network. Again, a mixture of political and market economic factors is not surprising. Briefly, and remaining in Britain, we may note the demonstration (Fulford and Hodder 1975) that Oxfordshire ware (a sort of British equivalent of Argonne ware) was distributed downstream along the Thames preferentially to the diocesan capital, London, and the Shore forts of Reculver, Richborough and Dover, perhaps travelling with grain supplies to these imperial installations. Indeed, some Oxfordshire wares along with some other south British products such as New Forest also occur along the Gallic coast (Blaskiewicz and Jigan 1994) in company with black-burnished ware. What these arguments seem to show is that the existence of the imperial political imperatives of army supply in the militarised areas of northern Gaul impacted on the range and volume of pottery distributions in this area in a way that would not have occurred in the absence of these requirements, demonstrating the importance of army supply with bulk, low-value goods as a factor in the economy at a more than local level. This is emphatically not to say that it was the only driver for the movement of these goods; it is clear that 'normal' market economics were at least as important overall, and certainly important the further one was from the Rhine and Channel military commands. But in this region we have clear evidence for the role both of the state and thus of relatively long-distance commercial pottery supply as integrative mechanisms over a wide area. One may perhaps close this section with a textual example to decorate the margins of the archaeology. Sulpicius Severus tells us (*Dialogues* II.3) that one day in the late fourth century his hero, Martin, the bishop of Tours, was travelling the roads of his diocese when he came upon a heavy-laden cart of the revenue (*fiscalis raeda*) drawn by a long line of mules (*ut saepe vidistis* 'as you have often seen' – and suggesting movement of heavy goods), which the bishop managed to startle, causing the soldiers or officials (*militantes viri*) to leap down and beat Martin with rods and whips until he fell over unconscious, to be rescued by his friends who had dropped behind. This vignette of how commonplace such transport was, and of the violence of the servants of the state, evokes the reality of the late Roman fiscal system in a way that potsherds perhaps fail to do.

Another relatively widespread pottery type in the West may also be an expression in part of the effects of state mobilisation of resources, the *terra sigillata hispánica tardía* (TSHT) of the north-central Meseta and the upper valley of the Ebro (for summary, see Juan Tovar 1997; Reynolds 2010: Ch. 2, Sect. 2.1). From its many production centres, TSHT was distributed (Figure 7.5) across a large area north of the Sierra de Guadarrama up to the western Pyrenees and across to the valley of the Duero/Douro (Reynolds 2010: Map 8). One important feature of this distribution was that it was an entirely inland one, hardly interacting at all with the coastwise distribution of north African products, especially ARS, which might otherwise have been seen as a competitor; this is an illustration of the geographical realities of the Iberian peninsula with the highlands of the Meseta relatively difficult of access from the lower coastal strips which surround them. The dispersed nature of the industry's production centres (the relative and absolute chronologies of these remain to be refined, so there may be shifting patterns at present obscured) and its presence in quantity at urban and villa sites argues strongly that it was in large measure market-driven, supplying the urban

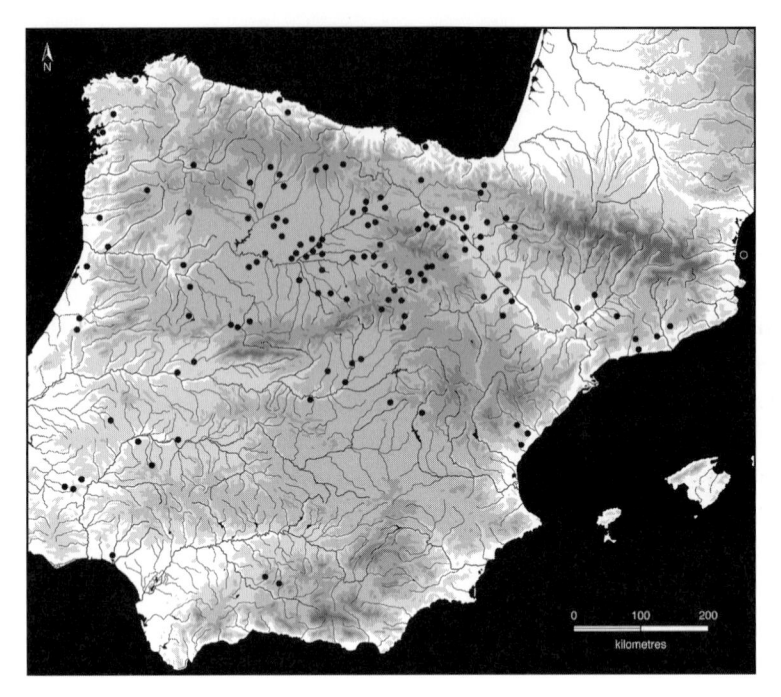

Fig. 7.5 Distribution of *terra sigillata hispánica tardía* (TSHT)

and rural populations with tableware of reasonable quality. But it is possible to hypothesise that there may have been more to it. The distribution overlaps, though not precisely, with a number of other patterns observed in previous chapters: the fortified urban sites of the north and north-west; the roads whose upkeep is attested to by large numbers of milestones (Chapter 3), and later on by the presence of garrison units, as attested to in the *Notitia Dignitatum*; and the significant, new, fourth-century grouping of villas in the northern Meseta (Chapter 5). If this area were, then, one where production and the economy were stimulated by imperial demands, both direct taxation and the more profitable *coemptio*, then this may underlie the emergence of numbers of large, relatively wealthy villas. It might also help explain the distribution of TSHT, not only through market mechanisms to the prosperous civil population of the area, but also because of the transport infrastructure of roads and carriage created by the political economy, facilitating the transport of pottery piggyback. It has to be admitted that this is an exercise in using epiphenomena to identify a phenomenon not otherwise clearly attested to, for we have little direct evidence for the large-scale involvement of this area in *annona* or other supplies (save possibly for horses); nonetheless, it is a plausible explanation for a concatenation of evidence and could stand as an example of how the effects of the political economy might be identified and of how they interacted with and augmented a market-driven pattern.

The market economy in the West: some examples

So far we have been considering pottery industries where there is good or circumstantial evidence for their benefiting from links to state-induced chains of movement of goods. Now we should look at evidence that other industries still operated essentially by a 'market' logic with little or no input from the distortions introduced by the state. To the north of the Pyrenees there developed from the fourth century, but flourishing particularly in the fifth, a series of centres producing vessels in a range of closely related forms and decorations, both of which were strongly influenced by those of ARS. Because of the Christian nature of some of the decorative motifs, earlier workers named them *dérivées de sigillées paléochrétiennes* (DSP) ('derivatives of early Christian sigillata') (Bonifay *et al.* 1998; Rigoir 1968; Rigoir and Meffre 1973). In the fourth century in Languedoc, these were predominantly fired in oxidising conditions to an orangey colour. But from about the turn of the fourth and fifth centuries, there came one of these ceramic fashion 'flips' which saw a turn to reducing firings and consequently to grey finishes, a change coinciding with the main period of production across the south of Gaul. These wares were made at a variety of centres, most probably including Marseille (Bonifay *et al.* 1998: 367) as a major producer for the 'Provençal' group, and Narbonne and possibly Carcassonne for the 'Languedoc' group, with a workshop also at Clermont-l'Hérault (Hérault) (Pomarèdes *et al.* 2005) and Bordeaux for the 'Atlantic' group. It is noticeable that the foci of production, insofar as they can be demonstrated, are mainly situated at or near major cities, and their distribution patterns show strong presences at other cities in their regions such as Arles and Nîmes for the south-eastern producers, or the cities of Novempopulana such as Saint-Bertrand-de-Comminges (Dieulafait 2006) for the Bordeaux producers. The distribution pattern and frequencies of DSP as at present apprehended correspond with a model of essentially commercial, market-driven movement; DSP appears to have been a regional fine ware produced at a number of centres and traded through urban centres to the urban population and to the rural populations around. Incidentally, this argues for the continued commercial functions of the cities of southern Gaul at this period. The known distributions can be explained in these terms without evidence for a particular input from the movement of goods as part of the political economy, especially for the main period of production in fifth century. For the fourth century, the reference in Ammianus (*Res Gestae* XVII.8.1) to Julian waiting for grain from Aquitaine before starting on campaign in the Rhineland, as well as the proposed movement of materiel up from north-western Iberia (cf. p. 129), shows that the political economy may have had some impact, though this cannot as yet be discerned through the distributions of DSP. As well as being widely distributed in south-western Gaul, 'Atlantic' DSP also occurs along the west coast of Gaul as far as Normandy (Blaskiewicz and Jigan 1994: 133 and Fig. 7; Rigoir 1968). This is probably linked to a coastal trade network involving the western seaboard of Iberia, including new *garum* manufactories in Galicia (Reynolds 2005: 393), and attested to by finds of north African products, both amphorae and ARS, in modern Portugal (Dias Diogo and Trinidade 1999; Quaresma 1999), with a scatter northwards as far as Britain (Williams and Carreras 1995), a trade that was to remain important well after the political disintegration of the West in the fifth century.

Another production in western Gaul was that of '*céramique à l'éponge*' from the Saintonge area north of the Dordogne and possibly also the Bordeaux area (Raimbault 1973), which achieved a wide distribution between the Loire and the Garonne (with coastal outliers as far as Normandy and southern Britain, perhaps by the same mechanisms as the African amphorae and ARS mentioned above) through what appear to have been market mechanisms. Something similar seems to have been happening in south-eastern Gaul with the widespread diffusion of the so-called *céramique luisante* tradition (Raynaud 1993), a regional fine ware that evolved out of and took over from the second- to third-century Claire B industry and shows many similarities in form and decoration to DSP. The excavation of production sites for this pottery at Conjux and Portout (Pernon and Pernon 1990) in Savoie hard by the upper course of the Rhône shows that its dominance in the lower Rhône corridor and into western Provence and eastern Languedoc was achieved by exploiting the river, though, as noted above, in the coastal areas it came under heavy competition from ARS. Even so, what we seem to have here is a widely diffused regional fine ware of the fourth to fifth centuries, attesting to the degree of commercial integration possible in south-eastern Gaul, its distribution facilitated by the river. In north-central Gaul we have already seen the importance of the market in the pattern of occurrence of the main regional pottery, Argonne. Overlapping with the southern edge of the Argonne distribution area was that of the rural pottery centre at

Jaulges/Villiers-Vineux in northern Burgundy (Brulet 2010; Jacob and Leredde 1985), again producing a range of utilitarian and some finer wares. The incidence of the products of this centre across a range of site types, essentially urban and rural rather than military *sensu stricto*, is again a demonstration of a functioning economy where demand for such products stimulated a supply.

Argonne, TSHT and DSP have been used as examples of productions covering large regions which were influenced in varying ways by supply and demand mechanisms; Argonne (and associated north Gaulish and British fabrics) clearly responded in considerable measure to the political economy both in supplies to sites of significance to the state (forts, cities and *fabricae*) and more generally to the advantages to be gained in the market economy from the infrastructure provided by state requirements, on the North African model. A case has been made that something similar could have been happening with TSHT alongside its more market-driven aspects. On the other hand, DSP across the south of Gaul, *céramique luisante* in the south-east, *céramique à l'éponge* in the centre-west, and Jaulges/Villiers-Vineux further north seem principally to have been produced and distributed through a commercial logic. But what they all have in common also is that they demonstrate the degree of integration of the economy in the later Roman period, especially the fourth century. From the point of view of the producer/supply, their coverage was extensive in terms of geographical area and could be intensive both in terms of production cycles and in terms of supply to particular destinations; from the point of view of the consumer/demand, these were products that were readily available in addition to more locally produced wares, and they were all of relatively good technical quality – what we now call 'fine wares' – indeed, all were derived from the red-gloss, fine-ware traditions of the High Empire (even if most DSP was reduced rather than oxidised in firing). This high degree of integration was achieved in part by the mechanisms of the political economy, which put in place the necessary fiscal and transport infrastructure to commercialise these goods over a much wider area than would otherwise have been possible. But it was also in part achieved by a continuing and vigorous market economy where surplus was negotiated for finished goods and for services, the goods and services being made by specialists, reflecting the division of labour and specialisation inherent in the developed Roman economy, and probably mediated from producer to consumer by merchants and middlemen (for the personnel of late Roman trade, see Whittaker 1983); again, these were specialists working within but also sustaining the frameworks of the late Roman exchange systems.

Local networks

As well as the long-distance and regional and super-regional networks that have just been discussed, it is important not to lose sight of the evidence for local commercial networks, the ones that operated at the scale of the individual city and its hinterland. The evidence for this is vast, far eclipsing in quantity the evidence for the longer-distance commerce. The problem is that it is so plentiful and familiar that it is difficult to grasp. It is the level of exchange manifested by the bulk of the pottery from any fourth-century Roman site anywhere in the West, pottery made not more than 50 km from the consumer site, and often much closer. It comprises the 'coarse ware' storage jars, cooking vessels, containers, dishes, bowls and jugs in everyday use at sites from the humblest to the grandest and characteristically making up 80 per cent or more of the ceramic assemblage from a site. A good example of this is the recent study of fourth-century assemblages from recent excavations at Eauze (Gers), probable capital of the province of Novempopulana (Nin 2006), where, apart from a tiny representation of imported fine wares, the assemblages consist of locally produced fine wares imitating ARS and other models that probably had a subregional extent to their distribution along with a range of locally produced coarse wares (including those handmade) that do not appear to penetrate far from Eauze. A similar pattern seems to be appearing for other major urban centres in this region of south-western Gaul (Dieulafait 2006). From some of the detailed studies that have been undertaken in Britain and elsewhere (e.g. Fulford and Hodder 1975; Hodder 1974) seeking to relate distribution patterns to distributive mechanisms, it seems very likely that much of this was accomplished through market centres, often the principal city of a territory, and sometimes through secondary centres such as the *agglomérations secondaires*, though this latter is much more easily identifiable for the High than the Late Empire in Gaul and Iberia, where, as stated earlier (p. 140), such settlements seem to have been much reduced in the later period. This does, nevertheless, attest to the continuing economic function of the cities, even in northern Gaul where such distributions are still visible in the late period (for examples, see Tuffreau-Libre and Jacques 1994). Alternatively, the articulation of the economy may be approached from the point of view of the consumer site, demonstrating the geographical range of the site's contacts and the relative quantities from longer- or shorter-range sources and their change over time (for a good example from Britain, see Going 1987: Ch. 12). This demonstrates that a market economy dependent on a rural population converting surplus into goods and services and probably also coin was still active and vigorous over much of the West, and it shows a basic level of integration which attracted to trading centres the more specialist personnel and their goods represented by the more archaeologically visible wares discussed above. As so often in archaeology, it is the recognisable minority of objects that have consumed the lion's share of the attention and analysis at the expense of the more mundane majority. In terms of the 'forms' of economic articulation presented earlier in the chapter, it is this type of activity that accords most closely with what was denominated as the 'peasant economy', essentially a short-range economy where either imbalances in resources were negotiated, generally through mechanisms of reciprocity, or access to specialist goods and services was made possible, at either the very short range of neighbouring settlements or the slightly longer range of local market centres, and this is where the peasant economy impinged upon the market economy, creating demand but also possibly acting as a sump to soak up (over-)supply of non-local commodities. Given that the agricultural peasantry made up the bulk of the population of the empire as a whole and of its constituent regions, the aggregate of these transactions was undoubtedly the largest form of economic activity in the empire. But the sheer scale of this form of the economy and of its material expression, especially in pottery, has meant that as yet it has not been accorded the study it needs, perhaps, in particular, in quantified relation to the expression of the other, more visible forms of the economy.

Coinage and the political and market economies

One prolific class of material that has not yet been considered, but certainly had something or other to do with economic activity, is the coinage. As with the pottery, this has been the subject of huge intellectual effort, particularly in the last forty years or so, at levels from the basic but essential cataloguing of the multitude of obverse and reverse types and of mint marks, to more discursive treatments of the place of coinage in the political, economic, fiscal and commercial structures. Here the concern will again specifically be with the role of the coinage as an integrative and facilitating mechanism in the operation of the late Roman economies of the West. Much of the recent work has been from the producer perspective; that is, the reasons and processes for the striking and putting into circulation of coin. Here, because the focus is on the archaeologically recovered data, the emphasis will be on the use and deposition of coins, particularly the bronze coinage, and thus how they entered the archaeological record and what this may indicate about use patterns; that is, the consumer perspective.

The producer end of the process can be briefly summarised as follows. The late Roman (essentially, fourth-century) state struck coins in gold, silver and billon (a copper alloy that shifted in composition across time) for essentially fiscal purposes, the redistributive aspect of the economy. Gold and silver were struck under the authority of the *comes sacrarum largitionum*, to a high and consistent degree of purity, at a series of mints related to the whereabouts of the emperor(s) (hence 'comitatensian' mints, from the imperial *comitatenses* or entourage), in order to discharge the financial obligations of the state, of which the largest single head of expenditure was the army, but there were also other heads such as the bureaucracy, the cities of Rome and Constantinople, and imperial patronage and munificence. Coin was the most familiar part of this, but, as we have seen elsewhere (esp. Chapter 5), precious metals could also take the form of items of apparel or of vessels and plate, some of which were formally presented on state occasions, blurring somewhat the distinction between redistribution and reciprocity. Once it had put these precious metals into circulation, the state was much exercised to retrieve them, which it did through the obligations to pay tax in these metals and by a variety of strategies to oblige people holding them to yield them up (the legal texts relating to this, of course, reflect the world as the central administration wished it to work, not necessarily as it actually did work). The archaeological effects of this are clear enough. Gold, intrinsically very valuable anyway, hardly ever appears in the form of coin as a site find and is rare in hoards (cf. Hobbs 2006), though gold objects do sometimes survive, particularly in plate hoards, attesting to the important social role of gold as a status marker. Silver, on the other hand, both as coin and as plate is much more common in hoards, and silver coins do turn up much more often than gold as site finds (again cf. Hobbs 2006). Clearly, silver coin was a much more widespread medium of economic activity; its lower intrinsic value than gold probably meant that it was more useful for higher-value but still frequent transactions, commercial or social, and more useful and practicable for accumulation as a wealth store. The processes of supply from the mints and recovery to be sent out again as supply mean that there was a lot of 'churning' of the precious metal coinage, so the coin from any particular region is often very mixed as regards the mints of origin, particularly for periods when there were or had been several emperors and/or imperial mobility, thus entailing striking at a variety of comitatensian mints. At periods of fewer emperors and few mints, supply could be dominated by a small number of mints (e.g. Guest 2005). These two circumstances make it difficult to reconstruct regional patterns of supply since the coins are either too mixed or too dominated by a single mint or very few mints. Nevertheless, from Diocletian's reforms of the mints onwards (see Hendy 1985), the late Roman state did put into circulation a single, uniform, precious metal coinage both as an essential aid to discharging its own obligations and as a medium for commercial transaction, albeit that this latter was a spin-off arising from the coinage's existence, and not a primary intention of the fiscal authorities.

The billon (copper alloy) coinage (probably referred to generically as *nummi*) was struck for rather different reasons within the fiscal cycle and thus circulated under a different set of constraints and possibilities. Unlike the precious metal coinage, the billon coinage was not the responsibility of the *comes sacrarum largitionum*, but of the praetorian prefects (for the Western provinces, the praetorian prefect of the Gauls), who had it struck at a series of mints across the empire as and when they saw fit (the late Roman state did not see it as any of its business to provide a constant supply of new coinage). In the prefecture of the Gauls, the mints were principally Trier, Lyon and Arles, as well as London briefly in the early fourth century and Amiens very briefly during the usurpation of Magnentius (350–3), though the Western provinces also received considerable quantities of billon from the mints in Italy, a smaller quantity from the Balkans and a little from the East. The purpose of striking this coinage was to have the means with which to buy back gold and silver coin through the *nummularii*, the money changers. The means by which these coins were put into circulation remain a matter for debate. It is clear that the individual mints did not strike to a constant volume, nor did they strike all issues to the same levels. There was thus a variable supply available to the authorities. Nor did the authorities supply all provinces equally; provinces nearer the frontiers received more billon coinage than those in the interior. For instance, the coinage of the House of Valentinian was prolific on the Rhine and in Britain, and scarce in the south-west of Gaul (see Depeyrot 2001: vol. II, 22). Nor was supply consistent year on year; there were periods of glut and of famine for particular provinces. This is probably the reason for the mixtures of coins from different mints to be found in individual provinces – the prefectoral authorities supplied what was to hand when required. Once the coin was injected into a province, it tended to stay there (cf. Fulford 1978). Nonetheless, this did mean that within a province there was a homogeneous circulating pool of coinage and thus integration at that scale; moreover, that coinage was drawn from the imperial system with its stated denominational system, allowing the use of coin across wide areas. Once the billon coin had performed its buy-back function, it was of little or no interest to the authorities, and, unlike the precious metal coinage, they had no means to retrieve it; if private individuals wished to use it for commercial or other transactions, then it seems that that was their business.

From the archaeology it is abundantly clear that billon was used in such ways – thus the state had provided a uniform currency across the West as part of its redistributive activities but with great utility in the market economy, and it is to the role of that currency as a facilitator of economic activity that we now turn. To put it another way: to what extent was the late Roman West monetised? This is, of course, to pose a question related much more to the point of view of the consumer than of the producer of the coinage – to the uses to which the coin was put once it had performed its designated fiscal functions. It is, of course, impossible to give a definitive answer to this question from the coins alone, especially from a single hoard or site, since all they represent is that fraction of the circulating coin pool that entered the archaeological record through loss, discarding or deposition. Fourth-century hoards tend to be biased towards the precious metal end of the coin spectrum, particularly silver, presumably because they were value hoards (deposited for whatever reason/s). Site finds, by contrast, are overwhelmingly billon; and even considering both deposition types together still gives a picture of two distinct coin pools and coin uses according to the metal. But it remains the case that sites, particularly the cities, have a tendency to produce quantities of billon coin, and by comparison with the first- and second-century coinage from sites, the fourth-century ones are much more numerous and of lower face value. This was a tendency that had started in the mid to later third century as the progressive debasement of the silver content of the *antoninianus* (radiate (?)double denarius) led both to a decline in its actual value (whatever the official tariff) and its increase in volume. The successive revaluations of the official coinage under Aurelian and Diocletian in the late third century had produced a billon coinage of much higher face value, but the low-value coin continued to circulate as, crucially, did the copious local imitations produced in the West and elsewhere ('barbarous radiates'); eventually, in the 330s, the official billon was reduced in module to something similar to the imitative coinage. All of this would seem to argue for these coinages and their imitations being token coinages for day-to-day commercial transactions. Indeed, and importantly, through the fourth century in periods of penury of official supply (or, occasionally, probably, the withdrawal of earlier coin), there continued to be regional outbreaks of copying, which must have been done to sustain the circulating pool of low-value, market-useful coins, some of which were of such low standards of production that they can only have been of token value (perhaps again used in rolls or bundles). Both billon hoards and site finds suggest that these coins could circulate for considerable periods, sustaining the availability of coin and serving as an awful warning to over-credulous archaeologists about dating. But taken together at the regional or provincial level, the aggregate of site finds demonstrates that there was a reasonably homogeneous pool of low-value coin, be it official issues or copies, whose presence and incidence strongly suggests a commercial function. It is important to note, though, that this pool did display regional variation, with a tendency for the coin pool in the provinces nearer the frontiers to be dominated by the smaller issues (what numismatists often refer to as Æ 4), whereas the provinces closer to the Mediterranean at times demonstrate a preference for the larger-module Æ 3 (see Reece 1973). So from the coins alone, it would be possible to argue that the economy of the late Roman West was in part monetised, in silver for more important transactions and in billon for the more day-to-day. The strong representation of billon, both official and copies, at cities supports the view of these coins as market-related, and thus supports the continuing commercial function of the cities. But it was very probably not just a matter of the use of coin for buying and selling but also for transactions such as the payment of wages, thus putting more coin into circulation and available to spend. This is by no means to claim universal monetisation; the evidence from many rural sites suggests a low and/or intermittent contact with coin. Reviews of the monetisation of the Roman economy based on textual evidence (e.g. Duncan-Jones 1994; Howgego 1982) tend, unfortunately for our purposes, to deal more with the High Empire than the Late Empire, but they indicate nonetheless that monetary transactions were a regular feature of economic life and at a range of values from sums representing more than the annual wage of a legionary to the trivial (cf. Howgego 1982: 16–22). This was in the period of the Augustan monetary system with its relatively large and valuable copper and copper-alloy denominations. Under the Late Empire with the much lower-value billon, the same must at the very least have held true; far more probably, these coins and their copies represent a far greater use of coin for low-value transactions. The substantial balance of probabilities is, therefore, that the coinage produced by the late Roman state served an important integrative function for the economy, not just by creating a 'single currency' over a huge area, allowing economic transactions to be undertaken at any range, but also by supplying (at least in part) the low-value coinage necessary for integration of the day-to-day economy, the 'market' and 'peasant' economies in the terminology adopted here.

The 'prestige economy'

'Prestige economy' here is taken to mean two things, both arising from the late Roman social and economic structure of landed proprietorship. One meaning is the movement of low-value goods for the purposes of the proprietor, essentially the transport of foodstuffs, oil or wine from production area to supply the proprietor or his dependants. Scattered documentary evidence (Whittaker 1983: 169–73) shows that this was happening, as is only likely, but whether it was on a scale and regularity to impact on the archaeological record is much more doubtful. It should be noted, though, that there was one institution whose importance was developing in the fourth century and was to become enormous from the fifth century on, the Church. Some individual churches were the recipients of substantial imperial patronage. One thinks above all of the great basilicas of Rome, especially St Peter's, which were endowed not only with gifts in precious metals, such as great, gold dishes or candelabra, but also with extensive landed estates. In this sense, bishops of Rome were among the great landowning aristocrats of the Western Empire and could transfer revenues from many provinces to Rome and spend them on great, richly decorated building complexes. It is unfortunate that we do not know the endowments of the great church of Trier, but since it must have been an imperial project, it, too, in all probability, received imperial donation(s) of property in Gaul if not elsewhere. The liturgies of the Church, of course, required wine, and certainly in subsequent centuries this may have accounted for some at least of the longer-distance movement of this commodity, especially to regions which did not provide their own, though in fact almost all the fourth-century West did produce wine (see papers in Brun and Laubenheimer 2001; see also Brown, A. G. *et al.* 2001). But the Church also had a 'moral economy' that demanded good works such as famine relief, which, as we know from fifth-century sources for Gaul, could be on a considerable scale (e.g. Harries 1992: esp. 90–1). Archaeological evidence that this affected such things as pottery distributions has not yet been detected (probably partly because it is not much looked for), but it may be worth bearing in mind as a mechanism to explain certain untypical distributions. But that a religious community's needs might have such an effect is demonstrated by the distribution of Calabrian wine amphorae of form Keay 52 bearing a stamp with a menorah on the handle, whose distribution to Rome and a limited number of other west Mediterranean sites, including sites in southern Gaul and Spain, has led to the suggestion that they were produced for (and by?) Jewish communities (Arthur 1989, 138–9; Reynolds 2005, 416–17).

The other meaning of 'prestige economy' is that, more usually, the landowning elite converted their surpluses into cash to enable them to pay for the lifestyle appropriate to their rank and status (or the ones to which they aspired) or they lent it out to others who needed liquidity to pay for such undertakings. Part of this aristocratic culture, as we noted in Chapter 5 (p. 262), was the reciprocal exchange of goods dictated by a variety of social situations. Often socially dictated also was the nature of the gift, as in the celebration of a consulship by a carved ivory diptych, but other occasions required simply the presentation of a gift of suitable magnificence or worth to express the donor's estimation of the recipient and to initiate or perpetuate a chain of reciprocal obligation, social capital to be drawn on and discharged as occasion demanded. Such mechanisms can, of course, be invoked to explain the presence of 'exotic' goods on sites far from their place of manufacture, particularly the commodities especially valued by the aristocracies such as plate, marble, sculpture, ivory and fine glassware – or possibly the craftsmen to produce them; other commodities such as mosaics; and, of course, the much less archaeologically visible gifts of such things as silks, paintings, fine furniture, books and honorific verses (cf., in Gaul, Ausonius for the fourth century and Sidonius Apollinaris for the fifth). The volume of such movements would be tiny (otherwise, of course, they would not have remained prestigious), but their role in cementing the social alliances and cultural integration of the aristocracy was critical.

Conclusions

The purpose of this chapter has not been to reopen the whole question of the nature and operations of the late Roman economy; instead it had a more limited brief, one firmly tied to the nature of the archaeological evidence available – pottery and coins above all. This chapter aimed to examine how the archaeological evidence in tandem with the textual has allowed a model to be created for the levels and forms at and in which the late Roman economy functioned. Particular attention was paid to the evidence that archaeology is particularly well suited to examine; that is, the evidence revealing the scale and the degree of integration of the late Roman economy across and within the West, the archaeologically visible economy standing proxy, as so often, for social and cultural formations. It has been clearly demonstrated that there was a considerable degree of integration, particularly at the higher levels of society, the wealthy and those attached to the imperial system itself and to the market economy mediated through the cities. Crucial to this integration were the redistributive mechanisms of the empire. By its very existence, the empire to a certain extent encouraged exchange by creating essentially secure conditions for transport and by putting in place infrastructures, such as roads and ports, and supporting such things as cities with their large groupings of consumers. But more importantly, its political economy demanded the suspension of some of the 'natural' economic laws of the ancient world through the imperative to move supplies, such as grain and oil, or other commodities, such as coin, over large distances through the mechanisms of the tax system. And piggyback on this fiscal infrastructure went, as we have seen, other goods, of which the most visible to us is pottery. The state also produced for its own purposes an abundant, trimetallic coinage central to the economic integration of the West through the provision of media for the effecting of large- or small-value exchanges over longer or shorter distances. Both the 'spine' created by the movement of goods at the state's behest and the lubrication provided by the presence of the currency stimulated the market economy that was long established and centred on the cities, and clearly still functioning strongly for the manufacture and distribution of goods. In addition, the reciprocal economies of the aristocracies, through socially conditioned activities such as gift exchange, and of the peasantries as they supplemented their own produce with goods and services, promoted the movement of goods, sometimes in significant quantities. The peasantry also participated in the market economy, as local pottery distributions reveal, both as part of their mechanisms for obtaining goods and services and to acquire coin for tax and rent and to participate in the monetised parts of the economy. As the textual evidence (albeit often of a rather moralising nature) shows, the system was far from perfect, involving violence, graft, extortion, arbitrariness, inconsistency and unpredictability (among other things); there was still famine and the range of goods available and frequency of access to them (or not) were still a function of social status, but at least it was a system, and as a result more people had more access to goods and services than they would have had if it had not existed (this is a quantitative, not a moral, statement). So we should always bear in mind the impact of this system upon the consumer, and not see it just from the producers' or mobilisers' points of view. To the archaeologist, the consumer is more easily identified at the level of the site – that is, an aggregate of individual consumers – but the message for the third and fourth centuries is consistently that the consumer, even in areas isolated from the main currents of commerce, had access to a range of manufactured goods and in quantities that were significantly greater than was the case in the pre-Roman period or was to be the case in the immediately succeeding centuries, as we shall see in Chapter 9. The extreme visibility of the late Roman period in the archaeological record is in itself a testament to this level of economic activity and integration as well as to the cultural forces shaping the forms those products took. It is also the disintegration of this economic nexus that is one of the defining archaeological features of the 'fall' of the Western Empire in the course of the fifth century and that will be considered in Chapter 9.

8 | Breakdown and barbarians

Introduction

Rather in the way that the last two chapters formed a diptych, concerning themselves with different but complementary aspects of the production, mobilisation and deployment of surpluses in the late Roman world, this chapter and the succeeding one will form a diptych relating to defining features of the fifth century and its archaeology. This chapter will concern itself essentially with the breakdown of the structures of imperial political, military and fiscal control in the West, on the one hand, and, on the other hand, the appearance of features of the archaeology which may (or may not) be related to the increasing presence and importance of 'barbarians' on the territories of the Western Empire. The following chapter will examine the consequence of these developments for wider economic and cultural formations across the West, which ran to a somewhat different tempo.

The archaeology of the fifth century on its own would tell us that there were major changes across the board in the Western provinces in this period; it sees massive alterations over a short timescale. Archaeologically, the fifth century marks an important threshold of development, one that sees important structural changes across the range of the evidence, thus marking a far more important horizon than the 'crisis' of the third century. Yet, like the third century, the fifth century was also a crisis, in the technical sense that it was a point at which the 'patient' recovered from or succumbed to the ills besetting it; in this case the universal perception is that it succumbed to a virulent attack of barbarians. This is, of course, a view derived from the textual sources, from their narratives, often with a strong moralising agenda, of military, political and administrative collapse and the replacement of the imperial system by the Germanic successor states of the early Middle Ages. In this chapter the traditional discourse of the 'fall of the Western Roman Empire' will not be ignored (it hardly can be), but it will be viewed from a different perspective, that of the archaeology, which may give us a rather different range, chronology and causation of events, in particular as regards the place of the various brands of barbarian peoples.

Chronological outline

The traditional narrative and structure for understanding the events of the fifth century has been derived from the historical and other textual sources (for a representative, recent and detailed treatment, see Heather 2005 and references). A much abbreviated version of events in the first half of the century is presented here to give a chronology and an outline of events in the short term. It must be emphasised that this is not because this narrative is 'true', and still less because the archaeology is simply there to ornament this narrative. It is because the narrative and the events it relates have given both the accepted chronological structure to the fifth century and a version of events. This chronology and these events have for a long time shaped the presentation and the discussion of the archaeological evidence, so that it is necessary to have an appreciation of the traditional narrative, even if the intention is to discard it and replace it with something else more responsive to the nature of the archaeological evidence and its significance(s).

On the last day of what is normally given as the year 406, in fact very probably 405 (Kulikowski 2000), large barbarian forces consisting of Alamanni, Alans, Sueves, Vandals and others crossed the frozen Rhine in the region of Mainz and penetrated deep into Gaul, encountering little opposition from imperial forces and heralding fifteen years of war and instability. This provoked the usurpation in Britain of Constantine III, who crossed to Gaul to try to restore order and to deny to the barbarians the passes into Spain. In both of these he was unsuccessful, surrendering to imperial forces at Arles in 411 and being done away with. But by this time the Alans, Sueves and Vandals had penetrated into Spain, where the Sueves carved out for themselves a territory in the north-west of the peninsula. The imperial authorities, under the direction of the very able patrician Constantius (later briefly emperor in 421), manipulated the Visigoths, fresh from their part in the sack of Rome in 410, into south-western Gaul and then into north-eastern Spain to try to defeat the other tribes, before eventually settling them in south-western Gaul in 418, or more probably 419, ceding them rights from Toulouse to the Atlantic. The Visigoths were intervening under Roman auspices in Spain from 422, but a more worrying presage of things to come saw them attacking the imperial seat in Gaul, Arles, as early as 425. In 429, the Vandals and many Alans crossed to north Africa, where they took Carthage in 439, depriving the Western emperors of their richest tax lands. In 433, military command of the West was conferred on Aetius, who tried to stabilise the position by force, defeating the

Burgundians and resettling them around Geneva and westwards in 436/7, defeating the Bacaudae (Drinkwater 1992) (a local uprising) in Armorica (Brittany) in 437, and in 439 attempting to subdue the Visigoths, who had been attacking Arles and Narbonne, an attempt that was unsuccessful under the walls of Toulouse but at least led to a reaffirmation of the original treaty of 419. The relatively peaceful 440s saw the various contestants with claims over territory in the West circling and manoeuvring; the imperial government under Valentinian III (425–55), represented in Gaul by Aetius, was contesting with the other factions also, the Visigoths, Alans (resettled by Aetius on the Loire in 442), Burgundians in central and southern Gaul, and the nascent Frankish power in the north. In Spain the remnants of the imperial authorities maintained a precarious hold on the Mediterranean littoral and adjacent inland areas, with the Sueves becoming more dominant in the north-west and expanding their territories. In 451 in Gaul, the contending parties sank their differences and united under the leadership of Aetius to face the invasion of Attila and the Huns, successfully facing them down at the battle of the Catalaunian Plains (near Troyes in central Gaul), a battle in which Theodoric I, king of the Visigoths, was killed. Aetius was to meet the fate of several successful late Roman generals by being assassinated, in this case by Valentinian III personally, in 454, Valentinian himself being assassinated in revenge the following year, all of this testament to the poisonous faction fighting on the Roman side, which could affect relations with the Germanic rulers.

As can be seen, two intertwined themes are central to this narrative: the increasing enfeeblement of the unified imperial power in the West and, as both cause and consequence, its lands and power being taken over by a series of kingdoms ruled by dynasties claiming Germanic descent and identity. To turn from this short-term 'kings and battles' history to how this all intersected with more medium-term processes, what we need to consider is how the military and political events acted upon the existing structures of the West, and, in particular, how they brought about 'The end of the Western Roman Empire'. Of course, what is generally meant by this expression is the end of imperial political, administrative and fiscal control, the end of the late Roman state and its structures, and it is that which we shall examine now. What happened to the populations of the West and their political, economic and cultural formations will be the concern of the next chapter. The process of the dissolution of the Roman state control over the territories and peoples of the West and its proximate causes can be fairly readily characterised and understood. As has been stated earlier (p. 19), the political, administrative and fiscal systems of the late Roman Empire depended in the last analysis on the army. It was the army that was there to hold the frontiers against external threat and sought to guarantee internal peace and stability. It underpinned emperors and their reigns over their peoples (or, alternatively, attempted to replace them), and it also underpinned the state's fiscal system; after all, it was the principal beneficiary of that very system. In order to do this, it had to have ensured sources of manpower, money and materiel. In the fourth century this balance held and the army maintained its manpower (though with increasing difficulty) and was paid and supplied, though, as we shall see, the 390s may well have marked a turning point for the Western armies. But certainly from 406, the Western Empire started to suffer not only military defeat but also, in crucial distinction to the 'third-century crisis', permanent, large-scale loss of territory. With territory went recruiting-grounds, taxpayers and resources, enfeebling the army and the state. The incoming Germanic peoples picked up on this weakness and sought to turn it to their advantage by taking further imperial territory. Increasing loss of territory translated into decreasing Roman ability to do anything to restore the situation, a vicious cycle, and by the 450s the once-mighty Western Empire was but one player among many in the campaigns and alliances. By the end of the 470s, it was not even that: military debilitation had resulted in political oblivion. This was the structural crisis of the Western Empire, one from which it did not pull through. Of course, this was not planned or predestined, either by the Romans or by the Germanic peoples. On the Roman side, such things as the settlement of the Visigoths in Aquitaine in 419 were doubtless seen as expedient and temporary – it got the Roman authorities off a particular hook. They could not know at the time that an allocation of land would turn into an independent kingdom. Nor, so far as we can tell from the Roman textual sources, was there any intention on the Germanic side to destroy the empire as such; rather, they wanted to establish their claim to parts of it. If in this process they had to ally themselves with or confront the imperial government, well, that was politics. One could say that the Western Roman Empire was one of the larger of history's victims of the law of unintended consequences.

The end of the Roman army in the West

Central to the existence of the Roman Empire was its army, which defended imperial territory, safeguarded the person of the emperor and ultimately underpinned the judicial and fiscal systems that sustained the emperor and the empire, and, indeed, the army. Its progressive debilitation and ultimate disappearance are therefore equally central to the study of the fate of the Western Empire, since it can be said that without a Roman army there could be no Roman Empire. The fate of the Roman army in the West and the processes by which it disappeared are difficult to pin down, particularly from the archaeological evidence; nevertheless, the attempt must be made, even if only to demonstrate the problems inherent in the exercise.

In Chapter 2 it was argued that the crucial distinguishing feature of the late Roman army was that it was a standing army, paid, housed, equipped and supplied by the state (the taxpayer), and commanded by officers appointed ultimately by and answerable to the emperor as part of the 'public' power of the state. It was a major institution of the Roman state, organised into functional types (*comitatenses* were the internal field armies, *limitanei/ripenses* the frontier armies) and into regional commands. Each command (as listed in the *Notitia Dignitatum*) consisted of a variable number of named units, units that had a long-term existence as organisations independent of the command of which they might form a part or of the soldiers or commanding officers who at any one time made them up (for instance, unit titles listed in northern Britain can be traced back some three hundred years before their appearance in the *Notitia*). The soldiers were defined by the state authorities through formal processes of recruitment, training, registering in and membership of units; subordination to officers and regional commanders; and receipt of pay, provisions and equipment. This 'etic' (external) definition overlapped with the 'emic' (internalised) self-definition of the soldiers inculcated and routinised daily through the forts in which they lived, the clothes they wore, the weaponry and armour they used, the oaths they took, the ceremonies they attended, the distinctive military language and laws they used, the unit to which they belonged and its *esprit de corps*, and their consciousness of membership of the wider 'imagined community' of the soldiery, set apart from the wider civilian population of the empire. This definition of the late Roman army has been recapped here, because, central to the argument that follows about how to model archaeologically the demise of this institution, will be precisely the fact that it was a distinctive institution, in particular one that was sustained by the state and was part of the 'public' power structures of the state. It will be proposed that crucial for our understanding of what happened to the army in the fifth century will be the idea that it progressively ceased to be sustained by the ever more enfeebled state, and that, as a result and in its place, there came about command over, and expressions of, military power that increasingly were the responsibility of individual commanders rather than the imperial command and control structures: military power increasingly became 'privatised'.

A key site which we may use as a case study because of its large suite of excavated evidence covering these years is the fort of Krefeld-Gellep (*Gelduba*) on the lower Rhine (cf. Figure 2.2), more particularly the cemeteries excavated between 1960 and 2000 under the direction of Renate Pirling (for a summary to 1985, see Pirling 1986; for the more recent work, see Pirling *et al.* 2000 with bibliography). The majority of the fourth-century inhumation graves exhibited the relatively simple Roman provincial burial rite common across northern Gaul and the Rhineland or Britain (cf. Chapter 2, p. 51) and contained a range of grave goods, most often pottery. Some male graves contained items of dress such as belt suites and crossbow brooches, suggesting that the dead may have been soldiers of the garrison at Krefeld. But the presence in one grave (Gr. 4755) not only of an elaborate, later fourth-century belt suite of Roman manufacture but also a bronze neck ring of a type originating east of the Rhine suggests contact with that area, though this supports the concept of a *Mischzivilization* with cultural traits borrowed from either side of the river. Likewise, in some female graves of the later fourth century, there were pairs of brooches, including *Tutulusfibeln*, with both the objects and the way of wearing them reflecting material and practice from east of the Rhine. Here was also one female grave, Gr. 4607, containing a mirror of a type common in the area known to the Romans as Sarmatia. Does this echo the *Sarmatae gentiles* of the *Notitia* (cf. Chapter 2, p. 92), or was it just a trinket? At Krefeld there was also metalwork indicative of contacts with Pannonia and some glazed pottery vessels, more common in Pannonia than the Rhineland (Swift 2000b: 79–82). The interpretative problem is whether the areas of origin of the objects reflect also and directly the areas of origin of the persons with whom they were buried, in which case they may be used as 'ethnic' markers, telling us something about the origins of the garrison of fourth-century Krefeld. Alternatively, of course, the objects may have reached Krefeld and been buried there by means which divorced them from their 'ethnic' significance. To complicate matters, Gr. 3007 contained bracelets both of Danubian and of British origin (Swift 2000a: 176, 2010), demonstrating the difficulties inherent in using objects rather than attributes such as burial rite (or eventually chemical and physical analyses) to determine geographical, let alone ethnic, origins. This was all in the fourth century when the site was a fort, normally thought to have housed a garrison of the regular, standing Roman army: it is a testament to a mix of material culture at one site associated with the late Roman army and thus to the heterogeneity of the personnel of that army.

From the turn of the fourth and fifth centuries, both burial rites and objects start to change, with the first appearance of graves containing weaponry and handmade ceramics of non-Roman origin (e.g. Gr. 2650), though this in itself says nothing about the origins and loyalties of the troops or warriors at Krefeld. But from about the end of the first quarter of the fifth century, we begin to see weapon burials with long swords (*spathae*), spearheads and knives, along with brooches and buckles of 'Germanic' (in the sense of origins east of the Rhine) type. At the same time there are female burials with mainly 'Germanic' brooch types and other dress elements. Both male and female burials had glass vessels (including cruder ones of forest glass, compared with the technically superior tradition of the Roman-derived products), but also pottery that was increasingly of 'Germanic' forms and handmade. These burials, though in the same cemeteries as the fourth-century ones, tended to cluster in groups. The excavators interpret these changes during the first half of the fifth century, taken together, as representing the arrival of families or kin groups from east of the Rhine, led by male warriors and in some sense supplanting the regular, Roman garrison of the previous century. In the excavators' opinion these were Franks. While not necessarily accepting such a precise ethnic identification (we shall examine the problems of the archaeology of 'fifth-century Franks' below), we can at the very least argue on the basis of the material culture and maybe features of the burial rite (e.g. deposition of weapons) that these burials express much closer links with the material culture and status and gender markers of peoples to the east of the Rhine. Again, in default of physical or chemical analyses, we cannot be certain, but there is a plausible case to be made that these changes represent people as well as objects from east of the Rhine. Given that Roman provincial pottery was still available, and used in some of the burials, the presence of handmade pottery of 'Germanic' type would seem to be a persuasive factor in favour of the people, as well as the pottery, being of Germanic origin, especially given the importance of pottery in the burial rites of the Germanic peoples at the time.

What cannot be established from their funerary rites is whether the menfolk buried at Krefeld in the fifth century were, by either 'etic' or 'emic' definition, 'Roman soldiers'. Was there a continuing Roman state or government that regarded the men of Krefeld as subject to its control, loyal to the emperor and due some sort of payment or support in exchange? Or were they subordinate to some form of officer who still regarded himself as loyal to the emperor, even if the emperor and his bureaucracy may not have been aware of the existence of either the men or their officers, and thus could be thought of as 'Roman' in that sense. Did they regard themselves as in any sense 'Roman' soldiers, loyal to the emperor and part of a wider community of the Roman soldiery? Or was their allegiance to an ethnic leader whose loyalties lay to himself and his followers, making it very hard to see Krefeld any longer as a 'Roman' military installation with a 'Roman' garrison and commander? To date, the Krefeld-Gellep cemeteries provide us with by far the fullest evidence in the West for developments through the second half of the fourth and the first half of the fifth centuries. What this example shows is that, whereas it is possible to demonstrate continued occupation at a site that in the fourth century was a Roman military installation, after the beginning of the fifth century it becomes progressively more difficult to reconstruct from the archaeology what the function and status of these groupings may have been, or their relation (if any) with what remained of the Roman state.

A comparable site, this time on the upper Rhine, is Kaiseraugst (Drack and Fellmann 1988: 300–12, 411–14). Within the fortification, there was probably a *principia*, and certainly, and unusually, a major bathhouse, a storehouse and a church. From within the fortification came the major, mid-fourth-century Kaiseraugst treasure (Cahn and Kaufmann-Heinemann 1984). Some 300 m south-east of the fortress lay a cemetery, of which some 2,000 burials have been excavated and which shows a similar sequence to Krefeld-Gellep. The burials of the second half of the fourth century either had no grave goods or were furnished with pottery and, in a few cases, items of dress, in the standard late Roman way. From the end of the fourth century began to appear burials with 'Germanic' grave goods, though, at the same time, there was built a small apsidal structure, quite probably a *cella memoriae*, so religious change is as evident in this cemetery as any ethnic change there may have been. The cemetery was to remain in use until the seventh century, by which time it held gravestones with Germanic names. But again, for the fifth century, the ethnic identities and the political loyalties of the changing population remain unfathomable, as also their relationship to the Roman state. On the middle Rhine, one may point to sites such as Alzey and to a lesser extent Altrip. The fort at Alzey (Oldenstein 1986) had been established under Valentinian I; it was square in shape with projecting towers, and the internal accommodation took the form of buildings along the inside face of the walls, leaving the centre of the enclosure largely free of buildings (Figure 8.1). The fort seems to have been partially destroyed around 400; this was ascribed to the Germanic invasion in 406. Thereafter, the damaged buildings were restored or replaced. The

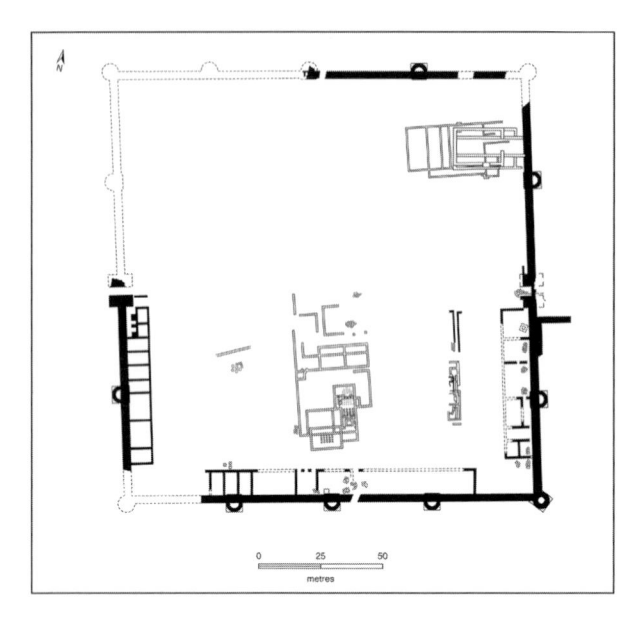

Fig. 8.1 Alzey fort, fourth-century (black) and fifth-century (outline) structures

material culture associated with this phase is of types much more closely linked with that from east of the Rhine, and is interpreted by the excavator as the installation of a Germanic garrison, possibly of Burgundians, but still under Roman command. Alzey was destroyed by fire in the middle of the fifth century.

A common feature of the archaeological sequences at these forts and in their cemeteries is the increase in the amount of 'Germanic' material from them after the start of the fifth century. In some of the cemeteries, this material comes from what seem to be male and female graves in restricted areas of burial, and this may well point to family groupings. Both here and in Chapter 2, there has been an insistence that any simple equation between an object and a specific identity or ethnicity, or between the presence of an object in a burial and the identity or ethnicity of the occupant of the grave, should be avoided. These arguments stand. But at the case-study sites and at many others with more partial documentation, what changes in the fifth century is the volume and range of this new material and its increasing dominance of the material culture record, either on its own or in combination with the latest types of Roman-derived material culture, especially belt fittings. Whereas at the level of the individual object or the individual occupation deposit or burial it is possible and desirable to be cautious about ethnic ascriptions, what is different in the fifth century is the *aggregate* level of these types of material culture, which form a significant proportion of the total by the end of the first half of the century and pretty much the total by the end of the century. The origins of this material culture lay ultimately east of the Rhine and north of the Danube, the 'Pontico-Danubian' area, the homelands of the Germanic peoples and of other non-Germanic peoples. It may be objected that this is simply to accept the agenda of Roman writers and their ethnic labelling, but the archaeology makes it abundantly clear that there was in the fourth century and on into the fifth a series of distributions of related material culture across these areas (e.g. the complex often referred to as the '*Elbegermanen*' [see Drinkwater 2007: Ch. 2; Drinkwater and Elton 1992]) that differentiated these peoples from those in lands directly subject to Roman imperial power. It becomes increasingly hard to sustain the interpretation of the large-scale arrival of this material culture at a large number of Roman military sites all along the Rhineland simply in terms of a continuing Roman provincial garrison and/or population as helpless fashion victims with a taste for Germanic goods. The presence of what may well be discrete groupings in the cemeteries with this sort of material, as against the continuing Roman provincial rites, as at Krefeld-Gellep, does look very much like the movement of people, not just of pots or brooches. This, of course, could have coexisted with the indigenous populations starting to redefine their identities and ethnicities in terms of the Germanic incomers, particularly given that these latter may have had a privileged position, one dependent on the martial prowess of the menfolk. So ethnic ascription from material culture remains problematic, and not all burials with 'Germanic' material need have been the burials of Germans from across the Rhine. Indeed, what these burials seem to show is the progressive 'Germanisation' of the groupings (incomers or indigenous) in aspects of their funerary practice such as, in particular, the preparation of the corpse and, in the case of women, above all by laying-out bodies in forms of clothing which, even if not making claims to specific ethnic identities, were certainly making claims not to follow Roman provincial practices. The increasing presence of triangular 'Germanic' combs may suggest the importance of hairstyles alongside the more obvious clothing, suggesting that a situation developed where markers of ethnicity (or at least of not becoming Roman) became more important, particularly at burial, than markers of relation to the Roman state and its army.

So, by the mid fifth century, it would seem that the peoples living and buried at a series of Rhineland forts increasingly used material culture of non-Roman origins, mainly from areas that Roman written sources classed as 'German'. Whether all these people were from those areas to the east of the Rhine and to the north of the Danube remains unknowable; it may be that some of them were from west of the Rhine but assimilated to this 'Germanic' identity (these matters are discussed more extensively later in the chapter). But the question posed in this section of the chapter is that of the processes by which the Western Roman army ceased to exist, or at least to be recognisable in the archaeology. Earlier it was argued that a 'Roman' army fulfilled certain 'emic' and 'etic' definitions as regards the internalised loyalties and practices of the soldiers, the institutional existence of the army and its units, and the political loyalty of the army to the emperor. The changes in the archaeology, particularly the material culture, suggest that during the fifth century the 'emic' definitions of the people at these sites moved away from that which had characterised the garrisons of the fourth century towards something which to Roman eyes would appear more 'barbarian'. But 'barbarians' served in the army of the fourth century at all levels, as was seen in Chapter 2, so that in itself is not a sufficient index of no longer regarding themselves as servants of the emperor, or being so regarded by others. What the archaeology at present cannot tell us is where the sense of the community to which individuals belonged lay or where their political loyalties lay. Did they regard themselves as soldiers of the emperor, or did they regard themselves as members of 'tribal' or other groupings and followers of individual leaders whose loyalties were negotiable? There is, though, one class of material which may be a strong indicator of an 'etic' definition – a definition made by the Roman authorities – and that is the coinage, which was closely tied to the question of army pay and loyalty.

Coinage in the early fifth century

In the previous chapter the striking of coinages by the late Roman state was explicitly tied to the political economy, specifically the payment/clawback system put in place by which precious metal was paid out to discharge the obligations of the state, above all to pay the army, and then recovered through a variety of means including the compulsory changing of gold and silver for base metal by the *nummularii*. In the West the bulk of state commitments was to the army, to its infrastructure, such as the *fabricae*, and to the bureaucracy, so this payment/clawback nexus was very closely allied to the army. At the turn of the fourth and fifth centuries, there were major, far-reaching changes to the state production of coinage, a horizon which perhaps has not received due attention (cf. Kent 1994). The precious metal coinage had therefore always been central to the state's meeting its obligations, especially as regarded the payment of the army. Silver coins, principally the *siliqua*, had been struck at the Western mints, mainly Trier but also Lyon and Arles, through the second half of the fourth century. At the turn of the fourth and fifth centuries, these mints ceased precious metal production, and henceforth the Western authorities struck gold (in small quantities) and more especially silver, principally at Milan. The usurper Eugenius struck a considerable silver coinage there in 393–4, but after his suppression at the battle of the Frigidus in early 395, there was an hiatus in production until 397. The five years between 397 and 402 saw a huge issue from Milan (rev. *Virtus Romanorum*). Thereafter the principal mint for precious metals in the West was Ravenna, particularly between 408 and 425, with sporadic production at Rome and Aquileia in 407–8 (cf. Guest 2005a: 74–6). But these later issues did not penetrate north of the Alps in any quantity. The usurper Constantine III (406–11) did strike in silver, as well as some gold, at mints such as Lyon, both before and after the death of Arcadius in 408, but not in large enough quantities or for long enough to reverse the overall trend. For the coinages in base metal, in the year 395 the Western *monetae publicae*, the mints supplying these coins, were reorganised, massively changing the scale and nature of the coinage produced and supplied. Trier, Lyon and Arles largely ceased to strike in base metals; in the West, only Rome continued to do so in any volume. This step change was succeeded by another in 402 when the three Gallic mints effectively ceased base metal production at the end of the *Victoria Auggg* issue in 402, and the succeeding *Salus Reipublicae*, *Urbs Roma Felix* and *Gloria Romanorum* (three emperors) issues of Rome hardly circulated north of the Alps.

So from about 402 the Western Empire was suddenly in a situation where it was no longer producing the coinages, particularly silver and base metal, that had been vital to its revenue and expenditure cycle, the expenditure, of course, directed principally at the army. It is important to recognise that this was developing before the failure of the Rhine frontier and the start of the barbarian land grabs from the end of 405 on, so it cannot be, in origin at least, an effect of these. Also, Italy seems to have been different, since silver was still struck at Ravenna, and bronze continued to be struck at and circulated from the Rome mint. One possible explanation is that 402 marked one of the pauses in the production of coin which are detectable in the fourth century, the intention having been to resume coining, but this never came about outside Italy because of the events of 406 and the following years when a combination of barbarian incursion and the usurpation by Constantine III meant no coins of the later issues would be supplied to such unstable areas. It is noticeable, though, that even after the suppression of

Constantine III in 411 and the re-establishment of a measure of imperial political and military control north of the Alps, the large-scale supply of coin to those areas was not resumed. In that case the imperial authorities presumably had to find other means of paying those soldiers and units still loyal to them. A logical, if extreme, response would have been the Western authorities deciding that they no longer needed to support these armies, but this would fly in the face of the fundamental importance of the army in maintaining the empire and the imperial system; it also ignores the textual evidence for something called a West Roman army in the first half of the fifth century. But, less controversially, one might propose that the state had chosen, or had been forced through circumstance, to change the ways in which it sustained and remunerated its armies. The fiscal system, insofar as it related to the armies, was designed in part to produce the wherewithal to pay them, but also the revenues to cover the costs of heads of expenditure such as the construction of military installations, the provision of weapons and equipment (through the *fabricae*), and the ensuring of foodstuffs and other supplies over and above those directly raised from and transported by the taxpayer. Interestingly, the trend over the latter part of the fourth century had increasingly been to adaerate these obligations – that is, to commute them for coin/bullion payments. If the Western Empire now no longer wished to raise the precious metals necessary for discharging these functions, then, presumably, the armies were to be supported in some other way(s), perhaps by more direct requisitions from the provincial populations, though we have no positive evidence for this. Logically, this would also entail the dismantling of the necessary bureaucracies under the *comes sacrarum largitionum* (precious metal revenues and payments), the *magister officiorum* (the *fabricae*) and the praetorian prefect of the Gauls (billon coinage and materiel). In fact, it is hard to trace these officers, save the praetorian prefect, in the written sources outside Italy much after the start of the fifth century. This picture of what may have happened to the Western armies from the end of the fourth century is provisional and needs more work and thought on the precise chronology of these changes and on the distributions of the various coin issues. But the major changes to the supply and circulation of coinage and the significance of those changes do have to be recognised and pursued. Either it was intended to be a temporary pause, one that was overtaken by events, or it marks a purposive shift in the imperial fiscal system beyond the Alps. Whichever it was, the result was that from the start of the fifth century the Western authorities could not or would not be in a position to maintain a standing Roman army of the traditional form. Some other expedients would have to be resorted to.

The archaeological evidence from military installations suggests that increasingly they were occupied by soldiers or warriors of 'Germanic' origin or by locals who were increasingly defining themselves in non-Roman ways. It could be proposed that this is the horizon at which the control of force passes out of the hands of the Romans and into those of the incomers as the latter supplanted the Roman army in what had been its garrison forts – a power and land grab. But the relationship of Roman provincial and Germanic material cultures and burials suggests rather that the two coexisted, at least in the first half of the fifth century. In this case one might propose a scenario whereby instead of a standing army with soldiers whose recruitment, routines of life, identity and ideological commitments were shaped by the Roman army and state, military force in the West was increasingly committed to 'barbarian' groupings for whose support the state did not have to take responsibility in the same way as it had for a 'Roman' army. In effect, it was an extension of the principle and practice of *foederati*, tribal detachments who fought for Rome but were not part of her standing armies. Presumably, the Roman state settled them in its forts and allocated them provincial land off which to support themselves on the understanding that they would fight for the emperor under the command of the senior officers (*comites rei militaris* and the like), who were, as we can see from the texts, still appointed to Gaul and Germany and to a lesser extent to Spain. This would echo the arrangements that we know were made for the settling and support of the Visigothic army and people in south-western Gaul in 419 (see below). Under this scenario the Western authorities would no longer have needed to mint much in the way of coin for the areas outside Italy (and North Africa), and that is precisely what we see.

The progressive loss of the recruiting grounds and the tax base of Germany, Gaul, Britain and Spain from 406 forced the imperial authorities to desperate measures, measures that for the first half of the fifth century seem to have had some success, to judge by the textual accounts of senior Roman generals, such as Constantius and Aetius, in managing to some extent to resist, control and resettle the incoming peoples (cf. p. 359), above all in Gaul, down to the middle of the fifth century. What the texts also show is the increasing importance of the personal charisma and military competence of these generals in persuading an increasingly heterogeneous range of troops and warriors to follow them. The public power of the Roman state was increasingly being supplanted by loyalty to a leader. This is the appearance of the type of retinue of warriors known to the sources as *bucellarii* (hard-tack men), men who followed a successful military leader because he fed them and his successes yielded booty. After that, the textual sources show the increasing fragmentation of Roman power, or at least the power of those commanders who legitimised themselves by use of the name and aura of Rome, in both northern and southern Gaul (Spain seems by then to have been a lost cause), with the newly emerging barbarian kingdoms (see below) taking over as the possessors of military force. The rulers of these kingdoms, and presumably the leaders of smaller war bands elsewhere in Gaul, were, of course, another expression of this 'privatisation' of military force as they jockeyed with each other and the last of the 'Roman' commanders for control of people and resources. How different would fifth-century, nominally imperial troops have looked from Germanic warriors of the same period, especially since Germanic troops and units had formed part of the regular Roman army since the fourth century? Were such identities fixed and immutable? The evidence strongly suggests not; individuals and units could segue from one identity to another within an essentially unchanged material culture. For the mixed garrisons of the forts of the Rhine frontier and the interior of the north of Gaul, it was but a short step in the later fifth century to incorporating themselves into the locally dominant ethnic grouping – Franks, Alamanni or whatever. A distant echo of such a process may be the tale related by Procopius (*Bellum Gothicum* V.12.13–19) of how the last Roman troops on the lower Rhine assimilated themselves to the Franks while keeping their unit identities.

Barbarians and breakdown

The part played by the transformation of late Roman military formations and garrisons in the creation of the successor peoples to the Western Empire in the course of the fifth century will now form part of a wider discussion of the archaeological evidence for the settlement in Roman territory of the various Germanic peoples in the course of the fifth century. Before we embark on a consideration of the archaeology, the current state of the debate on using evidence from historical sources to ascribe to aspects of the archaeology, above all burials and the objects from them, a particular 'barbarian' identity (Alan, Frank, Vandal, Visigoth, etc.) needs to be outlined. In dealing with the archaeology, rather than try to encompass all the peoples mentioned in the historical sources and all the evidence that has been used, a work which would run to several volumes, we will use the technique of case studies to open up the subject and indicate the range of evidence types and possibilities of interpretation. These case studies will be the Visigoths for the south of Gaul and the Iberian peninsula, and the Franks for the north and centre of Gaul. Other peoples such as Burgundians, Sueves and Vandals will be mentioned as and where appropriate and to give a brief indication of modern studies. First of all, the term that will be most frequently used below to denote these incomers is 'ethnic' with its correlates such as 'ethnicity'. This is currently the standard academic terminology, one that avoids other contentious terms such as 'tribe', 'people', '*Volk*', '*Stamme*' and so on, let alone the loaded concept, 'race', terms that lack precision in modern anthropological and ethnographic literature while at the same time giving the impression of a range of different sizes of population groupings in some sort of hierarchical organisation. 'Ethnic' and its correlates are used here simply to signify groups of people who were felt at the time or are considered now to be distinguishable from each other not on grounds of age, gender, status or religion but on grounds of having a matrix of attitudes and behaviours that set them apart from other neighbouring groups, and in particular set them apart from the Roman provincial cultures, which thus form a sort of 'background noise' against which the different ethnic groups stand out. In the cases we shall be looking at, these are also groupings that were mobile and thus ended up in areas to which they were 'foreign' in many senses of the word.

Over the last hundred years and more, the question of ethnic identity, what constitutes it and how it is expressed, has been the subject of intense debate, now conveniently and very accessibly summarised in Halsall 2007: Ch. 2. In the later nineteenth and early twentieth centuries, such identity was held to be 'primordial' or 'essential' – that is, innate and, indeed, genetic (to be anachronistic) – and expressed through such things as belief in a common descent, a common kingship and nobility, a common religion, a common language, common customs and a 'national dress'. An important feature of 'primordial' ethnic identity was not only that it defined the in-group but that it also defined (usually as inferior) out-groups. There was thus a strong belief in the works of early twentieth-century scholars such as Kossinna in the purity of each racial grouping and that they did not mix with other groupings; thus Alans did not mix with Vandals, for instance, let alone 'Germans' with provincial Romans, the latter view supported by many of the law codes issued by the successor kingdoms which distinguished strongly between 'German' and Roman provincial to the extent of forbidding intermarriage. Where such ideas about the 'essential' nature of ethnic identity and the need to maintain the 'purity' of the stock could lead was made catastrophically clear with the Nazis and the 'Aryan' identity and the position of that identity in relation to other, allegedly 'inferior' identities (*Untermensch*). Since World War II and in reaction to its ethnically created nightmares, a considerable and lively debate has taken place over the meaning of 'ethnicity' and 'ethnic' identity, and how to recognise such things – indeed, whether it is possible to recognise such things – in the archaeology. Ultimately, this comes down to whether objects, such as dress fittings, have an inherent ethnic identity and whether particular types of such objects would have been worn only by people of that ethnicity; thus an object betrays ethnic grouping.

Different modern nation states have developed different traditions of exegesis. In the German tradition the ascription of ethnic identities to features of funerary practice, such as deposition and especially object types, has been persistent, and publications regularly identify particular burials with specific ethnic groupings mentioned in the textual sources as being in certain areas at certain dates. This approach has been followed to a considerable degree in Spain (see below), where the influence of German workers has been strong, and to a lesser but still important extent in France, where emancipation of the archaeological evidence from the textual narratives has proceeded relatively slowly, and ethnic identification of burials and of grave goods still forms an accepted part of archaeological publication. The English-speaking tradition, along with some other European traditions, particularly the Dutch, has shown less fealty to the notion of ascribing ethnicities to burial practices and to objects; it has been more influenced by the development of postmodern (post-processual) concepts of the fluidity of identity and its signifiers. To workers in this tradition, objects have no inherent ethnic identity. The people who made them may have regarded themselves as belonging to a particular grouping, and so may the people who used or wore them, but not necessarily the same grouping, and the people who buried someone with such objects may have had their own views on the matter; none of them may have regarded an object or practice as belonging to a specific 'ethnicity'. There is great doubt over the extent to which any such 'ethnic' identities were expressed through particular items of dress, and, of course, individual objects might pass through many hands. In addition, were these objects used only to construct statements about 'ethnic' identity, or were other aspects of identity, such as age, gender or status, being signified? Moreover, the 'ethnic' identification often rests on an unstated assumption that 'Alan' objects were only worn and used by Alans, whereas it is clear from burials that objects from different 'ethnicities' can be found in the same grave. In an ethnicist reading, one would have to argue something such as that the deceased was the issue of a mixed marriage: it is equally possible to argue that the objects were chosen because the deceased or their buriers liked them and had no ethnic intention in their deposition. Of course, neither tradition of study exists in isolation from the other, and there has been cross-fertilisation; nonetheless, there remains a difference along the lines sketched above.

Let us summarise what developments in understanding of the mutability of identity have meant. First they showed that it was 'instrumental'; it could be changed if there was an advantage to do so. This led to the concept of 'situational' identity, one taken on as the optimal response to surrounding circumstances. The crucial realisation here was that ethnicity was not innate; rather it could be a result of birth but it could also be opted for and it could be changed. Ethnicity was something that happened in people's heads, not in their genes: it was 'cognitive'. This is not to say that this is in any way a weaker form of identity; human beings are capable of believing in such things passionately and to the death (others' or their own). Moreover, such supposed signifiers of identity as language and religion are nothing of the sort: the modern world contains plenty of examples of speakers of a common language or co-religionists who are very good at hating one another (sometimes bringing us back to 'the narcissism of small differences'). Halsall (2007: 40) makes the point that individuals' identities are also multilayered, and different aspects of them can be emphasised or downplayed in different circumstances. This necessarily means that identity is 'performative'; the chosen identity must be displayed and acted out to be realised and reified. All this might seem a recipe for a sort of Humpty-Dumpty ethnicity: ethnic identity means what I want it to mean. But there are important constraints. First, and in particular, that individuals have to negotiate their identity with others around them, and this may impose severe constraints on what they can opt for. Second, and relevant for us here, identity can be ascribed to individuals by others ('etic') as well as, or instead of, being ascribed by individuals to themselves ('emic'). An existing group may deny membership to someone wanting to join it, for any of a number of pretexts which seem to them entirely reasonable and compelling. Equally, a dominant group may ascribe to individuals or groups in a less powerful position an identity of its own choosing, one quite possibly not the choice of those thus identified. For the period we are concerned with, this can be particularly important, since it is clear that 'barbarian' identities were, at least in part, created as a reaction to how the Romans thought about other peoples (cf. Curta 2007), with Roman views instrumental in creating 'barbarian' groups' sense of self-awareness and self-definition (the Goths are a good example). These remarks in turn raise the important point that signifiers such as dress items were not just passive reflections of an existing identity (ethnic, status or other) but were also used actively to construct such identities, including constructing new, different identities that users had chosen to 'situate' themselves in and to 'perform', thus 'falsifying' their original identity as created for them by their parents and their wider social or ethnic grouping.

For late antiquity, work on the 'ethnic identities' of the period and what they may have meant and expressed has been particularly associated with the 'Vienna school' of Walter Pohl and his co-workers or the 'Toronto school' of Walter Goffart and his colleagues, which hold divergent views on how to interpret the nature and settlement of the 'barbarian' peoples. Both groups, though, have critically examined the textual sources for the various ethnic groupings of early medieval Europe, in particular the Goths, to see what they tell us about the ways in which ethnic identities were created and made evident, and why individuals or groups made the statements they did. They have shown that such identities were fluid and constantly being manipulated and recreated to fit the current situation, often under Roman influence, direct or indirect. The textual sources do allow us sometimes to approach what members of these groupings thought at the time, or more often what other people thought about them, above all what the Romans thought, since frequently what we have are Roman thoughts (with all their problems of ignorance and stereotyping) about societies that were often not in a position to give their side of the story to a distant Roman commentator working within an established frame of reference about 'barbarians'. In all these modern studies, great stress has been laid on the concept of 'ethnogenesis'. If we no longer accept fixed and immutable identities and their transmission down the generations, either for individuals or for groups, then there must be reasons for which and processes by which individuals and especially groups come to differentiate themselves from those around them and to construct ways of doing things that state these differences. Many of these ways of doing things, such as speech, will not be visible to the archaeologist; others, such as dress and appearance, may well be. It should be noted that, following the implicit framework of ancient commentators, the Roman provincial populations are not seen to have an ethnicity as such, other than provincial designations, though these do, of course, go back to perceived ethnic differences at the time of their incorporation into the empire. But by the Late Empire they are to an extent the 'norm' against which the ethnic groups are defined. As we shall see, this has led to a situation where their presence in the evidence and thus their contribution to the debate are often underestimated.

In what follows, the more sceptical approaches to ethnicity outlined above will be used in a discussion of the archaeological rather than the textual sources for 'barbarian identity'. This discussion will therefore concentrate on the material-culture correlates of a range of possible identities, such things as objects, building types and settlement types. Above all, it will consider the funerary evidence, since in preparing a corpse for disposal, the living can make powerful statements about how they see, or would like to see, the identity of the deceased, and this, of course, includes such things as gender, age and status as well as claimed or ascribed 'ethnicity'. In order not to get embroiled in a seemingly endless range of evidence and possible interpretations, the discussion will focus on the two 'peoples' mentioned above, the Visigoths and the Franks, who were crucial for the transformation of what had been the Western Roman Empire into the 'barbarian' successor kingdoms. Another major and well-documented (archaeologically as well as textually) people, the Alamanni, will not be dealt with in detail here because their main areas of activity and settlement were either on the periphery of our area of interest, in the Rhineland, or were outside the Rhine frontier altogether and thus fall outside the purview of this work: an excellent and up-to-date introduction to them, focusing primarily on the textual sources but with consideration of aspects of the archaeology, is provided by Drinkwater (2007), and there is a comprehensive introduction to their archaeology by Theune (2004). After a look at the Visigoths and the Franks as case studies, more general conclusions will be drawn as to the role of ethnic identity and interaction in the transformation of the Roman West.

The Visigoths in south-west Gaul and Spain

The Goths are the most intensively studied of the Germanic successor peoples in the Roman West, thanks to a rich documentary corpus including narrative histories, chronicles, letters and saints' lives written by men from the Roman world who came into direct contact with them or recorded their doings; in addition, and unusually, there are written sources produced by the Goths themselves – for the Visigoths in particular a series of law codes and the *acta* of a series of Church councils, emanating mainly from the Spanish kingdom in the sixth and seventh centuries. These have given rise to a compendious literature (for starters, see Collins 2004; Ebel-Zepezauer 2000; Heather 1991, 1996, 1999), since the abundance of the written sources has made the Goths the case study *par excellence* for a Germanic people in the late antique period, the *locus classicus* for the study of ethnogenesis. This same abundance has often concealed the fact that the archaeological record is much less coherent, and for the Visigoths tells a rather remarkable story.

Let us recap in outline the historical narrative for the arrival and settlement of the Goths in the West. The Goths, or, as they then were, the Greuthungi and Tervingi, were allowed across the Danube in 376 and two years later inflicted on Rome one of her worst military defeats at the battle of Adrianople, in which the Eastern emperor Valens lost his life (for general discussions of the earlier parts of the story of the Goths, see Heather 1991: Pt. II, 1996: Pts. I and II, 1999). In the latter part of the fourth century, they moved westwards, and in 410 under Alaric I they sacked Rome herself, a psychological shock to the entire Roman world. After the sack of Rome, they were manipulated out of Italy and into south-western Gaul, where, along with a group of Alans, they besieged Bazas (Landes), an event best known for causing the ruin of the poet Paulinus of Pella (grandson of Ausonius), before being cajoled into north-eastern Spain to act as imperial agents in the clearing out of other Germanic peoples who had got there in the aftermath of the collapse of the Rhine frontier and the failures of the usurper Constantine III. Finally, in probably 419 (traditionally 418), the patrician Constantius settled them in south-western Gaul from Toulouse down the Garonne valley to the Atlantic, granting *hospitalitas* rather than direct payment to support them. The terms on which the imperial authorities settled them have given rise to a huge literature concerning the precise meaning and significance of the term '*hospitalitas*', one of those many late imperial euphemisms for something in reality more brutal; did they receive two-thirds of the land, two-thirds of the tax revenues or something else? (Barnish 1986; Durliat 1997; Goffart 1980: Ch. 4, 2006: Ch. 7; Liebeschuetz 1997; but see also Halsall [2007: 422–47] for a full review of the debate). This process was christened 'accommodation' by Goffart (1980), in contradistinction to earlier visions of brutal replacement of Roman by German, making the whole process less threatening or violent, and 'pacifying' this piece of the past (for a critique of this tendency, see Ward-Perkins 2005: 5–10). By now the interests of these people clearly lay in the West beyond the Alps, leading them to be described in due course as the Visigoths (western Goths) in contradistinction to the groups which later settled to their east in Italy, the Ostrogoths (eastern Goths).

The settlement of the Visigoths was established under Roman suzerainty and quite possibly as a supposedly temporary expedient; originally, it is very unlikely that either Goths or Romans saw this settlement as implying the creation of an independent political entity rather than simply as a convenient solution to a particular problem. But the developing weakness of the

Western Empire meant that gradually the Visigoths came to regard themselves as free agents, and their leaders became kings with their seat at Toulouse. By the mid fifth century, the Visigothic kingdom had taken on a life and identity of its own, and its kings became important players in the political chess of the mid to late fifth century, with Aetius trying and failing to defeat them in 439. But the Visigoths put themselves under his command against the Huns at the battle of the Catalaunian Plains in 451. Afterwards, under Theodoric II, they intervened more deeply into Spain, defeating the Suevic kingdom in 456 and pinning it back into the far north-west; in Gaul they gained Narbonne in 462/3. In 466 Theodoric II was assassinated and replaced by Euric I, who pursued an overtly aggressive policy of expansion, capturing Pamplona, Zaragoza and Tarragona in 473, thus coming to dominate the northern third of Spain, and finally taking Arles and Marseille in 476 (the previous year he had taken Clermont-Ferrand, whose bishop, the author Sidonius Apollinaris, had organised the resistance to the Visigothic takeover, but Sidonius was sold down the river by the imperial authorities in an attempt to hold onto Arles and Marseille – not one of their more successful gambits). The political opposition of the Visigothic kingdom to what remained of the Western Empire was emphasised by the fact that the Visigoths were adherents of the Arian branch of Christianity rather than the Catholic profession of the imperial authorities; Euric I was militantly Arian and anti-Catholic. By his death in 484, the Visigoth Euric I not only controlled south-western Gaul but was also master of much of Spain save the Suevic enclave in the north-west. Under his son Euric II and Euric II's son Alaric II, the Visigothic kingdom was clearly the major player in the former Western provinces of the Roman Empire. But there was to be one more roll of the dice; in 507 the Franks from the north under Clovis brought the Visigoths of Toulouse to battle at Vouillé near Poitiers and defeated them, killing Alaric II. Thereafter the Visigoths regrouped in Spain; north of the Pyrenees they held only the coastal fringe along the Mediterranean in Septimania. From the early sixth century, the Visigothic kingdom in Spain acquired the trappings of statehood such as law codes, coinage and wars of succession.

South-west Gaul

The textual sources therefore clearly present us, in the case of the kingdom of Toulouse, with a Germanic group with a defined identity; a monarchical, aristocratic and warrior society; a defined, stable and expanding territory; in what proved to be the twilight year of the kingdom, a legal system (the *Breviarium* of Alaric, 506); an ecclesiastical structure (Council of Agde in 506); and, at the level of the kings at least, clear notions of where the interests of the Visigoths lay distinct from those, including the Romans, around them. So how is this reflected in the archaeology of south-western Gaul, its Germanic settlements, structures, burials and material culture? Not at all well – an important exception is James, E. (1977), as is perfectly well known, but often glossed over by omission through concentrating on the written sources. The homelands of the Goths have long been identified by archaeologists, working in a culture-historical paradigm, with the area of the second- to fourth-century Sîntana de Mureş-Chernyakhov culture in the region to the north-west of the Black Sea outside the Roman lower Danube frontier (see Heather and Matthews 1991 and references), where there was a range of material culture, including brooches, belts and pottery, that is relatively distinctive. This culture was later to be found further west into Roman territories, and is taken to be evidence for the migration of the Goths into the empire in the second half of the fourth century. Reviews of 'Germanic/Gothic' material culture in fifth-century south-western Gaul have repeatedly come up with little more than a handful of sites and material (Ebel-Zepezauer 2000; James, E. 1977, 1991; Périn 1991; Rouche 1979 – the blank on Ebel-Zepezauer's distribution map of 'Visigothic' metalwork [2000: Abb. 1] where the kingdom of Toulouse should be is striking – Stutz 2000). There is a small handful of material in the south-west of types deriving from the Sîntana de Mureş-Chernyakhov culture, consisting of four bone combs (Kazanski and Lapart 1995) of a very distinctive form, rectangular with a semicircular projection on the upper side. These items come from sites in a triangle formed by the cities of Agen, Auch and Eauze to the west of Toulouse, namely the villas of Montréal-Séviac and Moncrabeau-Bapteste (Lot-et-Garonne) between Eauze and Agen, and that at La Turraque, Valence-sur-Baïse (Gers), between Eauze and Auch. It should be noted that similar combs have also been recovered from Trier and other sites in the area (Cüppers 1984: 345), so, though they are of non-Roman type, they are not necessarily solely 'Gothic'. The combs are of interest, though, not just for the links they provide with the home areas of the Goths, but also for their function; they reflect the importance of hair-style, a recurrent indicator of barbarian identity among Roman writers. Current research in the *région* of Midi-Pyrénées is adding to this corpus (J.-L. Boudartchouk, pers. comm.), but it is unlikely to change radically the impression of relatively little 'foreign' material culture through the course of most of the fifth century. One other indicator of non-local individuals is the group of four or so burials of people with deliberate cranial deformation carried out in infancy (Crubézy 1990) from south of the Garonne and, unfortunately, not well dated. Traditionally linked with the Huns (see below, p. 381), such burials in Gaul are small in number and mainly of adult females, suggesting the marrying of individuals whose origins lay in central Europe into populations further west; if so, they are not a good indicator for Visigothic identity.

Telling is the archaeology of fifth-century Toulouse, seat of the kingdom. In terms of material culture, there is a group of six *Armbrustfibeln* from the city and its environs (Bach *et al.* 2002: 534, 536), but this is a type with a wide distribution within the Germanic culture-province, so it cannot be specifically linked to a Visigothic identity. There are also three brooches of the Duratón type (Bach *et al.* 2002: 535, 537), a type whose main distribution lies in Spain, where it has traditionally been a marker of 'Visigothic' settlement, though such easy equivalence is now under serious question (see below, p. 366). It is only at a horizon datable to the turn of the fifth and sixth centuries, immediately before the Frankish conquest, that more items of apparel of 'Germanic' type are recorded from the city; this is a horizon we shall return to below, since it is an important one all across what the texts tell us had become the Visigothic realm. By contrast, there is very little 'Germanic' visible in the ceramic assemblages of the fifth century from Toulouse, which remain dominated by utilitarian, local productions in the Gallo-Roman tradition along with DSP of both 'Atlantic' and Languedoc types and a tiny amount of African amphorae and ARS (Dieulafait *et al.* 2002), though again recent research has identified a number of pieces of pottery whose parallels lie in eastern Europe, but numerically they are a minute group compared with the overwhelming dominance of Roman provincial ceramics. This is true also of other assemblages in the region, such as that from the fifth-century deposits in the upper town of Saint-Bertrand-de-Comminges (Dieulafait 2006), where the ceramics remain resolutely Roman provincial.

When we turn to structures, rather than material culture, recent excavations in and around the walls of the city, combined with re-evaluation of antiquarian observations, have yielded a complex of sites in the north-western area (Figure 8.2). The largest and most striking of these is the site of the Hôpital Larrey just inside the north-western angle of the enceinte (for a summary, see De Filippo 2002). A building range probably some 90 m long by 30 m wide had a central entrance way with, to either side, large internal courts with, originally, large apsidal terminals against the sides of the entrance. Along the façades of the building were two long galleries or suites of rooms. Because of the later demolition of the building and

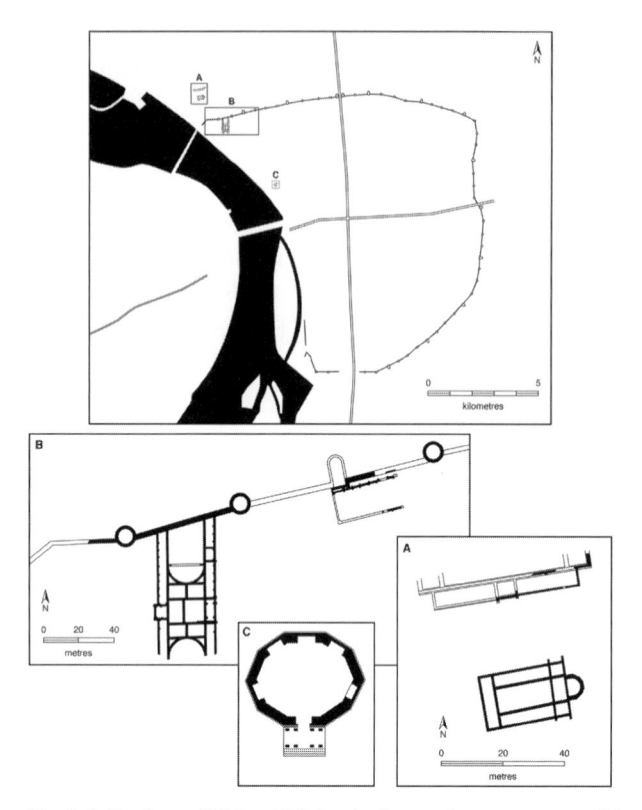

Fig. 8.2 Toulouse, 'Visigothic' sites in the north-western part of the city. A. Saint-Pierre-des-Cuisines; B. Hôpital Larrey building; C. Notre-Dame-de-la-Daurade

clearance of the site, the dating evidence was sparse but pointed to the first half of the fifth century. Another major structure of similar date lay a little to the north-west outside the walls, to the north of the later church of Saint-Pierre-des-Cuisines (Cazes and Arramond 2002), consisting of a roughly east–west gallery façade with central entrance way. Large-scale constructions of this date were rare anywhere in the West. This has led some to postulate that these structures reflected the new power at Toulouse and to suggest that the Hôpital Larrey site in particular may have been part of the palace of the Visigothic kings. Following on from this suggestion, it was then proposed that the core of the medieval church of Notre-Dame de la Daurade (Cazes and Scellès 2002), unfortunately destroyed in 1761 but of which engravings exist (Figure 8.3), was associated with the Hôpital Larrey site, lying as it did only some 250 m to the south-east. This church was a curious polygonal structure with an interior richly embellished by niches framed with marble colonnettes inlaid with gold mosaic, and the niches decorated

Fig. 8.3 Notre-Dame-de-la-Daurade, plans and view of the interior before demolition

in gold-ground mosaic with three registers of biblical personages and scenes. Clearly, this was one of the richest and most elaborate programmes of decoration known anywhere in the West at this date (the fifth century). Its function remains unclear. It has been posited to be a royal mausoleum, but its position within the walls makes this less likely. Many prefer to interpret it as the palace chapel of the Visigothic kings (mentioned in Sidonius Apollinaris's idealising account of his visit to the court of Theodoric II in 455 – *Epistulae* II.i), and the proposal that the iconography of the mosaics may have reflected Arian theology would fit since the Visigoths were still adherents of that heresy in this period. It should by now be clear that, first, there is no proof positive that these structures had anything whatsoever to do with the Visigothic kings, and that, second, the reason why they are so difficult to claim as 'Visigothic' is that in plan, layout and what is known of the decoration they were solidly Roman provincial, with, for example, the best parallel to the Hôpital Larrey plan to be found at the villa of Nérac (Lot-et-Garonne) to the north-west of Toulouse (Balmelle 2001: 390–3). This echoes the evidence from the countryside for the archaeological near invisibility of the Visigoths.

Why then this near invisibility for the first fifty years or so (a couple of generations) of the kingdom? This must relate to the experience of the Goths prior to their settlement in Aquitaine and to the circumstances of their settlement and subsequent integration. As has been pointed out on various occasions, prior to their arrival in Gaul, the Goths had spent some forty years touring the central areas of the Roman Empire: cultural influences can flow both ways, and in this case rather than Romans adopting 'barbarian' fashions, it appears that the Visigoths were 'Romanised'. After the sack of Rome in 410, they were clearly under the control of the patrician Constantius, who used them as a proxy for the much weakened Western Roman army in both Gaul and Spain. So by the time they were settled between Toulouse and the ocean, they were thoroughly accustomed to Roman ways (Alaric I's successor Athaulf had even been married to the emperor Honorius's sister Galla Placidia during the Goths' brief sojourn in Barcelona) and must have been using the Roman vocabulary and semiotics of rank and power alongside any of their own. Given that the Roman government formally settled them in the south-west with a treaty and with fiscal provision rather than their invading and taking over, they probably had more to gain from accommodation with the existing system in this very wealthy area, studded, as we saw in Chapter 5, with some of the largest and most splendid villas of the period, housing rich and powerful landowners. It looks as though the first couple of generations of Visigoths adapted to the existing Gallo-Roman style rather than the Gallo-Romans adapting to the Visigothic, so what the well-dressed Visigothic warrior of the mid fifth century wore and fought with is rather a difficult problem for the archaeologist. But as noted above, in the last third or so of the fifth century this started to change, and the 'Visigoths' become more visible in the archaeology, and it is this change and the reasons behind it that will be considered below in conjunction with the evidence from Spain (p. 375).

Spain

The Iberian peninsula in the fifth century saw, according to the texts, a whole range of different Germanic peoples, Alans, Sueves, Vandals (both Asding and Siling) and Visigoths, either passing through or carving out for themselves territories at the expense of the Roman state and the Hispano-Roman population, such as the kingdom of the Sueves centred on the late Roman province of Galicia and eventually, in the sixth century, the Visigothic kingdom encompassing the entire peninsula. The historical sources for the period are of varying forms and degrees of narrative reliability (the latter was often not their purpose) and have given rise to a huge literature of possible scenarios for what was going on and why, though it is generally agreed that many of the 'barbarian' peoples, such as the Vandals, left next to no trace in the archaeology, usually because they were too transient (see Arce 2005a, 2005b for a balanced and judicious treatment of the sources and of the history of the fifth century). The Visigothic period in Spain has received a great deal of attention from historians because of its central place in the creation of *hispanidad* through the forging for the first time of a state comprising the whole peninsula, a state, moreover, that was Christian – indeed, we know most about that state through the decrees of a whole series of Church councils. This state was to be overthrown by the Muslim Arabs from 711, leading to the nearly eight hundred years of the *reconquista* culminating in the expulsion of the Moors by *Los Reyes Católicos* in 1492, the crucible in which the Spanish 'national identity' was formed (cf. Collins 2004: Introduction). In addition, 'Visigothic' has also become a chronological and architectural/art-historical style, as well as an ethnic appellation, but that is for a period later than is our concern here. Because of our knowledge of the development of the Visigothic kingdom in the sixth and seventh centuries, there has inevitably been a certain amount of reading back from later conditions into the late fifth century (for instance, of the later legal bans on intermarriage between Goths and Romans, ironically recycling late Roman legislation which saw the problem from the other side) and of the use of the textual sources to condition study of the archaeological material. Here the intention is much more limited; it is to look at the development of what has been interpreted as a 'Visigothic' material culture, particularly in the northern part of the peninsula, in the fifth century and to relate this to developments in Septimania (roughly modern Languedoc-Roussillon) and in the Toulouse region.

The Iberian peninsula has yielded a large number of cemeteries that contain burials equipped with items of dress, equipment and personal adornment that were clearly not of Roman provincial types (Figure 8.4). These burials and cemeteries could be dated to the fifth to eighth centuries from the Roman-style objects in them and from parallels to the non-Roman material elsewhere in Europe (for a clear introduction to and summary of the archaeological evidence and the analyses thereof by a range of workers, see López Quiroga 2010: esp. Ch. 3). They were concentrated on the Meseta

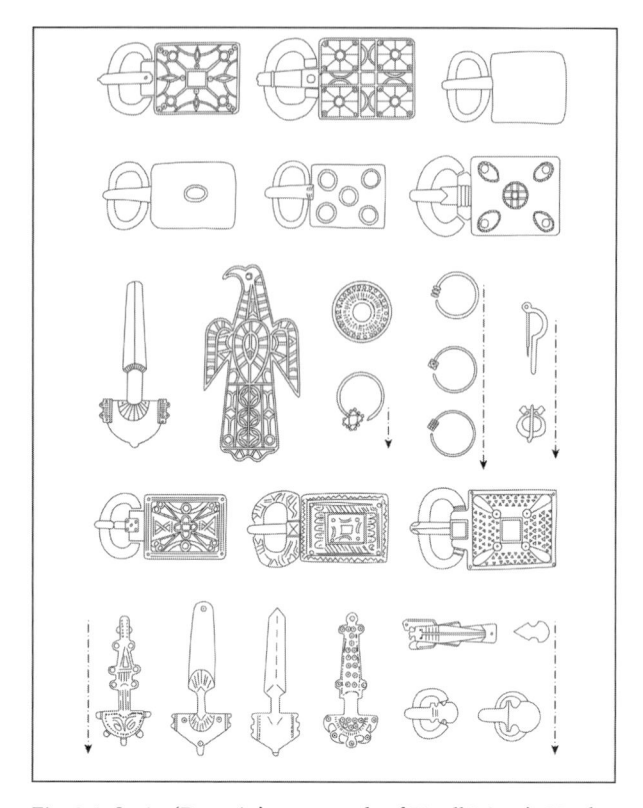

Fig. 8.4 Spain, 'Duratón' grave goods of Ripoll López's *Nivel 2*

of the central and northern parts of the peninsula, but there were examples of them more or less over the whole peninsula (cf. Ebel-Zepezauer 2000: Abb. 1) if we include the entire date range. Here our concern must be with the earlier part of the sequence, datable to the fifth century. In the 1940s, the excavation at two sites above all, Duratón (Segovia) and El Carpio de Tajo (Toledo), produced relatively large cemeteries with some graves containing numbers of 'barbarian' objects, associated for the most part with female burials and betokening a form of clothing different from that current among the female Hispano-Roman population. The objects were principally brooches, *Armbrustfibeln*, *Bügelknopffibeln* and *Blechfibeln* with some of the rarer *Adlerfibeln* (in the form of an eagle usually with cloisonné decoration). These were usually worn in pairs at or near the shoulders, suggesting females buried in a two-part tunic or *peplos*. Associated with these were elements of belts, most usually buckles, often with rectangular plates decorated in a variety of ways but most characteristically with polychrome cloisonné work. Another frequent find was necklaces, generally of glass beads but sometimes of other materials including amber; also occasionally found were earrings. It will be noted that what we have here are female graves with a distinctive, non-Hispano-Roman style of dress. The male graves were much less distinctive and in fact seem to be assimilated to Hispano-Roman traditions of burial (see below). In the intellectual framework prevailing at the time these cemeteries were excavated, particularly that created by German scholars such as Kossinna, these were seen as evidence for the movement of groups of ethnically distinct peoples of Germanic origin across Europe and settling ultimately in Spain. From that it was only a short step to accepting that these were the burials and cemeteries of the Visigoths, who, the texts stated, had moved over the Pyrenees in the latter part of the fifth century. For instance, a Spanish text, the *Chronica Caesaraugustana*, spoke of the settlement of the Goths between 494 and 497, and this was assumed to have been reinforced by refugees from north of the Pyrenees after the defeat of the kingdom of Toulouse at Vouillé in 507. Since at the time workers lacked independent dating for the burials, this gave a *terminus post quem* for the appearance of these burial rites and objects.

A major step forward came with the systematisation of the information on these burials accompanied by a re-examination of certain key sites such as El Carpio de Tajo, which was published by Gisela Ripoll López (e.g. 1985, 1991, 1998; English-language summary in Ripoll López 1999). She arranged the items of dress and personal adornment into a series of *Niveles* or levels (corresponding to the arrangement by *Stufen* of German workers such as Böhme), affording a chronotypology of the material with objects assigned to one or other of her *Niveles*, though because of the lack of independently datable material, it proved difficult to translate this relative chronology into an absolute one. Ripoll López's analysis is that there was Visigothic settlement from about 480 in the northern Meseta (corresponding to the expansion of the kingdom of Toulouse under Euric I), the cemetery evidence suggesting the importance of kin and the visible signs through dress suggesting a new, Visigothic identity. Further developments in the material culture and in the cemetery population through the sixth and on into the early seventh century were linked by Ripoll López to the historical record of the Visigothic kingdom in Spain, this burial tradition ultimately dying out in the early eighth century as the Visigothic kingdom succumbed to the Moorish invasions from 711. This approach has been criticised by a number of workers, such as Collins (2004: 174–86), for relying on *a priori* assumptions deriving from the historical evidence, in particular the absolute dating of the various *Niveles* by reference to supposed historical events of the fifth to eighth centuries (such as the dates for the entry of the Visigoths into the peninsula) and the relating of aspects of the burial rite to supposed earlier Gothic (or Tervingi/Greuthungi) practice (the Sîntana de Mureș-Chernyakhov culture), which thus restricted discussion of them to a Visigothic identity. Indeed, as he points out, there is little in the metalwork to argue directly that those buried with it were necessarily Visigothic (as we shall see below), and the literary sources attest to the presence of other non-Roman peoples in the peninsula.

More recently still, there has been further reconsideration of the date and significance of these burials. This was prompted partly by the excavation to modern standards of further cemeteries of this type, such as la Olmeda (Palencia), or sites in the province of Madrid such as Cacera de las Ranas or Gózquez de Arriba (the excavations in the 1940s were much more summary and major questions remain over how accurate the groupings of objects apparently from one burial actually are); partly by an improved knowledge of similar burials and material elsewhere in Europe; partly by the application of the more recent thinking about 'identity' and 'ethnicity' (including increased recognition of the other 'Germanic' peoples recorded as present in the peninsula); and partly by the recognition that these burials often form a minority in the cemeteries concerned (López Quiroga 2010: 199–268).

The dating of the objects from these burials has been greatly refined, partly by taking more account of the 'Roman' material from the graves and partly because of improved chronologies for their parallels elsewhere in Europe. It is clear that the earliest of this material dates to the first half of the fifth century and belongs to the horizon sometimes termed 'Pontico-Danubian' after its distribution in the area west of the Black Sea (*Pontus*) and in the lower Danube basin, linking through to the area of the Sîntana de Mureș-Chernyakhov culture. This material includes gold-and-garnet belt fittings from Portugal at Beja (cf. von Rummel 2007: 342–53) and the elaborate gold necklace from the Blanes site at Mérida. Another highly distinctive necklace, from Beiral (Algarve), has parallels in rich, non-Roman burials elsewhere in fifth-century Europe, as well as at Valleta del Valero (Lleida) in north-eastern Spain. A comb of a distinctive form, rectangular with a semicircular upper projection, from Castro Ventosa (León) again has parallels in the Sîntana de Mureș-Chernyakhov complex and also parallels those from north of the Pyrenees in the kingdom of Toulouse. By contrast, a necklace from Vigo (Pontevedra) has beads of amber of a distinctive mushroom form, otherwise known from the Elbe region (normally seen as the homelands of the Alamanni). These and a number of other objects without good archaeological provenance (including a sword from Beja) constitute what López Quiroga (2010: 112–32) terms his *Nivel* 1A, which he dates to the first half of the fifth century. In it he sees a strong military element, but notes that it is impossible to give any precise ethnic ascription to these objects, or, indeed, to tell whether they may have been worn by 'barbarians' in what was left of the late Roman army of the period.

In the second half of the fifth century, the presence of non-Roman material becomes more noticeable and widespread; this is the period of the early phases of classic cemeteries such as Duratón and El Carpio de Tajo – the *Nivel* 1B of López Quiroga (2010: 133–49). As well as the *Armbrustfibeln* and *Bügelknopffibeln* already well established from *Nivel* 1A, *Nivel* 1B is the heyday of the *Blechfibeln* of 'Smolin' or 'Kosino-Gyuilavan' type (named after sites in the Pontico-Danubian region) with expanded, silvered head plates and large foot plates. Other elements of the material culture, such as other brooch types and belt fittings, also derive from the area of the Sîntana de Mureş-Chernyakhov culture, showing the east European area of influence, an influence also present in the north of Gaul (Kazanski *et al.* 2008; Kazanski and Périn 2006), a region not usually regarded as a major focus of Visigothic settlement. The focus of distribution of burials containing this material remains on the Meseta of the centre and north of the interior of the peninsula, but extends into other regions also, as far as Andalusia in the south (cf. Ebel-Zepezauer 2000: Abb. 35), with the later examples of this material well evidenced in Septimania, the Languedoc-Roussillon littoral, where the Visigoths held out against the Franks after the defeat at Vouillé. This discussion has focused on the material culture because that is the most widely distributed and most intensively reported and studied aspect of these sites and the one that has been most important in constructing a Gothic identity for these burials. But a small number of burials demonstrate a practice that is also a strong link with the Pontico-Danubian region – the placing of the corpse(s) in niches cut into the side of the grave pit, a practice observable across much of eastern Europe, which has been linked with the 'Alano-Sarmatian' culture. Be that as it may, it was certainly alien to Hispano-Roman funerary practice (López Quiroga 2010: 151–6). It is not difficult to see why these burials were linked with Visigothic identity both in the 1940s and subsequently, since their distribution corresponds with important areas of the sixth-century Visigothic kingdom such as the Meseta and Septimania, with a peninsular distribution more generally, and the objects are clearly of non-Roman, 'Germanic' derivation. But it is now necessary to reassess the archaeological evidence and its possible meanings independently of the written sources and their pre-existing agenda.

There are a number of points about these burials and cemeteries that need to be made (I am most grateful to Gisela Ripoll for discussion on these points). First of all, in some of the cemeteries that have been excavated and recorded with sufficient care, from Duratón and El Carpio de Tajo on, the burials with distinctive rites and/or material culture normally form a minority of the total cemetery population. For instance, burials with dress elements form just under a third (31.57%) of the burials excavated at El Carpio de Tajo; the other two-thirds lack such material. At Cacera de las Ranas, the proportion was similar, 51 out of 145 recorded burials (35.17%) had dress fittings. Others, though, had much higher figures; 34 of the 52 burials (65.4%) from Herrera de Pisuerga contained grave goods. But much discussion of these cemeteries and the material from them has tended to concentrate on the contents of the furnished burials and to ignore the unfurnished ones, decontextualising the 'Visigothic' burials from much larger numbers of burials in the Hispano-Roman tradition and thus risking giving a false impression of a dominance in the funerary record that these burials simply do not have; they are a minority of known fifth-century burials in the Iberian peninsula. We shall return to the question of the relation with other burials. Of the furnished burials considered as 'Visigothic', the great majority seem to be female, though this is usually argued on the basis of the objects rather than of the osteological evidence, clearly running the risk of a circular argument. It is worth noting that there is very little pottery of 'Germanic' type from these cemeteries – we are dealing essentially with the evidence of dress. The most common elements are the pairs of brooches and belt buckles; more rarely, there are necklaces or strings of beads (which probably ran between the brooches), as well as earrings. Particularly notable are the more elaborate *Blechfibeln* and *Adlerfibeln*, whose disposition on the body was part of a suite of dress adornments. Comparison with other cemeteries of the period and with what is known of 'Roman' and 'barbarian' dress in the period (von Rummel 2007) strongly suggests that this was a female form of accoutrement, related to the fastening of a distinctively non-Roman dress form.

The stress placed on the form of dress of females in these cemeteries suggests both that they were of particular social importance and that their non-Romanness was important; a very specific set of statements about their identities was being constructed by the ways in which this material was being deployed. Given the links of the dress elements to the Pontico-Danubian region, it would seem overcritical to deny that non-Roman-provincial material culture was being used to make statements about these burials, though to move from this to specific 'ethnic' interpretations is almost certainly not possible. Both the Pontico-Danubian region and the Iberian peninsula contained a mixture of different 'ethnic' or sub-'ethnic' groupings, to judge by the textual sources (Alans, Goths, Sarmatians, Sueves, Vandals, etc.) and to judge archaeologically by the mixing of elements from different antecedent culture groups (e.g. Przeworsk, Sîntana de Mureş-Chernyakhov and Wielbark), rather than the racially pure *Stammen* of early twentieth-century views. The predominance of female accoutrements in these graves has caused sight to be lost, to a considerable extent, of what constituted a male grave (cf. Ebel-Zepezauer 2000: 130–2 – less than two pages in all). Unlike northern Gaul, it is not possible to identify a tradition of weapon burial in the Iberian peninsula (there is one weapon burial from the 'Visigothic' cemeteries). With the lack of this or the deposition of other grave goods that might be held to express a masculine identity, it would seem that either the menfolk of these women were not buried with gender-specific accoutrements, or these graves may comprise some of the simpler burials with just belt fittings, though it would be useful to know whether, for instance, the *Armbrustfibeln* and *Bügelknopffibeln* in many of these graves had retained the male gender significance their antecedents in the late Roman world had had. This will come with more research and publication that genders burials through osteology rather than objects. The visibility and presumably importance of females in the funerary world is very much at variance with the texts, which depict an almost exclusively male world, one with a strong military or warrior ethos (for similar problems of differential gender visibility in the burial record of fifth- and sixth-century 'Ostrogothic' Italy, see Barbiera 2010). So there remains then the question of why these particular female burials were invested with such distinctiveness. Since the emphasis here is on the non-Roman identity of the deceased through her dress, it may be that what we are seeing is an important matrilineal element in the social structures of these people(s), with the wives and mothers confirming the separateness of the identity of their husbands, sons and daughters. It may be no coincidence that, on the textual side, the law codes of the Visigothic kingdoms, from the *Breviarium* of Alaric in 506 down to the end of the sixth century, were exercised by the problem of intermarriage between Romans and (Visi-)Goths.

Another point worth making about these burials relates to the questions of social hierarchy and cemetery location. The social hierarchy expressed by these burials, especially from the middle of the fifth century, would seem not to be very developed, to judge both by the quantities of grave goods and by their materials (largely copper alloy with glass and paste insets). As yet there are no 'princely' burials from the peninsula what might betoken the upper reaches of a hierarchised society. Yet the picture presented unanimously by the texts is of a society ruled by a king with a nobility. The current absence of high-status burials is therefore worth remarking on. It may be that since the various incoming peoples were Christian we should be looking for such burials in and around the principal churches of cities such as Barcelona and Braga (and eventually Toledo) or at other forms of high-status settlement, about which we presently know little (see Chapter 9, p. 441). In this case, what we may be seeing in the rural cemeteries under consideration here are non-elite segments of the society. The increasing appreciation of the context of these burials in cemeteries where the majority may not follow this particular female burial rite also raises the question of the contribution of the indigenous, Hispano-Roman population. In particular, are the distinctive burials those of an element of the population 'foreign' to the cemetery, or might they represent the adoption by local families or kins of the self-representation of an incoming and important new strand in the population of the peninsula? Do we have here what Brather (2008: 429) characterises as *'politisch und nicht ethnisch gotisch'*, with groups within the indigenous communities choosing, presumably for reasons of self-advancement, to define themselves as these political and not ethnic Goths? It is also worth pointing out, following, for instance, Fuentes (cited in von Rummel 2007: 53), the coincidence of the heartlands of these 'Visigothic' cemeteries with those of the earlier, fourth-century, 'Duero' burial tradition, the *'cementerios tardohispanos con ajuares'* (p. 88), which had some similarities in its use of dress to distinguish certain individuals or groups; were the fifth-century traditions to an extent a development of already existing trends in Hispano-Roman burial practices in the Meseta region? On the other hand, it is worth remembering the small number of highly distinctive burials with the corpses in lateral niches; this is a central- and eastern European practice, not an Iberian one.

There is then the question of the relationship of the material culture from these Spanish cemeteries to that north of the Pyrenees, the area from which the Visigoths are reported to have arrived in the last third or so of the fifth century. As we have seen above, the visibly 'Visigothic' archaeology of the kingdom of Toulouse remained weakly developed through much of the fifth century. Some of the material, such as the small number of combs, does have the occasional parallel south of the mountains (e.g. the comb from Castro Ventosa), but this just demonstrates the weakness of the *comparanda*; one would not construct a story of a Visigothic kingdom in south-western Gaul which invaded the Iberian peninsula on the basis of four combs to the north of the Pyrenees and one to the south. There is little in the archaeology of the kingdom of Toulouse which could be said to be antecedent to, and the source of, developments south of the Pyrenees through the fifth century. In fact, recent research, as implied above, on the antecedents for the material in Spain points rather to the Pontico-Danubian region, well to the east rather than the north, and such distinctive items of 'Visigothic' dress as the *Adlerfibeln* seem to originate from there, possibly by way of Italy and the Ostrogoths rather than the Visigoths. It will be clear from the above that it is not possible to identify archaeologically the Visigothic settlement of the Iberian peninsula in any way that resembles that depicted in the various textual sources; and the same goes for the Sueves, Vandals and others. This is not to say that the texts recording Visigothic and other Germanic invasions, migrations and settlement are 'wrong'; they were representing something that seemed real (or at least plausible) to them at the time they were written. But they may have been partial in their view; they may have oversimplified a much more complex situation; or, if written outside the south-west of Gaul or the Iberian peninsula, they may not have had a clear appreciation of what actually went on. There is also the problem that most of the authors, if not all, were from the Roman tradition or even 'side' and that, therefore, precise ethnographic and chronological accuracy was not their primary concern. That there were Visigoths settling in the Iberian peninsula in the course of the later fifth century cannot be doubted. What can be doubted is the ability to recognise them in the ways traditionally employed.

The dating of this material now looks to start considerably earlier, by at least a generation, than the historical dates for the settlement of the Visigoths in Spain. It is, moreover, very difficult to identify any 'type fossils' in the material culture that point to a specifically Visigothic identity; the nearest one can get is the presence of material closely linked to the Sîntana de Mureş-Chernyakhov complex. Even so, this material is very much linked to the aspects of life (or death) to do with personal appearance; other aspects such as those represented by ceramics are very rare both north and south of the Pyrenees. So it would seem that what has been called 'Visigothic' identity was being constructed in very specific ways and in very specific contexts. Given that in the cemeteries burials with this type of material were often in a minority, it may be that this was just one of a range of possible strategies for making statements about the dead, and those statements may not be to do with what we term 'ethnicity' but rather with gender and status; this type of burial is heavily gendered. Other statements could have been made elsewhere in the funerary cycle, ones that are not so archaeologically visible; for instance, this may be where the affirmations of maleness were made but do not show up with the deceased in the grave. It is also worth recalling the question posed by Theuws (2009) of whether 'ethnicity' was something that mattered when preparing the dead for the tomb in antiquity, or is it just something that matters to us? Might the material thought of as 'Visigothic' – or even just 'Germanic' – simply have been useful for making statements about the dead that were not concerned with their ethnicity? There is another methodological problem that is not really acknowledged. There does not seem to be a complementary non-'Germanic' suite of dress and other items; there does not seem to be a Hispano-Roman *Tracht*, or, at least, not one that is visible to the archaeologist. If those burying the dead wanted to make certain statements about the deceased that involved using dress as a signifier, did they have an alternative to using what we style 'Visigothic'? So the positive visibility of 'Visigothic' markers may be being emphasised by the lack of competing markers.

Nevertheless, even without the textual evidence, the distribution of this material by the turn of the fifth and sixth centuries over most of the Iberian peninsula, with a concentration in the northern Meseta but starting to extend further – for instance, into the south (the former Baetica) and the north-east, with a marked concentration north of the eastern end of the Pyrenees in Septimania (the old Narbonensis) – would suggest an archaeological culture province with a certain unity in its material culture and funerary practices, if not in other aspects of life. Why did the production of such material and its deployment as signifiers in burials become so visible from the later fifth century? An explanation that may have value is that of political and social stress. In periods of uncertainty and change, self-definition and self-representation become more important as a means of staking out both 'emic' and 'etic' identities and thus the place of an individual or group in relation to others, and as a means of maintaining the internal cohesion of the group. Bearing this in mind, we may consider the material culture in relation to the historical narrative, reading the texts not for a precise depiction of 'what happened' but more for a general context within which different groups were operating. It was argued above that the relative archaeological invisibility of the Visigoths of south-western Gaul was due to the circumstances of their settlement and subsequent deployment; it suited them better to integrate with the existing Roman provincial culture than to stand out against it. But in the later fifth century circumstances seem to have changed to ones where identities mattered, though those identities were not necessarily 'ethnic'. South of the Pyrenees, they were confronted by groups such as the Sueves in the north-west of the peninsula or the Hispano-Roman populations with the remains of other Germanic peoples of passage. As noted above, even in the heartlands of the kingdom, at Toulouse itself, it is in the late fifth century that distinctive brooches and buckles begin to appear in any number, just at the point that the threat from the Franks became clear. It would seem unlikely to have been a coincidence that it was in the same year, 506, the year before the climactic campaign for the existence of the kingdom of Toulouse, that a set of laws defined Visigothic royal jurisdiction (the *Breviarium* of Alaric) and the first Church council reuniting all the bishops of the Visigothic lands at Agde was held. Surely Alaric II was trying to define 'Visigothic-ness' as never before (and, as we shall see below, it was precisely at this period that the 'Franks' also forged a series of archaeologically visible correlates to their proclaimed identity). In an instrumentalist reading of the use of material culture in constructing ethnicity, it can be argued that it was only in the later fifth century that the Visigoths, both as an ethnic group and as a political entity, had the need to make ever more public statements of their affiliations. To the archaeologist, this may appear above all through the medium of dress, in particular the *Tracht* in which the womenfolk of those who defined themselves as Visigoths were buried, making it clear where their ethnic loyalties (which were, of course, not necessarily the same as their ethnic origins) lay. On the other hand, the circumstances of the Visigoths' intrusion into the lands south of the Pyrenees and the fact that there they discovered a number of discrete ethnic groupings who contested their intrusion probably induced another kind of situational stress. The Visigoths found themselves in a milieu where in the mid to later fifth century they needed to define and display their identity in a way they did not need to north of the western half of the Pyrenean chain. The other area where, perhaps even more concentratedly than in Spain, they proclaimed their identity loud and clear was Septimania. This may be because the capture of Septimania had been in the face of bitter opposition from the moribund imperial authorities, and after the fall of Toulouse in 507 the Visigoths of the region were now the only ones of their people north of the Pyrenees who had retained political autonomy and were facing the growing power of the Franks. So both in the kingdom of Toulouse towards the end of the fifth century and in Spain from a couple of decades earlier, we may be able to see reasons why a hitherto archaeologically shy grouping increasingly found it necessary to make public statements about their ethnic affiliations, real or imagined. From the early sixth century, the rulers of Spain deployed Visigothic identity as a political tool to help legitimate their power, create an identity for their new state, and promote its cohesion (cf. Collins 2006: Ch. 9), albeit under Ostrogothic hegemony for much of the first third of that century. A united kingdom comprising all the peninsula was not achieved until the 570s. Whether this identity is the explanation for the dress of some female burials in rural cemeteries has, for now, to remain an open question.

The Franks and northern Gaul

The end of the preceding discussion of the Visigoths has introduced the Franks as another major 'barbarian' power player by the turn of the fifth and sixth centuries, and the study of their archaeology provides us with a salutary case study. The literary sources present us with a coherent if sketchy account of the early history of the Franks from the later third to the later fifth centuries (for discussions of the textual evidence for this period, see Feffer and Périn 1987: Chs. 1–3; James, E. 1988: Ch. 2; Rouche 1997). From the beginning, they seem to have comprised a number of different groupings such as the Chamavi, Bructeri or Salii, giving the impression of a confederation rather than a single ethnic identity: their name (recorded, of course, only from the Roman side), *Franci*, seems to be a Germanic word signifying 'fierce' or 'bold'. In addition, to the north of the lower Rhine, the Roman sources also name peoples, such as the Frisians and the Saxons, distinct from the Franks. The Franks are recorded by the Romans as making trouble for them in the later third century and again in the middle of the fourth. On the other hand, the *Notitia Dignitatum* lists several units of Franks serving in the Roman army, as far from home as Egypt, and some Franks rose to senior commands under the emperor, the *magister militum* Arbogast even creating an emperor, the usurper Eugenius. During this period they took over and settled the area of northern Gaul bounded to the north by the Rhine, to the west by the North Sea and to the east by the Maas/Meuse, and lying north of the Cologne–Bavai–Boulogne fortified road (cf. p. 47), the area known as Toxandria, which became the base of the Salian ('salt') Franks. We hear little of them in the late fourth and early fifth centuries, and it is not until the middle of the fifth century that we hear of them again, expanding southwards but also on good terms with Aetius and supporting him against the Huns in 451. Historically, the crucial period is the reign of the two kings Childeric (d. *c.* 481), who arguably forged a Frankish identity, and his son Clovis (*c.* 481–511), who defeated Syagrius, the last *soi-disant* sub-Roman commander in northern Gaul. In 486 at Soissons, Clovis converted to Christianity and was baptised at Reims – this is usually said to have happened in 496 – and he then went on to defeat the Visigoths of Toulouse at the battle of Vouillé in 507, thus gaining command of almost all of Gaul. Clovis has been a figure of immense importance in the construction of the identity of France as the king of the Franks who unified much of the later French national territory and converted his people to Catholic Christianity, cementing both by the calling of a Church council at Orléans in 511, the year of his death. His places of baptism and burial, Reims and Saint-Denis near Paris, were to become the royal coronation and mausoleum churches of medieval and later France (cf. Rouche 1997: vol. II). Not surprisingly, the scanty historical record has been much studied from this perspective of hindsight. Since the discovery of what is generally accepted as Childeric's tomb at Tournai in 1653, Frankish material culture has also been drawn on (famously, Napoleon I had golden bees modelled on those in Childeric's tomb sewn onto his imperial coronation robe of 1804).

But in fact, as with the Visigoths, the archaeology is far more equivocal and stands as a good case study of the relationship between what was happening on and in the ground and the external perspective of Romans at the time or of later chroniclers and historians such as the late sixth-century bishop, Gregory of Tours, in his *Historia Francorum*. If we look at the archaeology of the Rhineland, on both sides of the river, in the fourth century, we see a picture of a wide range and a mixture of different groupings, expressed especially through their material culture – what we have already encountered under Böhme's (1974) label of a *Mischzivilization* – a culture province characterised by a mixing of Roman provincial and 'Germanic' elements, with the Roman army playing a central role in its creation. This is echoed by Whittaker's characterisation of Roman frontiers as a zone rather than a line, where those in the zone had more in common with each other than with their 'parent' cultures to the rear (Whittaker 1994: Ch. 4). As well as the Roman provincial population and the units of the Roman army (cf. Chapter 2), there were two major Germanic groupings, the Franks on the lower Rhine and the Alamanni on the middle and upper Rhine. In fact, the Alamanni seem to have been as much a confederation of smaller groupings as were the Franks, and it is very difficult to identify anything in the archaeology east of the middle and lower Rhine that was distinctively 'Alamannic' rather than generically Germanic and being influenced by Roman provincial practice, in particular the huge culture grouping between the Elbe and the Rhine long characterised as the *Elbegermanen* (for discussion and a bibliography, see Drinkwater 2007: Ch. 2), but whose extent overlaps with the presumed homelands of the Franks as well as of the Alamanni (Drinkwater 2007: Ch. 3; Fuchs *et al.* 1997: 20–110; Theune

2004: 57–196). The confederate nature of the Alamanni agrees with the proposition that proximity over time to the Roman Empire encouraged socio-political change among the peoples along the frontier, especially the deepening of the hierarchy and the extension of control over a number of hitherto autarchic groups or peoples, and the names of some of the groupings within the Frankish complex are known as those of independent 'tribes' in the first and second centuries. This was in part promoted by the development of rulers or elites with access to Roman symbols of power (often buried with the dead) along with control of goods traded with or looted from imperial territory. The funerary evidence (Drinkwater 2007: Ch. 3; Steuer 1997) shows that a warrior identity was important on the male side, so warfare either with Rome or with neighbouring peoples, to bring them into subjection or to take tradable goods such as slaves, would have contributed to the socio-political modifications in train. This is, of course, a variant of the core-periphery and prestige-goods models proposed some time ago for later Iron Age north-western Europe (cf. Woolf 1990), but they seem to have value in this context also.

As for the Franks, the following discussion will avoid that precise ethno-cultural label, preferring instead to talk of the evidence for Germanic (and other) settlement, since, as we shall see, if we did not know that some of the inhabitants of these areas of northern Gaul were called Franks, it might be impossible to identify them archaeologically as a distinct group. Traditionally, the main way of trying to tie the historical Franks to the archaeology has been the presence in burials of a type of throwing axe with a long, curved blade, which has been linked with the textual mentions of the *francisca* as the defining weapon of the eponymous Franks. The problem is that the written sources for this weapon are all relatively late and sometimes distant geographically as well – for instance, the early seventh-century bishop of Seville, Isidore – and they have great difficulty in establishing whether the *francisca* was just a *securis*, axe, or a *bipennis*, a double-headed axe (which, of course, would not fit the archaeological '*francisca*' at all) (cf. Pohl 1998: 33–6). The distribution map of the single-bladed axe type usually labelled *francisca* (Hübener 1977) shows a spread across northern Gaul, particularly between the Seine and the Rhine, and eastwards into the Rhine–Danube re-entrant, thus corresponding broadly with the heartlands of the historical kingdom of the Franks but also with a large area historically labelled as belonging to the Alamanni. Unfortunately, the dating of these finds is not always secure, so it is not certain which may be of sixth-century date and thus part of the conscious creation of a Frankish identity (see below). So instead of accepting a predetermined textual narrative and agenda, we shall look at the evidence from the fourth and fifth centuries for the spread of an archaeological complex whose origins lay east and north of the Rhine and which it is thus reasonable to label 'Germanic'. The evidence will principally be that of settlement and building types, on the one hand, and material culture, particularly from funerary contexts, on the other hand.

Settlements characterised by the presence of buildings of north German rather than Roman provincial type begin to appear in the Roman Rhineland and northern Gaul in the course of the fourth century (for the sites from a recent survey, see Lenz 2005, with references; cf. Vermeulen 2001: 53–63), principally in Toxandria, but some are also now known further south. A detailed study of part of the lower Rhine (Van Es and Hessing 1994) shows a classic *Mischzivilization* with Roman-style military sites and elements of material culture coexisting with structures of Germanic type along with metalwork and pottery, with grave goods belonging to both traditions and showing again the importance of Roman official issue metalwork in Germanic graves. Perhaps the most diagnostic building type was the 'long house' (*Wohnstallhaus*) with opposed entrances in the long sides, and people housed at one end and animals at the other (cf. Hamerow 2002: Ch. 2); this type was already present in the third and fourth centuries at classic sites beyond the Rhine in Germany and the Netherlands such as Flögeln (Kreis Wesermünde) and Wijster (Drenthe) respectively. These 'long houses' are known from Toxandrian sites of the fourth century such as Gennep near Nijmegen (Gelderland) and Neerharen-Rekem (Limburg), but also, more unexpectedly, from the 1990s excavations on the site of Saint-Ouen-du-Breuil (Seine-Maritime) in Normandy north of Rouen (Van Ossel and Ouzoulias 2000: 149–51) (cf. p. 280). At these three sites and other similar ones, the 'long houses' were accompanied by satellite groups of *Grubenhäuser/fonds de cabane*/sunken featured buildings (SFB), often thought of as Germanic (especially by archaeologists in Britain, where they are seen as diagnostically 'Anglo-Saxon'), but in fact they are of much less definite origin (cf. Hamerow 2002: 31–5). In addition to these two very distinctive types, there were also rectangular, post-built structures, again usually with opposing doorways in the long sides, at a variety of sites, including late Roman fortifications, such as Krefeld-Gellep, or villas in northern Gaul, such as Marolles-sur-Seine (cf. p. 430) and Limetz-Ville – again accompanied by *Grubenhäuser* – or the Rhineland at Köln-Müngersdorf (Lindenthal, Nordrhein) and Voerendaal (Limburg). The number of sites with such structures continued to increase through the fifth century, in Toxandria (Thoen and Vermeulen 1998) but also in the parts of Gaul from the Seine valley northwards (Lenz 2005: 415–21;

Ouzoulias and Van Ossel 2001; Van Ossel 1992). With the exception of the *Grubenhäuser*, the origins of these building types and of the arrangement of the settlements lie north and east of the Rhine and can be seen chronologically to cross the lower Rhine frontier into Toxandria in the fourth century (and perhaps further south as at Saint-Ouen-du-Breuil), becoming established in northern Gaul in the course of the fifth century. As we have seen, the Germanic settlement in Toxandria was to an extent established with the connivance of the Roman authorities, and Germanic settlement further south in the course of the second half of the fourth century may well have been under Roman auspices as *laeti* or *gentiles*. As we shall see, whether these people all thought of themselves as Franks, even in Toxandria, is quite another matter.

The burial rites and material culture are even more ambiguous, particularly in terms of Roman-described ethnicities. Recent studies of fourth- to fifth-century metalwork have increasingly shown great variation in stylistic origins. This is in great measure due to the groundbreaking series of publications by Michel Kazanski and his co-workers, which demonstrates a mastery of the material not only from Gaul but also from a huge swathe of Europe from the Caucasus westwards, and also of publications in a range of modern languages. This has enabled the Gaulish material to be set in a much wider context and links to be made across much of temperate Europe; it is worth noting, though, that the exegetical framework for this major contribution remains strongly 'ethnic' within an essentially culture-historical framework. In addition, studies of pottery have also shown the presence of several types of handmade vessels in 'Germanic' rather than Roman provincial traditions: few if any of them can be or, even more interestingly, have been confidently labelled as 'Frankish' (though some are labelled '*mérovingien*', simply serving to confuse the issue). As we have already seen both in this chapter and in Chapter 2, even in the fourth century the literary evidence for northern Gaul and the Rhineland, such as the *Notitia Dignitatum*, refers to peoples such as the Sarmatians (cf. Lebedynsky 2002) and other 'Oriental' peoples (Kazanski 1986; cf. Kazanski and Legoux 1998; Kovalevskaya 1993) as well as Franks or Alamanni. With the events of the opening decade of the fifth century, a whole range of Germanic peoples, Alamanni, Alans, Burgundians, Franks, Gepids, Goths, Heruli, Saxons, Sueves and Vandals are mentioned (cf. esp. Jerome, *Ep.* CXXIII), and, by the middle of the fifth century, Huns also. There do appear to be indications in the material culture of changes in northern Gaul at this period; for instance, Swift (2000a: 213–19) has argued that a distinction is visible to east and west of the Maas/Meuse–Sambre line, with perhaps Germanic peoples to the west and a new line of defence along these rivers. Because of the literary sources for fifth-century Gaul, modern scholars of the archaeology have sought to assimilate elements of the funerary archaeology and material culture to the various historically attested peoples.

A good example of this is the Alans (Kouznetsov and Lebedynsky 2005: esp. Ch. 7), who crossed the Rhine with the other peoples in 405/6, and within ten years the texts mention them in the Rhineland, Aquitaine and Spain. Then silence for the Alans in Gaul until, in 440, some were settled by Aetius in the middle Rhône valley round Valence, and two years later in larger numbers in the Loire valley round Orléans, at the same time that Aetius was setting the defeated Burgundians to the east in Savoy (for their history and material culture, see below) as part of a programme of stabilising the situation against the Visigoths. Not surprisingly, attempts have been made to identify the area of Alan settlement. One means has been to use 'Alan' and its derivatives as a toponym element (e.g. Alainville) indicating Alanic settlement, but, given that none of these names are attested to before the ninth century and most much later, this is not a reliable method (Alemany 2006). More convincing is the linking of a small amount of burial evidence with sites more provably 'Alan', such as the objects from the rich female burial at Airan (Calvados) (Kazanski 1982) with parallels in the Ukraine, or at another Normandy site, Saint-Martin-de-Fontenay (Calvados) (Pilet 1980; Pilet *et al.* 1994), where, in a large rural cemetery in use from the fourth to the seventh century, there were a small number of burials of people with their crania deformed by binding in infancy, a practice associated by classical writers with the Alans and the Huns (cf. Bóna 2002: 25–6). It is one that is also found sporadically across eastern and central Europe from the Pontico-Danubian region westwards. The burials do contain some objects with links to the Caucasus, but do not contain objects such as cauldrons that were the hallmark of the Hunnic male burial (cf. Buchet 1988). It has been pointed out (Hakenbeck 2009) that such burials (and similar ones found south of the Garonne and noted above [p. 361]) are very small in number and, where the necessary osteological analysis has been undertaken, they are overwhelmingly those of adult females. It is again central and eastern Europe, the 'Pontico-Danubian' region, that is the focus of this practice for fifth-century Europe (its origins lie further east and earlier), suggesting that the outliers in Gaul may be women married out of their own 'culture' (Hakenbeck 2009: 77–9), so these individuals should not necessarily be taken as proxies for the movement of larger groupings. In fact, the archaeology of the peoples ancient sources chose to call the Alans, Huns and Sarmatians is in many respects very similar and can be traced back to their areas of origin in southern and south-western parts of the Russian Federation and into the Ukraine; it is normally related to culture provinces such as Przeworsk and Wielbark. By the time they get to Gaul, certainty over precise ethnicity is very difficult for us (if not for them). Even so, intentional cranial deformation would seem to be a very precise indicator of a set of beliefs about personal appearance and would require a detailed knowledge of how to perform the practice. It is a practice with no Roman provincial antecedents but with antecedents outside the empire, and thus one of the ways of proclaiming non-Romanness.

Just to complicate the picture in northern Gaul still further, there is a group of late fifth- to early sixth-century *Armbrustfibeln* and *Bügelknopffibeln*, principally in the basins of the middle Seine, the Marne and the Somme with a scattering further east (Kazanski *et al.* 2008: esp. Abb. 19; Wieczorek 1996: 353). These are labelled 'Visigothic' since their parallels lie in south-western Gaul and to an extent in Spain. This, of course, is perilously close to ascribing an ethnic identity to objects, something only their makers and users can have, objects being used to construct and reflect such identities. In this case, do we have to postulate Visigoths far from home, or simply the last resting place of much-travelled brooches? Moreover, further north, in Toxandria and along the Gallic side of the Channel, there is material, particularly pottery, whose closest parallels lie in south-eastern Britain. This has led workers – for instance, at the fifth-century cemetery of Vron (Somme) (Seillier 1989) – to characterise this as 'Anglo-Saxon', a descriptor that has also been applied to other pottery from the Netherlands down along the North Sea littoral (Vermeulen 2001: 67–8). This is because the literary authorities fix the Anglo-Saxons in Britain, and they are mentioned on the Gallic side of the Channel, so similar material from the Gallic littoral is ascribed a similar ethnicity. What the people who actually made and/or used this pottery thought of themselves as could have been very different. Of course, many of the other burials in the same cemeteries as the burials and objects noted above, and in other cemeteries without 'immigrant' rites and/or objects, continued the established, late Roman rite of inhumation with few or no grave goods; presumably, these were in large measure burials of the descendants of the Gallo-Roman population, but also perhaps of immigrants who had 'Romanised'. The purpose of this presentation of archaeological evidence that has been tied to a number of different ethnic groups, as described in the literature, has been to give some indication of how confused the archaeological picture for fifth-century northern Gaul, in the regions that were to become the heartlands of the Frankish kingdom, actually is.

So, as noted above, there is very little in the archaeology which can be firmly labelled 'Frankish' or 'Merovingian' rather than generically 'Germanic', or what is found can be related to other, non-Roman peoples, with some more specific ascriptions (but always to peoples other than the 'Franks'). It is not until one gets to the horizon represented by the burial of Childeric (d. *c.* 481) at Tournai (Périn and Kazanski 1996) that it becomes possible to talk of an increasingly coherent and distinctive set of burial practices in northern Gaul and to label them 'Frankish' if one so wishes. This burial was discovered, possibly under a barrow, in 1653 near the later church of Saint-Brice across the river from the late Roman fortifications. High-quality drawings of the principal contents were published two years later by a local doctor, Chifflet, though the objects themselves were mostly stolen and destroyed in 1831. The drawings show that it was a warrior burial with sword (in an elaborately decorated scabbard), spear and *francisca*. There was a large quantity of gold-and-garnet jewellery, some of it probably from horse harness, but most of it related to the occupant's clothing. The presence of a signet ring engraved with the name and image of Childeric identified the occupant of the grave and dates the burial to somewhere in the latter part of the fifth century. The form of the items of jewellery and the use of gold and garnet both link the burial to 'Germanic' material culture, but the presence also of an elaborate, openwork, gold crossbow brooch of latest Roman type and a purse of over one hundred gold and more than two hundred silver Roman coins shows another side to the burial. The crossbow brooch can be read, along with the gold-and-garnet dress accessories and the weaponry, as a version of late Roman military apparel, showing the importance of Roman military symbolism and the symbolic language of late Roman dress to Childeric as legitimating his position; indeed, some textual sources have him as some sort of Roman-approved governor as well as Germanic king. This may also be seen in his signet ring, suggesting the need to seal written documents in a late Roman official manner. More recent excavations (Brulet 1996) have reinforced the 'Germanic' aspects to the burial, with the discovery in the vicinity of the proposed barrow over the grave of three burials each containing several horses, twenty-one in all, as well as human burials. Horse burials of early medieval date are known from across central and western Europe (cf. Müller-Wille 1996), particularly between the Rhine and the Elbe (Figure 8.5), linked with high-status 'princely' or 'royal' burials, presumably because of the martial qualities of the horse and probably also because of its links to deities in the Germanic pantheon. The Tournai burial thus can be interpreted as a Germanic royal burial, yet it lies on former imperial lands reinterpreted in a Roman way

384 *Breakdown and barbarians*

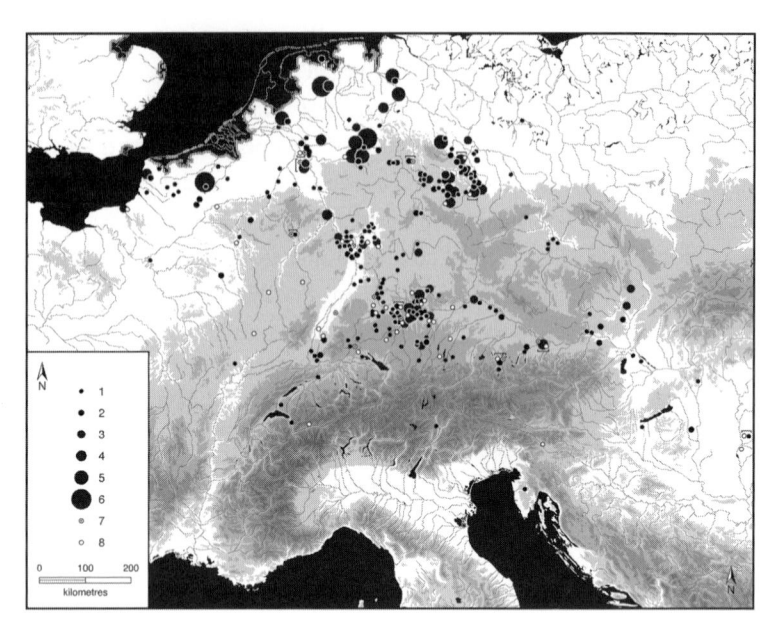

Fig. 8.5 Distribution of early medieval horse burials in Europe

which would have been comprehensible to the population of Gallo-Roman descent (cf. Halsall 2001). Childeric's son Clovis, who presumably oversaw the creation of his father's tomb, was to take the process to the next stage by converting the bulk of his subjects to Christianity. So it is really only from the late fifth-century horizon of the tomb of Childeric that we can begin to see the creation of a material culture in northern Gaul that is sufficiently homogeneous to be labelled 'Frankish' (Wieczorek *et al.* 1996), one that blended Roman provincial elements with a range of Germanic elements in terms of both material culture and the development of the characteristic *Reihengräberfelder* (cemeteries with graves in rows), though the Germanic elements continued to share many aspects with areas to which the literary sources ascribe different 'ethnic' labels such as Alamanni or Thuringians. The microregional study of the region of Metz (Halsall 1995: esp. Chs. 2 and 8) shows well that what is usually thought of as a Frankish or Merovingian cemetery with its clear structuring of grave goods by gender and by age developed there from the early sixth century, and not earlier (it is also worth noting the prevalence of grave goods in the burials of what was, nominally at least, a Christian population). The early sixth century was also the horizon when the Frankish law code ('Salic law') seems first to have been codified and when Frankish kings such as Theudebert (not a Roman-style name) started to strike coin in their own name rather than that of the emperor, suggesting that now they had confidence in their kingdom's own separate political identity both internally and by contrast with other powers.

The example of the north of Gaul shows that archaeology offers a very different range of evidence from the historical narrative, one which can be read only with great difficulty in terms of some sort of linear 'ethnogenesis' of any particular people, least of all the Franks as identified in the texts. From the later fourth century and on through the fifth century, the archaeology, especially of burial, can be read to demonstrate the presence of a variety of different groups, to which ethnic labels may be attached if desired. But this is to read it from a very particular perspective; it can and should also be read along axes such as status, gender, age, family and kin, as much as, or in conjunction with, ethnicity. If we did not have the textual evidence, it would probably be impossible to recognise 'the Franks' as a geographically and culturally distinct grouping in the archaeology; rather there would be a generic, 'Germanic' background in the burial rites and material, itself imposed on a more extensive Roman provincial rite, against which 'oddities' in the material culture or in practices, such as cranial deformation, would stand out. This is in no way to seek to deny that there were people who defined themselves, through their language and customs (*habitus*), through their religious beliefs, and through their beliefs about the genesis of their people and their ruling family or families, as 'Franks' and were recognised as such by contemporaries. Indeed, it might be argued that it was their lack of distinctiveness which was ultimately the key to their success; they had the flexibility to accept and be accepted by other groups, probably particularly the Gallo-Romans, when other groupings more jealous of their own identity died out or were subsumed from the end of the fifth century by the burgeoning Frankish political, cultural, religious and ethnic identity.

On their way to dominance, the Franks were to conquer and subsume the kingdom of the Burgundians, a people with a considerable presence in the historical record and therefore worth brief consideration here. They appear in a 'first' kingdom from 406 to 436 on the middle Rhine around Speyer and Worms, until it was suppressed by Aetius. Seven years later, he settled them in their 'second' kingdom in east-central Gaul between Lyon and Geneva, the region known as Sapaudia (Savoy), perhaps resuscitating them as a political and presumably military entity to act as a counterweight to the ambitions of the Visigoths. By the end of the fifth century, they had consolidated their hold over much of eastern and south-eastern Gaul, until conquered by the Franks in 534. The historical sources tell us of their kings, queens and other royal and noble personages. The kingdom issued coins, promulgated law codes and was clearly a recognised and recognisable political entity. Archaeologically, it might as well never have existed. From the areas it controlled comes only a handful of objects of 'Germanic' type, mainly brooches, some of which are of 'Alamannic' type (Escher 2005: vol. II). There is nothing there that can be said to be distinctively 'Burgundian', as opposed to 'Alamannic' or 'Visigothic' or, indeed, 'Frankish', apart from the coins, where gold was struck in the name of the emperor, and silver and copper in the name of the king (Grierson and Blackburn 1986: 74–7). The region appears as one in which there was a scatter of non-Roman objects and burials, but the majority of the archaeology remains of Roman provincial type. It would seem that though an ethnic self-definition was important to the ruling elite, it was not to the great majority of their subjects. To what extent, then, was the second Burgundian kingdom and its 'barbarian' identity one imposed by the Romans ('etic') rather than one internally generated ('emic') that did not spread far beyond the ruling dynasty and warrior elite, who used it as a tool to legitimate their rule over a population that was overwhelmingly Gallo-Roman?

Discussion: ethnicity, archaeology and history

It is worth briefly drawing out some of the arguments that have appeared in the discussions above of the archaeology of 'barbarian' or 'Germanic' settlement on the territories of the West in the fifth century and its relationship to historically described ethnic groupings and the origins of the early medieval kingdoms. The Visigoths and the Franks are the two groupings who were ultimately the most 'successful' of all the Germanic peoples recorded as taking over the territories of the Western Empire that are our concern here. Each was to create a large, powerful and stable kingdom on either side of the Pyrenees, encompassing essentially the lands of Hispania and Gallia respectively, with royal dynasties ruling over a people of mixed Germanic and Roman provincial descent, with civil and ecclesiastical structures (to a great extent taken over from the empire), taxes, laws (among other things distinguishing between 'German' and 'Roman' subjects), coinages and the apparatus of a functioning state, even if they had much less actual power than the late Roman emperors had had (cf. Wickham 2005: Ch. 3). Along the way they had defeated and incorporated Germanic and other peoples and kingdoms, sometimes relatively powerful ones such as the Sueves in Spain or the Burgundians in Gaul, as well as absorbing smaller groupings such as the Alans. This, of course, is essentially a historical narrative.

The archaeology presented above can now be seen to be far less clear-cut than used to be thought when its interpretation and use were controlled by the historical narrative. This is above all in the case of the Visigoths, whose archaeological ethnicity in fifth-century Spain was long held to be self-evident; on the other hand, discussion of the archaeological identity of the Franks has long had a tendency to take the burial of Childeric as its starting point and to avoid looking too hard at what came before. It is worth reviewing how this came about and what the archaeology has to contribute to the debate. Clearly, the 'traditional' narrative and the identification of the ethnicity of practices and, above all, artefacts were derived from the written texts because of their chronological and intellectual primacy. Archaeology was a johnny-come-lately, in its turn shaped by the pre-existing textual categories. The weaknesses of this approach are now widely recognised and acknowledged. But there are features of how the archaeological debate has developed that perhaps require further consideration, especially the domains of archaeological evidence within which the debate has been conducted. The 'ethnicity' debate has principally been sited within the domain of funerary archaeology linked with artefact studies, or, to put it another way, the preceding debate has almost entirely been about burials and grave goods; there are huge areas of the archaeological record not much implicated in or entirely untouched by the ethnicity question. In part this dominance of the funerary record can be attributed to the fact that artefacts tend to be well preserved in graves; in part to the fact that their disposition around the body can be read off in terms of dress, dress that is different from that of the numerically superior indigenous populations. After one has established differences, it has been but a short step to having recourse to the texts to label those differences. We have seen above how slippery such categorisations in fact are once 'essentialist' or 'primordialist' notions of ethnicity are discarded and replaced by 'situationalist' or 'performative' notions of ethnicity and other identities. We have also seen that often we are also dealing with strongly gendered representations, with female burials outnumbering male in certain regions such as Spain, suggesting, perhaps, that aspects such as descent and lineage were more important considerations than a simple category of 'ethnicity'. Leading on from this, it is also worth noting that the identification of 'ethnic' identity has often eclipsed other possible readings of the burial evidence such as status, age and, of course, gender. So even within the domain of funerary archaeology, the selection of evidence and approaches has been very partial. We may recall Theuws' (2009) disturbing question as to whether 'ethnicity' was something that people at the period actually felt was worth inscribing in the burial record. Or has our penchant for reading the funerary evidence in this way simply been a reflection of hugely important and contentious twentieth- and twenty-first-century political and cultural categories?

If we turn away from the study of certain aspects of the funerary record and certain classes of material culture to other domains of the archaeological record, the 'ethnic' reading of the evidence becomes decreasingly frequent, often because decreasingly possible. We may turn first to a domain where such identifications have been attempted – settlements and structures. As noted above (p. 379), certain types of structure, principally the 'hall house' and the SFB, have traditionally been assimilated to ethnic interpretations; they are the preferred residential and ancillary buildings of Germanic peoples. Now it is perfectly true that the hall building in its archetypal form of the *Wohnstallhaus* with accommodation for humans and for animals under the one roof does seem to have its origins in the regions of north-west Europe outside the Roman frontiers along the Rhine. It appears in increasing numbers south of the lower Rhine in the fourth century, often associated with the spread of the Franks into Toxandria. It also appears at some sites well to the south of Toxandria in the fourth century (e.g. Saint-Ouen-du-Breuil). But at such sites, though there may be a small amount of non-local ('Germanic') artefactual material, the great majority of the material culture is of Roman provincial types, producing a dissonance between any ethnic interpretations based on the structures and those based on the artefacts. In time, essentially from the sixth century on, rectangular, timber structures became widespread across Gaul north of the Loire (cf. Peytremann 2003: Ch. 5), often grouped into nucleated settlements or 'villages'. But by this time they are seldom interpreted in ethnic terms but more in terms of changing building technologies, developing structures of rural society and exploitation of agricultural resources. This raises the point that originally such structures in their builders' homelands outside the empire were not a statement of ethnicity but of particular forms of social structure and agrarian practice with their accompanying ideologies (cf. Roymans 1996a, 1996b). It can be envisaged that as people with their origins in the regions that employed this form of structure settled within northern Gaul, they might have constructed such buildings, but this may have been because it was what they were used to and it expressed their social formations and their agricultural regimes, not because they were thereby making an ethnic statement.

Indeed, the classic north German/Low Countries *Wohnstallhaus* is rare in northern Gaul; instead it is rectangular, post-built, timber structures (occasionally on sill beams) that predominate from the fourth century on, a form much less distinctive than the *Wohnstallhaus* and with antecedents in the Roman provincial building stock (Peytremann 2003: 290–7; Van Ossel 1992: Ch. 7). To judge by the activities attested to at such sites, they could fulfil a range of agrarian and artisan functions, so they might best be characterised as general-purpose agricultural structures. It has also been noted that the sunken-featured buildings, long thought to be 'Germanic', are in fact of much more equivocal origin since they are not a feature of the regions outside the Rhine frontier, and their origins cannot be tied to proven 'Germanic' settlements (cf. Hamerow 2002: 31–5). Furthermore, when we pass south of the Loire, let alone south of the Pyrenees, these supposed markers of Germanic ethnicity fade out to almost nothing, despite the historical attestations of the long-term presence of peoples of Germanic origin in these regions. We have already remarked upon the lack of 'Germanic' material culture in the realms of the kingdom of Toulouse, and this goes also for building types; indeed, it was noted that this region conserves the tradition of elite Gallo-Roman residences, apparently even for the Visigothic court. South of the Pyrenees, the few fifth- to sixth-century settlement sites we have, either installed within former Hispano-Roman villas or on new sites, as we shall see in the next chapter (p. 441), have little or nothing in their plans, building techniques or layout that suggests roots in northern or central Europe. There is hardly any archaeology of fifth-century 'Visigothic' structures and settlements. So over most of the area that concerns us and through the fourth and fifth centuries, there is little that we can read as betraying any ethnic identity. Whether that is how such structures were read at the time is even more debatable.

Modern archaeological identification of 'Germanic' and other non-Roman peoples, as we said above, has been largely done through burials and the grave goods from them. Certain forms of material culture, principally dress fittings, have been read in terms of proclaiming particular ethnic identities. The problems with doing this have been dilated upon at length above. Here the intention is just to point out that most of the archaeological domain of artefacts and material culture in this period is not susceptible to such interpretations. Let us take the most widespread artefactual material: pottery. Certain types of pottery have traditionally been interpreted as 'Germanic', based on their form and decoration, and sometimes their fabric. The classic manifestation of this is vessels that are handmade, in a limited repertoire of forms; this is principally the carinated, biconical 'urn', sometimes undecorated but over time produced with an increasingly elaborate range of incised and/or stamped decoration, sometimes with bosses pushed out on the surface. This is utterly unlike the Roman provincial repertoires in terms of technology and form; its fabric and decoration also are distinctive. Its antecedents lie outside the empire in the same regions of western Germany and the Low Countries that were home to the *Wohnstallhaus*; it is not difficult to see why this has been treated as the ceramic facies of incoming Germanic peoples. Such pottery appears within the empire in the fourth century – for instance, at Saint-Ouen-du-Breuil, where ceramics of this type (interpreted in terms of ethnicity) occur in small quantities alongside much larger quantities of Roman provincial pottery (interpreted in terms of trade). But it is in the fifth century that it becomes more widespread across northern Gaul and more common on individual sites. Many of these sites are cemeteries, and therefore these ceramics have been assimilated to ethnic identifications of the people buried with them and with other 'barbarian' material, as in the identification of 'Anglo-Saxons' buried on the Gallic coast of the Channel, partly on the basis of the forms and decoration of the vessels in the graves (Soulat 2007). Such interpretations, of course, are subject to the same strictures on the 'ethnic' identification of objects as are classes of material such as brooches and belt fittings; objects do not in themselves have an ethnicity. The cemeteries in which these types of 'Germanic' pottery occur are inhumation cemeteries, rather than the cremation cemeteries of the Free German homelands (or, indeed, of large areas of fifth-century eastern Britain), so the form of burial corresponds to indigenous Roman provincial practice. Some of the other material in the graves is of Roman provincial manufacture (decreasingly so through the fifth century), but again such material is not ascribed an ethnicity in the analyses of modern workers. Some of the graves discussed by Soulat (2007) also contain objects he characterises as 'Merovingian' (Frankish?) along with the 'Anglo-Saxon' material, raising problems for any neat ethnic interpretation. But comparable ceramics are also found on settlement sites, where interpretations are often as much in terms of functionality as of ethnicity; are these vessels for cooking, for the serving of food (communally? individually? and therefore related to social structure and practice?) or for other purposes? Are some of the vessels found in cemeteries specifically funerary, thus making them part of a rather different discourse about funerary practice? Is their increasing dominance through the fifth century not the consequence of any 'Germanisation' of material culture, but more a reflection of the breakdown of the large-scale manufacture and distribution of Roman provincial material, especially pottery, and the consequent move to simpler, more local production in styles that modern workers have called 'Germanic'? Nevertheless, it is undeniable that ceramics of these distinctively non-Roman types and of non-Roman antecedents did become widespread in Gaul north of the Loire during the fifth century (as they did also in eastern Britain). As with the dress accoutrements from Spain traditionally labelled 'Visigothic', while it may not be possible to follow such precise ethnic ascriptions, what this does seem to show is that some people in life and in death wished to present themselves in ways that were non-Roman. What this meant in terms of precise ethnicity and whether such people originated from east and north of the Rhine or from among the Roman provincial population are not questions that we can as yet pronounce upon with any degree of certainty.

South of the Loire and on into the Iberian peninsula, ceramics of 'Germanic' origin remain extremely rare. We have seen (p. 361) that there is a small quantity from Toulouse, seat of the Visigothic kingdom, through the fifth century. Interestingly, this all seems to be from occupation contexts and not from funerary ones, and this is true across the south-west of Gaul, where fifth-century burials, even those containing objects derived from the Sîntana de Mureş-Chernyakhov culture, have yet to yield any such pottery. The same largely holds true for fifth-century burials to the south of the Pyrenees, where the graves containing 'Visigothic' dress items very rarely contain 'Germanic' pottery. And, as with building types, so with ceramic types, fifth-century settlements to north and south of the Pyrenees, be they villas in the Roman provincial style or timber structures, were associated with Roman provincial products or local fabrics. As we shall see in the next chapter (p. 405), the fifth-century pottery of these southern regions is discussed essentially in economic terms as an indicator of commerce and of the integration, or not, of areas into wider exchange networks, even for areas that the texts tell us had passed under 'barbarian' dominion. Whatever the funerary or other significances of non-Roman forms and decorations of pottery to the north and the east of the Rhine and north of the Danube, these had been completely lost over the time and distance separating these 'homeland' regions from southern Gaul and Spain.

Another class of material with a wide distribution across the West throughout our period is glass. The chrono-typology of this material is now much better understood thanks to major recent publications (for an overview, see Foy 1995; for a more detailed study of north-eastern Gaul, see Feyeux 2003). Technologically and typologically, the Roman provincial production centres continued to operate through the third, fourth and fifth centuries. The forms characteristic of fifth-century and later cemeteries in northern Gaul were overwhelmingly concerned with the service and consumption of liquid. These comprise a limited range of flagons, but more especially a series of cup and beaker forms from the relatively simple hemispherical to the more elaborately decorated types, most famously 'claw beakers' and glass imitations of drinking horns. Again because of their presence in graves that have been labelled 'Germanic' in view of the other material culture in them, especially items of dress, these have been thought of as expressions of Germanic practice; indeed, the more inventive forms, in particular the 'claw beakers', have been seen as expressions of a 'Germanic' aesthetic as opposed to the more restrained canon of Roman provincial glass forms. In fact, the 'claw beaker' (and related forms) clearly developed out of and elaborated late Roman products; if one looks also at the volumes these vessels would have held, especially the flagons, they would seem more appropriate to the consumption of wine rather than any imagined Germanic beer drinking. And again, this ethnic association of late glass forms has always been a feature of the analysis of northern Gaul, with its cemeteries with a range of offerings, rather than of southern Gaul or Spain, where glass is rare in burials but overwhelmingly a find from domestic sites, where it is seen in functional terms with no ethnic overtones.

Currently, there are powerful new methods of physical and chemical analysis of human (and animal) bone being refined and becoming more widely available, and these should, in time, allow a whole new series of data sets to be interrogated. These, of course, are techniques involving the extraction and characterisation of such things as ancient DNA (including mitochondrial DNA), blood types and stable isotopes. Currently, the most promising of these seems to be stable isotope analysis. For our purposes here, there are two caveats that need to be entered. Suppose the analysis of a later fifth-century skeleton from a grave on the Spanish Meseta showed that the individual had spent his childhood in the Pontico-Danubian region. This would be of considerable interest but would not in itself say anything about his particular ethnicity, be it Alan, Goth, Hun, Suevic, Vandal or other, since all of these are recorded by historians as having been present at one time or another in this region. Given that the texts tell us that the Visigoths entered Spain from south-west Gaul, it would be very hard to argue that the individual was by birth a Visigoth, though, of course, he could have redefined himself as such at some stage in his life. There is also the 'second-generation problem' – the offspring of putative incomers to Spain from eastern Europe would have grown up in central Spain, and, if buried in the same cemetery as their parents, would have an entirely 'Spanish' isotopic signature, whatever they or others may have considered their ethnic identity to have been, and which might have been pronouncedly different from that of the indigenous population (an obvious modern parallel is that the children of Pakistani immigrants to Birmingham would have an English isotopic suite but be in several important ways culturally distinct from the majority English population).

Let us take a cautionary tale from an area within the compass of this book. Excavations in the 1960s on the fourth-century cemetery at Lankhills, Winchester, identified a number of burials whose rite differed from that of the Romano-British population and which the excavator identified as having originated in the area of Pannonia, on the middle Danube (Clarke 1979: Ch. 4, Sect. 2). Publication of work on a further tranche of the cemetery incorporated a programme of isotopic analysis on both 'local' and 'intrusive' burials (Booth *et al.* 2010: Ch. 5). In brief, there were individuals with local isotopic signatures and individuals with non-local ones. Of the groups defined by burial rite, some of the 'local' burials had non-local isotopic signatures, and others had local signatures: some of the 'intrusive' burials had local isotopic signatures, some had non-local ones. But the non-local ones suggested origins either in other parts of Britain, or, if from mainland Europe, the signatures suggested origins from the area of the western Mediterranean basin, not Pannonia. Only one burial had an isotopic signature suggesting an origin in central Europe, and the burial rite of the grave was not of the classic 'intrusive' type. Clearly, there was a significant mismatch between the groupings identified through burial rite and those identified through stable isotope analysis. It is only too likely that similar results will be replicated elsewhere, so this approach will not be a 'magic bullet' that will clarify the situation; more likely, it will add a further set of variables to analysis of the funerary archaeology.

'Barbarians' is a topic where there is a wide divergence between the textual and the archaeological evidence. The texts are specific about named peoples, named areas and named dates. The archaeology simply does not see these peoples in the way historians, either at the time or in later analyses, do. This is not to say that the events the ancient sources describe did not happen; the events, or at least something approximating to them, probably did happen, albeit that the sources probably greatly simplify much more complex chains of events, selecting among them for their particular moralising and other agendas. This is, though, to say that the material culture and other correlates, which have for so long been taken as more or less self-evident expressions of the presence of peoples of named 'barbarian' origins at certain times and in stated places, simply are not susceptible to being read in this way. In some areas at some times, we find building types and material culture types that are clearly not derived from Roman provincial practice and in most cases can be linked to antecedents either across the mid and lower Rhine or in the 'Pontico-Danubian' area. Clearly, these represent in some way the appearance on Roman territory of individuals or groups who defined themselves in some important ways through signifiers of 'non-Romanness'. This, of course, is an essentially negative definition and thus of limited use. It would be an exercise in hypercriticality to claim that such material culture and other aspects of the archaeology were not in some way making statements about particular forms of non-Romanness, and about particular identities proclaimed especially through dress (and probably other forms of bodily presentation such as hairstyles). These identities were in part to do with matters such as gender, status and age. But alongside this, there were very probably also claims to particular 'ethnic' identities. But as we have seen, such identities were not fixed and immutable; they were changeable according to situation and utility. Likewise, the archaeological material does not persistently recur in limited and bounded sets of associations of a type that would support the identification of particular ethnic identities in an old 'culture-historical' way; this material, too, is fluid and mutable, suggesting that the material correlates of these identities could be adapted, perhaps to suit the preconceptions of others. Rather than lamenting the loss of the old certainties, we should perhaps see this as an opportunity to refashion our perceptions of what was happening across the Western Empire in this period at both the macrolevel and the microlevel of the individual cemetery or settlement and at the subregional level, particularly in the northern part of Gaul, where 'non-Roman' signifiers both in life and in death were clearly important. But equally there remain large areas of the West, particularly in southern Gaul and Iberia, where the historical sources attest to the long-term presence of 'barbarian' peoples, probably in significant numbers, but they remain hard to pin down in the archaeology; clearly, it was possible to be a 'barbarian' while living in Roman-style buildings and using Roman-style material culture. Presumably, there were signifiers such as elements of bodily presentation or perhaps more especially language, nomenclature and a consciousness of belonging to a particular community defined by political loyalties and shared ideas, such as origin myths and lineages, or, indeed, particular types ('heresies') of Christianity, but these are signifiers that leave little or, more often no, trace that we are able to recognise in the archaeology.

9 | The fifth century and the dis-integration of the Western Empire

Introduction

In the previous chapter we looked at those elements of the archaeology that are most easily assimilated to the traditional, text-based narrative and processes of the 'fall of the Western Roman Empire', the elements dealing with the collapse of the structures that represented the political and military hegemony of the Roman state and their replacement by entities with a 'barbarian' or 'Germanic' identity (however arrived at) which came to control more or less effectively the territories and populations of the former Western provinces. These processes naturally entailed considerable disruption of the patterns of archaeological evidence, with that for the Roman state, particularly the army, becoming less and less visible and, the correlative of this, the evidence for incoming peoples and what is traditionally interpreted as their material culture, becoming more and more visible. But, of course, the Roman army and the incoming peoples (however calculated) formed only a minority of the total population of the Western provinces and operated within and upon the context of the established cultural and economic formations. It is the effect of the changes in political and military power on those cultural and economic formations that will be the concern of this chapter. To what extent was the fifth century, far more than the third, a period of archaeological 'crisis', or, less rhetorically, a period that saw a major threshold in the archaeology of the West involving the patterns and forms of deposition into and formation of the archaeological record, a period that marked the transitions from the classical world towards the medieval?

A central theme of this book, and the central theme of this chapter, is integration and dis-integration, particularly as visible in and explanatory of the archaeological record. In the previous chapters it has been argued that the existence of the Roman system provided a significant measure of integration, be it political, administrative, fiscal, economic or cultural, that would not otherwise have existed. The archaeological correlates of this integration are visible in a range of evidence types from churches to plate to pottery. But equally it was argued that this integration was superimposed on and modified a huge number of more local entities and traditions, so integration was very far from being homogenisation. Nevertheless, the archaeologies of the late Roman West and all the aspects of life and death that they represent would not have been the way they were without the integrating effects of membership of the Roman Empire. The focus of this chapter will be on what happened when those integrative mechanisms were removed, not all at once or at the same rate, and underlying differences asserted themselves, or new differences were created. As a consequence of the dis-integration of the West, societies and the resources at their command tended to become smaller in scale, and this is reflected in the archaeology, with a diminution and simplification of the quantity of archaeological material, be it settlements, structures or metalwork, and a corresponding loss of the more sophisticated end of the ranges of technologies for the transformation of raw materials and the production of finished goods, from houses to pottery. This quantitative decline – there is simply a lot less archaeology around in AD 500 than in 400 – can, of course, be, and traditionally has been, read as qualitative decline, and thus a comment on what became of the societies inhabiting or moving into the area of the former Western provinces. The last quarter-century or so in particular has seen the application of arguments and vocabulary designed to distance interpretative schemes from this simple linearity (often with an implicit moralising agenda) and to offer alternative interpretations such as asking whether the removal of imperial rule was something of benefit for the peoples of the former empire (arguments which, of course, carry their own strong moralising agenda from post-colonial discourse), or whether the depth and speed of 'decline' have been exaggerated because of overdependence on ancient textual sources (often with strong and explicit, frequently Christian, moralising agendas), meaning that archaeology may offer an alternative, less catastrophic vision.

Before we embark on a survey of the various areas of the West in the fifth century, something needs to be said about the archaeological resources for the study in order to appreciate the formidable problems of the evidence and thus of any interpretations proposed. From about the turn of the fourth and fifth centuries, the nature of the archaeological record undergoes major modifications. The tradition of building in mortared stone becomes less and less common, with the exception of churches, and gives way to construction with timber structural elements with daub and other infills, the structures being floored generally in beaten earth or clay, sometimes possibly wood. In cities and in the villas, such structures often colonised the standing remains or ruins of earlier, more solidly constructed public and private buildings and spaces. The archaeological traces of such structures are often fugitive and difficult to locate and understand, requiring a considerable level of technical expertise in the excavating. This means that in many older excavations such traces were certainly lost, with sometimes a record of later post-holes or pits penetrating earlier floors, showing that there had been such occupation, which was sometimes characterised (or dismissed) as 'squatter occupation'. Along with changes in the materials of construction, there often went major changes in what was being constructed. On the one hand, major classes of Roman-style buildings such as the urban *domus* or the rural villa largely disappear from the record by the end of the fifth century or not long thereafter. On the other hand, what increasingly dominates the rural landscape is nucleated settlements, which suggest a very different social structure to the villa; occasionally something similar may be discernible in the cities. As well as the forms of settlements, the forms of structures change, and this has provoked interpretations such as the tying of specific building forms to specific ethnic groups, particularly structures held to originate in 'Germanic' areas and thus to represent the ethnicity of their builders and occupants. In addition to the major changes in construction techniques and settlement and building forms, there was also a major change in the quantity and quality of artefacts, again from about the turn of the fourth and fifth centuries. In general, artefacts become much fewer. A particularly sore loss is that of base metal coins, produced in ever-decreasing quantities by the imperial mints after 395 (cf. p. 348) and with a progressively more and more limited circulation. Some imperial gold and silver coinage, along with gold and silver struck by such authorities as the Visigothic kingdom, did continue to circulate, but it is rare, especially as site finds, and even rarer in quantities or contexts where it is useful for dating. The consequences of this for dating at such a crucial juncture are apparent; the one independent dating medium almost ceases to operate. As yet, physical and chemical dating methods have been too expensive and too limited in application to make a significant difference to this situation. Over most of the West, pottery also underwent an accelerating downturn in production and distribution from the start of the fifth century, but in many regions of the West this production and distribution did at least continue, albeit in much smaller quantities. The problem is, though, that lacking the common association with coins characteristic of the earlier centuries, fifth-century pottery is very difficult to date with any precision; date ranges of up to half a century are not uncommon at this period. The absolute decline in the amount of archaeological record created in the fifth century still means that there are severe problems in detecting whether there was occupation at this date, with the related problem that absence of evidence in this context may not be evidence of absence. Even if occupation can be demonstrated, it is often very difficult to assess what it means in terms of an individual settlement, let alone in terms of a regional network of settlement and activity. It should be noted, though, that there is one important exception to this picture, particularly as regards building and related activities, the resources these imply and their cultural context; this is the Church.

Regional survey

It would be possible here to separate out and go over the evidence types discussed in previous chapters, towns, villas, rural settlement and the economy, outlining the changes that take place and discussing their significance, but this would make the fifth century simply act as a coda to the third and fourth. Here, because the central theme and exegesis is dis-integration, we shall return to another core consideration, regionalism. The archaeology of the West in the fifth century will be examined through looking at a series of different regions or super-regions, and, where appropriate, their constituent regions and areas, allowing us to juxtapose the different types of evidence to examine the differing ways in which the dis-integration of the West impacted on and helped alter the trajectories of development in these super-regions. The super-regions concerned are as follows: the Mediterranean littoral and its hinterland in both Iberia and southern Gaul, the interior of the Iberian peninsula, the interior of southern Gaul, and northern Gaul. These super-regions are in part defined by geography and resources, creating significant variabilities between neighbouring super-regions (the Iberian littoral and the Iberian interior are a good example of this); in part they are defined empirically by observable major variabilities in the archaeology between one super-region and another. Indeed, they are sometimes defined by the presence or absence of a sufficient body of archaeological evidence with which to work. In fact, we have already come across these super-regions several times in what has gone before, and their particularities have been noted and commented on. Only once this regional survey has been attempted will certain wider themes, such as urbanism or the elite, be discussed in more general terms.

The littoral of Iberia and southern Gaul

As already seen in Chapter 7, the super-region of the Mediterranean littoral is largely defined by its topography, which in turn influences its patterns of human exploitation. Consisting of a relatively narrow coastal strip along the Mediterranean, it is backed by tablelands and mountains relatively difficult of access, except along the courses of rivers. This is particularly true of Iberia, where really only the Ebro valley offered a major corridor of penetration into the interior. The topography is less marked north of the Pyrenees, where the Carcassonne Gap affords a relatively easy passage over to south-western Gaul, but from northern Languedoc round to the Italian border the situation more resembles that in Iberia, with the Rhône valley as the crucial corridor of communication into the interior of Gaul. But this is to be too terrestrial. If the topography of the coastal strip imposes severe constraints, that littoral fronts onto the exceptional 'connectivity' provided by the seaways of the Mediterranean. It is this feature that marks off this super-region from others in the fifth century, since the volumes and patterns of traded goods are unlike those anywhere else in the West, and it is this that needs to be considered first, as the defining feature, before considering other aspects of the archaeology.

The economic shifts in the western Mediterranean in the third century were outlined in Chapter 7, particularly in relation to the reorientation of the Baetican olive oil trade from the time of the Severi on. So also was the creation of the 'tax spine' (p. 316) from North Africa to Italy in the 320s, as central North Africa took over the bulk of the supply of *annona* grain and olive oil to Rome, with the transport system put in place by the state being used to privilege trade in North African products and manufactures across the western Mediterranean. In the archaeology these are most easily recognised as olive oil from its amphorae and the tableware in ARS (African red slip ware). Because of the state-engendered infrastructure, these products had achieved a degree of dominance over more local products across much of the western Mediterranean littoral through the mid and late fourth century, though the pattern is far from uniform, with, for instance, North African wine amphorae well represented at Marseille (probably related to the trade to Italy) but very rare or absent from sites on the Iberian coast. Of course, local productions of olive oil, wine and grain were still traded coastwise, as were manufactures, of which pottery is the most readily visible to us, but, as we have also seen (p. 318), there is considerable evidence that the African goods often out-competed local products, even in the homelands of the latter. It is important, though, not to be too supply-side oriented in the analysis of these patterns. Also crucial was the clear demand for these products, obviously in part because of the favourable pricing regimes made possible by state intervention, but also in part because the products themselves were desirable; in the case of ARS, we can tell this because of the multiple local imitative industries influenced by its forms and decorations, even such large-scale ones as DSP and TSHT. This shows that the distributions were, at least after the initial expansion into these markets of the North African goods, in important part demand-led.

This overall pattern held good through the first quarter of the fifth century, whatever the alarms and excursions further north and whatever short-lived incursions by Visigoths and others there were into the Iberian littoral and hinterlands. The crucial change came with the Vandals, who, since their arrival in Iberia in 409, had been doing very little that is textually or archaeologically visible in Baetica (Arce 1982, 2002b). In 429, they took it into their heads to invade North Africa under their king Gaiseric, and after much good luck on their side and much incompetence on the Roman side, they seized western and central North Africa, culminating in the capture of the great metropolis of Carthage in 439. This had crucial fiscal consequence for the Western Empire and economic consequence for the western Mediterranean trade nexus. The tax spine was broken (Wickham 2005: 711); on the one hand, the Western emperors could no longer exact the *annona* from North Africa to feed Rome, and, crucially for any hope of restoring the integrity of the Western Empire, they had lost their richest tax lands along with huge imperial estates and were ever thereafter much strapped for cash. On the other hand, the new Vandal kings and landowners were not going to supply the Romans' capital city on a not-for-profit basis. The aftershocks of this political and fiscal earthquake can be traced all around the western Mediterranean basin in a downturn in the presence of North African ceramics from around the middle of the fifth century (Fentress and Perkins 1988). But this was a reduction in scale, not an end to the commerce: on the one hand, the demand for North African produce and products was too firmly embedded in the populations around the western Mediterranean, perhaps especially the urban and the wealthier sections of society; on the other hand, the supply area, North Africa's rural economy and population and the wealth of its landowning classes (Roman or Vandal), was heavily dependent on the bulk production and export of agrarian surplus and manufactured goods, far too much so for the trade to be discontinued, even if it was now not founded on the *annona*. What is found instead is a series of reorientations of the patterns and volumes of commerce, involving not only North Africa and the western Mediterranean but also the eastern Mediterranean (for a clear, detailed and fully documented discussion, see Reynolds 2005, 2010, on which what follows is based albeit at a more generalising level).

The pattern that seems to develop at the port cities of the south Gaulish and Catalonian coast down as far as Valencia is a recrudescence of North African products after the mid-century downturn (Bonifay and Raynaud 2007: 105–7), especially oil amphorae and ARS along with cooking and other coarse wares. But now for the first time, Eastern products, principally wine amphorae from the Levant, make a significant showing in this area too, one where in the fourth century they had to all intents and purposes been absent. The reasons for this in part lie in the production and supply mechanisms in the East, but in part this would also seem to reflect local demand. It must be noted that in Catalonia these North African and Levantine products penetrate, at best, sporadically into the hinterlands, though presumably it was these hinterlands that produced the surpluses with which the elite and the urban populations paid for such goods. In southern Gaul, in the areas around the ports such as Narbonne and Marseille, for the latter of which we have good, quantified evidence (Bonifay et al. 1998; cf. Loseby 1992), the picture is not dissimilar, though some sites near Marseille, such as the refortified, coastal, hilltop centre of Saint-Blaise (Démians d'Archimbaud 1994: Pt. II, Ch. 2), did receive quantities of imports. Nevertheless, the general picture stands: North African supply persisted but its penetration compared with the fourth century had diminished; Levantine supply increased dramatically but its penetration was similarly limited. The coastal cities, though, seem to have remained sufficiently wealthy and populous to be able to demand, to be supplied with and to have the (presumably agrarian) resources to pay for their accustomed luxuries. In the latter part of the fifth century, this north-eastern Iberian/south Gaulish pattern of North African and Levantine imports persisted; indeed, at Marseille, the proportions of North African material steadily increased back towards pre-Vandal levels, the commerce consisting of amphorae and ARS and other commodities such as handmade cooking wares. By contrast, particularly in the later fifth century, the south-eastern part of the Iberian peninsula seems to have become part of a different nexus of commerce, still dominated by North African products, perhaps from different production centres from those of the northern circuit, but comprising a wide range of fabrics and forms and accompanied by a range of Levantine products (Reynolds 2005: 419–22, 2010: Ch. 3, Sect. 4.1). On some sites, such as Alicante, these ceramics occur in large quantities, and it is this facies of the produce and pottery trade which thrusts between the Pillars of Hercules to link the Atlantic façade of the Iberian peninsula to the Mediterranean nexus, in a way it had not been before, in the second half of the fifth and the first half of the sixth centuries. It was, of course, the northernmost extremity of this pattern that reached as far as sites in southwestern Britain, Ireland and round the Irish Sea.

If, then, the Mediterranean littorals of Iberia and southern Gaul would seem from pottery to have been economically still very active and linked into the supply and demand nexuses of the western Mediterranean for olive oil, wine, fish sauce, tableware and coarse wares, can we see this in the urban and rural settlement patterns and in other aspects of the archaeology? Unfortunately, the Iberian peninsula is the area of the West where archaeological evidence for urban developments in the fifth century is most at a premium (Arce *et al.* 2007; Kulikowski 2004: Ch. 9; Macias i Solé and Remolà Vallverdù 2005). This has in part been because of the priority given to the texts for this period and the narratives derived from them concerning the Germanic peoples in the peninsula such as the Sueves, and later in the century the arrival of the Visigoths and the origins of the Visigothic kingdom. Part of the rhetoric of these texts was the damage done by warfare and by siege to the Roman cities of the peninsula. In part the poor understanding has been because of the lack of major, intramural excavations, a situation now changing with large-scale projects to high technical standards. For southern Gaul the position is somewhat better, above all at Arles and Marseille as a result of a series of large-scale excavations with rich and well-studied artefact suites. In the area of Iberia that is our concern here, the most important sites are Valencia, Tarragona and Barcelona. At Valencia, the Almoina site (Gurt i Esparraguera and Ribera i Lacomba 2005: 208–13; Ribera i Lacomba and Rosselló Mesquida 2000: 165–85) covered the eastern part of the early imperial forum, which was destroyed and promptly reconstructed in the 270s. Through the fourth century the forum and associated public buildings continued to serve as an administrative and judicial centre for the city, with the possibility that part of the complex became Christianised as the place where the martyr Vincent was condemned. One earlier structure, a possible *collegium*, seems to have functioned in the fourth century as a building for food processing (Álvarez *et al.* 2005). The excavated part of the civic complex was destroyed in the early part of the fifth century, and the site then seems to have lain abandoned for a century or more until the construction, reusing stone from the earlier structures, in the mid sixth century of a major church (under the present cathedral) with eastern annexes including a baptistery and a mausoleum, and the accompanying development of an intramural cemetery (Gurt i Esparraguera and Ribera i Lacomba 2005: 213–30). It is tempting to interpret this as the appropriation by the new urban power, the Church, of the seat of the old temporal power, but, given the long interval between the destruction of the forum and the construction of the episcopal complex, there is a risk here of over-interpretation. Even so, the fact that the civic buildings were abandoned and their site became a wasteland makes important points about the physical and administrative structure of fifth-century Valencia. Other excavations in the city (Ribera i Lacomba and Roselló Mesquida 2000: 151–64) have shown that it was also the mid sixth century that saw the colonisation of the track of the former circus by buildings. To the same horizon can be attributed structures encroaching on a Roman *decumanus* and associated grain silos in the Banys de l'Amirall. Again, the fifth-century phase remains very difficult to characterise.

Another apparent instance of the deliberate colonisation of a former temporal structure by episcopal power lies up the coast at Tarragona (Figure 9.1), but, as at Valencia, the process was actually more nuanced and involved much more than just one area (Bosch Puche *et al.* 2005; Macias i Solé 2000). From the Flavian period on, the city of Tarragona had consisted essentially of two distinct areas: the first area comprised, on top of the hill, an immense complex of monuments, with at the summit a large colonnaded court containing a major temple (presumably of the

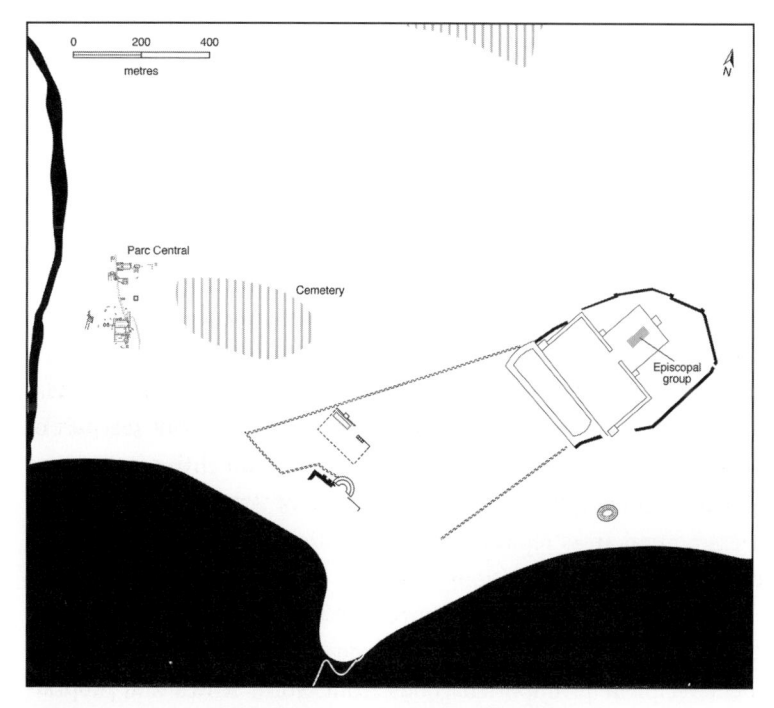

Fig. 9.1 Tarragona, main Christian areas in the fifth century

imperial cult), downhill from that another large colonnaded area interpreted as a 'provincial forum', and downhill again from that, and lying along its southern side, a circus; at the foot of the hill lay the second area: the city proper with its own public buildings and monuments. The monumental complex on top of the hill seems to have been maintained until the second quarter of the fifth century, when the main plaza started to be colonised by simple, domestic structures. Later in the century, cisterns for water storage were constructed (implying the failure of the aqueducts?). In the course of the sixth century, as at Valencia, the episcopal complex was established over part of the former temple, under the present, medieval cathedral (for this sequence, see Bosch Puche *et al.* 2005). From the fourth century, it would appear that the urban nucleus at the foot of the hill was progressively abandoned in favour of the harbour area outside the walls at the mouth of the river Francolí, with structures colonising the former public baths, the area characterised by a progressive decline in building techniques such as the disuse of mortar and ceramic tiles (Macias i Solé and Remolà Vallverdù 2005); why this settlement shift should have taken place is unclear, but it does argue for the importance of the exchange networks. Also outside the walls, necessarily, were three major religious sites (cf. p. 173): the basilica of Francolí with its baptistery; the basilica and associated buildings of Parc Central (interpreted as a monastery, but not certainly so – this was a major Christian complex which has been suggested to be the original episcopal area before the transfer to the hilltop); and, on the other side of the lower city, the church constructed in the amphitheatre to commemorate the martyrdom of Fructuosus, Eulogius and Augurius (TED'A 1990). It should be noted that the Francolí and Parc Central complexes were associated with extensive burial grounds, and there was another cemetery focused on the basilica of Fructuosus, all arguing for a continuing population, as does a ceramic sequence of local productions attesting to the interaction of the city and its hinterland (Macias i Solé 2003). At Tarragona, then, rather than a simple linear narrative of transition from late Roman to early medieval city essentially in the same place, or of the appropriation of the seat of the temporal power by the episcopal, we appear to have a much more profound remodelling, including a sort of centrifugality of urban form, with the former extramural areas replacing the intramural as centres of population and activity. But these populations and levels of activity seem still to have been significant, and we have seen above that Tarragona was part of a vital trade nexus through the fifth century; indeed, it seems to have been a prominent recipient of imported goods from North Africa and the East (Reynolds 2005).

At Barcelona (Arce *et al.* 2007: 314–16), sites such as the Plaça Sant Miquel and the calle Bisbe Caçador have revealed a large, well-appointed urban residence maintained and kept in good decorative order through the fifth century, suggesting the persistence of a wealthy urban aristocracy. The sites are a small sample, but, on the one hand, they do suggest for the fifth century that this was the period at which the armature and structures inherited from the High Empire were finally disused or dismantled as streets were built over and the former public monuments colonised and dismantled. On the other hand, there was continuing vitality, prosperity and a degree of wealth and social stratification similar to that from before the invasions in the early part of the century. The small amount of evidence available from the villas of the region (Chavarría Arnau 1996, 2006b, 2007: 114) seems to show at least the maintenance well into the fifth century of the structures and standards established in the fourth century, complementing the evidence from the urban sites. All in all, the economic vitality of the Iberian littoral in the fifth century seems to have reflected and supported a continuation of the standards of aristocratic life and display of earlier days. The fact that by the later fifth century this region was ruled by the Visigoths and North Africa by the Vandals seems to have had no effect on commercial currents; indeed, such ethnic designations are invisible in the archaeology of the economy. Nor are 'barbarians' at all easy to identify in the structures or material culture of the region (cf. Chavarría Arnau 2007: Ch. 4), more evidence for how thoroughly 'Romanised' both peoples, including crucially their elites, had become, especially in a region in close contact with developments in the traditional Mediterranean heartlands of the imperial culture.

A broadly similar picture can be painted for the cities of the Gallic section of the super-region, particularly for the two key cities of Arles and Marseille. Arles furnishes a good example of the way in which the monumental structures of the earlier city were turned over to new uses. In the heart of the city, the paved esplanade of the forum complex had been kept unencumbered for some four centuries, but early in the fifth century the surrounding colonnade was partially dismantled and simple, rectangular structures built over the stylobate and onto the paving (Heijmans 2004: 367–9; Sintès 1994: 182). To the north and just to the east of the imperial Baths of Constantine, the Commanderie Sainte-Luce site produced the only domestic building of any scale within the walls, dating to the turn of the fourth and fifth centuries (Heijmans 2004: 346–7). West of the probable imperial complex, a small excavation in the rue Truchet brought to light an instance of the colonisation of former public structures by small-scale domestic occupation. South of the late wall circuit (cf. p. 109) was an extensive area of occupation, revealed on several sites, many of them overlying some of the rich, earlier residences destroyed in the later third century (cf. p. 107). On the Esplanade site (Heijmans 2004: 350–3), this included a domestic structure to a larger scale than most, with two rooms and a courtyard fronted by a colonnade and dating to the turn of the fourth and fifth centuries (phase 6A). A little later (phase 6B), a new road or street was constructed along the eastern side of the building, deviating from the alignment of the earlier *cardo* to the west (Figure 9.2). The house seems to have been abandoned around the middle of the fifth century. Elsewhere in this zone, the evidence is for the partial reoccupation of the sumptuous, earlier residences which had been destroyed by fire, with some rooms

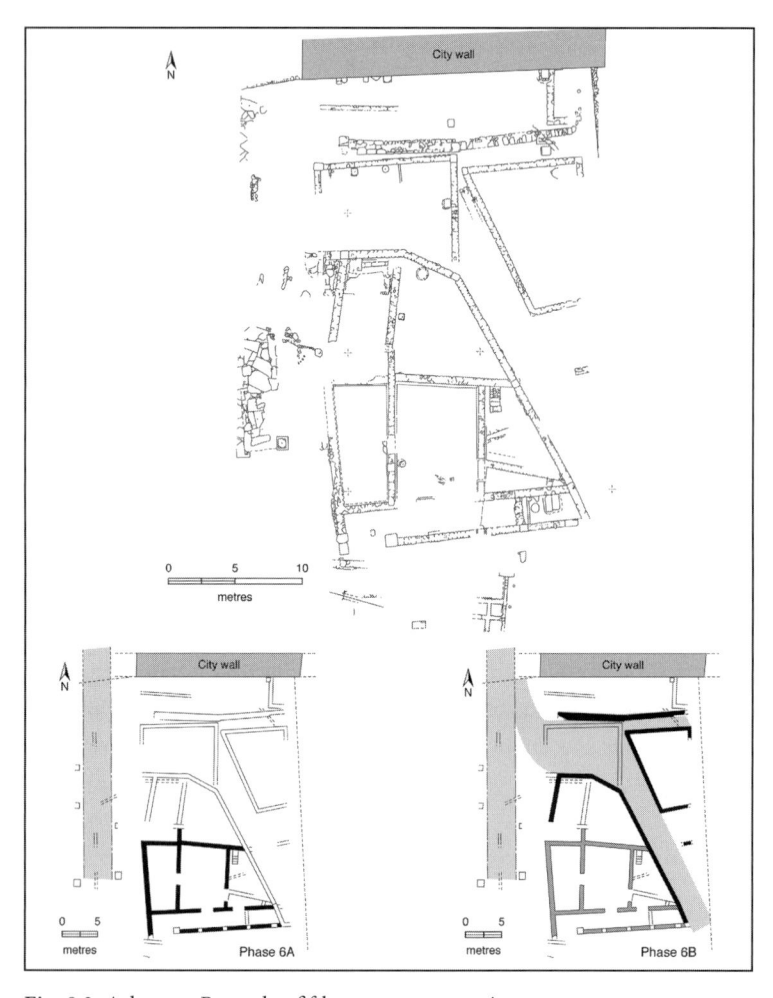

Fig. 9.2 Arles, rue Brossolet, fifth-century occupation

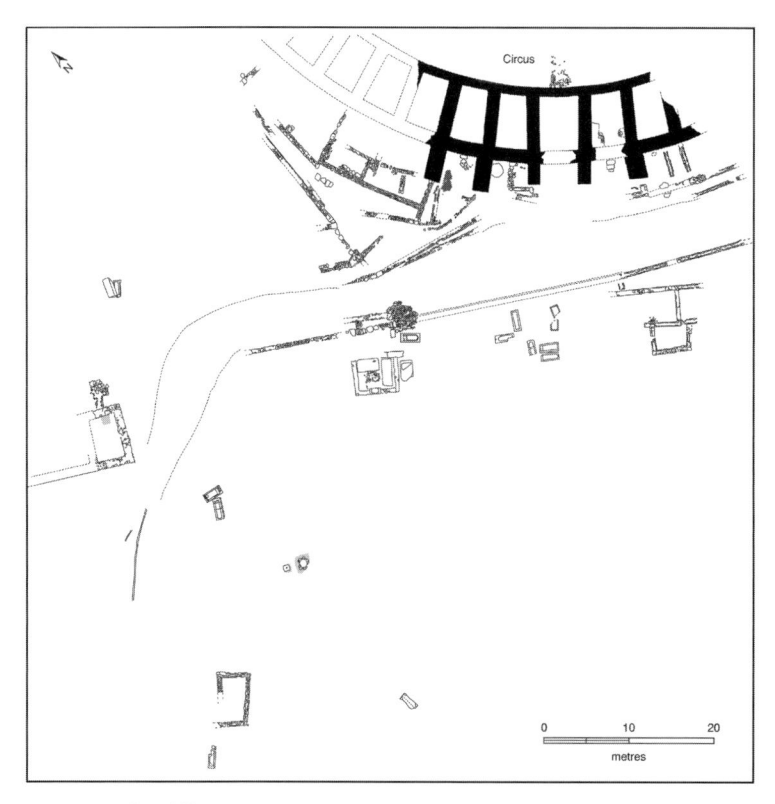

Fig. 9.3 Arles, fifth-century occupation round curved end of circus

cleared of their debris and the mosaic floors patched up, as, for instance, at the Crédit Agricole site (Heijmans 2004: 365–7). A remarkable situation has been revealed by the excavations at the south-western end of the circus (Heijmans 2004: 360–5), an area previously given over to burial (Figure 9.3). In the late fourth century, a wall was built some 30 m from the curved end, the *sphendone*, of the circus to define an area apart from the cemetery. Between the wall and the circus, a number of simple structures were built, including the reuse of earlier mausolea and breaking up of sarcophagi. This area was then covered by a thick build-up, onto which was laid a new road leading from the circus and past the cemetery to the Rhône. Subsequently, houses were created by colonising the cells which made up the curved end of the circus, supporting the seating banks, and by prolonging the lines of the buttresses at the outside end of the cells, thus creating two-room structures. Possibly similar late reuse of some of the cells along the northern long side of the circus was observed in earlier excavations. It is not known what was going on inside the circus, on the racetrack, at this date. Somewhere in the first half of the fifth century, possibly as the result of a major flood of the Rhône, this occupation was abandoned. In its place a new road was constructed outside the curve of the circus and leading to its interior through the cell on the long axis. Between this road and the façade of the circus were constructed new buildings. The circus and annexed structures were abandoned and dismantled from the later sixth century.

On the other side of the Rhône in the area of Trinquetaille, a similar pattern can be detected (Heijmans 2004: 353–8). On the one hand, excavations on the site of the ancient and modern cemetery revealed a large space surrounded by colonnades, which in the fifth century was probably densely occupied, to judge by the fragments of walls, floors and pits recovered. On the other hand, the excavation of the Verrerie and rue Pierre Brossolette sites revealed again instances of luxurious, earlier residences burnt down in the later third century and partially cleared and reoccupied in the fifth. It is interesting to note that almost any site excavated recently either within or outside the walled area has yielded evidence for this late occupation, suggesting that the population of Arles at the turn of the fourth and fifth centuries may actually have been increasing (some have linked this with the transfer of the seat of the praetorian prefecture of the Gauls from Trier to Arles at the start of the fifth century). On the other hand, the majority of the new buildings were simple one- or two-room structures or were parasitic within larger, earlier structures, suggesting a population of little wealth or status. These new areas were also associated with the laying out of new streets, respecting neither the alignment nor the quality of construction of the existing street grid, and there is some evidence from inside the walls (e.g. Commanderie Sainte-Luce) for encroachment on the earlier streets. Also evident is the colonisation of public buildings such as the forum and the circus. The amphitheatre of Arles (and its cousin at Nîmes) famously was filled with houses and became a defended quarter of the medieval city; the evidence both at Arles and from places such as the amphitheatre of Aix-en-Provence (Nin 2006) suggests that this process may well have originated in the fifth century. The impression of a still considerable population in the city is reinforced by the large cemeteries of fifth-century date outside the walls, most famously to the east and south-east in the Alyscamps but also across the river in the Trinquetaille area (Heijmans 2004: 260). The evidence for a continuing vitality and density of population is supported by the ceramic evidence, in particular the large quantities of North African and, later, Levantine imports – oil, wine, and tableware and cooking ware – arriving through the entrepôt at Marseille just down the coast (Reynolds 2005: 414–23). Emblematic of its position at the debouchement of the Rhône valley into the Mediterranean littoral, Arles also had large quantities of pottery from further north, particularly the *céramique luisante* from the upper Rhône. This vitality continued even after Arles was lost to the imperial authorities and fell under Ostrogothic suzerainty. Excavations have now revealed a major Christian basilica in the south-eastern angle of the walls, its construction dated to the sixth century (possibly under Bishop Caesarius) (Heijmans 2009).

Marseille from the fifth century on became the principal trading port of southern Gaul and thus up into the interior, acting as a gateway port for the commerce of the Mediterranean into the hinterland (Loseby 1992). In Marseille, unlike so many other cities of late Roman Gaul, the fourth and fifth centuries did not see a significant retraction of the occupied area. Instead, all excavations within the walled area have shown occupation of this period, with extramural occupation outside the east gate of the city spreading along the head of the inner harbour. The vitality of this city is confirmed by the number of large, fifth-century Christian churches and by the construction of an outer defensive wall in the area of the east gate in the last third of the century (Guyon 2005). This economic vitality can also be seen in the rural areas nearest to Marseille, with the presence of imported wares on a range of sites in western Provence and the lower Rhône corridor (Carru *et al.* 2001; Pellecuer and Pomarèdes 2001; Trément 2001). These sites included villas functioning in the fourth century and persisting well into the fifth. East of the Rhône, these tend to be relatively modest, workaday establishments presumably creating and processing the grain, oil, wine and animals needed to support Marseille and feed its exchange economy. It is possible therefore that the lack of ostentation at these sites may be because the wealth they created was being expended in Marseille itself (or in other cities such as Aix-en-Provence, Fréjus or Riez). West of the Rhône, in Languedoc, villas also continued to be occupied, but increasingly as functional estate centres rather than luxury residences. This is particularly clear at Roquemaure and Saint-André-de-Codols (cf. Chapter 7, p. 290), where the residential areas were abandoned while keeping the productive areas and adding to them. The always rather exceptional villa at Loupian (cf. p. 249) in fact saw its period of greatest elaboration of plan and decoration in the first half of the fifth century, but by the end of that century much of this had been suppressed, and the result was something much more functional. The evidence, largely from field survey but with some trial excavation, for non-villa settlements, concurs in general with the picture of continued occupation and economic activity through much of the fifth century.

East of the Rhône (Trément 1999, 2001), there is abundant evidence for dispersed settlement at a range of sizes above and below 1 ha. Though the number of settlements was well down on that for the second century, there were new settlements being created still in the fifth century, and this period does seem to have marked the beginning of a long period of stable settlement and population of the area. These settlements seem principally to have been mixed agrarian with not only evidence for cereals, olives and vines but also considerable evidence for the raising of stock and occasionally salt making, all at levels suggesting the production of considerable surpluses. A generally similar picture obtains west of the lower Rhône (Raynaud 2001), where the fifth century, though with many fewer settlements than the second century, again shows stabilisation and the beginning of a settlement pattern that was in essence to persist well into the early medieval period. A possible scenario for the considerable changes between the second and fourth/fifth centuries has already been outlined (p. 286), involving a settling back from an over-exploitation of the carrying capacity of the area. In this case, the fifth century would be part of the realignment of the productive capacity of the land to its longer-term capacity. Sites of this period have produced evidence for implication in the west Mediterranean commercial nexus, with finds of North African and Levantine amphorae and tableware; indeed, for the fourth century, imports were running at twice the level of those of the second. Rather than direct contact with the trade and traders, it is perhaps easier to envisage these commodities being obtained through urban centres (Arles and Marseille especially?) in exchange for the surplus produce of these territories. It should also be noted that the Mediterranean littoral and the lower valley of the Rhône in the fifth century were still supporting and were integrated with more localised ceramic industries such as the *céramique luisante* of the Rhône corridor or the *kaolinitique* and *pisolithique* wares of Languedoc and the Rhône delta (Bonifay and Raynaud 2007: esp. Fig. 80, p. 147).

The data available from Catalonia (e.g. Gurt i Esparraguera and Palet Martínez 2001) are congruent with the picture from Provence and Languedoc, though the systematic evidence from the *Ager Tarraconensis* (Prevosti and Guitart i Duran 2011: 397) shows a marked decline in the visibility of settlement because of the small amounts of pottery of the period yielded to field survey; also the pottery is increasingly local rather than imported. The main feature of the period defined for this survey as 'late antique' (the fifth to the seventh centuries) is the disappearance of the bulk of the villas, suggesting the collapse of the domanial system of exploitation. Some of the villas in their later phase show a change to more workaday activities and installations, suggesting that their agrarian functions become more important than their display ones, rather as was happening to the north of the Pyrenees in Languedoc and Provence.

One other field of expenditure worth drawing attention to, certainly for southern Gaul, is churches. Recent excavations have examined a number of relatively large basilican churches whose scale and furnishings (marble, mosaic and carved marble and other sarcophagi) attest to very considerable wealth being invested in their construction. These include the funerary basilicas of Saint-Victor, the rue Malaval at Marseille (Moliner 2006), with its remarkable marble *memoria*, and the Clos de la Lombarde at Narbonne (Solier 1991), as well as the new episcopal basilica on the island of Maguelone near Montpellier; there is also the unusual basilica near the Loupian villa (p. 186). Clearly, there was still considerable wealth to be extracted from the agriculture of the region; equally clearly, this was a new arena for aristocratic patronage and display.

The Iberian interior

If, then, the coastal areas of Iberia and southern Gaul demonstrated a considerable measure of continuing late Roman settlement and expenditure on established and new forms of display (villas, churches, and food and drink and its consumption), what of the areas away from the Mediterranean façade? Here we shall look at the interior of Iberia, in particular the northern Meseta and southern Portugal, first considering the very limited evidence for developments at the cities, and then discussing the more extensive and revealing suites of evidence from villas and other rural sites. In the interior of Iberia, the best excavation to date on an area of urban housing is that at the Morería in Mérida (see Alba Calzado 2005 for a summary). In Chapter 3 (p. 138), we saw that this area just inside the riverside walls was occupied by some thirteen residences, including a courtyard house of some pretensions in its plan and appointments, the 'Casa de los Mármoles'. One of the major pieces of evidence for the state of fifth-century Mérida is the inscription recording the restoration of the bridge over the Guadiana undertaken by Bishop Zeno with the Visigothic notable Salla in 483. Just a little downstream from the bridge, the Morería excavations revealed fifth-century additions (reusing stone from public buildings and funerary monuments) to the front of the Augustan walls, which virtually doubled their thickness. Within these strengthened defences, the houses on the Morería site demonstrate a number of common features (Figure 9.4) characterising their development in the fifth century (Mateos Cruz 2005: 130–8). Internal

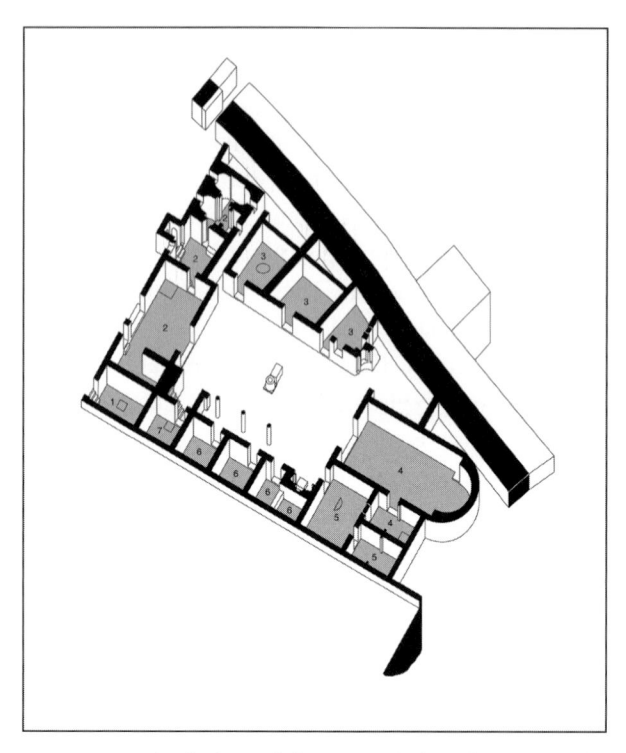

Fig. 9.4 Mérida, the 'Casa de los Mármoles' residence as subdivided in the fifth century

peristyles tended to be suppressed to create instead an internal courtyard onto which rooms now fronted. These rooms were no longer the spaces of varying use characteristic of the fourth-century residences but now attested largely to the compartmentalisation of the residences into multiple-occupancy buildings consisting of units of single rooms, or sometimes two or three, opening onto the streets or internal courtyards. Specific areas of the earlier residences such as baths or kitchens lost their particular functions and became simple spaces. The marble and other decoration of the residences were stripped away, and the floors and common areas tended to be of beaten earth. Hearths, ovens and small furnaces demonstrate the use of the rooms either for occupation or for small-scale artisan activity, including in one case bronze working. There was some evidence for areas reserved for animals. Elsewhere in the city (Mateos Cruz 2005: 139–47), simple one-room structures, or rows thereof, were inserted into former public spaces such as the 'Forum of the Colonia' or the precinct of the amphitheatre. Overall, the picture is of a fifth-century city still relatively intensively occupied, but at a far lower level of material comfort than earlier and with far less social differentiation; former aristocratic residences now played host to a series of families that had divided up the spaces which had previously served to house one family and its dependants. Previously, this might have been characterised as 'squatter occupation', but instead it can now be seen as a rational reapportionment of space in response to changing social frameworks in the population and in the function and priorities of a city, recalling somewhat what we have already seen for Arles. Historical sources speak of more than one attack on the city in the course of the fifth century, suggesting that the former capital of the *diocesis Hispaniarum* was still worth the taking.

The fate of the villas of the interior and south-east of Iberia was for a long time simply linked to the invasions of the Vandals, Sueves and others in the early part of the fifth century, followed by the warfare provoked by their territorial claims, and then the Visigothic takeover of the peninsula in the latter part of the century. These destroyed the economic prosperity, craft specialisation and aristocratic class on which such showcase residences depended. One mechanism by which the lives of these sites were sometimes apparently prolonged was their conversion into Christian sites, as attested to by the well-known site of the Villa Fortunatus (Huesca), where excavations in 1926–36 revealed a room in the south-eastern part of a peristyle villa which had been converted into a church, with a baptistery added later, probably associated with the laying of the eponymous mosaic where the name *Fortunatus* appears either side of a chi-rho. Such a channel of communication from classical antiquity to the Christian Visigothic kingdom and thus into the Catholicism of medieval and *reconquista* Spain was in tune with the ideology of the Franco period. More recent excavations and the reassessment of older excavations, along with an opening-up of intellectual horizons and thus of possible causes, have produced a more complex picture (Chavarría Arnau 2007; cf. López Quiroga 2006). In Chapter 5 (p. 251), we saw that at many villas of the eastern littoral the fourth and fifth centuries were marked by an increased emphasis on productive capacity, as evidenced by the insertion of *dolia* and presses into residential areas. This is not a pattern found in the interior or Portugal, apart from some traces at Carranque. Instead, the more general picture, as at the urban 'Casa de los Mármoles', is of the subdivision of space, the insertion of structures into and onto high-quality earlier floors, the use of timber and clay in place of stone, and a general diminution in the size and appointments of structures (Chavarría Arnau 2007: 129–33), the sort of evidence formerly characterised as 'squatter occupation' (cf. Lewit 2003, 2004). Three sites in the centre of the peninsula act as good examples. At El Val (Madrid) (Chavarría Arnau 2007: 74, 131, 233–5 and references), the rectangular, principal reception room saw a series of post holes dug through the extensive fourth-century mosaic floor. These post holes enclosed a rectangular space 14 by 9 m, a little smaller than the existing room, with other post holes defining subdivisions of the main space – there were also a hearth and an oven. The dating is not secure, and possibly lies in the second half of the fifth century. The interpretation of this structure, supposedly of North European 'longhouse' type and thus representing the settlement of Germanic peoples at the villa, is even more debatable; reconstruction by local people is equally possible. Similar evidence of post holes, along with slight walls, storage silos and detritus, has been found recently at Tinto Juan de la Cruz (Madrid), where again the presence of weaponry, including a Simancas-type dagger, has been used to propose a Visigothic presence (Chavarría Arnau 2007: 231–2 and references). At La Torrecilla (Madrid) (Chavarría Arnau 2007: 230–1 and references), meticulous excavation of a fourth-century, peristyle villa showed that in the fifth century, after a fire in the southern wing with the principal reception rooms, new, stone-and-mortar partition walls were constructed within the late Roman structure. These in turn were succeeded by slighter, drystone walls overlying rubble deposits. Both phases were associated with numerous storage silos. At El Val and at Tinto, there was a sixth-century cemetery; there was a small amount of supposed Visigothic material at Tinto, but none at El Val. The dominance of the textual tradition led to these burials being typed as 'Visigothic', and thus the successors to the fifth-century occupants, but in fact the archaeology can be made to support such a conclusion only with great difficulty; the burial grounds look much more likely to be those of the local population using the then available material culture.

These stratigraphic and functional sequences at these sites can be paralleled at many others and they raise a series of questions. Firstly, how long did high-status occupation in the late Roman style continue? It is at present difficult to be certain (Chavarría Arnau 2007: 115–16) because of the problems of the dating evidence, as several sites involved early, non-stratigraphic excavations. Nevertheless, there are a small number of new mosaics dated to the fifth century in the Ebro basin, as at Liédena, or further west, as at Navatajera (León), dated by association with late forms of TSHT and coins of the House of Theodosius. It seems likely that the traditions of aristocratic living and self-representation current through the fourth century continued into the first half of the fifth century. But it does appear that from the middle of the fifth century it is increasingly difficult to detect this sort of tradition of aristocratic display, though we must note the extraordinary and probably late fifth-century mosaic from Estada (Huesca) (Chavarría Arnau 2007: 195–6).

Secondly, is what succeeds to the late villas evidence for a complete redefinition of rural society and economy? We enter the world of the colonisation of villa buildings by timber structures: sometimes, as at El Val, respecting the existing structure; sometimes, as at La Torrecilla and Tinto, reordering it. The ways in which the pre-existing late Roman structures continued to govern the overall spatial patterning of the uses of the sites and of particular new constructions shows that it is far more likely that we are dealing with adaptation to new priorities rather than a clean sweep of what had gone before. This is, of course, not a purely rural phenomenon; it is just the rural version of the *habitat parasitaire* we have encountered at a number of cities in the fifth century. Moreover, as we have seen for La Torrecilla and Tinto, many of these villa sites became the location of cemeteries (some with 'Visigothic' material), dating from the later fifth and into the sixth and seventh centuries (Chavarría Arnau 2007: 134–7). This is quite widespread in the northern Meseta and very common in the north-west in Galicia. The cemeteries often are situated in the ruins of the villa; indeed, they mark the end of that form of habitat, but since they can often be associated with contemporaneous occupation of other areas of the site, they do not attest to the abandonment of the site as such. The insertion of burials into late Roman buildings is again a phenomenon not restricted to rural sites. It is well attested to on urban ones also, and the significance of the choice of abandoned Roman buildings for burial is one that is poorly, if at all, understood.

Thirdly, mention of burials and cemeteries leads to the model of the development of some sites into Christian foci and the related question of whether this is evidence for the alienation of landed estates to the Church. We have already seen (Chapters 3 and 5) that there is evidence for Christianity at some villas already in the fourth century, as is only to be expected, and this takes the form of buildings for worship, of burial places and mausolea, and of objects. We have already noted the Villa Fortunatus (p. 182 and Figure 4.15), where part of the main residential building was converted into a church or private chapel or oratory, which went through several successive phases including the addition of a baptistery (Chavarría Arnau 2007: 146). Interestingly, only a small number of burials are associated with the church, all inside it and in significant positions, suggesting important members of the community: the family that owned the villa? Other cases of the conversion of parts of the residential buildings of villas can be traced at sites such as the late fifth-/early sixth-century conversion of part of the baths of the villa at El Saucedo (Toledo) into a 15 by 8 m church. Probably rather more common was the creation of a church in the vicinity of a villa through adaptation of an existing building. An example of this is the basilica (cf. p. 183 and Figure 4.16) constructed close to the villa of Torre de Palma (Alto Alentejo) (Maloney and Hale 1996; Maloney and Ringbom 2005), over what may have been a temple of a traditional cult, though the early (fourth-century) date for this complex proposed by the excavators has been challenged (e.g. Chavarría Arnau 2007: 149–50). Interestingly, a very similar structure to that at Torre de Palma has been located by aerial photography near the villa of Las Calaveras (Valladolid); surface material dates from the fifth century on (Chavarría Arnau 2007: 152, 222–3). In the same region as Torre de Palma, the temple at the Milreu villa became the focus of a burial ground, one where later a baptistery was added. The very similar temple at São Cucufate was also turned over to funerary use, though, as there is no evidence for the religious affiliations of the burials, one must be careful in assuming they were Christian, a point which applies equally to other cemeteries annexed to mausolea or other structures proposed to represent the Christianisation of the villa owners. So there is evidence for Christian places of worship and burial grounds at some villas, some of them contemporaneous with the main occupation of the villa in the fourth or early fifth century, and some of them constructed later after the abandonment of the residential quarters. This is entirely to be expected in a context where the aristocracies of the Late Empire were increasingly leaving the traditional religions for the new, imperially sanctioned one. Much more debatable is whether there is sufficient evidence to propose or demonstrate a coherent pattern of conversion of family and buildings, one which then carried through into the Middle Ages, a question not helped by the many cases in which a medieval church has been found to overlie a Roman building and an assumption of cultic continuity is made without the detailed archaeological evidence that would be necessary to support this assumption. Even more difficult to tell would be cases where a villa or estate was alienated to the Church, since proprietorial rights do not show up well in archaeological evidence. Nevertheless, a religious vocation was clearly one of the range of possible 'after lives' of a late Roman villa in Iberia.

Fourthly, what can we tell of the economic basis of these sites from the later fifth century? The evidence from sites such as Congosto, La Torrecilla, Tinto Juan de la Cruz and others of silos for grain storage shows that they were still centres for agricultural production, probably producing a usable surplus. If so, then we have not an absolute collapse of the productive economy, but a relative, probably serious, one; in this case we would be looking not at a total impoverishment of the population but again a relative one, and one combined with a redirection of the objects of expenditure of such surplus as there was, away from the late Roman villa tradition. This argues for some sort of continuing elite or aristocracy and thus for a form of society where such a class played an important economic and social role through its command over people and resources and over the deployment of the latter, though this must have been on a far smaller scale and with markedly less social differentiation than in the fourth century.

That there was a continuing mobilisation of resources on the fifth-century Meseta by some sort of aristocracy, and thus some form of economic circulation and activity, is supported by the ceramic evidence of the latter part of the TSHT industry. In Chapter 7, this regional-scale industry was argued to be a marker both of the continuing vitality of a city-centred marketing nexus and of the stimulation supplied by demand from the aristocracy of the region and their involvement in the imperial fiscal system (cf. p. 323). The fate of the TSHT industries after the turn of the fourth and fifth centuries is very poorly understood. It does seem still to be present in dated deposits down to the middle of the fifth century at least, though in diminishing absolute quantities and with an increasingly restricted distribution (Paz Peralta 1991). From the mid fifth century on, the existence of this industry, of its forms and its distribution, becomes very difficult to trace, and we have the impression of an industry that has either ceased to operate or has devolved to very localised and derivative productions. The coincidence in this chronology with that for the villa culture of the northern Meseta is striking, again suggesting the importance of the demand engendered by the elite, their surpluses and their modes of expenditure, along with the effect of the termination of that demand. From the middle of the fifth century, both the surpluses available to the elite and their modes of expenditure appear to have changed radically and to the detriment of the TSHT industries, which seem to have been replaced by very local industries, as in the Duero valley (Larrén *et al.* 2003) or further north in the Basque country (Azkarate Garai-Olun *et al.* 2003), though it is worth underlining that there did continue to be such industries, and their localised distributions nevertheless attest to a persisting level of local and subregional economic activity and integration.

Southern Gaul

As we move north of the Pyrenees into south-western and south-eastern Gaul, some of the same patterns and rhythms may be discerned. An important city where there have been revealing recent excavations is Toulouse, which retained its long, early imperial wall circuit. At Place

Esquirol in the monumental centre of the *colonia*, the main temple or *capitolium* was systematically demolished and cleared away at the turn of the fourth and fifth centuries, as the abundant material from the destruction deposits attests to. The open area which had surrounded the temple underwent modifications, with the paving partially removed and a new street laid to the west of the surviving podium. At the turn of the fifth and sixth centuries, the presence of post holes, pits and other features indicates occupation of the simplest kind (Boudartchouk *et al*. 2002: 443–5). To the east, near the probable site of the episcopal complex, the rue Saint-Jacques/rue Sainte-Anne excavations (Catalo and Cazes 2002: 419–21) showed a section of one of the wide, north–south *decumani* maintained into the fifth century, but by the end of that century it was already suffering significant encroachment, which was to culminate in the early sixth century with the street reduced to a narrow alley on a rather different alignment to the earlier *decumanus* (Figure 9.5). Nevertheless, this encroachment consisted of residential buildings, even if to simple plans, attesting to a continuing occupation destroyed in the middle of the sixth century. The proximity of the episcopal group may explain the persistence of occupation in this part of the city.

Toulouse furnishes us with the best examples of what was happening to urban space and habitat in the fifth century in south-western Gaul. Other cities give occasional glimpses of what was happening in this period (Heijmans 2006a, 2006b), as, for instance, at Bordeaux, where the densely packed, large, richly decorated houses of central îlot Saint-Christoly in the fourth century gave way in places to simpler structures of a lower standard of construction and decoration, but nonetheless still elaborate compared with what was going on at Arles. In south-eastern Novempopulana, there is evidence for continuing occupation in the 'lower town' of Saint-Bertrand-de-Comminges during the fifth century, with mosaics being laid in one major residence and a church constructed close by (Guyon 2003). This was after the fortification of the 'upper town' early in the century, which arguably led to an intensification of occupation there (Esmonde Cleary and Wood 2005: 197–204) with, by the end of the fifth century, occupation in the 'lower town' increasingly restricted to discontinuous foci of activity (Esmonde Cleary 2007a: 139–40). Nevertheless, the small area enclosed within the hilltop defences at Saint-Bertrand and other 'urban' sites in Novempopulana, such as Oloron or Saint-Lizier (cf. Esmonde Cleary 2004), by comparison with the fortifications of central and northern Gaul, suggests that the view of what needed to be fortified had become similarly restricted to a strongpoint or *cité administrative*, a pattern reflected in the

Fig. 9.5 Toulouse, rue Sainte-Anne, development of street and occupation from the first to the end of the fifth century

fifth-century fortifications of the south-east (for these fortifications, see pp. 133–35).

As to villas in the south-west, essentially the provinces of Novempopulana and Aquitania II, the flourishing villa culture of the fourth century (see Chapter 5, p. 245) continued into the first half of the fifth. The type site for the consideration of late developments in the villas of the area is that of Séviac (cf. p. 218). By the late fourth century, this was a large villa arranged round a central, peristyle court, its colonnades and many rooms equipped with much marble and a variety of mosaics. From pavilions at the south-east and south-west angles ran curving colonnades linking the main residence to a bathhouse that had been progressively elaborated until, after a major reconstruction in the late fourth century, it was a substantial, elaborate, and lavishly equipped and decorated complex (Lapart and Petit 1993: 266–83), with a fragment of a glass cage cup (p. 234) witness to the richness of the portable equipment. Further mosaics, in a somewhat different tradition from the existing ones, were laid, probably in the first half of the fifth century (Balmelle 2001: 386–90), and the villa seems to have continued in use through the greater part of that century. The evidence of lightly constructed walls dividing the earlier rooms, post holes and hearths, some of them placed on earlier mosaics, suggests that by the later fifth century the nature of the occupation had changed substantially; unfortunately, features of this date are not well recorded or understood. Perhaps towards the end of the fifth century or early in the sixth, the south-east pavilion, consisting of a rectangular chamber with a southern apse, was modified (Lapart and Paillet 1991). A northern apse was added in which was installed a baptismal basin (Figure 9.6). Subsequently, a small rectangular extension was added to the centre of the eastern side of the chamber, soon replaced by a square 'nave' with a semicircular apse associated with other rooms. This would seem to have been a small Christian place of worship, including baptism. At the same general time, a simple church or chapel was built further to the east, consisting of a rectangular nave with a rectangular 'chancel'; perhaps this was for general liturgical use, with the baptistery complex reserved for that sacrament alone. A cemetery developed around this building, and when the complex with the baptismal basin went out of use, this cemetery expanded over the ruins of this part of the villa, with the rectangular chapel continuing in use until the later seventh or eighth century.

This sequence, for all the problems of lack of definitive publication and of shaky dating, has proved a focus for discussion of what it means in terms of the transition from antiquity to the early Middle Ages. Discussions have tended to concentrate on the Christian area in the south-east of the site, seeing it as a paradigm of a double shift – on the one hand, the move of the estate owners from the traditional religions to the new Christianity, and, on the other hand, a shift of the site from a substantial residence belonging to an aristocrat and inhabited by his household and retainers to more of a communal social structure, represented by the cemetery and its encroachment on the former elite space, with a material culture suggesting no marked gradations of status. The recovery from the baths courtyard of a 'Visigothic' bone comb with the semicircular projection characteristic of combs of the Sîntana de Mureș-Chernyakhov culture could add another layer to the debate over ownership: was it Gallo-Roman or a location where

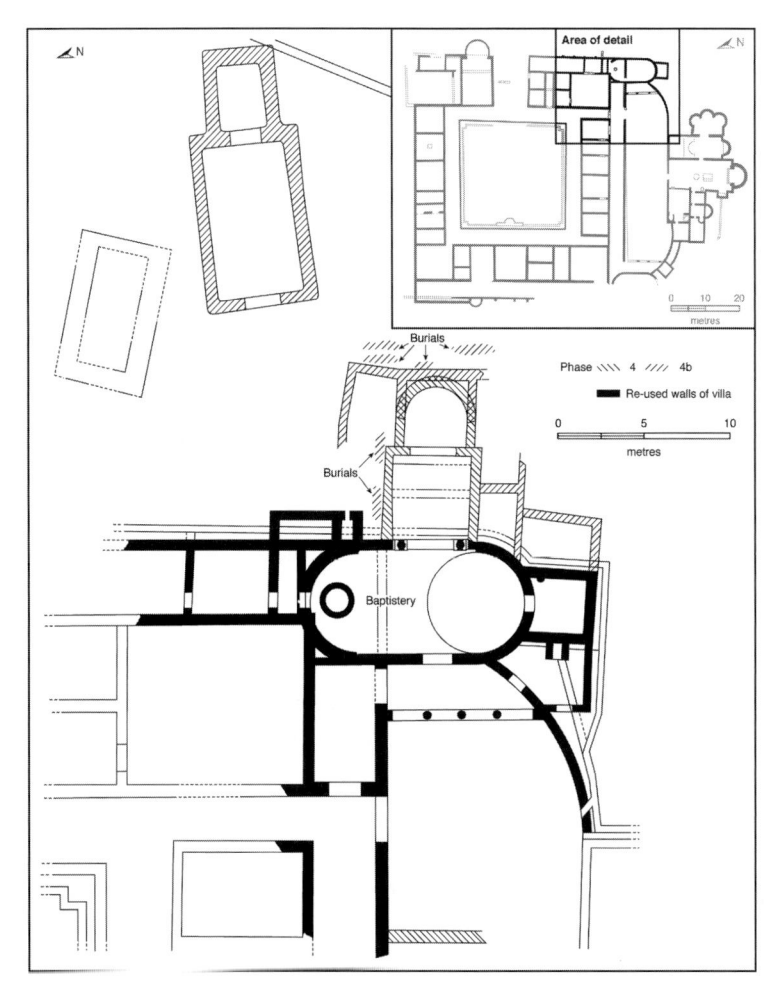

Fig. 9.6 (Montréal-)Séviac, fifth- to seventh-century Christian installations in the south-eastern angle of the villa

a Visigothic incomer was imposed on and supported by an existing aristocratic estate? It has also been seen as a paradigm of how an estate might have continued in being as property and as a productive unit even when the grand house lay in ruins. More recently, the fugitive traces of the late reorderings of the main buildings have been taken as emblematic of two different visions of social developments in this period of transition: the one (Lewit 2003) arguing for its still being a unitary residence in the hands of an aristocratic family, but one whose diminished circumstances led to a very different form of self-representation; the other (Bowes and Gutteridge 2005) arguing that, to the contrary, there is no trace of high-status occupation, so a single, aristocratic family cannot be posited – rather, the evidence for subdivision and for hearths suggests occupation by more than one group or family who divided up the shell of the building. This latter pattern would certainly accord with some of the suggestions put forward for south of the Pyrenees, such as those for the villa of La Torecilla or the urban 'Casa de los Mármoles' at Mérida.

But Séviac also demonstrates many of the pitfalls in trying to reconstruct the fifth-century and later development of the villa and its significance in this region. First, it is the only villa of the south-west to have been fairly fully and fairly carefully excavated (or at least its residential parts; the agricultural dependencies were, as usual, ignored). Thus our evidence set for other sites is much patchier, with the risk of assimilation to the Séviac 'model'. Secondly, the dating evidence is far less certain than desirable, especially for the mosaics on which so many of the later dates are based (cf. Balmelle 2001: 238–40). Down to the close of the fourth century, dating of features such as construction or the laying of mosaics does benefit from coins and pottery, though single coins are of dubious value. At some villas, later mosaics were superposed on existing ones, and these show the same sort of stylistic shift as seen as Séviac, suggesting that a mosaic repertoire dating to the first third of the fifth century can be identified. Further stylistic developments are then dated by reference to the North African and even Syrian mosaic repertoire (Balmelle 2001: 258–61), clearly leaving increasing margins of error. Thirdly, this is a testimony to another systemic problem, related in part to restricted excavation of sites, the lack of good, stratified and datable sequences which can be used to establish a regional chrono-stratigraphy, particularly for the regional fine ware, DSP. This is under way for DSP and for local coarse wares (e.g. Dieulafait 2006), but will take time to establish. A dating medium that is already beginning to prove its worth for this region is glass (Foy and Hochuli-Gysel 1995), but again further well-stratified deposits are needed.

Nevertheless, evidence from the re-excavation of villas such as Castelculier-Lamarque (Lot et Garonne) and Moncrabeau-Bapteste (Lot et Garonne) or re-evaluation of a classic site such as Montmaurin does show developments analogous to those observed at Séviac. At Castelculier (Jacques 2006: 79–92), the end of the fourth century also saw the elaboration of an architecturally ambitious set of baths with modifications into the first half of the fifth century. But towards the end of that century, the bath suite was demolished and much of it fed into a huge limekiln, leaving only a large, rectangular chamber with an apse. This latter could be interpreted as a church, but the internal arrangements of the apse look far from liturgical.

Even so, the late fifth century seems to be a major horizon of change at this villa, one of the first where there is good dating from DSP. At Moncrabeau-Bapteste (Jacques 2006: 92–101), re-excavation of the principal entrance showed late, probably fifth-century, post holes and other features, including a probable grain silo, penetrating the earlier, good-quality floors. The earlier excavations yielded fifth- and sixth-century pottery as well as two 'Visigothic' combs. The well-known site at Montmaurin, though claimed by its excavator (Fouet 1969) to have been destroyed by fire at the end of the fourth century, clearly survived it, and there are traces of late, slight walls and other features redefining the interior spaces. So, for the villas of this region of Gaul, it looks as though their major lines of development in the fifth century and later will be similar overall to those of their cousins of the northern Meseta, with the period of greatest elaboration in the later fourth century and persisting into the earlier fifth century, before gradual degradation, subdivision and changes to other uses, including funerary, set in from the second half of the fifth century.

Mention has been made of the importance in the fifth century in the south-west of the regional facies of DSP, the 'Atlantic' productions of Bordeaux and its immediate area, uniformly reduced, grey wares. Though the precise sequences and dating remain to be finalised, it is clear that the fifth century was the *floruit* of this ware and that it was widely available within south-western Gaul and also reached further – for instance, to the Atlantic coast of Iberia (perhaps connected with the long-distance Atlantic routes) and up as far as the Seine and the Paris Basin, albeit sporadically. This would seem to be good evidence for the existence of a considerable commercial nexus in south-western Gaul, probably in important part mediated through urban centres such as Bordeaux itself, Toulouse and Saint-Bertrand-de-Comminges, supporting the contention that these places still had important commercial functions. The evidence from cities such as Saint-Bertrand (Dieulafait 2006) or Toulouse (Dieulafait *et al.* 2002), not only for the DSP but also for more local wares, sometimes imitating DSP, again argues in favour of a continuing city-based, marketing pattern. To the east, in Languedoc, Provence and the Rhône valley, this was also the heyday of the *céramique luisante* industries (p. 318), with a wide distribution over the south-eastern quarter of Gaul; indeed, some of their forms and decorations are hard to tell apart from the south-eastern 'Languedocian' facies of the DSP industries, which were also flourishing through the early to mid fifth century in the hinterland of the North African-dominated littoral. If anything, these industries right across southern Gaul from the Atlantic to the Mediterranean seem to have been displaying even more vigour than the

TSHT of the northern part of Iberia. So southern Gaul could colourably be argued to have been enjoying a period of economic prosperity through at least the first half of the fifth century, and in the south-west some of the proceeds of this were still being expended on the traditional aristocratic theatre of display, the villa (and to an extent the urban *domus*). This, it should be noted, is at precisely the time when the south-west had fallen under 'barbarian' domination with the settlement of the Visigoths from 419 (cf. Chapter 8, p. 357). Whatever the precise legal and fiscal circumstances of this settlement under the terms of *hospitalitas* (cf. Chapter 8, p. 358), it is clear that the Visigoths were settled within an existing social and financial system which it behoved them not to disturb. Moreover, culturally, they were probably to a considerable degree Romanised, after forty years on imperial territory, and Christianised (albeit Arians). The archaeology, such as it is (p. 360), of their presence in the early to mid fifth century, and more particularly the archaeology of the villas and the economy, suggests that they at the least did not disturb unduly the *status quo*; indeed, they may actually have enhanced it. In this respect they were comparable with their contemporaries and descendants on the Mediterranean coasts of Iberia and, of course, their Ostrogothic cousins in Italy. The period of their increased cultural visibility, from the late fifth century, coincides with the end of the high villa culture of the south-west. This is most certainly not to propose a simple cause-and-effect argument, but rather to suggest a combination of changed circumstances at the end of the fifth century that will be looked at further below.

Northern Gaul

When we turn to the north of Gaul, the picture becomes hard to grasp because of the difficulties in recovering good stratigraphic sequences through the fifth century and then of dating them. As we shall see, this is perhaps even more of a problem at urban sites, whereas recent excavations on rural sites and complexes have started to give us a picture of developments. Perhaps the best way to approach the question will be to start with the evidence for the degree of economic activity and the importance and distances of exchange patterns to try to apprehend some sense of the vitality and levels of integration of the region, before going on to the problematic evidence for urban and rural settlement.

In the fourth century, the dominant regional fine ware was Argonne (p. 320), which was widely distributed from the Rhine to the Loire, most probably through a combination of movement along with the *annona* to the

Rhineland and of market-oriented commercial movement in the interior of northern Gaul, though even there the evident military units and *fabricae* may have affected the distribution mechanisms. Other industries such as Mayen (*Eifelkeramik*) also existed, in this case with a strong Rhineland bias, and the Jaulges/Villiers-Vineux industry and its imitators, supplying Burgundy and up into the Ile-de-France. In the latter part of the fourth century, two ceramic traditions that were to become very important in the following century were developing, *céramique granuleuse* and/or *céramique rugueuse*, a coarse, functional fabric produced in a range of forms and increasingly widely available. The start of the fifth century saw a range of developments. The Jaulges/Villiers-Vineux industry (Jacob and Leredde 1985) and its imitators ceased production, so far as can be ascertained, in the years soon after 400. On the other hand, Argonne continued to be produced, as can be demonstrated both by the relative chronology of new stamp types (including Christian symbols) (see Van Ossel 2011c) and by the absolute dating afforded by a limited number of datable deposits such as the destruction/abandonment deposits of the Barbarathermen at Trier (Böhner 1958) and the structures in the 'Grand Amphithéâtre' at Metz (Bayard 1990). The overall distribution range of these products remained extensive, covering much of the north of Gaul, though, so far as can be ascertained from a limited number of sites with quantified deposits (Van Ossel 1996), the amount of these products reaching the sites declined in the course of the first half of the fifth century. It seems that by the last third of that century the industry's output was on a much smaller scale than a century earlier and covering a far smaller area, with a limited range of products. Nevertheless, it does remain evidence for a regional or subregional level of contact and integration in northern Gaul.

Alongside Argonne, there is evidence for contact further afield in the form of DSP from the Bordeaux area, now being recognised on an increasing number of sites up as far as the Seine (cf. Van Ossel 2006: 326, 2011a); interestingly, this is generally dated to the mid to late fifth century as Argonne's distribution diminished (and the same time as DSP was gaining more of a foothold in northern Iberia [p. 477]). The small number of Mediterranean amphorae (North African and east Mediterranean) known from northern Gaul may suggest a continuing demand for their contents, which from their rarity must have been a status marker for the lay or ecclesiastical elites. But the bulk of ceramics datable to the fifth century consist of the *granuleuse/rugueuse* tradition, produced in and around the Paris Basin and suggesting a continuing level of trade and integration across much of northern Gaul through the fifth and into the sixth century, when the fabric was also produced in 'Merovingian' forms; that is to say, such forms as the biconical urn with stamped decoration. One other medium that may prove to be as useful, if not more so, for dating and evidence of contacts is glass. A comprehensive typology for the forms found on occupation sites and especially in burials in north-eastern Gaul has recently been published (Feyeux 2003), and a dating sequence has been established, though the implications of this, both for the dating of sites and for the social role of glass in habitation and burial sites, have yet to be worked through.

The artefactual material, pottery and glass, clearly shows that the northern part of Gaul remained to some extent integrated at a regional level (pottery and glass) and at a variety of subregional and local levels (pottery). From this material we can also derive a dating sequence, however approximate, through the fifth century and on into the sixth. What, then, of the types of sites, occupation in particular but also burial, from which it is recovered? Most difficult to understand are the former cities of the north of Gaul and the Rhineland. For a long time this was because it was assumed that they did not survive the invasions of the early fifth century in any significant form. More recent excavations and the re-evaluation of older sites and material are beginning to change this story, but only slowly; it is noticeable that the papers in a recent review of Roman cities in northern Gaul (Hanoune 2007) have very little to say about the fifth century (and not much about the fourth). Even for Trier we have little reliable archaeological information. After the city ceased to function as an imperial residence with the suppression of Maximus in 388 and after it lost the praetorian prefecture to Arles at the start of the fifth century, it nevertheless remained indisputably the largest and most magnificent city of northern Gaul. The study of fifth-century Trier, though, has been dominated by a handful of literary references, such as those by Salvian (*de Gubernatione Dei* VI.82–5) telling not only of the three sacks of the city but also that spectacles continued to be staged; both these facts suggest that the city remained a wealthy centre worth attacking. It is clear from the excavations of major monuments, such as that at the Barbarathermen in the earlier part of the twentieth century, that there were considerable deposits of material, principally pottery, associated with the disuse or 'destruction' of these complexes, probably somewhere towards the middle of the fifth century (Böhner 1958), but these deposits await full exploitation of their potential. Nor do we know what occupation there was later in the century within the city, an occupation whose traces are likely to have been ephemeral. One aspect of Trier's urban life, though, does show vigour, the Church, especially through the sequence of memorial inscriptions (Handley 2003: 46–56), which dominates the evidence from northern Gaul and speaks of imperial and royal officials as well as ecclesiastics. This is the class of evidence which does lend colour to the oft-expressed view that the former imperial residence did remain different through the fifth century.

Further up the Moselle at Metz, the evidence from the 'Grand Amphithéâtre' to the south-east of the walled area shows intense activity in the fifth century. Unfortunately, because of the early date of the excavations, it is not possible to be certain of the nature of this activity, whether it was domestic or whether there may have been a martyr church within the amphitheatre. Nevertheless, this site did yield a sequence of pottery, particularly Argonne ware with rouletted decoration, which can be placed in a relative sequence probably extending through the fifth century (Bayard 1990) and therefore of wider value, as in showing continued activity just within the walls of Melun (Seine-et-Marne) through the fifth century, one of the rare demonstrable instances of this (Van Ossel 2006). Inside the walls of Metz, little is known and there does not seem to have been a ceramic sequence similar to that from the amphitheatre (cf. Halsall 1995: Ch. 7). It is likely that the fifth century saw the construction of the episcopal church of St Stephen, and, as we shall see, church building is one of the few identifiable activities of any consequence in north Gaulish towns, as in their southern counterparts. Of the towns we examined in Chapter 2 where there was some evidence for their fourth-century forms, little can usually be said for the fifth century. At Arras (cf. p. 68), the rue Baudimont site (for a summary, see Jacques, A. 2007) sequence showed that after the destruction of the 'Germanic' sanctuary in the 380s there were two phases of buildings. The first of these was interpreted as barrack buildings in the style of the High Empire, though this is far from the only possible interpretation of the pattern of post holes, and the case should remain open; but associated deposits containing quantities of military or official equipment do support a possible military presence, as does the construction of a granary near the north gate of the 'city'. The second phase of the rue Baudimont late buildings saw the creation before the end of the fourth century of a probable stable and a series of smaller structures, more domestic in appearance, still associated with military equipment but also with items of female apparel. The abandonment of these structures is dated to the second quarter of the fifth century. Otherwise, there is the evidence for the gradual conversion of an apsidal room, which had started as part of a bathhouse, into a freestanding structure, either a church or perhaps part of the episcopal complex.

A more certain episcopal complex has been located at Rouen (Le Maho 1998), where an aisled basilica was constructed at the close of the fourth century (the time of the evangeliser bishop Victricius), curiously incorporating a pre-existing domestic bathhouse into its western façade (cf. p. 176 and Figure 4.13). On the south side, it had a colonnaded court or *atrium*, so there may have been another basilica under the medieval cathedral, forming a double church (or this may be later). But the episcopal complex apart, the intramural area of Rouen, despite a series of significant excavations, remains largely a blank for the period from the end of the fourth to the seventh century (Le Maho 2004), though there is a certain amount of fifth-century pottery from the city, including Argonne, DSP and Rhineland products, as well as more local *céramique granuleuse*. There would appear still to be some population and commerce, but the archaeology is hard put to identify the associated occupation deposits. Reims is another site where excavation under the medieval cathedral has located the site of the late Roman episcopal church and its baptistery (the one used for the baptism of Clovis?), installed in or over the large bathhouse completed as a gift of Constantine I (Neiss and Berry 1998). To the south of the city lay the church of Saint-Nicaise, recorded as having borne a dedicatory inscription of Jovinus, a *magister militum* under Julian and Valentinian (360s and 370s). The fate of Reims has tended to be linked to destruction by the Vandals in 406, as mentioned in 409 in a letter of Jerome, writing in Palestine (*Ep.* CXXIII.15), along with Amiens and Arras, so there is little that can be said about the fifth century, though recent excavations suggest a slackening in urban activity from the late fourth century (Neiss and Sindonino 2006: 105–12), a situation quite possibly echoed at Metz (Halsall 1995: Ch. 7, *pace* the comments of Bacharach 2002).

As will be appreciated, this sort of evidence is not a particularly firm foundation on which to base a vision of urban life, or death, in the fifth century. The one reasonably consistent feature is church building, particularly episcopal churches, and to the ones already mentioned we might add the example now known from inside the walls of Tournai (Verslype 1999). These would, of course, have required considerable resources to pay for them and access to the necessary masons and other craftsmen, showing the continuing ability to mobilise surpluses to expend on prestige projects. There is little other evidence that such specialists were readily available in the region; presumably, they were imported from further south where, as we have seen, the construction of churches and of walls was being undertaken at many cities. It is interesting to note that, like the episcopal church at Geneva described in Chapter 4, that at Tournai used *opus africanum* construction, very rare in Gaul, particularly the North. On the other hand, there are many northern Gaulish urban sites where no church building of this date is known, so one must avoid generalising in default of reliable evidence. Overall, the picture available is of little or no occupation or activity apart from the building of churches. It may be that, as posited in Chapter 2, these cities were as much imperial and military strongpoints as cities in the fourth century, with units in garrison and some installations such as *fabricae*. If so, then the collapse of imperial control in northern Gaul and the removal, or atrophy in place, of the army along with the end of support for the military infrastructure would probably have proved near catastrophic for the economy and functions of such places. This would seem a reasonable explanation for why they apparently differ so markedly in their histories of occupation and their functions from the cities of southern Gaul and Iberia in the fifth century. In one sense, though, the cities north of the Loire could be said to have a family resemblance to those further south; by the end of the fifth century, their chief monuments suggest they were for the production of militant Christians. It is, of course, true that these places were to become centres of administration in the Frankish kingdom of the sixth century onwards, hosting royal officials such as counts, as well as their bishops, but one should be chary of projecting this back into the fifth century, if we follow the argument in the previous chapter that the Frankish kingdom as such seems largely to have been invented in the years around 500.

Outside the urban sites, the main feature of the rural sites of the period is the disappearance of Roman-style site types, notably the villa, and construction techniques, notably the use of masonry. Instead there tends to be a pattern of dispersed, nucleated settlement, these settlements consisting of timber buildings to a variety of plans but including long, rectangular structures, semi-subterranean '*fonds de cabane*' or SFB, and post settings for what were probably above-ground granaries. Because these were long considered to be expressions of Germanic social and constructional traditions, such settlements were often regarded as 'Germanic', or, more specifically for this region, Frankish. But, as we have already seen in Chapter 6 (p. 280), when considering the evolution of the late Roman settlement pattern and buildings of northern Gaul, such associations between building type and ethnicity are far from easy to sustain. In fact what we seem to have is a general pattern starting from the fourth century of dispersed settlement in timber with types of building such as the long, rectangular 'hall' or the SFB already present from the late fourth century and in a variety of sizes and techniques (cf. Van Ossel 1997, 2006, 2010). A good example of longer-term occupation of a site with these building types being introduced piecemeal is afforded by the recent excavations at Marolles-sur-Seine (Seine-et-Marne),

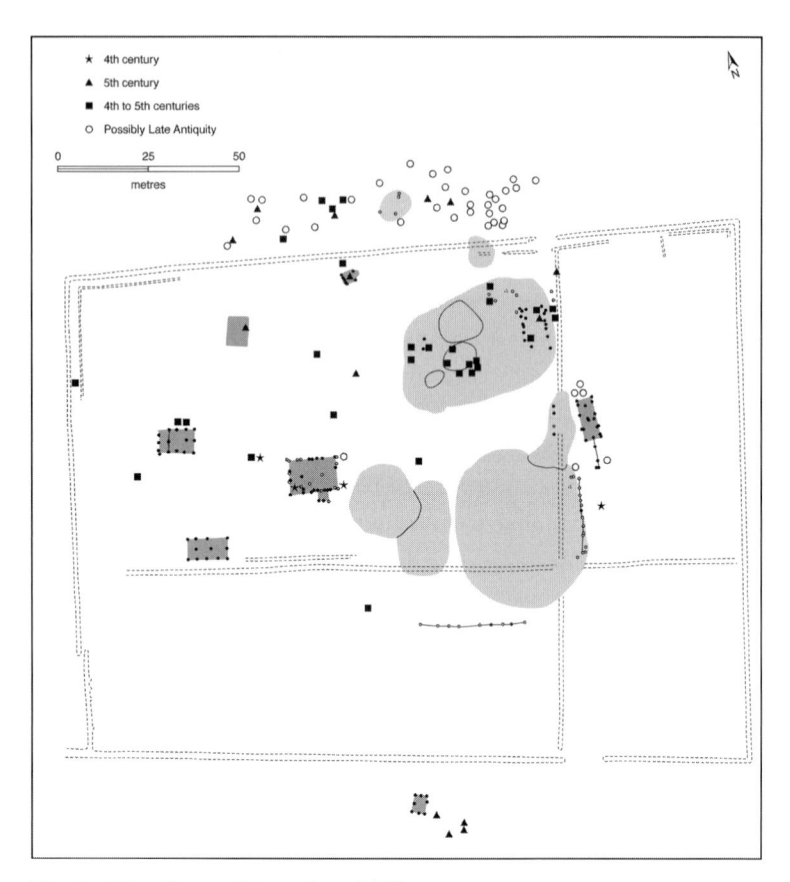

Fig. 9.7 Marolles-sur-Seine, plan of fifth-century occupation

where the occupation runs from the third to the late fifth century (Figure 9.7), with a range of building types and associated material culture (Séguier 2006). The differences in building type are certainly, in important part, to do with function, SFBs now generally being seen as specialised ancillary buildings dependent on a long, rectangular building, interpreted as the principal family residence. Individual settlements can be made up of groupings of these associated types, producing a 'village' (Lorren and Périn 1997; Périn 2004). Such settlement types do not suggest a marked social hierarchy, though the presence of pottery, some of which is of non-local types, and of glass shows that these sites and their populations were integrated into wider exchange networks. Again a good example is Marolles-sur-Seine with Argonne wares, *céramique rugueuse* and probably more local *céramique silicieuse* (Séguier 2006: esp. 265–8), along with quantities of glass. The loss of the habit of building in stone, the turn to timber, and the types of structures, along with the associated material culture, seem to betoken a simplification of social and economic formations and quite possibly also of the forms and relations of production, with a more 'peasant' form of society and economy becoming generalised across northern Gaul (cf. Van Ossel 2006, 2010), a contention which is in line with the cemetery evidence.

Many cemeteries of the fourth to sixth centuries have been excavated in the north of France and in the Low Countries, some associated with known settlements, though for most the associated settlement(s) remain unknown. Again, for a long time it was assumed from the presence of certain types of metalwork that these were 'Germanic' (cf. Chapter 8, p. 376), though, as with the houses of the living, this link has to be made with care. But as with the settlements, so with the cemeteries, the presence in some of the burials of goods from elsewhere in the north of Gaul or the Rhineland, and sometimes from further afield, attests to a continuing, if low, level of integration into wider exchange networks and to a degree, albeit not marked, of social stratification. Without going into too much detail on settlements and cemeteries, we may say that what is significant here is not just the evidence for continuing levels of rural population, some probably of 'Germanic' origin and most probably of indigenous descent, but also the evidence that there was still a continuing level of exchange at both local and longer-distance levels. This in its turn argues that agricultural surpluses were still being produced and mobilised in order to pay for these exotic goods. So, all in all, though the archaeology of the first half of the fifth century in northern Gaul may be lacunose – in particular for those key sites, the cities – it still demonstrates beyond a peradventure the persistence of economic activity, though with far less vitality and volume than regions further to the south and nearer the Mediterranean. The preceding sections have looked at a range of evidence types from major regions of the fifth-century West. In the course of this, certain themes, especially developments at cities and in urban ideologies, developments in the nature of aristocratic definition and self-representation, and developments in rural settlement and economy, have been evident. These themes will now be looked at to detect patterns of similarity and difference and their significance.

The city in the fifth century

All over the former Western provinces, modern study and analysis of cities in the fifth and sixth centuries, both historical and archaeological, has been dominated by a single topic – that of continuity or discontinuity from Roman to medieval. In general, historians, taking as their point of departure the texts with their mentions of aristocratic men and women, bishops, merchants, pilgrims and townspeople, have tended to see a greater measure of continuity from ancient to medieval than have archaeologists, who largely tend to remain resolutely unimpressed by an evidence suite characterised more by absence than by presence (cf. Ward-Perkins 1997). The fifth and sixth centuries have traditionally been seen as the period in which gradual degradation of the political, economic and cultural life of the towns proceeded steadily, attaining its nadir at the turn of the sixth and seventh centuries. The one important exception to this was the Church and its bishops, the saving grace of the ancient town, who tended its guttering flame through the Dark Ages. Here the question of continuity and discontinuity will obviously figure, but the principal thrust of the argument will be that in this period, as in any period, the development of the form of urbanism is contingent upon social, economic and cultural factors; thus the archaeology is expressive of and needs to be interpreted in the light of such factors. What do the important changes in the archaeology of towns in the West at this period show us about the wider changes to which they are responding but also helping to shape?

In Chapter 3, when discussing the cities of the southern half of Gaul and of Iberia, we noted some positive evidence for the continued use of some public buildings and monuments, some evidence which does not permit certainty as to whether a structure (e.g. a circus) was still in use or not, and some evidence for the disuse of structures. This, though, was within the framework of a street system where the streets were kept unencumbered and maintained, so the articulating structure of classic Roman urban form was still operative, as were many of the buildings and monuments that marked these places out as part of the Roman world. It was the fifth century that was to see the major, structural changes to this disposition. The street grids that had defined the overall shape and acted as the armature (cf. MacDonald 1986: Ch. 2) of such cities ceased to be maintained, at first in terms of physical structure with a decline in the maintenance of the street metallings, but subsequently, and more tellingly, in terms of the physical existence of the inherited street grids as they were colonised or abandoned in favour of something more convenient to the moment. For the monuments inherited from the High Empire, the recent review cited above of the fate of public buildings in the southern half of Gaul (Heijmans 2006a, 2006b) showed that across all major classes, fora, baths, temples and theatres/amphitheatres/circuses, the fifth century saw a consistent pattern of disuse, as attested to in particular by dismantling of the structure with its material removed for reuse elsewhere. A regular occurrence appears to have been the colonisation of former public spaces and buildings by new types of buildings. Occasionally this was churches, as with the construction of the episcopal church and baptistery over part of the former forum at Aix-en-Provence round about 500 (Fixot *et al.* 1985). More often the change was marked by the invasion of the structures by relatively flimsy buildings, *habitat parasitaire*, testimony both to the cessation of the original purposes of the structures and to the colonisation of public buildings and space by private housing. In addition, the old public structures often served as quarries for the construction of the new status monuments, the walls, in both the south-east and the south-west (Heijmans 2006a, 2006b). So in part the complex of changes consisted of the dismantling of the physical structures and thus the urban ideology inherited from the High Empire.

By contrast, there is no evidence for the construction of new civic buildings, nor even for large-scale works of upkeep and maintenance on existing ones, such as fora, baths or temples. Clearly, the urban vision that had produced and encompassed such structures and the forms of urban life and urban inhabitant they promoted were no longer seen as relevant. This must apply in particular to the forms of civic administration and political life once housed in such buildings, to the sense of identity through time they and their accompanying inscriptions and statuary expressed, and the sense of community enacted within them, and to the baths or temples as much as the fora. The two exceptions to this were, of course, the walls and in due course the churches. Indeed, given the symbolic importance of walls, their presence or absence may serve as a means of differentiating between those sites still considered significant, by their inhabitants at least, and those less highly regarded. As we have also seen, the advent of Christian buildings and topography was not a uniform process either in the form it took or in its chronology. Some cities, generally important ones such as imperial residences or provincial capitals (e.g. Arles, Mérida, Tarragona, Trier), show signs of significant Christian communities in the fourth century. But for others it seems not to be until the fifth or even sixth century that there is good archaeological evidence for an important Christian element in their populations and topography, a tendency probably becoming more or less universal by the middle of the sixth century when cities and their bishops were now creating the new Christian and often militarised citizen, of whatever claimed ethnicity.

Overall, the physical type of city inherited from the High Empire, and which had persisted in greater or lesser measure through the third and fourth centuries, was now definitely becoming derelict, and its streets and monuments were being adapted to other purposes. At one level this would seem to be a confirmation of the long-held, text-led view that the late Roman period saw the demise of civic government, institutions and values, and, so far as this goes, this would seem to be confirmed for much of the West by the archaeology of its fifth-century cities. But the significance of the changes also operates at a deeper level than just the institutional. In the preceding chapters, it has been a central tenet of all discussions of urban form that this was involved in the (re)production of citizens of particular types. If so, then what we are seeing in this period is that the type of citizen characteristic of the society of the first four centuries AD finally became obsolete. The citizen formed by being raised in the physical environment of the classical-style city – with its public and private spaces, its institutions of government and civic life, its places of entertainment, and its facilities for intellectual and social formation and bodily presentation – was no longer what was required. Increasingly, we are looking at cities, even in the old Mediterranean heartlands of the empire, whose defining features were their small size, their defences, their churches and the lack of much discernible archaeological differentiation in their social structures. They remained nuclei of population over and above that of contemporary rural settlement types, though how large these populations were remains a matter of guesswork; a city's population was probably in the hundreds, or low thousands of people at most. They probably represented some sort of administrative centralisation, though whether through a municipal administration or by direct royal or imperial appointees was probably changing markedly through the fifth century. They certainly discharged important functions as ecclesiastical centres marked by the appearance of episcopal groups as the major intramural building complexes. As already noted, there is little evidence yet for marked differentiation in buildings and occupation; the archaeology would be hard put to it to support the pictures of urban aristocracies painted by the texts, though what may have been happening was a displacement of status markers from the residence to such aspects as dress, hunting (rather than the ritualised versions of the amphitheatre or circus), munificence through largesse or feasting, armed retinues as power was privatised, and, of course, benefactions to the Church. There does remain a little evidence for craft specialisation, so cities may have remained centres for manufacture and commerce; this is supported by the evidence considered in Chapter 7 and to be presented below for city-based (or at least city-linked) patterns of distributions of artefacts. But it should be noted that it was only from the first half of the fifth century that the walls-and-churches model of the city, seen as the normative pattern of late Roman urbanism in so many studies, actually started to become dominant, let alone normative, culminating two hundred years after the supposed third-century 'crisis' of urbanism. Too often what was in fact a long-drawn-out process of civic/urban redefinition has been collapsed chronologically, and the walls-and-churches model, which was the 'end' of the process chronologically, has been seen as the 'end' in the sense of goal, producing a strongly teleological but inaccurate vision of what was going on, why and over how long a period.

The aristocracy in the fifth century

If the cities had been a major emblem of Roman culture, this was because the local aristocracies across the empire had conspired to make them so through euergetistic expenditure of surplus. Since the first century AD at least, they had been a major arena for aristocratic display through expenditure on public buildings and monuments, on private residences, and on the goods, services and culture that the cities made available. These in turn had served to define and display aristocratic status and to introduce the cultural innovations and modifications that allowed aristocratic competition to develop and to take new forms with which to attempt to out-compete other aristocrats. These forms, of course, had their rural as well as their urban vehicles for expression, particularly in the villas of the Late Empire. Through the fifth century, the cities seem decreasingly to have been a place for aristocratic display, as public buildings and monuments and private residences were increasingly abandoned, turned over to other purposes or served as quarries; much the same can be said for villas in those areas where they had been the socially dominant rural settlement type. Clearly, major changes were taking place in the nature of what it was to be an aristocrat and how this status was to be made manifest. These changes and the responses to them need to be considered and evaluated.

One of the obvious, major changes through the fifth century was simply that the Western aristocracies got a lot poorer. In Chapter 5 we noted that the texts are clear that the uppermost stratum of society, the senatorial super-rich, owned estates and properties in many provinces. With the political disintegration of the West in the fifth century, the ability to raise revenues from estates across a range of provinces would shrivel as the legal and administrative integration of the imperial system collapsed. In addition, as large tracts of the Western provinces fell piecemeal under 'barbarian' control, estates, properties and revenue were granted to or commandeered by the new masters. This would affect not only the super-rich, but even those of lesser but still substantial means with widespread properties. The ability to raise and transport revenues from more distant properties would be compromised, and the more aristocrats depended on such sources of revenue the more they would be impoverished. Even those of modest means would suffer as chronic warfare, brigandage and instability affected control over workforces and impacted on agricultural productivity. Paulinus of Pella, grandson of Ausonius and thus from a family that had prospered from its imperial connections, is a good case in point. Sheltering in reduced circumstances in Marseille, he was pathetically grateful to receive any payment from a Goth for family properties in Novempopulana; he would not have seen revenues from them again. Many others, presumably, were not so fortunate, as they lost not only revenues but also capital assets. Mention of the imperial connections of Paulinus's family also reminds us that important sections of the Western aristocracy had benefited from their service in and connections to the imperial court and bureaucracies, as we argued not only for Ausonius and the aristocracy of south-western Gaul, but also for those of the northern Meseta and southern Portugal in Iberia, of southern Britain, and of the areas immediately around the imperial residence at Trier. With the withdrawal of imperial presence and patronage north of the Alps at the start of the fifth century and with the breakdown soon after of the administrative and fiscal systems right across the West, what had been a major source not only of income but also of power, social advancement and aristocratic display ceased to operate. Of course, aristocracies raised in the vocabulary of late Roman power and its representation would cling onto such forms of power; there would have been a deal of inertia in the system. We can see this in the way in which for a couple of generations or so the villa system in particular continued to operate in both southern and central Gaul, in Iberia and to an extent elsewhere. Clearly, these aristocracies were still possessed of a degree of economic prosperity and they continued to expend their revenues on the traditional markers of late Roman aristocratic upbringing and display. But from the middle of the fifth century, it is clear that the means and the cultural will to maintain these forms were passing. It might have been expected that what would be detectable would have been a dwindling away of the traditional forms as ever more unsuccessful attempts were made to maintain the old ways on diminishing resources and with diminishing availability of the skilled personnel necessary. Instead it seems that there was a quite sudden 'flip' within the space of a generation or so from the mid fifth century to something else, with few villas being maintained in the old style. The question of what this new idiom was and why there should have been this change in the methods of elite display needs further consideration.

The evidence discussed above for the various super-regions in the West during the fifth century suggested that in all of them there continued to be the production and mobilisations of surpluses that were then expended on a variety of raw materials and finished products. Obviously, the evidence for the scale of surplus mobilisation and expenditure varied greatly across the geographical range, from the Mediterranean littoral to the interior of northern Gaul. But that it happened is clear indication of continuing social inequality and of the existence in certain regions, and particularly in the first half of the century, of a class, or at least of individuals, in a position to require the mobilisation of surpluses and to control their disbursement; that is, there continued to be elites or aristocracies. It is in the nature of elites to seek to display their social superiority in areas such as residence, dress, activities and consumption; the late Roman aristocracy were past masters at this (cf. Chapter 5). So why did the traditional markers of elite self-representation cease to be used and what replaced them and why? It was argued in Chapter 5 that central to the modes of elite self-representation across large areas of the fourth-century West were links with the imperial court and administration and with the old, senatorial aristocracy. All of these participated in forms of display centred on gradations of an elite culture defined by upbringing and education and expressed through one's residence; its décor, furnishings and fittings; dress; activities such as hunting or the entertaining of inferiors, equals or superiors; and mastery of the high aristocratic visual and linguistic culture exemplified by *paideia* and *ekphrasis*. Thus local aristocracies were as much dependent on imperial and senatorial exemplars for their means of cultural advancement as they were dependent on the imperial system for means of economic advancement. The removal of the imperial presence, followed by the removal of the imperial system from the West outside Italy, meant that the power of this complex of self-representation was severely weakened by the blow to the social and cultural rationale that underpinned it. Of course, the aristocracies of southern Gaul and Iberia retained links with the Mediterranean world and its aristocracies and would thus have been abreast of developments there (for textual examples, see Harries 1994: Pt. I; Matthews 1975: Chs. 12–14). This in part must account for the perpetuation of their fourth-century villa cultures down towards the middle of the fifth century, supporting the inherent tendency of these aristocracies to try to keep the existing system running. But the second half of the century saw, on the one hand, the final extinction of the imperial regime in Italy and, on the other hand, the growing definition of the successor states in Gaul and Iberia, the new sources of social and political power, often in opposition to the Roman and the Ostrogothic regimes in Italy. Thus the Roman-style aristocratic culture and its expression carried less and less worth in the new world that was developing. It can also not have helped the perpetuation of such a culture that it required huge resources of very specialised and equally expensive workers to reproduce, be it mosaicists, sculptors, goldsmiths, silversmiths or book-copyists; as resources became increasingly straitened and the times more uncertain, such specialists would have been harder and harder to train and maintain. Sidonius Apollinaris's evocation of the luxury villa, the *burgus*, of Pontius Leontius in mid-fifth-century Aquitania (*Carmina* XXII), written in as high and ekphrastic a literary style as would have graced the fourth century, is often cited as evidence for the perpetuation of the old high culture. We may leave aside the degree to which this is an exercise in rhetoric rather than a representation of reality, but less often referred to is Sidonius's comment on the baths of the villas of his two hosts, Apollinaris and Ferreolus: '*Balneas habebat in opere uterque hospes, in usu neuter*' ('Each of my hosts had baths being worked on; neither had ones in operation'), forcing them to provide a much more rough-and-ready approximation to a bath (*Epistulae* II.ii.8). The long-established, Roman-style means of aristocratic self-representation were breaking down because they no longer commanded respect or acquiescence in a world where other claims to elite status and other means of displaying that status were taking over.

Aristocratic display is a function of prevailing social and cultural norms. It represents wealth and status through access to and control of materials, objects and behaviours that set aristocrats apart from the majority and represent their wealth and status. But in order to do this, the display has to make sense in the power and wealth vocabularies of the time. If, in the second half of the fifth century, the Roman-style vocabulary of power was being abandoned, that was in part because it no longer commanded respect. But also, and perhaps more importantly, other claims to status and means of elite representation were taking over, offering functioning alternatives to the moribund culture expressed in the villas. This new type and representation of elite status was a militarised one, which elided across easily enough into a 'Germanic' context. The profession of arms had, of course, always been central to the identity of elite and non-elite Roman males since the earliest days of the Republic, but under the empire this identity had rather been submerged for the elite into the civilian language of aristocratic demeanour and its representation in cities and villas. But under the Late Empire, it regained a more prominent position as defence of the empire became ever more the central concern of the state. This was, of course, signalled at the highest level by the representation of the emperor as successful military leader and the recasting of the court and bureaucracy as a *militia*, an armed service in parallel with the army proper, with all the implications for dress and equipment that entailed. This gave an alternative, militarised language of power and assertion to that of the traditional senatorial aristocracies with their emphasis on cultural elitism. In Chapter 2 it was argued that the elites of the northern half of Gaul bought into this language in the course of the fourth century, resulting in the very different archaeological facies of elite culture to the north of the Loire compared with those to its south. In the fifth century the conditions of military stress, warfare and brigandage extended more widely across the West in tandem with the appearance of new 'barbarian' peoples whose kings and nobles were warriors first and foremost. The result was that an aristocrat became much more concerned with the safeguarding of his and his dependants' security and livelihoods. A good local leader was one who kept his followers safe, something which would in itself promote closer links between aristocrat and retinue. This was a civilian version of the phenomenon of the military *bucellarii* of the previous chapter, soldiers who followed their general not because he was appointed by an emperor but because he fed them and was a successful, booty-giving leader. Both civilian and military versions were in turn an expression of a wider trend, the privatisation of power. In place of the public institutions of the Western Empire now in its death throes, army, fisc, law and government, arose the private jurisdictions of the *potentes*, the powerful, administered at the point of the sword. The loyal and the favoured were rewarded; from the losers was taken even what they had.

In such a situation it is not surprising that, increasingly, the paraphernalia of force and violence (implied or actual) are to be found marking those who possessed or claimed status. This is perhaps most clearly to be seen in the interior of Iberia, where it develops out of an existing cultural trait and eventually develops into the expression of Visigothic identity. In Chapter 2 it was noted that as early as the fourth century in the northern Meseta and to the west and north there was a regional tradition of rural burial grounds, often associated with villas, as at La Olmeda, in which a minority of those buried were marked out by being buried with 'weapons', generally 'Simancas' knives but also lance fittings: the '*cementerios tardohispanos con ajuares*'. This 'Duero' tradition has been interpreted more in terms of hunting than strictly military weapons, but it does act, nevertheless, as a precedent for the interment of weapons as a status marker. Both in

Chapter 8 and earlier in this chapter (p. 429), we saw that associated with the structures succeeding the Roman-style villas of the northern Meseta, and also with the burials at or near the sites, were items of weaponry such as knives and spear fittings (Chavarría Arnau 2007: Ch. 4). Both on occupation sites and in burials, these were also associated with belt fittings, brooches and other items deriving ultimately from late Roman equipment worn by soldiers and other state servants. Still, only a minority of burials contained this equipment, so it can be argued that we are looking here at material that acted as a discriminator of the elite. In this reading, then, what we have in the interior of Iberia is the replacement of the ostentatiously civilian forms of late Roman aristocratic culture by one in which military identity and prowess were dominant. It also, of course, saw a displacement of much of the surviving evidence for this from the domain of the living to the arena of the burial and the cemetery. As discussed in the previous chapter, the security of the identification of particular styles of metalwork, or of the burials with which they were associated, as 'ethnically' Visigothic is very ambiguous. There is no reason why some of these burials should not represent a further stage in the militarisation of the Iberian elite, as they took on the material culture of the new, dominant military grouping in the peninsula, the Visigoths. The superposition of the extensive, 'Visigothic' cemetery of Duratón over a late Roman villa or next to the small villa of Tinto Juan de la Cruz (see below) could well be read as the replacement of one form and locus of elite display by another. North of the Pyrenees, similar, regionalised developments can be discerned. As noted in Chapter 8, it was only in the late fifth century, as the kingdom of Toulouse came under stress, that a 'Visigothic' identity became more important in south-west Gaul (to be superseded by a 'Merovingian', Frankish one). The ancestry of the people wearing or being buried with this material must, after nearly a century of cohabitation, have been very mixed. Similar questions can be asked about the people apparently making defiantly Visigothic statements of identity in Septimania.

There was, of course, one form of elite that did perpetuate the late Roman aristocratic vocabulary of masonry, marble and mosaic, and that was the Christian clergy – in particular, bishops. This has been described and discussed in Chapter 4. Here it is worth making the point that the construction and adornment of episcopal churches and groups were largely (as in the example of Geneva studied in Chapter 4) a feature of the fifth and into the sixth centuries, by which time the construction of rural churches was also getting under way. So in Iberia and southern Gaul, but less so, as we have seen, in northern Gaul, there remained a cadre of masons, mosaicists, sculptors and other architectural specialists who could build major basilicas and episcopal residences or smaller, rural churches and adorn them in the materials and styles derived from late Roman aristocratic display. What this means is that if the secular elites had wanted to perpetuate these idioms in their residences and elsewhere into the late fifth and sixth centuries, there was, at least to an extent, the expertise that could have been drawn on and augmented to keep the traditional villa (and *domus*) culture in being, even if to declining standards. That the elites across southern Gaul and Iberia did not exploit this possibility shows that the demise of the villa culture was not just a passive reflection of declining financial resources and technical expertise but also an active reinvestment of what resources there were in the new vocabularies of power and its representation. But the elites were not the only inhabitants of the fifth-century West. We must turn now to the scattered and partial evidence for non-elite settlement and life, particularly towards the end of the fifth and the beginning of the sixth century.

Rural settlement in the late fifth century

Iberia and southern Gaul

We start with the interior of the Iberian peninsula. In the discussion above of the fate of the great, fourth-century villas, several instances were noted of the construction in the second half of the fifth century of simple timber structures and other features such as silos on or close to the ruins of the villa. Sometimes these were associated with groups of burials. This has been taken to indicate the installation of a new type of settlement, traditionally seen as that of incomers or 'squatters', but now argued to be as likely to be the dwellings of a continuing rural population still exploiting the agricultural lands of the former or continuing villa estate. Preliminary publication on recent excavations in advance of major infrastructure and construction projects in the southern part of the province of Madrid (summarised in López Quiroga 2006) has yielded a range of settlement sites (cemeteries also) dating from the fourth to the seventh centuries. Taken as a whole, these seem to show that the middle of the fifth century marked a changeover period in the rural settlement pattern, with some settlements ending in the first half of the century and others starting in the second half. An emblematic site is that of Tinto Juan de la Cruz (López Quiroga *et al.* 2006: 56–8), where, in the first half of the fifth century, parts of a small villa were colonised by hearths and silos and other parts subjected to fire. The presence of weaponry associated with these deposits would permit a traditional explanation of barbarian takeover, but the excavators are more circumspect, allowing the possibility of change of use and of social and economic structure rather than of ownership and ethnicity. By the early sixth century, the site was abandoned and a 'Visigothic' cemetery established immediately to the north of the principal building of the villa. The sequence and dating are not dissimilar to those at the villa of El Val cited above (p. 413) from the same area. The new settlements of the latter part of the fifth century and later, such as Congosto, Gózquez, La Indiana, Pelícano and El Soto/Encadenado (Quirós Castillo and Vigil-Escalera Guirado 2006), were characterised by simple, sill-wall or sill-beam structures and post-built timber surface structures, often of one unit, but sometimes more. Accompanying these were sometimes sunken-featured buildings and usually grain silos. At Congosto (Figure 9.8), examination of the patterns of

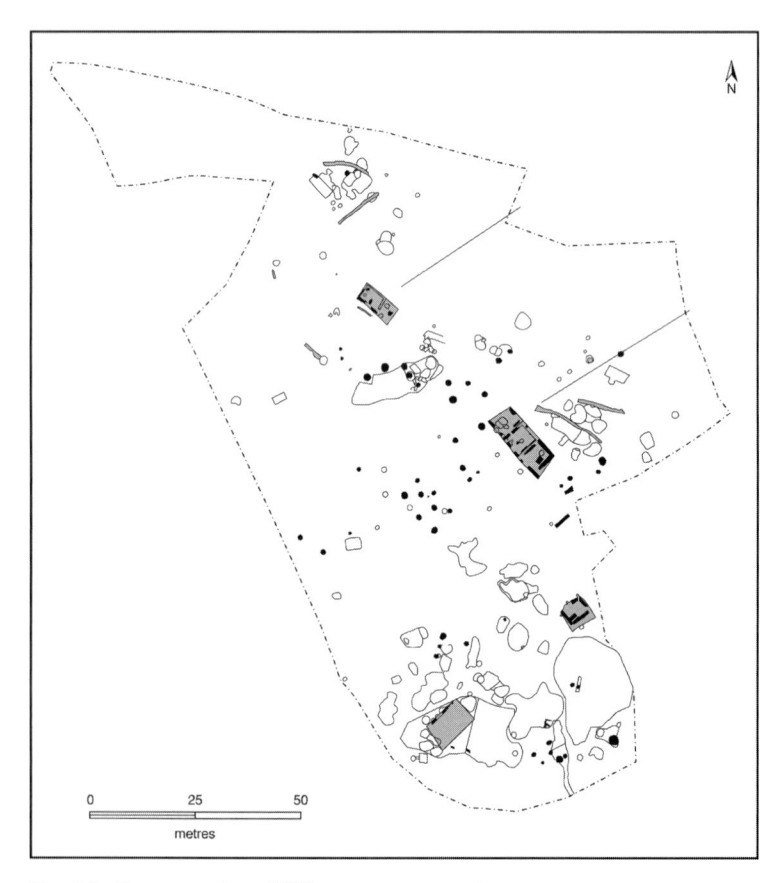

Fig. 9.8 Congosto, plan of fifth-century occupation

buildings and of the datable finds suggests a settlement consisting of a principal, stone-founded building with ancillary structures and silos, the whole shifting southwards over time. This settlement was occupied from the mid fifth to the mid seventh century. Other sites, exemplified best by Gózquez and El Pelícano, start in the second half of the fifth century, exhibiting a similar range of structures and activities to Congosto, and lasting until the later eighth century. The site at Arroyo Culebros (López Quiroga *et al.* 2006: 80–1) is notable for its battery of grain silos.

In the province of Álava in the Basque Country, the villa culture and economy characteristic of the northern Meseta spread into this area to the north, and, as on the Meseta proper, the evidence is that the villa buildings and the villa system were abandoned by or in the middle of the fifth century, coincident with the end of TSHT on sites in the area. As yet, no nucleated settlements of the type south of Madrid have been encountered, other than the late fifth-century site of La Erilla with structures and silos, but the existence of many groups of burials and cemeteries in this area (traditionally studied from an ethnic rather than a habitative perspective) argue that there must have been some form of settlement. However, an important example of another type of settlement has been excavated in the area, the *castrum*, or hilltop settlement, of Buradón, consisting of a church of the late fifth century associated with domestic structures and a cemetery from the sixth century. Interestingly, sites of the later fifth century in Álava yield DSP from southwest Gaul, though from the sixth they use local handmade wares.

If we put together the admittedly very scattered evidence, some observations can nevertheless be put forward. The fifth century onwards does seem to mark a caesura in both regions and coincides with the collapse of the villa systems and associated phenomena such as the demise of the TSHT industries. The evidence from the villas and their cemeteries suggests that some continued to act as a focus for settlement and often burial. But there is also, a little later, a horizon of the foundation of new settlements on sites not previously occupied. Socially, these seem to consist of small, probably family groupings, not very many to a settlement. Where associated cemeteries have been examined, there is little evidence for much social stratification, consistent with the evidence from the settlements themselves. These would seem to be 'peasant' settlements operating at a fairly low level of productivity; the sort of social formation posited in Wickham's (2005: Ch. 7) 'peasant mode'. But it is clear that these settlements and their inhabitants were not living in some autarchic, Bruegelian wonderland. The evidence of non-local goods such as pottery and glass makes it clear that they had access to such things, though quite probably through forms of socially mediated exchange such as gift or barter rather than by the operations of a market economy. The presence at so many of these sites of grain silos and at Gózquez of an olive press, as well as quantities of animal bone, suggests the possibility of some surplus production, though at a level almost unimaginably lower than that of the preceding villa economies. From the available evidence it is not possible to establish what sort of social hierarchy, if any, there was or what any tenurial relations (never very visible in archaeology) may have been. It may be that the settlements had a measure of social differentiation, or that they were dependent on a landlord or notable living elsewhere, or even, of course, on the Church. It is also worth making the point that none of this looks 'Germanic' as judged by building types or material culture, and the associated burials only sporadically have 'Visigothic' material in the form of dress accoutrements.

The Buradón *castrum* is an example of what appears to be a class of settlement whose numbers have been growing recently as a result of survey and excavation – the fortified hilltop settlement. These have been documented above all in the north and north-east of the peninsula, but this is not to say that they were confined to this region; it is more a function of the incidence of fieldwork. The type site of these northern hilltop settlements is El Bovalar (Lérida/Lleida) (Palol 1989), where a series of domestic structures was arranged round two courtyards, one side of one of which was formed by a church, and in the building separating the two open areas was an olive press (Figure 9.9). The dating evidence, such as it is, suggests an initial date in the latter part of the fifth century. The type of site represented by El Bovalar is open to debate. On the one hand, it could be seen as a 'normal' rural settlement with evidence for cereal and pastoral agriculture, grouped around and physically integrated with its church. On the other hand, it is this physical link with the church that has led to the proposition that what it represents is a small monastic establishment. Excavation of any associated cemetery might resolve this question. Other sites such Puig Rom (Girona), Las Muelas de Pan (Zamora), Alto de Yecla (Burgos), Tedeja (Burgos) or Villaclara (Burgos) seem to be broadly similar in location and type (cf. Chavarría Arnau 2005: 267–9). There are differences; for instance, Tedeja has notable defences and suggests a military character, whereas Alto de Yecla has been proposed as an aristocratic residence, and yet others, such as Las Muelas de Pan, have produced no military links and seem rather to have been agrarian settlements engaged in both cereal production and perhaps transhumance. As yet, it is debatable whether it is possible to sustain an argument that they represented, as some have suggested, a step in the settlement and social hierarchy superior to that of the open

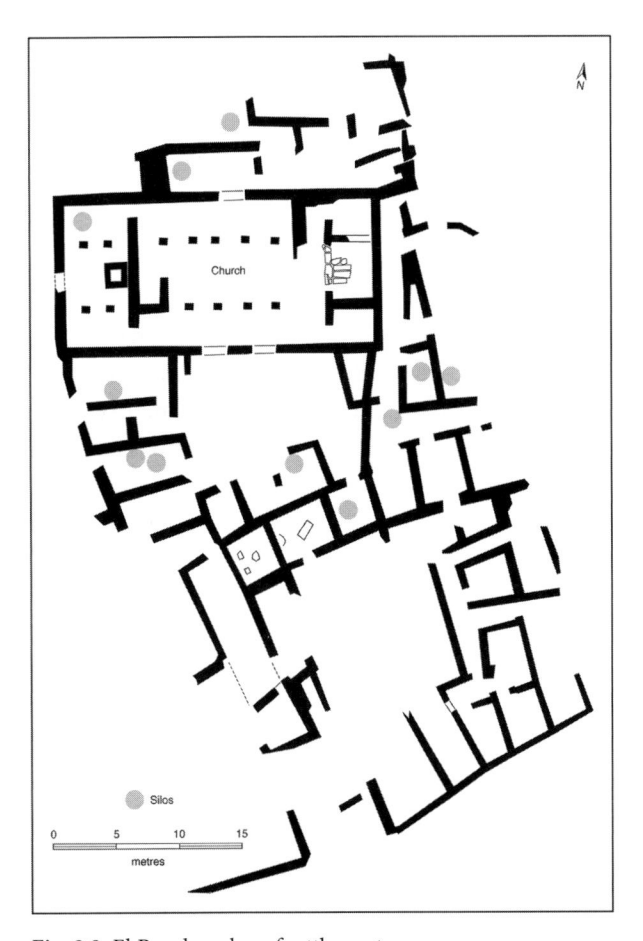

Fig. 9.9 El Bovalar, plan of settlement

settlements on the plain but still dependent on the authorities, episcopal or lay, in the cities. Nevertheless, the increasing (re-)occupation of fortified sites may suggest a perception of threat; it certainly suggests an increased emphasis on nucleation, possibly at the behest of a superior power, possibly as a communal action.

To the north of the eastern half of the Pyrenees, in Languedoc and up into Provence, the second half of the fifth century and the early part of the sixth century marked a major threshold in the development of the patterns and types of rural settlement, as an important recent article has made clear in a nuanced discussion, to which some violence may be done in what follows (see Schneider 2007, on which much that follows is based; cf. Schneider 2005). As we have already seen in Chapter 6, south-eastern Gaul, Languedoc in particular, has seen a quite exceptional amount of survey and analysis over the last quarter-century or so, and thus remains the region with the best data and most sophisticated treatments. For purposes of the argument here, one may divide the multiple forms of rural settlement into three main groups: villas, other lowland sites and upland sites. Surveys of the dating evidence for activity on the sites of villas in Languedoc (Pellecuer 1996) have suggested that of the 71 in existence by the second century, 50% still showed activity in the fifth century, but only 20% in the sixth and 7% later. A more detailed survey of those areas of Languedoc with relatively good data (Pellecuer and Pomarèdes 2001) showed that of 89 possible villas, 73% still showed activity in the fifth century, down to 42% in the sixth and 25% thereafter. Another survey (Buffat 2005) showed that of 198 sites which may have been villas in the territory of Nîmes, 37% still showed activity in the sixth century. At first glance, this might be taken to show a remarkable persistence of villa sites and thus of the domanial system expressed by the villa. But the phrase carefully utilised above was 'show activity', 'activity' being the operative word. The evidence is mostly surface scatters of pottery; excavations on sites such as La Ramière, Loupian, or Saint-André-de-Codols, as discussed above (p. 409), show that the classic villa layout and residence were disused by the end of the fifth century at the latest and that the subsequent occupation took a much more compact form, generally of relatively simple structures in wood. Thus, by the late fifth and sixth centuries, these sites of what must be regarded as former villas look pretty similar to other lowland settlements, as we have seen for areas of the Iberian peninsula. What the archaeology cannot tell us is what the system of land-ownership was by the sixth century, and whether the old landowning families retained their estate(s) or not. Many other lowland sites are also known, principally from surveys with a limited amount of excavation; it should be noted that these far outnumber the former villa sites, so the latter should not be focused on disproportionately because of the accident of their origins. Again, it seems to be the latter part of the fifth or the earlier sixth century that saw the establishment of many of these sites both in Languedoc and east of the Rhône in Provence. In this latter area, the surveys along the littoral of the Golfe de Fos and around the *étangs* of Saint-Blaise, Lavalduc and de Berre (Trément 1999) have shown that there was a phase of densification of settlement with new sites created at just this period. West of the Rhône, the key site remains Lunel Viel (Raynaud 1990, 2001), where excavation and survey show that the Roman-style secondary centre with its public buildings and large residences was progressively abandoned through the fourth century, but the location was not abandoned; occupation shifted a little to the east to the Verdier area and changed its character to something

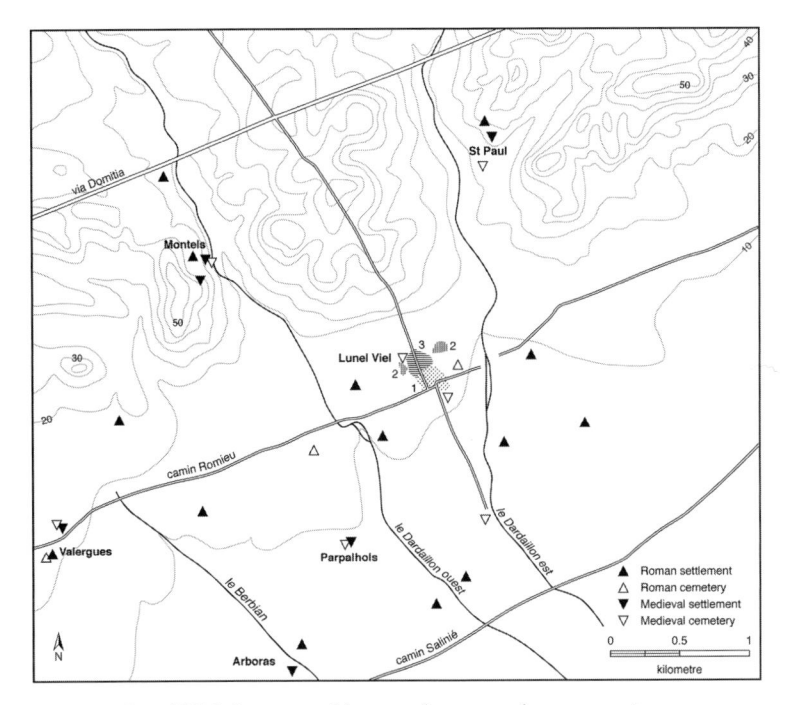

Fig. 9.10 Lunel Viel, Roman and later settlement and cemetery sites

more compact and largely in timber (Figure 9.10). By the sixth century, there was another zone of occupation in Saint-Vincent (under the later village). Both of these areas had an associated cemetery (cf. Raynaud 2010). In the countryside around the focus at Lunel Viel, there was a pattern of dispersed agricultural settlements, focused on the watercourses. A similar pattern of dispersed settlement of the fifth and sixth centuries is also known to the north of the emblematic Loupian villa, abandoned by the end of the fifth century. One of these areas was around the fifth-century basilica (p. 186), and the other a little to the east. Not far from Lunel Viel, excavations at Dassargues (Hérault) have again shown a pattern of dispersed and shifting occupation in timber structures (including sunken-featured ones) through this period. Overall, the picture is one of an active and dynamic settlement pattern and population on the lowlands in the fifth and sixth centuries.

As in Spain, so in Gaul, an innovation from the later fourth century on was the (re-)fortification of numbers of hilltop sites in both Languedoc and Provence, in a manner similar to that beginning to be seen south of the Pyrenees. Recent excavations have given a site to set alongside El Bovalar; this is the occupation at Roc de Pampelune (Hérault) (for a clear summary,

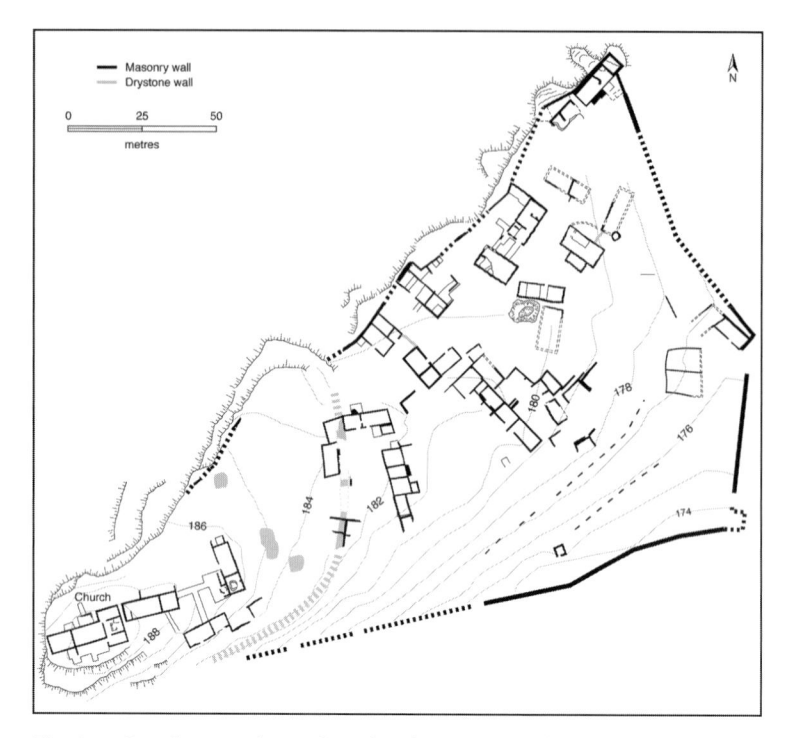

Fig. 9.11 Roc de Pampelune, plan of settlement and defences

see Schneider 2007: 27–9). The site lies in the uplands inland from and halfway between Loupian and Lunel Viel, occupying a roughly triangular hilltop of some 2.25 ha. that dominates a small basin in an area with little evidence for earlier activity (Figure 9.11). On the western, highest point of the Roc was a group of structures, including a church with a baptismal basin. A large terrace wall separated this from the main occupation consisting of a series of structures grouped around an open place with others grouped more informally around other spaces. The buildings were of stone with tiled roofs and some of the larger ones had evidence for an upper storey and for ancillary structures, suggesting a degree of social differentiation. There is a deal of evidence for agricultural activities at the site, including possible stables or sheepfolds as well as objects linked to shearing and weaving. But as well as this, there is considerable evidence for specialisation in metalworking, both iron and bronze, presumably exploiting the local woodlands for fuel. The site was in contact with the Mediterranean trade nexus, with plentiful North African material, the amphorae making up 40 per cent of the pottery. Obviously, one site cannot be regarded as typical; nevertheless, it does raise interesting issues. It was apparently an *ex novo* foundation, planted purposely and endowed with defences; this raises the question of the controlling authority for this operation. It was clearly not a *refuge* or *Fluchtburg* but a permanently occupied settlement of a type new to the area. It had both agricultural and specialised functions and created enough disposable surplus to be able to trade with the coast, arguably after paying some form of dues to the controlling authority. The presence of defences suggests that the public power of the late Roman state had given way to a private power able to fortify a site, though, interestingly, the Roc has yielded no weaponry or other evidence for military activity. Was the Roc the dominant site in the basin it overlooked, suggesting a degree of hierarchy in the settlement pattern and population?

It is now clear that the Roc de Pampelune is a representative of a much more widespread phenomenon across south-eastern Gaul, that of the reoccupation of prehistoric hilltop fortified sites or the construction of new ones from the later fifth century on (Schneider 2007: 34–8). Recent excavations on the hilltop fortification of La Malène (Lozère) on the border of Languedoc and the Cévennes, where a complex of buildings was erected in the late fifth century and lasted into the seventh (Schneider and Raynaud 2011: 27–9), give us another vision of such settlements in this period. The largest building was 48 by 7.50 m in plan and had an upper storey reusing Roman columns. The settlement also had a possible church and, somewhat surprisingly, a Roman-style bathhouse, supplied from a large cistern. East of the Rhône, another classic (re-)defended site is that of Saint-Blaise with its protohistoric fortifications refurbished and much of the interior occupied and containing a church (Démians d'Archimbaud 1994). This, of course, lies in the area of the densification of settlement at this time revealed by Trément's (1999) survey. The zone to the north and west of Saint-Blaise and up into the foothills of the western Alps has revealed a whole series of other fortified hilltop sites in the modern *départements* of Bouches-du-Rhône and Var and up into the lower valley of the Rhône itself. These sites vary considerably in precise topography, size and type of fortification and material recovered, and few have been excavated. Nevertheless, pretty uniformly, they appear to date from the latter part of the fifth century or the sixth. This threshold sees the creation of a new class of site, often in areas with little evidence for late Roman occupation. Because of the considerable disparities in size and other criteria, it would be unwise to see these sites as a unitary phenomenon, but some sort of phenomenon they were. Clearly, their fortifications give them a military capability, but it is unclear whether they were defended against external threat and troubled times, or whether in fact they were the threat in that they were local centres of control and force. This would again suggest that power and force were increasingly being privatised and that we may be looking at a developing landscape of lordships and local *potentes*; how these meshed with any city-based public power, the *castra* sometimes even lying within sight of the cities, is, currently, entirely unclear. But they also attest to the importance of militarisation of elites and populations, and if they were of some superior status, then they would be eloquent testimony to the new means of elite self-representation succeeding that of the villa aristocracy. And, of course, the turn of the fifth and sixth centuries is precisely the period at which, in Languedoc at least, we see the beginnings of what has traditionally been characterised as 'Visigothic' material culture in the cemeteries and on the settlements of Septimania (Hernandez and Raynaud 2006; Kazanski 1994). But if this material, particularly the belt suites, brooches and weaponry, is reinserted into the wider changes taking place at the time, then what we may be seeing is not due so much to ethnic change as to the growing militarisation of the region, particularly its aristocracy, who borrowed their paraphernalia from the surrounding Germanic peoples. Some, of course, would have been Visigoths, but not necessarily all.

Hilltop (re-)fortification is also increasingly being recognised as a widespread phenomenon in areas of central and eastern Gaul, such as the Massif Central and the Jura and across into what is now Switzerland. At present one can do little more than point to individual sites that have been excavated, but they probably stand as case studies for the range of other hilltop sites known in their area but not studied. A good example is 'La Motte', Ecrilles (Jura) (Gandel *et al.* 2008), where excavation has shown the hilltop to have been fortified for the first time at the turn of the fourth and fifth centuries. The material recovered included late Roman belt elements but also two silver-gilt brooches in the form of a bird, and a silver arm ring with expanded terminals. These latter have been compared with examples from the territory of the Burgundian kingdom, and because of the lack of other known occupation in the lowlands and the site's position overlooking axes of communication, a garrison of Burgundians has been proposed. But it would seem that the origins of the site lie rather too early for that, and the objects could, of course, be expressions of local prestige rather than of ethnicity. So it is possible that what we see here is a new form of militarised expression of the local elites through fortification and material culture. It is noted that Ecrilles is one of a number of late antique fortified sites in the Jura area, extending eastwards into what is now western Switzerland (cf. Marti 2000).

One other feature of the Roc de Pampelune which it shares with La Malène, El Bovalar and other excavated Iberian and south Gaulish *castra* is the presence of a church. The fifth century saw a gradually quickening pace of construction of churches away from the cities (Codou and Colin 2007). Sometimes, as at the complex of La Gravette at L'Isle-Jourdain between Toulouse and Auch (cf. p. 187), the church was built at a road station. But in south-eastern Gaul churches were being constructed at a range of settlements – for instance, at Saint-Maximin-la-Sainte-Baume (Var) over the mausoleum of what was probably a private estate – and as at this site and at the Roc de Pampelune, they very often contained baptismal basins, suggesting either foundation by the bishop or by a lay notable in collaboration with the bishop. This was still very far from being any sort of parochial system (see the papers in Delaplace 2005), but it did demonstrate the beginnings of the long-term Christianisation of the countryside. Of course, the traditional religions had had temples and shrines associated with and in settlements such as cities, small towns and villas, but seldom at simple, rural settlements. In addition, at both El Bovalar and the Roc de Pampelune, as well as other sites, the church was physically integrated not only into the settlement but also with the neighbouring buildings, creating a totally different spatial and social relationship between the church, its ceremonies and its clergy, and the population of the settlement.

It should be clear that the exceptional suite of data for south-eastern Gaul allows us to say that by the turn of the fifth and sixth centuries the human landscape and settlement of this region had been marked by profound changes compared with only a hundred years previously when the Roman-style pattern was still functioning. These changes included the abandonment of the villas (certainly as aristocratic show residences, possibly not as centres of working units) and their replacement by a range of other settlement types, quite probably reflecting unrecoverable changes in tenurial and productive relations, along with a substantial flattening of the social hierarchy. That there was still a hierarchy can be demonstrated partly by the differing sizes and elaboration of the settlement types, and partly by the evidence for resource mobilisation and its expenditure on traded goods from the Mediterranean. In addition there had been the introduction of a new and distinctive site type, the hilltop fortified site, probably attesting to the privatisation of military power and perhaps also to new steps in the settlement and social hierarchy between the peasant and the city, ones sustained ultimately by force. Alongside this was the commencement of the progressive Christianisation of the rural areas. So we are entering a world of private aristocratic power expressed through fortifications and military retinues, probably by the exploitation of dependent peasantries and associated with the growing presence of the Church: this would seem to be a world more familiar to and easily read by workers on the medieval period.

Northern Gaul

The other region of Gaul for which we have an extensive database is the north. Particularly since the excavation of the settlement at Brebières (Pas-de-Calais) in the 1960s, which was published in 1972, there has been a great deal of work on the questions of the transition from the Roman period landscape and the origins of the 'Merovingian village', aided by the extensive excavations in advance of TGV lines, motorways and the like (for a general survey and discussion, see Peytremann 2003). Two of the distinctive features of the settlements of the fourth and fifth centuries (and indeed later) in northern Gaul were the transition to construction in timber from the stone (or at least stone sill-walls) favoured in Gallo-Roman villas and the adoption of settlement plans characterised by grouped buildings, be they rectangular, post-built structures or sunken-featured buildings (cf. Van Ossel 2006, 2010), as discussed above (p. 379). Once considered to be the hallmarks of incoming Germanic peoples, it is now recognised that both features can be traced back into the fourth century, as discussed in Chapter 5. What we may therefore be seeing is the creation of new physical, social and tenurial structures of settlement, or even, in the opinion of some (e.g. Lorren 2006), the reassertion of earlier traditions suppressed by the domanial system, which was expressed by the villa. Clearly, the dating does not any longer allow an easy ethnic explanation for the changes. The dating does, though, suggest that again the later fifth and early sixth centuries may have been an important horizon for the creation of settlements and the establishment of the new settlement patterns and landscape (see Lorren 2006; Périn 2004; Peytremann 2003). The excavation of a type site such as Mondeville (Calvados) shows that the timber-built settlement originated in the late third or early fourth centuries (and from the beginning there were sunken-featured structures) and continued down to the end of the first millennium and later, with the construction of a church in the seventh or eighth century. This would seem to speak of a nucleation of population (several families?), possibly at the behest of a proprietor, or possibly through social cooperation.

Not only the physical structures but also the likely associated social structure differs considerably from those of a Gallo-Roman villa (of which there is one near the site). Though the material culture makes it clear that this was, as only to be expected, an agricultural settlement with evidence for the manufacture also of secondary products such as textiles, there is little evidence for an emphasis on the production of large-scale surpluses in the manner of the 'villa economy'. On the other hand, the surplus production and manufacture would certainly have allowed commerce with other settlements and further afield, or, if there were a single proprietor or 'lord', he could have derived rent and dues. As a result of the rescue excavations across northern France, over five hundred sites are known (Lorren 2006), the great majority, of course, only partially. From the same region has come also large numbers of cemeteries, again usually only known in part, but with a proportion of them that can be associated with accompanying settlements. These cemeteries, usually accorded the epithet '*mérovingien*' with all that implies in terms of ethnicity and date, not only demonstrate, as seen in Chapter 8, differences in burial rite and material culture that may or may not have 'ethnic' significance, but also, more generally, show, through the number, materials and technology of the grave goods, a degree of social stratification allied with statements related to age and gender. Like the settlements themselves, these seem to argue for a social structure based on the family (nuclear or extended) with males often marked by the presence of weapons, again attesting to the militarisation of the vocabulary of male self-representation. As well as militarisation, it is important to keep in view the horizon of the end of the fifth century as that at which, as argued in Chapter 8 (p. 383), a distinctive 'Frankish' identity was being created with its material correlates – what in the seventh century could reasonably be termed 'Merovingian' – so the populations of the region, whatever their origins, were subsuming themselves to the new, dominant power elite and its means of self-representation. As yet, it is not possible to identify separate elite or 'lordly' type(s) of settlement suggesting physical and social distancing of any proprietorial class from the generality of the population. Certainly, there does not seem to be a cadre of (re-)fortified hilltop settlements like those of southern Gaul and Iberia; the fourth-century hilltop fortifications of north-eastern Gaul and the Rhineland do not seem to last far into the fifth century. In fact, increasing evidence for social differentiation through building type, enclosures and satellite structures, and burial practice seems more to characterise the later sixth and seventh centuries (Lorren 2006; Périn 2004; Peytremann 2003), a period when the documentation also suggests increasing social differentiation and economic control. Though the detail of settlement types, some structures and material culture from northern Gaul in the later fifth and sixth centuries differs from that nearer the Mediterranean, similar patterns of settlement relocation and types, of social and economic structures at the settlements, of settlement variety, and of hierarchy seem to be discernible in the north. That, *mutatis mutandis*, similar patterns appear to be discernible from central Iberia to northern Gaul, in the decades either side of 500, suggests that the forms characteristic of the late Roman countryside had finally ceased to exercise any influence.

This chapter is part of a sort of diptych with Chapter 8, looking at the archaeology of the fifth century as a period of accelerated change and asking whether by the end of the century we have reached a 'threshold of change' marking the transition from a late Roman scheme of things to something else. The evidence cited above would seem to answer that question affirmatively and also to support the contention that the archaeology of the turn of the fifth and sixth centuries has ceased to be explicable in the terms normally used by Roman archaeologists and makes much more sense in the terms of the debates about the society, economy and culture of the early Middle Ages. If this be accepted, then the period around 500 can be seen not only as the end of a long period of transition in the archaeology of rural settlement and landscape but also, as argued earlier in the chapter, as a long period of transition in the form, fabric and function of cities. The changes that started to be discernible across a range of important classes of archaeological evidence for 'Roman' society, economy and culture at the very end of the second century, the year 200 in round numbers, thus reached a conclusion around 500, some three hundred years later. Interestingly, it has been proposed (e.g. Hamerow 2002: Ch. 7 and references) that it was another three hundred years later, centring on the late eighth century, that the next major realignment of settlement and economic patterns was to take place. In the next and final chapter, we shall examine the 'thresholds' round about AD 200 and 500, on whose existence this book is predicated, to see if they really do mark horizons of change in the archaeological record.

10 | Epilogue: AD 200–500, a coherent period?

This book has been predicated on the idea that the archaeology of the period between the turn of the second and third centuries and the turn of the fifth and sixth centuries forms a definable period, one with broad consistencies that serve not only to unite it internally but also to distinguish it in important ways from what went before and what came after. Of course, no archaeological (or historical) period can ever be entirely distinct from its preceding or succeeding periods, and that is not what will be argued here. Rather, it will be argued that these broad dates were 'thresholds' in the development of the archaeological record; that is, that they marked phases at which, on the one hand, important elements across a range of archaeological domains cease to develop as they had been doing, and, on the other hand, a range of important elements takes a different route, or else new elements entirely begin to make their appearance. The claim for thresholds around AD 200 and 500 was made in the Introduction, but it is now, with all the evidence and argument of the preceding chapters laid out, that we can attempt to substantiate this claim both by demonstrating internal consistencies in the period and by distinguishing it from the preceding and succeeding periods.

AD 200: an archaeological threshold?

In the conventional historiography of the Roman Empire, the turn of the second and third centuries passes almost unnoticed, a way station on the route from the 'fortunate age of Trajan and the Antonines', in Gibbon's (1776: Ch. 38) formulation, to the first blasts of the 'third-century crisis'. Yet, it is possible to argue, by contrast, that the archaeology of the period around the turn of the second and third centuries (if not the precise year AD 200) marks the end of one long period and the beginnings of something new. Indeed, it is implicit in the notion of the 'High' or 'Early' Empire, which, as we saw in Chapter 1, is essentially a shorthand for the first and second centuries, with AD 200 as roughly the end point. From the second century BC to the second century AD, the Mediterranean basin had been profoundly marked politically, culturally and economically by the unification of the entire area, along with parts of temperate Europe, under the aegis of Rome. The effects of this in the archaeology are highly visible, affecting principally the cultural and economic spheres; they have been the subject of much study and need only be summarised here. In brief, across the entire western Mediterranean and adjacent territories there appeared elements of a common culture, albeit one marked by strong regional variation. One aspect of this was the presence of the Roman army in the Western provinces, a presence that in the second century AD became highly localised as the fortified bases of the troops were strung out along the 'frontiers', essentially the Rhine and upper Danube and the northern part of Britain. More widespread was the adoption of certain Roman cultural norms and expressions that developed in particular from the first century BC on. The most celebrated of these, even at the time, was the spread of Roman-style cities across the West (Laurence *et al.* 2011). These are highly distinctive to the modern archaeologist with their variations on the themes of an orthogonal pattern of streets and certain classes of public building and monument (forum, baths, amphitheatre and so on), all derived ultimately from Italy (sometimes even from Rome), and all expressions not just of the acceptance of Roman values but also of the active desire to create Roman-style citizens through the urban phenomenon and its institutions such as law, upbringing and social practice. These were clothed in the architectural vocabulary that had developed at the end of the first century BC, and that is linked with the reign and programme of Augustus (Zanker 1988: esp. Chs. 4 and 8) and is instantly recognisable, now as then, as carrying a 'Roman' identity. The public buildings also exhibited other aspects of 'Roman' culture such as statuary, mosaics, wall painting and epigraphy. This last, the setting up of inscriptions, shows a peak in the first and second centuries AD (MacMullen 1982), and has been linked to the cultural and social need to show off the status both of individual cities and of individuals within those cities (Kulikowski 2004: Ch. 1; Woolf 1998: Ch. 4), and is clearly very closely linked to the spread of the Roman idea of the city and of Roman status for individuals. Many of these also carried over into the private sphere of housing, above all of the local elites, with their layouts, colonnades, gardens, mosaic pavements, painted walls, statues and all the other movable paraphernalia of Roman provincial identities and behaviours that they embodied. This in its turn had an impact on rural settlement with the appearance across the West of the 'villa' or at least Roman-influenced rural residences. These phenomena in their turn impacted on the economy of the West in defining ways. The army, of course, was a major consumer through the supplies it needed and with which it was supplied by the taxpayers, be it in coin or in kind. This in its turn, partly for reasons of the availability of supplies and partly for politico-cultural reasons connected to the preferences of the troops on the frontiers, engendered a network of long-distance supply networks on a large scale, acting as an overlay on a multitude of local economies. Allied with this was the production and distribution of coin, which, even if initially struck to discharge the debts of the state, soon became a medium of economic interaction for the civilian population at certain times and in certain regions. But more broadly the economic impact was the product of a system of proprietorial landholding designed to create surpluses for the proprietors and the need of those proprietors to expend those surpluses on creating and displaying their status, especially in arenas such as benefactions to their hometowns and the building of urban and rural residences in which their wealth and taste could be displayed and the next generation educated and trained up in the approved ways.

This pattern of development can be observed not only at towns, though they were supremely important as centres for the reception, adaptation and transmission of cultural behaviours, but also out in the vast rural tracts of the Western provinces. An important class of buildings that demonstrated much the same trajectory of development was temples, be they the 'Gallo-Roman' type of sanctuary north of the Pyrenees or the more classically inspired temple complexes of the Iberian peninsula. This was a question not only of the quantity of such sites, which reached a peak at this period (cf. Goudineau *et al.* 1994), but also of their elaboration, particularly the major urban temples of Gaul and Spain but also the extensive rural sanctuary complexes of Gaul, such as Sanxay, or of Spain, such as Munigua. Their overall extent, the complexity of their suites of structures and the elaboration of their architectural ambition all reached a climax at around the turn of the second and third centuries. In this they reflect and form part of a larger pattern of complexity embracing a whole series of arenas for making public declarations through architecture; this is not simply a reflection of religious architecture divorced from its wider cultural milieu. The epigraphic evidence from both Gaul and Spain makes it clear that such complexes were the recipients of the euergetism of the municipal elites, acting either individually or collectively, and that they were viewed as a proper place for competitive expenditure. Indeed, as has been noted, the major rural sanctuaries of Gaul seem to have formed part of the built identity of the *civitas* alongside the more conventionally Roman-style *civitas* capital. By the close of the second century, the development of elaborate rural residences, the villas, had also reached the culmination of its first major flowering both north and south of the Pyrenees. That the development of yet another form of expression of elite wealth and identity in the Roman style should coincide with the trajectories of cities and sanctuaries should occasion little surprise, since it seems that it was very much the same strata of society, often, indeed, probably the same families or individuals, who were engaged in this sort of self-affirmation. So, be it the densely clustered if decoratively unambitious villas of Picardy, the huge complexes of central Gaul, the richly decorated establishments of Provence or the elaborate villas of the Iberian littoral, the later second century was the time at which the cycle of development that had started back in the early first century AD, if not earlier, culminated.

One result of all this activity motivated by elite self-representation and display was increased pressure on agricultural production in the Western provinces in order to pay for the lifestyle to which the local elites wished to become accustomed. In part this may have entailed improvements, or at least changes, to the crops grown and animals reared; that is, to the technologies of production. It more certainly entailed both intensification and extensification of both arable and pastoral production to exploit further the carrying capacity of the various agrarian regions and resources of the West in order to mobilise greater surpluses. Allied to this, there may well have been changes in the social relations of production, with the landed class gaining more direct and heritable control over land, its yields and its workers, and those workers perhaps becoming more tied to their sites of production, sometimes as slaves but more often as dependent labour. Another result was the creation of the more complex series of crafts and skills required to service the cultural requirements of the elite; especially visible to us are such skills as those of the mosaicist or the sculptor, but also the stoneworker, the metalworker, the glassworker and the potter. But the less expensive products, building stone, metalwork, glass and pots, became available to a wider range of customers, who, partly motivated no doubt by emulation of their social superiors, increasingly consumed such products with a frequency and in ways that had not been possible before incorporation within the political, cultural and economic nexus of the Roman Empire.

It is the contention here that this enormous upsurge in cultural and economic activity slowed effectively to a halt by the end of the second century AD, and that from the early third century a reorientation of cultural values and economic expressions can be discerned. It has long been acknowledged that the creation of new cites in the Roman mode was essentially a phenomenon of the first century BC and the first century

AD, few demonstrably being created in the second century, with exceptions in outlying provinces such as Germania Inferior (e.g. *Colonia Ulpia Traiana*, Forum Hadriani). Within these and the earlier foundations, the late first and the second centuries saw the initial provision and subsequent elaboration of the range of public buildings and monuments that so characterise the 'Roman' city in the West. But by the later second century in the area under consideration here, the impetus to provide such structures had slowed almost to a standstill; many may still have been under construction, and it is entirely possible that some were never completed. Individual exceptions, such as the third-century 'Palais Gallien' amphitheatre at Bordeaux, do not disprove the general proposition. The late first and second centuries had also seen the increasing construction of private housing, both for the elites and, on a more humble scale, for the artisans and other non-elite members of the urban population. By the later second century, their development had led to the cities achieving their maximum built-up areas, with the residences of the elite often lavishly equipped with the trappings of wealth and display such as marble and mosaic. It would seem that by the second half of the second century urban development across much of the West had attained a peak which could not be sustained.

Along with this near cessation in the construction of public buildings and the beginning of the abandonment of some private buildings and contraction at the peripheries of cities came a slowdown in the rate of epigraphic activity; from the later second century on, the practice of setting up stone inscriptions dwindled rapidly (cf. MacMullen 1982). The construction of public buildings and the setting up on or in them of inscriptions were both practices very much dominated by local elites, who provided the funds for the provision of buildings, monuments and other facilities for their home city and wished to have these facts commemorated in a durable way which advertised not only their euergetism but also their status and honours. It can be argued (e.g. Kulikowski 2004: Ch. 1, esp. 26–7; Woolf 1998: Ch. 4) that, since the setting up of inscriptions was so intimately linked to the need to demonstrate status and thus to individual social insecurity, and since the need to proclaim the status of a city had similar roots, what we are seeing is in part the consequences of the settling down of the social order and the lessening of the need so insistently to proclaim it. This is probably to be linked with the decline of civic euergetism among local elites in the West, expressed in the decline in the provision of public buildings and facilities. It was argued in Chapter 3 that what was developing through the third century and on into the fourth was the increasing 'privatisation' of what had been the settings for much public interaction, with the elites retreating inside their residences, where control of access and interaction was much more easily arranged. Moreover, these residences were places where money could be spent more directly on the aggrandisement of the individual aristocrat through his surroundings. So what we seem to be seeing, both in the epigraphy and in the wider question of the decline in public benefaction, is a cultural shift away from some of the established means of elite self-promotion and display, possibly linked, as argued in Chapter 3, to levels of intra- and intercity rivalry whose expressions had escalated to unsustainable levels of cost. This was not necessarily the same, it should be noted, as a decline in the importance of towns *per se* as centres for such self-promotion and display; in many regions it was more about the start of a shift towards other modes of display. Nevertheless, there were regions where it does seem that the urban enterprise was starting to fail; in Chapter 3 we saw individual examples such as Javols and Jublains and also regions such as Normandy where the urban centres contracted through the third century, sometimes effectively to vanishing point. Other regions that may have seen a similar phenomenon include those of the mountain cities of the western Alps and the Pyrenees, and maybe also the Massif Central and Brittany. Evidence for the Iberian peninsula is, to date, not so readily available, but sites such as Labitolosa may conform to the same overall pattern. This is probably not just a function of environmental determinism, mountain areas often being poorer in expendable surpluses, because Normandy is a low-lying and agriculturally rich region. More likely, it is because there areas were by reason of their locations somewhat isolated from the main economic and social networks that encouraged and supported urbanism in regions more closely tied into these nexuses.

Overall, we saw a similar pattern for rural settlement and agricultural exploitation. In Chapter 6 we saw that there was a generalised pattern across Gaul and Spain that again suggests a substantial change in the trajectory of the development of rural settlement and the exploitation of the agrarian landscape. Again, the pattern varies by region, but certain common trends may be discerned. There is a marked diminution, sometimes a cessation, in the establishment of new sites. Of the sites already in existence, there is usually a fall in numbers. Sometimes (e.g. south-eastern Gaul and on into Catalonia) this seems to be a reduction of sites in marginal landscapes. Sometimes (e.g. central Gaul) this seems to be a reduction of smaller, less complex sites, be they of the 'farmstead' or 'villa' type, with an increasing focus on larger sites, which seem to become more dominant in the economic and social landscapes of such regions. For both these cases, it was argued that what we may be seeing, in part at least, is that the upsurge in activity across the early Roman period had attained its maximum possible extent; indeed, it may have gone beyond what was sustainable in more than the short term. For the abandonment of settlements on marginal land, it was argued that this represented a settling back from an overextended exploitation of the land to one more closely aligned with the agricultural carrying capacity of the land. If so, then this would probably have had an impact on the surpluses available for expenditure on other activities. More complex is the question of how to view the simplification of the settlement hierarchy in other areas. It does not seem to have been associated with any pattern of land abandonment, so it is unlikely that it can be laid at the feet of environmental factors. It does seem to be part of a wider pattern of reordering of the settlement hierarchy, with the largest and richest sites becoming more dominant. In this case what we may be seeing is the extension of control over land by the elite and the subordination of the least powerful, in terms of both social and tenurial relations and possibly also in terms of their physical location. This pattern of increasing dominance of the elite – 'the rich getting richer' – is one that was also argued to characterise the later third and fourth centuries in many regions, including central Gaul. So what we may be seeing here is changes in social relations (including those of production?). There are other regions of the West where the turn of the century marked a threshold of change for more immediate reasons, the obvious one being Baetica, where the actions of Septimius Severus and his family had a major impact on the ways the landscape was used, as is observable in the archaeology. At the other extremity of the study area, there is the unresolved question of when the pattern of intense villa settlement in northern Gaul, centred on modern Picardy but detectable elsewhere, began to break down both numerically and in the size of the individual establishments, towards the much less intense and more varied settlement patterns characteristic of the fourth century. Given that it is likely that the intensity of the colonisation of these areas was in important part a reflection of their role in supplying the Rhine armies, what we may be seeing is in part the impact of changes in the scale, nature, and supply requirements and patterns of the garrisons on the Rhine, quite apart from any impact of 'Germanic invasions' in the mid to later third century. Whatever may be the arguments about individual regions or types of settlement, cumulatively the picture is one of the marked deceleration or cessation of the growth of rural settlement and exploitation that had characterised the previous three centuries (longer in some regions) at about the turn of the second and third centuries; as in other aspects of the archaeology, a second-century peak had proved unsustainable.

Likewise, in Chapter 7, we noted that some important economic formations that had characterised the first two centuries AD also came to an end or changed markedly around the end of the second century or in the first part of the third century. Above all, this concerned the long-distance movement of goods engendered by the state's requirements to supply politically important groupings. We have just seen the way in which the Severi reoriented the olive oil supplies for the city of Rome away from Baetica. Equally well known is the decline in the volume of the long-distance supply of Mediterranean goods such as wine and olive oil to the armies in Germany and Britain from the later second century on. Part of the same pattern may be the 'decline' of the Gaulish samian industries, for which the military market had always been crucial, as evidenced by the long-term 'pull' of this market that caused the manufacturing centres to shift away from the Mediterranean and up, eventually, to the Rhineland. The reasons for this are complex, but important ones seem to be to do with what can broadly be characterised as 'import substitution', the growing ability of the provincial economies to satisfy the demands of the army, which were themselves very probably changing anyway. We may start with a rather unusual take on import substitution: recruitment. The epigraphic evidence shows (e.g. Mann 1983: esp. 63–8) that by the later second century the legions hardly recruited from Italy any longer, and a similar pattern holds good for many of the old Mediterranean recruiting provinces such as Narbonensis. Instead legionary recruitment in Europe increasingly took place from the frontier provinces and peoples. The same also seems to hold good for the auxiliary forces, to judge by the funerary epigraphy of provinces such as Britain and the Germanies. Thus provincial producers were increasingly substituting for Mediterranean imports. One consequence of this may have been a decreasing taste for Mediterranean dietary elements, such as olive oil, which had to be imported from the Mediterranean because of its climatic requirements, so local supply could not substitute for the imports. But other elements such as wine were increasingly being supplied from within the developing provincial economies (cf. the papers in Brun and Laubenheimer 2001), as also were herbs, spices and other foodstuffs that earlier had had to be imported from the Mediterranean (cf. Stallibrass and Thomas 2008: 9–11). Likewise, the meat component of the 'military diet', a diet that had once been formed by the interaction of incoming Mediterranean soldiery with local pastoral regimes and dietary preferences, seems, by this period, to have become indistinguishable from the local provincial one, as evidenced by animal bones from civil and military sites (King 1999), so again provincial tastes had won out over Mediterranean. The 'collapse' of the samian industries, once blamed upon 'Germanic invasions', may now be assimilated to a similar explanation. Indeed, in the later first century, the movement of production from the south Gaulish centres on the fringes of the Mediterranean world to the central Gaulish industries can be seen as this substitution process already under way. By the turn of the second and third centuries, the primacy was passing to the east Gaulish centres of the Rhineland. Even after those were reduced to little more than local centres, the red-slip tradition continued, above all in the Argonne production centres that flourished through the third and fourth centuries and well into the fifth century, along with other red-slip productions such as Jaulges/Villiers-Vineux in central Gaul or Oxfordshire in southern Britain, to say nothing of the huge ARS outputs of central North Africa, even if modern anglophone archaeology chooses not to qualify these with the name 'samian', thus imposing a discontinuity on what was essentially a continuous process of development and relocation of the red-slip industries. So rather than reading the end of the second and start of the third century as being defined economically by the 'decline' of the older, long-distance supply routes, it would probably be better to read this period as being the one in which the provincial economies had now developed to the extent where they could crowd out Mediterranean imports to a military market that was anyway probably less demanding of them. This may also help explain the decline in the volume of amphora-bearing shipwrecks in the western Mediterranean (also discussed in Chapter 7); indeed, yet again, what may need accounting for in the graph of such shipwrecks is not so much the 'decline' from the third century as the peak in the first and second centuries, which has been explicitly linked (Bowman and Wilson, A. 2009) with the economic transformations consequent upon the unification of the Mediterranean basin.

So the argument put forward here is that the decades either side of AD 200 represent a 'threshold' in the archaeological record by virtue of the ending of the phase of major cultural and economic unification and expansion consequent upon the conquest of the Mediterranean basin by Rome. A whole complex of developments in the archaeology had been made possible or encouraged by this. These had resulted in a series of peaks of activity across a range of domains of the archaeology of the West: towns, villas, rural settlement, the economy and commerce. As noted in earlier chapters, the risk for us is that we see the second half of the second century in teleological terms, as the 'norm', the fortunate state to which all had been tending, with the changes that succeeded it in the third century read in terms of 'decline'. As has been noted above on more than one occasion, it may well actually be the second-century peak that is abnormal and requires explaining and not the third-century realignments. Another way to look at this would be in Braudelian terms as a *conjoncture* where the *moyenne durée* of some three hundred years had come about as the result of the *histoire événementielle* of Rome's conquests with their cultural and economic consequences; from the end of the third century, the realities of the *longue durée* reimposed themselves, primarily in the economic sphere, with consequences for the substrates on which the particular cultural manifestations were based. It should also be pointed out that there are concurrent changes in other domains of the archaeology – for instance, the change from cremation to inhumation as the predominant burial form in the West – that were taking place at the same time but which it is not really feasible to read as a response to the unification of the west Mediterranean basin, save perhaps at the basic level that Roman law encouraged the separation of the living and the dead and that Roman society saw the rites concerned with the disposal of the dead as an arena in which statements about the identities of the deceased and their relicts might be made. Among the elites and at the cities in particular, these often took forms that were clearly influenced by metropolitan and Italian practice.

The changes around the turn of the second and third centuries have been analysed and discussed above in terms that are comfortable to the archaeologist, terms such as 'changes in the modes of elite self-display', 'carrying capacity' or 'import replacement'; these are explanations that allow for a variety of causes, some of which may be related, and others independent of each other. They are also concepts whose archaeological correlates can be modelled and ultimately tested; if, at present, this is rather imprecisely done, then at least the existence of the models can inform the future collection and analyses of data with the purpose of testing them. There is also one possible cause of major change towards the end of the second century that has not been invoked above but needs to be confronted: the 'Antonine plague'. The historical sources paint a picture of an extremely destructive disease pandemic appearing on imperial territory in 166, which apparently carried off a significant proportion of the empire's population, so it must thus have had a serious impact on the demographic and economic vitality of the empire. This is a field of study which archaeologists have conventionally tended to shy away from, partly because the evidence is textual and thus they have little to contribute, but, perhaps more importantly, because 'plague' (the inverted commas are there to indicate that there remains uncertainty over the precise nature of the disease and that it should not be assumed to be modern-style bubonic or pneumonic plague) and its consequences are very difficult if not impossible to pin down in the archaeological record and thus to model and test their impact. On the one hand, this 'plague' killed its victims in a short space of time (days at most); it is thus one of that category of virulent and lethal diseases that work so fast that they leave no trace in the osteology, which is all that archaeologists normally have of its victims: it is not as yet possible to tell if a particular individual was carried off by the 'plague'. On the other hand, even if archaeologists cannot identify 'plague' as the causative agent of an individual's death, can they identify wider changes in the archaeological record such as the ones referred to above as necessarily being down to the effects of the 'plague' rather than anything else? A valuable attempt to contextualise the 'plague' in terms of other, better-attested pandemics and to identify types of evidence that might be susceptible to such interpretation was made by Duncan-Jones (1999). He noted that, historically, such pandemics while associated with a high mortality, do not have a uniform incidence; crowded conditions such as army camps and cities are preferential situations for their spread, a point perhaps to be borne in mind when considering the relatively under-urbanised West (it did have important troop concentrations, though there is no mention of them having been seriously affected by the 'Antonine plague'). Duncan-Jones then tries to define a series of proxies which might yield evidence of the impact of the 'plague' such as coinage, inscriptions, documents from Egypt, military 'diplomas' (discharge certificates), brick stamps and marble quarry tallies. What unites these is, of course, that they all bear writing that makes them datable to a year or to a small number of years; they are thus not like the sorts of material normally available to the archaeologist where the date range of an individual building or burial or type of pottery is measured usually in decades, far too blunt a tool for the sort of relatively precise dating of the incidence of the plague or its immediate aftermath. Duncan-Jones' approach has been critiqued by Greenberg (2003), who notes, among other things, that the downturns noted by Duncan-Jones do not necessarily coincide with the arrival of the 'plague' – sometimes they start too early, or else they might also be ascribed to other causes – and that at present there is no way of discriminating between potential causes. But, more importantly, he lays out the sorts of reasons why archaeologists have tended to shy away from invoking the 'Antonine plague' as a causative mechanism for observed changes in the archaeological record. Put simply, no one has yet laid out a causative chain from the 'plague' to specific features of the archaeological record that either have to be explained or are highly likely to be explained as having been caused by such a disease and not by other factors. So there is no model relating medical cause to archaeological effect.

With no model, the hypothesis is untestable and thus unfalsifiable. So, currently, to invoke the 'Antonine plague' as an explanation of change in the archaeological record, certainly in the area covered in this book, is essentially to invoke it as a *deus* (or *pestis*) *ex machina*, waving a magic wand to solve a problem.

The discussion above has sought to establish that the decades at the end of the second century and the beginning of the third marked a 'threshold' in the development of the archaeological record. Perhaps the most important defining feature of this threshold is that it marked the cessation of a 300-year (or longer) period of archaeological trajectory related to and consequent upon Rome's conquest of the Western Empire. From then on, the archaeology tended to develop away from the norms of the second half of the second century; these developments, to be sure, took place at different rates and in differing ways in different regions of the West, but that there were certain cultural, economic and social commonalities expressed in the archaeological record has been the subject of the preceding chapters. By the fifth century these had to a certain extent come to cohere over wide areas of the West (see the two preceding chapters). It is now the task, therefore, to describe and justify the decades at the turn of the fifth and sixth centuries as marking another threshold that allows us to terminate this work at that point.

AD 500: an archaeological threshold?

Like the threshold argued for above, this threshold has two aspects: on the one hand, there is a series of 'ends' in the archaeological record and thus of the human activities they represent; on the other hand, there is a series of 'new beginnings' taking shape at about this time, ones that would have an important impact on into the sixth and seventh centuries, if not later. Whereas in the threshold around 200 it was the 'ends' that seem to be more important, around 500 there is a more equal balance between 'ends' and 'beginnings'. In this discussion we shall commence with some fairly clear 'ends', but as the discussion continues we shall increasingly balance these with some 'beginnings', and the consideration will close with areas in which this threshold marks points of departure towards the early medieval archaeology of the sixth and seventh centuries.

We start with the changes that betokened the end of the old order of the political and military hegemony of the Roman Empire. In Chapter 8 we saw that the archaeological evidence suggests that, from the early part of the fifth century on, it becomes progressively more difficult to recognise a standing army distinct from the rest of the population, in the way that the army had been distinctive in the Western provinces since at least the Caesarian conquests in the first century BC. To judge by the evidence of the forts of the Rhine frontier, the material culture of the people living and burying at these sites contained an increasing proportion of material originating from east of the Rhine or from the Pontico-Danubian region through the first half of the fifth century. But this was still overlaid onto a considerable proportion of material culture, both from fort interiors and from burials, of Roman provincial type. Allied with this was the precipitous decline in the supply of coin from the imperial mints, both precious and base metal, at around the start of the fifth century. What this meant for the standing army which the Roman state had maintained through the fiscal cycle embodied in that coinage is a debate yet to be had, but it would certainly seem to suggest a major shift in the relationship between the Western Empire and its troops. It would seem to betoken the end of a formal system of payment in coin; had the state moved more to an army paid in land and supplies? Were military garrisons and operations increasingly being confided to more local war leaders, some 'Roman' and others 'barbarian', whose men followed them because of their leadership rather than because of any particular loyalty to whoever was emperor of the West at any one time? From the middle of the fifth century, it is pretty much impossible to see anything in the archaeology that suggests a distinct and distinctive Roman military identity, rather than a series of war bands of shifting political loyalties. So the army by which Rome had gained and sustained her empire over half a millennium and more seems by the end of the fifth century to have been 'privatised' out of existence, replaced increasingly by the military forces of the 'barbarian' kingdoms, as we shall see below, just as the Western imperial office itself had been terminated and replaced by a 'barbarian' ruler in Italy in 476. By the end of the fifth century, anything recognisable as the political entity that had been the Western Roman Empire, underpinned by its army and its monopoly of legitimate force, had come to an end.

When we turn to the wider cultural formations of the West, one important index of change is the completion of a process that had been under way for the previous two centuries and more, the move away from the classical Roman-style provincial city with its public buildings, such as forum, baths and amphitheatre, to the late antique model of walls and churches. This move had been a long-drawn-out process with the widespread construction of walls as a defining monument at (former) cities starting in the later third century in northern Gaul and north-western and north-eastern Spain, and then becoming generalised probably from the turn of the fourth and fifth centuries across the southern half of Gaul and into Spain, where, until then, cities seem to have retained important aspects of their early imperial form. It was probably also from the later fourth century that the provision of urban churches became increasingly standard, both intramural episcopal complexes and extramural cemetery churches. This dual process of human and divine protection of these now much-shrunken cities had become more or less universal across the West (Britain excepted) by the end of the fifth century. As was argued in Chapters 3 and 4, these major changes in the physical form and monumentality of cities were not just a passive reflection of changing values but also served actively to promote the creation of the new form of citizen of the Roman Empire, militant and Christian. The former of these attributes, *militant*, also feeds into another growing theme in the period, the militarisation of aristocratic identity.

As with the rise of fortifications as a defining monument of the late antique town in the West, this militarisation was a phenomenon that emerged first in the northern part of Gaul in the aftermath of the troubles of the second half of the third century. With the increased presence, comings and goings, and importance of the army across this region, and not just along the Rhine; with the rhetoric, and often reality, of the emperor as military leader and guardian; and with even the paramilitary identity and dress of what we would call the civil service, it is not surprising that we may argue for a change in the vocabulary of elite identity towards the military and away from the traditional vocabulary embodied in such things as town houses, villas and grave monuments. In the fourth century this new ideology is most clearly seen in burial, with the spread across Gaul between Seine and Rhine of burials with the accoutrements of late Roman military dress, sometimes accompanied by knives, and much more rarely (for the fourth century) by weapons such as swords and shields. Conventionally viewed as 'Germanic weapon graves', these are in fact more likely to be, in the main, local elites using a new vocabulary of status display. Interestingly, such burials are not common either at forts or at towns, where we might expect garrisons of the regular army, suggesting again that this is a phenomenon of non-military persons adapting signifiers of military identity in ways different from the army's burial rites. Similar materials, particularly the dress elements, are found on villa and other rural sites, though whether they ended up there because they were worn by their inhabitants or by visiting soldiers or officials is not easy to say. There is also the question of the hilltop fortifications of eastern Gaul with their associated burials, the latter traditionally interpreted in ethnic terms but in fact linking in with the wider phenomenon of these furnished burials and again perhaps to be considered in the light of 'militarisation'. It was also noted that there is a comparable burial rite (the 'Duero' cemeteries) of the northern part of the Iberian peninsula, interpreted more in terms of the paraphernalia of hunting than of warfare. This interpretation has also recently been applied to the north Gaulish burials (there are sporadic burials of the same type in Britain also). But even if the 'weaponry' is not particularly martial in character and is related more to the ritualised violence of the hunt (which, it should be remembered, was a major aristocratic pastime and thus a status definer in the late Roman world), the use of military/official indicators of belonging and of rank was certainly being adopted in various regions. Of course, some of these men may have been soldiers at some time; the penetration into the ranks of the aristocracy of military men is a commonplace of late Roman society and of a certain amount of anguished, aristocratic social comment. Some ex-soldiers clearly returned east of the Rhine, and their status and identity were defined in death by their period of service to Rome. In the fifth century, it is clear that the proclamation of a 'military' identity became more and more important across much wider areas of the West. In the past this topic has been bedevilled by the 'ethnic' question, with the long-standing view that graves containing weapons and those containing material culture with its typological origins outside imperial territory were necessarily an expression (above all in death) of a 'Germanic' or, more widely, 'barbarian' identity. This subject in both its theoretical grounding and its evidential base was extensively discussed in Chapter 2 and especially Chapter 8, and the necessary link between burial rite/material culture and ethnic identity was broken. With this link broken, it is easier to see that burials that have hitherto been categorised as 'Germanic' or given more precise ascriptions such as 'Frankish' or 'Visigothic', can instead be seen as those of people to whom, for men, the concern was with displaying status, and in northern Gaul in particular, this was a status linked with weaponry and thus a warrior identity. Further south in Gaul, weapons as such were rarer, but dress elements derived from non-Roman regions, as well as from Roman provincial military-related dress, clearly proclaimed an identity where reference to martial qualities was clear, and in sharp contrast to fourth-century practices. In the Iberian peninsula, by contrast, we currently have a situation where there are very few archaeological correlates of male military or other elite status; instead it is female burials in the rural areas of the Meseta that carry particular ideological charges, but these are not (or at least not recognisably) martial. So, by the end of the fifth century, the archaeology across much of the West, especially of burial, makes a series of statements about the importance of this warrior identity for males and some form of non-Roman provincial identity for both males and females, whatever their ethnicity and whether or not the individual ever engaged in warfare.

This long-drawn-out process of increasing militarisation of elite identity had happened in tension with another complex of attributes relating to questions of elite self-representation: the persistence of an older tradition of aristocratic values displayed both at the towns of the southern part of Gaul and in the Iberian peninsula. In these towns it does seem that though the forms and values of the old 'public' town were increasingly falling into disuse, their replacement by display in the private sphere of the aristocratic residence was a feature of the fourth century and the earlier part of the fifth; it is just that at present we have much less excavated evidence for them than we do for their rural counterparts, the villas. The importance of villas was not a generalised phenomenon, but it was related to certain defined regions. This is the tradition exemplified in the person and writings of Ausonius and reflected in the villas of his native region of south-western Gaul, along with other regions such as the Meseta of Spain and across into modern Portugal, the Mediterranean littoral of the Iberian peninsula, the area around Trier, and the south of Britain; other areas see such villas, but not in the concentrations that are so marked in these regions. These villas harked back to earlier traditions of civilian aristocratic display, even if reworked for the times. In Chapter 5 particular emphasis was laid on the decorative elements such as mosaics, marble and metal sculpture, silver plate and other movables. As well as being in themselves indicators of wealth because of the intrinsic value of their materials, they also served a perhaps more important role in demonstrating the high culture and classical, Roman aristocratic learning, the *paideia*, of their owner. Their depiction of figures and scenes from classical Graeco-Roman mythology was designed to signal the degree of their owner's mastery of the complex codes of Roman elite education and his place in the web of social relations that bound the elites of the empire, senatorial or imperial, and provincial and local, together in a social and cultural *koine*. Even an unlettered military parvenu such as the emperor Valentinian I wanted his son to be formed in this culture – hence the appointment of Ausonius as tutor to the young Gratian, who was brought up at Trier, where the buildings of the imperial palace and of the villas in its hinterland were in this 'traditional' aristocratic style, even if the emperor paraded in them as generalissimo. Despite the difficulties of the dating evidence and of the quality of some of the earlier excavations, it would seem that this type of elite residence and display continued down into the first half of the fifth century in the southern half of Gaul and in Iberia; its fate in Britain and the Trier region was more summary. But it would seem, both in southern Gaul and on the Spanish Meseta, that the second half of the fifth century saw these complexes falling out of use as residences. Parts of them might still be inhabited or be colonised by what used to be termed 'squatter' occupation, and parts of them might be adapted for use as churches, but the major part of the buildings, along with the social and cultural messages of which they had been the material expressions, look to have been abandoned. This was probably partly due to functional reasons such as the decreasing availability of the craftsmen necessary for creating or maintaining the relatively sophisticated structures and decorative schemes, but it probably also reveals the move away from and final abandonment of this aristocratic lifestyle, its complex and expensive education, and the sorts of messages it sought to convey. Instead, across the West we see the move to simpler, wooden structures, which again have often been seen in ethnic terms but are better thought of as part of the complex of changes consequent upon the desuetude of Roman-style masonry construction. Another contributory factor may have been the increasing dominance of the Church and its unhappiness with the art inherited from a pagan world, which it had initially tolerated but which it increasingly sought to suppress. Paradoxically, it was nonetheless the Church that was to be the one institution that in fact perpetuated the old high culture and formal education in the Latin language, 'grammar' and 'rhetoric', even if modified for Christian consumption and use. The accomplishments of some of the clergy can be seen in the elaborate epitaphs in the old classical verse forms, such as the accomplished hexameters of the carefully lettered epitaph of Pantagathus from Vaison-la-Romaine, the elegiac couplets of the epitaph of Bishop Eutropius from Orange (Cavalier 2005: Nos. 215 and 210), or the elaborate verse inscription composed in the mid fifth century by Sidonius Apollinaris to be inscribed around the interior of the new episcopal church of his friend Bishop Patiens at Lyon. And, of course, church buildings, both in their masonry structures and in the marble, mosaic, glass and metalwork that adorned their interiors, also perpetuated the old, Roman, aristocratic tradition; given the aristocratic origins of an increasing number of bishops, this is perhaps understandable. Nevertheless, outside the particular case of the Church, it would seem that the late fifth century saw the end of the old means of elite display and their increasing replacement by a militarised aristocratic identity, one which was displayed in settlements and structures that were simpler than those of villas.

It was noted above that a concomitant of the decline of the old villa culture, both physically in its structures and socially and culturally in the messages it had embodied, and possibly also tenurially in the fragmentation of the late Roman pattern of estate holding, was that the tradition of building in wood that had always been there alongside the elite masonry techniques again became general. Study of such buildings and settlements has in the past often been in ethnic terms, attempting to ascribe a 'Germanic' identity; this has particularly been the case in the northern part of Gaul and in the Rhineland (and, of course, in Britain). Related to this has been the debate about the origins of the 'village', a term laden not just with social connotations but also with ones relating to lordship and possession as expressed in documents that are almost all of a later date than concerns us here but that have sometimes been projected back into the fifth century (for discussion of the phenomenon of villages and consideration of peasant societies, see Wickham 2005: Chs. 8 and 9). There were, of course, enormous differences across the regions encompassed in this book, from the south of Spain to the north of Gaul. These differences are further complicated by the very different amounts and traditions of work in the differing regions. Thus there are some regions where we benefit from a considerable amount of evidence through excavation, such as the north of Gaul and parts of the south-east of Gaul including the Mediterranean littoral across into Catalonia. Other regions, such as much of the centre and south-west of Gaul and almost the whole of the interior of the Iberian peninsula, are largely *terrae incognitae*, illuminated by the occasional individual instance of a detailed excavation or regional surface survey. The regions that do yield us enough evidence on which to try to base coherent discussions have been dealt with in Chapter 6 in particular and also in Chapter 9 for the fifth century, and it is not the intention to reprise that material. What is important here is, first, that even in the regions where the villa had dominated in the fourth and earlier fifth centuries, by the end of the fifth century the settlement pattern had shifted to this pattern of nucleated settlements in timber which, architecturally, were much simplified compared with all but the simplest villas. This architectural simplification must reflect a corresponding social simplification; some of these settlements have houses that are larger than others, sometimes with dependent structures, and sometimes standing within enclosures (particularly in northern Gaul). These are features that suggest a degree of social stratification, but with a much flatter social hierarchy than is evidenced by the old villa pattern (for examples and discussion, see Hamerow 2002; Peytremann 2003). On the other hand, one must bear in mind the importance of archaeologically invisible aspects such as furnishings, textiles and colour, as well as of the social activities (archaeologists do like to imagine these people indulging in much feasting) that took place in these technically simpler settings, and not assume that these places did not have their own signifiers of social gradients and access to prestigious goods and practices. Other regions exhibit somewhat different physical manifestations in terms of the plans of settlements overall and of the residential units within them; nevertheless, the arguments about social simplification still hold in large measure. For instance, the settlements in Provence, Languedoc and through to Catalonia are also marked by greater architectural simplicity: the buildings of sites such as El Bovalar, Lunel, le Roc de Pampelune or Saint-Blaise suggest a much simplified social structure in comparison with earlier villa landscapes in the region. Le Roc de Pampelune and Saint-Blaise share two features, however, that are of note as they foreshadow what will become wider spread phenomena from the sixth century on. One is that they are both defended. At one level, this could simply be read as a sign of insecure times, but, at another, it could be evidence for a landscape which was still, in part at least, owned by landed proprietors, only now they grouped their workers into 'estate villages' (some defended) rather than annexed to villas. The other common feature of the two sites, which they share with El Bovalar and in all probability Lunel, is that they have churches. As we saw also in Chapter 9, the wider provision of rural churches is also a phenomenon observable from the close of the fifth century. It was, of course, to continue into the sixth and seventh centuries and beyond, crystallising eventually into that most characteristic of medieval institutions, the parish. So the demise of the villa system towards the turn of the fifth and sixth centuries is also matched by the early development of social and ecclesiastical structures that were to become characteristic of the succeeding centuries.

Perhaps the clearest index of the dis-integration of the West by the end of the fifth century is in the economic sphere, particularly in its archaeological correlates for the range and scale of the movement of goods. In Chapter 7 it was argued that the existence of the Western Empire in the later third and fourth centuries had economic consequences that overlaid onto a large number of local economic systems some larger formations that were expressions of the state's needs but also served to make possible and to integrate economic activity at a scale that otherwise simply would not have occurred. This was what was termed the 'political (or imperial) economy', which responded to the political imperatives of the late Roman state, in particular the need to supply the city of Rome and the armies. We saw that the 'political economy' did impact directly on some areas under consideration here, essentially the Mediterranean littoral, and that, indirectly, the integration of economic activity it promoted may well have had consequences for the interior of Spain and Gaul, as expressed in the distribution patterns and volumes of some of the principal pottery industries. But the 'political economy' was not the sole driver of such distributions; it was also argued that there was a significant element of 'market economy' trading with the general population of the regions, but profiting from the enhanced reach made possible by the state-engendered transport systems. Moreover, the stability and largely peaceful conditions within imperial territories established conditions within which such large-scale production and long-distance commerce could profitably be carried out. Naturally, pottery is the best proxy available to archaeologists for such patterns, but the evidence for long-distance movement of and influence of luxury materials, principally marbles, and luxury crafts such as mosaic, along with more day-to-day materials such as items of dress, including brooches and belt suites, reinforces the picture of integration over long distances as well as more local production and diffusion. This economic activity, especially in its more mundane forms, was to an extent lubricated by the existence of a relatively plentiful, low-value, copper-alloy coinage. This is not to say that the economy was monetised in anything like the way modern, Western economies are; nonetheless, for those who had access to it, coin did facilitate exchange; this access was probably preferentially to the upper social strata, urban dwellers and probably also artisans, so probably the city-centred aspects of manufacture and exchange would have been enhanced by the use of coin. On the other hand, though coins are regularly found on non-villa rural sites, they are not found in quantities comparable with the cities, suggesting that they were used for transactions on a more occasional basis. The progressive weakening of the power of the Western Empire from the early years of the fifth century onwards had important consequences for the structures of trade across its territories. At one level, the stability and relatively peaceful conditions for trade guaranteed by the imperial system progressively diminished in the face of the irruptions of peoples from beyond the frontiers and the prolonged series of wars, large and small, for dominance over people, territory and resources throughout the fifth century. At another level, the elements of a command economy generated by the need to supply the army also collapsed, probably early in the fifth century, as goods were no longer moved in bulk over long distances. Implicated in this is the question of the cessation of the minting and supply of the low-value coinage north of the Alps from the very beginning of the century, followed soon after by the cessation in the minting and supply of the silver coinage that had been the staple for the payment of the army. It may have been that the state was already refashioning its fiscal relations with the army.

In northern Gaul the fifth century saw a progressive diminution in the quantity of pottery produced by major centres such as the Argonne and the Eifel, with the apparent extinction of the major Jaulges/Villiers-Vineux centre early in the century. In addition, the products that remained were traded over progressively smaller distances and in progressively smaller quantities. This was particularly so in the second half of the fifth century, so that Argonne, for example, which a hundred years earlier had been a major, super-regional supplier, now barely counted as a regional industry. Finds from sites and burials of the late fifth century in northern Gaul are predominantly of much more locally produced fabrics, some in forms and decorations deriving from the late Roman provincial repertoire, descendants, albeit on a smaller scale, of fourth-century industries such as the *céramique granuleuse/rugueuse* of the Paris Basin. Other local products, though, were often handmade and in forms and with decorative schemes clearly deriving from areas to the north-east of the lower Rhine. These have traditionally been discussed in ethnic terms as indicating the settlement of 'Germanic' peoples on provincial soil. To an extent this may be true, but it is also worth remembering that much of this pottery comes from graves and so may have as much to do with funerary practices as domestic, and some of the comparable pottery from settlement sites may be related more to domestic than to funerary use. It is also worth asking whether this was also an effect of changing practices in the preparation and consumption of foodstuffs and in drinking habits.

In the southern half of Gaul and in Spain, the picture was more varied and the trajectories rather different, but by the turn of the fifth and sixth centuries the picture was increasingly similar to that in northern Gaul. Initially, the political fragmentation of the Western Empire seems to have had remarkably little impact on the major industries and trading patterns in these areas. After the shock of the Vandal capture of North Africa and the breaking of the tax spine, the long-distance and relatively large-scale commerce in North African products, amphorae and red-slip wares seems to have re-established itself, perhaps not on the same absolute scale as before and with a greater presence of products from elsewhere in the Mediterranean, particularly the Aegean basin and the Levant. Clearly, established patterns of consumer demand persisted in the coastal cities, and producers responded to this, either in Africa or with other centres achieving greater penetration as African dominance slackened. This was, though, regionally variable, with Tarragona and its area receiving a high proportion of supplies from elsewhere in the Mediterranean, whereas Marseille and the Languedoc show a smaller proportion of long-distance imports, and some areas such as south-eastern Spain even less. Nevertheless, this circum-Mediterranean trade remained vigorous, and even after a downturn in the second half of the fifth century, it picked up again and experienced something of a boom around the turn of the fifth and sixth centuries (Reynolds 2010: Ch. 3). The Mediterranean littoral therefore bucks the trend of the overall argument here. But it is important at the same time to note that this commerce does not penetrate much beyond that littoral, nor, indeed, equally to all classes of site along that littoral; it is a highly directional trade concerning largely the urban centres. Moreover, this is not simply an artefact of more archaeological work at these places; rural sites have been surveyed and excavated also. By contrast, in the interior of the Iberian peninsula, the trajectory appears significantly different. The best-documented (and that is not the same as well-documented) industry is the TSHT (*terra sigillata hispánica tardía*) of the Meseta and adjoining regions, which had risen to regional or super-regional prominence in the course of the fourth century, possibly related to conditions created by the mobilisation of goods for army supply. Persisting into the first half of the fifth century, it seems to have collapsed around the middle of the fifth century, perhaps in tandem with the villas and their economy of the Meseta regions, which also seem to have gone into terminal decline at about the same date. Thereafter the pottery production and trade of at least the northern half of the peninsula was increasingly marked by small-scale centres with a limited distribution, related in part to the geographical constraints of the interior of the peninsula. The southern extremity of the peninsula did benefit increasingly from the commercial current westwards along the Mediterranean, supplying amphorae and fine wares which also went out through the Pillars of Hercules and up the Atlantic façade, reaching even as far as Britain (in minute quantities).

In the southern half of Gaul, away from the littoral, the first half of the fifth century was still a time of large-scale diffusion for a certain number of regional and super-regional production centres. The clearest example of this is the complex of products that goes under the generic name of DSP (*dérivées de sigillées paléochrétiennes*), which is known especially from the south-west of Gaul and became a major product at the very end of the fourth century. There were also Languedocian workshops (which tended to fire in oxidising conditions in preference to the reducing firings of the south-western, 'Atlantic', workshops). Neither of these centres seems to have been much troubled by the Visigothic settlement in Aquitaine or the subsequent wars in the south-east. Indeed, the Atlantic products seem to have benefited for a time from the disruptions to the regional producers of the northern half of Iberia, replacing them to some extent and even penetrating north of the Loire. There were also other relatively widely distributed wares of late Roman provincial types circulating into the first half of the fifth century, such as the coarse wares of the south-west or the *céramique luisante* of Languedoc. But again the second half of the fifth century seems to have been a period during which the volume and distribution of these centres declined. Of course, some, notably DSP, did continue to be produced and to circulate into the sixth century, but in a more restricted range of forms, in smaller quantities and over lesser distances than had been the case in the earlier fifth century.

The discussion above has essentially been in terms of ceramics, simply because they remain the archaeologist's best proxy. Luxury materials such as marble and mosaic collapsed along with the disappearance of the aristocratic market that had so long been their patrons, though the Church did continue to employ them (but in the case of marble there is clear evidence of reuse). The picture from the pottery, though, is consistent across almost all the former Western Empire. At the start of the fifth century, there were across the West several major fine-ware industries with a regional or super-regional distribution of their products. By the end, some of these had disappeared, some still had a regional distribution but on a much-reduced scale, and some had become essentially local producers. Alongside the major producers, there had always been many, local, technically unsophisticated producers supplying the needs of restricted areas for utilitarian pottery. By the end of the fifth century, it was this scale of production that had become predominant, sometimes in fabrics and forms derived from the Roman provincial repertoire, and sometimes in fabrics and forms recalling the 'Germanic homelands'. What all this attests to is the economic disintegration of the Roman West in the aftermath of the loss of political coherence and the associated demise of the 'political economy' of the state. From the point of view of the producer, this was a period of simplification of production techniques, the range and volume of products, and distribution networks. From the point of view of the consumer, this was a period of diminishing availability and choice. There was less pottery in absolute terms, and there were fewer products and forms available; mostly they came from producers situated near at hand, and they may have been acquired more through social mechanisms of exchange than through any 'market' mechanisms. This was a world of contracting horizons, and the reduction in and simplification of economic activity can stand as a proxy for the complexity – or, increasingly, the lesser degree of complexity – of social formations and cultural expressions. Nevertheless, there are two important exceptions to this picture. One is the Church, which, as we have already seen, remained capable of mobilising considerable resources of both economic and cultural capital and of deploying them to serve not only the continuation of a Christianised version of late Roman elite culture in its buildings, their fittings and the education of the clergy, but also, on occasion, to serve the 'moral economy' of the Church in areas such as famine relief and the ransom of prisoners. The other field in which we still find evidence for the long-distance movement of goods is in a particular area of the 'prestige economy'. Though the old, Roman aristocratic 'prestige economy' had collapsed, along with its enormous wealth, the networks of reciprocity, and the cultural values of the Roman aristocracies of the West, a new one was developing in the second half of the fifth century that was to have important consequences in the following century. This was the long-distance movement of items of dress in 'Germanic' taste from origins such as the Pontico-Danubian region of central and eastern Europe and also some areas of northern Europe into the heartlands of what had been the Western Roman Empire. The traditional 'ethnic' interpretations of such material was questioned in Chapter 8; instead it was proposed that what we find here is the development of a new vocabulary for the signifying of status, gender, age and even ethnicity in the funerary domain. In northern Gaul and the Rhineland, this material was also on occasion accompanied by weapons, such as swords and axes, and by armour, such as shields and helmets, whose origins also lay outside the empire (even if influenced by it), clearly signifying the importance of a warrior or martial identity for those buried with them. This brings us to the last topic to be considered here – not an 'end' but the important new beginnings taking place at the end of the fifth and through the sixth centuries; that is, the creation and acceptance of new political entities to replace the deceased Western Empire, in particular the Frankish and Visigothic kingdoms.

The replacement of the Western Roman Empire by a series of successor states ruled by royal families claiming Germanic descent and supported by a warrior nobility of similar claimed descent, as clearly proclaimed in their personal names, but nonetheless ruling over populations largely of Roman provincial descent, is one of the standard master narratives for the shift in conventional period divisions from Roman to early medieval, or for the origins of the Middle Ages, or for the origins of Europe. It is a standard master narrative because, historically, it is indisputable that such a shift in political authority occurred. Equally, it has been recognised for some time that a simple, linear narrative of this type obscured a much more complex situation with a range of actors, all with their own agendas and a much more complex web of cause and effect. For a long time the archaeology remained unproblematic (or unproblematised), with changes in the archaeological record, above all in aspects of material culture and to an extent in the built environment, being read as reflections of the historical narrative and the textual constructions of identity. The interest over the past few decades, as part of the postmodernist and post-colonialist enterprises, in questions of the construction of identity (both in literary and archaeological sources), and of the representation of identity in life and in death, has made clear the inadequacy of older approaches to the evidence and uncoupled the archaeological evidence from any simple, predetermined interpretation. As was discussed at greater length in Chapter 8, this has meant that for the fourth and fifth centuries problems of how to approach the identification of 'Germanic' and 'barbarian' identity have become far more open; in that chapter it was noted that certainty about the ethnic identity of individuals in the archaeological record is now rarely, if ever, possible. The chapter followed the trend in recent anglophone scholarship of replacing interpretations of that evidence, particularly burials, in terms of precise ethnic identities with interpretations in terms of status, gender and age. It argued that the material culture traditionally interpreted in ethnic terms might more accurately be interpreted in terms of making statements about identities that differed from those made in the Roman provincial burial tradition, identities that drew particularly from the ethnic and cultural mix in what is now termed the Pontico-Danubian region. But it was also argued that the new perspectives on how to interpret this material also made it difficult to identify 'Germanic' political entities on former Roman territory before late in the fifth century. It is this aspect of the arguments in Chapter 8 that is of relevance here.

In the historical sources, by the end of the fifth century, a number of 'Germanic' polities had come into being across the former Roman West, sometimes as the result of acts of the Roman government. By 500, there were two groups that predominated: the Franks and the Visigoths to north and south of the Alps. In their rise to dominance, the Franks had very recently defeated the Alamanni at the battle of Zülpich (traditionally dated to 496), were about to defeat and absorb the Visigothic kingdom of Toulouse in 506, and would do the same to the Burgundian polity in 534; in the meantime other ethnic groupings such as the Alans had briefly troubled the textual sources and possibly even the archaeology. A similar situation seems to have obtained south of the Pyrenees, where the Visigoths had arrived relatively late in the century and taken over a peninsula already home to a number of other ethnic groupings, particularly the Sueves, and then consolidated their hold. But it was argued that the archaeology on its own tells a far less precise story.

This is very much the case for northern Gaul, where it is very hard to argue, for the fourth and fifth centuries, that anything in the archaeology – either settlement and building types or funerary offerings or other material culture such as pottery – maps onto a definable and distinctive ethnic identity that can be correlated with the historical mentions of Frankish people. Archaeologically, there was indeed through the fifth century an increasingly important non-Roman provincial facies in the settlements/buildings, but its geographical and probably cultural origins were mixed, some of it deriving from the areas beyond the lower Rhine in the modern-day Netherlands, north-west Germany and southern Denmark, some of it from the Pontico-Danubian area, and much of it ending up irredeemably mixed, sometimes in the same grave. Moreover, though it is sometimes called 'Frankish' in modern scholarship, this tends to be a back-projection of the later political reality. In culture-historical terms, archaeologists have identified, with more or less plausibility, Alans, Alamanni, Anglo-Saxons, Burgundians Sarmatians and Visigoths, in the area of the future kingdom of the Franks, but nothing specifically Frankish. Instead it was proposed in Chapter 8 that the very end of the fifth and the beginning of the sixth centuries were a crucial time in the forging of a Frankish identity, crystallised in the burial of Childeric at Tournai with its fusion of Roman and Germanic symbols of power and authority; the presence in the grave of a personal signet ring suggests that Childeric needed to seal written documents produced for him by a Roman-style bureaucracy. From this point on, we start to see other trappings of a kingdom, in particular the adoption of a coinage which, while based on imperial prototypes, was now struck in the name of the king. Even so, other archaeological correlates of a distinct 'Frankish' identity are still not easy to pin down. If one looks at the regions where Frankish dominance is attested to from the early sixth century (e.g. Wieczorek et al. 1996: Pt. II), what is clear is that there was an increasing spread of relatively rich burials, including male burials with weapons and armour adorned with rich fittings of gold and gold-and-garnet settings and jewellery, along with female burials with a variety of brooches in various metals but also increasingly demonstrating status with gold-and-garnet jewellery. Many of the burials containing this sort of material are in the regular 'row-grave' cemeteries (*Reihengräberfelder*) that have long been thought of as 'Germanic', but, since they are largely rural and of an increasingly Christianised population, this may well be a misleadingly simple explanation. But also these cemeteries seem for the most part to have been new creations from the start of the sixth century on, again suggesting a horizon in the archaeological evidence. Moreover, these cemeteries and the very similar material culture were also used in regions historically attributed to peoples such as the Alamanni, the Bavarii or the Thuringi. But even so, the period around 500 can be depicted as a 'threshold' since, yet again, what we are seeing is the 'end' of Roman-derived practices – particularly in the domain of funerary archaeology – and the beginning of their replacement by something characterised by increasing social and gender differentiation through material culture, with specific aspects of masculinity, such as warrior equipment, or femininity, such as domestic equipment, being emphasised. This is a world very unlike the Roman provincial world of one hundred years previously, and, taken in conjunction with more direct evidence for consciousness of being a separate political entity, would alert us to a threshold of change even without the texts.

In the Iberian peninsula, something similar seems to be taking place at roughly the same time. The use of non-Roman funerary material that had been increasing in the centre and north of the peninsula since the middle of the fifth century was becoming more widespread across the peninsula, reaching down into the old Baetica in the south and up into Galicia in the north. Along with their geographical extension, the grave goods from the early sixth century on show a tendency to increase in size (e.g. buckles and their plates), elaboration, and the richness of their settings and decorative plates (cf. Ebel-Zepezauer 2000: Ch. 3; Ripoll López 1998). For all that, the traditional explanation for this material has been that it is 'Visigothic'; nevertheless, the objections raised to this reading in Chapter 8 remain valid. It is predominantly female in character (brooches above all, but belt suites less definitively), and it comes overwhelmingly from rural cemeteries. It therefore seems to lack a masculine counterpart to the female funerary deposits, and there is the problem of identifying the contemporaneous urban burial grounds and funerary rite. Linked with both problems is the lack of high-status male graves; perhaps kings and nobles were buried according to a Christian funerary rite and their graves marked by other characteristics, such as tombstones or funerary monuments in or beside major churches, as much as or more than the nature and richness of their grave goods. Nevertheless, the spread of the rural burials and their specific and increasingly elaborate contents across more and more of the peninsula does strongly suggest that, from the early sixth century, status (at least in death) was displayed in ways that were departing more and more from Roman provincial norms. So as with the Frankish areas of Gaul, so with Spain, identity in status and gender was increasingly being expressed in new, non-Roman ways. How this relates to the historical phenomenon of the Visigothic kingdom is, of course, uncertain, but it does seem that the peoples of the peninsula were increasingly devising for themselves an identity in their dress, and probably in other aspects not now visible to us, that, on the one hand, was becoming more uniform across the peninsula and, on the other hand, marked them off from the regions around them in Gaul, Italy and North Africa. So again the archaeology would tell us that the turn of the fifth and sixth centuries marked a threshold from which the archaeology of the Iberian peninsula more and more took on its own identity, influenced by external contacts and trends but not defined by them.

In seeking to define the periods around 200 and 500 as 'thresholds', this chapter has sought to justify the chronological parameters adopted by this book. Around 200, the development of a classic Roman-style archaeology slowed and ceased and started to turn into other expressions. Not everything changed at the same time, at the same rate and in the same ways (the impact of Christianity is the most obvious big exception); nevertheless, there are certain broad themes and similarities mapped in the individual chapters of this book and reprised in the discussion above that united wide geographical areas or social classes of the West and displayed a broad chronological unity also. Around 500, important aspects of the archaeology which derived from late Roman social, economic and cultural structures, in turn, slowed or ceased, and other formations came to the fore and developed on into the sixth and seventh centuries and even later. So what this chapter has also sought to do is to argue that in archaeological terms the three centuries between these two dates have an overall internal coherence and consistency that define the period and to an extent set it apart. It is these three centuries that I have chosen to call 'late Roman', because central to them is the remaking of Roman-style identities – often in ways widely different from under the Early Empire – under the impact of political, ideological, cultural and economic influences peculiar to the period. As new identities, increasingly divorced from Roman-style practice, new ideologies in religion and social order, and new economic formations came to the fore and took over from the early sixth century onwards, the peoples of what had been the Western Roman Empire moved archaeologically into a new period, one increasingly distinct from what had gone before and one in which they shaped their own responses to pressures and influences rather than being defined by the power of Rome, albeit that in so many respects, physical and mental, they still lived in its shadow.

Bibliography

Abad Casal, L. (1982) *Pintura romana en España*. Alicante

Abascal, J. M., Cebrián, R., Hortelano, I. and Ronda, A. M. (2008) 'Baños de la Reina y las villas romanas del Levante y de los extremos de la Meseta sur', in Fernández Ochoa *et al.*: 285–300

Abascal, J. M., Cebrián, R. and Sala, F. (2000) 'El vicus romano de "Baños de la Reina" (Calpe, Alicante)', in Ribera i Lacomba: 49–64

Adrian, Y.-M. (2006) 'Céramiques et verreries des IVe et Ve s. dans la basse vallée de la Seine: les exemples de Rouen, Lillebonne, Caudebec-lès-Elbeuf, Tourville-la-Rivière (Seine-Maritime)', in Ouzoulias and Van Ossel: 331–89

Agache, R. (1978) *La Somme pré-romaine et romaine d'après les prospections à basse altitude* (Mémoires de la Société des Antiquaires de Picardie, 24). Amiens

Alarcão, J. de, Etienne, R. and Mayet, F. (1990) *Les villas romaines de São Cucufate (Portugal)*. Paris

Alba Calzado, M. (2005) 'La vivienda en Emerita durante la antigüedad tardía: propuesto de un modelo para Hispania', in Gurt i Esparraguera and Ribera i Lacomba: 121–50

Alemany, A. (2006) 'La problemática de las fuentes sobre la presencia alana en la "Galia" e "Hispania"', in López Quiroga *et al.*: 307–15

Allen, J. R. L. and Fulford, M. G. (1996) 'The distribution of south-east Dorset black burnished category 1 pottery in south-west Britain', *Britannia* 27: 223–81

Almagro-Gorbea, M., Álvarez Martínez, J. M., Blázquez Martínez, J. M. and Rovira, S. (eds.) (2000) *El Disco de Teodosio*. Madrid

Almeida, M. J. de and Carvalho, M. (2005) '*Villa* romana da Quinta das Longas (Elvas, Portugal): la lixeira baixo-imperial', *Revista Portuguesa de Arqueologia* 8(1): 299–368

Álvarez García, N., Ballester Martínez, C., Carrión Marco, Y., Grau Almera, E., Pascual Berlanga, G., Pérez Jordà, G., Ribera i Lacomba, A. and Rodríguez Santana, C. G. (2005) 'L'àrea productive d'un edifice del fòrum de *Valentia* al baix imperi (segles IV–V)', in Gurt i Esparraguera and Ribera i Lacomba: 251–60

Amiel, C. and Berthault, F. (1996) 'Les amphores du Bas-Empire et de l'Antiquité tardive dans le sud-ouest de la France: apport à l'étude du commerce à grande distance pendant l'antiquité', in Maurin and Pailler: 255–63

Anderson, B. R. O'G. (1991) *Imagined Communities: Reflections on the Origin and Spread of Nationalism*. London

Anderson, J. K. (1985) *Hunting in the Ancient World*. Berkeley, Calif./Los Angeles/London

APDCA (Association pour la Promotion et la Diffusion des Connaissances Archéologiques) (1996) *Formes de l'habitat rural en Gaule Narbonnaise: spécial villa romaine*. Sophia Antipolis

Arce, J. (1982) *El ultimo siglo de la España romana (284–409)*. Madrid

(1997) 'Emperadores, palacios y *villae* (a propósito de la villa romana de Cercadilla, Córdoba)', *Antiquité Tardive* 5: 293–302

(ed.) (2002a) *Centcelles: el monumento tardorromano: iconografía y arquitectura*. Rome

(2002b) 'Los Vándalos en Hispania (409–420 a.D.)', *Antiquité Tardive* 10: 75–85

(2005a) *Bárbaros y romanos en Hispania (400–507)*. Madrid

(2005b) 'Antigüedad tardía hispánica: avances recientes', *Pyrenae* 36(1): 7–32

(2006) 'Obispos, emperadores o proprietarios en la cúpula de Centcelles', *Pyrenae* 37(2): 131–41

Arce, J., Chavarría Arnau, A. and Ripoll, G. (2007) 'The urban *domus* in late antique Hispania: examples from Emerita, Barcino and Complutum', in Lavan *et al*.: 305–36

Arce, J. and Delogu, P. (eds.) (2001) *Visigoti e Longobardi*. Florence

Arce, J. and Le Roux, P. (eds.) (1993) *Ciudad y comunidad cívica en Hispania: siglos II y III d.C. /Cité et communauté civique en Hispania* (Collections de la Casa de Velazquez, 40). Madrid

Arthur, P. (1989) 'Some observations on the economy of Bruttium under the later Roman Empire', *Journal of Roman Archaeology* 2: 133–42

Aupert, P. and Monturet, R. (2001) *Saint-Bertrand-de-Comminges II: les thermes du forum* (Etudes d'Archéologie Urbaine). Bordeaux

Aurrecoechea Fernández, J. (2001) *Los cinturones romanos en la Hispania del Bajo Imperio* (Monographies Instrumentum, 10). Montagnac

Azkarate Garai-Olun, A. (2002) 'De la tardoantigüedad al medioevo cristiano: una mirada a los estudios arqueológicos sobre el mundo funerario', in Vaquerizo: vol. II, 115–40

(2004) '*Reihengräberfelder* al sur de los Pirineos occidentales', in Blázquez Martínez and González Blanco: 389–414

Azkarate Garai-Olun, A., Núñez, J. and Solaun, J. L. (2003) 'Materiales y contextos cerámicos de los siglos VI al X en el País Vasco', in Caballero *et al*.: 321–70

Baccabrère, G. and Badie, A. (2002) 'Le rempart de bord de Garonne', in Pailler: 429–40

Bach, S., Boudartchouk, J.-L., Cazes, J.-P., Rifa, P. and Stutz, F. (2002) 'Le mobilier funéraire, témoin d'influences culturelles et d'une possible présence germanique', in Pailler: 533–43

Bacharach, B. S. (2002) 'Fifth-century Metz: late Roman Christian *urbs* or ghost town?', *Antiquité Tardive* 10: 363–81

Badie, A., Sablayrolles, R. and Schenck, J.-L. (1994) *Saint-Bertrand-de-Comminges I: le temple du forum et le monument à enceinte circulaire* (Etudes d'Archéologie Urbaine). Bordeaux

Balmelle, C. (1992) 'L'habitat urbain dans le sud-ouest de la Gaule romaine', in Maurin: 335–64

(2001) *Les demeures aristocratiques d'Aquitaine: société et culture de l'antiquité tardive dans le sud-ouest de la Gaule* (*Aquitania*, Suppl. 10). Bordeaux

Balmelle, C., Barraud, D., Brun, J.-P., Duprat, P., Gaillard, H., Jacques, P., Maurin, L., Petit-Aupert, C., Rigal, D., Robin, K., Poudié, P., Sillières, P. and Vernou, C. (2001) 'La viticulture antique en Aquitaine', *Gallia* 58: 129–64

Balmelle, C. and Van Ossel, P. (2001) 'De Trèves à Bordeaux: la marque des élites dans les campagnes de la Gaule romaine au IVe et Ve siècles', in Ouzoulias et al.: 533–52

Banaji, J. (2001) *Agrarian Change in Late Antiquity: Gold, Labour and Aristocratic Dominance*. Oxford

Barat, Y. (2003) 'Un établissement agricole en mutation: les transformations de la *villa* gallo-romaine de Richebourg (Yvelines) dans la seconde moitié du IIIe siècle', in Ouzoulias and Van Ossel: 7–29

Barat, Y. and Samzun, A. (2008) 'Découverte d'un établissement germanique du bas-empire (IVe s.) aux Essarts-le-Roi (Yvelines)', *Revue archéologique d'Ile-de-France* 1: 215–26

Baratte, F. (1981) *Le trésor d'argenterie gallo-romaine de Notre-Dame-d'Allençon* (*Gallia*, Suppl. XL). Paris

(1989) *Trésors d'orfèvrerie gallo-romains*. Paris

Barbet, A. (2008) *La peinture murale romaine en Gaule*. Paris

Barbiera, I. (2010) 'Le dame barbare e i loro invisibili mariti: le transformazioni dell'identità di generenel V secolo', in Delogu and Gasparri: 123–55

Barnish, S. J. B. (1986) 'Taxation, land and barbarian settlement in the Western Empire', *Papers of the British School at Rome* 54: 170–95

Barral i Altet, X. (1991) 'Les étapes de la recherche au XIXe siècle et les personnalités', in Duval: 348–68

Baucheron, F. and de Montjoye, A. (1996) 'Le groupe cathédral de Grenoble (Isère): essai sur les origines', *Antiquité Tardive* 4: 95–100

Bauer, F. A. and Witschel, C. (eds.) (2007) *Statuen in der Spätantike*. Wiesbaden

Bayard, D. (1990) 'L'ensemble du Grand Amphithéâtre de Metz et la sigillée d'Argonne au Ve siècle', *Gallia* 47: 271–319

Bayard, D. and Massy, J.-L. (1983) *Amiens romain: Samarobriva Ambianorum* (Revue archéologique de Picardie). Amiens

Beaujard, B. (2000) *Le culte des saints en Gaule: les premiers temps, d'Hilaire de Poitiers à la fin du VIe siècle*. Paris

(2006) 'Les cités de la Gaule méridionale du IIIe au VIIe s.', *Gallia* 63: 11–23

Beaujard, B. and Prévôt, F. (2004) 'Introduction à l'étude des capitales "éphémères" de la Gaule (Ier s.–début VIIe s.)', in Ferdière: 17–37

Bellet, M.-E., Cribellier, C., Ferdière, A. and Krausz, S. (eds.) (1999) *Agglomérations secondaires antiques en Région Centre* (17e suppl. à la Revue Archéologique du Centre de la France). Tours

Beltrán de Heredia Bercero, J. (2002) *From Barcino to Barcinona (1st to 7th Centuries): The Archaeological Remains of the Plaça del Rei in Barcelona*. Barcelona

Bénard, J., Mangin, M., Goguey, R. and Roussel, L. (eds.) (1994) *Les agglomérations antiques de Côte-d'Or*. Besançon

Bergmann, M. (1999) *Chiragan, Aphrodisias, Konstantinopel: Zur mythologischen Skulptur der Spätantike* (Palilia 7). Wiesbaden

  (2007) 'Die kaiserzeitlichen Porträts der Villa von Chiragan: Spätantike Sammlung oder gewachsenes Ensemble?', in Bauer and Witschel: 323–39

Bernhard, H. (1994) *Von der Spätantike zum frühen Mittelalter in Speyer: Bemerkungen zum Stand der archäologischen Forschung*. Speyer

Bernhard, H., Engels, H.-J., Engels, R. and Petrovsky, R. (1990) *Der römische Schatzfund von Hagenbach*. Mainz

Bertelli, C. (1999) 'Visual images of the town in late antiquity and the early Middle Ages', in Brogiolo and Ward-Perkins: 127–46

Bidwell, P. (1997) *Roman Forts in Britain*. London

Bintliff, J. (ed.) (1991) *The 'Annales' School and Archaeology*. Leicester

Bisconti, F. (1989) 'Le rappresentazioni urbane nelle pittura cimiteriale romana: dalla città reale a quella ideale', in Duval: 1305–21

Bishop, M. (2002) *Lorica Segmentata*. Vol. I: *A Handbook of Articulated Roman Plate Armour* (JRMES Monograph No. 1). Duns

Bishop, M. and Coulston, J. (2006) *Roman Military Equipment: From the Punic Wars to the Fall of Rome*, 2nd edn. London

Bishop, M. and Howard-Davis, C. (2009) 'The Roman militaria', in Newman: 687–92

Blanchet, A. (1900) *Les trésors de monnaies romaines et les invasions germaniques en Gaule*. Paris

Blaskiewicz, P. and Jigan, C. (1994) 'La céramique du Bas-Empire en Normandie', in Tuffreau-Libe and Jacques: 127–39

Blázquez Martínez, J. M. and González Blanco, A. (eds.) (2004) *Sacralidad y Arqueología: Thilo Ulbert zum 65 Geburtstag am 20 Juni 2004 gewidmet* (Antigüedad y Cristianismo; Monografias Históricas sobre la Antigüedad Tardía, 21). Murcia

Blin, O. (2000) 'Un sanctuaire de *vicus*: Jouars-Pontshrtrain (Yvelines)', in Van Andringa: 91–117

Bocquet, A. and Naveau, J. (2004) 'Jublains (Mayenne), capitale d'une cite éphémère', in Ferdière: 173–82

Böhme, H. W. (1974) *Germanische Grabfunde des 4. bis 5. Jahrhunderts zwischen unterer Elbe und Loire: Studien zur Chronologie und Bevölkerungsgeschichte*. Munich

(1985) 'Les découvertes du Bas-Empire à Vireux-Molhain: considérations générales', in Lemant: 76–88

(1986) 'Das Ende der Römerherrschaft in Britannien und die angelsächsische Besiedlung Englands im 5. Jahrhundert', *Jahrbuch des Römisch-Germanischen Zentralmuseums Mainz* 33(2): 469–574

(1996) 'Söldner und Siedler im spätantiken Nordgallien', in Wieczorek *et al.*: 91–101

Böhner, K. (1958) *Die fränkischen Altertümer des Trierer Landes* (Germanische Denkmäler der Völkerwanderungszeit, Serie B, Die fränkischen Altertümer des Rheinlandes, 1). Berlin

Bóna, I. (2002) *Les Huns: le grand empire barbare d'Europe IVe–Ve siècles*. Paris

Bonifay, M., Carré, M.-B. and Rigoir, Y. (eds.) (1998) *Fouilles à Marseille: les mobiliers (Ier–VIIe siècles ap. J.-C.)* (Travaux du Centre Camille-Jullian, 22/ Collection Etudes Massaliètes, 5). Paris

Bonifay, M. and Raynaud, C. (2007) 'Echanges et consommation', *Gallia* 64: 93–161

Bonnet, C. (1977) *Les premiers edifices chrétiens de la Madeleine à Genève: étude archéologique et recherches sur les functions des constructions funéraires.* Geneva

(1993) *Les fouilles de l'ancien groupe épiscopal de Genève (1976–1993)*. Geneva

(2006) 'Éléments de topographie chrétienne à Genève (Suisse)', *Gallia* 63: 111–15

Bonnet, C. and Beltrán de Heredia, J. (2000) 'El primer grupo episcopal de Barcelona', in Ripoll López and Gurt: 467–90

Bonnet, C. and Privati, B. (1991) *Le temple de Saint-Gervais*. Geneva

Booth, P. M., Simmonds, A., Boyle, A., Clough, S., Cool, H. E. M. and Poore, D. (2010) *The Late Roman Cemetery at Lankhills, Winchester: Excavations 2000–2005* (Oxford Archaeology Monograph, 10). Oxford

Bosch Puche, F., Macias i Solé, J. M., Menchon i Bes, J. J., Muñoz Melgar, A. and Teixell Navarro, I. (2005) 'La transformació urbanística de l'acròpolis de Tarracona: avanç de les excavacions del Pla director de la cathedral de Tarragona (2000–2002)', in Gurt i Esparraguera and Ribera i Lacomba: 161–5

Bost, J.-P., Roddaz, J.-M. and Tassaux, F. (eds.) (2003) *Itinéraires des saintes à Dougga: mélanges offertes à Louis Maurin*. Bordeaux

Boudartchouk, J.-L. (2005) 'Aux origins des paroisses rurales en Région Midi-Pyrénées: un pré-inventaire', in Delaplace: 135–49

(2006) 'La letter IV, 15 de Sidoine Apollinaire et la dédicace du baptistère d'Elaphius à *Castellum* (novembre–décembre 476 ou 477?): l'évêque de Clermont s'est-il-rendu à Chastel-sur-Murat?', *Revue de la Haute-Auvergne* 68: 547–68

Boudartchouk, J.-L., Arramond, J.-C. and Cazes, Q. (2002) 'Saint-Pierre-Saint-Géraud?', in Pailler: 490–1

Bouet, A. (2003a) *Les thermes privés et publics en Gaule Narbonnaise* (Collections de l'Ecole Française de Rome, 320). Rome (ed.) (2003b) *Thermae Gallicae: les thermes de Barzan (Charente-Maritime) et les thermes des provinces gauloises* (Suppl. 11 à la *Revue Aquitania*). Bordeaux

Bourdieu, P. (1977) *Outline of a Theory of Practice*. Cambridge

(1984) *Distinction: A Social Critique of the Judgement of Taste*. London

Bowersock, G. W. (1990) *Hellenism in Late Antiquity*. Ann Arbor, Mich.

Bowersock, G. W., Brown, P. R. L. and Grabar, O. (eds.) (1999) *Late Antiquity: A Guide to the Post-Classical World*. Cambridge, Mass.

Bowes, K. (2005) '"Une coterie espagnole pieuse": Christian archaeology and Christian communities in fourth- and fifth-century Hispania', in Bowes and Kulikowski: 189–263

(2006) 'Building sacred landscapes: villas and cult', in Chavarría Arnau *et al.*: 73–95

(2008) *Private Worship, Public Values, and Religious Change in Late Antiquity*. Cambridge

(2010) *Houses and Society in the Later Roman Empire*. London

Bowes, K. and Gutteridge, A. (2005) 'Rethinking the later Roman landscape', *Journal of Roman Archaeology* 18: 405–13

Bowes, K. and Kulikowski, M. (eds.) (2005) *Hispania in Late Antiquity: Current Perspectives*. Leiden and Boston

Bowman, A., Cameron, A. and Garney, P. (eds.) (2005) *The Cambridge Ancient History*, 2nd edn. Vol. XII: *The Crisis of Empire, A.D. 193–337*. Cambridge

Bowman, A. and Wilson, A. (eds.) (2009) *Quantifying the Roman Economy: Methods and Problems*. Oxford

Braat, W. C. (1973) 'Der Fund von Deurne, Holland', in Klumbach: 51–83

Brassous, L. (2011) 'Les enceintes urbaines tardives de la péninsule ibérique', in Schatzmann and Martin-Kilcher: 275–99

Brather, S. (2008a) 'Zwischen Spätantike und Frühmittelalter: Zusammenfassung', in Brather: 425–65

(ed.) (2008b) *Zwischen Spätantike und Frühmittelalter: Archäologie des 4. bis 7. Jahrhunderts im Westen* (57). Berlin

Braudel, F. (1972) *The Mediterranean and the Mediterranean World in the Age of Philip II*. New York

Bridger, C. (2008) 'Die Gräber der Spätantike', in Müller *et al.*: 583–94

Bridger, C. and Gilles, K.-J. (eds.) (1998) *Spätrömische Besfestigungsanlagen in den Rhein- und Donauprovinzen* (British Archaeological Reports, International Series, 704). Oxford

Brogiolo, G. P., Chavarría Arnau, A. and Valenti, M. (eds.) (2005) *Dopo la fine delle ville: le campagne dal VI al IX secolo* (Documenti di Archeologia, 40). Mantua

Brogiolo, G. P., Gauthier, N. and Christie, N. (eds.) (2000) *Towns and Their Territories Between Late Antiquity and the Early Middle Ages* (The Transformation of the Roman World). Leiden

Brogiolo, G. P. and Ward-Perkins, B. (eds.) (1999) *The Idea and Ideal of the Town Between Late Antiquity and the Early Middle Ages* (The Transformation of the Roman World), Leiden

Brown, A. G., Meadows, I., Turner, S. D. and Mattingly, D. J. (2001) 'Roman vineyards in Britain: stratigraphic and palynological data from Wollaston in the Nene Valley, England', *Antiquity* 75(4): 745–57

Brown, P. R. L. (1971) *The World of Late Antiquity*. London

  (1981) *The Cult of the Saints*. Chicago

  (1992) *Power and Persuasion in Late Antiquity: Towards a Christian Empire*. Madison, Wis. and London

Brulet, R. (1978) *La fortification de Hauterecenne à Furfooz* (Ardenne et Gaume Monographie, 12). Brussels

  (1990) *La Gaule septentrionale au Bas-Empire/Nordgallien in der Spätantike* (*Trierer Zeitschrift*, Suppl. 11). Trier

  (ed.) (1995) *Forts romains de la route-Bavay-Tongres: le dispositif militaire du Bas-Empire*. Louvain-la-Neuve

  (1996) 'Tournai und der Bestattungsplatz um Saint-Brice', in Wieczorek *et al*.: 163–70

  (2010) 'La sigillée du Bas-Empire de Jaulges-Villiers-Vineux', in Brulet *et al*.: 208–10

Brulet, R., Dewert, J.-P. and Vilvorder, F. (eds.) (2009) *Liberchies V: vicus gallo-romain*. Louvain-la-Neuve

Brulet, R., Vilvorder, F. and Delage, R. (eds.) (2010) *La céramique romaine en Gaule du nord: la vaisselle à large diffusion*. Leiden

Brun, J.-P. and Congès, G. (1996) 'Une crise agraire en Provence au troisième siècle?', in Fiches: 233–56

Brun, J.-P. and Gilles, K.-J. (2001) 'La viticulture antique en Rhénanie', in Brun and Laubenheimer: 165–79

Brun, J.-P. and Laubenheimer, F. (eds.) (2001) *Dossier: la viticulture en Gaule* (*Gallia*, Suppl. 58). Paris

Brunaux, J.-L. (ed.) (2009) *Les temples du sanctuaire gallo-romain de Ribemont-sur-Ancre*. St-Germain-en-Laye

Buchet, L. (1988) 'La deformation crânienne en Gaule et dans les regions limitrophes pendant le haut Moyen Age: son origine – sa valeur historique', *Archéologie Médiévale* 18: 55–72

Buffat, L. (2005) 'De la *villa* antique à la *villa* médiévale: L'évolution des centres domaniaux dans l'ancienne cite de Nîmes aux premiers siècles du Moyen Age', in Delestre *et al*.: 161–76

  (2011) *L'économie domaniale en Gaule Narbonnaise*, Monographies d'Archéologie Méditerranéenne, 29. Lattes

Burnett, A. (1987) *Coinage in the Roman World*. London

Burnham, B. and Johnson, H. (eds.) (1979) *Invasion and Response: The Case of Roman Britain* (British Archaeological Reports, British Series, 73). Oxford

Burnham, B. and Wacher, J. S. (1990) *The 'Small Towns' of Roman Britain*. London

Busson, D. (1998) *Carte archéologique de la Gaule 75 – Paris*. Paris

Butler, R. M. (1961) 'Late Roman town walls in Gaul', *Archaeological Journal* 116: 25–50

Caamaño Gesto, J. M. (1997) 'Los miliarios del siglo IV en Galicia', in Teja and Pérez: 407–24

Caballero, L. and Mateos, P. (eds.) (2000) *Visigodos y Omeyas: un debate entre la Antigüedad tardía y la Alta Edad Media* (Anejos de Archivo Español de Arqueología, 23). Madrid

Caballero, L., Mateos, P. and Retuerce, M. (eds.) (2003) *Cerámicas tardorromanoas y altomedievales en la Península Ibérica: ruptura y continuidad* (Anejos de Archivo Español de Arqueología, 28). Madrid

Cahn, H. A. and Kaufmann-Heinemann, A. (1984) *Der spätrömische Silberschatz von Kaiseraugst* (Basler Beiträge zur Ur- und Frühgeschichte, 9). Derendingen

Cameron, A. (1992) 'Observations on the distribution and ownership of late Roman silver plate', *Journal of Roman Archaeology* 5: 178–85

Cantino Wataghin, G. (2003) 'Christian topography in the late antique town: recent results and open questions', in Lavan and Bowden: 224–56

Carr, K. E. (2002) *Vandals to Visigoths: Rural Settlement Patterns in Early Medieval Spain*. Ann Arbor, Mich.

Carreté, J.-M., Keay, S. and Millett, M. (1995) *A Roman Provincial Capital and Its Hinterland: The Survey of the Territory of Tarragona, Spain, 1985–1990* (*Journal of Roman Archaeology*, Suppl. 15). Ann Arbor, Mich.

Carrié, J.-M. (1982) 'Le "colonat" du Bas-Empire: un mythe historiographique?', *Opus* 1: 351–70

 (1994) 'Les échanges commerciaux et l'état antique tardif', in Schenck: 175–211

Carroll, M. (1997) 'The late Roman frontier fort *Divitia* in Cologne-Deutz and its garrisons', in Groenman-van Waateringe: 143–90

 (2001) *Romans, Celts and Germans: The German Provinces of Rome*. Stroud

Carru, D., Gateau, F., Leveau, P. and Renaud, N. (2001) 'Les villae en Provence au IVe et Ve siècles', in Ouzoulias et al.: 475–501

Carver, M. (1993) *Arguments in Stone: Archaeological Research and the European Town in the First Millennium* (Oxbow Monograph, 29). Oxford

Casey, J. and Reece, R. (eds.) (1974) *Coins and the Archaeologist* (British Archaeological Reports, British Series 4). Oxford

Castellvi, G., Nolla, J. P. and Rodà, I. (eds.) (2008) *Le trophée de Pompée dans les Pyrénées (71 avant J.-C.): col de Panissars, Le Perthus, Pyrénées Orientales (France), La Jonquera, Haut Empordan (Espagne)* (Gallia, Suppl. 58). Paris

Catalo, J. and Cazes, Q. (2002) 'Rues Saint-Jacques et Sainte-Anne, un nouveau parcellaire aux abords du groupe épiscopal?', in Pailler: 419–21

Cattelain, P. and Paridaens, N. (2009) *Le sanctuaire tardo-romain du «Bois des Noël» à Matagne-la-Grande: nouvelles recherches (1994–2008) et réinterprétation du site* (Etudes d'Archéologie 2/Artefacts, 12). Brussels-Treignes

Caumont, A. de (1870) *Ere gallo-romaine: abécédaire ou rudiment d'archéologie.* Caen

Cavalier, O. (ed.) (2005) *La collection d'inscriptions gallo-grecques et latines du Musée Calvet.* Paris

Cazes, D. (1999) *Le Musée Saint-Raymond: musée des antiquités de Toulouse.* Paris
  (2002) 'Spiritualité et plastique: L'iconographie chrétienne vue au travers des sarcophages sculptés', in Pailler: 513–25

Cazes, Q. and Arramond, J.-C. (2002) 'Un autre grand edifice au nord de l'église Saint-Pierre-des-Cuisines', in Pailler: 451–53

Cazes, Q. and Scellès, M. (2002) 'La basilique Sainte-Marie: Notre-Dame-la-Daurade', in Pailler: 483–90

Chavarría Arnau, A. (1996) 'Transformaciones arquitectónicas de los establecimientos rurales en el nordeste de la *Tarraconensis* durante la antigüedad tardía', *Bulletí de la Reial Acadèmia Catalane de Belles Arts de San Jordi*, 10: 165–202
  (2001) 'Poblamiento rural en el *territorium* de Tarraco durante la antigüedad tardía', *Arqueología y Territorio Medieval* 8: 55–76
  (2004a) 'Osservazioni sulla fine delle ville in Occidente', *Archeologia Medievale* 31: 7–19
  (2004b) 'Interpreting the transformation of late Roman villas: the case of Hispania', in Christie: 67–102
  (2005a) 'Dopo la fine delle ville: le campagne ispaniche in epoca visigoda (VI–VIII secolo)', in Brogiolo *et al.*: 263–85
  (2005b) 'Villas in Hispania during the fourth and fifth centuries', in Bowes and Kulikowski: 519–55
  (2006a) 'Villas en *Hispania* durante la Antigüedad tardía', in Chavarría Arnau *et al.*: 17–35
  (2006b) 'Reflexiones sobre el final de las villas tardoantiguas en la Tarraconense', in Espinosa and Satiago: 19–39
  (2007) *El final de las villae en Hispania (siglos IV–VII d.C.)* (Bibliothèque le l'Antiquité Tardive). Turnhout

Chavarría Arnau, A., Arce, J. and Brogiolo, G. P. (eds.) (2006) *Villas tardoantiguas en el Mediterráneo occidental* (Anejos de Archivo Español de Arqueología, 39). Madrid

Chenet, G. (1941) *La céramique gallo-romaine d'Argonne du IVe siècle et la terre sigillée décorée à la molette.* Mâcon

Christie, N. (ed.) (2004) *Landscapes of Change: Rural Evolutions in Late Antiquity and the Early Middle Ages.* Aldershot

Christie, N. and Loseby, S. (eds.) (1996) *Towns in Transition: Urban Evolution in Late Antiquity and the Early Middle Ages.* Aldershot

Christol, M. (1997) *L'empire romain du IIIe siècle: histoire politique 192–325 après J-C.* Paris

Ciezar, P., Bertin, P., Pilon, F. and Van Ossel, P. (2006) 'Le mobilier céramique et numismatique du Bas-Empire provenant de deux caves de l'établissment antique de La Pièce du Gué au Mesnil-Amelot (Seine-et-Marne)', in Van Ossel: 185–208

Clarke, G. N. (1979) *Pre-Roman and Roman Winchester: Part II: The Roman Cemetery at Lankhills* (Winchester Studies, 3). Oxford

Codou, Y. (2000) 'Une mémoire de pierre: chantiers romans et monumenta paléochrétiens en Provence', in Codou and Lauwers: 561–600

(2005a) 'La christianisation des campagnes de Provence', in Delestre *et al.*: 53–62

(2005b) 'Le paysage réligieux et les paroisses rurales dans l'espace Provençal', in Delaplace: 82–97

Codou, Y. and Colin, M.-G. (2007) 'La christianisation des campagnes (IVe–VIIIe s.)', *Gallia* 64: 57–83

Codou, Y. and Lauwers, M. (eds.) (2009) *Lérins, une île sainte de l'antiquité au moyen âge* (Collection d'études médiévales de Nice, 9). Turnhout

Colin, M.-G. (2008) *Christianisation et peuplement des campagnes entre Garonne et Pyrénées IVe–VIIe siècles* (Archéologie du Midi Médiéval, Suppl. 5). Carcassonne

Collins, R. (2004) *Visigothic Spain 409–711*. Oxford

Cool, H. E. M. (2006) *Eating and Drinking in Roman Britain*. Cambridge

Cosh, S. and Neal, D. (2010) *Roman Mosaics of Britain*. Vol. IV: *Western Britain*. London

Croom, A. (2007) *Roman Furniture*. Stroud

Crubézy, E. (1990) 'Merovingian skull deformations in the southwest of France', in D. Austin and L. Alcock (eds.), *From the Baltic to the Black Sea: Studies in Medieval Archaeology*. London, 109–208

Cunliffe, B. (1988) *Greeks, Romans and Barbarians: Spheres of Interaction*. London

Cüppers, H. (ed.) (1984) *Trier Kaiserresidenz und Bischofssitz: die Stadt in spätantiker und frühchristlicher Zeit*. Mainz

(ed.) (1990) *Die Römer in Rheinland-Pfalz*. Stuttgart

Curta, F. (2007) 'Some remarks on ethnicity in medieval archaeology', *Early Medieval Europe* 15(2): 159–85

Cutler, A. (1993) 'Five lessons in late Roman ivory', *Journal of Roman Archaeology* 6: 167–92

Darmon, J.-P. (1994) *Recueil général des mosaïques de la Gaule: II – Lyonnaise – 5* (Xe Suppl. à *Gallia*). Paris

Daveau, I. (1997) 'Occupation des sols au Bas-Empire en Ile-de-France. Rupture et continuité: trois études de cas', in Ouzoulias and Van Ossel: 22–30

Deckers, J. G. (1989) 'Tradition und Adaptation: Bemerkungen zur Darstellung der christlichen Stadt', in Duval: 1285–1304

De Filippo, R. (2002) 'Le grand bâtiment du site de Larrey: la "question palatiale"', in Pailler: 445–50

Delaplace, C. (ed.) (2005) *Aux origines de la paroisse rurale en Gaule méridionale (IVe–IXe siècles)*. Paris

Delestre, X., Périn, P. and Kazanski, M. (eds.) (2005) *La Méditerranée et le monde mérovingien: témoins archéologiques* (*Bulletin Archéologique de Provence*, Suppl. 3). Aix-en-Provence

Delmaire, R. (ed.) (1990) *Carte archéologique de la Gaule 59 – Le Nord*. Paris
  (1994) *Carte archéologique de la Gaule 62/1 – Le Pas-de-Calais*. Paris
  (1995) 'Les enfouissements monétaires, témoignages d'insécurité?', *Revue du Nord – Archéologie* 77: 21–6
  (2004) 'Permanences et changements des chefs-lieux des cités au Bas-Empire: l'exemple du nord-ouest de la Gaule Belgique', in Ferdière: 39–50

Delogu, P. and Gasparri, S. (eds.) (2010) *Le trasformazioni del V secolo: l'Italia, I barbari e 'Occidente romano* (Seminari del Centro Iteruniversitario per la storia e l'archeologia dell'alto medioevo, 2). Turnhout

Démians d'Archimbaud, G. (ed.) (1994) *L'oppidum de Saint-Blaise du Ve au VIIe s. (Bouches-du-Rhône)* (Documents d'Archéologie Française, 45). Paris

Denis, J. (2006) 'Le baptistère de Limoges (Haute-Vienne)', *Gallia* 63: 125–9

Depeyrot, G. (2001) *Le numéraire gaulois du IVe siècle: aspects quantitatifs* (2 vols.). Mainz

Derks, T. and Roymans, N. (eds.) (2009) *Ethnic Constructs in Antiquity: The Role of Power and Tradition* (Amsterdam Archaeological Studies, 13). Amsterdam

Dey, H. (2009) 'Art, ceremony and city walls: the aesthetics of imperial resurgence in the late Roman West', *Journal of Late Antiquity* 3(1): 3–37

Dias Diogo, A. M. and Trinidade, L. (1999) 'Ânforas e sigillatas tardias (claras, foceenses e cipriotas) provenientes das excavações de 1966/67 de teatro romano de Lisboa', *Revista Portugusa de Arqueologia* 2(2): 83–96

Díaz, P. C. and Menéndez-Bueyes, L. R. (2005) 'The Cantabrian Basin in the fourth and fifth centuries: from imperial province to periphery', in Bowes and Kulikowski: 265–97

Dieulafait, C. (2006) 'Les céramiques', in Esmonde Cleary and Wood (2005): 275–94

Dieulafait, C., Boudartchouk, J.-L. and Llech, L. (2002) 'Production et échanges: quelques témoignages sur l'artisanat et le commerce', in Pailler: 463–70

Domergue, C. (1990) *Les mines de la péninsule ibérique dans l'Antiquité romaine*. Rome

Drack, W. and Fellmann, R. (1988) *Die Römer in der Schweiz*. Stuttgart/Jena

Dreier, C. (2011) 'Zwischwen Kontiuität und Zäsur: Zwei aktuelle Befunde zur Entwicklung der Stadt Metz nach der Mitte des 3. Jahrhunderts', in Schatzmann and Martin-Kilcher: 167–79

Drinkwater, J. F. (1987) *The Gallic Empire: Separatism and Continuity in the North-Western Provinces of the Roman Empire A.D. 260–274* (Historia Einzelschriften, 52). Stuttgart
  (1992) 'The Bacaudae of fifth-century Gaul', in Drinkwater and Elton: 208–17

(1996) 'The "Germanic threat on the Rhine frontier": a Romano-Gallic artefact?', in Mathisen and Sivan: 20–30

(2007) *The Alamanni and Rome 213–496: Caracalla to Clovis*. Oxford

Drinkwater, J. F. and Elton, H. (eds.) (1992) *Fifth-Century Gaul: A Crisis of Identity?* Cambridge

Duby, G. (ed.) (1980) *Histoire de la France urbaine: la ville antique des origins au IXe siècle*. Paris

Duffy, E. (1992) *The Stripping of the Altars: Traditional Religion in England c. 1400–1580*. New Haven, Conn.

Dunbabin, K. (2003) *The Roman Banquet: Images of Conviviality*. Cambridge

Duncan-Jones, R. (1978) 'Pay and numbers in Diocletian's army', *Chiron* 9: 347–75

(1990) *Structure and Scale in the Roman Economy*. Cambridge

(1994) *Money and Government in the Roman Empire*. Cambridge

(1999) 'The impact of the Antonine plague', *Journal of Roman Archaeology* 16: 108–36

Durliat, J. (1997) 'Cité, impôt et integration des barbares', in Pohl: 153–79

Duval, N. (ed.) (1989) *Actes du XIe Congrès International d'Archéologie Chrétienne: Lyon, Vienne, Grenoble, et Aoste (21–28 Septembre 1986)* (Collection de l'Ecole Française de Rome, 123). Rome

(ed.) (1991) *Naissance des arts chrétiens*. Paris

(ed.) (1995) *Les premiers monuments chrétiens de la France. 1. Sud-Est et Corse*. Paris

(ed.) (1996) *Les premiers monuments chrétiens de la France. 2. Sud-Ouest et Centre*. Paris

(ed.) (1998) *Les premiers monuments chrétiens de la France. 3. Ouest, Nord et Est*. Paris

Duval, N. and Caillet, J.-P. (1996) 'Introduction. La recherché sur les "églises doubles" depuis 1936: historique et problématique', *Antiquité Tardive* 4: 22–37

Duval, Y. (1988) *Auprès des saints corps et âme: l'inhumation "ad sanctos" dans la chrétienté d'Orient et d'Occident du IIIe au VIIe siècle* (Etudes Augustiniennes). Paris

Ebel-Zepezauer, W. (2000) *Studien zur Archäologie der Westgoten vom 5.–7. Jh. n. Chr.* (Iberia Archaeologica, 2). Mainz

Eckardt, H., Chenery, C., Booth, P., Lamb, A. and Müldner, G. (2009) 'Oxygen and strontium isotope evidence for mobility in Roman Winchester', *Journal of Archaeological Science* 36: 2816–25

Effros, B. (2002) *Caring for Body and Soul: Burial and the Afterlife in the Merovingian Period*. Philadelphia

Ellis, S. (1994) 'Power, architecture and decor: how the late Roman aristocrat appeared to his guests', in Gazda: 117–34

(2007) 'Shedding light on late Roman housing', in Lavan *et al.*: 283–302

Elsner, J. (1995) *Art and the Roman Viewer: The Transformation of Art from the Pagan World to Christianity*. Cambridge

(2007) *Roman Eyes: Visuality and Subjectivity in Art and Text*. Princeton, N.J.
Elsner, J. and Huskinson, J. (eds.) (2010) *Life, Death and Representation: Some New Work on Roman Sarcophagi*. Berlin/New York
Escher, K. (2005) *Genèse et évolution du deuxième royaume burgonde (443–534)* (2 vols.) (British Archaeological Reports, International Series, 1402). Oxford
Esmonde Cleary, A. S. (1989) *The Ending of Roman Britain*. London
  (2003) 'Civil defences in the West under the High Empire', in Wilson: 72–85
  (2004) 'The civitas-capitals of Novempopulana', in Ferdière: 183–9
  (2005) 'Beating the bounds: ritual and the articulation of urban space in Roman Britain', in MacMahon and Price: 1–17
  (2007a) *Rome in the Pyrenees: Lugdunum and the Convenae from the first century BC to the seventh century A.D.* London and New York
  (2007b) 'Fortificación urbana en la Britannia romana: ¿Defensa militar o monumento cívico?', in Rodríguez Colmenero and Rodà: 153–65
Esmonde Cleary, A. S. and Wood, J. (2005) *Saint-Bertrand-de-Comminges III: le rempart de l'Antiquité tardive de la ville haute* (Documents d'Archéologie Urbaine). Bordeaux
Estiot, S. (1996) 'Le troisième siècle et la monniae: crise et mutations', in Fiches: 33–70
Faider Feytmans, G. (1957) *Recueil des bronzes de Bavai* (Suppl. 8 à *Gallia*). Paris
Farnoux, C. (1987) 'Les fonds de cabanes mérovingiens Cisrhenans et leur contexte', *Amphora* 47: 1–48
Faulkner, N. (2000a) *The Decline and Fall of Roman Britain*. Stroud
  (2000b) 'Change and decline in late Romano-British towns', in Slater: 25–50
Favory, F. and Fiches, J.-L. (eds.) (1994) *Les campagnes de la France méditerranéenne dans l'Antiquité et le haut Moyen Age: études microrégionales* (Documents d'Archéologie Française, 42). Paris
Favory, F., Parodi, A., Poupet, P. and Raynaud, C. (1994) 'Lunel-Viel et son territoire', in Favory and Fiches: 236–45)
Feffer, L.-C. and Périn, P. (1987) *Les Francs* (2 vols.). Paris
Fentress, E. and Perkins, P. (1988) 'Counting African red slip ware', *L'Africa Romana* 5: 205–14
Ferdière, A. (ed.) (2000) *Archéologie funéraire* (Collections 'Archéologiques'). Paris
  (ed.) (2004) *Capitales éphémères: des capitales de cités perdent leur statut dans l'Antiquité tardive* (25e Suppl. à la *Revue Archéologique du Centre de la France*). Tours
Ferdière, A., Gandini, C., Nouvel, P. and Collart, J.-L. (2010) 'Les grandes *villae* "à pavillons multiples alignées" dans le provinces des Gaules et des Germanies: répartition, origines et fonctions', *Revue archéologique de l'Est* 59(2): 357–446
Ferdière, A., Marot, E. and Trintignac, A. (2009) 'Une petite ville romaine de moyenne montagne, Javols/*Anderitum* (Lozère), chef-lieu de cité des Gabales: état des connaissances (1996–2007)', *Gallia* 66(2): 171–225

Fernández-Galiano Ruiz, D. (ed.) (2001) *Carranque, centro de Hispania romana*. Alcalá de Henares

Fernández Ochoa, C. (1997) *La muralla romana de Gijón (Asturias)*. Gijón

Fernández Ochoa, C., García-Entero, V. and Gil Sendino, F. (eds.) (2008) *Las villae tardorromanas en el occidente del imperio: arquitectura y función*. Gijón

Fernández Ochoa, C. and Morillo Cerdan, A. (2005) 'Walls in the urban landscape of late Roman Spain: defense and imperial strategy', in Bowes and Kulikowski: 299–340

Fernández Ochoa, C. and Zarzalejos Prieto, M. (2001) 'Las termas públicas de las ciudades hispanas en el Bajo Imperio', in García Moreno and Rascón Marqués: 19–35

Feugère, M. (1993) *Weapons of the Romans*. Stroud

Février, P.-A. (1987) 'La mort chrétienne', in *Segni e riti nella chiesa altomedievale occidentale* (Settimane di studio del Centro italiano sull'alto medioevo, 11–17 aprile 1985, 33), 881–952. Spoleto

(1991) 'Naissance d'une archéologie chrétienne', in Duval: 336–47

Feyeux, J.-Y. (2003) *Le verre mérovingien du quart nord-est de la France*. Paris

Fiches, J.-L. (ed.) (1996) *Le IIIe siècle en Gaule narbonnaise*. Sophia-Antipolis

(ed.) (2002) *Les agglomérations gallo-romaines en Languedoc-Roussillon* (Monographies d'Archéologie Méditerranéenne, 13 and 14). Lattes

Fiches, J.-L. and Veyrac, A. (eds.) (1996) *Carte archéologique de la Gaule 30/1 – Nîmes*. Paris

Fichet de Clairfontaine, F., Delaval, E., Hincker, V. and Le Maho, J. (2004) 'Capitales déchues de la Normandie antique: état de la question', in Ferdière: 141–55

Finley, M. (1973) *The Ancient Economy*. Cambridge

Fixot, M., Guyon, J., Pelletier, P. and Rivet, L. (1985) *Les fouilles de la cour de l'archevêché: septembre 1984–janvier 1985* (Documents d'archéologie aixoise). Aix-en-Provence

Fouet, G. (1969) *La villa gallo-romaine de Montmaurin (Haute-Garonne)* (XXe Suppl. à *Gallia*). Paris

Foy, D. (ed.) (1995) *Le verre de l'Antiquité tardive et du haut Moyen Age: typologie, chronologie, diffusion*. Guiry-en-Vexin

Foy, D. and Hochuli-Gysel, A. (1995) 'Le verre en Aquitaine du IVe au IXe siècle', in Foy: 151–76

Frankovich, R., Patterson, H. and Barker, G. (eds.) (2000) *Extracting Meaning from Ploughsoil Assemblages* (The Archaeology of Mediterranean Landscapes, 5). Oxford

Frantz, A. (1988) *Late Antiquity A.D. 267–700* (The Athenian Agora, 24). Princeton, N.J.

Fremersdorf, F. (1957) *Das Römergrab in Weiden bei Köln*. Cologne

Frend, W. H. C. (1996) *The Archaeology of Early Christianity*. London

Fuchs, K., Kempa, M., Redies, R., Theuner-Großkopf, B. and Wais, A. (eds.) (1997) *Die Alamannen*. Stuttgart

Fuentes, A. (1989) *La necrópolis tardorromana de Albalete de las Nogueras (Cuenca), y el problema de las denominadas Necrópolis del Duero*. Cuenca

Fulford, M. G. (1978) 'Coin circulation and mint activity in the late Roman Empire: some economic implications', *Archaeological Journal* 135: 67–114

  (1992) 'Territorial expansion and the Roman Empire', *World Archaeology* 23: 294–305

Fulford, M. G. and Bird, J. (1975) 'Imported pottery from Germany in late Roman Britain', *Britannia* 6: 171–81

Fulford, M. G. and Hodder, I. (1974) 'A regression analysis of some late Romano-British pottery: a case study', *Oxoniensia* 39: 26–33

Gaimster, D., Redknap, M. and Wegner, H.-H. (eds.) (1988) *Zur keramik des Mittelalters und der beginnenden Neuzeit im Rheinland/Medieval and Later Pottery from the Rhineland and Its Markets* (British Archaeological Reports, International Series, 440). Oxford

Galinié, H. (ed.) (2007) *Tours antique et medieval: lieux de vie temps de la ville: 40 ans d'archéologie urbaine* (30ᵉ Suppl. à la *Revue Archéologique du Centre de la France*). Tours

Galinié, H. and Royo, M. (eds.) (1993) *Atlas des villes et des réseaux de villes en Région Centre*. Tours

Gandel, P., Billoin, D. and Humbert, S. (2008) 'Ecrille "La Motte" (Jura): un établissement de hauteur de l'Antiquité tardive et du haut Moyen Age', *Revue archéologique de l'Est* 57: 289–314

Gandini, C. (2008) *Des campagnes gauloises aux campagnes de l'Antiquité tardive: la dynamique de l'habitat rural dans la cité des* Bituriges Cubi *(IIᵉ s. av. J.-C. – VIIᵉ s. ap. J.-C.)* (33ᵉ Suppl. à la *Revue Archéologique du Centre de la France*). Tours

Gans, U.-W. (2006) 'Zur datierung der römischen Stadtmauer von Köln und zu den farbigen Steinornamenten in Gallein und Germanien', *Jahrbuch des Römisch-Germanischen Zentralmuseums Mainz* 53: 210–36

García-Entero, V. (2005) *Los balnea domésticos – ámbito rural y urbano en la Hispania romana* (Anejos de Archivo Español de Arqueología, 37). Madrid

  (2006) 'Los *balnea* de la *villae* tardoantiguas en *Hispania*', in Chavarría Arnau et al.: 97–111

García-Entero, V. and Vidal Álvarez, S. (2008) 'Los *marmora* y la decoración arquitectónica del edificio A de Carranque (Toledo): primeros resultados', in Fernández Ochoa et al.: 588–605

García Merino, C. (2008) 'Almenara de Adaja y las villas de la submeseta norte', in Fernández Ochoa et al.: 411–34

García Moreno, L. and Rascón Marqués, S. (eds.) (1999) *Complutum y las ciudades Hispanas en la Antigüedad tardía* (Acta Antiqua Complutensia, 1). Alcalá de Henares

  (eds.) (2001) *Ocio y espectáculo en la Antigüedad tardía* (Acta Antiqua Complutensia, 2). Alcalá de Henares

Gardner, A. (2007) *An Archaeology of Identity: Soldiers and Society in Late Roman Britain*. Walnut Creek, Calif.

Garmy, P. and Maurin, L. (1996) *Enceintes romaines d'Aquitaine: Bordeaux, Dax, Périgueux, Bazas* (Documents d'Archéologie Française, 53). Paris

Garnsey, P., Hopkins, K. and Whittaker, C. R. (eds.) (1983) *Trade in the Ancient Economy*. Berkeley, Calif. and Los Angeles

Gauthier, N. and Fixot, M. (1996) *Province ecclésiastique de Rouen (Lugdunensis Secunda)* (Topographie Chrétienne des Cités de la Gaule des origins au milieu du VIIIe siècle, 9). Paris

Gazda, E. K. (ed.) (1994) *Roman Art in the Private Sphere: New Perspectives on the Architecture and Decor of the Domus, Villa, and Insula*. Ann Arbor, Mich.

Geiberger, M., Stute, A. and Hoffmann, A. (eds.) (2005) *Imperium Romanum: Römer, Christen, Alemannen – Die Spätantike am Oberrhein*. Stuttgart

Gibbon, E. (1776) *The History of the Decline and Fall of the Roman Empire*, vol. I. London

Giddens, A. (1986) *The Constitution of Society: Outline of the Theory of Structuration*. Berkeley, Calif.

Gilles, K.-J. (1985) *Spätrömische Höhensiedlungen in Eifel und Hunsrück* (*Trierer Zeitschrift*, Beiheft 7). Trier

  (1998) 'Neuere Forschungen zu spätrömischen Höhensiedlungen in Eifel und Hunsrück', in Bridger and Gilles: 71–5

Godoy Fernández, C. (1995) *Arqueología y liturgia: iglesias Hispánicas (siglos IV al VIII)*. Barcelona

Goffart, W. (1980) *Barbarians and Romans A.D. 418–584: The Techniques of Accommodation*. Princeton, N.J.

  (2006) *Barbarian Tides: The Migration Age and the Later Roman Empire*. Philadelphia

Going, C. J. (1987) *The Mansio and Other Sites in the South-Eastern Sector of Caesaromagus: The Roman Pottery* (Chelmsford Archaeological Trust Report 3.2/Council for British Archaeology Research, 62). London

Goldsworthy, A. and Haynes, I. (eds.) (1999) *The Roman Army as a Community* (*Journal of Roman Archaeology*, Supplementary Series, 34). Portsmouth, R.I.

González, E., Ferrer, S., Herves, F. M. and Alacorta, E. J. (2002) 'Muralla Romana de Lucus Augusti: nuevas aportaciones a su studio y conocimiento', in Morillo Cerdan: 591–608

González, V., Ouzoulias, P. and Van Ossel, P. (2006) 'La céramique de l'habitat germanique de Saint-Ouen-du-Breuil (Seine-Matitime): quelques ensembles significatifs du milieu du IVe au début du Ve s.', in Ouzoulias and Van Ossel: 291–315

Goodburn, R. and Bartholomew, P. (1976) *Aspects of the Notitia Dignitatum* (British Archaeological Reports, International Series, 15). Oxford

Gorges, J.-G. (1979) *Les villas hispano-romaines: inventaire et problématique archéologiques*. Paris

(2008) 'L'architecture des *villae* romaines tardives: la création et le développement du modèle tétrarchique', in Fernández Ochoa *et al.*: 28–48

Gorrochategui, J. (1993) 'Las places votivas de plata de origen aquitano halladas en Hagenbach (Rhenania-Palatina, Alemania)', *Aquitania* 10: 25–47

Goudineau, C., Fauduet, I. and Coulon, G. (1994) *Les sanctuaires de tradition indigène en Gaule romaine*. Paris

Graen, D. (2005) 'Two Roman mausoleums at Quinta de Marim (Olhão): preliminary results of the excavations in 2002 and 2003', *Revista Portuguesa de Arqueologia* 8(1): 257–78

Greenberg, J. (2003) 'Plagued by doubt: reconsidering the impact of a mortality crisis in the 2nd c. A.D.', *Journal of Roman Archaeology* 16: 413–25

Greene, K. (1979) *Report on the Excavations at Usk 1965–1976: The Pre-Flavian Fine Wares*. Cardiff

Grierson, P. and Blackburn, M. (1986) *Medieval European Coinage: With a Catalogue of the Coins in the Fitzwilliam Museum, Cambridge*. Cambridge

Groenman-van Waateringe, W. (ed.) (1997) *Proceedings of the XVIth International Congress of Roman Frontier Studies*. Oxford

Guest, P. (2005a) *The Late Roman Gold and Silver Coins from the Hoxne Treasure*. London

(2005b) 'Review of Haupt 2001', *Britannia* 36: 514–15

Guggisberg, M. A. and Kaufmann-Heinemann, A. M. (2003) *Der spätrömische Silberschatz von Kaiseraugst*: die neuen Funde: *Silber im Spannungsfeld von Geschichte, Politik und Gesellschaft der Spätantike* (Forschungen in Augst, 34). Augst

Gurt i Esparraguera, J. M. and Palet Martínez, J.-M. (2001) 'Structuration du territoire dans le nord-est de l'Hispanie pendant l'Antiquité tardive: transformation du paysage et dynamique du peuplement', in Ouzoulias *et al.*: 303–29

Gurt i Esparraguera, J. M. and Ribera i Lacomba, A. (eds.) (2005) *VI Reunió d'Arqueologia Cristiana Hispànica: les cieutats tardoantigues d'Hispania: cristianització i topografia*. Barcelona

Gurt i Esparraguera, J. M. and Tenia, N. (eds.) (2000) *V Reunió d'Arqueologia Cristiana Hispànica/V Reunión de Arqueología Cristiana Hispánica*. Barcelona

Guyon, J. (2003) 'De *Lugdunum* des Convènes à *Convenae*, puis Saint-Bertrand: l'évolution urbaine de Saint-Bertrand-de-Comminges à la lumière des fouilles récentes', in Bost *et al.*: 131–49

(2005) 'Au-delà des Espagnes: un aperçu sur les groupes épiscopaux en Occident', in Gurt i Esparraguera and Ribera i Lacomba: 15–35

(2006) 'Emergence et affirmation d'une topographie chrétienne dans les villes de la Gaule méridionale', *Gallia* 63: 85–110

Hakenbeck, S. (2009) '"Hunnic" modified skulls: physical appearance, identity and the transformative nature of migrations', in Sayer and Williams: 64–80

Halsall, G. (1992) 'The origins of the *Reinengräberzivilization*: forty years on', in Drinkwater and Elton: 196–207

(1995) *Settlement and Social Organisation: The Merovingian Region of Metz.* Cambridge

(2000) 'Archaeology and the late Roman frontier in northern Gaul: the so-called "Föderatengräber" reconsidered', in Pohl and Reimitz: 167–80

(2001) 'Childeric's grave, Clovis' succession, and the origins of the Merovingian kingdom', in Mathisen and Shanzer: 116–33

(2007) *Barbarian Migrations and the Roman West 367–568.* Cambridge

(2008) 'Gräberfelduntersuchungen und das Ende des römischen Reichs', in Brather: 103–17

Hamerow, H. (2002) *Early Medieval Settlements: The Archaeology of Rural Communities in North-West Europe 400–900.* Oxford

Handley, M. (2003) *Death, Society and Culture: Inscriptions and Epitaphs in Gaul and Spain, AD 300–750* (British Archaeological Reports, International Series, 1135). Oxford

Hanoune, R. (ed.) (2007) *Les villes romaines du Nord de la Gaule: vingt ans de recherches nouvelles* (*Revue du Nord*, Hors série, Collection Art et Archéologie, 10). Lille

Harden, D. B. (ed.) (1987) *Glass of the Caesars.* Milan

Harlow, M. (2004) 'Female dress, 3rd to 6th century: the messages in the media', *Antiquité Tardive* 12: 203–15

Harries, J. (1992) 'Christianity and the city in late Roman Gaul', in Rich: 77–98

(1994) *Sidonius Apollinaris and the Fall of Rome.* Oxford

Hartley, E., Hawkes, J., Henig, M. and Mee, F. (eds.) (2006) *Constantine the Great: York's Roman Emperor.* York

Haupt, P. (2001) *Römische Münzhorte des 3. Jhs. in Gallien und den germanischen Provinzen* (Provinzialrömische Studien, 1). Grunbach

Heather, P. (1991) *Goths and Romans 332–489.* Oxford

(1996) *The Goths.* Oxford

(ed.) (1999) *The Visigoths from the Migration Period to the Seventh Century: An Ethnographic Perspective.* Woodbridge

(2005) *The Fall of the Roman Empire: A New History.* London

Heather, P. and Matthews, J. (1991) *The Goths in the Fourth Century.* Liverpool

Heijmans, M. (2004) *Arles durant l'Antiquité tardive: de la duplex Arelas á l'urbs genesii* (Collection de l'Ecole Française de Rome, 324). Rome

(2006a) 'La place des monuments publics du Haut-Empire dans les villes de la Gaule méridionale durant l'Antiquité tardive (IVe–VIe s.)', *Gallia* 63: 25–41

(2006b) 'Les habitations urbaines en Gaule méridionale durant l'Antiquité tardive', *Gallia* 63: 47–57

(2006c) 'La mise en défense de la Gaule méridionale au IVe–VIe s.', *Gallia* 63: 59–74

(2009) 'Les fouilles de l'enclos Saint-Césaire: la découverte d'une des plus grandes églises paléochrétiennes', *Bulletin de l'Association pour l'Antiquité tardive* 18: 26–30

Heijmans, M. and Pietri, L. (2009) 'Le "lobby" lérinien: le rayonnement du monastère insulaire au Ve siècle au début du VIIe siècle', in Codou and Lauwers: 35–61

Hendy, M. (1985) *Studies in the Byzantine Monetary Economy c. 300–1400*. Cambridge

Hernandez, J. and Raynaud, C. (2006) 'La Septimanie du Ve au VIIIe s.: archéologie du changement culturel', in Delestre et al.: 177–88

Hidalgo Prieto, R. (1996) *Espacio público y espacio privado en el conjunto palatino de Cercadilla (Córdoba): el aula central y las termas*. Seville

Hills, C. M. (2003) *Origins of the English*. London

Hobbs, R. (2006) *Late Roman Precious Metal Deposits c. A.D. 200–700: Changes Over Time and Space* (British Archaeological Reports, International Series, 1504). Oxford

(2010) 'Platters in the Mildenhall treasure', *Britannia* 41: 324–33

Hochuli-Gysel, A. (1996) 'Les verreries du Sud-Ouest de la Gaule, IVe–VIe s.', *Aquitania* 14: 231–6

Hodder, I. (1974) 'Some marketing models for Romano-British coarse pottery', *Britannia* 5: 340–59

Hoffmann, D. (1969) *Das spätrömische Bewegungsheer und die Notitia Dignitatum* (Epigraphische Studien, 7). Düsseldorf

Hope, V. M. (2001) *Constructing Identity: The Roman Funerary Monuments of Aquileia, Mainz and Nîmes* (British Archaeological Reports, International Series, 960). Oxford

Hopkins, K. (1980) 'Taxes and trade in the Roman Empire', *Journal of Roman Studies* 70: 101–25

Horden, P. and Purcell, N. (2000) *The Corrupting Sea: A Study of Mediterranean History*. Oxford

Horn, H. G. (ed.) (1987) *Die Römer in Nordrhein-Westfalen*. Stuttgart

Howgego, C. (1982) 'The supply and use of money in the Roman world: 200 BC – AD 300', *Journal of Roman Studies* 82: 1–31

Hübener, W. (1977) 'Waffennormen und Bewaffnungstypen der frühen Merowingerzeit', *Fundberichte aus Baden Württemburg* 3: 510–27

Huffstott, J. S. (1998) 'Votive (?) use of coins in fourth-century Lusitania?: the builders' deposit in the Torre de Palma basilica', *Revista Portuguesa de Arqueologia* 1(1): 221–6

Humphrey, J. (1986) *Roman Circuses: Arenas for Chariot Racing*. London

Hunold, A. (2011) *Die Befestigung auf dem Katzenberg bei Mayen und die spätrömischen Höhenbefestigungen in Nordgallien*. Mainz

Iglesias-Gil, J.-M. and Muñiz Castro, J. A. (1992) *Las comunicaciones en la Cantabria romana*. Santander

Ilkjaer, J. (2000) *Illerup Ådal – Archaeology as a Magic Mirror.* Mosegård

Jacob, J.-P. and Leredde, H. (1985) 'Les potiers de Jaulges/Villiers-Vineux (Yonne): étude d'un centre de production gallo-romain', *Gallia* 43: 167–92

Jacques, A. (2007) 'Arras-*Nemetacum*, chef-lieu de cité des Atrébates: bilan des recherches 1984–2002', in Hanoune: 63–82

Jacques, P. (2006) 'Nouvelles données sur l'habitat rural antique en Lot-et-Garonne', in Réchin: 77–121

James, E. (1977) *The Merovingian Archaeology of South-West Gaul* (British Archaeological Reports, International Series, 25). Oxford

(1988) *The Franks.* Oxford

(1991) 'Les problèmes archéologiques du Sud-Ouest wisigothique et franc', in Périn: 149–53

James, S. (2001) 'Soldiers and civilians: identity and interaction in Roman Britain', in James and Millett: 77–89

(2004) *Excavations at Dura-Europos Final Report VII: The Arms and Armour and Other Military Equipment.* London

(2011) *Rome and the Sword: How Warriors and Weapons Shaped Roman History.* London

James, S. and Millett, M. (eds.) (2001) *Britons and Romans: Advancing an Archaeological Agenda* (Council for British Archaeology, Research Report, 125). York

Janes, D. (1998) *God and Gold in Late Antiquity.* Cambridge

Johnson, M. J. (1997) 'Pagan-Christian burial practices of the fourth century: shared tombs?', *Journal of Early Christian Studies* 5(1): 37–59

Johnson, S. (1976) *The Roman Forts of the Saxon Shore.* London

(1983) *Late Roman Fortifications.* London

Johnston, D. E. (ed.) (1977) *The Saxon Shore* (Council for British Archaeology, Research Report, 18). London

Jones, A. H. M. (1964) *The Later Roman Empire 284–602.* Oxford

Joulin, L. (1901) *Les établissements gallo-romains de la plaine de Martres-Tolosane.* Paris

Juan Tovar, L. C. (1997) 'Las industrias cerámicas hispanas en el Bajo Imperio. Hacia una sistematización de la Sigillata Hispánica Tardía', in Teja and Pérez: 543–68

Kasprzyk, M. (2003) 'L'occupation des plateaux calcaires bourguignons durant l'Antiquité tardive: premiers résultats pour la region de Noyers-sur-Serein (Yonne)', in Ouzoulias and Van Ossel: 179–95

(2004) 'Militaires et fonctionnaires de l'Antiquité tardive à Escolives-Sainte-Camille (Yonne)?', *Revue archéologique de l'Est* 53: 239–52

(2005) 'Les cités des Eduens et de Chalon durant l'Antiquité tardive (v. 260–530 env.): contribution à l'étude de l'Antiquité tardive en Gaule centrale'. Thèse de doctorat du 3e cycle, Université de Bourgogne

Kaster, R. A. (1988) *Guardians of Language: The Grammarian and Society in Late Antiquity*. Berkeley, Calif.

Kazanski, M. (1982) 'Deux riches tombes de l'époque des grandes invasions au Nord de la Gaule: Airan et Pouan', *Archéologie Médiévale* 12: 17–33

 (1986) 'Un témoignage de la presence des Alano-Sarmates en Gaule: la sépulture de la fosse Jean-Fat à Reims', *Archéologie Médiévale* 16: 26–32

 (1991) 'A propos des armes et des elements d'harnachement "orientaux" en Occident à l'époque des grandes migrations (IVe–Ve s.)', *Journal of Roman Archaeology* 4: 123–39

 (1993) 'Les barbares orientaux et la défense de la Gaule au IVe–Ve siècles', in Vallet and Kazanski: 175–86

 (1994) 'Les plaques-boucles méditerranéennes des Ve et VIe siècles', *Archéologie Médiévale* 24: 137–98

 (1995) 'L'équipement et le matériel militaires au Bas-Empire en Gaule du Nord et de l'Est', *Revue du Nord – Archéologie* 77: 37–54

Kazanski, M. and Lapart, J. (1995) 'Quelques documents du Ve siècle ap. J.-C. attribuables aux Wisigoths découverts en Aquitaine', *Aquitania* 13: 193–202

Kazanski, M. and Legoux, R. (1998) 'Contribution à l'étude des témoignages archéologiques des Goths en Europe orientale à l'époque des grandes migrations: la chronologie de la culture Cernjachov récente', *Archéologie Médiévale* 18: 7–53

Kazanski, M., Mastykova, A. and Périn, P. (2008) 'Die Archäologie der Westgoten in Nordgallien: zum Stand der Forschung', in Brather: 149–92

Kazanski, M. and Périn, P. (2006) 'Les témoins archéologiques de la présence germanique et nomade en Gaule de la fin du IVe siècle aux alentours du VIIe siècle', in López Quiroga *et al.*: 191–212

Keay, S. J. (1984) *Late Roman Amphorae in the Western Mediterranean: A Typology and Economic Study. The Catalan Evidence* (British Archaeological Reports, International Series, 196). Oxford

 (1988) *Roman Spain*. London

 (ed.) (1998) *The Archaeology of Early Roman Baetica* (*Journal of Roman Archaeology*, Suppl. 29), Ann Arbor, Mich.

Kelly, C. (2004) *Ruling the Later Roman Empire* (Revealing Antiquity, 15). Cambridge, Mass. and London

Kent, J. P. C. (1974) 'Interpreting coin finds', in Casey and Reece: 184–200

 (1994) *Roman Imperial Coinage*. Vol. X: *The Divided Empire and the Fall of the Western Parts*. London

Kent, J. P. C. and Painter, K. S. (1977) *Wealth of the Roman World: Gold and Silver AD 300–700*. London

King, A. (1981) 'The decline of Samian ware manufacture in the North-West Provinces: problems of chronology and interpretation', in King and Henig: 55–78

(1999) 'Animals and the Roman army: the evidence of animal bones', in Goldsworthy and Haynes: 139–49

King, A. and Henig, M. (eds.) (1981) *The Roman West in the Third Century: Contributions from Archaeology and History* (British Archaeological Reports, International Series, 109). Oxford

Klumbach, H. (ed.) (1973) *Spätrömische Gardehelme*. Munich

Koch, G. (1982) *Römische Sarkophage* (Handbuch der Altertumswissenschaft, Abteilung, 6). Munich

Koehler, A. (1995) 'La villa romaine de Saint-Clément – La Bichère à Vert-Saint-Denis (Seine-et-Marne) durant l'Antiquité tardive', in Ouzoulias and Van Ossel: 95–115

Koppel, E. M. and Rodà, I. (2008) 'La escultura de las *villae* de la zona del noreste hispánico: los ejemplos de Tarragona y Tossa de Mar', in Fernández Ochoa *et al.*: 93–131

Kouznetsov, V. and Lebedynsky, I. (2005) *Les Alains: cavaliers des steppes, seigneurs du Caucase Ier–XVe siècles apr. J.-C.* Paris

Kovalevskaya, V. B. (1993) 'La presence alano-sarmate en Gaule: confrontation des données archéologiques, paléoanthropologiques, historiques et toponymiques', in Vallet and Kazanski: 209–21

Krause, J.-U. and Witschel, C. (eds.) (2006) *Die Stadt in der Spätantike – Niedergang oder Wandel?* (Historia Einzelschriften, 190). Stuttgart

Krier, J. (2011) '*Deae Fortunae ob salute imperi*: nouvelles inscriptions de Dalheim (Luxembourg) et la vie religieuse d'un *vicus* du nord-est de la Gaule à la veille de la tourmente du IIIe siècle', *Gallia* 68(2): 313–40

Krings, U. and Will, R. (eds.) (2009) *Das Baptisterium am Dom: Kölns erster Taufort*. Cologne

Kulikowski, M. (2000) 'Barbarians in Gaul, usurpers in Britain', *Britannia* 31: 325–45

(2004) *Late Roman Spain and Its Cities*. Baltimore and London

(2005) 'Cities and government in late antique Hispania: recent advances and future research', in Bowes and Kulikowski: 31–76

Landes, C. and Carrié, J.-M. (eds.) (2007) *Jeux et spectacles dans l'Antiquité tardive* (*Antiquité Tardive*, 15). Turnhout.

Lapart, J. and Paillet, J.-L. (1991) 'Ensemble paléochrétien et mérovingien du site de Séviac à Montréal-du-Gers', in Périn: 171–80

Lapart, J. and Petit, C. (1993) *Carte archéologique de la Gaule 32 – Le Gers*. Paris

Larrén, H., Blanco, J. F., Villanueva, O., Caballero, J., Domínguez, A., Nuño, J., Sanz, F. J., Marcos, G. J., Martín, M. A. and Misiego, J. (2003) 'Ensayo de sistematización de la cerámica tardoantigua en la Cuenca del Duero', in Caballero *et al.*: 273–306

Laubenheimer, F. (1990) *Le temps des amphores en Gaule: vins, huiles et sauces*. Paris

Laubenheimer, F. and Marlière, E. (2010) *Echanges et vie économique dans le Nord-Ouest des Gaules: le témoignage des amphores du IIe siècle avant J.-C. au IVe siècle après J.-C.* Paris

Lauffray, J. (1990) *La tour de Vésone à Périgueux: temple de Vesunna Petrucoriorum* (*Gallia*, Suppl. 49). Paris

Laurence, R., Esmonde Cleary, S. and Sears, G. (2011) *The City in the Roman West 200 B.C. – A.D. 200*. Cambridge

Lavan, L. (1999) 'Late antique governors' palaces: a gazetteer', *Antiquité Tardive* 7: 135–4

Lavan, L. and Bowden, W. (eds.) (2003) *Theory and Practice in Late Antique Archaeology* (Late Antique Archaeology, 1). Leiden

Lavan, L., Özgenel, L. and Sarantis, A. (eds.) (2007) *Housing in Late Antiquity: From Palaces to Shops* (*Late Antique Archaeology*, 3). Leiden

Leader-Newby, R. E. (2004) *Silver and Society in Late Antiquity: Functions and Meanings of Silver Plate in the Fourth to Seventh Centuries.* Aldershot

Lebedynsky, I. (2002) *Les Sarmates: Amazones et lanciers cuirassés entre Oural et Danube VIIe siècle av. J.-C. – VIe siècle apr. J.-C.* Paris

Leblanc, O. and Savay-Guerraz, H. (1996) 'Chronologie de l'abandon du site de Saint-Romain-en-Gal (Rhône)', in Fiches: 103–19

Leday, A. (1980) *La campagne à l'époque romaine dans le centre de la Gaule/Rural Settlement in Central Gaul in the Roman Period* (British Archaeological Reports, International Series 73). Oxford

Le Maho, J. (1998) 'Rouen, Cathédrale Notre-Dame', in Duval: 320–7

Lemant, J.-P. (1985) *Le cimitière et la fortification du Bas-Empire de Vireux-Molhain, Dep. Ardennes* (Römisch-Germanisches Zentralmuseum Mainz, Monographien 7). Mainz

(2001) 'Late Roman rural settlement in the southern part of the province Germania secunda in comparison with other regions of the Roman Rhineland', in Ouzoulias et al.: 113–46

Lenz, K. H. (2005) 'Germanische Siedlungen des 3. bis 5. Jahrhunderts n. Chr. in Gallien. Schriftliche Überliegerung und archäologische Befunde', *Bericht der Römisch-Germanischen Kommission* 86: 349–444

Lepelley, C. (1979–81) *Les cités de l'Afrique romaine au Bas-Empire* (2 vols.). Paris

(ed.) (1996) *La fin de la cité antique et le début de la cité médiévale: de la fin du IIIe siècle à l'avènement de Charlemagne*. Bari

Lequoy, M.-C. and Guillot, B. (2004) *Carte archéologique de la Gaule 76/2 – Rouen*. Paris

Letterlé, F. (ed.) (2001) *Carcassonne: études archéologiques*. Paris.

Leveau, P., Raynaud, C., Sablayrolles, R. and Trément, F. (eds.) (2009) *Les formes de l'habitat gallo-romain: terminologies et typologies à l'épreuve des réalités archéologiques* (Colloque AGER, 8). Toulouse

Lewis, M. J. T. (1966) *Temples in Roman Britain*. Cambridge
Lewit, T. (2003) 'Bones in the bath-house: re-evaluating the notion of "squatter occupation" in 5th–7th century villas', in Brogiolo *et al*.: 251–60
  (2004) '"Vanishing villas": what happened to élite rural habitation in the West in the 5th–6th c.?', *Journal of Roman Archaeology* 16: 260–74
Liebeschuetz, W. (1997) 'Cities, taxes and the accommodation of the barbarians: the theories of Durliat and Goffart', in Pohl: 135–51
  (2001) *The Decline and Fall of the Roman City*. Oxford
López Quiroga, J. (2005) 'Los orígenes de la parroquia rural en el occidente de Hispania (siglos IV–IX) (Provincia de Gallaecia y Lusitania)', in Delaplace: 193–228
  (2010) *Arqueología del mundo funerario en la Peninsula Ibérica (siglos V–X)*. Madrid
López Quiroga, J. and Martínez Tejera, A. M. (2006) 'El destino de los templos paganos en *Hispania* durante la Antigüedad tardía', *Archivo Español de Arqueología* 79: 125–53
López Quiroga, J., Martínez Tejera, A. M. and Morín de Pablos, J. (eds.) (2006) *Gallia e Hispania en el contexto de la presencia 'germánica' (ss. V–VII): balance y perspectivas* (British Archaeological Reports, International Series, 1534). Oxford
López Vilar, J. (2006) *Les basíliques paleocristianes del suburbi occidental de Tarraco: el temple septentrional i el complex martitial de Sant Fructuós* (Institut Català d'Arqueologia Clàssica, Documenta 4). Tarragona
Loridant, F. (2004) 'Décadence urbaine et Antiquité tardive à *Bagacum* et dans la *civitas camaracensium*', in Ferdière: 75–82
Lorquin, A. (1999) *Étoffes égyptiennes de l'Antiquité tardive*. Paris
Lorren, C. (2006) 'L'habitat rural en Gaule du Nord, du Ve au VIIe siècle: quelques observations et remarques suscitées par les données récentes de l'archéologie', in López Quiroga *et al*.: 9–18
Lorren, C. and Périn, P. (eds.) (1997) *L'habitat rural du haut Moyen Âge (France, Pays-Bas, Danemark et Grande-Bretagne)* (Mémoires de l'Association Française d'Archéologie Mérovingienne, 6). Condé-sur-Noireau
Loseby, S. (1992) 'Marseille: a late antique success story', *Journal of Roman Studies* 82: 165–85
  (1996) 'Arles in late antiquity: *Gallula Roma Arelas* and *Urbs Genesii*', in Christie and Loseby: 45–70
  (2000) 'Urban failures in late-antique Gaul', in Slater: 72–95
Luttwak, E. N. (1976) *The Grand Strategy of the Roman Empire: From the First Century A.D. to the Third*. Baltimore and London
Lysons, S. (1797) *An Account of the Roman Antiquities Discovered at Woodchester*. London
MacCormack, S. (1981) *Art and Ceremony in Late Antiquity* (The Transformation of the Classical Heritage). Berkeley, Calif., Los Angeles and London

MacDonald, W. L. (1986) *The Architecture of the Roman Empire*. Vol. II: *An Urban Appraisal* (Yale Publications in the History of Art, 35). New Haven, Conn. and London

Macias i Solé, J. M. (2000) 'Tarraco en la Antigüedad tardía: un proceso simultáneo de transformación urbana e ideológica', in Ribera i Lacomba: 259–71

  (2003) 'Cerámicas tardorromanas de Tarragona: economía de mercado versus autarquía', in Caballero *et al.*: 21–39

Macias i Solé, J. M. and Remolà Vallverdù, J. A. (2005) 'El port de Tarraco a l'antiguitat tardana', in Gurt i Esparraguera and Ribera i Lacomba: 175–87

MacMahon, A. and Price, J. (eds.) (2005) *Roman Working Lives and Urban Living*. Oxford

MacMullen, R. (1982) 'The epigraphic habit in the Roman Empire', *American Journal of Philology* 103: 233–46

Magallón, M. A., Sillieres, P., Fincker, M. and Navarro, M. (1995) 'Labitolosa, ville romaine des Pyrénées espagnoles', *Aquitania* 15: 75–103

Magnan, D. (2000) 'Un sanctuaire périurbain: La Bauve à Meaux (Seine-et-Marne)', in Van Andringa: 73–89

Maguire, H. (1999) 'The good life', in Bowersock *et al.*: 238–57

Maloney, S. J. and Hale, R. (1996) 'The villa of Torre de Palma (Alto Alentejo)', *Journal of Roman Archaeology* 9: 275–94

Maloney, S. J. and Ringbom, A. (2005) '^{14}C dating of mortars at Torre de Palma, Portugal', in Gurt i Esparraguera and Tenia: 151–5

Mango, M. M. and Bennett, A. (1994) *The Sevso Treasure, Part One* (*Journal of Roman Archaeology*, Suppl. 12). Ann Arbor, Mich.

Mann, J. C. (1983) *Legionary Recruitment and Veteran Settlement During the Principate* (UCL Institute of Archaeology, Occasional Publication, 7). London

Mar, R. and Verde, G. (2008) 'Las villas romanas tardoantiguas: cuestiones de tipología arquitectónica', in Fernández Ochoa *et al.*: 49–83

Marfil Ruiz, P. (2000) 'Córdoba de Teodosio a Abd al-Rahman III', in Caballero and Mateos: 117–41

Marlière, E. (2001) 'Le tonneau en Gaule romaine', *Gallia* 58: 181–201

Marrou, H. I. (1965) *Histoire de l'éducation dans l'Antiquité*. Paris

Marti, R. (2000) *Zwischen Römerzeit und Mittelalter: Forschungen zur frühmittelalterlichen Siedlungsgeschichte der Nordwestschweiz (4.-10. Jahrhundert)* (Archäologie und Museum, Band 41A). Liestal

Martin, J. (1727) *La religion des Gaulois*. Paris

Martínez Tejera, A. M. (2006) 'Arquitectura Cristiana en *Hispania* durante le Antigüedad Tardía', in López Quiroga *et al.*: 109–87

Mateos Cruz, P. (2005) 'Los orígenes de la cristianización urbana en *Hispania*', in Gurt i Esparraguera and Ribera i Lacomba: 49–62

Mathisen, R. and Shanzer, D. (eds.) (2001) *Society and Culture in Late Antique Gaul: Revisiting the Sources*. Aldershot

Mathisen, R. and Sivan, H. (eds.) (1996) *Shifting Frontiers in Late Antiquity.* Aldershot

Matthews, J. (1975) *Western Aristocracies and the Imperial Court AD 364–425.* Oxford

Mauné, S. (1996) 'L'habitat rural dans le Biterrois nord-oriental', in Fiches: 213–16

Maurin, L. (1992a) 'Remparts et cités dans les trois provinces du sud-ouest de la Gaule au Bas-Empire (dernier quart du IIIe siècle–début du Ve siècle)', in Maurin: 365–89

 (ed.) (1992b) *Villes et agglomérations urbaines antiques du sud-ouest de la Gaule: histoire et archéologie* (Aquitania, Suppl. 6). Bordeaux

Maurin, L. and Pailler, J.-M. (eds.) (1996) *La civilisation urbaine de l'Antiquité tardive dans le sud-ouest de la Gaule* (Aquitania, Suppl. 16). Paris

Mauss, M. (1954) *The Gift: Forms and Functions of Exchange in Archaic Societies* (trans. of *Essai sur le don*). London

Maxfield, V. (ed.) (1989) *The Saxon Shore: A Handbook.* Exeter

McLynn, N. (2005) '"*Genere Hispanus*": Theodosius, Spain and Nicene orthodoxy', in Bowes and Kulikowski: 77–120

Meates, G. W. (1979) *The Lullingstone Roman Villa.* Vol. I: *The Site.* Chichester

Mertens, J. (1972) *Oudenburg, Romeinse Legerbasis aan de Noordzeekust* (Archaeologicum Belgii Speculum, 4). Brussels

Mertens, J. and van Impe, L. (1971) *Het Laat-Romeins Grafveld von Oudenburg* (Archaeologia Belgica, 135). Brussels

 (1977) 'Oudenburg and the northern section of the continental *Litus Saxonicum*', in Johnston: 51–62

Meyer, E. A. (1990) 'Explaining the epigraphic habit in the Roman Empire', *Journal of Roman Studies* 80: 74–96

Middleton, P. S. (1979) 'Army supply in Roman Gaul: an hypothesis for Roman Britain', in Burnham and Johnson: 81–97

Mielczarek, M. (1993) *Cataphracti and Clibanarii: Studies on the Heavy Armoured Cavalry of the Ancient World.* Łódź

Moliner, M. (2006) 'La basilique funéraire de la rue Malaval à Marseille (Bouches-du-Rhône)', *Gallia* 63: 131–6

Monteil, M. (1996a) 'Nîmes: un état des lieux contrasté', in Fiches: 155–75

 (1996b) 'La ville romaine et wisigothique', in Fiches and Veyrac: 153–61

Monturet, R. and Rivière, H. (1986) *Les thermes de la villa gallo-romaine de Séviac.* Paris

Morillo Cerdan, A. (ed.) (2002) *Arqueología Militar Romana en Hispania* (Anejos de Gladius, 5). Madrid

Morris, I. (1992) *Death Ritual and Social Structure in Classical Antiquity.* Cambridge

Müller, M., Schalles, H.-J. and Zieling, N. (eds.) (2008) *Colonia Ulpia Traiana: Xanten und sein Umland in römischer Zeit* (Xantener Berichte Sonderband, Geschichte der Stadt Xanten, 1). Mainz

Müller-Wille, M. (1996) 'Königtum und Adel im Spiegel der Grabfunde', in Wieczorek *et al.*: 206–21

Naveau, J. (ed.) (1997) *Recherches sur Jublains (Mayenne) et sur la cite des Diablintes* (Documents Archéologiques de l'Ouest). Rennes

Neal, D. S. and Cosh, S. R. (2002) *Roman Mosaics of Britain*. Vol. I: *Northern Britain Incorporating the Midlands and East Anglia*. London

(2005) *Roman Mosaics of Britain*. Vol. II: *South-West Britain*. London

Neiss, R. and Berry, R. (1998) 'Reims, Cathédrale et baptistère', in Duval: 105–11

Neiss, R. and Sindonino, S. (2006) *Civitas Remi: Reims et son enceinte au IVe siècle* (Archéologie urbaine à Reims, 6). Reims

Nenquin, J. (1953) *La nécropole de Furfooz*. Bruges

Newman, R. (ed.) (2009) *The Carlisle Millennium Project: Excavations in Carlisle 1998–2001*. Oxford

Nielsen, I. (1990) *Thermae et Balnea*. Aarhus

Nin, N. (1996) 'Modalités du délaissement de l'agglomération d'Aix-en-Provence', in Fiches: 135–54

(2006) 'L'occupation du theatre d'Aix-en-Provence (Bouches-du-Rhône) durant l'Antiquité tardive', *Gallia* 63: 43–5

Noelke, P. (1984) 'Reiche Gräber von einem römischen Gutshof in Köln', *Germania* 62: 373–423

Nogales Basarrate, T., Carvalho, A. and Almeida, M. J. (2004) 'El programa decorative de la Quinta de Longas (Elvas, Portugal): un modelo excepcional de las *villae* de Lusitania', in Nogales Basarrate and Gonçalves: 103–56

Nogales Basarrate, T. and Gonçalves, L. (eds.) (2004) *Actas de la IV Reunión sobre Escultura Romana da Hispania*. Madrid

Nolla Brufau, J. M. (2007) '*Gerunda* y la defensa de la *via Augusta* en la Antigüedad tardía', in Rodríguez Colmenero and Rodà: 633–47

Nouvel, P. (2009) 'De la ferme au palais: les établissements ruraux antique de Bourgogne du Nord, IIe–IVe siècles p.C.', in Leveau *et al.*: 361–89

Ode, B. and Odiot, T. (2001) 'L'habitat rural de la moyenne vallée du Rhône au IVe et Ve siècles', in Ouzoulias *et al.*: 225–46

Oldenstein, J. (1986) 'Neue Forschungen im spätrömischen Kastell von Alzey: Vorbericht über die Ausgrabungen 1981–1985', *Bericht der Römisch-Germanischen Kommission* 67: 290–356

Otten, T. and Ristow, S. (2008) 'Xanten in der Spätantike', in Müller *et al.*: 549–82

Ouzoulias, P., Pellecuer, C., Raynaud, C., Van Ossel, P. and Garmy, P. (eds.) (2001) *Les campagnes de la Gaule à la fin de l'Antiquité* (IVe colloque de l'association AGER). Antibes

Ouzoulias, P. and Van Ossel, P. (eds.) (1995) *L'époque romaine tardive en Ile-de-France: les campagnes de l'Ile-de-France de Constantin à Clovis: pré-actes du colloque, Paris 14–15 décembre 1995*. Paris

(eds.) (1997) *L'époque romaine tardive en Ile-de-France: les campagnes de l'Ile-de-France de Constantin à Clovis* (Document de travail, 3). Paris

(2001) 'Dynamiques du peuplement et formes de l'habitat tardif: le cas de l'Ile-de-France', in Ouzoulias *et al.*: 147–72

(eds.) (2003) *Diocesis Galliarum* (Document de travail, 6). Paris

(eds.) (2006) *Diocesis Galliarum* (Document de travail, 7). *Les céramiques de l'Antiquité tardive en Ile-de-France et dans le Bassin parisien.* Vol. I: *Ensembles régionaux.* Paris

Özgenel, L. (2007) 'Public use and privacy in late antique houses in Asia Minor: the architecture of spatial control', in Lavan *et al.*: 239–81

Päffgen, B. (1992) *Die Ausgrabungen in St. Severin zu Köln* (Kölner Forschungen, 5). Mainz

Pailler, J.-M. (ed.) (2002) *Tolosa: nouvelles recherches sur Toulouse et son territoire dans l'Antiquité* (Collection de l'Ecole Française de Rome, 281). Rome

Painter, K. S. (1993) 'Late-Roman silver plate: a reply to Alan Cameron', *Journal of Roman Archaeology* 6: 109–15

(1997) 'Silver hoards from Britain in their late Roman context', *Antiquité Tardive* 5: 93–110

Palol, P. de (1989) *El Bovalar (Seròs; Segrià): conjunt d'època paleocristiana i visigòtica.* Barcelona

Parker, A. (1992) *Ancient Shipwrecks of the Mediterranean and the Roman Provinces* (British Archaeological Reports, International Series, 580). Oxford

Parsons, P. (2007) *City of the Sharp-Nosed Fish: Greek Lives in Roman Egypt.* London

Parthuisot, F., Pilon, F. and Poilane, D. (2008) 'L'ensemble cultuel central: structuration et périodisation provisoire', in Pilon: 53–63

Paxton, F. S. (1990) *Christianising Death: The Creation of a Ritual Process in Early Medieval Europe.* Ithaca, N.Y. and London

Paz Peralta, J. A. (1991) *Cerámica de mesa romana de los siglos III al VI d.C. en la Provincia de Zaragoza (terra sigillata hispánica tardía, African red slip ware, sigillata gálica tardía y phocean red slip ware).* Zaragoza

Pearson, A. (2002) *The Roman Shore Forts: Coastal Defences of Southern Britain.* Stroud

Pellecuer, C. (1996) 'Villa et domaine', in Fiches: 277–91

Pellecuer, C. and Pomarèdes, H. (2001) 'Crise, survie ou adaptation de la villa romaine en Narbonaise première? Contribution des récentes recherches de terrain en Languedoc-Roussillon', in Ouzoulias *et al.*: 503–32

Pellecuer, C. and Schneider, L. (2005) 'Premières églises et espace rural en Languedoc méditerranéen (V^e–Xe s.)', in Delaplace: 98–119

Périn, P. (ed.) (1991) *Gallo-Romains, Wisigoths et Francs en Aquitaine, Septimanie et Espagne.* Rouen

(2004) 'The origin of the village in early medieval Gaul', in Christie: 255–78

Périn, P. and Kazanski, M. (1996) 'Das Grab Childerics I', in Wieczorek *et al.*: 173–82

Pernon, C. and Pernon, J. (1990) *Les potiers de portout: productions, activités et cadre de vie d'un atelier au Ve siècle ap. J.-C. en Savoie*. Paris

Perring, D. (2002) *The Roman House in Britain*. London

Petit, J.-P., Mangin, M. and Brunella, P. (eds.) (1994) *Les agglomérations secondaires: la Gaule Belgique, les Germanies et l'Occident romain*. Paris

Petit, M. and Parthuisot, F. (1995) 'L'évolution de la villa da la Butte à Gravois à Saint-Germain-les-Corbeil (Essonne) au Bas-Empire at au haut Moyen Age', in Ouzoulias and Van Ossel: 127–33

Petts, D. (2003) *Christianity in Roman Britain*. Stroud

Peytremann, E. (2003) *Archéologie de l'habitat rural dans le nord de la France du IVe au XIIe siècle* (2 vols.) (Mémoires de l'Association française de l'Archéologie mérovingienne, 13). Condé-sur-Noireau

Pfanner, M. (1990) 'Modele römische Stadtentwicklung am Beispiel Hispaniens und der westlichen Provinzen', in Trillmich and Zanker: 59–116

Pietri, L. (1983) *La ville de Tours du IVe au VIe siècle: naissance d'une cité chrétienne* (Collections de l'Ecole Française de Rome, 69). Rome

Pilet, C. (1980) *La nécropole de Frénouville: étude d'une population de la fin du IIIe à la fin du VIIe siècle* (*British Archaeological Reports*, International Series, 83). Oxford

Pilet, C., Alduc-Le Bagousse, A., Buchet, L., Helluin, M., Kazanski, M., Lambart, J.-C., Martin, G., Pellerin, J., Pilet-Lemière, J., Vipard, P., Clet-Pellerin, M. and Van Vliet-Lanoë, B. (1994) *La nécropole de Saint-Martin-de-Fontenay: recherches sur le peuplement de la plaine de Caen du Ve siècle avant J.-C. au VIIe après J.-C.* (*Gallia*, Suppl. 54). Paris

Pilon, F. (ed.) (2008) *Les sanctuaires et les habitats de Châteaubleau (Seine-et-Marne). Diocesis Galliarum* (Document de travail, 8). Nanterre

Pirling, R. (1986) *Römer und Franken am Niederrhein*. Mainz

Pirling, R., Siepen, M., Noeske-Winter, B. and Tegtmeier, U. (2000) *Das römisch-fränkische Gräberfeld von Krefeld-Gellep 1989–2000*. Bonn

Piva, P. (1996) 'La "cattedrale doppia" e la storia de la liturgia', *Antiquité Tardive* 4: 55–60

Pohl, H. (ed.) (1997) *Kingdoms of the Empire: The Integration of Barbarians in Late Antiquity* (The Transformation of the Roman World). Leiden

(1998) 'Telling the difference: signs of ethnic identity', in Pohl and Reimitz: 17–69

Pohl, H. and Reimitz, H. (eds.) (1998) *Strategies of Difference: The Construction of Ethnic Communities, 300–800* (Transformation of the Roman World). Leiden

(eds.) (2000) *Grenze und Differenz im frühen Mittelalter* (Forschungen zur Geschichtes des Mittelalters, 1). Vienna

Polanyi, K. (1957) *The Great Transformation: The Political and Economic Origins of Our Time*. Boston

Polfer, M. (2001) 'Occupation du sol et évolution de l'habitat rural dans la partie occidentale de la cité des Trévires au Bas-Empire (IVe–Ve siècles)', in Ouzoulias *et al.*: 69–112

Pomaredès, H., Barberan, S., Fabre, L. and Rigoir, Y. (2005) *La Quintarié (Clermont-l'Hérault, 34): établissement agricole et viticulture, atelier de céramiques paléochrétiennes, DS.P (Ier–VIe siècles ap. J.-C.)*. Montagnac

Potter, D. (2004) *The Roman Empire at Bay AD 180–395*. London

Poulter, A. (ed.) (2009) *The Transition to Late Antiquity on the Danube and Beyond* (Proceedings of the British Academy, 141). London

Poyeton, A. (2003) 'L'établissement rural du Bois de Rosière à Bessancourt (Val-d'Oise)', in Ouzoulias and Van Ossel: 49–76

Precht, G. (1973) *Baugeschichtliche Untersuchungen zum römischen Praetorium in Köln* (Rheinische Ausgrabungen, 14). Cologne

Prevosti, M. and Guitart i Duran, J. (2011) *Ager Tarraconensis 2: el poblament*. Tarragona

Provost, M. and Jouannet, C. (1994) *Carte archéologique de la Gaule 63/1 –Clermont Ferrand*. Paris

Puig, F. and Rodà, I. (2007) 'Las murallas de Barcino: nuevas aportaciones al conocimiento de la evolución de sus sistemas de fortificación', in Rodríguez Colmenero and Rodà: 595–631

Py, M. (ed.) (1993) *Dicocer [1], Dictionnaire des céramiques antiques (VIIe s. av. N. è.-VIIe s. de n. è.) en Méditerranée nord-occidentale (Provence, Languedoc, Ampurdan)* (Lattara, 6), 1–624. Lattes

Quaresma, J. C. (1999) 'Terra Sigillata africana D e Foceense Tardia das *escavações* recentes de Mirobriga (Chãos Salgados, Santiago do Cacém)', *Revista Portuguesa de Arqueología* 2(2): 69–82

Quérel, P. and Feugère, M. (2000) *L'établissement rural antique de Dury (Somme) et son depot de bronzes (IIIe s. av. J.-C. – IVe s. apr. J.-C.)* (*Revue du Nord*, Les Hors série. Collection Art et Archéologie, 6). Lille

Quirós Castillo, J. A. and Vigil-Escalera Guirado, A. (2006) 'Networks of peasant villages between Toledo and *Velega Alabense*, north-western Spain (V–X^{th} centuries)', *Archeologia Medievale* 33: 79–128

Raepsaet-Charlier, M.-T. and Vanderhoeven, A. (2004) 'Tongres au Bas-Empire romain', in Ferdière: 51–73

Raimbault, M. (1973) 'La céramique gallo-romaine dite "à l'éponge" dans le nord-ouest de l'empire romain', *Gallia* 31: 185–206

Rascón Marqués, S. (1999) 'La ciudad de Complutum en la tardoantigüedad: restauración y renovación', in García Moreno and Rascón Marqués: 51–70

Rascón Marqués, S. and Sánchez Montes, A. L. (2000) 'Complutum: tradición y cambio en la Antiqüedad Tardía', in Ribera i Lacomba: 235–42

Raynaud, C. (1990) *Le village gallo-romain de Lunel-Vieil (Hérault): la fouille du quartier ouest (1981–1983)*. Paris

  (1993) 'LUIS. Céramique Luisante', in Py: 504–10

  (1996) 'Les campagnes rhodaniennes: quelle crise?', in Fiches: 189–212

  (2001) 'Les campagnes languedociennes aux IVe et Ve siècles', in Ouzoulias *et al.*: 247–74

(2006) 'Le monde des morts', *Gallia* 63: 137–56

(2010) *Les nécropoles de Lunel-Viel (Hérault) de l'Antiquité au Moyen-Age* (Revue Archéologique de Narbonnaise, Suppl. 40). Montpellier

Rebourg, A. (1993) *Carte archéologique de la Gaule 71/1 – Autun*. Paris

Réchin, F. (ed.) (2006) *Nouveaux regards sur les villae d'Aquitaine: bâtiments de vie et d'exploitation, domaines et postérités médiévales* (Archéologie des Pyrénées Occidentales et des Landes, Les Hors série, 2). Pau

Reddé, M., Brulet, R., Fellman, R., Haalebos, J. K. and Schnurbein, S. (2006) *Les fortifications militaires* (Documents d'Archéologie Française, 100). Paris

Redknap, M. (1988) 'Medieval pottery production at Mayen', in Gaimster *et al.*: 3–37

Reece, R. (1973) 'Roman coinage in Britain and the western empire', *Britannia* 4: 227–51

(1981) 'Coinage and currency in the third century', in King and Henig: 79–88

(1999) *The Later Roman Empire: An Archaeology AD 150–600*. Stroud

(2002) *The Coinage of Roman Britain*. Stroud

Remesal Rodríguez, J. (1998) 'Baetican olive oil and the Roman economy', in Keay: 183–99

Reynaud, J.-F. (1998) *Lugdunum Christianum. Lyon du IVe au VIIIe s.: topographie, necropolis et edifices religieux* (Documents d'Archéologie Française, 69). Paris

Reynolds, P. (2005) 'Hispania in the later Roman Mediterranean: ceramics and trade', in Bowes and Kulikowski: 369–486

(2010) *Hispania and the Roman Mediterranean AD 100–700: Ceramics and Trade*. London

Ribera i Lacomba, A. (ed.) (2000) *Los orígenes del cristianismo en Valencia y su entorno*. Valencia

Ribera i Lacomba, A. and Rosselló Mesquida, M. (2000) 'El primer grupo episcopal de Valencia', in Ribera i Lacomba: 165–85

Rich, J. (ed.) (1992) *The City in Late Antiquity*. London

Richmond, I. A. (1931) 'Five town-walls in Hispania Citerior', *Journal of Roman Studies* 22: 81–100

Rickert, F. (1989) 'Zu den Stadt- und Architekturdarstellungen des Ashburnham Pentateuch', in Duval: 1341–70

Rigal, D. (2004) 'Le temple gallo-romain de Cahors', *Aquitania* 20: 85–94

Rigoir, J. (1968) 'Les sigillées paléochrétiennes grises et oranges', *Gallia* 26: 177–243

Rigoir, J. and Meffre, J. F. (1973) 'Les dérivées des sigillées paléochrétiennes du Groupe Atlantique', *Gallia* 31: 207–63

Ripoll López, G. (1985) *La necrópolis visigoda de El Carpio de Tajo (Toledo)* (Excavaciones Arqueológicas en España, 142). Madrid

(1991) 'Materiales funerarios de la Hispania visigoda: problemas de cronología y tipología', in Périn: 111–32

(1998) 'The arrival of the Visigoths in Hispania: population problems and the process of acculturation', in Pohl and Reimitz: 153–87

(1999) 'Symbolic life and signs of identity in Visigothic times', in Heather: 403–31

(2001) 'Problemas cronológicos de los adornos personales hispánicos (finales del siglo V-inicios del siglo VIII)', in Arce and Delogu: 57–77

Ripoll López, G. and Arce, J. (2001) 'Transformación y final de las *villae* en occidente (siglos IV–VIII): problemas y perspectives', *Arqueología y Territorio Medieval* 8: 21–54

Ripoll López, G. and Gurt, J.-M. (eds.) (2000) *Sedes regiae (ann. 400–800)*. Barcelona

Ristow, S. (2009) 'Das Kölner Baptisterium am Dom und die frühchristlichen Tauforte nördlich der Alpen', in Krings and Will: 34–44

Rivet, A. L. F. (ed.) (1969) *The Roman Villa in Britain*. London

Rodríguez Colmenero, A. (2007) 'La muralla romana de Lugo, gran bastión defensivo en los confines del Imperio: análisis del conjunto', in Rodríguez Colmenero and Rodà: 217–53

Rodríguez Colmenero, A. and Rodà, I. (eds.) (2007) *Murallas de ciudades romanas en el occidente del imperio* (Lucus Augusti como paradigma). Lugo

Rodríguez Martín, F. G. and Carvalho, A. (2008) 'Torre Águila y las villas de la Lusitnia interior hasta el occidente atlántico', in Fernández Ochoa *et al.*: 310–44

Romo Salas, A. (2003) 'Recent excavations and sculptural finds in the colony of *Astigi* (Baetica)', *Journal of Roman Archaeology* 16: 286–99

Rorison, M. (2001) Vici *in Roman Gaul* (British Archaeological Reports, International Series, 933). Oxford

Rouche, M. (1979) *L'Aquitaine des wisigoths aux arabes, 418–781: naissance d'une region*. Paris

(ed.) (1997) *Clovis. Histoire et mémoire* (2 vols.). Paris

Roymans, N. (1996a) 'The sword or the plough: regional dynamics in the romanisation of Belgic Gaul and the Rhineland area', in Roymans: 9–126

(ed.) (1996b) *From the Sword to the Plough: Three Studies on the Earliest Romanisation of Northern Gaul* (Amsterdam Archaeological Studies, 1). Amsterdam

Sablayrolles, R. and Beyrie, A. (2006) *Carte archéologique de la Gaule 31/2 – Le Comminges (Haute-Garonne)*. Paris

Sapin, C. (ed.) (2009) *Les stucs de l'Aniquité tardive de Vouneuil-sous-Biard (Vienne)* (*Gallia*, Suppl. 60). Paris

Sayer, D. and Williams, H. (eds.) (2009) *Mortuary Practices and Social Identities in the Middle Ages*. Cambridge

Schallmayer, E. (ed.) (1995) *Der Augsburger Siegesaltar: Zeugnis einer unruhigen Zeit* (Sallburg-Schriften, 2). Bad Homburg

Scharf, R. (2005) *Der Dux Mogontiacensis und die Notitia Dignitatum: Eine Studie zur Spätantike Grenzverteidigung* (Ergänzungsbände zum Reallexikon der Germanischen Altertumskunde, 50). Berlin and New York

Schattner, T. G. (2002) *Munigua: cuarenta años de investigaciones*. Madrid

Schatzmann, R. (2011) 'Augusta Raurica: Von der prosperierenden Stadt zur enceinte réduite – archäologische Quellen und ihre Datierung', in Schatzmann and Martin-Kilcher: 65–94

Schatzmann, R. and Martin-Kilcher, S. (eds.) (2011) *L'empire romain en mutation: répercussions sur les villes dans la deuxième moitié du IIIe siècle/Das römische Reich im Umbruch: Auswirkungen auf die Städte in der zweiten Hälfte des 3. Jahrhunderts*. Montagnac

Scheidel, M. and Friesen, S. J. (2009) 'The size of the economy and the distribution of income in the Roman Empire', *Journal of Roman Studies* 99: 61–91

Scheidel, M., Morris, I. and Saller, R. (eds.) (2006) *The Cambridge Economic History of the Greco-Roman World*. Cambridge

Scheidel, M. and von Reden, S. (eds.) (2002) *The Ancient Economy*. Edinburgh

Schenck, J.-L. (ed.) (1994) *Économie antique. Les échanges dans l'Antiquité: le rôle de l'état* (Entretiens d'Archéologie et d'Histoire, 1). Saint-Bertrand-de-Comminges

Schlunk, H. and Hauschild, T. (1978) *Die Denkmäler der frühchristlichen und westgotischen Zeit* (Hispania Antiqua). Mainz

Schneider, L. (2005) 'Dynamiques spatiales et transformations de l'habitat en Languedoc méditerranéen durant le haut Moyen Age (VI–IX s.)', in Brogiolo et al.: 287–312

(2007) 'Rythmes de l'occupation rurale et formes de l'habitat dans le sud-est de la France entre Antiquité et Moyen Age (IVe–VIIIe s.): essai de synthèse', *Gallia* 64: 11–56

Schneider, L. and Raynaud, C. (2011) 'Etablissements perches de France méridionale (V^e–IXe siècles)', *Dossiers de l'Archéologie* 344: 24–9

Schönberger, H. (1969) 'The Roman frontier in Germany: an archaeological survey', *Journal of Roman Studies* 59: 144–97

Schulz, W. (1953) *Leuna: Ein germanischer Bestattungsplatz der spätrömischen Kaiserzeit*. Stuttgart

Schwarz, P.-A. (1998) 'Die spätrömischen Befestigungsanlagen in Augusta Raurica – Ein Überblick', in Bridger and Gilles: 105–11

Scott, S. (2000) *Art and Society in Fourth-Century Britain: Villa Mosaics in Context* (Oxford University School of Archaeology Monograph, 53). Oxford

Séguier, J.-M. (2006) 'Les mobiliers de l'Antiquité tardive (IIIe s.–Ve s.) de l'établissement rural du Chemin de Sens à Marolles-sur-Seine (Seine-et-Marne) dans leurs contextes', in Van Ossel: 227–75

(2011) 'La céramique du Bas-Empire du secteur Seine-Yonne: productions, typologie et proposition de classification chronologique des ensembles', in Van Ossel: 13–44

Seillier, C. (1989) 'Les tombes de transition du cimitière germanique de Vron (Somme)', *Jahrbuch des Römisch-Germanischen Zentralmuseums Mainz* 36: 599–634

(1994) 'La céramique romaine tardive de Gaule septentrionale en milieu funéraire daté (fin IVe–Ve siècle)', in Tuffreau-Libre and Jacques: 53–63

(1995) 'La présence germanique en Gaule du Nord au Bas-Empire', *Revue du Nord – Archéologie* 57: 71–8

(1996) 'Développement topographique et caractères généraux de la nécropole de Vron (Somme)', *Archéologie Médiévale* 16: 7–32

Seitz, G. and Zagermann, M. (2005) 'Spätrömische Festungen am Oberrhein', in Geiberger *et al.*: 204–9

Sfameni, C. (2006) *Ville residenziali nell'Italia tardoantica*. Bari

Shelton, K. J. (1981) *The Esquiline Treasure*. London

Simon, E. (1986) *Die konstantinischen Deckengemälde in Trier*. Mainz

Sintès, C. (1994) 'La réutilisation des espaces publics à Arles, un témoignage de la fin de l'antiquité', *Antiquité Tardive* 2: 181–92

Sireix, C. (2005) 'Bordeaux-*Burdigala* et la Bretagne romaine: quelques témoins archéologiques du commerce atlantique', *Aquitania* 21: 241–51

Sivan, H. (1993) *Ausonius of Bordeaux: Genesis of a Gallic Aristocracy*. London

Slater, T. (ed.) (2000) *Towns in Decline A.D. 100–1600*. Aldershot

Smith, J. T. (1997) *Roman Villas: A Study in Social Structure*. London

Solier, Y. (1991) *La basilique paléochrétienne du Clos de la Lombarde à Narbonne: cadre archéologique, vestiges et mobiliers* (Revue archéologique de Narbonnaise, Suppl. 23). Montpellier

Sommer, M. (1984) *Die Gürtel und Gürtelbeschläge des 4. und 5. Jahrhunderts im römischen Reich* (Bonner Hefte zur Vorgeschichte, 22). Bonn

Sotomayor, M. (2006) 'Centcelles sigue siendo un enigma', *Pyrenae* 37(2): 143–7

Soulat, J. (2007) 'Le mobilier de type anglo-saxon entre le Ponthieu et la basse vallée de la Seine', *Revue archéologique de Picardie* 3–4: 77–89

Srejović, D. (1993) *Roman Imperial Towns and Palaces in Serbia: Sirmium, Romuliana, Naissus*. Belgrade

Srejović, D. and Vasić, C. (1994) 'Emperor Galerius's buildings in *Romuliana* (Gamzigrad, eastern Serbia)', *Antiquité Tardive* 2: 123–41

Stallibrass, S. and Thomas, R. (2008) 'For starters: producing and supplying food to the army in the Roman north-west provinces', in Stallibrass and Thomas (eds.), *Feeding the Roman Army: The Archaeology of Production and Supply in NW Europe*. Oxford, 1–17

Stancliffe, C. (1983) *St Martin and His Hagiographer: History and Miracle in Sulpicius Severus*. Oxford

Steuer, H. (1997) 'Herrschaft von der Höhe: vom mobiles Söldnertrupp zur Residenz auf repräsentatiben Bergkuppen', in Fuchs *et al.*: 149–62

Stirling, L. (2005) *The Learned Collector: Mythological Statuettes and Classical Taste in Late Antique Gaul*. Ann Arbor, Mich.

(2007) 'Statuary collecting and display in the late antique villas of Gaul and Spain: a comparative study', in Bauer and Witschel: 307–21

Stutz, F. (2000) 'L'inhumation habillée à l'époque mérovingienne au sud de la Loire', *Mémoires de la Société Archéologique du Midi de la France* 60: 33–49
Stylow, A. U. (1990) 'Apuntes sobre el urbanismo de la Corduba romana', in Trillmich and Zanker: 259–82
Swift, E. (2000a) *Regionality in Dress Accessories in the Late Roman West* (Monographies Instrumentum, 11). Montagnac
 (2000b) *The End of the Western Roman Empire*. Stroud
 (2009) *Style and Function in Roman Decoration: Living with Objects and Interiors*. Farnham
 (2010) 'Identifying migrant communities: a contextual analysis of grave assemblages from continental late Roman cemeteries', *Britannia* 41: 237–82
TED'A (Taller Escola d'Arqueologia) (1990) *L'amfiteatre romà de Tarragona: la basilica visigòtica i l'església romànica* (Memòries d'Excavció, 3; Taller Escola d'Arqueologia). Tarragona
Teja, R. and Pérez, C. (eds.) (1997) *La Hispania de Teodosio*. Salamanca
Terrier, J. (2005) 'Bilan des recherches archéologiques sur les églises rurales en Suisse occidentale', in Delaplace: 72–81
Theune, C. (2004) *Germanen und Romanen in der Alamannia: Strukturveränderung aufgrund der archäologischen Quellen vom 3. bis zum 7. Jahrhundert* (Ergänzungsbände zum Reallexikon der Germanischen Altertumskunde, 45). Berlin
Theuws, F. (2009) 'Grave goods, ethnicity and the rhetoric of burial rites in late antique northern Gaul', in Derks and Roymans: 293–319
Theuws, F. and Alkemade, M. (2000) 'A kind of mirror for men: sword depositions in late antique northern Gaul', in Theuws and Nelson: 401–76
Theuws, F. and Nelson, J. (2000) *Rituals of Power: From Late Antiquity to the Early Middle Ages* (Transformation of the Roman World, 8). Leiden
Thoen, H. and Vermeulen, F. (1998) 'Phasen der Germanisierung in Flandern in der mittel- und spätrömischen Zeit', in Bridger and Gilles: 1–12
Toynbee, J. and Painter, K. (1986) 'Silver picture plates of late antiquity: A.D. 300 to 700', *Archaeologia* 108: 15–65
Tranoy, L. (2000) 'La mort en Gaule romaine', in Ferdière: Ch. 4
Trément, F. (1999) *Archéologie d'un paysage: les étangs de Saint-Blaise (Bouches-du-Rhône)* (Documents d'Archéologie Française, 74). Paris
 (2001) 'Habitat et peuplement en Provence à la fin de l'Antiquité', in Ouzoulias et al.: 275–302
Trément, F. and Dousteyssier, B. (2001) 'Elites et *villae* dans le térritoire de la cité arverne', *Bulletin AGER* 11: 17–24
Trillmich, W. and Zanker, P. (eds.) (1990) *Stadtbild und Ideologie: Die Monumentalisierung hispanischer Städte zwischen Republik und Kaiserzeit* (Bayerische Akademie der Wissenschaften, 103). Munich

Tuffreau-Libre, M. and Jacques, A. (eds.) (1994) *La céramique du Bas-Empire en Gaule Belgique et dans les régions voisines* (*Revue du Nord*, Les Hors série, Collection Archéologie, 4). Lille

Vallet, F. and Kazanski, M. (eds.) (1993) *L'armée romaine et les barbares du IIIe au VIIe siècle* (Mémoires de l'Association française d'Archéologie mérovingienne, 5). Paris

Van Andringa, W. (ed.) (2000) *Archéologie des sanctuaries en Gaule romaine*. Saint-Étienne

Van Dam, R. (1985) *Leadership and Community in Late Antique Gaul* (The Transformation of the Classical Heritage). Berkeley, Calif. and Los Angeles

Van der Leeuw, S., Favory, F. and Fiches, J.-L. (eds.) (2003) *Archéologie et systèmes socio-environnementaux: études multiscalaires sur la vallée du Rhône dans le programme ARCHEOMEDES*. Paris

Van Driel-Murray, C. (ed.) (1989) *Roman Military Equipment: The Sources of Evidence* (Proceedings of the Fifth Roman Military Equipment Conference) (British Archaeological Reports, International Series, 476). Oxford

Van Es, W. A. (1994) 'Volksverhuizing En Continuiteit', in Van Es and Hessing: 64–119

Van Es, W. A. and Hessing, W. A. M. (eds.) (1994) *Romeinen, Friezen en Franken in het hart van Nederland: van Traiectum tot Dorestad*. Utrecht

Van Ossel, P. (1992) *Etablissements ruraux de l'Antiquité tardive dans le nord de la Gaule* (*Gallia*, Suppl. 51). Paris

(1995) 'Insécurité et militarization en Gaule du Nord au Bas-Empire: l'exemple des campagnes', *Revue du Nord – Archéologie* 77: 27–36

(1996) 'La sigillée d'Argonne du Bas-Empire dans le nord de la Gaule: distribution, imitations et concurrences (IVe–Ve s.)', *Acta Rei Cretariae Romanae Fautorem* 34: 221–30

(1997) 'Structure, evolution et statut des habitats ruraux au Bas-Empire en Ile-de-France', in Ouzoulias and Van Ossel: 94–105

(2003) 'De la "villa" au village: les prémices d'une mutation', in Yante and Bultot-Verleysen: 1–19

(ed.) (2006) *Les céramiques de l'Antiquité tardive en Ile-de-France et dans le Bassin parisien*. Vol. I: *Ensembles régionaux*. Paris

(2010) 'Transformations et continuités aux contacts de trois cultures: les campagnes de la Gaule septentrionale au Ve siècle', in Delogu and Gasparri: 579–600

(2011a), 'Les sigillées du groupe Argonne dans le Bassin parisien au Bas-Empire: caractérisation, production et diffusion', in Van Ossel: 231–54

(2011b), 'Les cités de la Gaule pendant la seconde moitié du IIIe siècle: etat de la recherche et des questions', in Schatzmann and Martin-Kilcher: 9–21

(ed.) (2011c) *Les céramiques de l'Antiquité tardive en Ile-de-France et dans le Bassin parisien*. Vol. II: *Synthèses*. Diocesis Galliarum (Document de travail, 9). Paris

Van Ossel, P. and Defgnée, A. (2001) *Champion, Hamois: une villa romaine chez les Condruses* (Etudes et Documents Archéologie, 7). Luxembourg

Van Ossel, P. and Ouzoulias, P. (2000) 'Rural settlement economy in northern Gaul in the late empire: an overview', *Journal of Roman Archaeology* 13: 133–60

Vaquerizo, D. (ed.) (2002) *Espacios y usos funerarios en el occidente romano* (2 vols.). Córdoba

Vaquerizo, D. and Noguera, J. M. (1997) *La villa de El Ruedo (Almedinilla, Córdoba): decoración escultórica e interpretación*. Murcia

Ventura, A., León, P. and Márquez, C. (1998) 'Roman Córdoba in the light of recent research', in Keay: 87–108

Vermeulen, F. (2001) 'Les campagnes de la Belgique septentrionale et de Pays-Bas méridionaux au IVe et Ve siècles', in Ouzoulias *et al.*: 45–68

Verslype, L. (1999) 'La topographie du haut Moyen Age à Tournai: nouvel état des questions archéologiques', *Revue du Nord* 81: 143–62

Verstegen, U. (2006) *Ausgrabungen und Bauforschungen in St. Gereon zu Köln*. Mainz

Vidal, M. (ed.) (1992) *Incinérations et inhumations dans l'occident romain aux trois premiers siècles de notre ère*. Toulouse

  (1993) *Monde des morts, monde des vivants en Gaule rurale* (Revue Archéologique du Centre de la France, Suppl. 6). Tours

Vipard, P. (2007) 'Maison à *péristyle* et élites urbaines en Gaule sous l'Empire', *Gallia* 64: 227–77

Volbach, W. F. (1976) *Elfenbeinarbeiten der Spätantikeund des frühen Mittelalters*, 3rd edn. (Kataloge vor- und frühgeschichtiche Altertümer, 7). Mainz

Von Petrikovits, H. (1971) 'Fortifications in the north-western Roman Empire from the third to the fifth centuries A.D.', *Journal of Roman Studies* 61: 136–218

von Rummel, P. (2007) *Habitus Barbarus: Kleidung und Repräsentation spätantiker Eliten im 4. und 5. Jahrhundert* (Ergänzungsbande zum Reallexikon der Germanischen Altertumskunde, 55). Berlin

Wacher, J. S. (1995) *The Towns of Roman Britain*, 2nd edn. London

Walker, D. (1988) 'The Roman coins', in B. Cunliffe (ed.): *The Temple of Sulis Minerva at Bath. Vol. 2: The Finds from the Sacred Spring*. Oxford, 281–358

Walker, S. and Bierbrier, M. (1997) *Ancient Faces: Mummy Portraits from Roman Egypt*. London

Wallace-Hadrill, A. (1994) *Houses and Society in Pompeii and Herculaneum*. Princeton, N.J.

Ward-Perkins, B. R. (1997) 'Continuitists, catastrophists and the towns of post-Roman northern Italy', *Papers of the British School at Rome* 65: 157–76

  (2005) *The Fall of Rome and the End of Civilization*. Oxford

Weber, W. (1996) 'Trier: Antike Kirchenanlage im Bereich von Dom und Liebfrauen', *Antiquité Tardive* 4: 82–6

Weitzmann, K. (1977) *Late Antique and Early Christian Book Illumination*. London

Whittaker, C. R. (1983) 'Late Roman trade and traders', in Garnsey *et al.*: 163–80

(1994) *Frontiers of the Roman Empire: A Social and Economic Survey*. Baltimore and London

Wickham, C. J. (1984) 'The other transition: from the ancient world to feudalism', *Past and Present* 113: 3–36

(2005) *Framing the Early Middle Ages: Europe and the Mediterranean 400–800*. Oxford

Wieczorek, A. (1996) 'Identität und Integration – Zur Bevölkerungspolitik der Merowinger nach archäologischen Quellen', in Wieczorek *et al.*: 346–57

Wieczorek, A., Périn, P., von Welck, K. and Menghin, W. (eds.) (1996) *Die Franken, Wegbereiter Europas*. Mainz

Wightman, E. (1970) *Roman Trier and the Treveri*. London

(1985) *Gallia Belgica*. London

Wilkes, J. J. (1986) *Diocletian's Palace, Split* (Department of Ancient History and Classical Archaeology, University of Sheffield, Occasional Publication, 2). Sheffield

Wilkinson, P. (2011) 'An octagonal bath-house at Bax Farm, Teynham', *Journal of Roman Archaeology* 24: 408–22

Willems, W. J. H. (1989) 'An officer or a gentleman? A late Roman weapon-grave from a villa at Voerendaal (NL)', in Van Driel-Murray: 143–56

Williams, D. and Carreras, C. (1995) 'North African amphorae in Roman Britain: a reappraisal', *Britannia* 26: 231–52

Williams-Thorpe, O. (1988) 'Provenancing and archaeology of Roman millstones from the Mediterranean area', *Journal of Archeological Sciences* 15: 253–305

Wilson, A. (2009) 'Approaches to quantifying Roman trade', in Bowman and Wilson: 213–49

Wilson, P. R. (ed.) (2003) *The Archaeology of Roman Towns: Studies in Honour of John S. Wacher*. Oxford

Wilson, R. (1983) *Piazza Armerina*. London

(2006) 'Aspects of iconography in Romano-British mosaics: the Rudston "aquatic" scene and the Brading astronomer revisited', *Britannia* 37: 295–336

Witschel, C. (1999) *Krise – Rezession – Stagnation? Der Westen des römischen Reiches im 3. Jahrhundert n. Chr.* Frankfurt am Main

(2004) 'Re-evaluating the Roman West in the 3rd. c. A.D.', *Journal of Roman Archaeology* 17: 251–81

Woolf, G. (1990) 'World-systems analysis and the Roman Empire', *Journal of Roman Archaeology* 3: 44–58

(1992) 'Imperialism, empire and the integration of the Roman economy', *World Archaeology* 23: 283–93

(1998) *Becoming Roman: The Origins of Provincial Civilization in Gaul*. Cambridge

Wrede, H. (1972) *Die spätantike Hermengalerie von Welschbillig*. Berlin

Yante, J.-M. and Bultot-Verleysen, A.-M. (eds.) (2003) *Autour du "village": établissements humains, finages et communautés rurales entre Seine et Rhin*

(IVe–XIIIe siècles). Actes du colloque international de Louvain-la-Neuve, 16–17 mai 2003. Lovain-la-Neuve

Yegül, F. (2010) *Bathing in the Roman World*. Cambridge

Zanker, P. (1988) *The Power of Images in the Age of Augustus*. Ann Arbor, Mich.

Zimmer, J., Metzler, J. and Bakker, L. (1981) *Ausgrabungen in Echternach*. Luxembourg

Index

Aardenburg 322
abacus 224, 233
ad sanctos 163, 164, 166
adaeration 350
Adrianople 358
adventus 126
Aetius 339, 351, 359, 376, 385
Agde, Council of 360, 375
Agen 118, 360
agency 8
agglomération 289, 293, 318
agglomération secondaire see: 'small towns'
Agri Decumates 24, 30, 47, 85
agricultural exploitation/production 251, 265, 266, 289, 292, 416, 458
Airan 381
Aix-en-Provence 107, 109, 114, 118, 135, 137, 145, 159, 174, 180, 408, 433
Alamanni 24, 30, 31, 54, 77, 78, 80, 272, 279, 339, 352, 357, 368, 377, 378, 384, 479, 481
Alans 339, 358, 364, 381, 479
Alaric 358
Alaric II 359, 375
Albalete 88
Alberca, la 185
Aldenhover Platte 273
Alet (St-Malo) 52
Alf, river 272
Alicante 401
Almenara de Adaja 252
Alto de Yecla 444
Altrhein 48
Altrip 49, 345
Alzey 49, 72, 345, **346**
ambo 50, 155
Amiens 55, 70–2, 75, 93, 107, 300, 320, 322, 331, 428
amphitheatre (see also: Tarragona) 117–19, 148, 203
amphora/e 29, 226, 266, 297, 313, 314, 361, 401
    Dressel 20 310
    Gauloise 4 267, 296, 318
    North African 317, 399, 425, 448

Andalusía 369
Angers 125
Anglo-Saxon 279, 382, 390, 480
Angoulême 133
Annales 7
annona 123, 129, 132, 135, 293, 296, 309, 312, 315, 317, 324, 399, 400, 424
Antonine 'plague' 464–6
Antonines 19
antoninianus/-i 35, 332
Aphrodisias 228, 230
Aquileia 158, 349
Aquitaine 31, 132, 254, 326, 341, 364, 381
Arbogast 376
Arcadius 349
archery 56, 57
arcosolium 155, 167
Arian 359, 363, 424
aristocratic display/self-representation 12, 95, 198, 199, 214, 242, 244, 247, 260, 282, 295, 296, 297, 309, 414, 424, 431, 435, 436–9, 441, 460, 464, 470
Aristotle 99
Arles 32, 107–9, **109**, 114, 115, 117, 134, 137, 143, 145, 167, 168, 175, 201, 210–12, 317, 325, 331, 339, 359, 402, 405–9
    Alyscamps 212, 408
    amphitheatre 211, 408
    basilica **210**, 211
    'Baths of Constantine' 115, 210, 405
    circus 118, 211, 407, **407**
    Commanderie Ste-Luce 405
    Crédit Agricole 407
    Esplanade 109, 406, **406**
    forum 405
    Jardin d'Hiver 32
    theatre 211
    Trinquetaille 32, 107, 212, 408
armature 113, 144, 405, 432
Armorica/Brittany 306, 340, 460
armour 55, 57
army/soldiers, Roman 11, 44–55, 319, 341–8, 395, 456, 467, 474

Arras 68, 146, 427, 428
arrow 57
Arroyo Culebros 443
artisan 137
Arverni 285
Astorga 114, 126, 128, 130
Athaulf 364
Athens 124
atrium 155
Attila 340
Auch 133, 137, 147, 360
Augsburg 18, 30, 39, 48
Augst 31
Augustine of Hippo 163
aula (palatina) 171, 203, 222, 223, 225, 238, 239, 251
Aurelian 24, 31, 33, 35, 332
Ausonius 148, 207, 247, 335, 358, 470
Autun 64, 138
Avignon 134
Avitacum 116, 227
Avranches 91

Bacaudae 340
Bad Kreuznach 49
Baelo 114
Baetica 312, 316, 374, 400, 461
Baños de la Reina 238, 251
banquet/formal meal 223, 228
    women at 227
baptistery/baptism (see also: Aix-en-Provence, Barcelona, Fréjus, Geneva, Grenoble, Limoges, Loupian, Marseille, Riez, Saint-Maximin) 152, 153, 155, 158, 159, **160**, 171, 175, 176, 185, 187, 402, 415, 416, 420, 428, 451
'barbarian/s' (see also: identity) 12, 338, 348, 351, 393, 405, 439, 467
barbarous radiates 35, 332
Barcelona 126, 130, **131**, 139, 140, 145, 159, 171, 172, 235, 291, 364, 370, 372, 402, 405
barracks 49, 68, 212, 214, 269
barrel/s 266, 315
basilica 152
Basque country 417, 443
baths 191
    private 73, 115–17, 219, 404
    public 116–17, 219, 238, 252, 422, 438
Bauve, La 192
Bavai 51, 68, 71, 74, 107, 145, 320
Bavarii 481
Bayeux 72, 75
Bayonne 129, 132

Bazas 133, 358
Beauvais 75
Beiral 368
Beja 368
belt/*cingulum* 58, 78, 84, 87, 235, 259, 266, 343, 346, 366, 440, 450
Besançon 90
Béziers 134
Bignor 256
billon 33, 330, 331, 332, 350
bishop/s 117, 152, 175, 179, 198, 440
Bitburg 49
Biterrois/Béziers 289
Bituriges Cubi 258, 283–5, **283**, **284**, **285**
Blanzy-les-Fismes 261
Bois Rosière 273
Bonn 177
Boppard 49, 177
Bordeaux 95, 110, 114, 115, 118, 129, 132, 137, 145, 146, 148, 247, 322, 325, 418, 423
    'Palais Gallien' amphitheatre 118, **119**, 145, 459
Boulogne 51
Bourges 132, 258, 283, 285
Bovalar, El 444, **445**, 473
Brading 257
Braga 126, 128, 130, 370, 372
brandea 164
Brebières 452
Breviarium of Alaric 360, 371, 373, 375
Britain 5, 10, 51, 52, 62, 88, 93, 115, 118, 121, 122, 130, 135, 139, 140, 144, 145, 181, 190, 199, 215, 230, 256–8, 307, 310, 320, 322, 326, 328, 339, 343, 382, 402, 436, 462, 468, 469, 476
brooch 78, 84, 87, 235, **366**, 375, 386, 440
    Adlerfibel 366, 373
    Armbrustfibel 78, 85, 280, 361, 366, 369, 371, 372, 382
    Blechfibel 366, 369
    Bügelknopffibel 366, 369, 371, 372, 382
    crossbow brooch 58, 343, 383
    Duratón 361
    Gleicharmigefibel 85
    Schalenfibel 85
    Stutzarmfibel 280
    Tutulusfibel 78, 85, 343
    Zwiebelknopffibel 84
bucellarii 351, 439
buckle 58
Buradón 443
Burgo de Osma 127
Burgundians 339, 346, 353, 381, 385, 450, 480

Burgundy 259
burgus/burgi 43, 48, 50, 51, 76–9
   burgus of Pontius Leontius 438
burials/cemeteries 50, 77, 79–89, 160–6, 343, 415, 431, 440, 453, 480
   'Christian' 164, 165
   cremation 81, 464
   female 86, 347, 366, 370–1, 481
   graves with lateral niches 371, 372
   inhumation 81, 464
   'princely' 370, 372, 383
   weapon burials 81, 83, 468

Cacera de las Ranas 368
Cáceres 127
Cádiz 117
Caerwent 114
Cahors 114, 133
Caistor-by-Norwich 114
Calabria 313, 334
Cambrai 70
Canterbury 118, 135
Caparra 127, 130
capital, diocesan 433
Caracalla 20
Carcassone 134, 325
   Gap 399
Carmarthen 118
Carpio de Tajo, El 366, 367, 369
Carranque 184, **184**, 216, **216**, 234, 239, 240, 241, 245, 317, 413
carrying-capacity 112, 290, 296, 298, 410, 458, 461, 464
Cartagena 145
Carthage 339, 400
Cassel 70
Cassiodorus 124
Castelculier 219, 422
Castillejos, Los 223
Castro Ventosa 368, 371, 372
castrum 68, 443
Càstulo 127
catafract(ar)ii 57, 71
Catalaunian Plain 340, 359
Catalonia 9, 250, 254, 291, 401, 410, 473
catechumen 158
cella memoriae/memoria 156, 163, 177, 345, 411
cementerios tardohíspanos con ajuares 88, 252, 371, 372, 439
cemeteries: see 'burials'
Centcelles 182, **183**, 235, 251, 292
ceremony/ceremonial 205, 223, 342
Cerro de la Villa 239, 252

Chaourse 37
Chapelle-Vaupelteigne, La 259
Chastel-sur-Murat 187
Châteaubleau 192, **194**
Chaves 127
Cherbourg 322
Chichester 115
Childeric 376, 480
Chiragan 187, 228, **229**
chi-rho 59, 168, 181
Chora 93
Christian/ity (see also: Arian; burials/cemeteries) 11, 15, 81, 111, 117, 150, 151, 223, 245, 262, 415, 478, 480, 482
Chronica Caesaraugustana 367
church buildings 152, 162, 241, 411, 420, 451, 453, 473
   cemetery church 175, 181, 207, 468
   double church 157–9
ciborium 155, 158, 159
Cimiez 159
circus 117–19, 148, 203, 214, 403, 404
   faction 102
Cirencester 114, 118
civil service/bureaucracy, Roman 58, 198, 310, 348, 436, 439, 468, 480
Claudius II 33, 36
Clermont-Ferrand 133, 134, 359
Clermont-l'Hérault 325
Cléry-sur-Somme 299
clibanarii 57
Clion 258
clothing: see 'dress'
Clovis 359, 376, 384, 428
Cluses, Les 131
Cocosa, la 185, 241, 252
Codex Theodosianus 91, 116, 313
coemptio 310, 324
Coimbra 127
coinage (see also: hoarding) 304, 310, 329, 336, 348–50, 397, 457, 467, 474, 480
   Æ3 333
   Æ4 333
   circulation/supply 331, 350, 397
   debasement 20
   imitative/copies 332
   monetisation 332, 333
Colchester 118
collegium/ia 102, 166, 402
Cologne (see also: Köln-Deutz) 50, 51, 52, 62, 70, 74, 95, 209, 234, 260
   episcopal complex 176
   'Praetorium' 63

Römerturm 63
St Gereon 176, **177**
coloni 264, 269
colonisation/encroachment/subdivision (see also: 'squatter occupation'; parasitic occupation) 403, 405, 412, 413, 418, 420, 422, 432, 441
comb 347, 360, 368, 371, 372, 420, 423
Comes Argentoratensis 90
Comes Britanniae 53
Comes Hispaniarum 53
Comes litoris Saxonici 52, 90
Comes rei militaris 351
Comes Sacrarum largitionum 93, 254, 330, 331, 350
comitatenses 53, 91, 93, 330, 342
comitatus 53
commilito/nes 45
Commodus 20
Complutum 114, 115, 139
Condroz 77
Congosto 416, 442, **442**
Conimbriga 127, 130
conjoncture 7
Conjux 326
connectivity 306, 399
consistorium 203
Constans 183, 204
Constantine I 21, 22, 51, 53, 59, 73, 144, 202, 203, 207, 211, 234
Constantine II 204, 211
Constantine III 339, 349, 358
Constantinople 143, 185, 205, 207, 225, 229, 310
Constantius I 202
Constantius II 55, 200
Constantius Gallus 200
Constantius, patrician (Constantius III) 339, 351, 358, 364
consular diptych 59, 234, 335
Corbridge 233, 244
Córdoba 118, 212–14, 293
 La Cercadilla 139, 212, **213**, 219, 238
Coria 127
Courtrai 51
Coutances 91
cranial deformation 360, 381
Crispus 211
Crocus, king of Alamanni 108, 286
cryptoporticus 68, 212
cubiculum 217
Cuevas de Soria 251
cuneus 49, 53
Cynegius, Maternus 217

Dalheim 141
Dassargues 447
Dax 95, 129, 132, 137
decline 105, 110, 270, 273, 274, 311, 396, 460, 463
'defense-in-depth' 54
destruction (deposit/horizon) 31, 32, 426
Deurne 91
Die 134
'*Diocesis Galliarum*' 271, 275
Diocletian 6, 21, 22, 134, 213, 331, 332
disintegration (see also: integration) 10, 12, 395, 473, 477
DNA 86, 392
domestic architecture 136–40
dominus 220, 223, 226, 236, 237, 252, 268, 269, 288
domus 236–40, 397
Dorchester 118
Dover 322
dress/clothing 45, 79, 94, 226, 235, 304, 342, 365, 383, 389, 434, 474
 female 235, 370, 372
 military 55, 58, 60
 peplos 366
Duero burials 83, 88, 371, 372, 439, 469
Duero valley 417
Dunkirk II 48
Duratón (see also: brooch) 366, 369, 440
durée 7, 9, 151, 265, 464
Dury 260
dux Belgicae secundae 52, 90, 322
dux Britanniarum 52
dux Moguntiacensis 90
dux Sequanici 90
dux tractus Armoricani et Nervicani 52, 72, 90, 322

Eauze 124, 137, 255, 328, 360
Ebro 307, 399
Echternach 260, 272
Ecija 115, 293
economy (see also: coinage; trade) 297, 303
 imperial economy 308, 473
 market economy 307, 308, 313, 318, 325–7, 328, 332, 474
 moral economy 334, 478
 peasant economy 309, 329
 political economy 308, 309–25, 327, 336, 477
 prestige economy 309, 315, 334–5, 478
economic structure/s 307
 reciprocity 307, 336
 redistribution 307, 332, 336

Ecrilles 450
Eifel 76
ekphrasis 224, 227, 231, 244, 248
Elbe 85
Elbegermanen 347, 377
Elche 127
Els Munts 251
'emic' (see also: 'etic') 15, 342, 344, 348, 355, 374, 386
Emporiae/Empuriès/Ampurias 114, 291
encroachment, see: colonisation
environmental evidence 304
'epigraphic habit' 27, 101, 106, 111, 168, **169**
episcopal complex (see also: Aix-en-Provence; Barcelona; Geneva; Lyon; Marseille; Tarragona; Valencia) 152, 172, 174, 214, 403, 468
Equites catafractarii Ambianenses 71
Erilla, La 443
Escolives-Sainte-Camille 259
Esquiline treasure 233
Essarts-le-Roi 281
Estada 414
Estrées-sur-Noye 260
ethnicity (see also: identity) 353, 386, 387, 405, 433, 452, 469
ethnogenesis 356, 385
'etic' (see also: 'emic') 15, 342, 344, 348, 355, 374, 386
euergetism 105, 112, 179, 435, 457, 459
Eugenius 349, 376
Euren 260
Euric 359
Euric II 359
Evora 121, 127
Evreux 72, 75
Exeter 115
extensification (see also: intensification) 287, 295, 301, 458

fabrica/e 56, 64, 71, 73, 84, 89, 93, 149, 206, 211, 285, 319, 320, 348, 350, 425
Famars 70
familia 155, 179
Fausta 211
fifth century, chronology 339, 397
fiscal system/taxation 4, 11, 253, 254, 282, 296, 310, 323, 324, 330, 340, 350, 417, 467
'tax spine' 312, 313, 318, 319, 399, 400, 475
Flögeln 379
foederati 50, 53, 78, 79, 82, 262, 351
fonds de cabane see: SFB
food 226, 334, 390, 462, 475

forum 114, 180, 402
Forum Hadriani 459
francisca 378, 383
Franks/Frankish 13, 54, 80, 279, 340, 344, 352, 353, 357, 359, 361, 376–86, 387, 429, 453, 469, 478, 479
  Bructeri 376
  Chamavi 376
  Salian 48, 52, 77, 279, 376
Fréjus 115, 137, 159, **161**, 174
Frigidus, battle of 349
Frisian 376
frontiers 43, 44, 47, 456
  frontier zone 5, 54, 377
Furfooz 77
furniture 231

Gaiseric 400
Galerius 200
Galicia 127, 267, 326, 365, 415
Galla Placidia 364
Gallic Empire 24, 26, 33, 65, 202
Gallienus 24, 33, 36
Gamzigrad 200
Gap 135
garden 205, 224, 238
Garonne 358
garum 226, 313, 317, 326
Geneva 134, 153–7, **154**, 160, 187, 234, 340, 385
  episcopal complex **154**, 158, 179, 428
  La Madeleine 156
  Saint-Germain 156
  Saint-Gervais 156, 163, 165
Gennep 379
gentiles 380
'German/ic' 13, 79, 80, 262, 279, 280, 340, 344, 345, 346, 352, 360, 361, 378, 386, 388, 392, 395, 397, 414, 429, 431, 444, 452, 469, 472, 478, 479
Gerona 126, 131
Gijón 126, 129
gladius 57
glass 234, 300, 303, 335, 344, 391, 422, 426, 443
Goths 357
  Greuthungi 358
  Tervingi 358
Gózquez (de Arriba) 368, 442, 444
Gratian 204, 207, 247, 470
grave goods 165
Gregory of Tours 377
Grenoble 134, 159
Gresham's law 35

Grubenhaus see: SFB
Guadalquivir 292–4
Guerchy 259

habitus 8, 12, 45, 104, 385
Haccourt 299
Hadrian's Wall 52
Hagenbach 31
hairstyle 347
Hambach, forest of 272
Hamois 260, 272
Hayton 231
Helena 203
helmet 56, 83
Herculaneum 237
Herrera de Pisuerga 370
hilltop fortifications 76–9, 89, 320, 445, 449, 453, 468, 473
historiography 5, 22, 23, 105, 110, 170, 171, 190, 250, 264, 354, 365
hoarding
   coinage 21, 25, 32–7, **38, 39**, 42, 332
   non-recovery 33, 34, 39
      reasons for 35–9
   plate 34, 232–4
Holcombe 239, 256
horse 267, 324
   horse burial 383, **384**
hospitalitas 358, 424
house-church 174
Huns 340, 361, 376, 381
   Hunsrück 76
hunting 83, 241, 252, 266, 434, 439, 469

identity 13, 14, 87, 368, 479
   'barbarian' 355
   Christian 151
   'cognitive' 355
   ethnic 14, 80, 84, 86, 281, 343, 345, 353–7, 389, 394
   'instrumental' 355
   military 42, 46, 54, 262, 352, 468, 469
   'performative' 355, 387
   Roman 456, 467
   'situational' 355, 356, 387
Ile de France 271
Illerup Ådal 57
'imagined community' 45, 50, 151, 178, 189, 342
imperial residence 200–15, 266, 433
import substitution/replacement 462, 464
Indiana, La 442
Inestrillas 127
inflation 21

inscriptions 25, 26, 101, 156, 426, 433, 456, 459, 462
integration (see also: disintegration) 10, 395, 425
   cultural 262
   economic 305, 318, 323, 326, 327, 333, 335, 431
intensification (see also: extensification) 287, 295, 298, 301, 458
Ireland 402
Iruña 126, 129
Isidore of Seville 124, 378
Isle-Jourdain, L' 187, 451
Italy 5, 18, 48, 135, 174, 206, 349, 358, 373, 437
Iuthungi 18
ivory 234, 335

Javols 107, 460
Jerome 428
jewellery 34, 85, 234, 366, 383
Jewish 334
Jouars-Pontchartrain 193, 195
Jublains 66–8, 72, 74, 460
Julian 73, 77, 79, 132, 190, 200, 257, 273

Kaiseraugst 31, 49, 145, 177, 345
   cemetery 345
   treasure 233, 345
   Whylen 51
Keynsham 256
Köln-Deutz 49, 50, 63, 72, 202
Köln-Müngersdorf 379
Konz 209, 260
Krefeld-Gellep 31, **51**, 83, 343–5, 347, 379

Labitolosa 111, 460
laeti 53, 78, 79, 91, 380
landscape 240, 242, 269, 270, 275
Langmauer 207, **208**
Languedoc 287, **288**, 445, 473
late antiquity 6, 102, 264
late Roman 6, 482
Lectoure 133
Le Mans 68, 124, **125**
León 126, 128
Lérins 189
Lescar 133
Leuna-Hassleben 81
Levroux 285
Liberchies 195
Liédena 214, 252, 269, 414

light/ing 225
Ligugé 189
Lillebonne 107
limes Hispanicus 88, 130
Limetz-Ville 379
limitanei 53, 93, 342
Limoges 110, 132, 159
Lincoln 115
Lisbon 115
Lisieux 72, 75
Littlecote 256
London 114, 115, 144, 331
long house, see: *Wohnstallhaus*
lorica hamata 57
'*lorica segmentata*' 57
lorica squamata 57
Loupian 185, **186**, 249, **249**, 290, 317, 409, 411, 446, 447
Low Ham 257
Lucy-sur-Cure 259
Lufton 239, 256
Lugo 123, 126, 127, **128**, 130
Lullingstone 181, 235, 241
Lunel Viel 289, 446, **447**, 473
Lyon 168, 175, 331, 349, 385, 471

Maastricht 51, 70, 146
　Wyck 70
macellum 114, 172
magister equitum per Gallias 53, 91
magister militum praesentalis 57, 91
magister officiorum 93, 204, 350
Magnentius 273, 331
Magnus Maximus 204, 247, 426
Maguelone 165, 411
Mainz 24, 48, 50, 64, 339
　Kastell 51
Malène, La 449
marble 116, 184, 205, 217, 221, 231, 303, 315, 335, 474
Marcus Aurelius 19
Marialba 185
Marmoutier 188
Marolles-sur-Seine 278, **278**, 379, 429, **430**
Marseille 115, 137, 145, 159, 174, 180, 317, 325, 359, 399, 401, 402, 409, 436, 475
　rue Maraval basilica 411
　St-Victor basilica 411
Martin of Tours 163, 175, 189, 190, 323
martyrium 163, 173
Massif Central 460
Matagne-la-Grande 194, **195**

Matagne-la-Petite 195
materiality 15
Maurik 48
mausoleum 167, 181, 184, 222, 241, 402
Maxentius 214
Maximian 21, 24, 30, 134, 213
Meaux 193
Mediana 200, 208
Meinerswijk 48
Melania the Younger 268
Melun 427
menorah 334
mentalité 7, 199, 275, 290, 296, 297, 301, 312
Mérida 118, 121, 126, 144, 168, 368, 411
　bridge 411
　'Casa de los Mármoles' 138, **138**, 411, **412**
　Santa Eulalia 174
　walls 411
Merovingian/*Mérovingien* 380, 383, 390, 426, 453
Meseta 9, 88, 251, 253, 307, 365, 369, 374, 411, 415, 417, 436, 469, 476
Metz 32, 73, 74, 144, 320, 384
　Grand amphithéâtre 74, 425, 427
　St-Pierre-aux-Nonnains 74, **74**
Mienne-Marboué 261, 262
Milan 62, 143, 201, 205, 349
Mildenhall 233
milestone 129, 324
militarisation 12, 13, 31, 42, 60–2, 87, 93, 103, 122, 282, 438, 440, 450, 453, 468, 470
Milreu 185, 219, 222, 416
mint (financial) 93, 330, 349
mirror 343
Mischzivilization 54, 142, 343, 377, 379
Missorium (of Theodosius) 55, 203, 226, 232, **232**
monasticism 188, 239, 444
Moncrabeau(-Bapteste) 239, 360, 422
Mondeville 452
Montlevicq 259
Montmaurin(-Lassalles) 216, 219, **220**, **221**, 237, 238, 422
mosaic 140, 205, 217, 237, **246**, 256, 304, 414, 474
Moselle 76, 148, 266
Muelas de Pan, Las 444
Munigua 111, 457

Naissus 201
Nantes 91, 126

Narbonne 134, 145, 174, 325, 340, 359, 401, 411
Navatajera 414
navicularii 310
navy 91
Neerharen-Rekem 379
negotiatores 310
Nérac 241, 364
Niederemmel 59
Nîmes 107, 110, 114, 115, 120, 134, 137, 287, 325, 408, 446
Nismes 77
non-villa settlement 269–92, 409, 454, 460, 474
Norba 130
Normandy 271, 322, 326, 381, 460
Notitia Dignitatum 4, 45, 52, 53, 57, 61, 68, 71, 79, 86, 88, 90–3, 129, 206, 254, 322, 324, 342, 376, 380
Notitia Galliarum 67, 106
Notre-Dame-d'Allençon 37
Novempopulana 134, 135, 436
numerus 53, 71
nummularii 331, 348
nummus/-i 331
Nydam 57
nymphaeum 219, 222, 225, 241, 252

Oedenburg-Altkirch 209
olive oil 266, 291, 293, 312, 334, 399, 462
Olmeda, la 89, 219, 239, 251, 368, 439
Oloron-Ste-Marie 133, 418
oppidum/-a 295
opus Africanum 428
Orange 118, 134, 471
Orléans 381
Ostrogoth/ic 358, 371, 372, 376, 409, 424, 438
Oudenburg 48, 50, 52, 83, 322

paganism (see also: traditional religions) 150
paideia 4, 199, 243, 247, 253, 256, 257, 262, 437, 470
Palat 239
Pamplona 359
Pannonia 84, 343, 393
Pantelleria 313
'parasitic' occupation (see also: colonisation, 'squatter occupation') 408, 415, 433
Paris 72, 91, 93, 107, 146, 320
   Cluny Baths 73
   Île de la Cité 72
   St-Denis 377

Paris Basin 9, 273–9, **276**, **277**, 322, 423, 425
   Bassée, la 275
   Marne-la-Vallée 275
   Mauldre-Vaucouleurs 275
   Pays de France 17, 275
   Seine-Yonne interfluve 276
   Sénart 275
parish 181, 451, 473
Paulinus of Nola 247, 248, 255, 268
Paulinus of Pella 247, 358, 436
'peasant mode' 443
Pelagonius 267
Pelícano, El 442
Pepys, Samuel 37
Périgueux 110, 114, 132, 137, 146
   amphitheatre 118
   'Tour de Vésone' temple 114, 120, 145, 146
   walls 124, **126**
periodisation 7
Persian 19, 24
Pevensey 322
Pfalzel 207, **209**, 260
Philia 244
Piazza Armerina 214, 225, 242
Picardy 94, 260, 271, 300, 322, 458, 461
pileus Pannonicus 56
pilum 57
plumbata/martio-mattiobarbulus 57
Poitiers 110, 132
Pollentia 127
Pompeii 237
Pont d'Oly 241
'Pontico-Danubian' 347, 368, 370, 371, 372, 373, 381, 393, 467, 478, 479
Portchester 322
Portugal, southern 251, 254, 411, 436
Postumus 18, 24, 30, 38
pottery/ceramics (see also: amphora/e) 303, 361, 389, 397, 399, 443, 474
   Argonne ware 280, 311, 319, **320**, 326, 424, 427, 428, 463, 475
   ARS (African red slip ware) 312, 313, 317, 323, 326, 361, 399, 400, 401, 463
   Black-Burnished ware 280, 322
   céramique à l'éponge 326
   céramique granuleuse/rugueuse 322, 425, 428, 475
   céramique kaolinitique 410
   céramique luisante 318, 326, 409, 410, 423, 477
   céramique pisolithique 410
   céramique siliceuse 430
   coarse ware 328, 401

pottery/ceramics (cont.)
  DSP (*dérivées des sigillées paléochrétiennes*) 325, 361, 400, 422, 428, 443, 476
    Atlantic 325, 423, 425
    Languedoc 325, 423
    Provençal 325
  East Mediterranean 401
  Eifelkeramik/Mayen ware 321, **321**, 425, 428, 475
  Jaulges/Villiers-Vineux 326, 425, 463, 475
  New Forest ware 322
  non-Roman 344, 370, 372, 380, 389, 475
  Oxfordshire ware 322, 463
  samian/*terra sigillata* 21, 29, 300, 311, 319, 462
  TSHT (*terra sigillata tardía hispánica*) 253, 323, **324**, 400, 414, 417, 423, 443, 476
Praefectus laetorum 83
  Praefectus Laetorum Batavorum Nemetacensium 68
  Praefectus Laetorum Nerviorum 70
Praetorian prefect/ure 137, 185, 186, 206, 211, 217, 254, 255, 331, 350, 408, 426
Primuliacum 186, 188
'privatisation' 14, 343, 352, 434, 439, 459, 467
Probus 24, 26, 30, 33, 36, 37
Provence 287–90, 445, 458, 473
Przeworsk culture 371, 372, 382
public/private 14, 140, 144, 225, 236, 237, 238, 342, 351, 439, 449, 451
Pueblanueva, Las Vegas de 185, 241
Puig Rom 444

Quinta das Longas 226, 230, 252
Quinta de Marim 222

radiate coins 35
Raetia 18
Ramière, La 249, 446
Ravenna 349
Reculver 322
region/regionality 9, 102, 143, 199, 215, 245, 250, 253, 262, 271, 286, 305, 398, 426, 456
  super-regions 398
Reihengräberfeld 384, 480
Reims 64, 72, 73, 75, 175, 320, 376, 428
  St-Nicaise 428
relics 164
Rennes 93, 126
res privata 198
Rethel 37
Rheinzabern 29

Rhône valley 399
Ribemont-sur-Ancre 191, **192**, **193**
Richborough 322
Richebourg 273
Riez 159, **162**, 174
ripenses 53
Roc de Pampelune 447, **448**, 473
Rome 5, 143, 200, 205, 207, 309, 339, 349, 358, 473
Roquemaure 409
Rouen 72, 91, 279
  episcopal complex 175, **176**, 427, 428
Rubricaire 67
Rufinus 255

Sabinillas 251
sacramentum 45
Sagunto 127
Saintes 110, 132, 146
  amphitheatre 118
saints, cult of 164
Salic law 384
Saloninus 24
Salvian 426
Sant Julià de Ramis 131
Sanxay 457
São Cucufate 185, 216, 221, **222**, 239, 266, 268, 416
Sapaudia (Savoy) 385
sarcophagus 166, **167**, 212, 304
Sarmatia/n 92, 93, 343, 380, 480
Saucedo, El 415
Saxon Shore 52, 257, 322
Scheldt 38
Schola provincialium 71
scholae 55
sculpture (see also: statuary) 228, 244, 335
seasonal 227, 265
Semnones 18
senate 198, 248, 435
Senones 285
Septimania 365, 369, 374, 375, 450
Septimius Severus 20, 312, 461
Serdica 201
sermo militaris 45, 342
Severus Alexander 20, 24
Séviac (Montréal-Séviac) 187, 216, 218, **218**, 239, 268, 360, 419–22, **421**
Seville 293
Sevso treasure 233, 242
SFB (sunken-features building/*fonds de cabane*/ *Grubenhaus*) 279, 379, 388, 429, 452
shield 56, 83

shipwreck 313, 314–15, **314**, **316**, 463
Sidonius Apollinaris 116, 134, 175, 187, 227,
    335, 359, 363, 438, 471
siege 123
Silchester 114
siliqua 349
Silistra 58, 84
silo (grain) 403, 442, 444
silver plate (see also: *missorium*) 55, 224, 227,
    330, 335
Simancas knives 88, 414, 439
Sîntana de Mureş-Chernyakhov culture 360,
    368, 369, 371, 372, 373, 391, 420
slave/servant 227, 240, 268, 378, 458
'small towns' 25, 27, 97, 135, 140–2, 187, 328
social stress 374, 440
Soissons 75, 376
solea 155
Soto/Encanadeno, El 442
Souzy-la-Briche 259
spatha 57, 344
spear 383
Speyer 31, 385
Split 200
'squatter occupation' (see also: 'parasitic'
    occupation) 397, 413, 471
St-André-de-Codols 249, 290, 409, 446
St-Bertrand-de-Comminges 110, 115, 118, 121,
    133, **133**, 137, 147, 325, 361, 418, 423
St-Blaise 289, 401, 446, 449, 473
St-Georges-de-Montagne 230
St-Germain-lès-Corbeil 273, **274**, 279
St-Giniez, *pierre écrite* 186
St-Lézer 133
St-Lizier 133, 418
St-Marcel/*Argentomagus* 285
St-Martin-de-Fontenay 381
St-Maurice de Gourdans 36
St-Maximin(-la-Sainte-Baume) 185, 451
St-Ouen-du-Breuil 279–81, **280**, 379, 388, 390
St-Quentin 70
St-Rustice 225
St-Séver 219
Ste-Marguerite-sur-Mer 261
stable isotope analysis 86, 88, 304, 392
statuary 224, 433
Steleco 261, 262
stibadium 224, 225, 227, 232, 242
Stilicho 59
Strabo 306
Strasbourg 47
street systems/grids 113, 121, 432
stucco 231

succession, imperial 20
Sueves 339, 340, 353, 359, 364, 402, 479
Suèvres 259
Sulpicius Severus 186, 189, 190, 247, 323
sword 57, 83, 383
Syagrius 376

Tarragona 115, 117, 118, 121, 126, 145, 167,
    168, 230, 291, 359, 402, 403–4, **403**, 475
  Ager Tarraconensis 291, 410
  amphitheatre church 163, **163**, 404
  episcopal complex 173, 179, 196, 404
  Francolì 173, **173**, 404
  Parc Central 173, 404
'tax spine' see: fiscal system
Tedeja 444
temple/sanctuary 68, 114, 118, 119–21, 141,
    161, 180, 190, 196, 211, 241, 403, 418,
    427, 457
Tetrarchy 19, 21, 22
Tetrici 24
textile 235, 266, 472
Teynham 256
theatre 117, 191
Theodoric I 340
Theodoric II 359
Theodosius I 55, 217, 255
Thessalonica 205
Theudebert 384
third-century crisis 6, 18–41, 42, 76, 96, 102,
    103, 111, 141, 264, 271, 286, 294, 295,
    301, 310, 338, 341, 435, 455, 461
Thuringi 384, 481
Tiermes 127
timber construction 278, 284, 286, 388, 396,
    413, 429, 441, 452, 471, 472
Tinto Juan de la Cruz 414, 416, 440, 441
Toledo 115, 371, 372
tombstones 55, 71, 471
  Christian 168–70, **169**, 207
Tongeren/Tongres 51, 64, 70
torc/neck ring 55, 207, 343
'Toronto school' 356
Torre Águila 219, 252
Torre de Cardeira 219
Torre de Palma 182, **183**, 241, 252, 416
Torre Llauder 251
Torrecilla, La 414, 416
Toulouse 118, 120, 134, 137, 318, 339, 358, 359,
    361–4, 391, 417, 423, 440
  Hôpital Larrey 361, **362**
  Notre Dame de la Daurade 362, **363**
  Place Esquirol 417

Toulouse (cont.)
  rue St-Jacques/Ste-Anne 418, **419**
  St-Pierre-des-Cuisines 362
Tournai 51, 70, 377, 383, 428, 480
Tours 95, 107, 146
Toxandria 48, 52, 77, 80, 85, 279, 376, 379, 382, 388
trade
  cabotage 313
  local 328–9
  long-distance 21, 25, 28, 110, 300, 310, 457, 462
  Mediterranean 254, 317, 400, 410, 475
  North African 316
tradition 147, 190, 247, 248, 255
traditional religions 150, 164, 190–7, 217
Trajan 19
'transformation' 101
'tributary mode' 308
triclinium 224
triconch 224, 225, 249, 252, 256, 259, 261
Trier 62, 74, 79, 95, 117, 139, 143, 148, 152, 168, **201**, 234, 247, 272, 320, 331, 360, 426, 436
  Barbarathermen 425, 426
  'Basilika' 202, **202**, 211, 212, 223
  double church 157, **157**, 168, 201, 203, 205, 334
  'Kaiserthermen' 202, 203, **204**, **205**
  St Irminen storehouse 207

urbanism
  Christian 177–80
  continuity/discontinuity 432
  urban change/form 25, 26, 101, 106, 112, 122, 147, 151, 281, 297, 402, 404, 432, 454, 456, 467
  urban 'decline' 101
  urban fortifications 26, 62, **62**, 65, 89, 122–36, 148, 324, 433, 467
  urban functions 74, 75, 97–101, 104–5, 116, 147, 428, 434
  urban ideology 113, 121, 122, 123, 136, 180, 433, 468, 470
  urban society 104
  urban 'type' 98, 99, 142
  urbanism, 'parasitic' 98, 121, 142, 149

Vaison-la-Romaine 115, 471
Val, El 267, 413, 442
Valdetorres del Jarama 230, 238
Valence 134, 381
Valence-sur-Baïse, La Turraque 360

Valencia 114, 115, 126, 145, 172, 179, 401, 402
Valentine 187, 239, 241
Valentinian I 51, 55, 203, 204, 209, 247, 345, 470
Valentinian III 340
Valerian 24
Valleta del Valero 368
Vandals 13, 339, 353, 364, 400, 405, 428
Vandoeuvres 187
Vannes 91
vasa diatreta/cage cup 234, 420
Venantius Fortunatus 121
Vergilius Romanus 226, 232, 235
Vermand 70
Vert-St-Denis 278
Verulamium 118
'very special dead' 163, 189
vexillation 19, 53
via Domitia 135
Victorinus 24, 202
Victricius of Rouen 428
'Vienna school' 356
Vienne 107, 109, 115, 120, 134, 168
Vieux 107
Vieux-Rouen-sur-Bresle 261
Vigo 368
villa 28, 94, 181, 215, 285, 299, 397, 413, 446, 457
  pars rustica/productive area 265
  pars urbana/residential area 265, 269, 299
  villa economy 267, 444, 453
Villa Clara 444
Villa Fortunatus 181, **182**, 413, 415
village 388, 430, 452, 472
Vireux-Molhain 78
Visigoth/ic 13, 133, 339, 341, 351, 353, 357–76, 382, 387, 405, 414, 421, 424, 439, 442, 450, 469, 476, 478, 479, 481
  kingdom 359, 397, 402
Voerendaal 87, 379
Vouillé 359, 367, 377
Vouneuil-sous-Biard 231
Vron 382

wall painting 231
'water feature' 224
Waziers 36
weapons (see also: burials/cemeteries; weapon burials) 55, 82, 87, 207, 344, 440, 478, 480
Weiden bei Köln 95
Welschbillig 55, 207, 226, 233, 260

Weser 85
Wielbark culture 371, 372, 382
Wijster 379
Winchester
   Lankhills 88, 393
wine 227, 266, 291, 313, 334, 392, 462
Wohnstallhaus/long house 379, 388, 414
women's quarters 239
Woodchester 231, 256

Worms 385
Wroxeter 114, 115

Xanten/*Colonia Ulpia Traiana*/*Tricensima* 63, **64**, 177, 459

York 202

Zaragoza 115, 117, 126, 129, 359